MULTILATERALIZING REGIONALISM

Regional trade agreements (RTAs) have proliferated around the world
in the past two decades, and now virtually all the members of the
WTO are party to at least one. Besides tariffs and rules of origin
regulating trade in goods, many RTAs now include provisions on
services, investment, technical barriers to trade and competition rules,
as well as a host of issues not directly related to trade. The geographical reach of RTAs is expanding, with transcontinental agreements
spreading forcefully alongside intra-regional agreements.

'Multilateralizing Regionalism' was the title of a major conference
held on 10–12 September 2007 at the WTO in Geneva, and the bulk of
the chapters in this volume were first presented at that conference.
Together, the conference papers achieve two things. First, they marshal
detailed new empirical work on the nature of the 'spaghetti bowl', and
the problems it poses for the multilateral trade system. Second, they
contribute fresh and creative thinking on how to 'tame the tangle' of
regional trade agreements.

RICHARD BALDWIN is Professor of International Economics at the
Graduate Institute, Geneva. He is also Policy Director at the Centre for
International Policy Research, London, and editor-in-chief of *VoxEU*.

PATRICK LOW is Director of Economic Research and Statistics at the
WTO Secretariat and an Adjunct Professor at the Graduate Institute,
Geneva.

MULTILATERALIZING REGIONALISM

Edited by

RICHARD BALDWIN AND PATRICK LOW

CAMBRIDGE
UNIVERSITY PRESS

CAMBRIDGE UNIVERSITY PRESS

Cambridge, New York, Melbourne, Madrid, Cape Town, Singapore, São Paulo, Delhi

Cambridge University Press
The Edinburgh Building, Cambridge CB2 8RU, UK

Published in the United States of America by Cambridge University Press, New York

www.cambridge.org
Information on this title: www.cambridge.org/9780521738101

First published 2009

Printed in the United Kingdom at the University Press, Cambridge

A catalogue record for this publication is available from the British Library

Library of Congress Cataloguing in Publication data
Multilateralizing regionalism / edited by Patrick Low, Richard Baldwin.
p.   cm.
Includes bibliographical references and index.
ISBN 978-0-521-50601-4 (hbk.)
1. Trade blocs.   2. International trade.   3. Regionalism.   4. Commercial policy.
5. Commercial treaties.   I. Low, Patrick, 1949-   II. Baldwin, Richard E.   III. Title.
HF1418.7.M85 2009
382′.91–dc22
2008053208

ISBN 978-0-521-50601-4 hardback
ISBN 978-0-521-73810-1 paperback

CONTENTS

v

CONTRIBUTORS

PATRICIA AUGIER
Centre d'Économie et de Finances Internationales (CEFI), Aix-en-Provence

RICHARD BALDWIN
Graduate Institute of International and Development Studies, Geneva

CLAUDE BARFIELD
Resident Scholar, American Enterprise Institute, Washington, DC

OLIVIER CADOT
University of Lausanne

THERESA CARPENTER
Graduate Institute of International and Development Studies, Geneva

INKYO CHEONG
Inha University, Korea

JO-ANN CRAWFORD
World Trade Organization, Geneva

PETER DRAPER
South African Institute of International Affairs and European Centre for
International Political Economy

ANTONI ESTEVADEORDAL
Inter-American Development Bank, New York

SIMON EVENETT
University of St Gallen, Switzerland

CARSTEN FINK
World Bank, Washington, DC

ROBERTO V. FIORENTINO
World Trade Organization, Geneva

MICHAEL GASIOREK
University of Sussex, UK

JEREMY HARRIS
Inter-American Development Bank, New York

BERNARD HOEKMAN
World Bank, Washington, DC, and Centre for Economic Policy Research (CEPR), London

GARY HUFBAUER
Peterson Institute for International Economics, Brandeis University

MARION JANSEN
World Trade Organization, Geneva

ALEJANDRO JARA
Deputy Director-General, WTO Secretariat, Geneva

MASAHIRO KAWAI
Asian Development Bank Institute, Tokyo

CHARLES LAI-TONG
Centre d'Économie et de Finances Internationales (CEFI), Aix-en-Provence

PHILIP I. LEVY
American Enterprise Institute, Washington, DC

XUEPENG LIU
Kennesaw State University, GA

PATRICK LOW
World Trade Organization, Geneva

CATHERINE MANN
Peterson Institute for International Economics, Brandeis University

SÉBASTIEN MIROUDOT
OECD Trade and Agriculture Directorate, Paris

MARCELO OLARREAGA
University of Geneva

JOOST PAUWELYN
Graduate Institute, Geneva

MZUKISI QOBO
Stellenbosch University and South African Institute of International Affairs

JIM ROLLO
University of Sussex, UK

JEFFREY SCHOTT
Peterson Institute for International Economics, Brandeis University

MATTHEW SHEARER
Inter-American Development Bank, New York

KATI SUOMINEN
Inter-American Development Bank, New York

CHRISTELLE TOQUEBOEUF
World Trade Organization, Geneva

GANESHAN WIGNARAJA
Asian Development Bank Institute, Tokyo

L. ALAN WINTERS
University of Sussex and Centre for Economic Policy Research (CEPR),
London

FOREWORD

Regionalism is much debated in contemporary trade policy discourse. This is hardly surprising, considering that well over 200 regional agreements with highly varied content and a rich array of geographical configurations are in existence, with dozens more agreements in the making. The phenomenon has accelerated notably in the last several years. The growth in the number of agreements reflects both a growing number of agreements per country and an increase in the number of countries emerging onto the trading scene.

A vast quantity of writing on the subject of regionalism now exists, and one might be tempted to ask what yet another conference volume on the subject can add. The chapters in this volume pose a number of questions that have not previously been addressed, notwithstanding the proliferation of scholarly literature. The focus here is not upon why so many regional agreements have sprung up – that question has dominated many a debate, and lots of interesting explanations have been offered of both an economic and a political nature. Rather, this volume looks ahead and asks how policymakers, traders and businesses view and react to the explosion of regionalism. It also ponders the nature of the relationship between the multilateral trading system and regional agreements.

Are we in a world in which regional agreements will continue to multiply, eventually reaching some critically high number that will place the trading system in a stable equilibrium, where hundreds of criss-crossing agreements coexist in some fashion with the WTO? My view is that most people think not. Proliferation is breeding concern – concern about incoherence, confusion, unnecessary business costs, instability, and unpredictability in trade relations.

This is not to argue that regionalism is all bad, nor that it will simply disappear in time. On the contrary, many regional initiatives have made important contributions to economic welfare, and doubtless to political stability as well. Governments will continue to sign such agreements. But we need to consider where this proliferation is leading us in terms of trade and international economic relations, and perhaps revisit our approach to trade cooperation in a more general sense.

A key idea underlying most of the chapters in this volume is that the tangle of overlapping trade agreements will increasingly generate an interest in multilateralizing regional arrangements by joining them up into larger entities that bring us much closer to a multilateral system of trade arrangements. The question, then, is what forces and interests might push trade relations in a multilateralizing direction.

And what forces and interests might push in the contrary direction – where the discrimination inherent in regional arrangements is viewed favorably by interest groups that benefit from it? If the latter interests prevail, we may expect continuing pressure upon governments to go more regional and resist multilateralization, or at the very least to defend existing regional arrangements against greater inclusiveness. This volume throws new light on these fascinating and important issues.

As suggested above, the debate about whether regionalism is a good or a bad thing per se has long been sterile. It misses the point. We need to look at the manner in which regional agreements operate, and what effects they have on trade opening and on the creation of new economic opportunities. We also need to reflect on whether regionalism is causing harm to multilaterally based trading relationships. Many different kinds of agreements exist and much will depend on their design and intent. These self-same questions will also be relevant in considering the prospects for multilateralizing regionalism. Regionalism might be hurting multilateralism, either by bolstering discriminatory interests, or by fostering protection behind enlarged closed markets. Another concern is whether building on the stock of regional agreements distracts from multilateral processes.

But let us turn the question around and ask what the WTO might do to help avoid a situation in which negative aspects of regional agreements prevail, and ultimately to promote multilateralization. The first element here is that governments need to pay proper attention to their multilateral interests. We neglect the unique advantages of an inclusive, non-discriminatory multilateral trading system at our peril. It is these self-same governments that own the WTO and that enter into regional trading arrangements. It is for them to bring this debate home.

What the WTO can do for international trade in the first instance is to close the Doha Round quickly and successfully. Apart from the intrinsic benefits of completing the Round, this would help to refocus governments' attention on their broader global trade interests. It would also further reduce the scope for discriminatory trade policy in the future.

Second, the 2006 decision to fast-track the transparency mechanism negotiated in the Doha Round (Decision on Transparency Mechanism for Regional Trade Agreements), and make it operational on a provisional basis, is a significant potential contribution to helping us understand what is really going on in so many different regional trade agreements. In my view the decision to anticipate this outcome from the Doha Round reflects a growing level of concern regarding the consequences of a continuing regionalization of trade relations.

Third, an examination of the multilateral rules governing regionalism has long been on the GATT/WTO's negotiating agendas and work programs. Such efforts should continue. It would be useful to look systematically at the characteristics and design of regional agreements not only in terms of legal compliance questions, but also in terms of whether their architecture is more or less likely to foster multilateralization in the future. Perhaps we should think in terms of best practices in this regard.

I welcome the initiative behind this volume to explore the emerging relationship between regionalism and multilateral trade arrangements, and in particular the idea that governments could do more to multi-lateralize regional agreements for the broad benefit of the international trading community, as well as to explore new ways of ensuring that regional agreements are not designed so as to close off opportunities for more broadly based trade cooperation.

Pascal Lamy
Director-General, World Trade Organization

ACKNOWLEDGEMENTS

The September 2007 conference at which most of the chapters in this volume were originally presented was jointly organized by the Graduate Institute of International and Development Studies (HEID), Geneva, and the WTO Secretariat, with the assistance of the Centre for Economic Policy Research (CEPR). The editors are grateful to Theresa Carpenter, Paulette Planchette and Souda Tandara-Stenier for their valuable assistance in organizing the conference, as well as to staff of CEPR. They would also like to thank staff at CUP and Frances Nugent for their untiring efforts in preparing the volume for publication, and to Frances Nugent for her excellent editing skills. The editors would also like to express appreciation for financial support from HEID, the Swiss government (SECO), the NCCR Trade project (IP3), the UK's Department of Industry and Trade, the World Bank, the Inter-American Development Bank, the Asian Development Bank, and CEPR. The WTO provided support in kind.

Opinions expressed in the chapters and any errors or omissions therein are the responsibility of their authors and not of the editors of this volume, nor of the institutions to which they are affiliated.

Introduction

RICHARD BALDWIN AND PATRICK LOW

The last two decades have seen an explosion of regional trade agreements, some of them involving several countries, many of them bilateral. Some have been local, within regions, others have stretched across regions. Some have involved deep integration, going beyond the WTO, while others have been quite light and superficial. All in all, some 350 of these agreements exist.

This proliferation of regional agreements has created a spaghetti bowl of criss-crossing arrangements, with little attention to coherence among agreements or to the implications of so many regimes for trade costs, efficiency, and the conditions of competition in global markets. The chapters in this volume, prepared for a conference held at the WTO in September 2007, are primarily focused on a core question concerning the prospects for gains in efficiency and coherence in international trade relations that might emerge from a process of multilateralizing regionalism. In thinking about this process of potential coalescence of dozens of regional agreements around the world into a more coherent whole, the conference did not attempt to analyze in any systematic way the economic, political, or political economy reasons why the incidence of regionalism has exploded in recent years. The reasons are many and plenty of analyses have been undertaken along these lines.

Against the background of proliferating regionalism and the assumption that today's international trading arrangements are far from optimal, it is as well to ask what is meant more precisely by the notion of multilateralizing regionalism. Most obviously, a process of multilateralization is promoted through the non-discriminatory extension of preferential trading arrangements to additional trading partners. Such extension can occur in two ways – either through the inclusion of new members in existing agreements, or by replacing existing agreements with new ones that extend to new members. There is no a priori way of judging the relative merits of these two approaches. Much depends on the preexisting architecture of the preferential arrangements and the

1

economics and politics that might drive an interest in "taming the tangle" of multiple overlapping agreements.

Major elements of the underlying analytical framework for looking at the multilateralization builds on recent work by Richard Baldwin.[1] The starting point of Baldwin's analysis is that a good deal of trade liberalization has occurred in recent years in most parts of the world. This liberalization has been multilateral, regional, and unilateral. More open trading arrangements have fed on themselves through political economy forces increasingly disposed to further trade opening – Baldwin's so-called juggernaut effect – and countries have participated in more open trade arrangements, in part so as to avoid being left behind – the domino effect.

A key component of the analysis rests on the growing phenomenon of production sharing – also referred to as unbundling, off-shoring, or fragmentation. This is a world in which production processes are spread through multiple jurisdictions across the world. The political economy effects of this fragmentation have been significant – blunting the old distinctions between "us" and "them" that used to drive trade policy. Producer interests that previously sought to protect their local markets from outsiders now worry about market access conditions and trade costs in a range of other markets as well. Hence the growing political economy forces that favor more open markets. But in the last few years trade policy has been dominated by regional initiatives, with their discriminatory and potentially distorting side-effects. Higher trade costs have also accompanied regionalism – in the Baldwin analysis this is in large measure a rules-of-origin story.

The basic proposition emerging from this analysis is that against a background of diminishing trade protection, brought about in part through an "untamed tangle" of criss-crossing preferential trade agreements and their associated higher trade costs, an interest is emerging in multilateralization – that is, in a process that would rationalize trade relations on a more global basis. The argument is not that regionalism will go away. Rather, it is the more modest but nevertheless important proposition that there may be growing interest in moving away from the spaghetti bowl.

In considering this, it is natural to ask not only how regionalism itself might evolve into something different, but also what role the WTO might play in promoting a more inclusive and coherent trading system,

---

[1] The most complete summary available of this work is to be found in Baldwin (2006).

freer of economic distortions. Whatever else the GATT/WTO has achieved over the six decades of its existence – and many would agree that these achievements have been significant – the fact remains that to all intents and purposes, the WTO has been something of a passive observer as regionalism has exploded. So while at least some governments have shown growing signs of asking where all this regionalism is taking us, a key question is what the WTO might do in the new and complex world of international trade relations. What should its role be? Regionalism is not going to just disappear, but along with all the other things the WTO does, can it contribute to making regionalism more multilateral-friendly? Several of the chapters and commentaries in the volume have touched on this question.[2]

The conference volume is divided into four main sections, dealing respectively with the evolution of regionalism, prospects and past experiences with multilateralization, sectors and themes relevant to multilateralization, and regional perspectives on the issues.

In the introductory section of the volume (Part I), Carpenter takes a historical perspective on regionalism, tracing the growth over time of the attractiveness of this brand of trade cooperation. She identifies three main phases of regionalism in the postwar period, and emphasizes the variety of motivations for regional trade agreements. This is followed by a chapter by Fiorentino, Crawford, and Toqueboeuf analyzing the current landscape of regional agreements. This chapter shows in stark fashion just how pervasive regionalism has become and emphasizes some of the trends in recent years, notably a strong preference for free trade areas over customs unions, agreements among countries that are not contiguous, a strong preference for bilateral agreements, significant geographical overlap with countries belonging to several different agreements, and considerable diversity in the scope and coverage of different agreements.

The chapter by Fiorentino *et al.* also examines the GATT/WTO's role in the surveillance of regional agreements, making the point that the multilateral trading system has proved ineffectual in this role. The chapter notes an important new departure in the WTO's approach to regional agreements, however, with the introduction of a new transparency mechanism as a provisional "early harvest" outcome of the

---

[2] In addition, Richard Baldwin and Philip Thornton recently published a short monograph (Baldwin and Thornton, 2008), based on the conference, which focuses particularly on the question of a possible WTO contribution to the multilateralization process.

Doha Round. The new mechanism emphasizes a non-litigious approach to establishing a uniform and complete information base that will allow the WTO membership to acquire an improved understanding of regional trade agreements. This exercise is not intended to undermine the WTO's legal basis for dealing with preferential trade agreements, but rather to strengthen it.

The first chapter in Part II – on prospects and past experience with multilateralization – is by Baldwin, Evenett, and Low. The chapter considers how far the logic of multilateralization – driven in Baldwin's earlier analysis by political economy forces, trade costs, and the unbundling of production across nations – extends to non-tariff measures. The focus is on trade in services, government procurement, competition policy, investment, technical barriers to trade, and trade remedies. The fundamental question is what determines the balance of interests that gives rise either to a spaghetti bowl phenomenon or a relative lack of discrimination. The overall conclusion of the chapter is that the spaghetti bowl is often not as apparent where non-tariff measures are concerned as it is in the case of tariff regimes supported by rules of origin. A determining factor is how far discriminatory outcomes are the result of intentional as opposed to incidental protection. The degree of success of multilateralization initiatives in the areas examined depends on the domestic balance of interests, and non-discrimination often requires reciprocity from RTA partners.

The chapter finds that outcomes in some areas benefit from an "MFN [most favored nation] dividend," where regulatory reform undertaken at the regional level applies to all trade, either by design or because it is simply inefficient to seek to discriminate among alternative trade or investment sources in the relevant policy domains. In other areas, however, where reciprocity is important, the question arises whether a plurilateral or "club" approach might be required in the context of multilateralization. This clearly raises a systemic issue for the multilateral trading system, although in some cases – such as the mutual recognition of professional qualifications or conformity assessment in relation to product standards – the WTO already has to deal with the reality that governments will not enter into such arrangements on a fully non-discriminatory basis. This calls for a nuanced approach to non-discrimination, where a distinction is necessary between opportunity (the absence of *ex ante* exclusion) and outcome (the possibility of *ex post* exclusion). Overall, the authors emphasize the tentative nature of their analysis and the need for further research involving a broader range of actors in the trading system, particularly to determine the intensity of the spaghetti bowl effect in different policy areas.

The chapter by Gasiorek recounts the context in which the Pan-European Cumulation System (PECS) came into existence in 1997, and explains how, by allowing "cumulation" among many countries in the determination of origin, a spaghetti bowl of hub-and-spoke arrangements was rendered down into a more integrated and less discriminatory set of market arrangements. The answer to the question whether this experience could be generalized as a means of multilateralizing fractured regional arrangements is not entirely encouraging. The reason for this is that cumulation has to be based on a set of shared FTAs with identical rules of origin, or the arrangements would require a value-added origin rule where tariffs are charged only on those components that do not originate in the qualifying region. These requirements are rather stringent in the complex world of multiple and laboriously negotiated rules of origin. An additional point is that even if this were possible, it would amount to partial multilateralization, possibly with additional discriminatory implications for third parties.

The chapter by Mann and Xuepeng Liu is not much more sanguine regarding the idea that another documented multilateralization episode – the establishment of the Information Technology Agreement in the aftermath of the WTO's first Ministerial Conference in 1996 – could serve as a model for moves towards multilateralizing regional approaches to trade policy. The authors argue that the IT sector was something of a special case, as was the timing of the ITA initiative. Information technology and the products associated with it are the bread and butter of innovation, productivity growth, diversification and development. Widespread interest in acquiring high-quality IT at low prices provided a significant incentive for governments to agree to a duty-free, open-ended sectoral deal, albeit one that required a high degree of reciprocity. Moreover, according to the authors, the political incentive to move in this direction was bolstered by the "hype" attached to IT in the early 1990s.

Part III examines a number of sectors and themes relating to the multilateralization question. The first chapter, by Fink and Jansen, is a detailed consideration of how far the notion of multilateralizing regionalism might be applicable in the field of trade in services. Service transactions are more complex than those involving goods and they tend to be heavily regulated in order to deal with market failures associated with information asymmetries, economies of scale and scope, and network externalities. In some service sectors distributional issues may also arise. The core issue is how far these policy interventions in RTAs are discriminatory. The authors argue that rules of origin tend to be relatively liberal in most cases, except in respect of Mode 4 dealing with the movement of natural persons. In the case of Mode 3 transactions involving commercial presence, however, the use of quotas on market access gives first-comers an advantage that renders rules of origin irrelevant. A particular feature of some RTAs with provisions on services is the so-called non-party MFN clause, which guarantees all preferential service suppliers the same conditions of access under different RTAs. This arrangement automatically fosters multilateralization. Similarly, as noted earlier, certain regulations by their nature automatically apply on a non-discriminatory basis, thus imparting a kind of MFN dividend. One area where discrimination is likely to be inherent, however, is that of mutual recognition agreements. Here a question is whether multilateral surveillance might mitigate the negative effects of discrimination. Overall, the authors argue that in many instances RTAs involving service trade are likely to be mildly discriminatory, although there are exceptions to this and more research is required in this area.

The chapter by Estevadeordal, Harris, and Suominen on multilateralizing preferential rules of origin notes that rules of origin can inhibit trading opportunities for third parties, limit trading opportunities within RTAs by choking off access to competitive inputs, and increase transaction costs for countries and companies seeking to trade across more than one RTA. In this sense, both restrictiveness and divergence in rules of origin matter. Rules of origin may be expressed in terms of wholly obtained or produced products, a change in tariff classification, exceptions and additions to a change in a tariff classification, value content or technical requirements, and practices with respect to these different approaches vary widely among RTAs and across regions. The authors report on the relative restrictiveness of different sets of rules of origin, showing quite a bit of variation. They also note that the greater the degree of restrictiveness, the more divergence matters. At the limit, divergence does not matter if rules of origin are non-binding, but the costs of divergence occur both in relation to customs procedures and corporate practices. The chapter identifies a number of strategic options for lessening the negative impacts associated with rules of origin, including multilateralization, regional convergence, and bilateral reform. They conclude that multilateral guidelines for rules of origin are desirable, that fully harmonized rules are neither practical nor desirable, that some regional convergence (the authors call this "lasagna noodles") could simplify multilateral negotiations, and, of course, that all the problems would go away if MFN tariffs were reduced to zero.

Pauwelyn examines legal avenues towards multilateralizing regionalism. Starting from the observation that Article XXIV of the GATT and Article V of GATS are largely inoperative, the author argues for the application of the principles of general international law. The core proposition of the chapter is that there should be no assumption of hierarchy between WTO law and law established in RTA agreements – in other words, we should move away from notions of hierarchy towards mutual accommodation. Without mutual accommodation, problems inevitably arise as a result of overlapping and sometimes contradictory laws, differing obligations among parties, and competing fora for settling disputes. The author develops eight basic rules of interpretation and practice. These include the notion that all treaties are in principle equal and binding only on those agreeing to them, a presumption against conflict, the possibility that treaties can explicitly regulate against overlap, that treaties are valid unless declared otherwise, that treaties most recent in time prevail over earlier ones, that the most specific treaty prevails and that WTO and RTA panels can consider both WTO and RTA law. The chapter then examines a range of particular legal situations to demonstrate how these principles would operate in practice.

Turning to the regionally based chapters – Part IV of the volume – Draper and Qobo discuss African regionalism and argue that prospects are poor for any multilateralization of regionalism in terms of the Baldwin framework. The impetus simply does not exist for the juggernaut and domino effects to take hold, and much of Africa is excluded from unbundling or production sharing. On the contrary, many African governments feel defensive and vulnerable when it comes to trade policy, owing in part to structural imbalances and inequitable rules governing agricultural trade. Unilateral trade policy reforms are not widely embraced, regional agreements are often partial and shallow, and the general posture on the international scene is preoccupied with preference erosion, residual interest in import substitution, policy space and special and differential treatment, and the need for external resource flows. Problems besetting the continent include supply-side capacity limitations, economic sparseness, challenges of governance and very high trade costs. The economic logic of what Africa needs – improved infrastructure, further liberalization in some areas, investor protection, trade facilitation, rationalized regional arrangements, competition policy, stronger institutions, and "aid for trade" – does not always sit comfortably with prevailing policy postures. These are among the challenges that must be met before the multilateralization of regionalism could become a reality.

The chapter by Estevadeordal, Shearer, and Suominen on multilateralizing RTAs in the Americas notes that, by 2013, the spaghetti bowl of the Americas should have rendered 80 percent of trade free of duties. But the spaghetti bowl is large, dense, and complex, and considerable architectural heterogeneity exists among agreements. Moreover, there are exceptions to the general state of openness within the region, such as tariff rate quotas in agriculture and restrictions on textiles and apparel, food, chemicals. and footwear. Restrictive rules of origin also dampen the trade effects of RTAs. Many RTAs in the region have fairly comprehensive provisions in various other areas, such as services and investment. A possible move towards multilateralization could be transcontinental free trade in the Americas (FTAA), but this seems unlikely in the near future. Other approaches could include policies towards convergence within the region, bearing in mind the short-term risk of polarizing the region with respect to the rest of the world. Case-by-case liberalization of individual RTAs may be a possibility, for example through enlarging cumulation zones, selectively relaxing rules of origin, and further liberalizing products where these have already been liberalized within RTAs to major exporters.

The chapter by Kawai and Wignaraja argues that the proliferation of RTAs in Asia is a defensive response to regionalism elsewhere, as well as a reflection of slow progress in global trade talks. Other factors include the IT revolution and the growth of production sharing. The authors argue that RTA formation in Asia can be complementary to the WTO process and benefits the region in a number of ways. These benefits will tend to be higher with elements of WTO-plus in the RTAs. The focus of the chapter is on an ASEAN+3 configuration (with China, Japan, and the Republic of Korea) and an ASEAN+6 bloc (with India, Australia, and New Zealand added). The larger configuration, which moves towards an East Asian FTA, is more likely to mitigate "noodle bowl" effects and yield the largest gains for the region. This approach will encourage the participation of low-income countries in freer trade arrangements, reduce trade-related business costs, and promote trade and investment. The authors also argue that commercial relations with the United States and the EU are important, and an East Asia–North America FTA and an East Asia–EU FTA could be on a future agenda.

Hufbauer and Schott also look at Asia-Pacific regionalism and argue that, notwithstanding fears in certain quarters that rapid growth in regionalism is eroding the WTO system, there are ways in which current and future Asia-Pacific FTAs could complement the WTO. Among the ways that this could happen are the various Asia-Pacific Economic Cooperation (APEC) initiatives aimed at developing best practices in regional agreements and through a proposal to harmonize MFN tariffs to the lowest rates of FTA partners. For its part, the best thing that the WTO could do would be to continue to lower MFN tariffs. One approach to this could be to harmonize MFN tariffs down to the lowest level prevailing among members of a regional agreement. WTO members seem to have little appetite for modifying the deliberately fuzzy multilateral rules on RTAs, although the new transparency mechanism is a timid step in the right direction. The best idea in the mechanism is the requirement to notify all changes to FTAs. In short, this chapter sees perhaps some prospect of a move towards multilateralization within the region, should a free trade area in Asia and the Pacific (FTAAP) emerge, although variance among RTAs in the region raises questions about how probable this is.

The chapter by Hoekman and Winters looks at "deep" regional integration questions from a developing country perspective. The authors are not very optimistic about overall prospects for the multilateralization of developing country RTAs – which they suggest has not really happened and in some cases might not in any event be a good idea. Nor do they see regional agreements offering an effective path to deep integration in developing countries. However, as far as the temporary movement of labor is concerned – a central focus of the chapter – it is clear that bilateral progress dominates multilateral action. Among the reasons for this are linkages between trade and migration, a lack of symmetry in the market for reciprocity, the binding nature of multilateral commitments, the need for mutual trust, and the role of culture in a globalized world. Further progress might be forthcoming with more explicit cooperation between origin and destination countries and more technical and adjustment assistance for developing countries.

The chapter by Rollo also has a regional flavor in that it considers the challenges facing developing countries in negotiating RTAs, given the second-best nature of such arrangements. Developing countries with resource constraints are likely to be at a particular disadvantage in assessing the costs and benefits of RTA proposals. The Sussex Framework is a relatively low-cost but robust analytical tool for making such assessments. The chapter argues there is a case for public or low-cost provision of such analytical tools, and that the WTO might in principle provide such services. But the author goes on to argue that perhaps this could cause a conflict of interest for the WTO and that there may therefore be a case for establishing an Advisory Centre on RTAs, modeled along the lines of the Advisory Centre.

References

Baldwin, R. E. (2006) "Multilateralising Regionalism: Spaghetti Bowls as Building Blocks on the Path to Global Free Trade", *The World Economy* 29, 11: 1451–518.

Baldwin, R. E. and Thornton, P. (2008) *Multilateralising Regionalism: Ideas for a WTO Action Plan on Regionalism*, London: Centre for Economic Policy Research.

PART I

Background to Regionalism

A historical perspective on regionalism

THERESA CARPENTER

This chapter explores the development of regionalism from a historical perspective, with a view to understanding how the world ended up with some 350 regional trade agreements (RTAs) (so far) of varying degrees of coverage, complexity and efficacy. Understanding the history of regionalism may shed light on how to multilateralize it; and an understanding of the factors that led nations to conclude trade agreements outside the multilateral trading system may help to identify some lessons for dealing with the increasing proliferation of RTAs.

Motivations for regionalism can be varied and several. The report of the First Warwick Commission (2007) identifies a number of important reasons why governments may become involved in regionalism. The most important of these reasons can be summarized as seeking enhanced market access; furthering foreign policy objectives; and influencing the domestic policies of trading partners, for example in the field of intellectual property or migration. Other, secondary reasons include the CNN effect, whereby the short-term publicity associated with signing an agreement may be more important than the substance of the agreement; and the 'laboratory motive', whereby it is possible to experiment with different forms of international rule-making or trade liberalization, perhaps prior to undertaking such liberalization or commitments on a multilateral basis. In the story that follows, we bear these motivations in mind. It is beyond the capacity of this piece to examine in detail which motives are most important in which agreements, but we provide evidence that each of these motives governs some agreements.

1   What is regionalism?

First, a short digression: what is meant by the term 'regionalism'? We use the term in this volume to indicate certain types of trade agreements. The WTO's working definition of regionalism seems to be any trade agreement that involves two or more countries but fewer than all members. It is useful to have an understanding of the complex variety of types of agreement that are covered by this understanding of 'regionalism'. There can be several signatories, as in the case of the EC/EU; or just two, such as the bilateral trade agreement between India and Sri Lanka. The agreements may involve countries that are of close geographical proximity, such as MERCOSOR and SADC; or maybe in different parts of the globe, as in, for example, the agreements between the EU and Chile, Switzerland and Morocco, and the US and Jordan.

In addition, there are other trade policies that may be either unilateral, such as the liberalization policies pursued by Singapore and Hong Kong, China; or are narrow in the scope of products covered, such as the Information Technology Agreement (ITA). These agreements fall outside our definition of regionalism because they are not discriminatory, but an awareness of them is useful to complete the picture.

Aggarwal (2001), from which Table 1.1 is adapted, offers a useful classification of varieties of trade governance and policy. The types of agreement we are primarily interested in fall within table cells 8, 9, 10 and 11. The agreements that fall within these cells all cover a wide variety of products and are between two or more countries, but not so many that they can be considered multilateral. The codes of the Tokyo Round, the concept of which some commentators (such as Pauwelyn, 2005), are suggesting should be revived as an alternative to the single undertaking for either the current or subsequent trade rounds, would fall into the multilateral column, as the goal of such codes is universal rather than exclusive membership.

There is a justification for what may appear at first glance to be a rather haphazard and idiosyncratic definition of regionalism: all the agreements that fall within table cells 8–11 either are (or probably should be) notified to the WTO under Article XXIV (for agreements that involve one or more of the developed countries); or under the Enabling Clause (for agreements that are limited to developing countries). In this way the focus of regionalism is defined directly by the scope of WTO rules. To borrow a phrase from Finger (1993), who said that anti-dumping is trade protection that you can get away with under the anti-dumping agreement, regionalism can be understood to be discriminatory trade policy that you can get away with under Article XXIV. By way of contrast, notice that the examples of agreements that fall into cells 2, 3, 4 and 5 include examples of agreements that may be inconsistent with GATT rules.

Table 1.1. *Varieties of trade governance*

Product scope	Number of participants					
		Bilateral		Minilateral		
	Unilateral	Geographically concentrated	Geographically dispersed	Geographically concentrated	Geographically dispersed	Multilateral
Few products (sectoral)	1 Trade policy of some Asian countries in some products	2 US–Canada Auto pact	3 US–Japan Voluntary Export Restraints (VERs)	4 European Coal and Steel Community	5 Multifibre Arrangement	6 ITA Tokyo codes
Many products	7 Trade policies of Singapore and Hong Kong, China	8 Mexico–Guatemala India–Bhutan	9 US–Jordan Chile–Rep. of Korea	10 EU MERCOSOR ECOWAS CARICOM NAFTA	11 Protocol relating to Trade Negotiations among Developing Countries (PTA) Tripartite Agreement	12 GATT (1947) WTO (1995)

2   Discriminatory trade policy and Article XXIV

Article I of the GATT states that trade concessions granted to one member are supposed to be applied immediately and without conditions to all other members. Despite this commitment to Most Favoured Nation (MFN) treatment by all members, since the birth of the GATT over 550 trade agreements granting selected preferences to some partners have been made; some 330 of these are currently in force, of which two-thirds have been notified to the WTO by members. How did the world get into this plethora of regional trade agreements that has been so ineloquently named 'the spaghetti bowl'? This chapter traces the development of regionalism, seeking to highlight the main motivation of key players at various milestones since 1948.[1]

Exceptions to the MFN clause are allowed under Article XXIV of the original GATT,[2] which allows 'the formation of a customs union *or of a free trade area*' (emphasis added) under specific conditions, the essence of which is that closer integration between the parties to an agreement is considered beneficial, so long as 'the purpose is not to raise barriers to the trade of other contracting parties'. Why was Article XXIV allowed into the GATT in the first place, and how was the term 'free trade area' reputedly allowed to creep in at the last minute? It can be reasoned that provision was made for customs unions, partly because there were a number of customs unions that were operative at the time of the drafting of the GATT (including Switzerland–Liechtenstein); and partly because a customs union would have to be allowed because it recreates some important elements of single-nation characteristics (Bhagwati, 1999).

Scholars that have traced the negotiating history of the GATT have identified three stories as to why the words 'or free trade area' were added alongside customs unions as a permissible exception to the MFN clause. One relates to the idea that European regionalism was viewed as a prerequisite for peace on the war-torn continent. This is unlikely, as the main trading ties of key European nations at the time were with countries with whom they had strong historical ties, rather than with each other. Another story relates to a free trade agreement that was supposedly being negotiated between the United States and Canada.

---

[1] For a description of trade policy prior to 1948, see Irwin (1993).
[2] The other instruments by which exceptions to MFN are permitted are the Enabling Clause and Article V of the General Agreement on Trade in Services.

Other possible explanations are the existing Italy–Vatican PTA; and an agreement between Lebanon and Syria.

3   The first wave of regionalism

The first wave of regionalism refers to the period prior to 1986.

Early European regionalism

The formation of the European Economic Community (EEC) in 1958 was a watershed in the history of regionalism. European regionalism was born out of a French desire for security. France first sought to expand her trading prospects with an approach to her wartime ally, Great Britain.[3] In 1955, two ideas were mooted by France: the first was the possibility of a union between France and Britain; the second was the request by France to join the British Commonwealth. These approaches to Britain can be set against the backdrop of the events in Egypt, Algeria and Israel/Jordan: in Egypt, Nasser had nationalized the Suez Canal; in French Algeria there was a separatist rebellion; and tension was growing along the border between Israel and Jordan. After Britain decided to pull out of Suez, the battle against President Nasser was lost, and all talk of union died too. A year later, France teamed up with Germany, building on the European Coal and Steel Community established in 1952, which placed the French and German steel industries under a common authority in order to lessen the likelihood of war between France and Germany, and the EEC was born.[4]

The Treaty of Rome clearly did not comply with the spirit of Article XXIV, in that it excluded an entire sector – agriculture. Despite this obvious flaw, the EC agreement was allowed to pass in the GATT because of the United States' interest in having a strong, peaceful Western Europe in the post-war era. The Cold War was, at this time, heating up. The accommodation of the EC's imperfect union is referred to by some commentators (e.g. Jackson, 1993) as a breakdown of the GATT's legal discipline. A debate on what constituted 'substantially all trade' began, as excluded countries were concerned about what were termed 'systemic issues', meaning that they feared that the proliferation

---

[3] Details reported at http://news.bbc.co.uk/2/hi/uk_news/6261885.stm.

[4] The original six members of the EEC were Belgium, France, Germany, Italy, Luxembourg and the Netherlands.

of regional trade agreements and the corresponding disregard for the rules could harm the multilateral system.

The establishment of the EC, with its plan to move to a common external tariff in 1968 (ten years after the Treaty of Rome entered into force), led to the almost simultaneous development of another European bloc, the EFTA.[5] Afraid of being left out, a group of non-EC European nations, led by the UK, formed EFTA. This rival bloc was less successful than the EC. Gradually five of the seven original members of EFTA, except Switzerland and Norway, migrated to the EC. This can be explained by the domino theory of regionalism (Baldwin, 1993; Baldwin and Reider, 2007). Prior to this, the UK had hoped that in joining EFTA it would retain sovereignty over trade policy, but would benefit from a larger market. This was not to be, and finally, after careful analysis, the UK concluded that joining the EEC was in its best interests.

Early regionalism among developing countries

The EC and EFTA are just two of fifty-seven trade agreements that were concluded during the period 1955 to 1974. Important geopolitical events and movements during this period include decolonization, the rise of the Non-Aligned movement, and the promotion of the development paradigm known as import substitution industrialization, which was developed during the interwar period, under the influence of the early work of Raul Prebisch and the Economic Commission for Latin America and the Caribbean (ECLAC).

These developments gave rise to a spate of agreements between developing countries. Some of these were ideologically motivated, and had very little content in the way of trade concessions. For example, the trade concessions embodied in the Tripartite Agreement between Egypt, India and Yugoslavia, whose leaders were the pioneers of the Non-Aligned movement, amounted to a 50 per cent tariff reduction for 193 products.

However, this period saw the foundations laid for what have become the main regional groupings, including ASEAN, which was formed in 1967 with five members. Initially the formation of ASEAN was related primarily to security motives. A trade dimension, in the form of inclusion lists, was added eleven years later.

---

[5] The original seven EFTA members were Austria, Denmark, Norway, Portugal, Sweden, Switzerland and the UK.

Early Latin American regionalism

The idea of Latin American integration has deep roots in the region's political and economic culture that date as far back as Latin American independence during the early nineteenth century, but Latin American schemes of economic integration blossomed during the 1960s and 1970s. During those years, Latin American countries actively pursued a policy of industrialization behind high tariffs and most of them engaged in an active developmental approach.

As the easy stage of light manufacturing was accomplished, Latin American leaders championed the idea of economic integration largely as a way to address the bottlenecks related to the limited size of their national markets, particularly as subsequent stages of development involved capital-intensive industries. This led, for example, to the creation of the Central American Common Market, the Caribbean Community, and the Andean Community.[6] It also led to pan-Latin American integration initiatives, notably the LAFTA (Asociación Latinoamericana de Libre Comercio) and later on the ALADI (Asociación Latinoamericana de Integración), which envisioned the establishment of a Latin American free trade area and common market, respectively, through the granting of regional or bilateral economic preferences among members.[7]

Developments in the early 1980s

European regionalism expanded and deepened. The first expansion of the EC involved the accession of the UK, Ireland and Denmark in 1973,

---

[6] This does not imply that political considerations are irrelevant, but for reasons of space we limit this discussion to economic factors. Three of the four customs unions in the Americas were created in the 1960s and 1970s: the Central American Common Market (CACM) created in 1961, the Andean Community created in 1969, and the Caribbean Community and Common Market (CARICOM) created in 1973. The fourth one, the Common Market of the South (MERCOSUR), was created in 1991 and entered into force in 1995.

[7] Established in 1960, the ALALC counted eleven members: Argentina, Bolivia, Brazil, Chile, Colombia, Ecuador, Mexico, Paraguay, Peru, Uruguay and Venezuela. The Andean Pact, which was established nine years later, was supposedly an early example of a subregional 'building block' towards regional free trade. Born in 1980, the ALADI built on the legacy of the ALALC, but adopted a more flexible approach to achieving free trade among nations as it allowed subregional and bilateral partial scope agreements on top of regional preferences. Today the ALADI serves as an umbrella agreement for many bilateral FTAs and customs unions in the Americas, notably the MERCOSUR.

bringing the total number of countries to nine. The second expansion in 1981 added Greece to the fold.

During the early 1980s Latin American countries were hard hit by the debt crisis, which triggered an early wave of market-oriented reforms. Top priorities on the external agenda included eliminating policy-induced biases of the import substitution industrialization development strategy, and adopting a decisive export-oriented trade strategy, complemented by friendly policies towards foreign investors – all elements that underscored the success of Asian economies. While regionalism was not a policy option for early reformers, it was brought back with important transformations to the regional agenda in the late 1980s.

4   The second wave of regionalism

The 'second wave' of regionalism, as Bhagwati (1999) termed it, began in the mid-1980s. The seeds of the Uruguay Round had been sown in November 1982 at a ministerial meeting of GATT members in Geneva, where ministers intended but were unable to launch a major new negotiation. In 1986, the Round was launched. What had changed in those four years? Two idiosyncratic events that precipitated the launch of the Round and the second wave of regionalism can be noted.

These two events are simultaneous developments in regionalism in Europe and North America. In Europe, the EC was expanding and deepening: the third expansion of the EC to include Spain and Portugal, together with the laying of plans for completing the move to a Single European Market for goods, services, capital and labour. This led to two concerns among the rest of the world: first, that the EC would be less interested in pursuing multilateral negotiations within the GATT; and, second, a fear of 'Fortress Europe' – the idea that the EC would become less open to trade with outsiders. In North America the efforts to recreate a free trade area joining Canada and the United States finally succeeded, and the CUSFTA came into being.

Two elements were different in the second wave compared with the first wave. The most important development was that the United States had clearly changed track, transforming from a staunch multi-lateralist stance to embracing and beginning to negotiate preferential agreements. The second element was the planned deepening of integration in Western Europe, which is acknowledged to have paved the way for the inclusion of services in the Uruguay Round.

In Latin America, the 'new' regionalism was decisively 'open' regionalism, for it was accompanied, at least initially, by unilateral and multilateral liberalization. Among South American ALADI members, the new regionalism still maintained traces of the old regionalism, notably its efforts to foster non-traditional exports to Latin American markets and its thematic focus on achieving market access for regional goods. Most Latin American and Caribbean (LAC) countries took on RTA negotiations between each other with renewed enthusiasm and deeper liberalizing ambition. Existing regional pacts were revamped and relaunched, while a new regional scheme took place in the Southern Cone, the MERCOSUR.

The shift in US policy towards regionalism and Mexico's initiative to join the US and Canada in the NAFTA – which posed a major challenge to Latin American countries – were key factors that shaped the content and landscape of the new regionalism in the Americas (Ethier, 1998; Salazar Xirinachs, 2002). NAFTA proposed a revolutionary approach to regionalism in the Americas, as it envisaged a North–South RTA between highly asymmetric partners, with limited or no special treatment for the less-developed partner. Prior to NAFTA, Latin American integration had only involved agreements among developing countries, and these had often included special and differential treatment (e.g. the ALADI). Additionally, NAFTA went far beyond market access as it included 'deep' commitments in an entirely new set of trade disciplines, which responded to the Mexican focus on attracting investment (Lawrence, 1996).

Following the announcement of NAFTA negotiations, many Latin American countries expressed interest in negotiating a similar agreement with the United States. As a response, in 1990 the United States launched the 'Enterprise for the Americas Initiative' with the goal of achieving free trade in the western hemisphere by 2000. Four years later negotiations on the Free Trade Area of the Americas (FTAA) started. However, negotiations were marked by slow progress due to intractable obstacles in agriculture, and anti-dumping on the US side, as well as the defensive position of leading South American nations concerning industrial products and the 'new areas of trade' (chiefly investment and intellectual property rights).

As the FTAA negotiations faltered, the United States and many Latin American countries – notably Chile and Central American countries – embraced bilateral negotiations within the Americas. Meanwhile Mexico, which had been actively negotiating trade agreements in the Americas throughout the 1990s, turned to path-breaking FTA negotiations with transcontinental partners,[8] initially from Europe and later from Asia.

MERCOSUR countries, led by Brazil, consolidated their network of arrangements in South America by negotiating FTAs and subsequently granting associated member status to Andean countries as a first step towards the South American Union of Nations (UNASUR).[9] While the idea of a South American FTA had already been presented by the Brazilian authorities back in 1994, it materialized only in December 2004. The strong reaction against liberal reforms of the 1990s that spread unevenly throughout the Americas led to the dilution of the commercial component of UNASUR and to placing more emphasis on other aspects of the integration agenda, such as physical integration, energy, and social and cultural integration.

5   The third wave of regionalism

The third wave of regionalism has occurred since the conclusion of the Uruguay Round. Some of the more recent agreements can be explained as either the deepening or widening of existing agreements, such as the plethora of agreements that have occurred between the EU and new European nations. The new factors here are the sheer number of countries that want to be associated with the success of Europe.

The current situation is one where, for some customs territories, only the least favoured nations pay the MFN tariff; others pay a preferential tariff or none at all. This has led to a climate of competition among nations to establish preferential arrangements with selected trade partners, in order to avoid a situation where paying the MFN tariff is to be one of the least favoured nations. This situation has led to a third wave of regionalism, with several important countries actively pursuing a smorgasbord of new agreements with a variety of potential partners.

Australia–US agreement

We include this agreement as a special case. Typically it could be expected that the 'CNN motive', if it exists, would prevail only in the

---

[8] This claim is within the Latin American context. The United States and Canada had already negotiated transcontinental FTAs back in the 1980s and 1990s with Israel.
[9] As illustrated in Table 1.1, Chile and Bolivia had become associated members of MERCOSUR in the early and mid-1990s.

types of countries whose public spaces are adorned with portraits of their unelected leaders, rather than in liberal democracies. This is seemingly not the case, as the motivation for this agreement is widely acknowledged to be not a particularly good one for Australia, but the prime minister at the time is reported to have wanted an agreement, and hence one was signed.

6   Other factors explaining the growth in regionalism

That regionalism has grown is indisputable. Whether or not this is a good or bad thing for the multilateral trading system is the subject of many scholarly papers, and the arguments will not be rehearsed here. It is worth drawing attention to two numerical factors that help explain the growth in the number of trade agreements. First, over the period under consideration, the number of independent countries who are state actors and potentially eligible for membership of the GATT/WTO has grown from 70 in 1949 to 195 in 2008. An increase in the number of countries by a factor of less than three leads to an increase in the potential number of bilateral trade agreements by a factor of eight. Figure 1.1 illustrates the concurrence of the increase in the number of GATT/WTO members and new trade agreements. It is worth noting that the 1960s, which is the period corresponding to one of the peaks in regionalism in Figure 1.1, saw thirty-two African nations achieve independence; and that thirty-three countries have been created since 1990. Twenty of these were formed due to the break-up of the former Soviet Union (fifteen new countries in 1991) and the former Yugoslavia (five new countries in 1992). Many of these new nations have engaged in trade agreements with each other and with the EU, and this accounts for the second peak in Figure 1.1 in the 1990s.

Second, international trade has grown both in absolute terms and as a proportion of GDP. If there is more trade, then more trade agreements might be expected, both in number and in depth of coverage.

The third factor is the apparent simultaneity of expanding and deepening regionalism, and the development of the multilateral system. The explosion of regionalism in the second wave described above was not necessarily detrimental to the multilateral system, as had been feared during what turned out to be the closing years of the Uruguay Round. The Uruguay Round was concluded, with its achievement of the Single Undertaking, despite the NAFTA and the European single market.

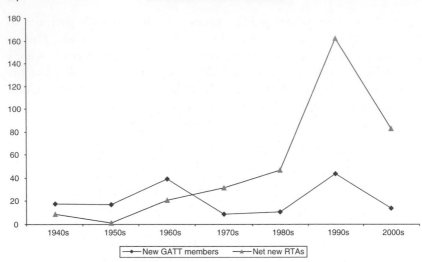

Figure 1.1 New GATT/WTO members and net new RTAs by decade
Source: Author's calculations based on Hufbauer dataset and information from WTO
website.

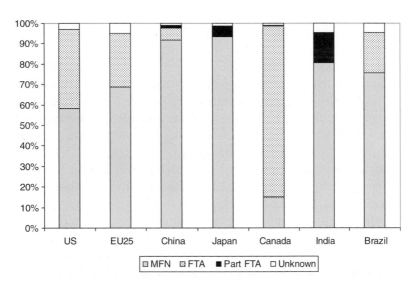

Figure 1.2 MFN and preferential treatment of exports, by exporter (selected
countries)
Source: Baldwin and Carpenter (2007).

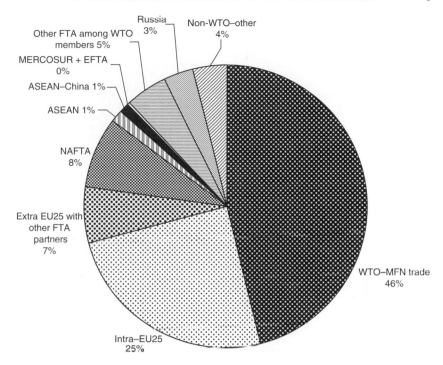

Figure 1.3 World trade by trade governance region
Source: Baldwin and Carpenter, 2007.

Finally, in assessing the importance of regionalism and its potential impact on the multilateral trading system, it is important to note that multilateralism is of primary importance to many of the key players. Figure 1.2 shows the proportion of exports that are subject to MFN rather than preferential tariffs at their destination markets for a selection of countries. For example, almost 60 per cent of US exports are subject to MFN tariffs. The proportion is even higher for exports from the EU to third countries. Only Canada enjoys preferential tariffs for the majority of its exports. Figure 1.3 illustrates that over 45 per cent of world trade is conducted with MFN tariffs. Figure 1.4 illustrates that almost 60 per cent of goods entering the EU do so under zero MFN tariffs; and that 21 per cent of goods, for which the MFN tariffs are greater than zero, are not the subject of any preferences. Together these illustrations demonstrate that multilateralism is still of considerable importance, and that as tariffs are eroded the value of preferences wanes.

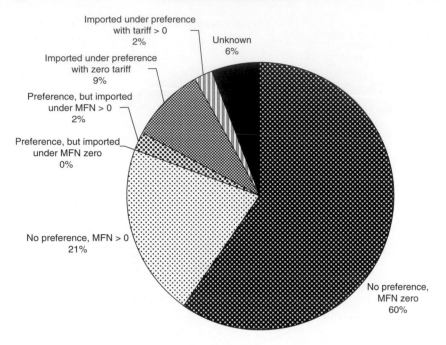

Figure 1.4 Imports to the EU by type of tariff
Source: Baldwin and Carpenter, 2007.

7   Lessons from history

Are there any lessons to be learned from the brief historical analysis that has been conducted in this chapter? We have seen that the motivations for regionalism are multilayered and complex. Only if the multilateral system can respond to satisfy these desires could the interest in regionalism be lessened. And, as noted above, regionalism shows no sign of abating; on the contrary, over 150 trade agreements are currently being proposed or negotiated.[10]

If there is something to learn, it is that a growth in regionalism appears to go hand in hand with developments in multilateralism. In

---

[10] Author's calculation, based on data gathered from national government websites in March 2008. This figure includes agreements being proposed or negotiated by the EU (twenty-nine); India (twenty-two); Republic of Korea (sixteen); China (fifteen); USA (thirteen); Australia (twelve); Japan (eleven); New Zealand (nine); Brazil (five); and other Asian countries (twenty-four).

fact the two elements of trade policy, incompatible as they may appear on the surface, have actually expanded simultaneously. It would seem, just as the spate of new agreements that were negotiated and concluded during the Uruguay Round did not prevent the successful conclusion of that Round, that it is unlikely that the current developments in regionalism will be a sticking point in any conclusion of the Doha Round.

References

Aggarwal, V. K. (2001) 'Economics: International Trade', in P. J. Simmons and C. Oudraat (eds.), *Managing Globalized Issues: Lessons Learned*, Washington DC: Carnegie Endowment for International Peace.

Baldwin, R. (1993) 'A Domino Theory of Regionalism', CEPR Discussion Papers 857, London: Centre for Economic Policy Research.

Baldwin, R. and Carpenter, T. (2007) 'Exploding the Myth of Exploding Regionalism', mimeo.

Baldwin, R. and Rieder, R. (2007) 'A Test of Endogenous Trade Bloc Formation Theory on EU Data', CEPR Discussion Papers 6389, London: Centre for Economic Policy Research.

Bhagwati, J. (1999) 'Regionalism and Multilateralism: An Overview', in J. Bhagwati, P. Krishna and A. Panagariya (eds.), *Trading Blocs: Alternative Approaches to Analyzing Preferential Trade Agreements*, Cambridge, MA: MIT Press.

Ethier, W. J. (1998) 'The New Regionalism', *The Economic Journal* 108 (449): 1149–61.

Finger, J. M. (1993) *Antidumping: How It Works and Who Gets Hurt*, Ann Arbor: University of Michigan Press.

First Warwick Commission (2007) *The Multilateral Trade Regime: Which Way Forward?*, University of Warwick.

Irwin, D. (1993) 'Multilateral and Bilateral Trade Polices in the World Trading System: An Historical Perspective', in J. de Melo and A. Panagariya (eds.), *New Dimensions in Regional Integration*, Cambridge: Cambridge University Press.

Jackson, J. H. 'Regional Trade Blocs and GATT', *The World Economy* 16: 121–31.

Lawrence, R. (1996) *Regionalism, Multilateralism and Deeper Integration*, Washington DC: Brookings Institution.

Pauwelyn, J. H.B. (2005) 'The Transformation of World Trade', *Michigan Law Review* 104: 1–66.

Salazar-Xirinachs, J. M. (2002) 'Proliferation of Sub-Regional Trade Agreements in the Americas: An Assessment of Key Analytical and Policy Issues', *Journal of Asian Economics* 13 (2): 181–212.

2

The landscape of regional trade agreements and WTO surveillance

ROBERTO V. FIORENTINO, JO-ANN CRAWFORD
AND CHRISTELLE TOQUEBOEUF

1 Introductory remarks[1]

Regional trade agreements (RTAs) have become so prominent in recent years that they permeate much of the discourse on international trade. The current scale of RTA proliferation is unprecedented both in quantitative and qualitative terms. A bewildering range of geographical configurations and varying policy content characterize the new agreements. This trend is likely to continue. The embrace of RTAs by virtually every trading nation carries systemic implications for the multilateral trading system, most notably through increased discrimination and complexity in trade relations and by undermining the transparency and predictability of trade relations.

Trends in the establishment and development of RTAs and the role of the WTO in relation to regionalism are the subject matter of this chapter. In the first section we look at the changing global landscape of RTAs. The aim is twofold: to provide an update of RTA developments and to draw out the main trends and characteristics of RTA proliferation through the inclusion of quantitative and qualitative indicators. The focus of the second section is on the role and functions of the WTO in respect of RTAs. Here we provide a historical account of the relationship between RTAs and the GATT/WTO and we look at how this

---

[1] This chapter has been prepared under the authors' own responsibility and without prejudice to the positions of WTO members and to their rights and obligations under the WTO Agreement. Figures, tables and geographical groupings included in this chapter do not imply any judgement on the part of the WTO as to the legal status or frontier of any territory. The authors are indebted to Clemens Boonekamp, Patrick Low, Rohini Acharya and colleagues in the Regional Trade Agreements Section of the Trade Policies Review Division for their helpful comments and suggestions on a previous draft.

relationship has evolved, in particular as a result of the Doha Development Agenda (DDA) negotiations on WTO rules and procedures in respect of RTAs. We conclude by providing a detailed overview of the new Transparency Mechanism for RTAs and offer some thoughts on the functioning of this Mechanism.

2   A kaleidoscope of regional trade agreements

Unless otherwise stated, the data presented here take account of all bilateral, regional, and plurilateral trade agreements of a preferential reciprocal nature that have been notified to the GATT/WTO. The primary focus is on free trade areas (FTAs) and customs unions (CUs) in the area of trade in goods, and economic integration agreements (EIAs) in the area of trade in services. Details on partial scope arrangements have been included where possible.[2] This part of the chapter draws heavily on previous surveys by the authors.[3]

The main trends and characteristics of RTAs

RTAs are not new as a concept and several integration schemes can be traced back to well before the establishment of the GATT. However, while past waves of regionalism were centred on a few RTAs, regionally based and limited to a handful of countries, today all but one WTO member (Mongolia) are engaged in negotiations of multiple RTAs with a variety of partners at the regional and extra-regional level. The growth and development of RTAs today is fast-paced, complex and global, and mapping RTAs has become an increasingly difficult task.

---

[2] The information gathered in this study is based on notifications to the WTO, RTA documentation submitted to the Committee on Regional Trade Agreements (CRTA), WTO accession documents, Trade Policy Reviews and other public sources. In this sense the information may not be exhaustive, since while it is possible to account accurately for all notified RTAs, for the non-notified RTAs, agreements under negotiation and those being proposed, information is often scarce or inconclusive.

[3] This chapter reproduces in part, updates and expands a previous survey by the authors, R. Fiorentino, L. Verdeja and C. Toqueboeuf (2007), 'The Changing Landscape of Regional Trade Agreements: 2006 Update', WTO Discussion Paper No. 12. This is itself an update of an earlier WTO Discussion Paper, J. Crawford and R. Fiorentino (2005), 'The Changing Landscape of Regional Trade Agreements', WTO Discussion Paper No. 8.

Quantifying the proliferation of RTAs

The most obvious trend observed over the last fifteen years is the ever-increasing number of RTAs. Between January and December 2007 a further eighteen notifications of RTAs were made to the WTO, raising the total number of notified RTAs in force to 197. A large number of other agreements are at different levels of implementation though not yet notified, under negotiation or at the proposal stage.

WTO statistics tend to overstate the total number of RTAs since they are based on notification requirements that do not reflect the physical number of RTAs.[4] On the other hand, to focus on the 'actual' number of agreements results in non-exhaustive and inaccurate figures since it is practically impossible to verify data for the many RTAs that have either not yet been notified or are at different phases of implementation. Irrespective of the methodology, however, the degree of RTA proliferation is not difficult to discern. The following three figures substantiate this observation.

Figure 2.1 lists the total number of RTAs notified over time to the GATT/WTO. As of December 2007 the figure was 386 RTAs, of which 197 are currently in force. We should note that a net reduction in the total number of RTAs does not necessarily imply a reduction in the global volume of preferential trade nor a decline in the trend of RTA expansion. Indeed, the two significant drops in the total number of RTAs shown in Figure 2.1 are both due to the consolidation of RTA networks in the European region – the first in 2004 resulting from the enlargement of the European Communities (EC) from fifteen to twenty-five members and the corresponding repeal of sixty-five RTAs, and the second in 2007 resulting from the EC enlargement to twenty-seven members and the consolidation of the RTA network among countries of the Balkans in an enlarged CEFTA.[5] Thus the net reduction in the total number of RTAs in Figure 2.1 must be read as an expansion of existing RTAs rather than a slowdown in the trend of RTA formation.

---

[4] RTA notifications to the WTO include those made under GATT Article XXIV, GATS Article V, the Enabling Clause, as well as accessions to existing RTAs; it should be noted that the notification requirements contained in WTO provisions require that RTAs covering trade in goods and services be notified separately. For a complete list of RTAs notified and in force to the GATT/WTO see www.wto.org/english/tratop_e/region_e/regfac_e.htm.

[5] See the section in this chapter on Europe for further explanation, and the list of acronyms in Table 2.2.

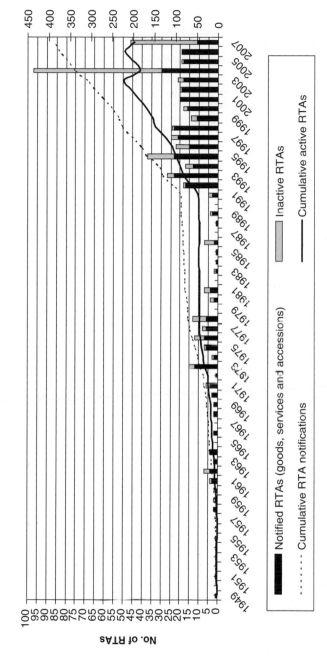

Figure 2.1 All RTAs notified to the GATT/WTO (1948–2007) by year of entry into force

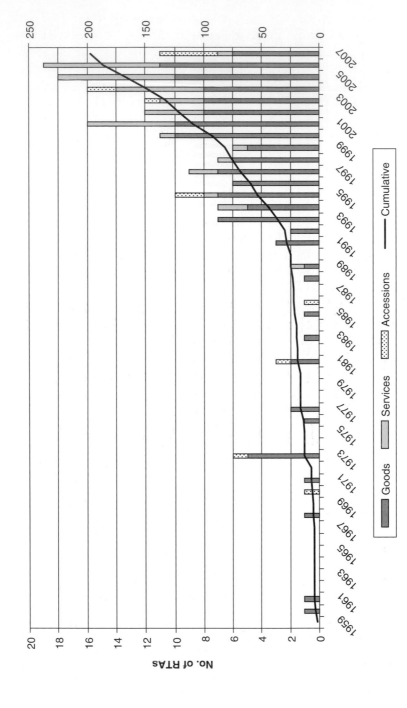

Figure 2.2 RTAs notified to the GATT/WTO (1948–2007) in force, by year of entry into force

Figure 2.2 breaks down the number of RTAs notified and in force by type of notification, thus allowing us to differentiate between the number of actual agreements and RTA notifications.[6] Out of the total, 138 RTAs cover trade in goods, 47 cover trade in services, and the remaining 12 are accessions to existing RTAs, involving either goods or services. The relevance of EIAs has continued to grow in 2007, currently representing 25 per cent of total notifications of RTAs. Their significance is likely to increase further in the future if we consider that approximately 70 per cent of the RTAs being negotiated contain provisions on trade in services.

Figure 2.3 looks at RTA proliferation on a chronological basis by differentiating between two time periods, the GATT and the WTO years. The latter is the period we associate with the current wave of RTAs, and indeed the figure indicates a large increase in RTA activity over this period. Of the total number of RTAs notified to the GATT/WTO up to December 2007, 124 agreements were notified during the GATT years and 262 during the WTO years, corresponding to an annual average RTA notification rate of twenty for the WTO years compared to less than three during the four and half decades of the GATT. Also significant is the fact that of the RTAs notified to the GATT, only thirty-one remain in force today, reflecting in most cases the evolution over time of the agreements themselves, as they were superseded by new ones between the same signatories (most often with deeper integration), or by their consolidation into wider groupings.

Taken together, Figures 2.1, 2.2 and 2.3 leave us in no doubt as to the unprecedented scale of RTA expansion since the early 1990s. The magnitude of the phenomenon is even more significant if we consider the number of RTAs in force but not yet notified (approximately seventy), those signed but not yet in force (approximately thirty), and the RTAs currently being negotiated (approximately seventy). If all of these agreements are implemented by 2010 we will be looking at a global landscape of 350 or more agreements.[7]

---

[6] The total number of notified RTAs in force minus EIAs in services and accessions to existing RTAs gives us the number of physical agreements, i.e. 138 agreements.

[7] Not every RTA under negotiation will automatically increase the number of RTAs in force, given that some will supersede or expand existing RTAs. It should be noted that the conclusion of these agreements may actually result in a net reduction in terms of the total number of RTAs in force due to the consolidation effect that some of these agreements may have. Besides the case of the EC enlargement mentioned earlier, this pattern may also be observed in Latin America where FTAs currently under negotiation should replace and consolidate a myriad of bilateral partial scope agreements.

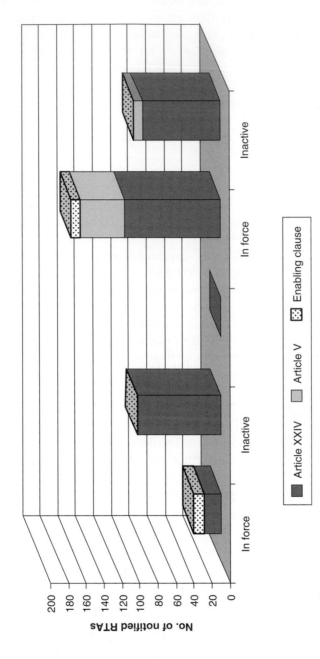

Figure 2.3 RTAs notified to the GATT/WTO (pre-1995) and WTO (post-1995)

Table 2.1. *Notified RTAs in goods and services by date of entry into force and type of partner, as of December 2007*

Year range	Developed only		Developed–Developing		Developing only		Total	
	Goods	Services	Goods	Services	Goods	Services	Goods	Services
1958–1964	2	1			1		3	1
1965–1969					1		1	0
1970–1974	5		1		2		8	0
1975–1979			2		1		3	0
1980–1984	2		1		1		4	0
1985–1989	1	1	1		2		4	1
1990–1994	7	1	3	1	7		17	2
1995–1999	16	1	7	1	7	4	30	6
2000–2003	2	1	19	7	18	6	39	14
2004–2007	3	3	20	15	15	8	38	26
Total	38	8	54	24	55	18	147	50
	46		78		73		197	

Qualifying the proliferation of RTAs

The second trend discernable from the current wave of RTAs relates to the geopolitics of such agreements and more precisely to the choice of preferential partners. RTAs appear to be changing established patterns of trade both in terms of choice of partners and the regimes governing such trade. RTA dynamics over the last fifteen years point to an increase in North–South RTAs and their gradual replacement of long-established non-reciprocal systems of preferences, and more recently to an increasing number of South–South RTAs – a development that appears to be tied to the emergence of several major RTA hubs in the developing world. Table 2.1 shows a breakdown of RTAs notified and in force by type of partner on a chronological basis. This may be an indication of evolving trade patterns, although further empirical research is needed to substantiate any claims along these lines.

Table 2.1 reveals significant trends. The major clusters of RTAs are North–South and South–South RTAs, each accounting for 37 per cent of the total number of notified RTAs in goods (see Figure 2.4). Significantly, most of the agreements falling under these two categories are recent; as shown in Table 2.1, of the fifty-four North–South RTAs and the fifty-five South–South RTAs, forty-six and forty agreements respectively date to 1995 or later. These two clusters combined represent over 80 per cent of the total number of agreements that have entered into force since 1995. These agreements are therefore the backbone of today's RTA proliferation and are likely to remain so if we consider that 97 per cent of the RTAs in the making fall under these two categories (see Figure 2.5).

These developments are significant in a number of ways. With respect to the North–South cluster, the forging of such agreements implies, for most developing country partners, foregoing non-reciprocal systems of preferences under schemes like the Generalized System of Preferences (GSP) and other unilateral initiatives covered by WTO waivers in favour of reciprocal trade regimes. This is required by the WTO provisions applying to RTAs.[8] For those developing countries benefiting from WTO waivers, such as the one covering the Cotonou Agreement, this

---

[8] Given that the legal cover of the Enabling Clause only applies to preferential agreements concluded among developing countries, RTAs in goods involving developed and developing WTO members may only fall under GATT Article XXIV and therefore are subject to the requirements contained therein.

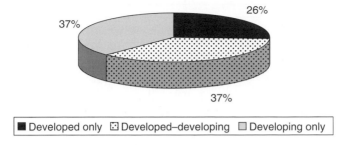

Figure 2.4 Notified RTAs (goods) in force by type of partner, as of December 2007

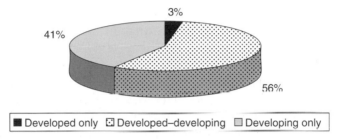

Figure 2.5 RTAs signed and under negotiation by type of partner, as of December 2007

transition is in part driven by compatibility requirements with WTO rules. In other cases the choice is based on a conscious trade policy strategy underpinned by domestic reforms and trade liberalization at the bilateral and multilateral level. Regardless of the motivations, the point is that, through RTAs, the nature of North–South trade relations appears to be evolving towards a framework of reciprocity with relatively ambitious scope in trade policy coverage. In this respect it is interesting to note that approximately half of the notified North–South RTAs provide for the liberalization of trade in services and most of the others foresee the negotiation of a services chapter in the future.

Another significant development is the rapid emergence of a South–South cluster of RTAs which is substantially different from the early agreements falling under this category. The latter typically consisted of plurilateral integration initiatives at the regional level, often with limited trade coverage (i.e. partial scope agreements); most RTA groupings in

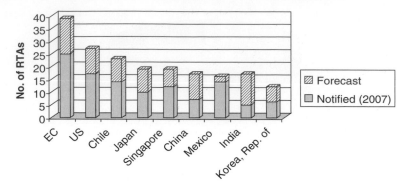

Figure 2.6 Number of RTAs in force, signed and under negotiation by selected countries

Africa and Latin America can be placed here. Recent RTAs, however, suggest a departure from past practice, with the emergence of comprehensive agreements (several RTAs include a services chapter), often on a bilateral basis and in several cases not geographically bound – RTAs such as Republic of Korea–Chile, India–Singapore, and Chile–China are good examples. The trade policy scope of these agreements and the fact that several of them have been notified under Article XXIV of the GATT 1994 (and Article V of the GATS where it applies) points to a growing interest in South–South trade and a readiness by some of these countries to commit to comprehensive trade liberalization, albeit on a gradual basis and with a selected number of partners.

Also related to these clusters is the emergence of several RTA hubs. While in Europe and North America these are well established (i.e. the European Communities and the United States), in other continents, and especially in the Asia-Pacific region, the competition for RTA 'shopping' appears to be wide open. Figure 2.6 lists current and future RTAs for selected WTO members.

A third trend which is closely related to the geopolitics of RTAs referred to above is the increasing number of cross-regional agreements. These represent the most distinctive feature of the current proliferation of RTAs since they suggest a shift from the traditional concept of regional integration among neighbouring countries – a core element of previous RTAs waves – to preferential partnerships driven by strategic political and economic considerations that are to a large extent unrelated to regional dynamics. Figure 2.7 shows the scale of this development. While 44 per cent of the RTAs notified and in force are

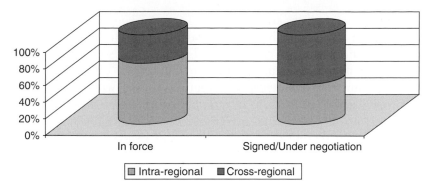

Figure 2.7 Cross-regional RTAs, as percentage of total RTAs, and intra-regional, as of December 2007

cross-regional, this figure increases to 67 per cent for the agreements signed and under negotiation.[9]

The trend towards cross-regional RTAs raises some interesting questions and makes us ponder to what extent the premise of RTA formation among 'natural' trading partners still applies. The data in the figure would confirm that RTAs have traditionally been agreed among geographically contiguous countries with already well-established trading patterns; prime examples include the NAFTA in North America, the EC and EFTA in Europe, ASEAN and SAFTA in Asia, UEMOA, SADC and SACU in sub-Saharan African, and CARICOM, the CACM and MERCOSUR in South and Central America and the Caribbean.[10] All of these, as well as most of the other existing regional groupings, have their origins in former waves of regionalism and to this day efforts are ongoing to deepen and strengthen intra-regional integration.

Thus, cross-regional RTAs could be seen as a drive to look further afield once more local regional prospects have been exhausted. This impression is borne out by some of the other RTA indicators explored below, which reveal a predominance of bilateral as opposed to plurilateral

[9] The definition of geographical groupings in this chapter reflects that used in the WTO International Trade Statistics Report (2007). Accordingly the term 'cross-regional' refers to those RTAs concluded among countries from the following regions: North America, South and Central America and the Caribbean, Europe, the Commonwealth of Independent States (CIS), Africa, the Middle East, and Asia. For the list of countries falling under each of these regions, see WTO International Trade Statistics Report (2007).

[10] For the full title and membership to these and other RTAs referred to in this chapter see the list of acronyms in Table 2.2.

initiatives. The former are typically FTAs as opposed to the more cumbersome and regionally based customs unions. However, the sharp increase in the number of cross-regional RTAs may also indicate a shift from regional priorities due to frustration in several cases at the slow pace of existing regional integration initiatives. Indeed, with the exception of Europe where the process of integration is firmly rooted in the EC, all other regions manifest growing asymmetries between regional integration processes and the scope and depth of the cross-regional RTAs to which individual countries are parties. This is especially the case with regional integration schemes among developing countries, since these are often less comprehensive in terms of trade liberalization and coverage of trade-related areas than those found in cross-regional, and particularly North–South, RTAs. In this sense and perhaps as a further facet of globalization, RTAs have broadened their *raison d'être* and are being used as tools to overcome regional constraints and open new trade opportunities in the global market.

Another significant aspect of this proliferation is the evolving configuration of RTAs. Figure 2.8 indicates a decreasing propensity for plurilateral RTAs and a net increase in the number of bilateral RTAs. With a few exceptions, the bulk of RTAs in the making are based on bilateral RTA configurations rather than plurilateral RTAs. Bilateral agreements account for 76 per cent of all RTAs notified and in force, and 93 per cent of those signed and under negotiation.[11]

This preponderance of bilateral configurations has several explanations. From a geopolitical perspective, the opportunities for region-wide RTAs are fewer, since, as argued earlier, many of these agreements have already been established during past waves of regionalism. New initiatives either revamp existing regional schemes (i.e. SAPTA to SAFTA) or consolidate such schemes into broader integration arrangements. Another reason for an increase in bilateral RTAs is the apparent shift from using RTAs as instruments of regional integration to vehicles for strategic market access. The latter tendency strengthens the drive for bilateral RTAs, especially in the case of cross-regional RTAs.[12] Finally,

---

[11] Bilateral agreements may include more than two countries when one of them is itself an RTA (e.g. EC (27)–Turkey (1) is a two-party RTA comprising twenty-eight countries). A plurilateral agreement refers to an RTA in which the constituent parties exceed two countries (e.g. EFTA, MERCOSUR, AFTA, SADC).

[12] The majority of cross-regional RTAs are bilateral agreements, i.e. two parties (see note 13). One exception is the Trans-Pacific Strategic Economic Partnership (SEP-4) between Brunei, Chile, New Zealand and Singapore.

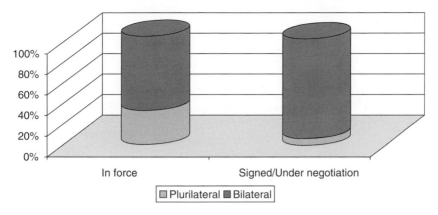

Figure 2.8 RTA configurations as of December 2007

some cross-regional RTAs can best be understood in predominantly political terms, but this aspect of preferential trade arrangements is beyond the analytical reach of the present chapter.

A related development is the emergence of atypical RTA configurations. The simple bilateral (i.e. two countries) and plurilateral configurations are being supplemented by agreements in which one of the parties is itself an RTA. Such agreements have been in the making for some time and their number is increasing. Another emerging pattern involves bilateral RTAs where each party is a distinct RTA. The advent of such agreements points to a consolidation of established trading relationships. But the fact that several such agreements have been under negotiation for numerous years and that none, thus far, has entered into force underscores the complexity of such negotiations.[13]

Another characteristic of the proliferation of RTAs is revealed by distinguishing among FTAs, CUs and partial scope agreements. Figure 2.9 categorizes RTAs in force along these lines and Figure 2.10 focuses on RTAs signed or under negotiation but not yet in force and/or notified to the WTO. The data show that FTAs account for 82 per cent of all

---

[13] Examples include EC–MERCOSUR, EC–GCC. Prospective ones may include EC–ASEAN and EC–CAN. One such agreement between EFTA and SACU was signed between late June and early July 2006, but according to available information is not yet in force. Another such agreement is the one between SACU and MERCOSUR, which was signed in December 2004; however, the limited scope of the agreement prompted a reopening of negotiations, which are currently underway.

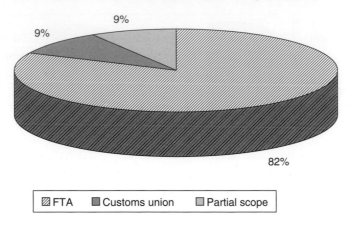

Figure 2.9 Notified RTAs in force as of December 2007, by type of agreement

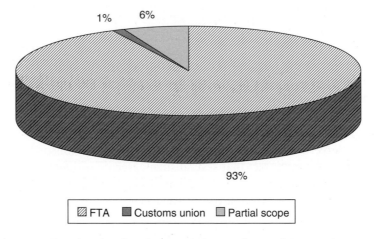

Figure 2.10 RTAs signed and under negotiation as of December 2007, by type of agreement

RTAs notified and in force, while partial scope agreements and CUs each account for 9 per cent. Of the projected RTAs, 93 per cent are intended to be FTAs, 6 per cent partial scope agreements and only 1 per cent CUs.

The preference for FTAs is a reflection of the defining characteristics of the current RTA race. Key attributes of the proliferation appear to be speed, flexibility and selectivity, and the FTA is, in most cases, the configuration that best meets these needs. Although the negotiation of an FTA may take years to conclude,[14] evidence suggests that the time from the launching of negotiations to their conclusion has been shrinking in recent years, especially for agreements among like-minded countries.[15]

Customs unions involve a higher degree of commitment and coordination, not least because of the establishment of a common external trade policy as opposed to reliance on rules of origin that define the preferential trading area. In addition, CUs often aspire to reach beyond the realm of trade, to include such features as political integration, economic and monetary union, and supranational institutions. Moreover, to the best of our knowledge, all CUs are among contiguous countries. Finally, while the parties to an FTA have, in principle, full flexibility with regard to their individual choice of future FTA partners,[16] participation in a CU, if played by the rules, limits the individual parties' choice of future RTA partners, since a proper functioning of the union requires that any agreement with a third party includes the CU as a whole.[17] In the current trading climate of demand for flexible and speedy RTAs, the preference for FTAs over CUs is easily explained.[18]

---

[14] An example of protracted negotiations is the FTA between the EC and MERCOSUR which has not yet been concluded after ten years. It should also be noted that these are complex negotiations involving two CUs.

[15] A case in point is the FTA between the EFTA states and the Republic of Korea which took one year to negotiate after only four rounds of negotiations.

[16] Some limitations may apply in the form of an MFN clause whereby parties to the agreement commit to extending to each other any more favourable treatment that they may grant to a third party in a future agreement. Some geographically bound FTAs also show a propensity to negotiate agreements with common parties. Examples would include the EFTA states, Australia and New Zealand and ASEAN members. However, we should be careful in making any generalizations since many other agreements do not contain such features.

[17] The requirement in a CU of a common external tariff and harmonization of the parties' commercial policies does not in principle allow a 'go alone' policy whereby one party negotiates a preferential agreement with a third party. Such a situation would disrupt the functioning of the CU, since products from the third party could enter the union at a preferential rate through the bilateral RTA, implying a loss of tariff revenues for the other members of the union. Examples of such a situation include SACU (the FTA between the EC and South Africa) and the GCC (the FTA between the United States and Bahrain).

[18] It is interesting to note that the current predominance of FTAs over CUs does not appear to reflect the original spirit of the multilateral trading rules. A perusal of the drafting history of Article XXIV of the GATT (which contains the legal provisions for the conclusion of FTAs, CUs and interim agreements leading to the formation of FTAs or CUs) reveals that it was not until the Havana Charter that provisions for the formation of FTAs were included in what became GATT Article XXIV. The previous charters only spoke of CUs and interim agreements leading to the formation of CUs.

As for partial scope agreements, their limited trade coverage, poor implementation record, and limitations with respect to the choice of partners due to WTO rules,[19] makes them less attractive to countries that are committed to comprehensive trade liberalization. Nevertheless, we may see a slight increase in the number of partial scope agreements due to a novel approach to RTAs being employed by several large developing countries in South–South agreements. Several of these agreements are based on a staged approach to trade liberalization whereby a framework agreement is signed that entails as a first step the conclusion of a partial scope agreement, often accompanied by an 'early harvest programme', and as a second step a commitment to future FTA negotiations.[20]

The global landscape of RTAs: state of play and future developments

The proliferation of RTAs can be associated with a combination of geopolitical developments dating back to the late 1980s and early 1990s. The most important include multilateral and regional dynamics as well as individual countries' policy choices. At the multilateral level, the protracted Uruguay Round (1986–94) had prompted several countries to pursue preferential deals as an insurance against an eventual failure of the multilateral trade negotiations. At the regional level the fragmentation of the former Soviet Union and the disbanding of the Council for Mutual Economic Assistance (COMECON) generated a new cluster of RTAs between transition economies and the EC and EFTA states as well

---

This suggests that the perception of regional economic integration, and the means to achieve it that the drafters of Article XXIV had in mind, were not likely to be along the lines of the proliferation of FTAs that we are witnessing today. It is also interesting to speculate how different the current landscape of RTAs would be if the provisions of GATT Article XXIV only applied to CUs with no related provision for the formation of FTAs.

[19] Under the WTO, the only legal provision applicable to a North–South RTA covering trade in goods is Article XXIV of the GATT 1994. This provision provides among other requirements a comprehensive trade liberalization schedule based on tariff elimination. Partial scope agreements providing for reduction and/or elimination of duties on a limited number of products are unlikely to be found compatible with such provision. Partial scope agreements are allowed under paragraph 2(c) of the Enabling Clause; however, the recourse to such a provision is only available to developing country members.

[20] Examples of such agreements include the recently notified China–ASEAN agreement and many of the RTAs being negotiated by India.

as among transition economies themselves.[21] At the country level, the predominance of Europe in RTAs began to be challenged by the RTA policy of countries that had traditionally been less enthusiastic about such preferential agreements. In the 1990s we saw the establishment of NAFTA, MERCOSUR and AFTA which had a domino effect on other countries' decisions to pursue RTAs. We also saw the emergence of a policy of 'additive regionalism' whereby countries such as Chile, Mexico and Singapore began to forge preferential relationships with their major trading partners. Albeit sporadic in their manifestation, these combined developments have sowed the seeds for the surge in RTAs that we are witnessing today.

More significantly, this process of action–reaction, whereby the creation of discriminatory arrangements by one country is matched by an equal reaction (often defensive) by other countries, seems to have become irreversible, almost as if RTA proliferation has reached a critical point from which there is no turning back. These layers of discriminatory treatment have flourished under a multilateral framework of laws and regulations (GATT and now WTO) that is underpinned by the fundamental principle of non-discrimination. While the propensity to enter into RTAs may increase at times when the WTO is not making much progress on the multilateral agenda, a question beyond the scope of this chapter is whether regional or selective approaches to trade relations are simply an inevitable accompaniment of multilateralism in an increasingly globalized world. The sections below map developments in regionalism in different areas of the world.

Europe

Europe is the region with the largest number of RTAs, accounting for a large share of the agreements in force and notified to the WTO. The main regional groupings are the EC and the EFTA states. South-eastern Europe has recently become the third European trading group, having consolidated the network of bilateral FTAs negotiated under the auspices of the Stability Pact into a plurilateral agreement termed CEFTA plus.[22] Existing ties between this sub-region and the EC are being

---

[21] Transition economies include the countries of the former Soviet Union, Eastern and Central Europe, the Baltic States and the Balkans.

[22] The official name of the agreement is the 'Agreement on Amendment of and Accession to the Central European Free Trade Agreement (CEFTA 2006)'; (see list of acronyms in Table 2.2 for membership of the agreement).

further institutionalized. EC accession negotiations are continuing with Croatia and Turkey,[23] and a Stability and Association Agreement (SAA) between the EC and Serbia and Montenegro is in progress.[24] The year 2007 saw further consolidation of the existing intra-European RTA networks. In addition to the CEFTA plus, the other major event was the enlargement of the EC from twenty-five to twenty-seven members with the accession of Romania and Bulgaria.[25] Future intra-European RTA initiatives will include FTA negotiations between the EC and Ukraine, once the latter has acceded to the WTO.

In the Mediterranean basin, the EC and its Mediterranean partners are working towards the establishment of a Euro-Mediterranean FTA by 2010. This is set to become one of the world's biggest marketplaces, grouping as many as forty countries (including the EFTA) under a free trade area.[26] The EC has so far signed EuroMed Association Agreements with all the Mediterranean partners,[27] and the EFTA states and Turkey, by virtue of their association with the EC, are following suit.[28] The EuroMed FTA, once completed, will provide for diagonal cumulation of origin among the EC, the EFTA states, Turkey, the Faroe Islands and the Mediterranean countries; a PanEuroMed Protocol on cumulation of origin has been adopted for this purpose. Other EC initiatives under the EuroMed framework include liberalization of trade in services and investment,[29] deepening agricultural liberalization, regulatory convergence, and a strengthening of the legal and institutional framework.

---

[23] The Former Yugoslav Republic of Macedonia (FYROM) is also a candidate country, but accession negotiations have yet to begin.

[24] In the sub-region, the EC has SAAs with Albania, Croatia, FYROM and Montenegro, and it is negotiating one with Bosnia-Herzegovina.

[25] As a result of these two consolidations, thirty-five notified RTAs have been repealed, which explains the net reduction in total number of notified RTAs registered in 2007. See WTO Documents WT/REG/GEN/N/5 for CEFTA and WT/REG/GEN/N/4 for EC enlargement.

[26] The Mediterranean partners are Algeria, Egypt, Israel, Jordan, Lebanon, Morocco, the Palestinian Authority, Syria, Tunisia and Turkey.

[27] The Association Agreement with Syria has yet to enter into force.

[28] The EFTA states have FTAs with all the EuroMed partners except Algeria (although FTA negotiations were launched in November 2007) and Syria. As for Turkey, it has FTAs with all the EuroMed partners except Algeria, Jordan and Lebanon, with whom it is currently negotiating.

[29] At the sixth EuroMed Trade Ministerial Conference in October 2007, Israel, Morocco and Jordan accepted the EC's invitation to launch services negotiations.

Beyond its immediate neighbourhood, the EC has ongoing FTA negotiations with MERCOSUR and the GCC. In 2007, the European Commission was given a negotiating mandate for a new generation of FTAs with the Republic of Korea, India and ASEAN. Negotiations with each of these parties were launched between May and June 2007. As for the much talked-about EC–ACP Economic Partnership Agreements (EPAs),[30] the EC had to downscale its ambition for comprehensive EPAs by 31 December 2007 and settle for interim market access arrangements designed primarily to safeguard Cotonou trade preferences for non-LDCs in the absence of the WTO waiver. On 20 December 2007, the EC adopted a market access regulation to grant duty- and quota-free access to the EC market for ACP countries from 1 January 2008, with transition periods for sugar and rice. This applies to those ACP countries that have concluded negotiations on agreements establishing or leading to the establishment of EPAs.[31] Countries that have neither initialled an agreement nor have access to the Everything But Arms (EBA) regime for LDCs are expected to export to the EC under the GSP regime.[32]

As for the EFTA states, in 2007 they successfully concluded nine years of FTA negotiations with Canada, and launched FTA negotiations with Colombia and Peru in addition to the ongoing negotiations with the GCC and Thailand. An FTA with India also seems to be on the agenda. An interesting development in 2007 was Switzerland's decision to break ranks with its EFTA partners and launch negotiations for a comprehensive economic partnership agreement with Japan, which is Switzerland's third-largest trading partner after the EC and the United States.

The Americas

The western hemisphere continued to be a major zone of RTA activity in 2007. The United States has concluded and implemented ten FTAs

---

[30] The EC is negotiating with seven different groups of ACP countries: ECOWAS plus Mauritania; CEMAC plus DRC and Sao Tomé and Principe; the East African Community (EAC); East and Southern Africa (ESA); the SADC group; the CARIFORUM (CARICOM plus Dominican Republic) and the Pacific Islands.

[31] At the current state of negotiations, the Caribbean is the only region that has initialled a full EPA covering both goods and services. See http://ec.europa.eu/trade/issues/bilateral/regions/acp/index_en.htm for further information on the EPA process and status.

[32] As of 20 December 2007, these are Nigeria, Republic of the Congo, Gabon, and the following Pacific countries: Cook Islands, Federated States of Micronesia, Nauru, Niue, Palau, Marshall Islands and Tonga. South Africa will export under the Trade, Development and Cooperation Agreement (TDCA).

since 2004 and its RTA network is further expanding.[33] The United States is reputedly negotiating FTAs with Malaysia, Thailand, SACU and the United Arab Emirates.[34] It has an FTA with Oman which is pending implementation and four more pending congressional approval. These are the FTAs with Peru, Colombia, Panama and the Republic of Korea.[35] Canada, like the United States, has intensified its focus on RTAs in recent years.[36] The year 2007 saw the conclusion of longstanding FTA negotiations with the EFTA states and the launch of FTA negotiations with Colombia, Peru and the Dominican Republic. These are in addition to its ongoing FTA negotiations with the Central America Four,[37] Singapore and the Republic of Korea. A feasibility study is underway for an FTA with Jordan.

Mexico's participation in RTAs is longstanding and the country currently has twelve FTAs covering forty-six preferential partners (counting EC-27 and EFTA-4) across the Americas, Asia and Europe.[38] With a view to expanding its RTA network further, Mexico is currently negotiating FTAs with the Republic of Korea and with Singapore.

The RTA landscape in Central and Latin America is a prime example of a spaghetti bowl of preferential agreements. The region has four CUs at various stages of implementation (CACM in Central America, CARICOM in the Caribbean, CAN and MERCOSUR in Latin America), a Latin America integration framework (LAIA/ALADI) which aims at a region-wide common market,[39] and a myriad of bilateral agreements with intra-regional and extra-regional partners. In Central America the members of CACM, in addition to their CUs, have concluded FTAs with Chile, Mexico and the United States, and are negotiating with Canada and Panama. As for Panama, it has FTAs in force with Singapore and

---

[33] These are FTAs with Chile, Singapore, Australia, Morocco, CAFTA-DR (see list of acronyms in Table 2.2 – the agreement has not yet entered into force for Costa Rica) and Bahrain. Furthermore, the United States has earlier FTAs with Israel and Jordan and with Canada and Mexico as a party to the NAFTA.

[34] The FTA negotiations with Ecuador have been suspended for the time being.

[35] All of these FTAs have been amended by including provisions on labour, the environment, and other trade matters to reflect the bipartisan trade agreement reached in May 2007 between the Administration and the Congressional leadership.

[36] To date, Canada has relatively few RTAs. These are with Costa Rica, Chile, Israel and the United States and Mexico as a party to NAFTA.

[37] El Salvador, Guatemala, Honduras, Nicaragua.

[38] In addition, Mexico is a party to the LAIA, the GSTP and the PTN.

[39] ALADI has twelve members (see list of acronyms in Table 2.2). ALADI promotes trade liberalization through regional and partial scope agreements.

Chinese Taipei, has signed FTAs with the United States and with Chile, and is considering an FTA with MERCOSUR. In the Caribbean, in addition to its FTAs with Costa Rica and the Dominican Republic, CARICOM is negotiating an FTA with Canada and is considering a further one with MERCOSUR.

Further south, the Andean Community members, while working as a group towards an FTA with MERCOSUR, are pursuing several other FTAs on an individual basis. Peru has signed FTAs with the United States, Chile and Thailand,[40] and is negotiating FTAs with Canada, China, the EFTA states and Singapore. Colombia, for its part, has signed FTAs with Chile and the United States and is negotiating with EFTA. Ecuador is negotiating an FTA with Chile. MERCOSUR has signed several framework agreements aimed at the establishment of FTAs, but to date they do not appear to have led to any concrete outcome.[41] MERCOSUR's only ongoing FTA negotiation is with the EC. In 2007, Chile notified FTAs with Japan and China, and with New Zealand, Brunei and Singapore as parties to the Trans-Pacific Strategic Economic Partnership (SEP-4). It approved its partial scope agreement with India, launched FTA negotiations with Australia and Malaysia, and concluded a feasibility study for an FTA with Turkey, while the FTA negotiation with Thailand is ongoing.[42]

Asia-Pacific

Countries in the Asia-Pacific region are consolidating their drive towards regionalism at an accelerated pace. Historical reservations about RTAs have long gone and a network of regional and cross-regional RTAs is clearly emerging. Notwithstanding the existence of sub-regional groupings,[43] most of the RTAs being created are bilateral, with some instances of collective RTA negotiations, mainly involving ASEAN. As a result, overlapping memberships are on the increase and so is

---

[40] Peru and Thailand have signed an early harvest agreement with a view to signing a fully fledged FTA.

[41] The countries concerned are Egypt (2004), the GCC (2005), India (2004), Morocco (2004) and SACU. MERCOSUR has engaged in negotiations with SACU, but it appears that the last round was held in 2006.

[42] In addition, Chile has FTAs with CACM, Canada, the EFTA states, the EC, Republic of Korea, Mexico and the United States. It has several more RTAs under the ALADI framework.

[43] In Asia these include ASEAN, APTA (formerly the Bangkok Agreement), and the South Asian Association for Regional Cooperation (SAARC). In the Pacific they include the CER between Australia and New Zealand, and the Pacific Islands Forum.

the complexity of intra-regional trade relations.[44] Rationalization of these bilateral relationships into region-wide integration schemes is, however, on the agenda, with several initiatives being either pursued (ASEAN+3)[45] or suggested.[46]

East Asia features some of the most notable RTA developments in recent years. Japan is a newcomer on the RTA scene, having notified its first FTA in late 2002. Since then it has notified five FTAs, signed two and is negotiating a further eight. In 2007 alone, Japan launched FTA negotiations with Australia, India, Switzerland and Viet Nam.[47] The Republic of Korea has not been idle either, having signed a major FTA with the United States in 2007, and launched FTA negotiations with the EC and feasibility studies for FTAs with Australia, China, MERCOSUR and New Zealand.[48] As for China, it has notified five FTAs since 2003 and has recently concluded one with Pakistan. Furthermore, it has ongoing FTA negotiations with five partners and is considering two more with India and the Republic of Korea.[49] Chinese Taipei is also further expanding its FTA network, having signed FTAs with several Central America countries.[50]

South-East Asia is also proving to be a major RTA negotiating theatre both at the regional and extra-regional level. ASEAN members are working towards the creation of an East Asian Economic Community by 2015, which aims to form a single market with the progressive

---

[44] Examples include APTA and BIMSTEC (Bangladesh, Bhutan, India, Myanmar, Nepal, Sri Lanka and Thailand), both of which include countries that are members of ASEAN and SAFTA.

[45] The ASEAN + China, Republic of Korea and Japan process was institutionalized in 1999 at the ASEAN+3 Summit held in Manila. The process aims to strengthen and deepen East Asian cooperation and foresees the establishment of a region-wide FTA. In this regard, ASEAN has already concluded an FTA with China and is negotiating one with Japan and one with the Republic of Korea.

[46] Japan has proposed a Comprehensive Economic Partnership for East Asia (CEPEA) which adds India, Australia and New Zealand to ASEAN+3. A similar proposal has been made by India under the name of the 'Pan-Asia Free Trade Area'.

[47] Japan has FTAs with Chile, Malaysia, Mexico, Singapore and Thailand, two signed FTAs with Brunei and the Philippines, and ongoing FTA negotiations with ASEAN, the GCC, Republic of Korea, and Indonesia, in addition to those mentioned above.

[48] In addition the Republic of Korea has FTAs with Chile, the EFTA states and Singapore and ongoing FTA negotiations with ASEAN, Canada, India, Japan, and Mexico.

[49] China is a member of APTA and it has FTAs with Hong Kong, China; Macao, China; ASEAN; Chile; and Pakistan. It is negotiating FTAs with the GCC, Singapore, Australia, New Zealand and Iceland.

[50] These are El Salvador, Honduras, Guatemala, Nicaragua and Panama.

elimination of tariff and non-tariff barriers, liberalization of services and investment, and free movement of professionals. In addition, ASEAN is negotiating FTAs with its major trading partners. Besides its notified agreement with China, FTA negotiations are under way with Australia, New Zealand, the Republic of Korea, Japan, India and the EC. At the same time, some ASEAN members are further pursuing their own bilateral initiatives. Singapore is party to eleven FTAs and is negotiating a further seven.[51] Malaysia has an FTA with Japan and a partial scope agreement with Pakistan; it is negotiating with Australia, New Zealand and the United States, and is conducting a feasibility study with India. As for Thailand, in addition to its FTAs with Australia, New Zealand and Japan, it is negotiating FTAs with Bahrain, the EFTA states, India, Peru and the United States, and is considering several others.[52]

In South Asia, RTA initiatives have traditionally been limited to the region's immediate neighbourhood in the form of SAFTA and a few partial scope agreements. In recent years, however, Pakistan, and in particular India, have embarked on ambitious RTA programmes aimed at concluding preferential agreements with their major trading partners.[53] India has to date notified two FTAs, one with Sri Lanka and more recently one with Singapore. Furthermore, India has concluded RTAs with Afghanistan, Chile, MERCOSUR, SACU and Thailand. It is negotiating with ASEAN, the EC, the GCC, the Republic of Korea and Japan, and it is considering RTAs with Australia, China, EFTA, Malaysia and New Zealand. By the end of December 2007 Pakistan had not notified any RTAs, but it has partial scope agreements with Mauritius and Sri Lanka and has signed FTAs with China, and more recently with Malaysia. Pakistan is negotiating RTAs with the GCC, Indonesia, MERCOSUR and Singapore, and is considering several others.

Turning to the Pacific, the main RTA actors here are Australia and New Zealand. Besides their Closer Economic Relations Agreement of 1983, both countries have reacted to the global spread of RTAs by negotiating their own. Australia has FTAs with Singapore, Thailand and

---

[51] Singapore is a member of ASEAN and a party to the GSTP. It has FTAs with Australia, EFTA, Japan, Jordan, Republic of Korea, India, New Zealand, Panama, the Trans-Pacific SEP and the United States, and it is also negotiating FTAs with Canada, China, the GCC, Mexico, Pakistan, Peru and the Ukraine.

[52] The negotiations with India and Peru provide for an 'early harvest'.

[53] In the case of India and Pakistan, several of the agreements concluded by them appear to be partial scope agreements and not necessarily FTAs.

the United States, and ongoing negotiations of six FTAs, with three more at a proposal stage.[54] New Zealand has FTAs with Singapore and Thailand and is a party to the Trans-Pacific SEP. It is also engaged in five FTA negotiations and is considering two more.[55] As for the Pacific islands, besides their PICTA FTA,[56] they are all engaged in negotiating an EPA with the EC. However, to date it appears that only Papua New Guinea and Fiji (out of fourteen island countries) have initialled the agreement.

Central Asia

Integration initiatives in Central Asia have been mainly directed at re-establishing the economic links that existed before the fall of the communist bloc. However, most early attempts to reproduce those links through plurilateral initiatives (i.e. the CIS FTA) have not materialized and although the CIS institutional framework is still present, preferential liberalization has been achieved through an overlapping network of bilateral agreements and other plurilateral initiatives. The latter include the Single Economic Space between Belarus, Kazakhstan, Russia, and Ukraine, the EurAsian Economic Community between Belarus, Kazakhstan, Kyrgyzstan, Russia and Tajikistan,[57] and the Central Asian Cooperation Organization, whose members are Kazakhstan, Kyrgyzstan, Russia, Tajikistan and Uzbekistan.[58] Other regional organizations include ECO,[59] whose members, among other initiatives, signed the ECO trade agreement (ECOTA) in 2003 providing for tariff reductions, and agreed in 2005 on the common objective of forming an FTA in the future.[60]

---

[54] Australia is negotiating with ASEAN, Chile, China, the GCC, Japan and Malaysia and is undertaking feasibility studies with Republic of Korea, India and Indonesia.

[55] Its FTA negotiations include ASEAN; China; the GCC; Hong Kong, China; and Malaysia and it is considering FTAs with the Republic of Korea and India.

[56] Pacific Island Countries Trade Agreement (PICTA).

[57] The EAEC emerged from a CU between Russia, Belarus and Kazakhstan with the later accession of Kyrgyzstan and Tajikistan. Ukraine and Moldova have been granted the status of observers.

[58] CACO replaces the Central Asia Economic Union, which was composed of Kazakhstan, Kyrgyzstan and Uzbekistan. When Tajikistan joined in 1998, it was renamed the Central Asian Economic Cooperation. Its final name, CACO, was adopted in 2002, and Russia joined the group in 2004.

[59] ECO, which was founded originally in 1985 by Iran, Pakistan and Turkey, was later joined by Afghanistan, Azerbaijan, Kazakhstan, Kyrgyzstan, Tajikistan, Turkmenistan and Uzbekistan.

[60] ECO Vision 2015.

North Africa and the Middle East

The most significant developments in North Africa and the Middle East include the Agadir Agreement between Egypt, Jordan, Morocco and Tunisia, which entered into force in 2007, the Pan-Arab FTA notified to the WTO in 2007, and the GCC which has established itself as a customs union. Besides these regionally based initiatives, several countries in the region are developing closer links with Europe as part of the EuroMed process. Some countries have also begun looking further afield for market access opportunities. Examples include Jordan's FTAs with Singapore and the United States, as well as the one under consideration with Canada. More significant, however, is the impressive RTA agenda of the GCC, which is currently negotiating ten FTAs with key trading partners around the world.[61]

Sub-Saharan Africa

Among all regions of the world, Sub-Saharan Africa has focused most on the traditional concept of regional integration based on far-reaching economic and political integration among geographically contiguous countries.[62] The ambitious goals of most African RTAs (CUs, common markets and economic and monetary unions), their low level of intra-regional trade, poor implementation of several agreements, and overlapping memberships tend to underline the dominant role played by regional politics in the design of the region's RTAs. Sub-Saharan intra-regional dynamics have become intimately intertwined with extra-regional preferential trade relations. These have been based, until recently, on non-reciprocal preferences under schemes such as the GSP, the African Growth Opportunity Act (AGOA), and the EC-ACP programmes. Most countries in the continent benefit from such preferential schemes, the exception being countries in North Africa and South Africa, which have forgone unilateral preferences for reciprocal RTAs with partners in Europe – and more recently in the western hemisphere, Asia-Pacific

---

[61] These include: Australia, China, EFTA, the EC, Japan, India, New Zealand, Pakistan, Singapore and Turkey. With respect to the United States, negotiations are being conducted on a country-by-country basis rather than as a customs union. So far, Bahrain and Oman have concluded FTAs with the United States, while the UAE is negotiating one.

[62] The Sub-Saharan region contains eight major regional integration schemes all with ambitious integration objectives: six of these aim to become economic unions (CEMAC, EAC, ECCAS, ECOWAS, SADC, UEMOA); one a common market (COMESA); and one a CU (SACU).

and the Middle East. The shift to reciprocal preferences is being extended to most Sub-Saharan countries, with the EPAs replacing the long-standing unilateral preferences granted by the EC under its ACP policy.

The EPA process has taken centre stage in African RTA developments in recent years and it is likely to affect significantly intra-RTA dynamics. The EPA process is supposed to build upon and strengthen existing regional integration arrangements. While this may be the case in Western and Central Africa, where negotiations are taking place with the ECOWAS and CEMAC configurations (with the sole inclusion of Mauritania in ECOWAS and Sao Tomé and Principe and the Democratic Republic of Congo in CEMAC),[63] it may not be so apparent in Eastern and Southern Africa where the EPA negotiations foresee three configurations (Eastern and Southern Africa (ESA), the East African Community (EAC) and SADC 'minus'), with members from four distinct regional integration schemes.[64] Considering that each of these RTAs is already a customs union (EAC and SACU), or planning to become one (SADC and COMESA), it is expected that the ESA and SADC EPAs may face compatibility challenges with the integration agendas of the existing RTAs.[65] Nevertheless, the countries of Eastern and Southern Africa (with a few exceptions) have initialled EPAs, while no regional interim agreement had been reached by the end of 2007 with either ECOWAS or the CEMAC EPAs.

3   RTAs and the WTO: an ill-defined relationship

RTAs and the WTO share the common objective of trade liberalization. The former are discriminatory in intent, the latter is not. The pursuance of similar objectives through different approaches has created a lack of definitional clarity in terms of where regional agreements stand in relation to the WTO. This lack of clarity has become a more significant

---

[63] The UEMOA has been a functioning monetary union since 1994; the ECOWAS, comprising all UEMOA members plus other West African countries, has decided to merge with UEMOA. On 1 January 2005, ECOWAS launched the CET to become a CU, providing for three years of transition period.

[64] The COMESA, the SADC, the EAC and the SACU.

[65] Examples of overlapping or misaligned membership include SADC members Malawi, Mauritius, Zambia and Zimbabwe, which have chosen to negotiate with ESA; COMESA members Angola and Swaziland (the latter is also a SACU member) which have opted for the SADC EPA configuration; and South Africa as part of the SADC configuration, along with its existing FTA with the EC.

policy issue as regionalism has grown in importance. The GATT and now the WTO have seen a gradual erosion of the MFN principle over the years due to the emergence of several layers of preferential trade regimes. Much has been written about the motivations behind preferential trade agreements and it is beyond the scope of this chapter to review this literature. Another strand of the lengthy regionalism debate has involved the question of the legal compatibility of regional agreements with GATT/WTO obligations. In what follows, we shall focus not so much on this legal issue, but rather on the surveillance role of the WTO, with particular reference to the recent transparency decision taken in the context of the Doha Round negotiations.

GATT/WTO surveillance of RTAs: some history

The core GATT/WTO rules permitting departures from MFN in order to establish reciprocal preferential trading agreements are found in GATT Article XXIV for agreements in trade in goods, and in GATS Article V for agreements in the area of trade in services. The criteria are fundamentally three: (a) transparency, (b) a commitment to a substantial degree of free trade among the signatories, and (c) the avoidance of additional discrimination against non-party trade. Paragraph 2(c) of the 1979 Decision of the GATT Council on Differential and More Favourable Treatment (Enabling Clause) waives developing countries' obligations under GATT Article I (MFN) when concluding preferential arrangements among themselves. In practice, a limited degree of transparency has become the primary requirement attached to RTAs concluded under the Enabling Clause.

GATT Article XXIV provisions confronted their first real test with the notification in 1957 of the Treaty of Rome establishing the European Economic Community. The working group set up to consider the agreement could not reach a clear-cut conclusion with respect to the consistency of the agreement with the relevant GATT rules (GATT Article XXIV). In retrospect, the inconclusive nature of the deliberations on the establishment of the Treaty of Rome came to symbolize a continuing de facto recognition of the inoperability of the conditions contained in GATT Article XXIV. The subsequent examination of customs unions and free trade areas notified to the GATT did not yield any clearer assessments of full consistency with the rules,[66] and friction

---

[66] The only exception to this was the examination of the Czech Republic–Slovak Republic customs union.

arising between GATT members in these areas was largely dealt with in a pragmatic fashion. During the Uruguay Round, in an endeavour to clarify GATT Article XXIV, members agreed to the *Understanding on the Interpretation of Article XXIV of the GATT 1994* (the Understanding).[67] The Understanding sheds some light on certain issues (of a rather procedural nature), but it did not provide any substantive clarification or interpretation of the essential requirements contained in the Article.

The increase in the number of RTAs during the late 1980s and early 1990s was beginning to create administrative bottlenecks in the newly established WTO, since, according to GATT practice, a working group was established for each notified RTA mandated for examination. To deal with this situation, in February 1996, the Committee on Regional Trade Agreements (CRTA) was established with the mandate to verify the compliance of notified RTAs with the relevant WTO provisions and, among other things, to consider the systemic implications of such agreements and regional initiatives for the multilateral trading system. At the time of the launch of the Doha Round in November 2001, the CRTA had made no progress on its mandate of consistency assessment, owing to the endemic questions of interpretation of the provisions contained in Article XXIV of the GATT 1994.[68] Members had not been able to reach consensus on the format nor the substance of the reports on any of the examinations entrusted to the CRTA. Stalemate in that area had also resulted in little or no progress in the other areas falling under the CRTA mandate. Concerns over the increasing number of RTAs and a malfunctioning multilateral surveillance mechanism prompted ministers meeting at the Fourth Ministerial Conference in Doha in November 2001 to include negotiations on WTO rules and procedures applying to RTAs under the DDA.

DDA negotiations on WTO rules on RTAs

The Doha Ministerial Declaration contains two references to RTAs.[69] Paragraph 4 of the Preamble reaffirms members' commitment to the WTO as the unique forum for global trade rule-making and liberalization, while acknowledging the role that RTAs can play in promoting

---

[67] The Understanding is an integral part of the 'The Final Act Embodying the Results of the Uruguay Round of Multilateral Trade Negotiations'.
[68] Similar problems of interpretation apply to EIAs under GATS Article V.
[69] WTO Document WT/MIN(01)/DEC/1.

the liberalization and expansion of trade and in fostering development. The negotiating mandate is contained in Paragraph 29 of the Declaration, which calls for the clarification and improvement of the disciplines and procedures under existing WTO provisions applying to RTAs, taking due account of the developmental aspects of these agreements.

The mandate of the Declaration on RTAs, as well as its language, is significant in several ways. It should be noted that, with the exception of the Understanding, never before had the original GATT/WTO rules applying to RTAs been subject to multilateral negotiations. Their inclusion in the Doha negotiating mandate marked a shift by members from a position of denial to one of acknowledgement of a need to engage on the issue. The positive language of the mandate also denotes a shift from thinking of RTAs in terms of a dichotomy (the building v. stumbling blocks debate) to one of synergy, whereby the focus is on building the RTA/WTO relationship on a mutually beneficial basis.

Accordingly, the objective of these negotiations is to clarify and possibly improve the relevant RTA disciplines and procedures under existing WTO provisions with a view to resolving the impasse in the CRTA, exercising better control of RTA dynamics, and minimizing the risks to the integrity of the multilateral trading system associated with the proliferation of RTAs. Unlike other areas of the DDA negotiations, the substantive and procedural problems related to RTAs had been known for years. These are reflected in the inability of the CRTA to conduct the examination of the RTAs under its purview in accordance with its mandate,[70] and by the weak role played by the Committee on Trade and Development (CTD) in providing comprehensive information on RTAs notified under Paragraph 2(c) of the Enabling Clause. This facilitated the issue identification phase of the negotiations, which had been virtually completed by the end of 2002.[71] Supported by a number of submissions, participants were quickly able to distinguish, as a working hypothesis, those issues that were more 'procedural' in nature from those that had a higher 'systemic' or 'legal' content.

From October 2002, the Negotiating Group on Rules primarily focused its work on procedural issues, which became known as 'RTA

---

[70] The CRTA is mandated, for individual RTAs, to (multilaterally) come out with an assessment of their consistency with the rules.

[71] Upon request, the Secretariat circulated a background note summarizing the discussions held in the CRTA, TN/RL/W/8/Rev.1 of 1 August 2002 (*Compendium of Issues Related to Regional Trade Agreements*).

transparency'. By mid 2003, some submissions relating to 'systemic' issues had been tabled, though discussions remained rather academic in this area. In March 2004, the group resumed its work with discussions on RTA transparency and 'systemic' issues being held in parallel. A chairman's roadmap[72] and submissions by some members served as a basis to engage the group in a more in-depth consideration of systemic questions. However, the debate only gained momentum from March 2005, once various specific proposals had been tabled by participants (Australia and the EC). Discussions on RTA transparency continued to evolve on the basis of informal notes by the group's chairman, and in July 2006 members reached a formal agreement on a Draft Decision on a Transparency Mechanism for Regional Trade Agreements. The Decision has been applied on a provisional basis since December 2006 while awaiting the conclusion of the Doha Round.[73]

Meanwhile, discussions on systemic issues have made some progress. However, the scope of issues under consideration is wide, complex and politically charged. Discussions have focused on a core set of issues, in particular the clarification of the 'substantially all the trade' (SAT) concept, the length of transition periods, and the inclusion of special and differential (S&D) treatment provisions in Article XXIV of the GATT 1994. The elements of SAT that have attracted most of the group's attention are the pros and cons of SAT tests based on trade and tariff lines, their respective benchmarks, how to combine them, the level of HS[74] disaggregation for the calculations, the non-exclusion of 'major sectors', and the relationship of 'other restrictive regulations of commerce' (as well as preferential rules of origin) with SAT. Most technical elements have not yet been fully explored. With respect to the permitted transition period for RTAs, views diverge on the definition and scope of application of the 'exceptional cases' that would allow the parties to an RTA to go beyond the ten-year transition period mandated by the Understanding.

The issue of S&D treatment permeates all aspects of these discussions. The scope and extent of S&D to be included in Article XXIV of the GATT 1994 remains unclear and several members hold that the question should be addressed at a later stage of the negotiations, once the issues

---

[72] *Roadmap for Discussions on RTAs' 'Systemic' Issues* and *Rev.1*, dated 26 April 2004 and 22 June 2004, respectively.

[73] General Council Decision of 14 December 2006; WTO Document WT/L/671.

[74] Harmonized Commodity Description and Coding System of tariff nomenclature.

of SAT and transition periods are clarified. However, the future of these discussions is uncertain as sharp differences remain. Some members are rather reluctant to negotiate on 'systemic' questions, having concerns over a potential dilution of existing RTA rules. Other members are seeking to modify RTA disciplines, though with different objectives, ranging from pure 'clarification' of some existing provisions (making them stricter, in principle) to added flexibility. Lack of formal negotiating submissions on these questions, combined with relatively slow progress in other negotiating areas has resulted in the group not meeting since February 2007. New impetus will be needed to move these questions forward.

The Transparency Mechanism for RTAs

The Decision on a Transparency Mechanism for Regional Trade Agreements (TM) has resulted in a number of important procedural changes in the treatment of RTAs within the WTO framework. The TM, which applies to all RTAs, whether notified under GATT Article XXIV, GATS Article V or the Enabling Clause, is being implemented on a provisional basis in accordance with Paragraph 47 of the Doha Ministerial Declaration, and will be replaced by a permanent mechanism to be adopted as part of the Doha Round of trade negotiations. An explanation of the key elements of the TM, together with an assessment of its first year of operation, is outlined below.

The TM introduces the concept of an early announcement for RTAs, either under negotiation or signed, but not yet in force. Members participating in RTA negotiations should provide basic information in the form of a press release or similar which is made available on the WTO website. Once the RTA has been signed, members are to convey information, such as the scope and date of signature, relevant contact points, and/or website addresses to the WTO. As of December 2007, early announcements of nine signed RTAs and twenty-four RTAs under negotiation had been received from members and posted on the WTO website.[75]

The system of early announcements has increased the transparency of RTAs, allowing members and the public to make use of a centralized source of information on RTAs under negotiation or signed, but not

---

[75] See www.wto.org/english/tratop_e/region_e/early_announc_e.htm. RTAs notified subsequently are removed from this list.

yet in force. Nonetheless, only about a third of the RTAs under negotiation or already signed have been announced early to the WTO. Of
roughly seventy RTAs currently under negotiation, twenty-four have
been announced early. Likewise, of twenty-eight RTAs which have been
signed, but are not yet in force, only nine were announced early. Clearly
WTO members will need to make a greater effort to inform the Secretariat of ongoing RTA negotiations in order to render this information
as comprehensive as possible.

The TM strengthens existing provisions on notification by stipulating
that notification is to take place 'as early as possible . . . no later than
directly following the parties' ratification of the RTA or any party's
decision on application of the relevant parts of an agreement, and before
the application of preferential treatment between the parties'. Of the
twenty notifications of RTAs made during 2007, five were received
before the RTA entered into force. By way of comparison, according to
figures for 2006, nine of the twenty-five notifications were made before
the RTA's entry into force. This suggests that there is still room for
improvement and that while some members have made efforts to provide
timely notification of their RTAs, others have yet fully to integrate the
new obligations relating to notification.

Under the TM, the WTO Secretariat is charged with the preparation
of a factual presentation of all notified RTAs covering trade in goods
and/or services. The factual presentation, which replaces the standard
format furnished by the parties to an RTA, is a detailed summary and
contains data on the trade environment of the RTA parties, a description of the RTA's regulatory features, and details of the tariff, trade and
regulatory liberalization envisaged over the transition period of the
RTA. It is factual and is prepared on the Secretariat's own responsibility,
in full consultation with the parties, and cannot be used as a basis for
dispute settlement procedures or to create new rights and obligations for
members.

The purpose of the factual presentation is to produce objective,
homogeneous reports containing no value judgements which are used
by members in their consideration of an RTA under review. Prior to the
adoption of the TM, RTAs were transmitted to the CRTA for examination following the adoption of terms of reference by the Council for
Trade in Goods (for RTAs notified under GATT Article XXIV) or the
Council for Trade in Services (for RTAs notified under GATS Article V).
The emphasis in the TM on 'consideration' rather than 'examination'
stems from the fact that in the ten years of the CRTA's existence not a

single examination report of an RTA was approved by members. This was owing to various factors including differing interpretations of key provisions of the existing legal texts, members' inability (or, in some cases, unwillingness) to provide adequate statistics, and political difficulties stemming from the need to produce a consensual report acceptable to all members, including the RTA parties under review.

During 2007, a total of thirteen factual presentations were completed by the Secretariat, eleven of which were used as the basis for consideration of the relevant RTAs in the CRTA.[76] This number falls somewhat short of that envisaged in the work programme for the CRTA established in March 2007, and is caused by a number of factors, including delays in the receipt of statistical data from parties, data discrepancies in members' submissions, and delays in the receipt of comments from the parties. Most of these are teething problems which should be resolved as members become more familiar with the process and adept at producing the required statistical data. Members have expressed satisfaction with the operation of the TM so far, noting that the provision of consistent, timely and objective information in the factual presentation has increased the quality of information available and has aided the consideration process.

According to the TM, consideration of a notified RTA is to be concluded within one year of the date of notification of the RTA in a single formal meeting. Any additional exchange of information is to take place in written form. Given that, prior to the adoption of the TM, RTAs were often subject to multiple rounds of examination over a period of years, the adoption of the new Mechanism has greatly streamlined the CRTA's work.

With respect to subsequent notification and reporting, the TM supplants the largely dysfunctional RTA biennial reporting schedule by providing that the required notification of changes affecting the implementation or operation of an RTA should take place as soon as possible after changes occur.[77] At the end of the RTA's implementation period, the parties should submit a short written report on the realization of liberalization commitments in the RTA. During 2007,

---

[76] Details can be found at www.wto.org/english/tratop_e/region_e/trans_mecha_e.htm.

[77] The biennial reporting schedule applied only to those RTAs for which an examination report had been adopted during the GATT years. The majority of RTAs in force which have been notified since then were not subject to any reporting mechanism prior to the adoption of the TM.

notifications of changes on four RTAs were received and posted on the WTO website.[78] So far, no reports on the realization of liberalization commitments have been received.

Under the new Mechanism, the CRTA is the body responsible for RTAs notified under GATT Article XXIV or GATS Article V. RTAs notified under the Enabling Clause are the responsibility of the CTD, convening in a dedicated session. A number of RTAs have been considered in the CRTA under the TM during the first year of its operation. None has yet been considered in the CTD as the first notification of an RTA under the Enabling Clause was made in October 2007.[79] This RTA will be considered in the CTD during the course of 2008.

Prior to the adoption of the TM, notifications and terms of reference for the examination of RTAs were dealt with in different bodies.[80] RTAs notified under GATT Article XXIV were subject to mandatory examination, those under GATS Article V were subject to possible examination, while those under the Enabling Clause were not examined, but could be subject to consultations in the CTD, if requested by members. Under the TM, all RTAs are subject to consideration using a factual presentation prepared by the Secretariat. By streamlining the bodies responsible for the implementation of the Mechanism, procedural time lags should be reduced and the process of transparency enhanced.

RTAs for which the CRTA had already concluded the factual examination prior to the adoption of the TM are subject to a factual abstract prepared by the Secretariat.[81] The factual abstract is a short summary (two or three pages) of an RTA with a description of its key elements. Factual abstracts are to be made publicly available on the WTO website. Of the sixty or so RTAs subject to the preparation of a factual abstract by the Secretariat, fifteen have been completed and posted on the WTO website.[82] The rest are in preparation and will be made available shortly.

The Mechanism makes provision for the Secretariat to establish and maintain an updated electronic database on individual RTAs which is easily accessible to the public. The database, which will include relevant

---

[78] See www.wto.org/english/tratop_e/region_e/notif_changes_e.htm.

[79] The FTA between Turkey and Egypt.

[80] RTAs notified under GATT Article XXIV were notified to the Council for Trade in Goods, those under GATS Article V to the Council for Trade in Services and those under the Enabling Clause to the CTD.

[81] The requirement of factual abstracts also applies to RTAs notified under the Enabling Clause.

[82] See www.wto.org/english/tratop_e/region_e/factual_abstracts_e.htm.

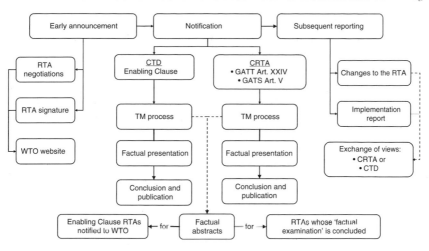

Figure 2.11 WTO process for RTAs according to the Decision on RTA Transparency

tariff- and trade-related information, and give access to all written material related to announced or notified RTAs available at the WTO, is currently under construction. Phase 1, which provides an ID card for each notified RTA, should be made public during the course of 2008.

Experience of the Transparency Mechanism thus far

The availability of factual presentations has reinvigorated the CRTA and members have expressed their satisfaction with the quality of information made available. Nonetheless, a few teething problems are evident. Some countries have had difficulty in providing the mandated data in the required format and in a timely fashion, and the quality of data submissions provided by members varies. The time periods foreseen in the Mechanism, particularly for comments from the parties to the first draft of the factual presentation and for members' questions and replies, have been deemed by members to be too short and have been lengthened.

Some other issues have arisen, such as the periodicity of data to be used in the factual presentation. The Mechanism makes it clear that the parties should provide import statistics for the most recent three years preceding the notification of the RTA and that the WTO Secretariat may also use data available from other sources. Nonetheless, some members are reluctant to sanction the use of post-entry-into-force data in the factual presentation, as they fear a misinterpretation of the data. This issue needs to be discussed further among members.

With regard to future work, the Mechanism makes provision for members to review, and if necessary modify, the Decision in light of the experience gained from its provisional operation, and to replace it by a permanent mechanism adopted as part of the overall results of the Doha Round, in accordance with Paragraph 47 of the Doha Declaration. Members are also charged with reviewing the legal relationship between the Mechanism and relevant WTO provisions related to RTAs.

At the time of its adoption in December 2006, the Chair of the General Council noted that members intended to conduct an initial review of the Mechanism within one year. However, by the end of 2007 members considered that there had not yet been enough experience with the Mechanism to conduct a proper review and therefore postponed it to a later date.[83] Also pending is discussion on the legal relationship between the TM and the existing WTO provisions related to RTAs. For the moment, members have taken a pragmatic approach to the adoption of ad hoc procedural changes where necessary. It is clear that in the longer term efforts will need to be made to accommodate the Mechanism into the existing WTO legal framework on a more permanent basis.[84]

---

[83] See the Report (2007) of the CRTA to the General Council, WTO Document WT/REG/18.
[84] See Tables 2.1A and 2.2A in the Appendix for a comparison between the Decision on RTA Transparency and the existing WTO provisions applying to RTAs.

Table 2.2 *List of acronyms of notified RTAs*

Abbreviation	Full title	Member countries
AFTA	ASEAN Free Trade Area	Brunei Darussalam, Cambodia, Indonesia, Laos, Malaysia, Myanmar, Philippines, Singapore, Thailand, Viet Nam
APTA	Asia-Pacific Trade Agreement (Bangkok Agreement)	Bangladesh, China, India, Republic of Korea, Laos, Sri Lanka
ASEAN	Association of South East Asian Nations	Brunei Darussalam, Cambodia, Indonesia, Laos, Malaysia, Myanmar, Philippines, Singapore, Thailand, Viet Nam
CAN	Andean Community	Bolivia, Colombia, Ecuador, Peru, Venezuela
CARICOM	Caribbean Community and Common Market	Antigua and Barbuda, Bahamas, Barbados, Belize, Dominica, Grenada, Guyana, Haiti, Jamaica, Montserrat, Trinidad and Tobago, St Kitts and Nevis, St Lucia, St Vincent and the Grenadines, Surinam
CACM	Central American Common Market	Costa Rica, El Salvador, Guatemala, Honduras, Nicaragua
CAFTA-DR	Dominican Republic–Central America–United States	Dominican Republic, El Salvador, Guatemala, Honduras, Nicaragua, United States
CEFTA	Central European Free Trade Agreement	Albania, Bosnia and Herzegovina, Croatia, Former Yugoslav Republic of Macedonia (FYROM), Moldova, Montenegro, Serbia and United Nations Interim Administration Mission in Kosovo
CEMAC	Economic and Monetary Community of Central Africa	Cameroon, Central African Republic, Chad, Congo, Equatorial Guinea, Gabon
CER	Closer Trade Relations Trade Agreement	Australia, New Zealand

Table 2.2 (*cont.*)

Abbreviation	Full title	Member countries
CIS	Commonwealth of Independent States	Azerbaijan, Armenia, Belarus, Georgia, Moldova, Kazakhstan, Russian Federation, Ukraine, Uzbekistan, Tajikistan, Kyrgyz Republic
COMESA	Common Market for Eastern and Southern Africa	Angola, Burundi, Comoros, Democratic Republic of Congo, Djibouti, Egypt, Eritrea, Ethiopia, Kenya, Madagascar, Malawi, Mauritius, Namibia, Rwanda, Seychelles, Sudan, Swaziland, Uganda Zambia, Zimbabwe
EAC	East African Community	Kenya, Tanzania, Uganda
EAEC	Eurasian Economic Community	Belarus, Kazakhstan, Kyrgyz Republic, Russian Federation, Tajikistan
EC	European Communities	Austria, Belgium, Bulgaria, Cyprus, Czech Republic, Denmark, Estonia, Finland, France, Germany, Greece, Hungary, Ireland, Italy, Latvia, Lithuania, Luxembourg, Malta, Poland, Portugal, Romania, Slovak Republic, Slovenia, Spain, Sweden, Netherlands, United Kingdom
ECO	Economic Cooperation Organization	Afghanistan, Azerbaijan, Iran, Kazakhstan, Kyrgyz Republic, Pakistan, Tajikistan, Turkey, Turkmenistan, Uzbekistan
ECOWAS	Economic Community of West African States	Benin, Burkina Faso, Cape Verde, Cote d'Ivoire, Gambia, Ghana, Guinea, Guinea-Bissau, Liberia, Mali, Niger, Nigeria, Senegal, Sierra Leone, Togo
EEA	European Economic Area	EC, Iceland, Liechtenstein, Norway
EFTA	European Free Trade Association	Iceland, Liechtenstein, Norway, Switzerland
GCC	Gulf Cooperation Council	Bahrain, Kuwait, Oman, Qatar, Saudi Arabia, United Arab Emirates

Table 2.2 (*cont.*)

Abbreviation	Full title	Member countries
GSTP	General System of Trade Preferences among Developing Countries	Algeria, Argentina, Bangladesh, Benin, Bolivia, Brazil, Cameroon, Chile, Colombia, Cuba, Democratic People's Republic of Korea, Ecuador, Egypt, Ghana, Guinea, Guyana, India, Indonesia, Islamic Republic of Iran, Iraq, Libya, Malaysia, Mexico, Morocco, Mozambique, Myanmar, Nicaragua, Nigeria, Pakistan, Peru, Philippines, Republic of Korea, Romania, Singapore, Sri Lanka, Sudan, Thailand, Trinidad and Tobago, Tunisia, United Republic of Tanzania, Venezuela, Viet Nam, Yugoslavia, Zimbabwe
LAIA/ALADI	Latin American Integration Association	Argentina, Bolivia, Brazil, Chile, Colombia, Cuba, Ecuador, Mexico, Paraguay, Peru, Uruguay, Venezuela
MERCOSUR	Southern Common Market	Argentina, Brazil, Paraguay, Uruguay
MSG	Melanesian Spearhead Group	Fiji, Papua New Guinea, Solomon Islands, Vanuatu
NAFTA	North American Free Trade Agreement	Canada, Mexico, United States
OCT	Overseas Countries and Territories	Greenland, New Caledonia, French Polynesia, French Southern and Antarctic Territories, Wallis and Futuna Islands, Mayotte, Saint Pierre and Miquelon, Aruba, Netherlands Antilles, Anguilla, Cayman Islands, Falkland Islands, South Georgia and South Sandwich Islands, Montserrat, Pitcairn, Saint Helena, Ascension Island, Tristan da Cunha, Turks and Caicos Islands, British Antarctic Territory, British Indian Ocean Territory, British Virgin Islands
PAN-ARAB	Pan-Arab Free Trade Area	Bahrain, Egypt, Iraq, Jordan, Kuwait, Lebanon, Libya, Morocco, Oman, Qatar, Saudi Arabia, Sudan, Syria, Tunisia, United Arab Emirates, Yemen

Table 2.2 (*cont.*)

Abbreviation	Full title	Member countries
PATCRA	Papua New Guinea–Australia Trade and Commercial Relations Agreement	Australia, Papua New Guinea
PTN	Protocol Relating to Trade Negotiations among Developing Countries	Bangladesh, Brazil, Chile, Egypt, Israel, Mexico, Pakistan, Paraguay, Peru, Philippines, Republic of Korea, Romania, Tunisia, Turkey, Uruguay, Yugoslavia
SACU	Southern African Customs Union	Botswana, Lesotho, Namibia, South Africa, Swaziland
SADC	Southern African Development Community	Angola, Botswana, Lesotho, Malawi, Mauritius, Mozambique, Namibia, South Africa, Swaziland, Tanzania, Zambia, Zimbabwe
SAPTA/SAFTA	South Asian Preferential (Free) Trade Arrangement	Bangladesh, Bhutan, India, Maldives, Nepal, Pakistan, Sri Lanka
SPARTECA	South Pacific Regional Trade and Economic Cooperation Agreement	Australia, New Zealand, Cook Islands, Fiji, Kiribati, Marshall Islands, Micronesia, Nauru, Niue, Papua New Guinea, Solomon Islands, Tonga, Tuvalu, Vanuatu, Western Samoa
Trans-Pacific SEP	Trans-Pacific Strategic Economic Partnership	Brunei Darussalam, Chile, New Zealand, Singapore
TRIPARTITE	Tripartite Agreement	Egypt, India, Yugoslavia
UEMOA/ WAEMU	West African Economic and Monetary Union	Benin, Burkina Faso, Côte d'Ivoire, Guinea Bissau, Mali, Niger, Senegal, Togo

Appendix: Comparison between the 'Transparency Mechanism for Regional Trade Agreements' (WT/L/671) and existing WTO-related provisions

Table 2.1A. *Transparency Mechanism and WTO-related provisions*

Transparency Mechanism	Related provisions in the WTO Agreements		
	GATT XXIV & Understanding (U)	Enabling Clause	GATS V
A. Early announcement:			
a) "Members participating in new negotiations … of an RTA shall endeavour to so inform the WTO."	No equivalent provision	No equivalent provision	No equivalent provision
b) "Members parties to a newly signed RTA shall convey to the WTO … information on the RTA …"			
B. Notification:			
3. "The … notification of an RTA … shall take place as early as possible. As a rule, it will occur no later than directly following the parties' ratification of the RTA or any	XXIV:7(a) - "Any contracting party deciding to enter into [an RTA] shall promptly notify the Contracting Parties'	Para 4(a) - "Any contracting party taking action to introduce an arrangement … shall … notify the CONTRACTING PARTIES"	V:7(a) - "Members which are parties to [an RTA] shall promptly notify any such agreement … to the Council for Trade in Services"

Table 2.1A. (*cont.*)

Transparency Mechanism	Related provisions in the WTO Agreements		
	GATT XXIV & Understanding (U)	Enabling Clause	GATS V
party's decision on application of the relevant parts of an agreement, and before the application of preferential treatment between the parties."			
4. "In notifying their RTA, the parties shall specify under which provision(s) of the WTO agreements it is notified. They will also provide the full text of the RTA ... and any related schedules, annexes and protocols ..."	XXIV:7(a) - "Any contracting party deciding to enter into [an RTA] ... shall make available to [the Contracting Parties] such information regarding the proposed [RTA] as will enable them to make such reports and recommendations to contracting parties as they may deem appropriate"	Para 4(a) - "Any contracting party taking action to introduce an arrangement ... shall ... furnish [the CONTRACTING PARTIES] with all the information they may deem appropriate relating to such action"	V:7(a) - "Members which are parties to [an RTA] ... shall also make available to the Council such relevant information as may be requested by it"

Table 2.1A. (*cont.*)

Transparency Mechanism	Related provisions in the WTO Agreements		
	GATT XXIV & Understanding (U)	Enabling Clause	GATS V
C. *Procedures to enhance transparency*			
6. "The consideration by Members of a notified RTA shall be normally concluded in a period not exceeding one year after the date of notification..."	*No equivalent provision*	*No equivalent provision*	*No equivalent provision*
7. "To assist Members in their consideration of a notified RTA:			
a) the parties shall make available to the WTO Secretariat data as specified in the Annex ...; and			
b) the WTO Secretariat, on its own responsibility and in full consultation with the parties, shall prepare a factual presentation of the RTA."			

Table 2.1A. (*cont.*)

Transparency Mechanism	Related provisions in the WTO Agreements		
	GATT XXIV & Understanding (U)	Enabling Clause	GATS V
9. "The factual presentation ... shall be primarily based on the information provided by the parties; ... In preparing the factual presentation, the WTO Secretariat shall refrain from any value judgement."			
D. *Subsequent notification and reporting* 14. "The ... notification of changes affecting the implementation of an RTA, or the operation of an already implemented RTA, shall take place as soon as possible after the changes occur. Changes to be notified include, *inter alia*, modifications to the preferential treatment between the parties and to the RTA's disciplines ..."	XXIV:7(c) - "Any substantial change in the plan or schedule referred to in paragraph 5(c) shall be communicated to the Contracting Parties, which may request the contracting parties concerned to consult with them if the change seems likely to jeopardize or delay unduly the formation of the [RTA]"	Para 4(a) - "Any contracting party ... subsequently taking action to introduce modification or withdrawal of the differential and more favourable treatment so provided shall ... notify the CONTRACTING PARTIES and furnish them with all the information they may deem appropriate relating to such action"	V:7(a) - "Members which are parties to [an RTA] shall promptly notify ... any enlargement or any significant modification of that agreement to the Council for Trade in Services. They shall also make available to the Council such relevant information as may be requested by it."

Table 2.1A. (*cont.*)

Transparency Mechanism	Related provisions in the WTO Agreements		
	GATT XXIV & Understanding (U)	Enabling Clause	GATS V
15. "At the end of the RTA's implementation period, the parties shall submit to the WTO a short written report on the realization of the liberalization commitments in the RTA as originally notified."	U:9 - "Members parties to an interim agreement shall notify substantial changes in the plan and schedule included in that agreement to the [CTG] and, if so requested, the Council shall examine the changes"		V:7(b) - "Members which are parties to any agreement ... which is implemented on the basis of a time-frame shall report periodically to the [CTS] on its implementation. The Council may establish a working party to examine such reports if it deems such a working party necessary"
16. "Upon request, the relevant WTO body shall provide an adequate opportunity for an exchange of views on the communications submitted under paragraphs 14 and 15."	U:11 – "... Any significant changes and/or developments in the [RTA] should be reported as they occur. – [RTAs] shall report periodically to the [CTG]; as envisaged by the CONTRACTING PARTIES to GATT 1947 in their		

Table 2.1A. (*cont.*)

	Related provisions in the WTO Agreements		
Transparency Mechanism	GATT XXIV & Understanding (U)	Enabling Clause	GATS V
	instruction to the GATT 1947 Council concerning reports on regional agreements (BISD 18S/38), on the operation of the relevant agreement"		
E. Bodies entrusted			
18. "The ... ("CRTA") and the ... ("CTD") are instructed to implement this Transparency Mechanism ... The CRTA shall do so for RTAs falling under Article XXIV of GATT 1994 and Article V of GATS, while the CTD shall do so for RTAs falling under paragraph 2(c) of the Enabling Clause ..."	*Council for Trade in Goods and CRTA*	*CTD*	*Council for Trade in Services and CRTA*

Table 2.1A. (*cont.*)

	Related provisions in the WTO Agreements		
Transparency Mechanism	GATT XXIV & Understanding (U)	Enabling Clause	GATS V
F. Technical support for developing countries			
19. "Upon request, the WTO Secretariat shall provide technical support to developing country Members ... in the implementation of this Transparency Mechanism ..."	*No equivalent provision*	*No equivalent provision*	*No equivalent provision*
G. Other provisions			
20. "Any Member may ... bring to the attention of the relevant WTO body information on any RTA that it considers ought to have been submitted to Members in the framework of this Transparency Mechanism."	*No equivalent provision*	*No equivalent provision*	*No equivalent provision*

Table 2.2A. *WTO-related provisions and the Transparency Mechanism*

	Mandatory related provisions in the WTO Agreements			Related procedural practice	Transparency Mechanism
	GATT & Understanding (U)	Enabling Clause	GATS		All Three Provisions
	U:7 – "All notifications made under paragraph 7(a) of Article XXIV shall be examined by a working party in the light of the relevant provisions of GATT 1994 and of paragraph 1 of this Understanding. The working party shall submit a report to the [CTG] on its findings in this regard."	Para 4(b) - "Any contracting party taking action to introduce an arrangement ... shall ... afford adequate opportunity for prompt consultations at the request of any interested contracting party with respect to any difficulty or matter that may arise"	V:7(a) – " ... The Council may establish a working party to examine such an agreement or enlargement or modification of that agreement and to report to the Council on its consistency with this Article."	Prior to the application of the TM, RTAs notified under GATT Article XXIV and GATS Article V were sent to the CRTA for examination; those notified under Paragraph 2(c) of the Enabling Clause would be considered by the CTD.	RTAs notified under GATT Article XXIV and GATS Article V are sent to the CRTA (those under Paragraph 2(c) of the Enabling Clause to the CTD) for consideration by Members.

PART II

Multilateralization: Prospects and Past Experience

3

Beyond tariffs: multilateralizing non-tariff RTA commitments

RICHARD BALDWIN, SIMON EVENETT
AND PATRICK LOW[1]

1 Introduction

World trade is now influenced markedly by a 'spaghetti bowl'[2] of regional trade agreements and, given the strong current interest in negotiating more such initiatives, this influence will almost certainly become heavier over time. Regionalism, it seems, is here to stay. The economic inefficiencies created by reciprocal, preferential trade agreements are well appreciated, and add to the corrosion of multilateral principles that unrestrained regionalism gives rise to. But are there any countervailing tendencies that are reinforcing the principle of non-discrimination in international trading relations? Baldwin (2006b) argues that specific changes in the global economy – especially the spatial unbundling of the manufacturing process and attendant offshoring of tasks – have changed the political economy of the spaghetti bowl of preferential tariffs. Indeed, some nations have demonstrated an interest in 'taming the tangle'. These changes also open the door to new WTO-led initiatives that could further multilateralize, or at least plurilateralize, the spaghetti bowl of reciprocal preferences.

The goals of this chapter are threefold: (i) to consider whether the spaghetti bowl problem also exists for six non-tariff barriers (NTBs) and so-called behind-the-border policy measures; (ii) to examine the ways in which regional trading agreements have become vehicles for reducing discrimination in international trade and the political economy dynamics underlying these developments; and (iii) to elaborate on and explore the

---

[1] The chapter represents the opinions of the authors, and is the product of professional research. It is not meant to represent the position or opinions of the WTO or its members, nor the official position of any staff members. Any errors are the fault of the authors.

[2] Jagdish Bhagwati initially introduced this phraseology.

merits of potential WTO initiatives that could channel the evident momentum behind reciprocal, preferential trade negotiations towards reinforcing the principle of non-discrimination in international commercial relations.

The chapter starts by considering what multilateralization actually means in relation to policy choices made in the context of regional agreements. This is followed by a section reviewing the economic and political–economic logic of two major episodes of multilateralization that occurred in the 1990s. The subsequent section considers whether the spaghetti bowl problem extends to non-tariff barriers by reviewing research on NTB provisions in regional trade agreements (RTAs). We focus on six NTB areas: trade in services, government procurement, competition policy, investment performance measures, technical barriers to trade, and trade remedies. After this, the chapter extracts the lessons of the six case studies and then discusses a number of ways in which the WTO might engage in keeping these regional NTB commitments as multilateral-friendly as possible.

2   How preferential arrangements can be multilateralized

The notion of multilateralizing preferential agreements can be defined with more or less precision. The fundamental idea is obvious – a process of multilateralization occurs when existing preferential arrangements are extended in a non-discriminatory manner to additional parties. Full multilateralization would mean that all international trade policy obligations would apply to all trading nations on a non-discriminatory basis. Our discussion of multilateralization does not imply the attainment of a fully non-discriminatory international regime – such a regime has never existed and probably never will. What we are interested in is the enlargement of preferential trade policy zones through the reduction of discrimination among countries and/or the reduction of overlap in arrangements among sets of countries. This could be done either by superimposing new, more multilateralized arrangements on existing agreements, or by extending existing agreements. For the purposes of the present discussion, this distinction is not important, but it may matter when considering the practicalities of concrete multilateralizing actions. In any event, the process of multilateralization is likely to involve a combination of additional liberalization and rationalization.

A related consideration is how particular trade policies can be designed within the framework of RTAs to promote multilateralization.

We identify five ways that the design of RTA provisions will favour multilateralization.

1. The geographical expansion of FTAs (such as EU enlargement) or of a set of policies applied across more than one agreement.
2. The inclusion in FTAs of *de jure* MFN provisions in respect of particular policies. An example of this would be investment performance requirements that applied to any foreign investor regardless of national origin.
3. Rules agreed to within an FTA, which by their nature apply on a de facto basis. This could be the case, for example, with regulatory reform in a customs administration that was negotiated under an FTA, where the nature of the new policy makes discrimination undesirable and/or infeasible.
4. The inclusion of third-party MFN clauses in FTAs, which ensure that signatories to existing FTAs do not undermine the acquired benefits of preferred parties by extending more favourable treatment in subsequent FTA arrangements. Such clauses exist, for example, in some RTAs in relation to services and government procurement.
5. The inclusion in FTAs of provisions that prevent actions allowed under WTO agreements from being taken in a manner that results in discriminatory treatment. An example here would be where an FTA partner took a safeguard action and applied the relevant measures to FTA partners and non-partners alike.

This taxonomy is useful in thinking about the design features of FTAs, either in relation to the redesign of existing arrangements, or the establishment of new ones. Examples of these kinds of policy design are identifiable in our discussion below of multilateralizing NTBs found in FTAs.

3   Multilateralization of tariff preferences

The last ten years have witnessed a significant reduction in tariffs worldwide. The tariff liberalization, however, resulted from a tangle of unilateral, bilateral and plurilateral initiatives – the famous spaghetti bowl effect. During the same period, the world has also witnessed two multilateralizations of the tangle of tariffs and the attendant miasma of rules of origin. This section, which draws heavily on Baldwin (2006b), discusses the problems with the spaghetti bowl, the two multilateralization initiatives and the political economy forces that drove them. The chapters in this volume by Giosarek and Mann and Liu also provide useful insights into these episodes of multilateralization.

The goal of this section is to establish a baseline for comparing how the spaghetti bowl has developed with respect to non-tariff barriers, and how multilateralization has or could proceed in the field of non-tariff barriers.

The preference spaghetti bowl and its multilateralization

As far as tariff preferences are concerned, there are three key economic aspects to the spaghetti bowl.

1. The preferential tariffs themselves

Preferences – that is, geographically discriminatory tariffs – produce well-known economic inefficiencies. These can be so great that even the countries benefiting from the preferences may end up worse off – a result known as Viner's Ambiguity (Viner, 1950). Third parties are almost surely harmed by such preferences. Note that the size of 'margin of preference' matters; if a nation's MFN tariff is zero or almost zero, an RTA cannot create much discrimination.

2. Rules of origin (ROOs)

Preferential tariffs always involve 'rules of origin' since customs officers must be able to identify where an imported good is made in order to know which tariff to apply. ROOs often act as a subtle form of protection. In particular, ROOs often prevent firms from choosing the most efficient international supply network, since they fear that their exports may lose 'origin status' and the preference it confers. In this way, ROOs can act like 'frictional' trade barriers; they raise the cost that firms face when they sell across an RTA border.[3]

3. Rules of cumulation (ROCs)

Rules of origin always involve 'rules of cumulation' – namely rules where value can be added and still count as local. The most common ROC – bilateral cumulation – allows firms to count the value that is added in either of the two nations. Permissive ROCs can mitigate the protectionist content of ROOs by expanding firms' choices when it comes to their international supply networks. See Box 3.1 for how ROOs and ROCs interact with preferences.

---

[3] Of course firms always have the option of paying the MFN tariff, so the tariff equivalent of the frictional barrier is limited to the height of the MFN tariff.

BOX 3.1 RULES OF ORIGIN AND DIAGONAL CUMULATION:
WHEN DUTY-FREE TRADE IS NOT FREE TRADE

Consider a simple thought experiment. Think of a network of bilateral FTAs among nations A, B and C, and compare this to a world where each of the three nations embraced MFN free trade. In both cases, tariffs worldwide would seem to be zero. However, if the FTAs have restrictive ROOs and/or bilateral ROCs, the three bilaterals are likely to produce trade that is less than fully free. The point is that ROOs would prevent firms from setting up the most efficient international supply networks. Bilateral cumulation, as opposed to diagonal or full cumulation, can similarly distort the purchase pattern of intermediate inputs in a way that does not occur under MFN free trade.

Some definitions:

- Bilateral cumulation is where inputs originating in one country are considered as originating in the other. This is a feature of all FTAs.
- A diagonal cumulation 'zone' is to bilateral cumulation as customs unions are to FTAs. Under diagonal cumulation, a set of nations adopts a common set of ROOs, i.e. the zone becomes what might be called a 'ROOs union'. Once a product enters the diagonal cumulation zone, its origin is determined by the common ROOs and it can therefore never lose its origin status by crossing a border inside the zone. This relaxes the constraints on firms' choice of suppliers compared to bilateral cumulation, but it still favours suppliers inside the cumulation zone.
- Full cumulation is rare, usually limited to customs unions. Any value added inside the zone, regardless of whether it involves a component bought inside or outside the area, counts toward domestic value-added. This matters, since origin status is normally an all-or-nothing proposition. For example, some of the value that is added to a component in a diagonal cumulation zone may not be counted if it is not sufficient to grant a component origin status.

What is wrong with the spaghetti bowl?

This discriminatory tariff liberalization is inferior to multilateral liberalization on three main counts:

- Economic inefficiency. Multiple tariff rates introduce economic inefficiency into the trade system, with this problem being especially severe in industries with complex international supply networks.
- Stumbling blocks. The existence of preferences may help or hinder moves towards multilateral liberalization. To the extent that preferences hinder multilateral tariff cutting, RTAs are a problem for the global trade system.

- Hegemony. The world of trade negotiations is governed by something of the law of the jungle, where nations with big markets have more leverage than those with small markets. The WTO's rules – especially the non-discrimination provisions – tend to mitigate the power of current and future trade hegemons (the US, the EU, Japan, China, India and Brazil). The jungle law is much more in evidence when large countries sit down with small ones than it is in a WTO context.

How can the tangle of tariff preferences be multilateralized?

Logically, there are two ways of eliminating the spaghetti bowl as far as tariffs are concerned.

1. Set all nations' MFN tariffs to zero. This eliminates the distortions of 'geographically discriminatory import taxes' by eliminating the discrimination. It simultaneously eliminates the distortions of non-harmonized ROOs and bilateral cumulation since it eliminates the incentive to prove origin.
2. Switch to diagonal rules of cumulation. If a group of nations has a complete set of bilateral FTAs among them, they can reduce the distortionary effect of ROOs and bilateral ROCs by switching to a harmonized set of ROOs and diagonal cumulation.[4] This reduces distortions of the international economic production pattern within the zone, but does little to improve the efficiency of the global production pattern.

Two real world examples   The world has seen both types of multilateralization. They both happened in 1997. The first was the Pan-European Cumulation System (PECS);[5] the second was the Information Technology Agreement (ITA). Both started from a situation where the MFN tariffs were low. The PECS example involved a tangle of preferences and rules of origin – a spaghetti bowl situation.[6] The ITA case

---

[4] Roughly speaking, switching to diagonal cumulation creates what might be called a ROOs customs union, in that it imposes common external ROOs and means that a product can never lose origin status by crossing an internal border.

[5] PECS is sometimes referred to as the PanEuroMed zone after it was enlarged to include a number of Mediterranean nations.

[6] Note, however, that a concept like the Effective Rate of Protection is necessary to understand the true importance of preferences. Since the nominal tariff is applied to the full value of the good and the good can lose origin status due to minor shifts in the location of production, the nominal margin of preference often radically underestimates the extent to which a particular slice of the value-added chain is protected.

entailed agreement among a subset of the WTO membership to eliminate tariffs and to extend zero tariff treatment on a non-discriminatory
basis, including to those countries that retained tariffs on information
technology products.

As we shall argue, the initial conditions (i.e. low MFN tariffs) meant
that the gains and losses from 'taming the tangle' in the case of the PECS
were fairly small to begin with, so a modest shift in the political economy
forces against maintaining the tangle could result in its sudden elimination. This modest shift was provided by the unbundling, or fragmentation, of manufacturing. This same unbundling phenomenon was also
responsible for tariff elimination between certain countries under the
ITA arrangements. This section considers the basic economic and political economy logic behind the two episodes of multilateralization of
regionalism.

The political economy of the spaghetti bowl and its multilateralization

The multilateralization of regionalism involves the removal of trade
barriers. Understanding this sort of trade liberalization – as is true
of all trade liberalization – involves some mental gymnastics. One
has to explain why it became politically optimal to remove trade
barriers that governments had previously found politically optimal to
impose.

The place to start the gymnastics is with an understanding of the
political economy logic that produced the spaghetti bowl in the first
place.

Political economy forces that created the spaghetti bowl

The spaghetti bowl of RTAs did not emerge by mistake. The politically
optimal structure of a bilateral RTA depends upon the comparative
advantages of the two nations and the particular political strengths of
various interest groups at the time the deal is signed. Since these forces
are usually different for every bilateral relationship, it is natural that
RTAs vary greatly – especially as concerns their list of product exclusions, and ROOs that reduce the degree of liberalization implied for
certain products.

This logic accounts for one of the major stylized facts about ROOs –
their hub-and-spoke nature where large trading powers like the United
States and the EU tend to have similar ROOs and exclusions for all their
bilateral RTAs. This is to be expected, since they have the negotiating

leverage to more or less dictate the terms of their ROOs.[7] Powerful vested interests that secure exclusions or protectionist ROOs for one RTA typically obtain them for all.

Asymmetry of the spaghetti bowl

While the hub-and-spoke nature of the spaghetti bowl arose from well-understood protectionist interests, its economic implications are subtle. If a firm is located in the hub market, the world does not really look like a spaghetti bowl. Due to the hub-and-spoke pattern of ROOs and ROCs, a firm located in the hub faces only one set of ROOs for its exports in the hub-and-spoke zone. For example, US–Mexico, US–Canada and US–Chile exports all use what are known as NAFTA rules of origin. The situation is quite different for a firm located in one of the spoke nations. A Mexican firm faces different ROOs for its exports to various partners since the EU–Mexico FTA uses the EU rules of origin, the US–Mexico FTA uses NAFTA rules of origin, and the Japan–Mexico FTA uses a third set. In short, the economic costs of the spaghetti bowl syndrome falls disproportionately on firms located in the spoke economies.

Two costs in particular are worth highlighting since they play a big role in driving multilateralization. The first is the cost of adapting production techniques so that the firm's product meets the criteria of multiple rules of origin (or that of the RTA with the most stringent ROOs). The second is that bilateral cumulation hinders efficient sourcing of parts. For example, if a good needs 50 per cent of its value added in, say, the US or Mexico, Mexican firms can source from either market. However, if a Mexican firm sources from the US, the value added will not count towards origin status when it comes to its exports to the EU, thus discouraging the Mexican firm from buying from the lowest-cost supplier.

In a nutshell, rules of origin serve their protectionist intent in a way that creates more problems for firms located in spoke nations than for firms located in hub nations.

Political economy logic of the Pan-European Cumulation System (PECS)

Given the political economy logic discussed above, the emergence of a spaghetti bowl syndrome in Europe in the 1990s should have been

---

[7] For example, EU total imports exceed 3 trillion dollars, while the import markets of its regional partners are a tenth or a hundredth as large.

expected. What may not have been expected is the volte-face that occurred in 1997 with the implementation of the PECS. To understand the shift, it is necessary to identify the changes that rearranged the political economy forces that produced the European spaghetti bowl in the first place. The focus here is on the globally observed phenomenon of 'unbundling' of manufacturing processes (Baldwin 2006a), which is sometimes called fragmentation, or slicing up the value-added chain.

As competition from low-wage nations mounted in the 1990s, and the coordination of distant activities became easier and cheaper, EU firms unbundled their manufacturing processes and offshored the production of some components to low-wage/low-productivity nations, especially those in nearby Central Europe. This shift of manufacturing from 'hub' to 'spoke' meant that EU firms started to suffer more from the asymmetric effects of the spaghetti bowl. Moreover, the downsizing of production in the EU (due to both unbundling and offshoring and the rise in competition from emerging nations such as China) meant that there was less EU-based production to benefit from the protectionist ROOs.

'Us' becomes 'them'   These changes induced some EU firms (maybe even some of those that pushed for the asymmetric spaghetti bowl in the first place) to become advocates of taming the tangle. They pushed the EU (i) to harmonize rules of origin so as to avoid the cost of meeting the actual and documentary requirements of multiple sets of rules of origin, and (ii) to allow diagonal cumulation, so their factories in the 'spoke' economies could source inputs from a wider range of nations without fear of losing origin status. Of course, a complete analysis of the situation would require examination of the changes in the political economy alignment in the 'spoke' economies as well, but given the hugely asymmetric export dependence of the spoke economies on the EU, the latter was in the driving seat when it came to reform. The switch was made even easier, since most of the spoke countries hoped to become EU members in just a few years.

Nations inside this zone of harmonized preferences tended to be more attractive to FDI from the EU, so the formation of PECS started a domino effect. Turkey joined PECS in 1999, and it is being extended to the EuroMed FTAs gradually with a completion deadline of 2010. Joining PECS requires nations like Tunisia to sign identical FTAs with PECS rules of origin with all of the other PECS members. The diagonal cumulation only comes into effect when the new member completes its system of FTAs.[8]

Political economy logic of ITA

The same sort of political economy logic can account for the emergence of the ITA which eliminated the spaghetti bowl problems in a different way. Instead of keeping the tariff preference and harmonizing the ROOs and ROCs, the ITA made ROOs and ROCs non-operative by granting duty-free treatment to imports from all destinations.

The political economy forces driving this policy move were, however, quite similar to those behind PECS. By the mid 1990s, tariffs were quite low on electronic components all around the world due to an ad hoc collection of multilateral, regional and unilateral tariff cuts. In fact, the EU was the only major trader to charge significant tariffs on such goods. Since the tariff cutting in IT goods was not conducted under the aegis of the GATT, trade was marked by a spaghetti bowl.

From the mid 1980s onward, the production of IT goods witnessed a massive unbundling of production and an attendant explosion of the trade of parts and components. This big increase in unbundling/out-sourcing – together with the acceleration of the product cycle – turned the spaghetti bowl's hindrance of efficient sourcing from a headache into a problem for IT manufacturers all around the world. 'Us' and 'them' became blurred. In this setting, it is fairly easy to see why major producing firms wanted to 'tame the tangle'.

Lessons: spaghetti bowls as building blocks

The key elements in both instances of multilateralization are:

- ROOs and bilateral ROCs act as frictional (i.e. cost-raising) trade barriers since they raise the costs of competitors located in other RTA nations. The hub-and-spoke pattern makes this asymmetrically costly for firms producing in spoke nations.
- Unbundling the manufacturing process erodes political support for existing ROO/cumulation protection since it downsizes the import-competing industries that benefited from them. Additionally, unbund-ling creates new political economy opponents of the ROO/cumulation protection system since the firms that offshore production facilities to

---

[8] See ec.europa.eu/taxation_customs/customs/customs_duties/rules_origin/preferential/ for details.

'spoke' economies find themselves on the 'wrong' side of the ROO/ cumulation protection.

4   Multilateralizing FTA commitments on non-tariff barriers

Does the spaghetti bowl problem extend to non-tariff barriers? Most RTAs address non-tariff barriers in varying degrees, and therefore raise similar questions about the prospects for multilateralizing regionalism. Indeed, it is striking that many WTO members accepted RTAs that include disciplines whose discussion they firmly rejected at the multilateral level. This section considers the extent to which RTAs have created a spaghetti bowl in six areas of deeper RTA commitments: trade in services, government procurement, competition policy, investment performance measures, technical barriers to trade, and trade remedies. It also considers the extent to which such RTA commitments have been or could be multilateralized.

Multilateralization of preferential agreements on trade in services

Trade in services is growing rapidly and nations increasingly view access to world-class services as an essential aspect of competitiveness. The rapid multiplication of FTAs has been accompanied by an explosion of regional commitments on services liberalization, the so-called GATS-plus arrangements (Fink and Jansen, Chapter 6 of this volume; Roy, Marchetti and Lim 2006). This section considers the spaghetti bowl problem with respect to service provisions in FTAs and discusses how they might be multilateralized.

Barriers to trade in services

Barriers to trade in services are distinctive from those on imported goods since trade in services is different. Trade in goods happens when a product is made in one nation and sold in another. Trade in services is a richer phenomenon. Some service trade resembles goods trade in that the producer and the consumer remain on opposite sides of the border – think of internet translation services. In the idiom of the WTO General Agreement on Trade in Services (GATS), these are known as mode 1 (cross-border) transactions. However, many service trades require, or are facilitated by, the physical proximity of producer and consumer. Either the consumer goes to the producer – e.g. someone travels for medical treatment – or the producer goes to the consumer – e.g. a foreign bank establishes a local branch. These types of trade in services are mode 2 (consumption abroad) and mode 3 (commercial presence) respectively.[9] In addition to the need for or desirability of proximity, many service transactions involve intangible products. Intangibility makes it hard to determine what crossed the border and when, so governments have found it difficult or impossible to impose border measures like tariffs. Moreover, intangibility has led governments to pursue their regulatory goals (protecting consumers, etc.) by regulating service providers rather than the service itself.[10]

GATS+ RTAs

RTAs in services can provide preferential market access in two main ways. The first is to ensure that service providers from RTA partners are treated as local suppliers when it comes to regulation and taxation. This extends national treatment in a preferential manner in areas where the nation has not yet committed to national treatment in the GATS. The second is to provide better market access to the partner's service suppliers. Since governments typically regulate service providers instead of the services themselves, one part of market access concerns the recognition of professional qualifications for individuals and regulatory certification for firms. Just as in the case of technical barriers to trade (TBTs – see below), complexity and trust are dominant considerations, so preferential service provisions share many of the features of the preferential TBT agreements discussed below.

'Third party' MFN   Fink and Molinuevo (2008) distinguish a third type of provision that concerns current and future non-discrimination with respect to national treatment and/or market access. In particular, some RTAs explicitly rule out discrimination among RTA members (so-called regional MFN). Another type of MFN provision concerns the preferences that a nation may grant to third parties in the future. Colloquially, this commitment says: 'whatever preference we give to someone else in the future we automatically give to each other'. This provision, called 'non-party MFN' in the jargon, is somewhat akin to

---

[9] There is a fourth GATS mode on temporary movement of service providers (natural persons) which is akin to guest worker programmes but is distinguished from migration; it is rarely addressed in PTAs, so we shall leave it aside in this chapter.

[10] In goods, this would be akin to regulating clothing producers instead of setting norms for clothes.

unconditional MFN in the pre-GATT era. It means that current RTA partners will never have less than the best preferential access, so maybe it should be called 'most preferred access' status. In some service RTAs, most-preferred-access status is guaranteed (so-called 'hard' third-party MFN commitments). In others, there is only the soft commitment that the RTA partners will consider favourably requests for the extension of future preferences to service providers from current RTA partners. See Fink and Molinuevo (2008) and Dee, Ochiai and Okamoto (2006) for details.

ROOs   Service RTAs include rules of origin that establish which services and/or service providers are eligible for preferential treatment. These rules of origin are quite different from the ROOs associated with preferential tariffs.

When it comes to cross-border service trade (mode 1) officials must determine where the service came from. Given the statistical and conceptual difficulties of measuring intermediate inputs in services, ROOs for mode 1 trade tend to be extremely simple. If the provider of the service is located in an RTA partner nation, then the service is considered as originating in that nation and thus eligible for preferences.[11] Rules of origin for mode 2 trade also tend to be simple or absent. A control point occurs at the immigration post of the exporting nation (i.e. as the consumer physically enters the exporting/producing nation), so the issue of the exporters' origin is immaterial and the origin of the consumer is readily verified if necessary.

The rules of origin for trade in services that involve a local presence (mode 3) face a very different challenge. When a government extends preferences to service providers in its RTA partner, it is necessary to establish which service providers are eligible for the preferences. For example, which banks can extend mortgages to home owners? For a variety of reasons, most service RTAs include very liberal rules of origin when it comes to mode 3 services. Most service RTAs in East Asia, for example, extend RTA benefits to firms ('juridical persons' in the jargon) that are constituted or otherwise organized under the laws of one of the

---

[11] In principle, these weak ROOs could produce trade deflection. For instance, a service provider in one RTA partner might be outsourcing the service jobs to providers located in third nations. Typically this is a minor issue since either the mode 1 market access barriers are low or non-existent at the MFN level, so pure trade deflection is not commercially attractive, or trade in the type of service is forbidden on an MFN and preferential basis, e.g. online gambling.

RTA partners and that have substantive business operations in the same nation.[12] These ROOs avoid the difficult question of a firm's nationality, or the nationality of the people who control the corporation. For mode 3 trade, service suppliers from third nations can profit from the market opening negotiated under the RTA. The only requirement is that they establish a legal presence and a certain level of commercial activity in one of the RTA partners. The exception that proves the rule is China's RTA with Hong Kong, China. This contains quite strict provisions intended to exclude service providers that are not owned and controlled by residents of either Hong Kong, China or the mainland.

Note that liberal ROOs are required by GATS Article V.6 for RTAs involving developed country WTO members.[13]

Multilateralization

As the chapter by Fink and Jansen in this volume argues persuasively, the preferential agreements concerning trade in services have not created a spaghetti bowl in the way tariff preferences have. In essence, the special features of most service FTAs have provided what might be called 'multilateralization on autopilot'. The 'leaky' ROOs automatically multilateralize the preferential market access to a certain extent, since third-nation service providers can free-ride on the preference by paying the cost of establishing a presence in one of the partner's markets. Unless all of the partners have equally restrictive MFN market access restrictions, the liberal ROOs tend to have the effect of lowering all RTA partners' MFN market access to that of the most liberal member (plus the extra establishment cost). Likewise, the hard and soft most-preferred-access clauses (i.e. third-party MFN) tend automatically to tame the tangle.

The options for multilateralizing service RTAs are quite similar to those for preferential TBT agreements, which are discussed on p. 113.

---

[12] This is not to say these nations make it easy for foreign firms to establish a judicial presence, but any firm that does manage to do so in one FTA partner will enjoy the preferences, e.g. national treatment with respect to taxes and regulation.

[13] The article requires that a service supplier that is a 'juridical person' (i.e. legally established) with 'substantive business operations' in any other PTA member nations must be granted the preferential treatment; in short, the rule of origin must be based on where the firm operates rather than its nationality. Fink and Jansen (in the present volume) assert that this requirement may have been included in the GATS for political economy motives that resemble the 'spaghetti bowls as building blocks' argument. That is, in a world of large multinational service providers, 'us' is 'them', and so allowing strict rules of origin would be likely to harm the commercial interests of the most influential service providers around the world.

The first point is that the WTO should encourage the use of 'leaky' ROOs in future RTAs concerning trade in services. The second point is that the WTO should encourage the adoption of global standards for the regulation of service providers as a way of reducing the tension between the protectionist and legitimate motives driving service sector regulation. The positive example here comes from the Decision on Disciplines on Domestic Regulation in the Accountancy Sector that was agreed by the WTO Working Party on Professional Services in 1998. The Working Party on Domestic Regulation is already engaged in the task of exploring whether the success of international standardization in accounting could be reproduced in other service sectors.

Much of the liberalization of services by developing nations – especially the ones that are rapidly industrializing – resembles the unilateral tariff cutting that they are also engaging in. As in tariff cutting, these nations appear unwilling to bind their very low applied rates in the multilateral setting. GATS-plus commitments in services are especially marked in sectors that directly affect their attractiveness to FDI that boosts export competitiveness. Examples include trade-related financial services (insurance, letters of credit, etc.), distribution services (express package delivery and courier services), construction, business services and telecommunications. The GATS-plus RTAs – especially in North–South RTAs – provide the developing country in such an arrangement with a means of locking in market opening and thus giving assurances to investors that the reforms will remain in place. Of course, GATS scheduling would also play this role, but this route suffers from free-riding because of MFN. This line of reasoning suggests that the WTO might create lock-in mechanisms that help developing nation members to consolidate their policy reforms without going all the way to GATS scheduling.

Finally, the ongoing process of unbundling and offshoring is likely to foster the liberalization of trade in services. The combination of falling communications costs and the unbundling of manufacturing and service sectors should create an incentive for nations to abandon idiosyncratic service standards as a way of boosting the competitiveness of their own exporters and improving the attractiveness of their nations as destinations for foreign direct investment.

Government procurement

Government procurement is big business. It is not uncommon for developing and industrialized country governments to spend 15 to

20 per cent of their GDP on goods and services (Audet, 1998; Trionfetti, 2000). In a world where there are fourteen economies in the trillion dollar-plus category and forty economies in the hundred billion dollar-plus range,[14] government procurement represents a substantial commercial opportunity.

In many nations, these opportunities are systematically denied to foreign firms. Indeed, nations have never agreed to liberalize government procurement markets on a fully MFN basis. Liberalization to date has involved a degree of exclusiveness in the RTA context as well as in the WTO context.

Liberalization initiatives: the GPA and RTAs

The WTO's Government Procurement Agreement (GPA) is a plurilateral agreement (or club) whose objective is to open up its members' procurement markets on a preferential basis to other club members. Roughly speaking, the GPA rules out most discrimination, but only as concerns club members.[15] The exclusion of non-members from international procurement opportunities is permitted and occurs frequently. Indeed, the GATT explicitly excludes government procurement from coverage, which explains why the MFN rule is not infringed by the GPA.

The GPA was revised during the Uruguay Round of trade negotiations and a number of WTO members joined the Agreement. Other WTO members can seek to join this Agreement, and negotiate their terms of entry accordingly, but only a minority have done so. Currently, counting the European Communities as a single member, this plurilateral accord has twelve other members (mostly industrialized countries). Countries that have joined the WTO (including China) in recent years have been pressed to join the GPA as part of the accession terms, and as they do a number of 'exogenous shocks' will affect the magnitude of procurement covered by the GPA's disciplines.

---

[14] Measured in purchasing power parity terms. Data taken from the World Bank's World Development Indicators for the last year available (2005).

[15] The application of price preferences against non-domestic bidders is disallowed between GPA members, thereby creating a margin of preference over non-members. Other measures in the Agreement seek to limit or eliminate discrimination against suppliers whose governments are parties to the GPA. The state bodies whose procurements were covered as a result of their inclusion in the negotiations were bound in the resulting agreement, adding to transparency and predictability. Taken together, these measures confer substantial commercial advantages over suppliers from jurisdictions that are not members of the GPA.

ROOs and foreign subsidiaries   The GPA forbids discrimination in public procurement processes against foreign subsidiaries based in a GPA signatory. It also rules out the application of special rules of origin for procurement; GPA members must apply the same set of rules of origin to determining preferences in public procurement as they do in determining preferences in tariff rates.

Procurement in RTAs   Like the GPA, the government procurement provisions in RTAs typically open state purchasing to foreign competition on a preferential – often bilateral – basis. A description and taxonomy of the content of the government procurement chapters of almost thirty FTAs can be found in Bourgeois, Dawar and Evenett (2007: section 4). The provisions vary considerably across agreements in detail and content. The most detailed contain provisions on the scope and coverage of disciplines; the definition of government procurement, associated entities, and related matters; the methods and manner in which state purchases can be conducted; rules of origin; the allowable rules on the qualification of suppliers; time limits employed in state procurement procedures; and institutional matters.

Third-party MFN   As in many GATS-plus RTAs, many RTA procurement provisions require third-party MFN guarantees so as to limit the extent to which preferential procurement is undermined by subsequent RTAs. Specifically, these procurement-related provisions require that each party's government purchases treat the other party's

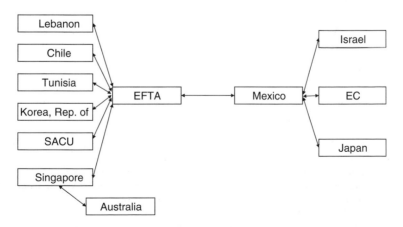

Figure 3.1 FTAs with most-preferential-access provisions on procurement

commercial entities no worse than those entities from any other third party. This implies that if nations A and B sign an FTA with such a provision and B subsequently signs an FTA with nation C that grants the latter's firms more generous access to B's procurement market, B must unconditionally extend the more generous access to firms in A. Note that this provision is a one-way ratchet towards liberalization; if B's new RTA grants C *worse* access than it gave A, then A's access does not change.

As in services FTAs, there is also a 'soft' variant of the most-preferential-access clause. This implies that the better access is not automatically granted, but rather negotiated. This is something like the distinction between conditional and unconditional MFN (using the pre-GATT meaning of MFN).[16] Some RTAs trigger such negotiations, or, more weakly, consultations following the conclusion of an FTA with a third party that includes more generous access to national procurement markets than the original FTA.

Interestingly, some nations have included such provisions for pro-curement-related matters but not for other forms of trade in their FTAs, suggesting that there is something particular to the nature of compe-tition in procurement markets (perhaps the rents in such markets are on average higher or exporters in procurement markets are more concen-trated and potentially better at lobbying for their own interests). Such provisions can be seen in defensive terms – allowing an FTA partner to claim back some of the lost profits brought about by greater competi-tion in another country's procurement market through rights to sell to a greater number of government entities or on less onerous terms. As Figure 3.1 shows, these clauses have been used by middle-sized trading nations and blocs, notably EFTA and Mexico.

Multilateralization

From the multilateralization perspective, it is important to stress the importance of rules of origin. The GPA forbids discrimination against non-party subsidiaries in GPA nations. At first sight, this may seem to be a 'leaky' ROO of the type seen in many services RTAs. However, this simply means that 'origin' of the company does not matter but the origin of goods sold to governments does, and this is determined by the standard ROOs. For example, if a US government office puts out a large tender for printing equipment, the procurement provisions in NAFTA

---

[16] On the pre-GATT meaning of MFN and the broader history of the MFN concept, see Yanai (2002).

allow firms in Mexico to bid on the contract if the printing equipment is considered to be made in Mexico under the standard NAFTA ROOs – even if the firm is the Mexican subsidiary of a Japanese corporation. Since the ROOs may differ for each RTA among GPA members, and each GPA member has its own non-preferential rules of origin, preferences under the GPA tend to create a spaghetti bowl of preferential access – at least as far as trade in goods is concerned.[17] When it comes to services, the application of typical 'leaky' service ROOs tends to lessen the spaghetti bowl problem due to the 'automatic multilateralization' property of 'leaky' ROOs.

There have been, however, some distinct developments in the government procurement disciplines contained in RTAs that either extend or facilitate the extension of preferential market access. If more of these provisions are adopted in RTAs, and, as we shall argue, there are identifiable incentives for certain parties to include them, then a considerable widening of access to state procurement markets may be possible. In turn, this may eventually make it easier to negotiate a multilateral WTO accord on government procurement-related matters.

As mentioned in the services section, these third-party MFN or most-preferential-access clauses automatically reduce the geographical discrimination implied by proliferating RTAs; they are thus multilateralization on autopilot – or perhaps one should say 'plurilateralization' since the deeper preferences are only granted to the existing set of RTA partners.

Third-party MFN provisions foster liberalization in another way. They allow one nation to free-ride on the negotiating clout of future RTA partners. Continuing with the example, a most-preferential-access clause means that A can free-ride on C's negotiating clout with B. In this respect one can understand why nations with small procurement outlays may wish to include this provision in their FTAs if they expect that their FTA partners will subsequently negotiate another FTA with a larger country that is likely to demand and receive greater preferential access to state contracts. Interestingly, we found several such provisions in FTAs between smaller states in Eastern Europe (South-Eastern Europe in particular) and in the Mediterranean. Many of these states have gone on

---

[17] The difference can be illustrated by analogy to EFTA. EFTA is a 'free trade lake' since it is a club where members extend duty-free treatment to all members *and* apply the same rules of origin to all EFTA members. If each EFTA member were free to impose different ROOs on imports from different EFTA members, the implied market access would look like a tangle of 'canals' rather than a 'lake'.

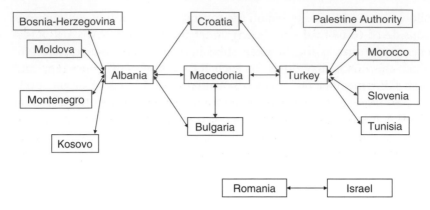

Figure 3.2 South-eastern European FTAs with most-preferential-access provisions on procurement

to negotiate FTAs with the European Union, which certainly does have plenty of negotiating clout. Figure 3.2 suggests that Albania, Macedonia, and Turkey have pursued such strategies in the past.

Domino effects Another mechanism through which preferential market access is extended – and perhaps eventually multilateralized – is through domino-like effects triggered by the consequences of lower exporter profits that follow from selective market opening (Baldwin, 1993). Arguably such an effect can be discerned in the GPA enlargement that followed the EU's expansion to twenty-five members.

The incumbent fifteen EU members were members of the GPA but the ten members who joined were not. EU membership granted the ten newcomers preferential access to the EU15 procurement markets, so EU enlargement meant other GPA members faced heightened competition in the EU15 from the ten newcomers and heightened competition in the ten from the EU15 incumbents. According to the domino logic, the non-EU GPA members accelerated GPA membership for the ten new-comers in order to offset this new 'trade diversion'.[18] The EU enlarge-ment changed the array of vested interests in a way that fostered a GPA

---

[18] Indeed, the United States Trade Representatives' 2004 Annual Report on Foreign Trade Barriers explicitly acknowledged that 'negative commercial consequences in some instances' may follow EU enlargement. Moreover, the same report states the US desire to see the new EU member states bound by the provisions of the WTO GPA, which would effectively open the latter nations' state purchases to US exporters.

enlargement.[19] The representative of Israel noted that '[h]is delegation hoped that this was the beginning of a process whereby parties to the Agreement would bring in more countries, and not stop at a one-time historic moment' (WTO, 2004), suggesting that the dynamics involved were of a more general nature and not EU-specific.

Thinking ahead, the accession of a large trading nation like China – which is obliged to eventually join as per its accession agreement – is very likely to trigger a similar domino effect as other nations seek to offset the resulting discrimination their firms would face relative to GPA members.

Competition policy

Since Adam Smith (and possibly before) it has been recognized that the benefits of international commerce can be reduced by the exercise of market power. Rents have provided a powerful rationale for state measures to promote competition in markets and, by the same token, strong incentives for corporations to lobby for and against such measures. In a multilateral trading system where the reciprocal exchange of market access is central, fears about the impact of anti-competitive practices have often been expressed in terms of nullifying or impairing previously negotiated improvements in access to foreign investment. Moreover, as FDI has grown, concerns about the anti-competitive conduct of incumbent firms in countries receiving FDI, in particular the conduct of state-owned or state-influenced firms, has further raised the profile of competition-related matters in trade negotiations. Finally, as international market integration has progressed, more and more countries have enacted and begun enforcing national competition laws, although the relationship between these two trends is not very well understood.

Despite the economic logic linking trade and competition policy, attempts to agree binding multilateral disciplines have failed. The inter-war experience in Europe – where cartels were a serious barrier to trade

[19] Four of the ten newcomer states had already applied for GPA membership, but the accession procedures were taking many years and involved bilateral negotiations with (in principle) every existing GPA member. In view of the EU enlargement, the GPA committee agreed to an expedited administrative procedure. At a meeting on 23 April 2003 a consensus of the existing GPA members was reached in favour of accession. On 8 December 2006 the GPA committee also agreed to allow in Bulgaria and Romania following their EU accession.

(Wurm, 1993) – led to the inclusion of competition policy provisions in the Havana Charter. The US Congress baulked at ratifying it, not least because of concerns about the proposed disciplines on monopolies and the like. More recently, in 2004 WTO members decided not to launch negotiations on a multilateral framework on competition policy. There is, therefore, no comprehensive set of binding multilateral rules on competition law and its enforcement.

There are, however, provisions in the TRIPs, TRIMs and GATS agreements that refer to anti-competitive conduct. Moreover, some scholars argue that the national treatment provisions in the GATT apply to the legislated content as well as to the application of competition law. As a result, it would not be difficult for non-WTO-related initiatives on competition law and policy to go beyond existing multilateral disciplines in this area.

Competition policy in RTAs

While binding disciplines at the multilateral level are largely lacking, progress has been made in RTAs.[20] Solano and Sennekamp (2006) review the competition chapters of eighty-six FTAs. The overwhelming majority of these are of the North–South type. The provisions they found were on adopting, maintaining and applying competition laws; coordination and cooperation between competition enforcement bodies; provisions addressing specific forms of anti-competitive behaviour; competition principles reflecting core principles, including non-discrimination, due process and transparency; provisions to exclude or alter the recourse to trade remedies; dispute settlement; and measures involving special and differential treatment for developing countries.

For our purposes, it is also noteworthy that Solano and Sennekamp identify two broad models for competition provisions in RTAs:

- a 'European' model that focuses on measures to adopt and apply competition law and specific measures addressing anti-competitive conduct; and
- a 'North American' model that principally contains provisions on coordination and cooperation between competition enforcement agencies.

---

[20] The focus here on binding disciplines is to be distinguished from the development of non-binding international accords on competition law and its enforcement that have been developed under the auspices of UNCTAD, the OECD and the International Competition Network.

Anderson and Evenett (2006) evaluated the Solano and Sennekamp study and argued that the latter omitted potentially important competition-related provisions that were not included in the competition chapters of RTAs. The overlooked provisions often referred to ensuring that monopolies, state-owned enterprises, and formally privatized firms do not engage in anti-competitive conduct. Moreover, the telecommunications chapters of many RTAs made specific reference to anti-competitive conduct.[21] Furthermore, some RTAs contain competition-specific provisions relating to the granting of public subsidies to individual firms competing in national markets (so-called state aids provisions in EC parlance). These competition provisions can be thought of as 'taming the state' and are quite different in conception and specificity[22] from many of the substantive disciplines relating to national laws concerning private sector anti-competitive conduct.

The foregoing remarks are particularly relevant here because of the alleged spread of the so-called NAFTA competition provisions throughout parts of Latin America. The NAFTA model contains at least the following elements: provisions concerning the adoption and maintenance of 'measures' (which are not necessarily laws) to proscribe anti-competitive conduct (Article 1501); measures relating to the conduct of monopolies and state enterprises (Articles 1502 and 1503); and specific provisions relating to monopolies in the telecommunications sector (Article 1305). We have examined whether these particular NAFTA provisions could be found in the RTAs concluded in the ten years after NAFTA was signed and in agreements where at least one party was located in North America and Latin America (see Figures 3.3 and 3.4).[23]

Figures 3.3 and 3.4 show how two important competition-related NAFTA provisions on telecommunications have spread within and outside the Americas in the ten years since the NAFTA was signed. (Article 1305.1 of the NAFTA proscribes telecommunication monopolies from engaging in anti-competitive conduct.) It is clear that Mexico

---

[21] Here a common concern is the terms upon which rivals can access an incumbent firm's distribution network.

[22] The specificity of these provisions is a strong indication that they were drafted with the advice of and in consultation with the affected private sector interests. These may well be provisions deliberately designed to tackle known and serious problems facing commercial interests that operate or plan to operate abroad.

[23] We are interested in the extent to which other nations have adopted the use of these specific provisions, which were originally proposed for inclusion in NAFTA by the US. For this reason we ignore the FTAs signed by the US in the ten years after NAFTA.

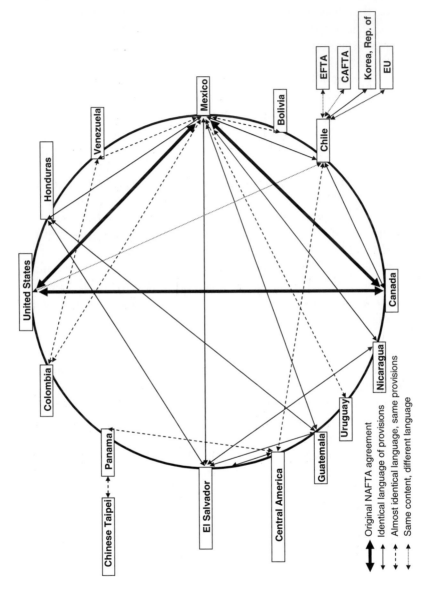

Figure 3.3 Spread of NAFTA Article 1305.1

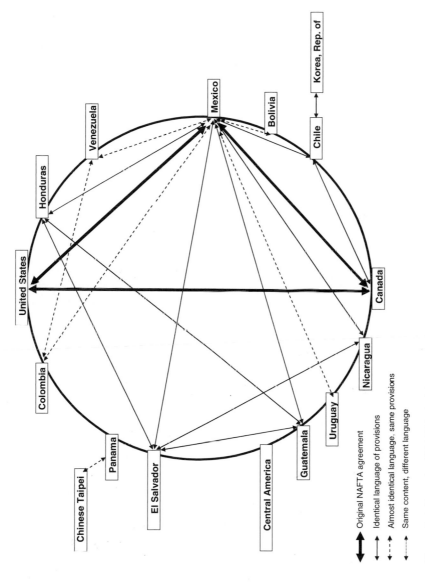

Figure 3.4 Spread of NAFTA Article 1305.2

Legend:
- Original NAFTA agreement
- Identical language of provisions
- Almost identical language, same provisions
- Same content, different language

and Chile have included this provision in a number of the FTAs that they have signed. The spread of this provision is such that Asian economies, such as Chinese Taipei and the Republic of Korea, are now supposed to abide by the strictures contained in Article 1305.1 of NAFTA.

Article 1305.2 of NAFTA refers to steps that each party shall take to prevent anti-competitive conduct by telecommunications firms. This article has spread widely within Latin America, as evidenced by Figure 3.4. Comparing the figures suggests that Article 1305.2 may not have spread as far as Article 1305.1; even so, sixteen nations have signed up to FTA provisions identical or similar to Article 1305.2.

Multilateralization

As far as multilateralization is concerned, it is important to note that very few RTAs have explicitly discriminatory provisions; RTA provisions on competition policy generally insist on core principles that include non-discrimination, due process and transparency. Thus although the commitments are made in preferential trade deals, their effect is multilateral. A US firm in Turkey has the same rights before Turkish competition authorities as an EU firm, even though Turkey's competition policy was the result of bilaterals with the EU (Kulaksizoglu, 2006). In nations without explicit competition policy, discrimination based on nationality can be a problem. (CARICOM is the exception that proves the rule; it contains conditional MFN rules on mergers and acquisitions that favour CARICOM firms.) This suggests that the spaghetti bowl may not be much of a problem with respect to competition policy.

The so-called NAFTA model, with its greater reliance on state-to-state actions could open the door to spaghetti bowl problems; only parties to the RTA are granted rights. For example, NAFTA gives the US government a mechanism for encouraging the Canadian government to take action, while EU governments have no such mechanisms. In practice, discrimination is not thought to be a major issue; the distinction between the discriminatory impact of the two models is minor in practice.

The spread of the NAFTA-style telecommunications provision can be thought of as multilateralizing regionalism in two respects. First, the number of countries that have signed RTAs with such provisions indicates that a pervasive norm has been established. As more RTAs with these provisions are signed the norm will grow in country coverage. Second, harmonization to a single regulatory regime for telecommunications liberalizes trade in the same way that adoption of an international standard liberalizes TBTs. A common set of rules that governments apply to private firms in many nations tends to foster competition and trade. Moreover, since the regulator regime principle concerns the relationship between the regulating government and all firms, it cannot be considered preferential.

In this light, it is useful to reflect upon the political economy forces driving the spread of what are effectively multilateral disciplines via RTAs.

Political economy drivers In the case of the European model, a crucial point is that the EU offers many tiers of preferential market access to its trading partners (Baldwin and Wyplosz, 2005: chapter 12). The highest – so-called single-market access – is limited to nations that have, inter alia, adopted EU competition policy norms and practices. Nations that are heavily dependent on the EU market often adopt EU internal policies, including competition policy, on a 'voluntary' basis, locking in such reforms in their EU bilaterals.[24] In these cases, it is the usual domino effect that drives the EU's partners to seek to offset the discrimination implicit in the lower levels of EU access.[25]

The spread of NAFTA competition policy provisions in the telecoms sector documented above seems to be driven by two political economy factors. First, during the 1990s, many Latin American nations deregulated and privatized telecoms. Many of these countries may have found North South RTAs a particularly useful commitment device or, more weakly, a means to signal their intent to get serious about competition in the telecoms sector.[26]

Second, the same decade saw a considerable international consolidation in the telecommunications, utilities and banking sectors, as well as greater openness in Latin America to foreign investors in these and other sectors. Such foreign investors would no doubt like to have seen region-wide rules to discourage anti-competitive conduct by incumbent firms, but in the absence of any progress towards completing the Free Trade Areas of the

---

[24] EFTA nations (all of whom have adopted EU competition norms) follow a policy of shadowing EU bilaterals so that EFTA-based firms face the same competitive conditions as EU-based firms. This phenomenon, which creates what might be called an RTA union, means that the number of RTAs with EU-like competition policy is doubled almost automatically.

[25] See Baldwin (1997) on how the domino effect worked with respect to single-market access.

[26] Alternatively, they may have regarded the provisions as unimportant and so accepted them rather than offer further concessions to induce a trading partner to drop demands for competition provisions.

Americas (FTAA), tough binding rules in a web of bilateral RTAs may well have been the next-best alternative. Moreover, since expansion by a subsidiary within Latin America might have been represented successfully as benefiting the subsidiary's host country, the host government might have been induced to demand competition provisions be included in RTAs with other countries. Given that one of the key sectors involved – telecommunications – became very concentrated in Latin America in the late 1990s, a small number of foreign investors had plenty at stake.[27] Given that similar consolidation has taken place across the globe in the banking, financial services and utilities sectors (to name but a few), greater pressures for measures against the anti-competitive conduct of incumbent firms (that may well be state-backed or state-influenced) will grow. The substantial cross-border corporate consolidation witnessed in recent years blurs the distinction between 'us' and 'them', creating in this case pressures for the wider application of national treatment in national commercial legislation and associated regulations.

In sum, because non-discrimination is one of the core principles of competition policy that is typically part of RTA competition provisions, the proliferation of RTAs has done little to create a spaghetti bowl effect. Moreover, as the spread of certain competition-related provisions of the NAFTA agreement demonstrates, RTAs may well over time broaden support for particular multilateral initiatives on competition law and its enforcement. This is not to imply, however, that the competition provisions in existing RTAs are carbon copies of one another, or that there is no room for further entrenching non-discrimination principles in the competition chapters of RTAs.

Investment performance requirements

Despite the economic significance that many policymakers attach to FDI, three attempts to negotiate wide-ranging international disciplines have ended in failure.[28] The General Agreement on Trade in Services does,

---

[27] At the end of the period of consolidation, Telefonica (of Spain) and Bell South (of the US) were by far the two largest firms operating in the Latin American telecommunications markets.

[28] Specifically the inclusion of the proposed investment chapter in the Havana Charter, the collapse of negotiations over a Multilateral Agreement on Investment (MAI) at the OECD in 1998, and the July 2004 decision by WTO members not to negotiate a Multilateral Framework on Investment during the course of the Doha Round of multilateral trade negotiations.

however, contain investment liberalization provisions through its scheduling options under mode 3 (commercial presence). Notwithstanding the absence of a comprehensive international investment regime, there are multilateral disciplines on selected investment matters including those related to trade-related investment measures (such as rules on performance requirements contained in the WTO's TRIMs agreement) and in services (as part of the GATS agreement). Many observers agree, however, that most of the innovation in designing international disciplines is taking place in preferential agreements such as bilateral investment treaties (BITs) and RTAs (Sauvé, 2006: 327). At the end of 2005, some 2,495 BITs had been signed and dozens of FTAs included investment provisions, in particular those FTAs between industrialized and developing countries (UNCTAD, 2006; Lesher and Miroudot, 2006).

In this case study, we focus mainly on commitments to ban so-called performance requirements on foreign investors – whether those requirements are trade-related or not.[29] Before proceeding along these lines, however, it is worth noting that GATS provisions on mode 3 access for foreign investors, as well as such access provisions in RTAs and BITS, are mostly of a non-discriminatory nature (see Fink and Jansen in this volume), and therefore pose little threat of a spaghetti bowl phenomenon or obstacle to multilateralization, if investment rules were to prosper as a subject for multilateral negotiation. On the other hand, some investment liberalization commitments on access effectively involve rationing – the commitment is to permit a limited number of suppliers into the domestic market. In this case incumbent firms, from wherever they come, clearly have an advantage, and multilateralization would not offer significant additional market access benefits.

Preferential provisions

NAFTA provides good examples of the sort of investment disciplines that can be included in RTAs. Chapter 11 of the NAFTA agreement covers a wide range of matters including the definition of investment, the standards of treatment of investors, expropriation, and consultation and dispute resolution mechanisms (Heindl, 2006). In particular, Article

---

[29] Performance requirements include measures requiring foreign investors to export a given percentage of goods or services, to achieve a given level of domestic content, to accord preferences to goods or services in a specific territory or from a certain group of suppliers, to use or exchange certain amounts of foreign currency, to restrict sales of goods produced or services delivered by the foreign investor, or to require an investor to be an exclusive supplier.

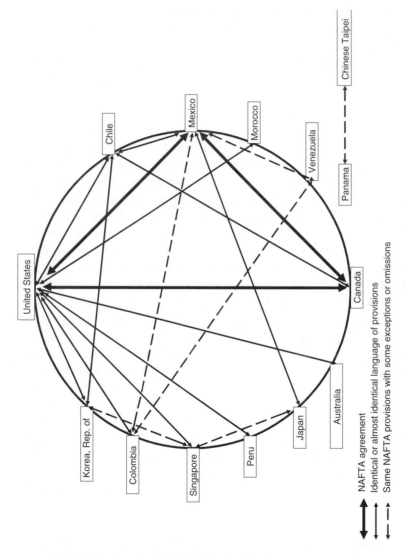

NAFTA agreement
Identical or almost identical language of provisions
Same NAFTA provisions with some exceptions or omissions

Figure 3.5 Spread of NAFTA performance requirements provisions in FTAs

1106 of Chapter 11 contains strict provisions on performance requirements that are often regarded as having gone beyond the measures
contained in the TRIMs agreement, not least by offering a more
extensive list of prohibited measures than in the latter agreement but
also by requiring the abolition of these requirements against any foreign
investor, even those from countries not party to the NAFTA (OECD,
1996; Wilke, 2002).

There is evidence that certain investment provisions have spread
across RTAs, in particular NAFTA's investment provisions (Gantz,
2004; Gangé and Morin, 2006; Reiter, 2004). To explore these matters
further, we examined how many FTAs contained a clause that was
identical or very similar to that found in Article 1106 of NAFTA.

Figure 3.5 shows the extent of the spread of NAFTA's restrictions on
performance requirements in Latin America and beyond. Fourteen
countries have effectively agreed to repeal and never apply performance
requirements against foreign investors from any jurisdiction. Another
country (Uruguay) has agreed to do likewise, but in the context of its
recent BIT with the United States. This reform is effectively multilateralized, even though the vehicle for doing so is traditionally asso
ciated with preferential treatment and discrimination.

We also checked whether clauses similar to Article 1106 can be
found in US and Canadian BITs, which are traditionally associated with
including measures on performance requirements that go beyond the
TRIMs agreement (OECD, 2005). A further thirty-six countries were
found to have committed to forgo the application of performance
requirements against US or Canadian investors, but are not committed
to treat non-party foreign investors similarly. In terms of FDI covered,
however, the FDI inflows into countries that have liberalized on an
MFN basis were three times as large as those into countries that liberalized on a preferential basis.[30] The fact that in less than fifteen years a
quarter of worldwide FDI currently flows into countries which operate
under the same liberalized regime for performance requirements is
striking (see Tables 3.1 and 3.2), and provides a firm basis for the

---

[30] For the sake of completeness we also checked an UNCTAD compendium of national
investment regimes to see which countries had eliminated preference requirements on a
unilateral basis. The results are reported in the penultimate column of Table 3.1. Two
countries were said to have eliminated their performance requirements in totality (those
with a tick in this column) and two other countries were found to have 'generally'
liberalized their performance requirement (those with a 'G' in this column).

Table 3.1. *RTAs and BITs that forgo the use of performance requirements (PR) entirely*

	Performance requirements (PR) eliminated because of:				
	FTA	BIT with US	BIT with Canada	Unilateral	FDI average 2003–5 ($m)
Countries committed to eliminate PR entirely					
Australia	✓			✓	5,855
Canada	✓			G	14,323
Chile	✓				6,049
Colombia	✓				5,022
Japan	✓			✓	5,638
Korea, Rep. of	✓				6,272
Mexico	✓				16,971
Morocco	✓				2,144
Panama	✓	✓			820
Peru	✓				1,838
Singapore	✓				15,093
Chinese Taipei	✓				1,325
United States	✓			G	91,655
Uruguay		✓	✓		449
Venezuela	✓				2,378
Total:					**175,834 (24.1 per cent)**

further spread and multilateralization of rules to ban the use of such requirements on foreign investors.

It is noteworthy that few EU member states and no large emerging markets (such as Brazil, India or China) have agreed to eliminate performance requirements, either unilaterally, bilaterally or multilaterally. More generally, multilateralization of a ban on performance requirements on foreign investors is an option for WTO members, although if recent debates are anything to go by, a controversial one (Sauvé, 2006; Ferrarini, 2003).

Like preferential access to goods markets, preferential access to investment locations can introduce differentials to corporate cost structures and so distort FDI flows from the global optimum. Worse still, preferential access offered to foreign investors may trigger a 'race to the bottom' when it comes to subsidies and other benefits that have high

Table 3.2. *RTAs and BITs that forgo the use of performance requirements (PR) bilaterally*

| | Performance requirements (PR) eliminated because of: | | | | |
	TA	BIT with US	BIT with Canada	Unilateral	FDI average 2003–5 ($m)
Countries committed to eliminate PR bilaterally					
Albania	✓				257
Argentina	✓				3,529
Armenia	✓		✓		198
Azerbaijan	✓				2,840
Bahrain	✓				810
Bangladesh	✓				501
Bolivia	✓				12
Bulgaria	✓				2,588
Cameroon	✓				6
Costa Rica			✓		615
Croatia	✓		✓		1,697
Czech Republic	✓				6,022
Egypt	✓				2,590
El Salvador			✓		345
Ecuador	✓				1,543
Estonia	✓				1,607
Georgia	✓				430
Grenada	✓				58
Honduras	✓				281
Jamaica	✓				641
Jordan	✓				873
Kazakhstan	✓				2,648
Kyrgyzstan	✓				89
Latvia	✓				541
Lebanon			✓		2,444
Moldova	✓				152
Mongolia	✓				136
Poland	✓				8,395
Romania	✓		✓		5,039
Senegal	✓				61
Slovakia	✓				1,308
South Africa			✓		2,637

Table 3.2. (*cont.*)

		Performance requirements (PR) eliminated because of:			
	TA	BIT with US	BIT with Canada	Unilateral	FDI average 2003–5 ($m)
Trinidad and Tobago	✓				614
Tunisia	✓				668
Turkey	✓				4,757
Ukraine			✓		3,649
Total					**60,582 (8.3 per cent)**

opportunity costs in developing nations. Not every argument, however, points to welfare reductions from preferential investment rules. For one, in a second-best world the offer of such preferences by a trading partner may induce a government to eliminate costly restrictions and obligations on foreign investors. In sum, then, it is inappropriate to issue a blanket condemnation of the investment provisions in FTAs or BITs.

Multilateralization

As far as multilateralization is concerned, it is important to note that many of the RTAs include MFN clauses which automatically multilateralize the disciplines and thus spread the benefits offered by a trading partner to foreign investors from a given jurisdiction to other jurisdictions. Admittedly, these MFN clauses are not so prevalent that they have eliminated all forms of discrimination; even so, they are probably more prevalent than some might appreciate (OECD, 2005). Table 3.1 gives some very concrete examples. Given the multilateralization-via-RTAs effect, it is useful to think about the political economy driving the spread of investment provisions in RTAs and BITs.

Unbundling – specifically, here, the creation of those complex international supply networks that require FDI – fundamentally alters the political economy of performance requirements within nations. A growing number of national firms that are internationally competitive in supplying a single part or component, or in undertaking a step in the production process, will support performance requirements that shield less efficient domestic input suppliers, knowing that the latter raise the total cost of supplying overseas markets from their country, putting off foreign investors in the first place, and limiting the demand for the former firms' products. Once again 'us' fragments and some domestic commercial interests align themselves with 'them'. This logic has become pervasive in a number of developing countries that employ investment provisions in RTAs as a means of promoting the attractiveness of their economies as export centres. Reiter (2004) argues that these considerations drove Mexico, Chile and, to a lesser degree, Singapore to include tough disciplines on foreign investment in their myriad of RTAs – a strategy which has been quite successful.[31]

Unbundling is growing in prominence globally, and spreading to a wider range of manufacturing and service sectors. As a result, export performance and inward investment are increasingly tied. In East Asia, for example, the rapid rise of regional trade in parts and components was closely associated with the rise in regional investment in manufacturing (Ando and Kimura, 2005). Just as this unbundling and competition for unbundling encouraged a 'race to the bottom' on MFN tariff cutting, it likewise encouraged nations in the region to commit to certain liberal investment policies, such as forgoing the right to performance criteria. While these commitments have typically been made in the context of RTAs and BITs, the logic of making such commitments is not primarily bilateral – it is to improve the attractiveness of the nation as a location for all foreign investors. For their part, outsourcing firms clearly prefer a larger diversified pool of potential investment locations where there are few, if any, conditions imposed on their operations. In short, there may well be an interest on the part of both home and host countries in multilateralizing the investment provisions in their network of RTAs and BITs. The WTO should consider using its power as fair broker and convenor of negotiations to facilitate this sort of multilateralization, or more precisely plurilateralization, of investment provision.

Technical barriers to trade

The steady lowering of tariffs has redirected attention to non-tariff measures.[32] TBTs have been one of the most important categories.

---

[31] Reiter (2004) also reports that Mexico sought to include expansive investment provisions in its FTA with the EC. However, for a variety of internal reasons the EC was not able to accede to Mexico's demands in this respect.

[32] This point is not new. The last time 'globalization' was in fashion – when it was called internationalization and interdependence – Robert Baldwin (1970: 2) wrote: 'The

Technical barriers to trade are different

With the goal of protecting the health and safety of consumers, animals and plants, protecting the environment, and protecting consumers from fraud, most governments regulate the sale of most goods. Such regulation is an essential part of good governance. However, the resulting standards, regulations and rules can act as protectionist measures when they unjustifiably raise foreign firms' costs. The WTO rules try to avoid the protectionist use of standards by insisting that they be applied in a non-discriminatory manner and are no more restrictive of trade than necessary to achieve the underlying public policy objective. It is useful to distinguish two forms of TBTs: (i) the content of the product norm (i.e. the precise standard, regulation, rule),[33] and (ii) testing (i.e. testing procedures that are necessary to demonstrate that a product complies with a particular norm, also called 'conformity assessment procedures').[34]

Complexity and the 'trust issue' Product regulation is intrinsically complex and this complexity is the key to the distinctiveness of TBT reform (Baldwin, 2000). First, it implies that protectionism is finely interwoven with good governance regulation.[35] Second, it means that reducing the protectionist content of product regulation without lowering regulatory quality requires trust; liberalizing governments must believe that the other government is capable of establishing and enforcing highly technical rules in a transparent and credible manner. This

---

    lowering of tariffs has, in effect, been like draining a swamp. The lower water level has revealed all the snags and stumps of non-tariff barriers that still have to be cleared away.'

[33] Many authors break the norms into standards (usually defined as voluntary norms, like the GSM standard for cell phones), and regulations (mandatory norms, like prohibition of lead paint on toys).

[34] The extent to which a particular regulation or testing procedure is a trade barrier is extremely difficult to ascertain. Much product regulation is highly technical and thus its impact can only be understood by industry experts. Since these experts usually work for companies whose bottom lines are affected by the rules, it can be difficult or impossible to get unbiased advice.

[35] It is often asserted that TBT liberalization engages sovereignty issues, which tariff cutting does not, but this is incomplete reasoning. Many tariffs are used for valid policy goals – e.g. protecting jobs of low-wage workers – but the WTO rejects the raising of bound rates as a legitimate means of attaining such goals since tariffs are not the least-trade-restrictive means. The transparency of tariffs makes this an easy distinction to make. It is radically more difficult to determine objectively whether TBTs could be less trade restrictive and accomplish their valid policy goal. In short, the key difference between regulatory protection and tariffs is obscurity, not sovereignty.

'trust issue' plays an important role in understanding why TBT liberalization is so different from tariff liberalization.

TBT commitments in FTAs

Piermartini and Budetta (2006) have undertaken a survey of the TBT provisions in a representative sample of seventy FTAs. They found that fifty-eight of these include TBT provisions. Importantly, these include all the largest regional arrangements. Since the internal trade of NAFTA and the EU alone account for about a third of world trade – and both have important TBT commitments – the TBT commitments in RTAs clearly matter for the world trade system. We distinguish three ways that TBT regimes can facilitate trade:

1. harmonizing norms so that only one norm applies to all the RTA partners;
2. establishing mutual recognition arrangements among parties such that all national standards are accepted in all jurisdictions; and
3. making it cheaper and/or faster for firms to certify that their products meet the norms of the RTA partner, including through mutual recognition of national conformity assessment procedures.

Piermartini and Budetta (2006) also list RTA commitments concerning transparency (e.g. prior notification of new norms, sometimes with a right to comment before the norm is adopted), institutional cooperation (e.g. establishment of a committee to discuss standards) and dispute resolution.

The two deepest RTAs in the world – the EU and the Australia–New Zealand Closer Economic Relationship (CER) – involve substantial harmonization and mutual recognition of product norms and testing.[36] Although the EU's rules affect a very large share of world trade (nations that embrace the European norms account for about 40 per cent of world imports), the EU and CER provisions do not create a spaghetti bowl. Indeed, empirical evidence suggests that the EU's single market

---

[36] The EU and EFTA extend mutual recognition in norms and testing to each other quite broadly in the European Economic Area agreement. The EU also encourages its other nearby trade partners (e.g. its bilaterals with Mediterranean nations) to unilaterally adopt EU norms, but the EU does not grant mutual recognition of norms or testing. See Baldwin (2000) for an examination of the various harmonization efforts that have been made in Europe, and Piermartini and Budetta (2006) for an overview of TBT provisions in RTAs around the world.

programme increased access at least as much for third-party firms (Mayer and Zignago, 2005).

Apart from the European and CER arrangements, the main liberalizing elements of regional TBT agreements concern the mutual recognition of testing facilities in certain sectors such as pharmaceutical and electrical equipment. In Mutual Recognition Agreements (MRAs) signed between the United States and the EU, for example, the EU recognizes the right of certain US laboratories to certify that goods meet EU norms and thus can be sold in the EU. Likewise, the United States recognizes the right of certain EU laboratories to certify goods as meeting US norms. This is a cost-lowering arrangement, since in the past all US norm testing had to be done in the United States, and all the EU testing in the EU.

No rules of origin   From the world perspective, it is very important to note that the typical testing-MRA does not contain rules of origin. The MRA in essence expands the list of laboratories that can certify that a product meets a particular norm, without requiring that the origin of the product be established. Consider, for example, a US laboratory that has been named under the US–EU MRA as capable of certifying that that product meets EU requirements; this US laboratory can then be used by a Canadian firm that wishes to export its goods to the EU.

The lack of ROOs has the effect of automatically multilateralizing the preferential TBT liberalization. For example, the EU–US MRA might seem to put Mexican firms at a disadvantage in the EU market. However, the fact that Mexican firms can use US laboratories to demonstrate that their products are in conformity with EU norms goes a long way to reducing the discriminatory effect of the MRA. To see the point by analogy, we can compare it to an FTA between countries A and B that has no ROOs. Without ROOs, third nations, say nation C, can always take advantage of A's duty-free access to B by trans-shipping their goods via nation A. While this does put firms in nation C at somewhat of a disadvantage compared to firms from nation B, the disadvantage is limited – it can never exceed the trans-shipment cost. Similarly, having a testing laboratory in the US provides US firms with an edge that Canadian firms do not have, but the advantage is limited to the extra cost of having Canadian products tested in the United States.

In short, weak rules of origin can be thought of as 'automatic multilateralizers' in that they greatly reduce the spaghetti bowl problem.

Multilateralization

While economists widely agree that multilateral tariff cutting would be superior to the equivalent preferential liberalization, the situation for TBTs is much more nuanced – a fact that is recognized explicitly by the WTO's TBT Agreement.

First, global TBT liberalization is not necessarily optimal. The EU and the EEA are the only entities that have made substantial progress in eliminating TBTs across the board. This was achieved through a combination of harmonization to a European standard on essential norms, and mutual recognition on the rest (Baldwin, 2000; Vancauteren, 2002). Given the wide gaps in income levels and governance capacity, a similar liberalization is unthinkable at the global level. There is no reason to believe that Europe's norms – or any other for that matter – would be optimal for the rest of the world, or vice versa (Bhagwati and Hudec, 1996).

Second, the most common form of bilateral cooperation on TBTs compromises MRAs in the area of testing, not in respect of the norms themselves. Since these do not have rules of origin attached, they are systematically less trade-distorting than preferential tariffs. As mentioned above, one can think of testing MRAs as acting something like preferential tariffs without rules of origin.

Third, the 'trust issue' makes deep liberalization at the multilateral level impossible. The WTO's TBT Agreement recognizes as much by encouraging MRAs among members. It encourages members to adopt international standards wherever possible, but imposes no harmonization requirement. Thus the TBT Agreement does not impose the same strictures on preferential cooperation in respect of TBTs as it does on preferential tariffs, or liberalization of trade in services. There is no requirement, for example, that testing-MRAs apply to a wide range of sectors. Nor is there any explicit requirement that MRAs do not raise barriers against third-party goods.

Fourth, TBTs are cost-raising, i.e. frictional barriers, and the simple economics of frictional barriers tells us that preferential liberalization is systematically less harmful to economic efficiency than preferential liberalization of tariffs. For example, Viner's Ambiguity – which tells us that in the case of preferential tariffs even the members of a bilateral agreement may lose – disappears in the frictional barriers case (Viner, 1950).

Modalities   The distinctive features of TBTs imply that multilateralization is both less necessary (since MRAs are less distortionary than FTAs) and much more difficult (the trust issue). Nevertheless, it is useful to think about modalities for multilateralization. The first point is that the lack of rules of origin in testing-MRAs came about for practical reasons (Baldwin, 2000), not due to WTO rules. Thus one step would be to encourage or require future testing-MRAs to continue the practice of eschewing ROOs. The second is that the transparency provisions in RTAs could be multilateralized, especially those concerning prior notification on new standards and regulations. Indeed the WTO itself might play a role in this.

Since deep TBT liberalization is unlikely to extend beyond advanced industrialized nations, the pattern of preferences is more like a two-tier system than a spaghetti bowl. A third way to multilateralize TBT liberalization would be to counter the exclusionary impact of a two-tier system directly. The WTO could actively seek to offset any anti-developing nation bias arising from regional TBT liberalization. The WTO TBT Agreement already contains hortatory language encouraging members upon request 'to be willing to enter into negotiations for the conclusion of agreements for the mutual recognition of results of each other's conformity assessment procedures',[37] the implication being that excluded parties should be given a chance to make a case for inclusion. Statements are also included about providing technical assistance to developing nations. The WTO could more explicitly promote the TBT equivalent of GSP. For instance, industrial nations might directly or indirectly subsidize conformity assessment procedures for products made in developing nations, or pay for the establishment of certified testing facilities. Similarly, the current TBT Agreement contains disciplines to ensure that certification fees are not too high for foreign firms. To offset the cascading effects of discriminatory TBT liberalization, the WTO might encourage subsidization of fees charged to firms based in developing nations.

Finally, a TBT would be less of a trade barrier if national norms were more similar. Thus one way to multilateralize TBT liberalization is to encourage harmonization of standards. This is already part of the TBT Agreement – and the objective of numerous standardization bodies worldwide – but it would seem that the WTO could help by raising the issue of standards harmonization at the political level and perhaps facilitate negotiation of harmonization across sectors, including across the services and manufacturing sectors. The existing international

---

[37] Paragraph 6.3 of the Agreement on Technical Barriers to Trade.

forums for standards do almost nothing to encourage the sort of cross-sector compromises that the WTO system is so good at.

Unbundling and political economy forces The multilateralization of preferential tariffs was, according to the arguments on pp. 86–8, driven by the unbundling and offshoring of manufacturing. Unbundling confused the 'us' and 'them' distinction and this in turn made it easier to cooperate on taming the tangle. Just as the spaghetti bowl came to be a building block with respect to tariffs, ever widening unbundling may lead firms to lobby for a multilateralization of TBTs, especially in regions where trade in parts and components is particularly intense. While the trust issue limits the applicability of the logic, this reasoning may account for the fact that it has been relatively easy to liberalize TBTs in electrical machinery and electronic components in East Asia (although in this case the main vector for liberalization was the widespread adoption of international standards).

More generally, the role of unbundling may help explain why international standards have been adopted in some industries but not others. In the cases of cell phone protocols and high-definition video, for example, firms still seek idiosyncratic standards in order to garner an advantage in their local markets. However, in industries where production is highly fragmented, the loss of scale economies and organizational simplicity is high enough for all firms to want to agree on common standards – at least for parts and components. As unbundling proceeds and spreads to more industries, opportunities for further regional TBT harmonization are likely to arise. The WTO could use its role as honest broker and convenor of negotiations to help ensure that this regional liberalization is woven constructively into multilateral liberalization efforts.

Trade remedies

The number of countries that have enacted and used trade remedies – anti-dumping measures, countervailing duty measures and safeguards – has grown sharply since the 1980s (Prusa, 2005). The application of these measures has seen duties applied to affected imports at levels many times the prevailing MFN tariff rate, and considerable uncertainty has been created by the mere threat of such remedies during the associated investigations (Blonigen and Prusa, 2001). Trade remedies have been subject to multilateral GATT/WTO disciplines since the beginning, but liberalization at the multilateral level has proved slow. As in so many other areas, RTAs have provided another vehicle for the reform trade remedies.

Trade remedy provision in RTAs

Teh, Prusa and Budetta (2007) provide an illuminating overview of the trade remedy provisions in a representative sample of seventy-four RTAs. Only nine of these RTAs forbid the use of anti-dumping measures among the parties.[38] Likewise, only five RTAs rule out the use of countervailing duties and safeguard measures.[39] These agreements are essentially limited to the deepest regional integration initiatives, i.e. the EU and its neighbours, and the CER, where the abolition of remedies is accompanied by deep political cooperation (or even supranationality) on competition and state aid policies. Some RTAs include provisions that allow for greater discrimination across trading partners in the application of trade remedies. For instance in fourteen RTAs, parties have agreed to exempt other parties from any global safeguards that they impose under the respective WTO agreement. (This is an example of exactly the opposite of multilateralizing regionalism, with RTAs undermining an established non-discriminatory multilateral norm.)

Other provisions in RTAs appear to reduce the probability that an exporter from a party is found to have traded unfairly in the first place or to have caused injury to an import-competing sector. On the face of it the latter provisions might be welfare-improving. However, care is needed here. A welfare analysis of these latter RTA provisions ought to take account of the fact that the pre-RTA application of trade remedies

---

[38] As in most areas of deeper integration, the European Economic Community was the pioneer in the preferential liberalization of trade remedies. Right from its founding in 1958, the Community forbade members from imposing anti-dumping or countervailing duties on each other's exports. Instead, the Community adopted a common competition policy and a common state aid policy. The idea was that the common policies – implemented by the supranational European Commission and overseen by the supranational European Court of Justice – would satisfy members' legitimate needs to discipline unfair competition by firms located in other member states, or trade distorting subsidies provided by other members (see Baldwin and Wyplosz (2005) for details). This practice of substituting common competition and state aid policies for trade remedies was extended to other rich Western European nations via the 1992 European Economic Area Agreement. This switch potentially liberalizes markets since it involves meeting legitimate regulatory goals with less trade-distorting measures.

[39] None of these FTAs requires a party not to use a trade remedy against all of its trading partners, which would, of course, represent the greatest multilateral benefit from the FTA provisions in question.

was very often discriminatory. Second-best considerations, and the possibility that commitments to forgo or discourage the use of trade remedies against RTA trading partners, may increase the probability that non-parties to an RTA are subject to trade remedies.

There is one feature of trade remedy provisions in many RTAs that is fairly prevalent, even if it is not global. Many RTAs include provisions that stipulate that any anti-dumping or safeguards investigation of firms located in an RTA party must be notified to a 'joint committee' of the RTA parties, and that consultations between the parties may follow and an amicable solution possibly be found. Although this does not reduce the application of remedies *de jure*, it is likely to do so *de facto*. What was previously a purely unilateral act (investigating trade remedies and taking measures) now becomes a matter that automatically invokes the possibility of trade diplomacy in the first instance. Reminders from trading partners of the totality of the benefits of the bilateral trading relationship may discourage the application of trade remedies in the first place. Teh, Prusa and Budetta (2007) note that these provisions are commonly found in RTAs with the EU. Our investigation has revealed that there are plenty of RTA agreements with non-EU members that include provisions for notifying a joint committee when trade remedies are undertaken,[40] although it should be said that many of these RTAs have parties that are in Europe (generously defined) or in the Mediterranean.

Figure 3.6 identifies the fifty-two RTAs notified to the WTO which have joint committee provisions relating to the application of trade remedies.[41] Interestingly, many of these RTAs involve countries in Eastern Europe and the Mediterranean. It also shows that these joint committee clauses proliferated after 2000 and now extend across the

---

[40] Moreover, the fact that the Republic of Korea sought similar provisions in its FTA with the US (establishing a consultation process for anti-dumping investigations) suggests that the potential benefits of such provisions have been perceived outside Europe too. The US could not agree to the Republic of Korea's request. It was argued by some US observers that, had the Korean request been accepted, it would have allowed Korea to interfere unjustly in the application of US anti-dumping law, which was precisely the point of the request.

[41] With the admission of the Central European states (and signatories of the CEFTA agreement) Romania and Bulgaria to the European Union, admittedly the total number of currently operative agreements with joint committee provisions is less than fifty-two. As will become clear soon, however, we would argue that the original pre-EU accession FTAs are interesting precisely because they included these joint committee provisions at exactly the time when Eastern Europe was seeking to establish itself as an attractive location for outsourcing and for the production of parts and components.

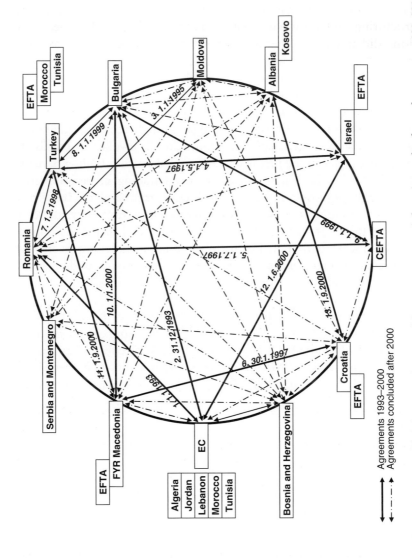

Figure 3.6 FTAs with joint committee provisions to oversee anti-dumping and safeguard measures, 1993–2007

→ ← Agreements 1993–2000
→ ← Agreements concluded after 2000

Mediterranean as well.[42] Since the threat of remedies hinders unbundling and efficient regional supply networks – the 'EuroMed Factory' – the RTA provisions on remedies helped guard the benefits of lower tariffs from being reversed by trade remedies. The above argument might also partly account for the fact that, despite all the economic restructuring and unemployment witnessed in Eastern Europe, these nations did not become heavy users of trade remedies such as anti-dumping.[43]

Multilateralization

The effect of production unbundling and offshoring on the level of corporate support for harmonizing and liberalizing preferential rules of origin was discussed earlier. Here we argue that pervasive unbundling and the associated international outsourcing of parts and components may well have implications for the spread of certain trade remedy provisions found in RTAs and, perhaps, eventually for securing greater support for new multilateral rules on trade remedies. Indeed, the spread of joint committee provisions among EuroMed RTAs suggests that unbundling and offshoring have expanded the constituency pushing for trade remedy reform. There are three reasons for this:

1. RTAs may reduce tariffs to zero but keeping them at zero is important. Countries wishing to attract export-oriented FDI appreciate that their cost advantages can be readily offset by punitive trade-remedy tariffs. This creates a demand for trading partners to forgo, or at least to limit, recourse to trade remedies. A related motive affects incentives in the investing company's home nation.
2. After production unbundling, countries may find themselves applying trade remedies against imports shipped by the foreign subsidiaries of 'their' multinational firms. In other words, unbundling blurs the distinction between 'us' and 'them'. Indeed, governments that seek to form a coalition for the reform of remedies may seek an RTA-related commitment to counter domestic demands for trade remedy investigations in those industries where some firms have unbundled production and others have not.

---

[42] In Figure 3.6, those jurisdictions outside the circle are ones which have FTAs with joint committee provisions with the country closest on the circle. For example, EFTA, Morocco and Tunisia have FTAs with joint committee provisions with Turkey.

[43] Of the Eastern European nations destined to become EU members, only Poland became a moderate user of anti-dumping measures; see Evenett and Vermulst (2005).

3. Firms seeking to source parts and components from abroad do so with cost minimization and security of supply in mind, amongst other considerations. Trade remedies that disrupt prior contractual arrangements are particularly unwelcome, especially in sectors with very thin profit margins and little room to pay extra tariffs. Another critical factor to bear in mind is that outsourcing firms want to source parts and components made to specified standards from the cheapest possible location. Given unforeseen fluctuations in exchange rates and unanticipated cross-country differences in wage growth (and, more generally, in the growth of production costs), a firm engaged in outsourcing is not content with measures that discourage the use of trade remedies in any one bilateral trade relationship, but in as many bilateral trading relationships as possible. This underlies producer support for the spread of a common or similar set of rules on the application of trade remedies.

Very few RTAs have abolished trade-remedy tariffs. Although these include the largest RTA, they are not indicative of an appetite for multilateral initiatives that forgo the use of trade remedies. Many other RTAs, however, adopt subtle reforms that may hinder the use of remedies – especially in cases where production has been unbundled and offshored within the region, so the distinction between 'us' and 'them' is blurred. Such RTA clauses add a diplomatic component to an otherwise unilateral action. Some WTO members may resist this pressure, arguing that it involves an intrusion into their independent rights to enforce so-called fair and unfair trade laws. Nevertheless, as outsourcing continues, the balance of commercial interests seeking security from imports and those seeking security of supply chains will likely shift, facilitating the potential multilateralization of measures to limit the application of trade remedies.

5   Lessons from the case studies

The case studies provide useful perspectives on the factors propelling the spread of common RTA provisions towards multilateralization. The discussion makes clear that precise circumstances differ from one policy instrument to another. We now examine how the process of multilateralization in the field of non-tariff measures is similar to or differs from the case of tariffs. Table 3.3 identifies key characteristics of tariffs and the six policy areas covered by the case studies. The comparison of these characteristics underlies the observations that follow.

The first observation concerns the departure from non-discrimination at the border (MFN) and inside the border (national treatment). In the case of tariffs, RTAs are the principal point of departure from MFN. RTAs are an important source of discrimination for government procurement and investment measures. However, in both cases other international agreements have introduced important elements of discrimination too. In contrast, the principal sources of discrimination in trade remedies and competition law are unilateral: that is, the discrimination follows from the acts of a single national government. In the former, these are acts of commission (e.g. the imposition of anti-dumping duties). In the latter, it could be sins of commission (e.g. explicitly discriminatory national competition laws) or sins of omission (e.g. the absence of rules against anti-competitive conduct by firms that sustain discriminatory practices). The purpose of making these distinctions is to point out that RTAs are not always the source of discrimination and, as we have seen, in some cases certain RTA clauses can be an antidote to discrimination, and the spread of those clauses may contribute to the restoration of a non-discriminatory multilateral norm (such as desisting from the discriminatory application of national competition law).

The second observation is that, in the case of some of the policy instruments considered here, no role is played by rules of origin that is comparable to the case of the preferential liberalization of tariffs (as explained on pp. 88–92). Rules of origin are, of course, conditions that must be met before a firm can enjoy the preferential benefits contained in a trade agreement. In the case of some instruments, governments may not want to differentiate between foreign suppliers (in which case they offer MFN) or they may find it too costly and cumbersome to discriminate and so measures are *de facto* MFN. A national government, for example, may take on obligations in an RTA to introduce and enforce a pro-competitive regulatory regime for the financial services sector. That government may then decide that it is too costly to maintain two regulatory regimes (one for firms that hail from the RTA parties and another for other firms), and in this case the benefits of the new regulatory regime are effectively multilateralized. Our case study of service sector provisions in RTAs pointed to research which had identified similar outcomes in other circumstances. The underlying and perhaps more fundamental point being made here is that trade agreements can contain commitments both on market access and on rules and that, while rules of origin can in principle be applied to both, in fact they are not applied uniformly.

The fact that rules of origin do not create spaghetti bowl effects for some of the policy instruments considered in our case studies does not mean there are no triggers for multilateralizing the RTA provisions associated with those instruments. Our third observation from Table 3.3 is that there are a number of triggers or factors conducive to multilateralization. Unbundling of production across national borders, in particular across regions, has probably contributed to the spread of certain RTA provisions on trade remedies and on performance requirements for foreign investors. Other prevalent changes in corporate strategy observed in the last ten to fifteen years have been important too, such as cross-border consolidation. Moreover, multilateralization has probably been facilitated by long-standing domino effects, at least in the area of government procurement practices, which to date are not subject to a comprehensive WTO agreement.

The fourth observation is that the measure which 'tames the tangle' – the vehicle for multilateralization, so to speak – differs markedly across the policy instruments. In some cases, the measures needed are entrenched in RTAs, and so long as they are observed then the outcome is non-discriminatory. For example, a commitment not to apply performance requirements on foreign investors on an MFN basis can be entrenched in an RTA. Once implemented, any prior discrimination of this form will have been eliminated. In other cases, however, a legal measure must be complemented by some factors. Requirements on parties to create joint committees and to notify trading partners and consult with them before imposing trade remedies do not on their own prevent nations from discriminating against foreign suppliers on this basis. Discrimination is only avoided if sufficient pressure is brought to bear by trading partners on an RTA party considering the imposition of a trade remedy (or there is the expectation that sufficient pressure will be brought to bear after notification). Pressure may not always be successful, pointing to a potential weakness of this particular vehicle for multilateralization. A lesson for policymaking here is that a broad view ought to be taken of the different possible vehicles of multilateralization. An implication for analysts is that we need to learn a lot more about how different vehicles work, how well they work, and how to make them work better.

The fifth observation is that the current existence of a comprehensive set of multilateral rules for a policy instrument may well reveal something about the political economy forces that are likely to influence any trajectory towards multilateralization. A case in point is the GATS

Table 3.3 *Multilateralizing regionalism: tariffs and behind-the-border measures compared*

	Tariffs	Services	Government procurement	Competition law	Investment performance requirements	TBTs	Trade remedies
Principal source of observed bilateral discrimination	Discriminatory tariffs, protectionist ROOs, bilateral ROCs	Preferential market access	Preferential access to bidding on government contracts	Rare (e.g. CARICOM merger rules)	Preferential application of performance criteria	Mutual recognition; norms and testing	Discriminatory tariffs (AD, CVD and safeguards)
Agreements creating discrimination	RTAs	RTAs, MRAs (qualifications)	RTAs, national practices, WTO GPA	RTAs (rarely)	BITs, RTAs	RTAs, MRAs (testing)	National implementation, Article VI
ROOs create spaghetti bowl	Yes	Slight ('leaky ROOs')	Yes for goods, slight for services ('leaky ROOs')	No	No	No	No
Political economy trigger for multilateralization	Unbundling	Unbundling (mode 3) and RTB unilateralism and struggle for hub status	Dominoes and accession of new WTO members to WTO GPA	Cross border M&A and consolidation (e.g. telecoms)	Unbundling	Unbundling	Unbundling

Table 3.3 (*cont.*)

	Tariffs	Services	Government procurement	Competition law	Investment performance requirements	TBTs	Trade remedies
In practice, how is discrimination tamed?	Common ROOs, diagonal ROCs, zero MFN tariffs	Leaky ROOs, third-party MFN, application of 'concessions' on an MFN basis	Expanding WTO GPA (strong), third-party MFN clauses (weaker), leaky ROOs in services	Formal competition law implemented without nationality bias	MFN commitments in RTAs (e.g. NAFTA 1106)	Lack of ROOs on MRAs, harmonization to international standards	Joint committee clauses and diplomatic pressure
Severity of spaghetti bowl	Severe	Modest	High in RTAs, modest in GPA	Slight	Slight	Modest	Slight
Existing comprehensive multilateral WTO rules?	Yes (GATT)	GATS	No	No	Partial (TRIMs and GATS)	TBT Agreement	Yes (GATT and GATS)

insistence on 'leaky ROOs' and the fact that most GATS-plus RTAs have adopted this – even many of the South–South RTAs that are only loosely bound by GATS disciplines. At the moment, the extent of agreement among WTO members on the ultimate goal of multilateral disciplines in trade in goods is probably greater than it is in the area of trade remedies. This may change, and the evolving international reorganization of production, which has been emphasized throughout this chapter, could well be an important factor in this regard. Whatever the future, though, there are probably good political economy reasons that account for the present set of multilateral rules, and these ought not to be overlooked when assessing the potential for multilateralization of a particular policy instrument.

The last observation is that the 'end point' of multilateralization is easier to discern than others. This may not just be a matter of different views among interested parties. In some cases there is still disagreement among dispassionate experts about what the globally optimal set of multilateral rules would be for an organization like the WTO, whose members' circumstances are extremely diverse. Having said that, there may be some existing policy measures (such as multiple, costly rules of origin) for which it is almost inconceivable that there is a justification, and multilateralization of measures to improve matters in these respects is desirable. Still, there is a role here for further normative analysis.

The analysis of multilateralizing regionalism and consideration of its policy implications is still at an early stage. We would argue that the key dimensions of the multilateralizing regionalism are now clearer, not least the vehicles for multilateralization and the factors influencing this process. We turn next to the near- and longer-term implications of this analysis for possible WTO initiatives.

6   Concluding remarks

The proliferation of RTAs has had a varied impact on non-tariff barriers (NTBs), creating spaghetti bowls for some types of NTBs but not others. Moreover the scope for multilateralizing the RTA commitments is likewise diverse. This section first sets out a framework for organizing our thinking about various outcomes and prospects for multi-lateralization; it then proposes a number of areas where WTO engage-ment might help 'tame the tangle' and help ensure that commitments in future RTAs are better woven into the fabric of the multilateral trading system.

An organizing framework

The two key concepts are 'intentional versus incidental protection' and 'the level of self-balancing'.

Intentional versus incidental protection

Some policy measures are explicitly intended to make foreign firms less competitive, i.e. to protect domestic producers. Tariffs and anti-foreign procurement rules are the classic examples. This is what we call 'intentional protection'. Other policy measures are explicitly intended to achieve regulatory goals such as guarding the health and safety of consumers. Given the realities of special-interest politics, such regulation is often implemented in ways that protect domestic firms. This is what we call 'incidental protection'; it is not accidental – powerful vested interests are likely to have promoted the protectionist content – but it is incidental in that the protection is not the stated goal. It is no accident that intentional protection tends to prevail where market access conditions are at the core of the policy intervention, whereas much regulatory intervention is most likely only to throw up incidental protection.

This distinction goes a long way to understanding the types of NTBs where RTAs have created a spaghetti bowl.

- Intentional-protection instruments come equipped with features that make geographical discrimination easy: rules of origin are the classic example. It is not surprising that powerful vested interests use these features to create important differences among RTAs. When this occurs in many nations, the world gets the spaghetti bowl effect.
- Incidental-protection instruments may or may not come with features that ease geographical discrimination. It is relatively easy to design a safety regulation that favours domestic products over all foreign products. Take the example of elevators. In the absence of anything more subtle, the regulation could name the domestic elevator company's unique selling advantage in its safety regulation, thus shutting out all competitors. It is much harder to design a regulation that meets safety goals and favours domestic products over imports from third parties but not over those from the RTA partner. Moreover, the greater the number of RTA partners, the more difficult it is to generate the desired incidental protection. In short, incidental-protection instruments are much easier to use on an MFN basis than they are on a

geographically discriminatory basis. For this reason, RTAs tend not to produce spaghetti bowl effects for incidental-protection instruments.

We can use this distinction to understand why – according to our judgements in Table 3.3 – the explosion of RTAs has created a spaghetti bowl only in some areas. Perhaps the most interesting example concerns procurement. In our judgement, RTAs have created a spaghetti bowl when it comes to the government procurement of goods but not with respect to government procurement of services. Standard rules of origin apply to the goods that governments buy, so the vested-interest process creates a spaghetti bowl. As discussed earlier, however, intangibility rules out this tactic when it comes to government purchases of services. It is difficult or impossible to determine how much of the value-added of a loan made by a Canadian bank is actually added inside Canada.[44] Preferential agreements on government procurement therefore use a simple rule of origin based on where the seller of the service is established. If the preferences are high enough, third-party firms would use this 'leaky' ROO to profit from the preferences by establishing a distinct commercial presence in one of the RTA partners. A very distortionary spaghetti bowl cannot emerge.

RTAs have not created much of a spaghetti bowl effect in remedies, competition policy or TBTs since the protectionist content of these instruments is incidental to their main policy goal and, in most cases, the instruments lack features that make nation-specific discrimination feasible. One systematic, anti-spaghetti-bowl factor is the difficulty of ascertaining the nationality of a modern corporation.

The level of self-balancing

The concept of self-balancing is best explained with an example. Unilateral tariff cuts may not be politically optimal even when the same cut is politically optimal on a reciprocal basis. Under reciprocity, domestic exporters who want better foreign market access must counterbalance the political resistance of import-competing firms who oppose domestic tariff cuts. In this example, the domestic policy reform – e.g. tariff cutting – is self-balancing only when reciprocity realigns the array of political economy forces inside each nation.

This concept can help us think about which multilateralization initiatives are not entirely unthinkable. For instance, the ASEAN nations

---

[44] The same problem plagues value-added taxation of services.

are implementing a regional free trade agreement and thus cutting tariffs on each other's imports. Most of the ASEAN countries, however, multilateralize their preferential tariffs by lowering their applied MFN rates in tandem with their preferential rates. Obviously, they could have maintained geographical tariff discrimination via ROOs but they chose not to. In this case, the unilateral tariff cut on third-party imports is self-balancing *within each nation*. That is, the pro-protection and anti-protection forces inside each nation are such that government finds it politically optimal unilaterally to extend the preferential tariffs to third nations.[45] A similar example occurs in some BITs where nations have made MFN commitments in agreements that only involve bilateral reciprocity (see Table 3.2). Again, it must be that this unilateral third-party liberalization was self-balancing within the nations themselves.

As our discussion of the six case studies makes clear, there are surprisingly many instruments where the liberalization comes in the form of bilateral RTA commitments but is implemented on a non-discriminatory basis. For example, some nations have used GATS-plus RTAs to lock in service sector liberalization that is intended to enhance their competitiveness, for example by lowering the cost and improving the quality of distribution and communication services. Since the balance of political interest favours improved competitiveness, the government finds it optimal to give access to the best service providers in the world: the bilateral market access 'concession' is extended – unconditionally – to third parties.

Self-balancing can also occur at the bilateral level. An example is the third-party MFN clauses in bilateral RTAs, some GATS-plus RTAs, and procurement agreements. These commit the parties to granting to each other any 'concession' made in future RTAs. Here we see that although unilaterally extending the additional concessions is not yet politically optimal – i.e. such a reform is not self-balancing within each nation – the nations find it politically optimal to commit to exchanging third-party concessions in the future. In essence, the level at which a reform is 'self-balancing' determines whether the reform will be undertaken unilaterally (internal self-balancing), bilaterally (bilaterally self-balancing), plurilaterally or multilaterally. EU and US agriculture reform is a good

---

[45] The basic idea is that unilateral tariff cuts are a means of competing for FDI, and the ASEAN nations are engaged in race-to-the-bottom tariff cuts; see Baldwin (2006c) for details.

example of policy action that can only be self-balancing at the global level.

Club-of-clubs concept   For the purposes of this chapter, the interest in the self-balancing notion lies in its ability to help us analyse whether the NTB provisions in RTAs could be multilateralized. In particular, it suggests that some form of reciprocity is a key element in making such initiatives viable. This in turn suggests that multilateralizing initiatives might make use of the 'flexible integration' or club-of-clubs concept. Note that the EU has formally used the 'clubs within the club' approach (the clubs are called Closer Cooperations, or Enhanced Cooperations) to address the tension between deeper integration and member diversity since the 1997 Amsterdam Treaty.[46] The driving force behind the EU's admission of the club-of-clubs concept was the fact that subgroups of members, frustrated by the slow progress of integration in some areas, decided to proceed on their own (e.g. the Schengen Accord). The EU had the choice of continuing as an innocent bystander and having no influence, or engaging, and bringing some order to the process. The WTO now faces a similar choice.

Why in RTAs but not in a multilateral setting?

The self-balancing concept helps to organize thinking about why many nations – especially developing nations – are willing to make commitments on NTBs in the context of RTAs – especially North–South RTAs – when they refuse to engage in negotiations on such matters at the WTO level. According to this thinking, when developing nations negotiate in the multilateral setting, there is very little reciprocity – in part due to the general presumption of special and differential treatment in MTNs and in part due to the inability of small importers to affect the overall package much. This means that there is very little self-balancing. An example helps illustrate the point.

Consider a developing country government that is contemplating locking in a commitment to apply national treatment in a particular type of traded service. Consider the politics of doing it in a reciprocal RTA with a developed country versus doing it in the Doha Development Agenda (DDA). If the developed nation partner is very interested in

---

[46] For more on the concept and its limitations and alternatives, see Dewatripont *et al.* (1995) and the recent discussion of how flexible integration might be applied to the WTO in Lawrence (2006).

such service sector market access, the service sector reform may be balanced with preferential market access in, say, clothing exports. More specifically, the reciprocity in the RTA shifts the array of political forces within the developing nation towards reform. The RTA's reciprocity allows the developing nation's government to line up domestic exporters to counter the protectionist pressures from domestic service providers. Since there is very little direct reciprocity in the DDA for many developing nations, the reforms that are politically optimal in an RTA may not be politically optimal in a multilateral negotiation.[47] Some scholars call this the 'free-riding phenomenon' but the term is too blunt to capture the way in which the level of the agreement affects the array of political economy forces inside the participating nations.[48] The free-riding is not done by the governments; it is done by the pro-trade forces inside each nation which feel that they will not profit from bringing pro-reform pressure on their own government. This distinction is crucial when thinking about the level and nature of multilateralization initiatives. It also suggests that some form of mandatory GPA-like reciprocity will often play a role.

Examples of possible multilateralization initiatives

What sort of multilateralization initiatives are suggested by our analysis?

Tariff multilateralization

The case for multilateralizing tariff preferences was made in the last section. In terms of our framework, the ITA and PECS became self-balancing arrangements when the unbundling of manufacturing and offshoring to 'spoke' economies created enough politically influential winners in each nation to counter the politically influential losers in each nation. Since unbundling and offshoring are proceeding apace, and the range of goods and service sectors affected is spreading, it would seem that future PECS-like or ITA-like initiatives might be self-balancing. The notion of self-balancing suggests that some form of strong reciprocity is necessary. Such reciprocity was obviously a part of PECS – nations were either in PECS and thus benefiting from the taming of the tangle, and

---

[47] Roy, Marchetti and Lim (2006) document the fact that developing nations' GATS offers in the DDA are frequently less forward-leaning than the commitments they have made in their service RTAs.

[48] In academic economic journals, it is often called the 'terms of trade externality'.

changing their policies to make it happen, or they were outside. This reciprocity meant, for example, that the Turkish government could harness the political influence of domestic exporters to counter the resistance of domestic import-competing firms that stood to lose from the elimination of idiosyncratic ROOs and bilateral cumulation. The reciprocity in the ITA came from the requirement that at least 80 per cent of the world's production be covered – a stipulation that meant that the deal would die if exporters in all the major producing nations did not counterbalance the protectionist pressures in their own nations.

Given the massive two-way trade in components in East Asia, the relatively harmonious state of ROOs and the very low level of applied tariffs, it would seem that a WTO initiative to implement a PECS-like taming of the tangle in East Asia would have some chance of success. If the initiative also resulted in a WTO binding of the zero-applied MFN tariffs, the initiative would be a big contribution to making regionalism more multilateral-friendly.

Services

The spaghetti bowl aspects of GATS-plus RTAs are modest compared to those affecting preferential tariffs. One of the reasons is that these RTAs include automatic multilateralizers, such as third-nation MFN and leaky ROOs. While the leaky ROOs are already required by the GATS for developed nations, the fact that most developing nations have adopted them suggests that there is willingness to commit to more discipline than currently exists in the GATS. Of course, developing countries already have the ability to do this unilaterally by declaring themselves developed nations in the WTO, but this is politically inconceivable. What might be closer to a self-balancing outcome would be a GPA-like 'club' that would commit the members – developed and developing alike – to using this sort of liberal, or leaky, ROO in all the current and future GATS-plus RTAs; other disciplines and rules might also be considered for inclusion in this GATS-plus club. The self-balancing aspect of this would stem from the signal that such a commitment would send to current and future investors. Membership of the GATS-plus club would show that members were unswervingly devoted to making sure that investors would always have access to the most competitive services.

Procurement

Like services, NTBs related to government procurement of goods are not subject to anything like the spaghetti bowl problems facing preferential tariffs, so the gains from a multilateralizing initiative are likely to be lower. There are, however, indications to suggest that such an initiative could be self-balancing at the regional or global level. First, some RTAs that address procurement include hard or soft versions of third-party MFN, which, as discussed on p. 94, can be thought of as a form of automatic multilateralizer. This suggests that nations are already sensitive to the dangers of a spaghetti bowl problem emerging. Averting such problems with bilateral third-party MFN clauses, however, is obviously inferior to a plurilateral commitment to a similar clause. The WTO's GPA provides an example. GPA members must extend 'most preferred access' to each other. This automatically avoids a spaghetti bowl inside the GPA club. GPA enlargement would be the neatest solution from a logical point of view, but given the current accession rules, it would be very difficult in practice (entrants have to negotiate an exchange of concessions with each incumbent). Short of this, more modest regional arrangements might also help. For example, an initiative to multi-lateralize the third-nation MFN clauses depicted in Figures 3.1 and 3.2 might provide a starting point; this would establish a second GPA-like club with more modest commitments. The WTO might also consider hard-law or soft-law rules that encourage/require nations to include third-nation MFN clauses in RTAs that provide preferential procurement access.

Competition policy

This is one area where RTAs have substantially advanced the removal of potential and actual protection. There are, however, a number of well-known barriers to agreeing disciplines at the WTO level. In the absence of progress on this issue, one idea would be to attempt a clubs approach that committed all club members to the core principles of good competition policy. As with the GATS-plus club suggested above, membership would be a signal of good governance and thus one step toward improving the investment climate in member nations.

Investment

The more than 2,500 bilateral investment treaties in force cover virtually all important foreign direct investment flows. Given the similarities of these agreements – at least in terms of the set of BITs centred on the major FDI providers – the United States, EU and Japan – it would seem that this area was ripe for a multilateralization initiative. To avoid the pitfalls encountered by earlier attempts to establish multilateral disciplines, the multilateralization initiatives might start with regional GPA-like agreements that would begin with the 'lowest common denominator' of the BITs concerned. The gain from such multilateralization initiatives would be modest in terms of liberalization, but perhaps more important in terms of administrative simplicity and transparency and engagement of the WTO. Given that trade and investment are increasingly tied – the developments in East Asia being the prime example – getting the WTO into this policy area may be important to ensuring that future developments would remain multilateral-friendly. It would also tend to reduce the hegemonic influence of the large investing nations.

TBTs

Most of the RTA liberalization in TBTs is limited to bilateral testing-MRAs in specific sectors. The list of covered sectors, however, is not too dissimilar among nations; it consists largely of sectors where large firms are engaged in two-way trade so that the MRAs are self-balancing at the bilateral level. As noted above, these testing-MRAs do not impose rules of origin. This fortunate outcome, however, is a matter of convenience, not WTO discipline. One initiative would be to turn the *de facto* reality into *de jure* commitment by amending the TBT Agreement to include disciplines on rules of origin. A less ambitious but more easily self-balancing initiative would be to merge the set of bilateral MRAs into a plurilateral MRA club. Given the absence of ROOs, the practical benefit of this would come mainly in the form of administrative simplicity and transparency. More generally, getting the WTO more closely engaged with this approach in TBTs would increase the chance that future developments would be multilateral-friendly.

Remedies

Substantial reform of anti-dumping and countervailing duties is an enormously difficult endeavour, since it is not self-balancing. The pattern of remedy usage and the pattern of trade in the products most affected make a self-balancing agreement in remedies difficult, even at the multilateral level. Trade-offs between remedies reform and concessions in other areas seem to be necessary. Short of this level of ambition, however, the RTA provisions that have been adopted on remedies – e.g. notification and consultation provisions (the joint committee approach) – suggest that something less ambitious might be done. We argued that the remedy commitments in RTAs were driven by unbundling and regional offshoring. Even if such a thing were infeasible at the WTO level, it might be self-balancing in GPA-like clubs in regions with dense international supply networks.

Final caveat

As the old saying goes, 'the difference between theory and practice is different in practice than it is in theory'. The ideas in this chapter will plainly need practitioners' input to bring them closer to practical proposals. We hope, however, that we have at least stimulated thinking on ways of engaging the WTO more pro-actively in making sure that the broad range of regional liberalization initiatives remain as multilateral-friendly as possible.

References

Anderson, R. and Evenett, S. J. (2006) 'Incorporating Competition Elements into Regional Trade Agreements', paper prepared for the Inter-American Development Bank and World Trade Organization project entitled 'Regional Rules in the Global Trading System'.

Ando, M. and Kimura, F. (2005) 'The Formation of International Production and Distribution Networks in East Asia', in T. Ito and A. Rose (eds.), *International Trade*, NBER–East Asia Seminar on Economics, vol. XIV, Chicago: University of Chicago Press (first version, NBER Working Paper No. 10167).

Audet, D. (1998) 'Government Procurement: A Synthesis Report', *OECD Journal of Budgeting* 2 (3): 156–203.

Baldwin, Robert E. (1970) *Nontariff Distortions of International Trade*, Washington DC: Brookings Institution.

(1993) 'A Domino Theory of Regionalism', NBER Working Paper No. 4465, Cambridge, MA: National Bureau of Economic Research.

(1997) 'The Causes of Regionalism', *The World Economy* 20 (7): 865–88.

(2000) 'Regulatory Protectionism, Developing Nations and a Two-Tier World Trading System', in S. Collins and D. Rodrik (eds.), *Brookings Trade Forum*, Washington DC: Brookings Institution, pp. 237–93.

(2006a) 'Globalisation: The Great Unbundling(s)', Report to the Finnish Prime Minister's Office, August 2006, available at: http://hei.unige.ch/~baldwin/PapersBooks/Unbundling_Baldwin_06-09-20.pdf.

(2006b) 'Multilateralising Regionalism: Spaghetti Bowls as Building Blocks on the Path to Global Free Trade', *The World Economy* 29 (11): 1451–518, available at: http://hei.unige.ch/~baldwin/PapersBooks/multilateralism.pdf.

(2006c) 'Managing the Noodle Bowl: The Fragility of East Asian Regionalism', Centre for Economic Policy Research Discussion Paper No. 5561, available at: www.cepr.org/pubs/dps/DP5561.asp.

Baldwin, R. E. and Wyplosz, C. (2005) *The Economics of European Integration*, London: McGraw-Hill.

Bhagwati, J. N. and Hudec, R. (eds.) (1996) *Fair Trade and Harmonization: Prerequisites for Free Trade?*, Cambridge, MA: MIT Press.

Blonigen, B. and Prusa, T. J. (2001) 'Antidumping', NBER Working Paper No. 9265, Cambridge, MA: National Bureau of Economic Research.

Bourgeois, J., Dawar, K. and Evenett, S. J. (2007) 'A Comparative Analysis of Selected Provisions in Free Trade Agreements', report prepared for DG Trade, European Commission. August.

Dee, P., Ochiai, R. and Okamoto, J. (2006) 'Measuring the Economic Effects of the Service Provisions of Preferential Trade Agreements', chapter prepared for the IADB–WTO project on 'Mapping Regionalism'.

Dewatripont, M., Giavazzi, F., Harden, I., Persson, T., Roland, G., Sapir, A., Tabellini, G. and von Hagen, J. (1995) *Flexible Integration: Towards a More Effective and Democratic Europe*, Monitoring European Integration, vol. VI, London: Centre for Economic Policy Research, available at: www.cepr.org/pubs/books/P076.asp.

Evenett, S. J. and Vermulst, E. (2005) 'The Politicisation of EC Anti-dumping Policy: Member States, their Votes, and the European Commission', *The World Economy* 28 (5): 701–17.

Ferrarini, B. (2003) 'A Multilateral Framework For Investment', in S. J. Evenett and SECO (eds.), *The Singapore Issues and the World Trading System: The Road to Cancun and Beyond*, Bern: World Trade Institute.

Fink, C. and Molinuevo, M. (2008) 'East Asian Free Trade Agreements in Services: Key Architectural Elements', *Journal of International Economic Law* 11(2): 263–311.

Gangé, G. and Morin, J.-F. (2006) 'The Evolving American Policy on Investment Protection: Evidence from Recent FTAs and the 2004 Model BIT', *Journal of International Economic Law* 9 (2): 357–82.

Gantz, D. (2004) 'The Evolution of FTA Investment Provisions: From NAFTA to the United States–Chile Free Trade Agreement', *American University International Law Review* 19: 679–767.

Heindl, J. (2006) 'Toward a History of NAFTA's Chapter Eleven', *Berkeley Journal of International Law* 24 (2): 672–86.

Kulaksizoglu, T. (2006) 'Competition Policy in Turkey', MPRA Paper No. 179, available at: mpra.ub.uni-muenchen.de/ 179/.

Lawrence, R. (2006) 'Rulemaking amidst Growing Diversity: A Club-of-Clubs Approach to WTO Reform and New Issue Selection', *Journal of International Economic Law* 9 (4): 823–35.

Lesher, M. and Miroudot, S. (2006) 'Analysis of the Economic Impact of Investment Provisions in Regional Trade Agreements', OECD Trade Policy Working Paper No. 36. TD/TC/WP(2005)40/FINAL, Paris: OECD.

Mayer, T. and Zignago, S. (2005) 'Market Access in Global and Regional Trade', CEPII Working Paper 2005-02, Paris: CEPII.

OECD (1996) 'Performance Requirements', note by the Chairman, DAFFE/MAI(96)4, Paris: OECD.

(2005) 'Novel Features in OECD Countries' Recent Investment Agreements: An Overview', Secretariat paper prepared for a symposium entitled 'Making the Most of International Investment Agreements: A Common Agenda', Paris: OECD.

Piermartini, R. and Budetta, M. (2006) 'Mapping of Regional Rules on Technical Barriers to Trade', chapter prepared for the IADB–WTO project on 'Mapping Regionalism'.

Prusa, T. (2005) 'Antidumping: A Growing Problem in International Trade', *The World Economy*, 28 (5): 683–700.

Reiter, J. (2004) 'Investments in RTAs', mimeo, Brussels, 6 December.

Roy, M., Marchetti, J. and Lim, H. (2006) 'Services Liberalization in the New Generation of Preferential Trade Agreements (PTAs): How Much Further than the GATS?', WTO Economic Research and Statistics Division.

Sauvé, P. (2006) 'Multilateral Rules on Investment: Is Forward Movement Possible?', *Journal of International Economic Law* 9 (2): 325–55.

Schott, J. (1988) 'The Free Trade Agreement: A US Assessment', in J. Schott and M. Smith (eds.), *The Canada–US Free Trade Agreement: The Global Impact*, Washington DC: Institute for International Economics.

Solano, O. and Sennekamp, A. (2006) 'Competition Provisions in Regional Trading Agreements', OECD Trade Policy Working Paper No. 31, Paris: OECD.

Teh, R., Prusa, T. and Budetta, M. (2007) 'Trade Remedy Provisions in Regional Trade Agreements', paper prepared for the Inter-American Development Bank and World Trade Organization project entitled 'Regional Rules in the Global Trading System'.

Trionfetti, F. (2000) 'Discriminatory Public Procurement and International Trade', *The World Economy* 23: 57–76.

UNCTAD (2006) *World Investment Report*, Geneva: UNCTAD.

Vancauteren, M. (2002) 'The Impact of Technical Barriers to Trade on Home Bias: An Application to EU Data', Université Catholique de Louvain, available at: www.ires.ucl.ac.be/DP/IRES_DP/2002-32.pdf.

Viner, J. (1950) *The Customs Union Issue*, New York: Carnegie Endowment for International Peace.

Wilke, W. (2002) 'The Origins of NAFTA Investment Provisions: Economic and Policy Considerations', mimeo.

Wonnacott, P. (1987) *The United States and Canada: The Quest for Free Trade*, Washington DC: Institute for International Economics.

WTO (2004) 'Minutes of the Meeting Held on 23 April 2003', Committee on Government Procurement, GPA/M/22, 11 May.

Wurm, C. (1993) *Business, Politics and International Relations: Steel, Cotton and International Cartels in British Politics, 1924–1939*, Cambridge: Cambridge University Press.

Yanai, A. (2002) 'The Function of the MFN Clause in the Global Trading System', APEC Study Center, Institute of Developing Economies, Working Paper 01/02, No. 3.

Comment

SÉBASTIEN MIROUDOT

The chapter by Baldwin, Evenett and Low asks whether the 'spaghetti bowl' of regional trade agreements also exists beyond tariffs and in particular in six NTB areas: technical barriers to trade, trade in service preferences, trade remedies, government procurement, competition policy and investment performance requirements. It is difficult to do justice to the rich content of the study and to say something specific about each type of non-tariff barrier in the space allocated for the discussant comments. One conclusion of the analysis is precisely that there are differences between these six areas. What is interesting is the comparative approach taken – the assessment of the severity of the spaghetti bowl for each type of provision and how multilateralization has or should proceed.

Two important ideas are acknowledged in the chapter. First, the role of 'unbundling' or the fragmentation of world production in explaining why RTAs include 'deeper commitments'. A new trade theory has recently emerged that takes into account the heterogeneity of producers, the role of foreign direct investment and this unbundling. The implications for the political economy of regional trade agreements are only beginning to be investigated.

A certain number of countries now use regionalism not only to increase their volume of trade or to offer a preferential treatment to some of their partners, but also to attract investment, to develop their service sector, and to be part of global value chains. Countries are not only interested in the static gains from trade – on which the Vinerian analysis relies – but also in dynamic productivity gains. With such an objective in mind, there is no rationale for discriminatory treatment between foreign partners. RTAs can be seen as tools to increase incentives for firms and individuals to be more productive by allowing foreign competition in the economy and encouraging technological spill-overs.

Moreover, the reforms which are at stake in these areas, dealing with investment, competition rules, standards or trade in services, cannot easily be used to create preferential treatment. These reforms can to a certain extent discriminate between foreign and domestic producers, but are generally not tailored to offer specific advantages to certain partner countries. As described in the chapter, the protection offered in these areas is more often 'incidental' rather than 'intentional'.

As a consequence, whether there is or is not a 'spaghetti bowl' issue regarding deeper RTA commitments is not related to the number of agreements signed and their proliferation. The criteria should be whether trade (or investment) distortions are introduced by 'behind the border' measures. In the case of international investment agreements (such as bilateral investment treaties), there are thousands of agreements in force (as opposed to a few hundred RTAs). But this does not automatically create a systemic issue as long as no distortion is introduced and agreements do not lead to welfare losses for third parties.

In this sense, it is a useful exercise to compare NTB areas and to establish a typology of the potential severity of the 'spaghetti bowl' for each of them, as it is done in Table 3.3. For technical barriers to trade (TBTs), for example, one can agree that RTAs rarely discriminate. Technical regulations, voluntary standards and related conformity assessment procedures can be trade barriers, but the majority of agreements do not include provisions going beyond the WTO Agreement on Technical Barriers to Trade, and when they do, they have harmonization requirements that encourage convergence towards international standards.[1] In this area, RTAs are thus more like building blocks and there is no real spaghetti bowl problem.

However, in the case of services, one can wonder if the authors are not over-optimistic when they say that the spaghetti bowl aspects are 'fairly modest'. The way service trade (and investment) is liberalized in RTAs includes MFN exceptions and national treatment limitations that can be discriminatory. It is true that rules of origin are more liberal for trade in services and investment, but studies on the coverage of service provisions in RTAs generally highlight important differences in the level of commitments in different agreements.[2] Moreover, the 'third party MFN rule' that is mentioned in the chapter is not so common in services RTAs. Agreements that are modelled after the GATS, for example, generally include a regional economic integration organization (REIO)

[1] Lesser (2007) and Piermartini and Budetta (2006).
[2] Houde et al. (2007) and Roy et al. (2006).

exception clause, similar to GATS Article V, that prevents the application of the MFN principle to third-party agreements.

In addition, trade in services is more and more intertwined with trade in goods, so that 'leaky' rules of origin for services might not create such a liberal regime when associated with stricter rules of origin for goods that hinder imports of essential inputs by service providers. There are also complementarities between modes of supply of services, such as mode 3 (the commercial presence) and mode 4 (the presence of natural persons) where the rules of origin can lead to a discriminatory treatment on the basis of the nationality of the service supplier. Empirical studies are needed to assess whether rules of origin in services create distortions.

Regarding investment provisions, the chapter focuses on performance requirements. Here there is no important spaghetti bowl problem, and it is likely that it is the same for provisions on investment protection and operational measures that were traditionally found in bilateral investment treaties and are now more often found in trade agreements. However, the liberalization provisions that are found in RTAs[3] can discriminate between partners. The debate is similar to the one on services highlighted above, as about 90 per cent of the limitations to national treatment and MFN treatment listed in RTA schedules deal with investment in services.

Last, the chapter from Baldwin, Evenett and Low highlights the fact that multilateralizing regionalism is also relevant for deeper RTA commitments and that there is a diversity of options available to do it. First and foremost, it is in the RTAs themselves that provisions can be added to facilitate the multilateralization of commitments. A good example is the third-party MFN rule that grants to parties of other agreements signed by the same country the commitments made in newer agreements. More generally, any non-discriminatory provision can easily be extended to new parties and leaves the door open for multilateral rules if there is a need for them and countries are ready for it. As long as RTAs are not used to discriminate between partners, but to go further on specific areas to supplement WTO rules, they are more likely to be 'building blocks' rather than 'stumbling blocks'. And it is likely to be the case in most of the NTB areas covered in the chapter.

---

[3] With the exception of US BITs and some BITs signed by Canada, it is only in RTAs that commitments are found on national treatment and MFN treatment in the pre-establishment phase.

When it comes to NTBs, RTAs can serve as laboratories for future multilateral rules. The liberalization of service trade and investment, and the reforms implied, can sometimes be more easily implemented through a progressive opening to foreign competition with a few selected partner countries. However, this implies a convergence in the provisions signed and in the different 'models' of agreements.

As a step towards multilateralization, plurilateral agreements or initiatives are worth considering. The examples of the ITA agreement or government procurement agreement are interesting to look at. One can also think about the WTO reference chapter on telecommunications. When there are enough countries interested in going further in a specific area or sector, a plurilateral initiative at the WTO is certainly more helpful than an RTA, as any WTO member can join. Of course, such initiatives could undermine the single undertaking but, as explained in the chapter, plurilateral commitments as well as autonomous liberalization can be self-balancing and do not automatically weaken multilateral trade liberalization.

References

Houde, M.-F., A. Kolse-Patil and S. Miroudot (2007) 'The Interaction Between Investment and Services Chapters in Selected Regional Trade Agreements', OECD Trade Policy Working Paper No. 55, COM/DAF/INV/TD(2006)40/FINAL, Paris: OECD.

Lesser, C. (2007) 'Do Bilateral and Regional Approaches for Reducing Technical Barriers to Trade Converge towards the Multilateral Trade System?', OECD Trade Policy Working Paper No. 58, TAD/TC/WP(2007)12/FINAL, Paris: OECD.

Piermartini, R. and M. Budetta (2006) 'A Mapping of Regional Rules on Technical Barriers to Trade', paper prepared for Inter-American Development Bank and World Bank Meeting on 'Regional Rules in the Global Trading System', held in Washington, DC on 26–27 July 2006.

Roy, M., J. Marchetti and H. Lim (2006) 'Services Liberalization in the New Generation of Preferential Trade Agreements (PTAs): How Much Further than the GATS?', WTO Staff Working Paper, ERSD-2006-07.

4

Multilateralizing regionalism: lessons from the EU experience in relaxing rules of origin

MICHAEL GASIOREK, PATRICIA AUGIER
AND CHARLES LAI-TONG[1]

1 Introduction

Over the last fifteen years or so the world trading system has witnessed the dramatic emergence and rise of regional or preferential trading agreements (RTAs/PTAs). This appears to be a significant shift away from the principle of multilateralism that the world trading system has been built around since the Second World War. There are a number of posited reasons for this emergence of regionalism, which between them suggest that liberalizing trade regionally rather than multilaterally may be easier to achieve, and that regional agreements may be able to 'reach the parts that multilateralism cannot reach' – i.e. that they might be able to go significantly further in key policy areas.

Two interrelated issues arise in considering this emergence of regionalism. The first is whether it is indeed the case that, for the individual countries involved, such agreements are likely to be welfare improving. There is a large literature that clearly shows that the answer to this question is inherently ambiguous. There is also a new and emerging literature which suggests that agreements which successfully combine elements of deep integration (i.e. the parts that multilateralism struggles to reach) *may* be significantly more welfare enhancing. The second issue

[1] The authors gratefully acknowledge funding from the UK Department of Trade and Industry for this chapter, and the usual disclaimers apply: the views expressed in this chapter are those of the authors and not of the DTI, and responsibility for all errors and omissions is ours. We would also like to thank participants at the 'Multilateralizing Regionalism' conference, Geneva, September 2007, for helpful comments and discussion. In particular we would like to thank Marcelo Olarreaga, Olivier Cadot, Peter Holmes and Richard Baldwin. We would also like to thank Sherman Robinson for useful feedback. Finally, we would also like to thank Stefania Lovo and Jedrzej Chwiejczak for their excellent research assistance on this chapter.

concerns the inherent compatibility, or lack of it, between the multi-lateral system and regionalism – the extent to which regional agreements are 'stepping stones' towards greater multilateralism or 'stumbling blocks' – where stepping stones are seen as being much more likely to yield higher welfare gains than stumbling blocks. In particular there is a serious concern about the growing 'spaghetti bowl' of criss-crossing agreements distorting trade down bilateral channels.

For reasons that will be explained below, rules of origin (ROOs) are an extremely detailed and necessary feature of *all* preferential trading agreements (except customs unions). Essentially ROOs imply con-straints on firms concerning where they can source their intermediate inputs. By impacting on firms' choices regarding their sourcing of intermediates, ROOs have two consequences. First, they open up the possibility for ROOs to be used for protectionist purposes, and thus they can undermine the process of regional integration they were originally intended to support. Second, because the ROOs are complex and spe-cific to each given RTA/PTA, they have an extremely powerful natural impetus towards strengthening the spaghetti bowl effect.

The aim of this chapter is to focus on the issue of ROOs in the multilateral context. In the first part of the chapter we detail why ROOs are necessary and the forms they take, and explain why they can undermine the process of regional integration, as well as their relation-ship to the multilateral process of trade liberalization. In 1997, the European Union 'relaxed' the application of their rules of origin with regard to a group of countries, largely those of Central Europe. This provides a natural experiment, which enables us to identify the impact on trade of this change in policy. The second part of the chapter sum-marizes the empirical evidence from Augier, Gasiorek and Lai-Tong (2005) which identifies the impact on aggregate trade of this policy change; and then we provide new empirical evidence at the sectoral level of the impact of the policy change. In the third part of the chapter we turn to a discussion of some possible policy options designed both to minimize the spaghetti bowl effect, and to maximize the benefits of regionalism for developing countries.

2   Why do we need ROOs?

By their very nature PTAs grant tariff reductions or exemptions on imports from the preference-receiving countries. Those preferences can either derive from the formation of a free trade area, or can be granted

unilaterally under schemes such as the Generalized System of Preference, Everything but Arms, or the current preferences granted by the
EU to the African, Caribbean and Pacific states, or by the US to a
number of African countries under the African Growth and Opportunity Act (AGOA).

ROOs are then needed in order to establish whether a given good is
genuinely eligible for the preferential reduction of or exemption from
customs duties conferred by the PTA/RTA arrangements. Suppose the
preferential tariff on the export of an Ethiopian good to the EU is zero.
When the good is exported to the EU, the EU needs to ensure that the
good really does originate from Ethiopia and is not being rerouted via
Ethiopia by some third country which does not have the same degree of
preferences. That rerouting of goods is known as trade deflection. In
order to prevent trade deflection, rules which confirm the true originating status of the good are required.

ROOs can also be required in non-preferential contexts, where a
country needs to have proof of where a given good originated. For
example, where anti-dumping duties are being levied against the exports
of a given country on a given product/industry, then it is clearly
necessary to correctly ascertain in which country the exported good
originated. ROOs are also needed for statistical purposes in determining
the geographical source of imports. Under the auspices of the 1994
WTO Agreement on Rules of Origin, WTO members have agreed in
principle to harmonize these non-preferential rules, but discussions on
this are still ongoing and agreement has not yet been reached.

Within the preferential context, each RTA or PTA that is signed
contains a protocol or chapter to the main agreement, which identifies
the criteria which confer originating status on the exported good. Those
criteria are typically identified at the HS four-digit level (and sometimes
HS six-digit) level,[2] such that the protocols detailing the applicable rules
are typically over 100 pages long, and considerably longer than the main
agreement itself. ROOs have long been perceived as being very technical,
and this appears to arise largely from the high level of disaggregation at
which they are defined and from the criteria combinations employed.[3]

---

[2] Harmonized Commodity Description and Coding System tariff nomenclature.
[3] Details of the NAFTA rules of origin can be found at: www.nafta-sec-alena.org/
DefaultSite/index_e.aspx?DetailID=188; and an example of the EU rules of origin as
applied in the EU–Egypt Free Trade Agreement can be found at: http://eur-lex.europa.eu/
LexUriServ/site/en/oj/2006/l_073/l_07320060313en00010115.pdf.

The principle for determining originating status is that *substantial transformation* needs to have occurred. The idea here is that for a good to be treated as being, say, Ethiopian, there has to have been a sufficient amount of processing in Ethiopia. Hence, for example, it would not be enough to simply import a good from China, package it up, and then try and export it as an Ethiopian good.

Typically one or more of three criteria are used in determining whether there has been substantial transformation or not:

(a) The *change in tariff classification rule:* whether the transformation of the good results in a different tariff classification line between the inputs and the manufactured product. That change in tariff classification line is typically either at the chapter, heading, or sub-heading level of the HS classification system.

(b) The *value content rule:* whether or not the value of the imported intermediate(s) exceed(s) a certain percentage of domestic value-added.

(c) The *specific production process rule:* whether a particular specified production process has been employed or not.

These criteria are often given singly for a given product category, but can also be employed together. In the latter case the rules will sometimes specify an either/or choice (e.g. to be granted originating status the producer must fulfil either criteria (a) or criteria (b)), and sometimes the rules may specify that both criteria need to be met.

In addition to the above, all preferential trading agreements allow the partner countries to use each other's goods as inputs into the production process. Hence if countries A and B sign a free trade agreement, country A can use intermediates from country B, and vice versa, without having to comply with the above criteria. This is known as *bilateral cumulation.*

What is clear from the above is that the objective of ROOs is straightforward, and that they are needed in support of any preferential trading arrangement in order to prevent fiscal fraud. The rules themselves, however, are very complex and therefore potentially more easily subject to regulatory capture and protectionist pressure.

The impact of rules of origin on patterns of trade

As ROOs are formulated in the context of trade liberalizing preferential agreements, they are, in principle, intended to support a process of (regional) trade liberalization. Nevertheless, de facto, ROOs may result in a far less substantial degree of trade liberalization than might, on the face of it, be implied by the preferences which have been granted. There are two principal reasons for this. The first reason concerns the administrative and bureaucratic costs and difficulties involved with administering rules of origin regimes, and the second concerns the possible trade diverting or trade suppressing properties of rules of origin.

With regard to the former, for a good to be granted originating status the exporting firm needs to be able to provide detailed documentary evidence in order to obtain the relevant certification. This requires firms to operate detailed and precise records of their use of intermediate inputs, as well as requiring knowledge of the certification procedures. Evidence on the administrative costs ranges from about 1–7 per cent, depending on the time period and country examined. There is also anecdotal evidence, though not much formal empirical evidence, to suggest that, due to reasons of cost or simply a lack of organizational capacity, certification may not be acquired even where there may be eligibility. In this context it is interesting to note that, for example, in 2005 tariffs were levied on 20 per cent of all the products that were eligible to be preferentially exported duty-free to the EU by Egypt.[4]

With regard to the second reason, the classical analysis of the impact of a PTA focuses, of course, on the possibilities of trade creation and trade diversion. Trade creation arises when more efficiently produced imported goods from the new partner country replace less efficiently produced domestic goods. Trade is 'created' and yields welfare gains. Trade diversion occurs when sources of supply switch away from more efficient non-partner countries to less efficient partner countries. This arises because the less efficient partner countries have tariff-free access within the PTA and therefore may be able to undercut more efficient non-partner countries. Trade diversion therefore reduces welfare. The net welfare impact of a PTA will depend on the relative size of the two effects. These impacts arise because of the asymmetric preferences being granted to countries as part of the regional agreement.

There is a growing literature that shows that the ROOs underlying these agreements can also materially impact on trade flows – and thus can also be used for protectionist purposes. Hence, in addition to the 'classical' effects, there may be further significant trade diversion and/or trade suppression arising from the nature of the ROO, which are put in

---

[4] Own calculations based on the European Commission's database on utilization rates.

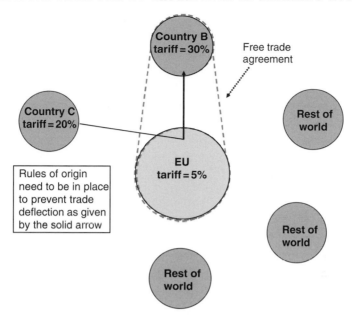

Figure 4.1 ROOs and trade deflection

place. In effect, where ROOs are constraining or restrictive in this sense, their effect is to establish barriers to trade between the PTA countries and the non-PTA countries.

Consider the following simple characterization as depicted in Figure 4.1: suppose there are a number of countries – the EU, countries B and C and those making up the rest of the world. In Figure 4.1, the EU is depicted as a hub, with trading relations with a number of spokes. Assume initially that country B exports shirts to the EU using inter-mediates (fabric) from country C, where the exports are subject to the EU's tariff, set at 5 per cent. Now, assume that the EU signs a PTA with country B with given ROOs. ROOs are now necessary to ensure that country C does not export the fabric to country B but via the EU. If it could do so it would pay a 5 per cent tariff on export to the EU, and the fabric could then be shipped on to country B with no further tariff.

Suppose now that under the ROO the shirt which B exports to the EU does not qualify as originating there – either because the proportion of intermediates from C is too high, or because a required production process has not been utilized, or because there has not been the requisite change in the tariff heading. The producer in country B now has a choice between (a) continuing to import the fabric from C, in which case tariffs

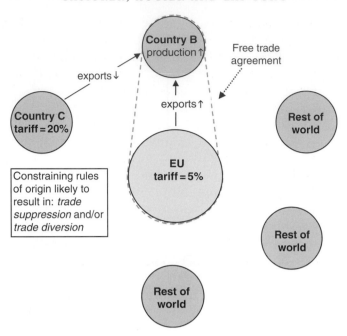

Figure 4.2 The impact of constraining ROOs – supply switching

still have to paid on export to the EU, or (b) to source the fabric from within the FTA under the bilateral cumulation provision. Note that in the absence of the PTA with the EU, the preferred source of supply was country C, which in turn implies that country C is the more efficient supplier of fabric. The producer is therefore faced with a choice of 'supply switching' by using more expensive fabric, either locally produced (which implies trade suppression) or from the EU (which implies trade diversion) each of which is welfare reducing, and in return obtaining tariff-free access to the EU; or not to take advantage of the preferences and continue with the more efficient supplier (country C), and then also continue to face tariffs on exports to the EU. This is depicted in Figure 4.2.

With 'supply switching' the ROOs have served to strengthen the bilateral trade link between country B and the EU (between the hub and the spoke) at the expense of trade between B and C (between the spokes). This is precisely the strengthening of the 'spaghetti bowl' effect discussed earlier. Both where there is supply switching and where the preferences advantage is not utilized the ROOs have reduced the liberalization impact of the FTA on EU firms. This is because with supply switching the ROOs have raised firms' costs; and in the case where the preferences are not utilized effectively the good has been excluded from the FTA.

In summary, in comparison with a non-binding ROO, a binding ROO will always raise the cost of production and hence the price of the imported good within the preferential area, which thus effectively offsets part of the bilateral tariff cut. This could be called the liberalization abatement feature. If the ROO also leads the spoke to switch away from a third-country supplier, then it is as if the spoke had raised its MFN tariff on the intermediate good.[5] This could be called the external protection feature.

ROOs for protection

The preceding discussion shows that, where they are constraining, ROOs will either directly impact on trade flows through supply switching, or will effectively result in certain industries being excluded from the preferential agreement. The determination of ROOs is also, to put it mildly, technically opaque: ROOs are determined product by product at a very detailed level of disaggregation; they apply one or more of three different criteria (change in tariff classification rule, value-content rule, and specific production-process rule); and they can then be supplemented with further complex rules (de minimis, no duty drawback, etc.). The combination of their technical opacity together with their direct impact on production suggests that with ROOs there is clearly the scope for regulatory capture, as there is potentially a strong incentive for firms/industries within the participating countries to influence the underlying ROO in their favour (see, for example, Flatters and Kirk, 2003; Dattagupta and Panagariya, 2002; Grossman and Helpman, 1995).

Indeed the very use of the combination of different criteria as opposed to simply one criterion in many agreements is clearly driven in good part by differing producer interests applying pressure on governments in the formulation of the rules. For example, in the NAFTA agreement it is the change in the tariff classification rule that is principally used. However, US car manufacturers were concerned that Mexico would be used as a base for assembly operations, which would then expose them to competition from imports. Hence the tariff classification was supplemented

---

[5] See Krishna (2005) for a more formal treatment of this point.

with the value-content rule where the imported cars must contain a minimum of 62.5 per cent of originating materials (Ramirez, 2004; Morici, 1993).

In the context of EU agreements it is typically the case for textile imports that the change in tariff classification rule is employed. However, as opposed to allowing a single change in the tariff classification line, the transformed good must have moved at least two tariff classification lines in order to be considered originating. A similar rule applies with NAFTA, but instead of a double transformation rule, there is a triple transformation rule. Clearly a double or triple transformation rule is likely to offer more protection than a single transformation rule. In more recent years the textile industry in Europe, fearful of the consequences of liberalized trade in textiles under the Agreement on Textiles and Clothing, has been influential in encouraging the adoption of greater flexibility in the EU's ROOs through the introduction of more widespread diagonal cumulation arrangements (Gasiorek *et al.*, 2002). Diagonal cumulation is discussed below, but essentially the arrangements widen the range of countries where textiles and clothing goods can be produced, and from which EU producers can source their intermediates while still obtaining tariff-free access to the EU market.

When are ROOs likely to matter more?

It is clear that ROOs can impact on trade, and are therefore likely to be subject to protectionist pressure. If we go back to the earlier example, it is worth recalling that having signed a PTA between country B and the EU, the country B producer had a choice between 'supply switching' or not taking advantage of the preferences. This in turn raises the question of what are the circumstances under which it is more likely that the ROO would tend to be constraining and thus have an impact on trade flows and costs of production. In the first instance, given that ROOs influence the sourcing of intermediate goods, the first impact would be on intermediate goods trade. However, given that constraining ROOs impact on firms' costs, there will then be a second impact on final goods trade. Bearing this in mind, there are a number of criteria that can be identified where it is likely that rules of origin are most likely to be constraining. These are:

- the more restrictive the ROO in terms of any of the three rules identified above;

- the higher the intermediate share in production;
- the higher the intermediate imports relative to final goods imports in a given sector;
- the higher the tariffs that would be applied if the ROO requirements for tariff-free access were not met;
- the lower the import tariffs between non-cumulating countries;
- the bigger the cost difference between cumulating (be this bilaterally or diagonally) and non-cumulating countries;
- the smaller the country – for small countries it may be more difficult to competitively source intermediates domestically;
- the higher the export share in the final good production;
- the higher the share of exports of the final good destined for a free trade area;
- the greater the possibilities of sourcing substitute intermediates from within the free trade area.

3 Cumulation and rules of origin in a multilateral world

In the current plethora of PTAs there is little consistency in the underlying ROOs across the different agreements.[6] Hence, for example, a Moroccan firm wishing to export a given product will have different ROO requirements and different administrative procedures depending on whether it is exporting the good to the United States, to Europe or to PAFTA.[7] This in turn makes it harder for firms to organize international supply chains. A firm wishing to export a product into different PTA partner country markets, and wishing to take advantage of the preferences granted, needs to ensure that it has satisfied the ROOs applicable to each of these markets. In certain cases this is likely to be unproblematic. In other cases it is likely to constrain firms' actions and choices. For example, where there are different value-added thresholds, firms may end up choosing to produce according to the strictest ROO and therefore at higher cost for all markets; alternatively firms may choose to focus primarily on one export market – either because the ROO is the least constraining, or because the market is sufficiently important.

---

[6] There are some similarities across families of agreements, with US agreements typically making more use of the change in tariff classification rule, while EU agreements have more variety in the use of the three criteria. These issues are discussed in more detail in the chapter by Estevadeordal, Harris and Suominen in this volume.

[7] PAFTA is the Pan-Arab Free Trade Area.

Hence not only is it possible that ROOs for any *given* PTA reinforce bilateral/regional trading relationships, but the lack of compatibility between the ROOs across *different* PTAs makes the organization of production and international supply chains more complicated for firms. Hence, ROOs and overlapping ROOs can serve to encourage trade between (key) PTA partners at the expense of less important PTA partners or non-PTA partners, and this is likely to be a key factor driving the spaghetti bowl phenomenon in international trade. It is also worth pointing out that with the increasing fragmentation of production this problem is likely to be greatly exacerbated.

For the EU this issue became increasingly significant in the 1990s, as it engaged in bilateral agreements with a number of countries both from Central and Eastern Europe and from the Southern Mediterranean. It became apparent that the EU's spaghetti bowl of criss-crossing agreements was restricting firms' ability to source intermediate goods from the cheapest source. In 1997 the EU introduced a common set of ROOs, known as the pan-European rules of origin, which in principle the EU wished to apply in all its PTAs with Central and Eastern European countries and with regard to EU–Southern Mediterranean trade.[8]

A big advantage of having a common set of ROOs is that it is then possible to break down the barriers to spoke–spoke trade – and this can be achieved via something called *diagonal cumulation* (of rules of origin). Diagonal cumulation was a key principle introduced in the pan-European rules. Essentially, ROOs typically provide some limit on the amount of intermediate inputs that a country can import from a non-PTA partner country. Diagonal cumulation makes it easier to import such goods and still satisfy the rules of origin. This is explained more fully below where we return to the example given earlier.

Why diagonal cumulation matters

Suppose the EU signs two PTAs with two (sets of) countries denoted B and C. Shirts originating in B would have tariff-free access to the EU, as would fabric originating in C. However, a shirt produced in B, using imported fabric from C, which does not meet the rules granting originating status for B's exporters to the EU, would then be subject to tariffs on exports to the EU. Note that the fabric directly exported from C to the EU would be granted preferential access, but a good exported

---

[8] Formally these ROOs are now referred to as the Pan-Euro Mediterranean rules of origin.

BOX 4.1 EXPLAINING CUMULATION

In principle there are three types of cumulation – bilateral, diagonal and full. These are described below:

1. *Bilateral cumulation:* Applies to trade between two trading partners. Bilateral cumulation means that materials originating in one country can be considered as materials originating in the other partner country (and vice versa). All PTAs allow for bilateral cumulation.

2. *Diagonal cumulation:* Applies to trade between three or more trading partners normally linked by FTAs with identical rules of origin. Under diagonal cumulation the participating countries bilaterally agree, in all the FTAs concluded among each other, that materials originating in one country can be considered to be materials originating in all the other countries. Hence, in terms of the example in the text, suppose that the intermediate good imported by B was deemed to originate in country C. Country B could *cumulate* its own value added with the intermediate input from C in determining originating status on the export of the final product to the EU.

3. *Full or total cumulation:* Again this applies between three or more countries, but involves more flexibility than diagonal cumulation. This is because it allows intermediate processing to be split in any way between all the parties to the preferential agreement, provided that when added together all the materials/processing used throughout the area are sufficient to meet the origin rule. Returning again to our example used for diagonal cumulation: suppose now that the intermediate input from country C did not qualify as originating from C. With full cumulation the producer in country B can cumulate the proportion of C's value-added together with its own value-added in determining originating status.

---

from B using C's fabric would not. Such a system of bilateral hub–spoke agreements with constraining rules of origin is thus likely to greatly encourage hub–spoke trade at the expense of spoke–spoke trade.

An obvious way of resolving this arbitrary and unnecessary discrimination is to agree that if the fabric from country C were granted originating status when exported to the EU, that fabric could then be used in the production of shirts in country B and the shirt would count as originating from country B, and could hence be exported to the EU duty-free. Country B is thus allowed to *cumulate* its production with the intermediate input from C in determining originating status on the export of the final product to the EU. This is precisely the principle of diagonal cumulation, which is part of the pan-European rules of origin introduced in 1997, and which we refer to in this chapter as the Pan-European Cumulation System (PECS). In 2002 the EU decided to extend PECS to include the Barcelona countries, and in 2003 the new protocol on ROOs was endorsed at the Palermo trade ministerial conference.[9] So with respect to the EU, the picture is one of a group of EU partner countries (CEFTA, EFTA and the Baltic states) becoming part of a unified system of diagonal cumulation in 1997, and a group of other countries currently not part of the system but hoping to join in the near future.[10] With respect to non-EU PTAs diagonal cumulation is, for example, also present in the Canada–Israel agreement, as well in the NAFTA and CAFTA agreements.[11] Full cumulation is only present in ANZCERTA and SPARTECA. Outside the EU, therefore, the norm is to allow only for bilateral cumulation.

While the solution appears obvious, in practice it requires certain strict conditions to be fulfilled in order for it to be applied. In particular in order to be able to participate in the PECS system of diagonal cumulation, the participating countries must sign FTAs among themselves, and those FTAs must be based on exactly the same ROOs as those of the PECS. Hence, for country B to be able to use the fabric of country C, it must first sign an FTA with country C, and that FTA must contain the PECS ROOs.

The logic behind the need for identical ROOs is quite simple – to prevent trade deflection. Assume that both countries B and C have signed an FTA with the EU and between themselves, and all of the agreements have the PECS ROOs. Suppose that in the PECS system in order for a fabric to be considered as originating in a particular country the producer must use domestic yarn. Hence, if country B imports fabric from country C, which is produced using country C yarn, then the good is treated as originating in country C. Country B can then use that fabric in the production of shirts which are then exported to the

---

[9] Note that in order to do so, a given Mediterranean partner is required to sign FTAs with all the other pan-European countries, and adopt identical (i.e. the pan-European) ROOs. The signing of the Agadir Agreement (2004) between Jordan, Egypt, Morocco and Tunisia has in part been stimulated by the desire to adopt the PECS, as is the case with the Morocco–Turkey FTA, also signed in 2004.

[10] See the *Official Journal of the European Communities*, C-Series (C229), 29 September 2007, p. 3 for a table showing which country pairings are currently part of the PECS system.

[11] Note that diagonal cumulation in CAFTA is complicated as there are different ROOs applicable between the original CACM countries, those that joined later, and then also those that applied when the Dominican Republic joined.

EU duty-free. If country C had used yarn from the rest of the world, then the fabric would not have been considered as originating from country C; if the country B producer had then used that fabric to produce shirts, they would not have been considered as originating in country B, and thus tariffs would be payable on exports to the EU.

Alternatively, suppose that the FTA between country B and country C applies different ROOs, such that country B considers the fabric to originate from country C even though the yarn comes from the rest of the world, on the basis that country C has, for example, used a particular production process. If country C exported the fabric directly to the EU it would not be considered as originating from country C and hence tariffs would be payable. However, if country C exported the fabric to country B, country B would accept the good as originating in country C, and could then try and export the shirt to the EU without paying tariffs. We now have a situation where the intermediate good, when exported directly, is liable to a tariff, but when used in another country's production process is not. Trade in fabrics is here being deflected to the EU, via country B.

In order to be applicable, therefore, diagonal cumulation requires that all participating countries sign FTAs, and that those FTAs contain identical ROOs. Under those circumstances, diagonal cumulation encourages the use of materials and processing within the preferential area(s) while maintaining a common standard for treating third-country non-preferential inputs. It therefore gives countries a wider choice of suppliers – all those participating in the system of diagonal cumulation – from which intermediates can be sourced.

If a system of diagonal cumulation is then introduced, once again returning to our earlier example, there are a number of possible effects which can be identified, and which are summarized in Figure 4.3.

Spoke–spoke trade (e.g. between countries B and C)

Here there is likely to be a combination of *trade creation* and *trade reorientation*. Trade creation occurs as, for example, country B is now able to source more intermediates from country C instead of supplying the good domestically. This reverses the trade suppression caused by the original ROO. Trade reorientation occurs as country B switches its supply of fabric away from the EU and towards country C. This reverses some of the trade diversion arising from the original ROO. Given the original impact of the constraining ROO, this is likely to be the most significant direct effect.

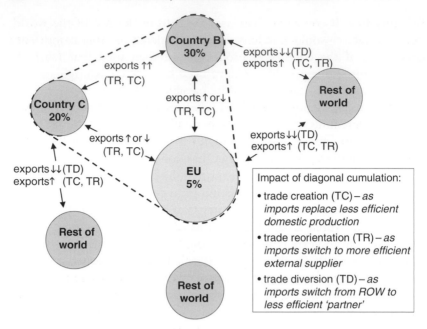

Figure 4.3 The impact of diagonal cumulation

Hub–spoke trade

Here it is important to distinguish between flows from the hub to the spoke, and from the spoke to the hub. With regard to the hub–spoke trade, to the extent that country B reorients its sourcing of fabric away from the EU to country C, then there would be a negative impact. With regard to spoke–hub trade, it is possible that the EU could be reorienting its sourcing of intermediates towards country B for final goods destined for country C. Hence there could be some increase of spoke–hub trade flows.

Spoke–ROW trade

Here there are two possible effects. First, there may be trade diversion as country B chooses to import more from country C as opposed to the ROW. The reason for doing so is that the country C intermediate inputs can be cumulated, while the ROW inputs cannot. Second, to the extent that country B increases the proportion of fabrics imported from country C, this may also enable it to import more intermediates from the ROW while still being granted originating status on exports to the

EU. If those imports replace more expensive partner country (e.g. EU) imports, then we have trade reorientation; if they replace domestic production, then we have trade creation.

Hub–ROW trade

This case is analogous to spoke–ROW trade discussed above. There could be some trade diversion away from EU imports from the ROW if the EU switched to spoke suppliers. However, there could also be some trade creation or trade reorientation.

Evidence on the constraining impact of ROOs

The preceding discussion has shown that ROOs are likely to materially impact on trade flows, and that allowing for diagonal cumulation is in turn likely to partially offset that impact. Empirically, it is extremely hard to obtain unambiguous results on the constraining or distortionary nature of ROOs, and this is principally because ROOs are de jure instigated at the same time as the very processes of regional integration they are designed to 'support' and therefore it is extremely hard to disentangle the different effects.

Many studies either cite Herin (1986) – who calculated that MFN tariffs were paid on 21.5 per cent of EFTA's imports from the EC, and 27.6 per cent of EC imports from EFTA, because of the failure to meet the origin requirements – or give anecdotal evidence. More recently there have been studies by Estevadeordal and Suominen (2004), Mattoo, Roy and Subramanian (2002), Brenton and Manchin (2003), Gasiorek et al. (2002), Augier, Gasiorek and Lai-Tong (2004, 2005), Cadot, Estevadeordal and Suwa-Eisenmann (2004) and Flatters and Kirk (2003).

In the context of the NAFTA agreement, Estevadeordal (1995) shows that ROOs tend to be more restrictive the greater the difference between US and Mexican tariffs; and that there is a strong correlation between restrictive ROOs and those sectors with long phase-out periods for tariff liberalization. The conclusion, therefore, is that restrictive ROOs tend to be more prevalent in those industries which also seek greater tariff protection. Cadot et al. (2004), also in the context of US–Mexico trade, show that ROOs have a negative impact on the volume of preferential trade. Mattoo et al. assessed the African Growth and Opportunity Acts and suggest that the benefits to Africa would have been approximately five times greater without the restrictive ROOs that were in place (in particular with regard to yarn). Flatters and Kirk (2003) argue that the

SADC rules of origin were heavily influenced by highly protectionist domestic industries, and then illustrate this with detailed examples from a number of sectors.

Brenton and Manchin (2002) show that with respect to the Baltic states' exports to the EU tariffs are in reality paid on a substantial proportion of supposedly tariff-free General System of Preferences (GSP) imports. They argue that a significant part of the explanation for this derives from the restrictive ROOs applied by the EU. In a similar vein, Inama (2003) provides some preliminary estimates of the possible impact of constraining and/or complex ROOs. For the total imports of Canada, the EU, Japan and the USA he calculates the rate of GSP utilization. This is defined as the ratio of imports into these countries actually benefiting from preferential customs duties divided by the value of imports that in principle are entitled to GSP preferential treatment. This rate of GSP utilization fell from 55.1 per cent in 1995 to 38.9 per cent in 2001. This low level of utilization suggests that, even where there are GSP preferences, developing countries appear to have difficulties in actually realizing tariff-free access to developed country markets, and that a key explanatory factor lies with ROOs. Gasiorek *et al.* (2002) use a variety of methodologies (interviews, descriptive statistics, econometric modelling, computable general equilibrium (CGE) modelling) to assess the possible impact of the *cumulation* of ROOs for the Barcelona group of countries.

The impact of the PECS system of diagonal cumulation

The introduction of the pan-European system in 1997 provides a natural experiment, which can then be utilized in order to directly focus on the possible impact of ROOs. If ROOs were constraining as described above, then the introduction of the PECS system of diagonal cumulation should have materially impacted on trade flows after 1997. In several papers Augier, Gasiorek and Lai-Tong (2004, 2005) have explored this issue in the context of a gravity model of international trade.

The principle underlying the gravity model is that in the first instance bilateral trade flows between any given pair of countries will depend on the level of economic activity in both the exporting and the importing country, and the level of trade costs between the two countries. Hence the larger the exporting country the more it is likely to export. Similarly, the larger the importing country the more it is likely to import. Clearly those flows will also be affected by trade costs – be these tariffs, quotas or distance between the countries. This basic model is then augmented in several ways. As well as using GDP to capture activity levels, the respective populations of the countries are usually included. This serves to capture not simply economic size, but also per capita income levels. Other variables are designed to capture institutional arrangements between countries (such as RTAs), or cultural affinities between countries (such as a common language). In our work we have added a further variable designed to capture the impact of the introduction of the PECS system on trade flows between the newly cumulating countries, and between these countries and the ROW.[12]

In Augier, Gasiorek and Lai-Tong (2004) the impact of rules of origin and the lack of cumulation were examined at the sectoral level for the textile industry. The result suggested that ROOs do indeed serve to restrict trade flows between countries and that trade between non-cumulating countries could be lower by up to 50–70 per cent. In Augier, Gasiorek and Lai-Tong (2005), we focused on trade in all goods, trade in intermediate goods, and trade in manufactured goods. The results suggested that the introduction of cumulation served to increase trade between spokes by between 7 and 22 per cent, and that trade was potentially lower between those countries that were not part of the PECS system by up to 70 per cent. Our estimates are based on trade flows between thirty-eight countries – all the EU countries, three EFTA countries (Iceland, Norway and Switzerland), the CEFTA countries, the Baltic States, six countries taking part in the Barcelona process (Turkey, Jordan, Israel, Egypt, Tunisia and Morocco), as well as the US, Canada, China, Japan and Australia.

The statistical analysis we used to establish a lower bound on the impact of ROOs is a technique called difference-in-differences analysis. This compares the behaviour of two groups of bilateral trade flows. The 'treatment' group includes all the bilateral trade flows that should have been boosted by the PECS. The 'control' group is made up of the bilateral trade flows that should not have been affected by the PECS. In essence, the procedure is to compare how much treatment-group trade flows arose as a result of cumulation (this is the first difference) and compare this with the change in flows for the control group (the second difference) – hence the term difference-in-differences.

---

[12] It is worth noting that Estevadeordal and Suominen (2004) also use a gravity model in their estimates of the impact of ROOs. Unlike our work, however, they construct a restrictiveness index which ranges between 1 and 7, designed to capture differing degrees of restrictiveness across a range of different PTAs. Their results also suggest that rules of origin restrict trade flows.

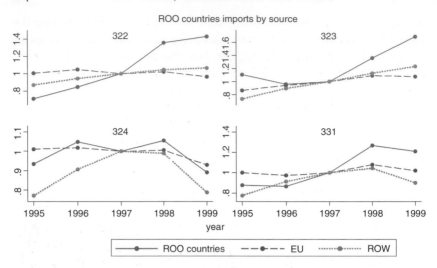

Figure 4.4 Changes in PECS countries trade flows
Source: Graphs by ISICRev2.

Consider Figure 4.4. Here we are plotting the imports in 1997 between those countries that could have been directly affected by the cumulation of ROOs (the ROO countries), and their imports from other sources. We do this for four sample industries. If the cumulation of ROOs indeed had an impact then we would expect trade between newly cumulating countries to rise by more than trade between these countries and third countries. Figure 4.4 is quite striking, as it suggests that in at least three cases – International Standard Industrial Classification (ISIC) numbers 322, 323 and 331 – there was indeed a difference in the evolution of trade between the newly cumulating countries.

Of course, the introduction of cumulation was not the only thing that changed between the pre-1997 and post-1997 periods; hence we use the gravity model to control for other factors as well as for all sorts of other unobservable pair-specific factors (e.g. historical ties, business networks, etc.). Our statistical method therefore compares the change in trade flows for the treatment group – i.e. those countries where spoke–spoke trade is most likely to be affected – with the change in trade flows for a control group – i.e. those countries where we would not expect cumulation to impact on trade flows.[13]

---

[13] There are different ways in which the control group can be defined, and in Augier, Gasiorek and Lai-Tong (2007) we explore the sensitivity of the results to three different control groups.

More recently we have extended this analysis by estimating the impact of the PECS system at the sectoral level, and hence obtaining estimates of the impact of the PECS for twenty-seven industries. We do this for two slightly different variants of the gravity model, and Table 4.1 summarizes the results for these two variants.[14]

In Table 4.1 we report on the estimated size of the percentage impact on spoke–spoke trade which occurred as a result of the introduction of the PECS system of diagonal cumulation in 1997. Out of twenty-seven industries for which we have run the regressions, the coefficient is positive in fifteen industries in each of the variants reported here. The industries where the coefficient is consistently positive are: food manufacturing, textiles, wearing apparel, leather and products of leather, wood and cork products, furniture, other chemical products, rubber products, plastic products, pottery, iron and steel basic industries, non-ferrous metal basic industries, fabricated metal products, electrical machinery, and transport equipment. We see that the results indicate that spoke–spoke trade increased by 14–72 per cent across the different industries and variants. The biggest impact of cumulation is on wearing apparel, leather products, fabricated metal products and electrical machinery. Here it is worth noting that wearing apparel and leather products are two of the industries where ROOs are typically considered to be restrictive and protectionist.

It is also important to note that, a priori, one would not expect ROOs to be constraining in all sectors, and we should not therefore expect a positive coefficient for all sectors. Consider an industry where the EU's MFN tariff rate is zero – there is then no need for a ROO (as there is no 'penalty' for failing to meet that rule), and hence one would not expect the ROO to be constraining. By extension therefore, where EU MFN tariffs are 'low' one would expect the impact of cumulation to be lower.

In order to explore whether there is any prima facie evidence that the industries with higher MFN tariffs have a larger impact on cumulation we report on some scatter plots (together with a trend line), where we have correlated the EU simple MFN tariff, for the year 2000, with the

---

[14] The difference between the two variables concerns how we measure economic activity in each country. In variant 1 we use sectoral production in the exporting country and apparent consumption in the importing country, whereas in variant 2 we use the GDPs of the respective countries.

Table 4.1. *Impact of PECS on spoke–spoke trade*

| ISIC | Industry | Percentage change in spoke–spoke trade | |
		Variant 1	Variant 2
311	Food manufacturing	**39.10**	**35.93**
313	Beverage industries	0.70	−7.50
314	Tobacco	62.09	19.36
321	Textiles	**41.62**	**47.55**
322	Wearing apparel, except footwear	**55.74**	**62.91**
323	Leather and products of leather	**72.46**	**70.23**
324	Footwear	17.12	**19.01**
331	Wood and cork products	**24.23**	**22.63**
332	Furniture and fixtures	**27.63**	**24.86**
341	Paper and paper products	15.37	14.80
342	Printing, publishing	11.63	**19.12**
351	Industrial chemicals	6.61	5.87
352	Other chemical products	**31.39**	**38.96**
353	Petroleum refineries	14.57	25.23
355	Rubber products	**49.93**	**53.73**
356	Plastic products	**41.76**	**35.53**
361	Pottery, china and earthenware	**23.49**	**20.56**
362	Glass and glass products	16.42	10.74
369	Non-metallic mineral products	3.05	1.21
371	Iron and steel basic industries	**42.48**	**32.58**
372	Non-ferrous metal basic industries	**43.33**	**34.31**
381	Fabricated metal products	**60.16**	**36.89**
382	Machinery except electrical	3.15	8.33
383	Electrical machinery apparatus	**68.54**	**53.42**
384	Transport equipment	**56.67**	**63.23**
385	Professional and scientific equipment	**14.22**	13.77
390	Other manufacturing	**19.36**	12.75

Note: bold types indicates where the coefficients are statistically significant.

estimated impact of diagonal cumulation by sector, for both sets of experiments. These scatter plots can be seen in Figures 4.5 and 4.6. From these it can be clearly seen that there is indeed a positive correlation between the height of the EU tariff and the underlying effective degree of restrictiveness of the ROO.

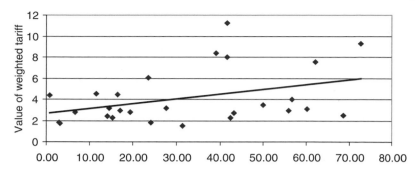

Figure 4.5 Correlation between EU MFN weighted tariff and impact of cumulation (variant 1)

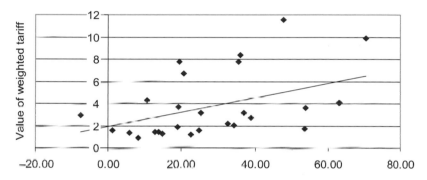

Figure 4.6 Correlation between EU MFN weighted tariff and impact of cumulation (variant 2)

4 Minimizing the negative impact of ROOs

It is worth recalling that ROOs are a necessary feature of all preferential trading arrangements, except customs unions, and are there, in principle, in order to support the process of greater regional integration. However, constraining ROOs are likely to distort trade in addition to the classic trade-creating and trade-diverting impact of a given process of regional integration. In doing so they contribute very strongly to the spaghetti bowl effect – encouraging trade between partner countries at the expense of non-partner countries. In addition, because ROOs are specific to each preferential trading arrangement, they are likely to make it more diffi-cult/costly for firms to establish international supply chains, and this also further contributes to the spaghetti bowl. It seems clear then that ROOs are likely to contribute to regional trading arrangements as stumbling blocks as opposed to stepping stones to multilateral liberalization.

Are there ways of minimizing the potential negative impact of preferential ROOs – in terms of their potential distortionary impact and in terms of their reinforcing of the spaghetti bowl effect? One obvious answer to this question is that eliminating or at least greatly reducing MFN tariffs would go a long way to minimizing the problem. Preferential ROOs are only required because of differences between tariff levels between countries, and the height of each partner country's MFN tariff represents the 'penalty' for not satisfying the ROO. Harmonizing tariffs (as in a customs union) takes away the need for ROOs, and reducing MFN tariffs reduces the potential penalty and reduces the incentive for firms to care about whether or not they can satisfy the originating requirements. Clearly, however, as long as countries maintain positive MFN tariffs, and as long as they wish to grant each other improved preferences for partner country output, there will be a need for ROOs.

A key feature of ROOs is that once they have been agreed it is typically relatively hard to subsequently negotiate any changes in them. This is not uniformly so as, for example, successive minor changes have been made to the NAFTA rules of origin. This is particularly the case when the ROO is based on change in the tariff classification rule, as there is a relatively limited amount of relaxation that can be achieved. This is not the case with the value-added rule, where a relaxation can be achieved by changing the domestic value-added requirement from, say, 45 to 30 per cent. In considering ways of minimizing the impact of ROOs it is then also important to consider how negotiable/flexible those ROOs might be, thus opening up the possibility of future relaxation.

There is also another issue that arises in this context concerning the impact that restrictive ROOs have on developing countries. ROOs primarily impact on the possibilities for firms in terms of their sourcing of intermediates. Typically, for developing countries the domestic intermediate supply possibilities are narrower, and hence they may need to rely more on imported intermediates. In turn, this makes it more difficult for them to satisfy the ROOs and thus to take advantage of preferences notionally granted to them. The relative administrative costs of meeting the ROOs are also likely to be higher for such countries. These concerns are frequently raised by developing countries in their negotiations with developed countries, and have, for example, proved contentious in the current EPA negotiations between the EU and the African, Caribbean and Pacific (ACP) countries. In turn, the EU has acknowledged that its ROOs are problematic for developing countries. In the 2003 green paper, it committed itself to introducing more 'development-friendly' ROOs, which would be primarily based on the value-content criterion. However, despite this commitment, the EU is finding it difficult to agree upon these new ROOs, and discussions with the Commission are ongoing.

Another possible solution would be to harmonize ROOs across PTAs. This would at least deal with the international supply chain issue, though not necessarily with the problem of the distortions caused by ROOs. Here it is worth remembering that ROOs are needed for both preferential and non-preferential reasons. With regard to non-preferential ROOs, since the mid-1990s there have been extremely difficult and long drawn-out discussions at the WTO attempting to agree upon a harmonized set of rules of origin. These negotiations are by now well advanced and appear to be largely (though not uniquely) based on the change in tariff classification rule.[15] In the current proposed harmonized rules, in most cases any change of tariff classification, and effectively therefore any assembly operation, is sufficient to grant originating status. For statistical purposes, or for determining origin for issues such as anti-dumping, this basic principle may be sufficient. But it is extremely unlikely to be acceptable to countries as a basis for conferring preferential access to their markets. There are certain 'families' of agreements[16] where some harmonization may be possible, such as those centred around the EU or the US. However, harmonizing across these agreements does not seem likely.

A further way of approaching the issue is to consider the relative merits and demerits of the underlying rules themselves – the change in tariff classification rule, the value-content rule, and the specific production processes rule, and therefore whether a change of criteria might reduce the distortionary impact. There are a number of issues here that are typically raised in the literature with regard to this, and which are discussed below. However, the picture which emerges from this literature is that each of the criteria has its advantages and disadvantages and none of the criteria emerges as being less distortionary or less problematic.

Tariff classification rule

The advantages of the tariff classification rule are that it is seen as transparent, predictable and has supposedly lower administrative costs

---

[15] See WTO (2007).

[16] See the chapter by Estevadeordal in this volume for a discussion of families of agreements.

associated with it. On the other hand, tariff schedules were not designed in order to determine issues of origin, and goods can undergo substantial transformation, in particular in processing and assembly operations, yet remain in the same tariff heading. This can be particularly true as production processes and the development of new products change more rapidly than the updating of tariff schedules.

Value-content rule

This rule essentially specifies a minimum amount of domestic value-added that is required in order to ensure that substantial transformation has taken place. By focusing on the proportion of domestic value-added (which may vary across industries) the value-content rule avoids some of the arbitrariness inherent in the tariff classification rule. Critics of the value-content rule point to difficult and complex accounting procedures required to prove origin, which make the system more costly; to the fact that it may discourage local final goods producers from reducing their costs as this then raises the proportion of (imported) intermediate inputs; and to the uncertainty that can be generated by changes in input costs and exchange rate changes.

Specific production processes rule

In this case the ROOs are determined in terms of specific industrial operations, and this is sometimes referred to as a 'technical test' for proof of originating status. Again, this criterion is relatively transparent and predictable, but it has the potential disadvantage of obsolescence – as developments in production techniques overtake the specified rules – as well as being highly subject to political economy capture by firms/industries influencing which specific processes may be deemed acceptable.

Hence the tariff classification and specific production processes rules have the advantage of greater transparency, and are probably less costly to implement. However, they do have some major drawbacks. Clearly the specific production processes rule is not one that can be widely applied across a range of industries primarily on the grounds of obsolescence, and the complications of detailing all possible acceptable production processes. A major drawback of the tariff classification rule is the often-mentioned one that tariff schedules were not designed with origin issues in mind.

However, more importantly, the change of tariff classification rule is harder to implement where there are more complex production processes, involving more than one imported intermediate input. Suppose a given firm imports two intermediates – one that meets the change in tariff classification rule and one that does not. Under the current EU PECS rules, where there is a change of tariff classification rule, *all* intermediates need to meet that rule, even if the contribution to the production process of the intermediate not meeting the rule is very small. In contrast, in the draft harmonized non-preferential ROOs being discussed at the WTO, it is required that just one of the imported intermediates needs to meet the rule – even if its contribution to the production process may be very small. Hence here it is possible for the firm producing the final good to simply use a single intermediate which satisfies the rule, and through this to grant originating status to the final product. Hence, with more complex production systems, one would need a supplementary criterion, such as the value-added rule, to be applied in these more complex cases. In conclusion, the change in tariff classification rule is not well suited to more complex production systems.

The potential big disadvantage of the value-added rule is the higher cost typically associated with it. However, in addition to the rule avoiding the problem of arbitrariness, there is another important advantage: in principle the value-content thresholds can be varied and hence are negotiable. In the same way that successive tariff cutting rounds have reduced tariffs, with a value-content rule it is possible to negotiate over the thresholds. This is typically not possible with the change of tariff classification rule, or the specific production processes rule. It is also the case that if the value-content rule were applied more widely, this would open up the possibility of multilateralizing cumulation, and this is discussed more fully in Proposition 2 below.

With respect to the different criteria, the principal issue is over the use of the change in tariff classification rule versus the value-added rule. One step forward that could be taken in this regard would be for the greater adoption of dual rules. For each given product a change in both tariff classification rule and value-added rule would then be specified and producers could choose either (as opposed to both) of these rules. This would introduce more flexibility into the system, and would make it more likely for compatibility across different PTAs to be possible. However, it would not address the fundamental issue of the degree of restrictiveness of the rule itself, nor extend cumulation possibilities to more countries.

From the preceding it is clear that, in order to multilateralize regionalism, alternative mechanisms and/or solutions to deal with the problem of ROOs need to be found. In the rest of this section we identify and discuss three ways. These are (a) extending and making more flexible the principle of diagonal cumulation; (b) moving towards full cumulation with value-added tariffs; and (c) only applying rules of origin when they really matter. Each of these is considered in more detail below.

Proposition 1: Flexing those PECS – applying the 'preferential partner' principle

The main issue/distortion for the multilateral system arising from ROOs is that they serve to strengthen the spaghetti bowl effect and make it very inflexible. The evidence from this chapter on PECS is that cumulation can potentially make a big difference by widening the sourcing possibilities for firms while maintaining tariff-free access to partner country markets. In doing so cumulation is likely to reduce the distortions created by restrictive rules of origin.[17] The question then is: how easy is it to generalize this across different regional trading arrangements?

The way diagonal cumulation is currently formulated requires each of the participating countries to have signed at least one bilateral FTA, and for those FTAs to contain identical ROOs. Suppose we take the EU, Morocco and Egypt as an example. Prior to the implementation of the Agadir Agreement both Morocco and Egypt had FTAs with the EU, with (almost) identical ROOs, but did not have an FTA with each other. Hence, both countries could export duty-free to the EU, but could not cumulate each other's intermediates for origin purposes. This was made possible by the Agadir Agreement (2004), which established an FTA between these countries (as well as Egypt and Jordan), and applied the Pan-European rules of origin. In principle, then, Egypt and Morocco can now take advantage of the PECS. As explained earlier, the reason for requiring identical ROOs is that trade deflection could occur if Morocco and Egypt agreed to much laxer ROOs with each other than are in operation with the EU. In turn, in order to have ROOs it is necessary for the countries to have negotiated an FTA.

---

[17] As discussed earlier, it is also possible for cumulation to result in trade diversion with respect to non-cumulating countries. On balance, we feel that this is unlikely, partly because increasing the number of cumulating countries is more likely to increase the possibility of including the more efficient suppliers, and partly because cumulation is likely to increase the share of originating inputs which will then allow a higher share of non-originating inputs, with a consequent net decline in the domestic input share. Ultimately this is an empirical matter.

Hence, trying to multilateralize cumulation *under current arrangements* would be extremely difficult, because of the need for FTAs with identical ROOs. In the pan-European context it was conceivable that the Central and Eastern European countries and the countries of North Africa would agree to have the same ROOs in their agreements with the EU and with each other. However, it is hard to imagine, for example, the US and the EU currently agreeing to using the same ROOs.

Closer reflection suggests that these conditions are not really necessary and that diagonal cumulation should be possible even if countries do not have an FTA, and thus do not have ROOs with each other, and even if the bilateral FTAs which the EU has respectively with Morocco and Egypt contain different rules of origin. The new principle that we propose is that any preferential partner can use the intermediates of any other preferential partner, providing that for each imported intermediate the ROO applicable to the country supplying the intermediate is used. Hence, if we return to the previous example, suppose that the EU–Egypt and the EU–Morocco ROOs were different. Egypt would be allowed to use Moroccan intermediates, providing that the definition of what constituted a Moroccan good is the same as that applied in the EU–Morocco FTA. If that were the case then there could be no trade deflection via ROOs, which is what the current requirements for diagonal cumulation are designed to avoid. Similarly, Morocco could use Egyptian intermediates, providing that the definition of what constituted an Egyptian good was the same as that applied in the EU–Egypt.[18]

It is important to note that adoption of this principle does not even require all the participating countries to have signed FTAs with each other. In terms of the above example, the principle can be applied even if Morocco and Egypt have no FTA with each other. Of course it may well be in their interests to sign an FTA in order to obtain cheaper imports from each other, but it is not necessary for the application of diagonal cumulation. Should they choose to sign an FTA with each other, again it may be in their interests to have ROOs which are similar to those applied in either of the bilaterals with the EU – but it is not necessary.

This proposal is essentially analogous to the national treatment principle, but is perhaps more appropriately entitled the 'preferential

[18] Note that currently in the agreement between MERCOSUR and the Andean Community diagonal cumulation is in principle allowed. However, it appears that each of the bilateral pairings has different rules of origin, making that cumulation impossible in practice. This would not be the case under the preferential partner principle.

partner principle'. It would be relatively easy to implement and would immediately extend cumulation possibilities to all countries with over-lapping PTAs. The proposal would also go a long way towards extending the range of countries from which firms can source their intermediates and would thus significantly reduce the spaghetti bowl effect.

The preferential partner principle is the minimum that we suggest countries with overlapping FTAs should adopt, and that should also be adopted by the developed countries in formulating their preferential regimes (Generalized System of Preferences, Everything but Arms, Economic Partnership Agreements) with developing countries. How-ever, it could also be taken a step further by countries instead adopting the equivalent of the MFN principle. Suppose again that the EU has bilateral agreements with Morocco and Egypt which contain different ROOs. In this case the principle would be that the Egyptian firm, in using a Moroccan intermediate in the production of a final good exported to the EU, can use either the originating rule applicable between the EU and Egypt, or the one applicable between the EU and Morocco. We call this the MFN-ROO principle, and it effectively means that the firm can choose whichever ROO it can satisfy more easily.[19] This would not only extend the possibilities for cumulation – as with the preferential partner principle – but would also relax the underlying constraint implied by the ROOs by allowing firms to choose the least constraining ROO across the overlapping FTAs for which the MFN-ROO principle has been agreed.

Proposition 2: Full cumulation with value-added tariffs

The proposal for preferential partner treatment outlined above has the very strong merit that it allows for the extension of cumulation in a straightforward and practical fashion. However, the proposal does not really address the issue of the underlying restrictiveness of the ROOs that are applied, nor the issue of introducing flexibility and ease of negoti-ability into the rules. But there is a way of addressing this problem, which is on the face of it more complex, but certainly feasible and merits serious consideration. This proposal involves three stages: first switching to the value-content rule in determining origin; second, allowing for the pos-sibility of 'value-added tariffs' and thirdly introducing 'full' as opposed

---

[19] Note that we have called this the MFN principle; in certain contexts this is perhaps more analogous to the principle of mutual recognition.

to diagonal cumulation. Cumulation would then be possible even if countries had different (value-content) ROOs.

1. Switch to a value-content rule. The first part of this proposal involves countries adopting the value-content rule as the key criterion in determining originating status. Even if stages 2 and 3 of this proposal are not implemented, or are implemented later, in our view there are two overriding advantages of the value-content rule. The first is that it is much more suited to a world of vertical fragmentation with complicated supply chains. The second is that value-content thresholds are inherently flexible and negotiable. In the same way that tariffs have been reduced through negotiation over time, it is conceivable that value-content thresholds could also be reduced in this fashion.

2. Use a value-added tariff rule in determining tariffs. This is a proposal that was first made by Lloyd (1993). The principle here is that the tariff is levied in proportion to the amount of non-originating inputs. For example, suppose the EU signs a PTA with country B, where country B used non-originating intermediates which comprised 60 per cent of the final price of the good. The good would then be subject to the export tariff (on the final good) weighted by the 60 per cent share of non-originating intermediates. Hence if the tariff were 10 per cent, the tariff levied would be 6 per cent. In the original Lloyd formulation, tariffs would be paid on any portion of the non-originating intermediate inputs. However, this rule could easily be combined with a minimum value-content rule, which confers originating status. Failure to meet the minimum originating requirement would no longer result in such a binary penalty system, thus giving producers a greater incentive to source their intermediates from the cheapest suppliers. Indeed, with a value-content-based ROO, a valued-added tariff has great merit in its own right, precisely because it moves away from the binary system of the firm paying the tariff or not depending on a particular threshold.

3. Introduce full as opposed to diagonal cumulation. Suppose that Morocco is importing intermediates from Egypt, which are then used in the production of a final good exported to the EU. Under diagonal cumulation, if the intermediate is deemed as originating from Egypt then the value of the intermediate can be cumulated with Moroccan value-added for originating purposes when the final good is exported to the EU. If the intermediate good is not deemed as originating in Egypt then its value cannot be cumulated with the Moroccan value-added, even if

there were some Egyptian value-added in the intermediate. Full cumulation overcomes this, and means that even if the intermediate imported from Egypt does not meet the originating requirement, and is thus not considered as Egyptian, providing it has some Egyptian inputs then the value of those Egyptian inputs can be cumulated with the Moroccan value-added for originating purposes when the final good is exported to the EU.[20] If the value-content rule is widely used, and if value-added tariffs are levied, then it is entirely possible for countries to have different ROOs (different value-content rules). Whether a tariff is levied on export to the EU or not will then depend on the relevant proportions of value-added from the different suppliers. There would also no longer be incentives for fiscal fraud – for firms to tranship goods (trade deflection) in order to reduce tariff costs.

The proposal outlined here is transparent, flexible and negotiable. Importantly it would both minimize the distortionary impact of ROOs as well as deal with the multilateral problems arising from the increasingly overlapping nature of RTAs. This would seem to be the most effective, if not the only, way of truly multilateralizing cumulation and hence multilateralizing regionalism.

Proposition 3: Applying ROOs only when necessary

The final proposal is particularly relevant for developing countries, and directly addresses the underlying justification for preferential ROOs. Recall that preferential ROOs are needed in order to prevent trade deflection. Trade deflection to the EU or the US (or any other developed country), via one of its preferential partner countries, can only occur where the partner country (e.g. Nigeria) has a lower import tariff than that of, for example, the EU or the US. If the partner country tariffs are higher than EU tariffs, than there is no incentive for trade deflection and therefore no need to apply rules of origin to prevent fiscal fraud.

This leads to a fairly simple proposal analytically – wherever the preference-receiving country has a higher tariff on the intermediates used in the production of the exported good there should be no need to prove originating status, and hence ROOs should not even be an issue. Indeed this principle could be extended to allow for tariffs to be lower

---

[20] Under the Cotonou Agreement, the ACP states have a system of full cumulation with all other ACP states.

than that of the preference-giving country but up to some margin, e.g. by up to 5 percentage points. This proposal does not entirely obviate the need for ROOs, as it will still be necessary for certain goods, or categories of goods, to prove originating status – but for those export goods where it can be established that the tariffs on intermediates are higher, then there should be no need for that proof of origin.

Of course, to the extent that ROOs are de facto there for protectionist reasons as opposed to prevention of fiscal fraud, then in practice it may be more difficult to achieve agreement on this. Nevertheless, if the EU, for example, is serious in its stated policy of making ROOs more 'development-friendly' then this would be a major step forward. It should be pointed out that, where there is a symmetric agreement (as is being proposed under the EPAs), the developing country may still be concerned about trade deflection into its market via the EU.[21] Hence ROOs will be a necessary part of the agreement – the issue is the circumstances under which the developed country chooses to enforce them. Having an asymmetry in ROO enforcement should not be problematic, and indeed the developed country firms should be able to meet the administrative burden of ROOs more easily than developing countries.

The point is that trade deflection only matters when the tariff levied by the preference-receiving countries is lower than the tariff of the preference-granting country. In the context of trade between developed and developing countries how frequently is this the case? We have taken the World Bank's division of countries into low income, low to middle income, upper-middle income and high income. For each country within these groups we have calculated the number of HS six-digit tariff lines for which these countries' MFN and applied tariffs are less than that of the EU or the US. We have also examined the number of cases where the tariffs are less than that of the EU and the US by more than 5 and 10 percentage points, and the share of trade so covered. The results are summarized in Table 4.2 where we present the averages for each country grouping.

If we focus on the first two columns we see that low-income countries have lower MFN tariffs than those of the EU in only just over 14 per cent of cases, and in just under 17 per cent of cases when considering applied tariffs. The numbers are slightly higher at just under 21 and 23 per cent respectively when comparing with US tariffs. When we look at the

---

[21] Clearly this issue does not arise in the case of unilateral preferences such as GSP and EBA.

Table 4.2 *The incidence of tariffs by country grouping less than EU and US tariffs*

	Low income		Low to middle income		Upper-middle income		High income	
	MFN	Applied	MFN	Applied	MFN	Applied	MFN	Applied
Total number of tariff lines	5,202	3,187	5,192	3,787	5,199	4,046	5,197	4,518
Percentage of tariff lines less than EU tariff	14.24	16.77	27.35	29.12	31.88	37.70	43.39	50.64
Percentage of tariffs less than US tariff	20.87	22.99	32.40	35.95	39.27	46.18	47.89	59.47
Percentage of tariffs less than EU and US	12.68	13.89	25.33	27.22	30.1	34.77	42.59	46.31
Percentage of tariffs less than EU and US by up to 5 per cent	7.00	7.76	14.07	15.08	16.13	17.66	23.54	23.75
Percentage of tariffs less than EU and US by between 5 and 10 per cent	3.55	3.65	7.29	7.81	7.54	9.10	10.08	11.67
Percentage of imports for tariffs less than EU and US	19.08	19.88	27.48	29.12	33.54	37.37	46.22	45.44
Percentage of imports for tariffs less than EU and US by more than 5 per cent	12.39	12.62	19.43	20.37	24.40	25.39	32.75	31.03
Percentage of imports for tariffs less than EU and US by between 5 and 10 per cent	3.75	3.97	4.13	4.54	4.58	6.09	6.47	7.19

percentage of imports for which the low-income country tariffs are less than both those of the EU and the US, we see that this represents just under 20 per cent of their imports. We also look at the number of cases where the tariff is lower by up to 5 percentage points, and between 5 and 10 percentage points. Here we see that the number of tariff lines, and the proportion of imports so covered, dramatically drops. Most low-income country tariffs are thus less than 5 percentage points lower than the EU tariff. What this suggests is that for these countries the EU and the US, for example, does not really need to be concerned about the possibilities for fiscal fraud arising from lower tariffs in the countries to which they have unilaterally extended preferences. The table also shows that the number of tariff lines where the partner country tariffs are lower than those of the EU and the US rises as we move through to higher-income countries, as do the share of trade covered. Nevertheless for low- to middle-income countries it is also the case that the number of tariff lines, and the share of trade which that implies, are relatively low.

5   Conclusions

In this chapter we have outlined the ways in which ROOs can constrain firms' choices with regard to the sourcing of intermediate inputs, and hence can serve to distort trade. The chapter has also provided empirical evidence at the sectoral level of that distortionary impact. Hence formal empirical evidence as well as anecdotal evidence strongly suggest that ROOs materially impact on trade flows. In doing so it is also clear that they are key components of the spaghetti bowl phenomenon, which makes it less likely for countries which are not party to the same trade agreement to trade with each other. If agreement could be reached on identical ROOs across trade agreements, then diagonal cumulation could be used to relax the constraining impact of those ROOs – however, only within the countries that are party to those trade agreements. This is unlikely to happen. Instead in this chapter we make three very specific policy recommendations, each of which would greatly contribute to multilateralizing regionalism. These three proposals are, first, to adopt the preferential partner principle for diagonal cumulation. This would immediately extend the possibilities for diagonal cumulation across a much wider range of countries than is currently the case without changing the existing preferences countries have already granted to each other. Second, we propose in the longer run to switch to the more widespread use of the value-added rule, to introduce the application of value-added tariffs, and to allow for full cumulation. We argue that this would also go a long way towards reducing the spaghetti bowl phenomenon and introduce both more flexibility and more negotiability into rules of origin arrangements. Finally, we propose that developed countries could do a lot to make ROOs more development-friendly by acknowledging that fiscal fraud can only occur where partner country tariffs are lower, and that therefore wherever they are higher there should be no need to enforce the ROOs.

References

Augier, P., Gasiorek, M. and Lai-Tong, C. (2004) 'Rules of Origin and the EU-Med Partnership: The Case of Textiles', *The World Economy* 27 (9): 1449–73.

(2005) 'The Impact of Rules of Origin on Trade Flows', *Economic Policy* 20 (43): 567–624.

Brenton, P. and Manchin, M. (2003) 'Making EU Trade Agreements Work: The Role of Rules of Origin', *World Economy* 26 (5): 755–69.

Cadot, O., Estevadeordal, A. and Suwa-Eisenmann, A. (2004) 'Rules of Origin as Export Subsidies', paper presented at the IDB-CEPR-DELTA/INRA conference 'Rules of Origin in Regional Trade Agreements: Conceptual and Empirical Approaches', Washington DC, February.

Dattagupta, R. and Panagariya, A. (2002) 'Free Trade Areas and Rules of Origin: Economics and Politics', working paper.

Estevadeordal, A. (2000) 'Negotiating Preferential Market Access: The Case of the North American Free Trade Agreement', *Journal of World Trade* 34 (1): 141–61.

Estevadeordal, A. and Suominen, K. (2004) 'Rules of Origin: A World Map and Trade Effects', paper presented at the IDB-CEPR-DELTA/INRA conference 'Rules of Origin in Regional Trade Agreements: Conceptual and Empirical Approaches', Washington DC, February.

European Commission (2003) 'Green Paper: On the Future of Rules of Origin in Preferential Trade Agreements', Brussels, December.

(2004) 'Green Paper: The Future of Rules of Origin in Preferential Trade Agreements', a summary report of the results of the consultation process, Brussels, August.

Flatters, F. and Kirk, R. (2004) 'Rules of Origin as Tools of Development? Some Lessons from SADC', Southern African Development Community, available at: www.msu.edu/~olsonuk/politicalEconomy/SADCInfo.htm.

Gasiorek, M., Augier, P., Evans, D., Holmes, P. and Lai-Tong, C. (2002) 'Study on the Economic Impact of Extending the Pan-European System of Cumulation of Origin to the Mediterranean Partners' Part of the Barcelona Process', report prepared for the European Commission.

Grossman, G. and Helpman, E. (1995) 'The Politics of Free-Trade Agreements', *American Economic Review* 85: 667–90.

Herin, J. (1986) 'Rules of Origin and Differences Between Tariff Levels in EFTA and the EC', EFTA Occasional Paper No. 13.

Inama, S. (2003) 'Trade Preferences for LDCs: An Early Assessment of Benefits and Possible Improvements', UNCTAD Paper ITCD/TSB/2003.

Krishna, K. (2005) 'Understanding Rules of Origin', NBER Working Paper No. 11149, Cambridge, MA: National Bureau of Economic Research.

Lloyd, P. J. (1993) 'A Tariff Substitute for Rules of Origin in Free Trade Areas', *The World Economy* 16 (6): 699–712.

Mattoo, A., Roy, D. and Subramanian, A. (2002) 'The Africa Growth and Opportunity Act and its Rules of Origin: Generosity Undermined?', *The World Economy* 26 (6): 829–51.

Morici, P. (1993) 'NAFTA Rules of Origin and Automotive Domestic Content', in S. Globerman (ed.), *Assessing NAFTA*, Vancouver, BC: Fraser Institute.

Ramirez, J. A. (2004) 'Rules of Origin – NAFTA's Heart but FTAA's Heartburn', *Brooklyn Journal of International Law* 29 (2): 617–62.

WTO (2007) Committee on Rules of Origin – Draft – Consolidated Text of Non-Preferential Rules of Origin – Harmonization Work Programme – Note by the Secretariat, WTO reference G/RO/W/111.

5

The Information Technology Agreement:
sui generis or model stepping stone?

CATHERINE MANN AND XUEPENG LIU[1]

1   Introduction

The Information Technology Agreement (ITA), negotiated in 1996, is a remarkably successful sectoral agreement. Broad coverage of products was achieved ex ante, rather than by building up coverage over "rounds" of negotiations tariff line by tariff line. A schedule for staged reductions of tariffs to zero was achieved ex ante, rather than tariff-reduction formulas becoming subjects for negotiation in themselves in subsequent rounds. Multilateral country coverage was achieved nearly ex ante, in that the initial set of countries agreed on the rules, many additional countries joined bandwagon-style in the initial months following inception of the agreement, and nearly half of all WTO member countries have joined as of 2007.

How extensive was the trade liberalization? Has it led to relatively larger economic benefits, such as trade growth and improvements in economic well-being, for the signatories? There is substantial research on the gains to countries of the effective use of information technology for growth and domestic development. There is surprisingly little research on the explicit role of the ITA for promoting trade or other measures of economic well-being. Research presented in this chapter points to relatively faster trade growth for ITA signatories. Broader-based economic gains require more than just trade liberalization.

As a unique agreement, with economic benefits, can the ITA offer lessons for trade negotiations more generally? Are there lessons for how the ITA was negotiated and brought to fruition that can be a model for

[1] Thanks to Deniz Civril for her assistance in research. This chapter has been financed by the State Secretariat for Economic Affairs (SECO). The views expressed in the chapter are the views of its authors and do not necessarily reflect the views or positions of SECO and Switzerland.

other sectoral or bilateral agreements? Can such agreements be pieced together to achieve multilateral liberalization on a broad product and services basis? Or is there something unique about information technology products, and was the timing of the negotiations particularly fortuitous? In other words, is the ITA a model stepping stone or *sui generis*?

2   Backdrop to the Information Technology Agreement

Economics of IT products: implications for trade liberalization

Information technology (IT) products are special and their special characteristics make trade liberalization more potent for trade and economic gains. IT products have three features that are key for this economic potency: price elasticity, income elasticity, and contribution to productivity growth.[2]

The first key feature of IT products is that they are price-elastic. Thus, a 10 percent decline in the price generates a greater than 10 percent increase in demand for the product (Flamm, 1997; Bayoumi and Haacker, 2002). Thus tariff reductions should serve to expand the global market more than one-for-one as compared to tariff reductions on price-inelastic products, where the market does grow, but not disproportionately.

The second key feature of IT is that investment in IT is income- and development-elastic. A 1 percent increase in income raises demand for IT products by more than 1 percent. Moreover, as development proceeds in a country, the demand for IT products rises disproportionately; higher income countries have a greater IT intensity in the economy. Therefore, to the extent that tariff reductions yield broad-based economic gains, the market for products demanded elastically should expand relatively more than for products that are not income-elastic.

The third key feature of IT is its role in generating productivity growth. If the economy has an appropriate domestic business climate and labor markets, IT investment contributes to overall macroeconomic gains by accelerating productivity growth, directly via capital deepening and indirectly through accelerated total factor productivity growth. For economies that have gained the most from IT products, it is not just investment in IT that matters, but also transformation of business process and products, and labor market practices in the workplace;

---

[2] This section draws on chapter 1 of Mann (2006).

this transformation can be measured by total factor productivity growth.[3]

How do these special characteristics relate to the tariff reductions obtained under the ITA? The characteristic of price elasticity means that the tariff reductions associated with the ITA should have had a disproportionate impact on the global trade for these products. The characteristic of enhanced contribution to productivity growth means that the tariff reductions could feed through to accelerate productivity growth, directly by increasing investment in IT products and indirectly through the channel of faster total factor productivity growth.

Finally, the elasticity of IT investment with respect to income growth and stage of development gives a third channel through which the ITA could generate economic gains. The faster productivity growth coming from tariff reductions raises a country's income and enhances development, which feeds back to further raise the demand for IT products. Trade liberalization in these products which enhance productivity should shift out the economy's production frontier.

In the context of trade liberalization, these key features of elastic investment demand and elastic price of IT could matter both economically and politically. Price reductions associated with trade liberalization for products with these three characteristics suggests that trade liberalization increases the size of the domestic and global economic pie more than would be the case of trade liberalization in products with unitary elasticity and with little feedthrough to productivity acceleration.

Countries that are net importers of products – whose prices decline on account of tariff reductions or other factors – gain the most, because their terms of trade are improving the most. But net exporters will also gain from trade liberalization by trading partners to the extent that tariff reductions expand their markets abroad. With larger potential economic gains both globally and domestically, there are greater resources to mitigate the costs of any adjustment and resource reallocations that occur when trade is liberalized.

Globalized production and trade in IT products in the run-up to ITA

Even before the ITA was negotiated and signed, trade and foreign investment in IT products were already highly globalized. Moreover, the fragmentation of the supply chain was well in train. Both situations

---

[3] For further discussion, see chapter 3 in Mann (2006).

raised the stakes for securing a liberal and non-preferential trade environment. Thus, to some extent the ITA can be seen as an effort to ensure and improve on the status quo of what was already a relatively integrated and globalized marketplace.

First, consider global trade patterns: as of 1990, Japan had 20 percent of the global export market for IT products, US had 19 percent and the UK and West Germany had 15 percent between them (8 percent and 7 percent, respectively). Other European countries accounted for an additional 14 percent of trade (4 + 4 + 3 + 3 for France, Netherlands, Italy, and Ireland). East Asia accounted for 19 percent (7 + 6 + 4 + 2 for Singapore, Chinese Taipei, Republic of Korea, and Malaysia). Hong Kong, China and China together accounted for less than 2 percent of the export market. The distribution of imports was similar, except for Japan's very low import share (4 percent). The United States and Europe accounted for about the same shares (see Mann, 2006, Table 3.2a).

In addition to globalized trade, there was already substantial foreign direct investment in the electronics sectors. For example, there was a well-established US FDI presence in Europe, and production in Asia based on US FDI platforms was coming on stream for the US and global marketplace. As of 1991, the value of US assets abroad in the computer industry was US$60 billion, with about US $40 billion in Europe and a bit less than US$20 billion in Asia (excluding Japan) (Mann, 1994). These global networks impacted the pattern of trade and the prices of computer products in the United States (Mann, 1997). For Japan and France as well, FDI outflows supported a globalized production network for IT. In sum, in the years well before the ITA was broached, the United States, the European Union, and Japan had significant trade and investment interests. Their business communities had a stake in continued access to production locations and liberal trade.

Not only were trade and direct investment well established, but an important hallmark of IT production – fragmentation into an international supply chain – was also well advanced prior to the ITA. The increasingly complex nature of the international supply chain further engendered a demand to ensure a liberalized trading environment. In particular, preferential trade relationships with their dependence on strict rules of origin (ROOs) would be expensive and potentially limiting to the continued globalization of the supply chain based on comparative advantage of production. Rules of origin could be imposed retroactively, leading to losses for firms if they had to shift production. Moreover, regional agreements and ROOs would limit the scope for further international supply chain management going forward.

Was the potential for trade diversion associated with IT products any worse than the general issue of trade diversion caused by rules of origin? In fact, the IT supply chain is characterized by a greater dependence on international supply chains. One way to measure the importance of the supply chain is the share of "parts and components" or "intermediate goods" in trade. This share gives us an idea of how a sector is vertically integrated internationally. Using US import data for 1996–2006 and classifying them into the broad economic categories of final consumption goods, capital goods, and intermediate goods, we find that the share of intermediate products is about 60 percent for IT sectors but only 44 percent for other products.

Another example is China, which has been playing an increasingly important role both for international trade in general and for trade of IT products in particular. Processing trade accounts for a large percentage in Chinese trade. This type of trade usually involves large imports of parts and components by China for processing. The final products are usually shipped back to foreign countries. Based on the data from the China Customs Administration, the share of imports for further processing varies considerably across sectors. During the period from 1996 to 2006, the share of processing trade in ITA sectors was as high as 73 percent as compared to only 29 percent in other sectors.[4]

These two examples from major traders suggest that the international supply chain is especially important for IT products. Trade in IT sectors would be seriously hurt by the rules of origin common to preferential trade arrangements. Therefore multilateral trade liberalization based on the most favored nation (MFN) principle is especially important for IT sectors.

Technology hype and trade skirmishes in the run-up to the ITA

The latter half of the 1990s was a heady time for the information technology sector. It was the darling of Wall Street, media, politics, and international institutions. Over and over again pundits emphasized IT's potential to radically transform business, society, and economic

---

[4] Discussions on the vertical integration of trade and FDI in East Asia can be found in Kimura and Ando (2005) and Kimura (2006).

development. International policymakers and institutions, in particular, took up the cry for IT in economic development.

For example, the G7 meetings included explicit note of IT's transformative role in the communiqués from Naples (1994) and Halifax (1995), and shepherded in the "The G7 Information Society" conference held in Brussels in February 1995, which encouraged the implementation of a series of pilot projects to promote innovation and the spread of new technologies. Additional major conferences were held in South Africa (1996), further touting the role for IT in development. At that conference there were some rumblings of strategic trade policy and industrial policy to support the domestic development of this sector that is so key for economic well-being. The potential for trade and investment protection began to rise.

At nearly the same time, the new institutional group – the Asia Pacific Economic Cooperation (APEC) forum, which originated in 1994 with the seminal goals of free trade among the members by 2010/2020 – reflected on these Bogor goals, and APEC's business advisory groups considered the growing importance of IT trade in the Asia-Pacific region (documented in the previous section). Against the background of the IT hype, the APEC ministers in 1996 at their Subic Bay summit returned a very specific communiqué: "In recognizing the importance of the information technology sector in world trade, Ministers endorsed the efforts at WTO to conclude an information technology agreement by the Singapore Ministerial Conference and urged all other members of the WTO to work toward that end." The outcome at the WTO meeting in Singapore would be the Information Technology Agreement (ITA).

In conjunction with international governmental support, industry's own institutional support fed into the ITA (Fleiss and Sauvé, 1997). In 1994 and 1995, the US Information Technology Industry Council (ITI), the European Association of Manufacturers of Business Machines and Information Technology Industries (EUROBIT), and the Japanese Electronic Industry Development Association (JEIDA) all worked to get the Brussels meeting (called by the G7 in 1995) to support a liberalization of trade among the industrial countries in computer hardware (including peripherals and parts), computer software, and semiconductors and integrated circuits.

Getting Europe on board was seen as important since, although they were at the Brussels event, they were left out of the Subic Bay declaration (not being Asian or Pacific). Moreover, European business was being left out of other bilateral IT agreements. For example, the US and Japan had been skirmishing over semiconductors for years. Under the threat of a dumping case, in 1986 Japan agreed to voluntarily restrain exports of semiconductors to the United States (mostly DRAMs). More importantly, although questionably explicit, the parties agreed to target a 20 percent market share in Japan for foreign (e.g. US) semiconductors. At that time, the Europeans brought a case in the GATT against both the US and Japan, arguing the agreement was price-fixing (Johnson, 1991). Although the initial agreement was to last only five years, it was renewed (Baldwin, 1990). It was set to expire in 1996, but at the margins of the APEC meeting it was renegotiated and renewed, again without European input. This Semiconductor Agreement went in the opposite direction from free trade on an MFN basis, and thus ensured European interest in an ITA at the Singapore Ministerial Conference.

In sum, during the period leading up to the ITA, business was already operating on an international production basis, and politicians and international groups viewed IT as full of economic promise. But the prospects for fragmenting the globe on a preferential basis seemed greater than ever, and the pressures for domestic protection for infant industries and domestic development were obvious.

3 The outcome: The ITA and the WTO

ITA negotiations vs. multilateral negotiations

The ITA was formally concluded at the Singapore Ministerial Conference of the World Trade Organization (WTO) in December 1996.[5] As noted in previous sections, the ITA is notable for both economic and political economy reasons. The run-up to the ITA occurred against the 1990s hype about the role of information technology in economic growth, trade, and development, including in forums such as the G7 and APEC, among others. However, in the negotiating process it represented a departure from the standard GATT approach even as it embraced the key GATT/WTO principle – free trade on a most-favored-nation basis.

---

[5] This section draws in part on the Asia Pacific Economic Cooperation Forum (1997) and the World Trade Organization's "Introduction: Information Technology Agreement," available at: www.wto.org/english/tratop_e/inftec_e/itaintro_e.htm (accessed March 22, 2006). www.wto.org/english/docs_e/legal_e/itadec_e.htm is the full text of the agreement (accessed October 28, 2007).

The negotiation of the ITA departed in several ways from common strategy in most multilateral trade negotiating rounds. First, it was a sectoral agreement that was negotiated outside a multilateral trade round, and was not explicitly part of a single undertaking, the Uruguay Round having been completed in 1994. The broad outlines of the agreement were broached by business advisory groups and interested country partners – including the United States, Japan, Canada, and Mexico – in the context of the Brussels meeting in 1995 and the 1996 summit at APEC, not at the WTO. The November 1996 meeting of APEC ministers in Subic Bay provided both explicit tariff-cutting formulas and product coverage for an agreement, as well as the momentum for the actual ITA, which was agreed upon by a subset of WTO members at the Singapore Ministerial Conference the following December. Not all WTO members signed on at Singapore, however, and in this too the ITA differs from a standard multilateral negotiation.

A second way in which the ITA differed from a standard WTO agreement was that it was provisional as signed. A key provision of the Declaration on Trade in Information Technology Products – the official term for the agreement made in Singapore – was that it would not come into effect unless participants representing approximately 90 percent of world trade in the covered products notified their acceptance of the ITA by April 1, 1997. At the signing in Singapore, only twenty nine countries or economic regions, accounting for about 83 percent of global trade in IT products, acceded to the agreement. These included Australia; Canada; Chinese Taipei; fifteen European Community members; Hong Kong, China; Iceland; Indonesia; Japan; Republic of Korea; Norway; Singapore; Switzerland (including Liechtenstein); Turkey; and the United States. However, before the April 1 deadline, fifteen more countries or economic entities joined, bringing the coverage of trade up to the required 90 percent, and the declaration came into force. The seventy ITA members now account for 97 percent of trade.

Third, under the ITA, countries agreed to bring tariffs on trade in covered products in six categories to zero by 2000, either immediately or by equally staged tariff reductions in four tranches from July 1997 to January 2000. These tariff reductions were on an MFN basis – even those not party to the ITA would receive the tariff reductions. The six categories are computers, software, telecom equipment, semiconductors, semiconductor manufacturing equipment, and scientific instruments. It is notable that these categories do not map explicitly into HS nomenclature. Moreover, not only were specific HS products covered, but there was a "positive list" of specifically named products covered by the agreement wherever they were classified in the HS (this is the so-called Appendix B list). So the covered products included, to some extent, products by their functionality, not just specifically by HS code. Finally, although the final list of covered products was subject to some negotiations amongst the parties, the negotiating strategy was not principally the "request/offer" approach common to trade liberalizing negotiations.

In contrast to a standard multilateral trade round, there was no generalized "special and differential" treatment, although provision for extending the final tariff-cutting phase to 2005 was agreed at the initial signing. Only a few countries took extensions for some products, including, for example, India, Malaysia, and Indonesia. China joined in 2003, as part of its WTO accession. Brazil, Mexico, and South Africa remain among the non-acceding countries. Notably, Mexico ranks in the top ten global exporters and importers of IT products (Mann, 2006, Table 3.2ab). Mexico may not have acceded to the agreement at the time, so as to keep its preferred NAFTA status. Subsequently, Mexico undertook reforms (so-called "ITA-Plus"), yielding commitments similar to the ITA.

In several respects, though, the ITA negotiations had troubles similar to those of previous multilateral negotiations. For example, negotiators decided to avoid "third rail" issues of culture (CD-ROMs and video are not included), and to "overlook" certain nascent domestic industries that countries may have sought to protect (consumer electronics).

Finally, negotiators tabled the discussion of non-tariff measures (NTMs) (business decided that achieving zero-for-zero tariff reductions on a broad range of products with the majority of trading partners was better than getting into the morass of NTMs). However, upon inception of the ITA, and under WTO auspices, the Committee of Participants on the Expansion of Trade in Information Technology Products was organized. This committee was charged with addressing issues of product classification and non-tariff measures, as well as working to broaden the product coverage under a so-called ITA II.

In sum, the key aspects in which the ITA negotiations differed were in terms of the initial venue for negotiations, with a subset of countries and business groups explicitly driving the process; the broad and functional product set; and up-front agreement on tariff-cutting formulas. The key area where the outcome was superior to bilateral or regional negotiations was that tariff reductions were on an MFN basis, regardless of whether the trading partner was a signatory to the ITA.

Fitting the ITA in the WTO

How do the commitments that countries made under the ITA fit with other commitments they have made under WTO auspices? First, the ITA was the first agreement negotiated following the completion of the Uruguay Round in 1994. Key aspects of the Uruguay Round potentially relevant for IT products are: GATS (trade in services), TRIPS (intellectual property issues), and the streamlined dispute settlement mechanism. To what extent did the ITA build on or otherwise embrace these aspects of the Uruguay Round and the WTO?

First, with respect to services, an important point of ambiguity for both the WTO and the ITA is software. At the time of the ITA, software tended to be delivered in physical form (for example, on a disk drive or diskette); software as a tradable service was just starting to be conceived. Although software is included in the list of six broad categories of covered products, it is not addressed specifically in the Appendices of coverage of the ITA. Even in Appendix B, which covers products by description rather than by HS code, software is not specifically addressed except as embodied in a tangible product.

Now, software as a tradable service butts up against the WTO (and technically the ITA as well) in all domains of the agreement: as embodied in a traded good (disk drives, shrink-wrapped boxes), and along all modes of the General Agreement on Trade in Services. Software can be delivered as mode 1 or mode 2 (via download using the internet), as mode 3 (multinational affiliate set up to engage in software design), and as mode 4 (cross-border movement of software engineers). But all discussions regarding the ITA take place in the Council on Trade in Goods.

Second, many of the computer products covered under the ITA have important attributes of intellectual property to which TRIPS would apply – software, for one, but also chip design and patents on telecommunications and semiconductor manufacturing equipment. The ITA made no mention of intellectual property, perhaps in recognition that TRIPS was already in place.

Third, with respect to dispute settlement, the Ministerial Declaration on Trade in Information Technology Products agreed upon in Singapore included language referencing Article XXIII of the GATT:[6]

---

[6] See www.wto.org/english/docs_e/legal_e/itadec_e.htm.

6. The participants understand that Article XXIII of the General Agreement will address nullification or impairment of benefits accruing directly or indirectly to a WTO Member participant through the implementation of this Declaration as a result of the application by another WTO Member participant of any measure, whether or not that measure conflicts with the provisions of the General Agreement.

7. Each participant shall afford sympathetic consideration to any request for consultation from any other participant concerning the undertakings set out above. Such consultations shall be without prejudice to rights and obligations under the WTO Agreement.

8. Participants acting under the auspices of the Council for Trade in Goods shall inform other Members of the WTO and States or separate customs territories in the process of acceding to the WTO of these modalities and initiate consultations with a view to facilitate their participation in the expansion of trade in information technology products on the basis of the Declaration.

The ITA embraced the new (at the time) WTO dispute settlement mechanism and several disputes have been brought under the WTO system covering DRAMs (three cases), integrated curcuits (one case) and computer equipment (one case). The most extensive set of disputes is over DRAMs. Recall that the US–Japan Semiconductor Agreement was one of the motivators for the ITA to begin with. Yet disputes over DRAMs continue, not with respect to tariffs, but with respect to subsidies and countervailing duties – measures that are consultative under the Subsidies and Countervailing Measures Agreement of the WTO.

In sum, there have been limited disputes on IT products, and none regarding tariffs. The disputes have focused on reclassification of a product (EU–US, 1996, network computer equipment), preferential tax treatment (China–US, integrated circuits, 2004), and subsidies and countervailing duties (EC, US–Republic of Korea, DRAMS, 1997, 2003).

There are, however, ongoing informal discussions regarding ITA-covered products that now have broader functionality than when the original agreement was signed. This issue of the evolution of functionality was embodied in the ITA language, but has become a stumbling block for the broadening of the ITA to an ITA II, a point that will be discussed later in this chapter.

4   Is the ITA a model stepping stone?

Overview of sectoral agreements

Sectoral agreements date back to the 1950s. The early sectoral arrangements were usually not to promote freer trade, but rather as a protectionist response to domestic pressures (e.g. voluntary export restraints, VERs[7]). However, since the 1980s, sector agreements have shifted from a protectionist bent to sector-by-sector liberalization. One of the earliest sectoral trade liberalization agreements was for trade in civil aircraft. It entered into force in 1980 to promote world trade in civil aircraft, parts and related equipment.[8]

The most important movement in sectoralism during the GATT Uruguay Round was the so-called "zero-for-zero" tariff reduction arrangements. (The reciprocal elimination of tariffs in a sector is often referred to as a "zero-for-zero" agreement.) During the Uruguay Round, the United States, Canada, the European Union, and Japan agreed to eliminate tariffs on a reciprocal basis, immediately or over a period of time of up to fifteen years, on most products in a number of sectors (agricultural equipment, beer, construction equipment, furniture, medical equipment, paper, pharmaceuticals, steel, brown spirits, and toys) as well as to harmonize tariffs on chemicals.

These agreements came into force on January 1, 1995 for most initial signatories. Australia, New Zealand, Switzerland, Norway, and the Republic of Korea also participated in the majority of the zero-for-zero tariff initiatives. By eliminating all tariffs in an entire sector, the zero-for-zero sectoral approach addressed the issue of tariff peaks (defined as tariffs greater than 15 percent in the Uruguay Round) and tariff escalation (higher tariffs on products as the level of processing increases), albeit only in those sectors identified above. In some cases, better market access was achieved through specific requests and offers. As with the ITA, the commitments undertaken under these sectoral agreements in the GATT/WTO are on an MFN basis. Therefore the benefits accrue to all other WTO members.

About two years after the "zero-for-zero" arrangements, the ITA came into force at the end of 1996. Since then, the ITA has been serving as a model for sectoralism. The Global Agreement on Basic Telecommunications was negotiated in 1997, and it covers over 95 percent of trade in telecoms since 1998. The Financial Services Agreement (FSA) followed closely in December 1997 to liberalize trade in banking, insurance, and securities. It came into effect in April 1999 and covers

---

[7] Such VERs were not GATT agreements, but rather were grey-area measures undertaken by some large trading partners, including the US, the EU, and Japan in autos, and, as noted, DRAMs.

[8] By now, about thirty countries have signed this agreement.

over 95 percent of trade in these sectors (Aggarwal and Ravenhill, 2001).[9] In addition, there also exist some other sectoral agreements, such as on tropical and natural resource-based products, agricultural products, textiles, and clothing products. The progress made in liberalizing trade in these sectors is rather limited.

Although negotiated as "zero-for-zero," progress on actual tariff reduction of these agreements has been uneven across countries. As noted by Hoda (2002), the negotiations on tariff peaks did result in a considerable reduction, but not the elimination of rates above 15 percent in the developed countries. The overall target for reduction by one-third for industrial tariffs was reached by all developed countries and exceeded by some. A major objective of the developed countries in these negotiations was to persuade the developing countries to increase the scope of their tariff bindings (maximum permitted tariffs) and to bring the binding level closer to the applied rate (the actual tariff).

The ITA has come closer to achieving the "zero-tariff objective." From tariff rates on IT products averaging 7.5 percent (up to 40 percent for developing ITA members) before the ITA, the weighted average tariff was only 3.5 percent in early 2000s (see Table 5.1).

Sectoral agreements as stepping stones

Most of the existing literature on "stepping stones or stumbling blocks" focuses on regionalism (regional trade agreements, RTAs) vs. multilateralism (the GATT/WTO). Nevertheless, this literature does offer insights that are applicable to the question of sectoralism as a stepping stone.

As summarized by Baldwin (2006), regionalism can act as a stumbling block for several reasons. First, RTAs may dampen enthusiasm for multilateral negotiations under the GATT/WTO, as well as diverting negotiating resources. Second, the formation of large trading blocs increases the hazard of inter-bloc trade war and may raise costs of trade through detailed rules of origin. Third, some RTAs especially "South–South" agreements may hinder multilateral liberalization by protecting import-substituting industries. To this list it is worthwhile to add a fourth point that is particularly related to sectoralism: hiving-off sectors

---

[9] Although with limits on foreign direct investment, the effective liberalization of financial services remains difficult to measure and controversial.

Table 5.1. *Tariffs before ITA vs. tariffs after ITA for selected countries*

Country	Year	Weighted tariff (%)	Year	Weighted tariff (%)
Albania	1997	12.4	2001	7.3
Australia	1997	3.3	2004	1.0
Canada	1997	0.9	2003	0.1
China	1997	14.2	2004	2.6
Costa Rica	1995	3.7	2002	0.3
Czech Republic	1996	4.1	2003	0.7
Egypt	1995	17.1	2002	12.6
El Salvador	1997	1.7	2002	0.6
Estonia	1995	0.0	2003	0.0
European Union	1997	3.0	2002	0.3
India	1997	30.5	2001	17.5
Indonesia	1996	6.8	2002	2.8
Japan	1997	0.1	2003	0.0
Korea, Rep. of	1996	7.9	2002	1.2
Latvia	1997	0.7	2001	0.0
Lithuania	1997	0.1	2003	0.0
Malaysia	1997	3.7	2002	2.4
Malta	1997	8.6	2003	5.7
Mauritius	1997	43.3	2002	12.9
Morocco	1997	11.6	2003	11.6
New Zealand	1997	4.6	2004	0.9
Norway	1996	1.2	2003	0.0
Panama	1997	10.5	2001	7.8
Philippines	1995	12.7	2003	1.2
Poland	1997	6.7	2003	0.8
Singapore	1995	0.0	2003	0.0
Switzerland	1997	0.0	2004	0.0
Chinese Taipei	1996	4.7	2003	0.8
Thailand	1995	11.5	2001	7.3
Turkey	1997	4.2	2003	0.2
United States of America	1997	2.4	2004	0.3
ITA members		**7.5**		**3.5**
Non-ITA members		**16.2**		**11.2**

Notes:
[1] Data sources: UNCTAD TRAINS.
[2] Years are the latest available years in each dataset, accessed in 2004.
[3] Weighted tariff is the simple average of HS six-digit weighted average tariffs applied on all ITA products.
[4] The tariffs for "ITA members" are the simple average tariffs for all ITA members.
[5] The tariffs for "Non-ITA members" are the simple average tariffs for all non-ITA members. The tariffs for each individual non-ITA member are not shown here due to limited space.

that may be easier to liberalize may dampen the momentum for broad-based liberalization.

Using the framework from analyzing RTAs as stumbling blocks, do sectoral agreements pose similar problems, and what about the ITA in particular? The first problem of RTAs may also exist for sectoral agreements. The shift of negotiating attention and effort from multilateralism to sectoralism may delay the process of the multilateral negotiation. As noted by Aggarwal and Ravenhill (2001), sectoralism is politically and economically hazardous. From a political perspective, sectoral agreements buy off winners in those sectors and reduce the support for future multilateral negotiations that would benefit a significantly broader group of industries and consumers. From an economic perspective, by liberalizing only specific, highly competitive sectors, sectoral trade agreements may lead to a perverse incentive to invest in or discourage exit from the least efficient areas of the economy and hence create more distortions.

The second and third problems identified by Baldwin (2006) for RTAs are, however, less likely to be an issue for sectoral agreements, so long as the agreement is on an MFN basis. Under these circumstances, sectoral agreements are a good approach to eliminating the tariff spikes and the political rents associated with the protection of import-competing industries.

Therefore, it is a key feature of the ITA that its members are committed to duty-free imports on an MFN basis. So long as a country is a WTO member, it enjoys the benefits of lowered tariffs from the parties to the sectoral agreement even when it has not signed the sectoral agreement itself. Moreover, the "external" tariffs on the imports from non-WTO members did not increase under the ITA, which can mitigate trade diversion. Finally, there are no rules of origin. This treatment afforded to the non-members avoids opposition from countries with inefficient producers. The distortion from this special treatment of non-members is small if these non-members' trade accounts for a small percentage of total world trade in these sectors.

Therefore, for a sectoral agreement to be successful by expanding global trade and avoiding the inefficiencies of free-riding non-signatories there are two key criteria: the sector should be large, and the share of trade by parties to the agreement should be high, preferably close to 100 percent.[10]

---

[10] This feature is similar to the "substantially all the trade" requirement of RTAs according to the GATT Article XXIV – a feature often not met by RTAs.

Table 5.2. *Trade shares and coverage of some selected sectoral agreements*

Sectoral agreements	Share of world trade (%)	Export coverage (%)	Import coverage (%)
ITA	13.25	95	95
Civil aircraft	12.63	n/a	n/a
Chemicals	9.99	82.57	68.79
Steel	2.52	72.54	63.77
Paper	2.25	71.16	71.63
Pharmaceuticals	1.52	86.83	73.50
Medical equipment	1.11	89.73	74.30
Construction equipment	0.97	84.84	64.00
Furniture	0.79	72.44	85.53
Toys	0.73	32.84	69.73
Agricultural equipment	0.25	88.24	74.94
Brown spirits	0.16	86.63	78.17
Beer	0.08	79.76	85.97

Notes: Share is the import share of a sector among total world imports over the period 1988–2003; import (export) coverage is the share of the import (export) covered by these agreements in 1994, except for the ITA which is calculated for 2002, based on the trade data from the UN COMTRADE.
Data sources: Bora and Liu (2006), Hoda (2002), WITS, WTO Secretariat.

First, with regard to sector size: the liberalization in a certain sector cannot make a significant contribution to trade liberalization unless the size of the sector is large enough. Trade shares of some of these agreements in total world trade for 1988–2003 are shown in Table 5.2. Based on the product definitions provided by the WTO, most sectors account for less than 3 percent of total world trade, except the ITA (13.25 percent), and the agreements on civil aircraft (12.6 percent) and chemicals (10 percent).[11]

Second, with regard to the coverage of total trade: because a sectoral agreement is usually signed by a small group of countries, it is important to make sure that the major producers and traders are covered by the

---

[11] The trade data exclude intra-EU trade because most of the European Union members were in the same customs union and free trade area since the beginning of our sample (1988). Therefore it is better to treat the intra-EU trade as trade within a country. For the same reason, we also drop all the intra-EU bilateral trade in our regressions in the empirical section.

agreement. The last two columns of Table 5.2 list the export and import coverage of these selected agreements. Most of the trade in these sectors is covered by these agreements, among which the ITA has the highest coverage (95 percent).

In sum, sectoralism can be a fruitful avenue to overall free trade, but the sectors have to be large and the membership widespread. The high coverage of trade and the relatively large size of the sector in world trade are key elements leading to the success of the ITA and make it a possible stepping stone to broad-based trade liberalization, particularly if countries see the domestic economic gains of importing and using IT investment throughout the domestic economy.

IT in bilateral agreements: towards making BTAs stepping stones?

The United States has embraced RTAs and bilateral trade agreements (BTAs) in which information technology plays an important role. Can the implementation of the IT provisions in those regional and bilateral agreements push them more toward being stepping stones rather than stumbling blocks?

US trade policy moved from full support of multilateral efforts to the near total embrace of bilateral and regional agreements in the mid 1990s. From 2001 to 2006, the number of US R/BTA partners or imminent partners went from three to twenty-nine (Ludema, 2007). Besides NAFTA (involving Canada and Mexico, which came into force in 1994) and the BTA with Israel (1985), the US has implemented R/BTAs with Jordan (2001), Chile (2004), Singapore (2004), Australia (2005), Morocco (2006), Bahrain (2006), and CAFTA-DR (Costa Rica, El Salvador, Guatemala, Honduras, Nicaragua, and the Dominican Republic). Other agreements negotiated and signed, albeit not ratified, include those with Colombia, Peru, and Oman. Negotiations continue with Ecuador, Panama, Republic of Korea, Malaysia, Thailand, United Arab Emirates, and the Southern African Customs Union (South Africa, Botswana, Lesotho, Namibia, and Swaziland).

Even before the current wave, the US BTAs were seen as a way to prevent piracy and counterfeiting, to push for the implementation of international laws and to protect US interests, particularly related to IT. Such agreements were a way to negotiate with countries with high tariffs and subsidies and then, under the umbrella of the WTO, to extend the commitments of TRIPS, ITA, and the Basic Telecommunication Agreement. Quoting from Charlene Barshefsky in 2001: "As formal barriers began to diminish, trade negotiations moved into more arcane fields such as harmonizing technical standards, so that a semiconductor chip built in Costa Rica and a hard drive assembled in Southeast Asia, for example, can run programs written in India for a computer designed in North Carolina."

Recent US BTAs have explicit chapters that follow a common template for information technology, including that the country accede to the ITA as well as commit to extension along the following lines:

- Eliminate tariffs on all information technology products (hardware and software) and components, infrastructure equipment, medical equipment, and scientific instruments. Medical equipment represents an extension of product coverage beyond the ITA.
- Ensure that as products covered by the ITA evolve technologically they retain zero-duty treatment, and that the product coverage continues to expand. Both of these points are areas of controversy for ITA II.
- As part of the Doha Round Non-Agricultural Market Access (NAMA) negotiations, countries should agree on sectoral tariff elimination that would apply to IT products, including those products not currently covered by the ITA.

Some public statements from the United States government imply that the ITA not only commits countries to duty-free trade in IT products, but also the elimination of non-tariff measures. For example, the United States International Trade Commission (USITC) report on the US–Colombia agreement states that: "Colombia has agreed to sign the WTO Information Technology Agreement (ITA), which requires signatories to remove tariff and nontariff barriers to trade in IT products."[12] Even if the actual language of the text of the agreement includes only tariff elimination on products under ITA I, the fact that the public statements include topics under consideration in ITA II reveals the potential power of these BTAs to change the weight of negotiations at the WTO on the ITA II and NTM issues. That is, to the extent that a country has already agreed with the United States to remove NTMs and to broaden the coverage of the ITA to ITA II products, then they may be more amenable to coverage of NTMs in the context of the WTO.

Indeed, Rob Portman, when he was USTR, explicitly gave to the BTAs the job of expanding product coverage of the ITA to ITA II and beyond.

---

[12] See www.usitc.gov/publications/pub3896.pdf.

In the last six weeks ... we launched new free trade agreement talks with two major economies in Asia: the Republic of Korea and Malaysia. In those accords, we will look at phasing out tariffs on consumer electronics not covered by ITA. These free trade agreements will also address investment, distribution, telecom and financial services, and help make consumer electronics companies' supply chains more efficient.[13]

The US push toward bilateral agreements, the nature of the negotiating template, and the expanding verbal coverage of products and NTMs under those agreements has the potential to change the weight of negotiations at the WTO on these ITA II issues. That is, if countries have already agreed to these parameters in their BTA with the United States, they may be more likely to join with the US negotiators at the WTO when similar issues arise in the WTO context. This could increase the potential for widening product coverage in the context of ITA II, thus expanding the scope of multilateral freer trade.

5   Empirical analysis of the impact of ITA

Did the ITA cut tariffs?

Has the ITA made a difference to global trade in technology products and to countries that are members? Theory and practical experience tell us that reducing tariffs leads to more trade, and that trade should grow more for the countries that cut tariffs the most. In fact, empirical evidence of the ITA has been difficult to ascertain. A key issue is that the tariff reductions took place in the context of dramatic increases in global trade in IT products associated with the technology boom up to 2000 (and the subsequent crash). It is difficult to pick out the changes in trade due to changes in tariffs alone.

From the perspective of average tariffs, the ITA made a difference. Table 5.1 using the UN TRAINS (UN Trade Analysis and Information System) database shows the tariffs of ITA products for selected countries before and after the ITA. The tariffs for individual non-ITA members are not listed, to save space, but their average tariffs are reported at the bottom of the table. Overall the average tariffs of non-ITA members were much higher than those of members both before (16.2 percent vs. 7.5 percent) and after the ITA (11.2 percent vs. 3.2 percent). Although the

---

[13] Remarks by Ambassador Rob Portman, United States Trade Representative, before the Consumer Electronics Association at the Ronald Reagan International Trade Center, Washington DC, March 15, 2006.

tariffs in non-member countries also dropped, the percentage change is much smaller than that in ITA members (25 percent vs. 57 percent). For the top four IT product exporters,[14] the reduction in tariffs in levels is the biggest in China, from 14.2 percent to 2.6 percent. The tariff the US and the EU dropped from 2–3 percent to almost zero. The room for further tariff reduction in Japan is very limited because Japan had almost achieved zero tariffs on IT products even before the ITA.

A related issue is how far the ITA sectors were characterized by preferential trade arrangements before the ITA. This will determine the extent to which the ITA "multilateralized" regional agreements that were already in force. Based on the UN COMTRADE data, at least 30 percent of the ITA trade (exports and imports) in 1996 was covered by certain regional trade agreements.[15] This implies that a significant part of the tariff reduction under the ITA was not just de novo MFN tariff-cutting, but rather tariff-cutting in the context of regional agreements. Thus the ITA did help to multilateralize regional trade in IT products.

Did the ITA promote trade in IT products?

Looking at just growth in trade, by the end of 2005 the share of IT products was 19 percent, excluding intra-EU trade (Finger, 2007). It was a significant amount compared to agricultural products (8.4 percent) and automotive products (7.2 percent). The world exports of IT products rose from $600 billion in 1996 to more than $1,500 billion in 2006. The growth of exports in IT products exceeds the growth of export in manufactures. Computers, semiconductors and telecoms make up approximately 80 percent of world exports of IT products.[16]

However, is this growth in trade due to the ITA or due to the way in which the technology itself and reductions in transportation costs allowed the fragmentation of the supply chain in IT production, which would increase the amount of trade? Moreover, given the high elasticity of investment demand for IT products, rising GDP alone would have increased trade in these products.

In principle, the ITA should promote the use of information and communication technology products (ICT) in developing countries. The

---

[14] The ranking is based on the 2002 UN COMTRADE data.

[15] The list of these RTAs can be found at: www.wto.org/english/tratop_e/region_e/region_e.htm.

[16] See also WTO (2007).

ITA can help with non-competitive environments, poor infrastructure, institutions, human capital and policies, but alone it may not be enough to promote trade. In fact, Joseph and Parayil (2006) did not find a significant change in the world demand for ITA products after the ITA was signed. Moreover, they determined that some non-ITA members were superior export and import performers in ITA products compared with ITA members.[17]

An alternative econometric approach (Mann, 2006) finds that being a member of the ITA is statistically associated with imports of IT products, controlling for domestic expenditures on IT. In addition, given that many IT products are intermediates in the supply chain of other IT products, being a member of the ITA should reduce tariffs on imported intermediates and thereby increase the competitiveness of IT exports. Indeed, econometric evidence suggests that being a member of the ITA may play this role.

A systematic assessment: Bora and Liu (2006)

The most systematic approach to estimating the impact of the ITA on trade is Bora and Liu (2006), from which this section is adapted. They estimate the effect of the ITA on bilateral trade flows of IT products using a gravity model framework, paying particular attention to the differences in ITA and WTO membership so as to capture their roles for both trade creation and trade diversion effects.

In Bora and Liu, the key variables of interest are constructed from the ITA and WTO memberships.[18] As discussed above, the nature of the ITA is that if the importer is an ITA member, then it will offer its ITA tariff rates to all WTO members, whether the exporter is an ITA member or not. This leads to the following four dummy variables of interest:

---

[17] One problem with the analysis is that some non-ITA members had fairly low tariffs on IT products due to preferential policies. For example, even before China joined the ITA, more than half of China's imports of manufactures were destined for processing in special zones and re-exported, and were exempt from duties.

[18] Bora and Liu assume that all ITA members are also WTO members. The issue of ITA membership prior to WTO membership (e.g. Estonia, Lithuania, Chinese Taipei) is also considered. Accounting for this issue does not affect the results. For countries that might have received special tariff treatment before WTO membership (such as the "permanent normal trade relationship" between China and the US), not explicitly considering this as a regional trade agreement would only serve to bias the results toward an insignificant impact of the ITA.

- The first variable is one if the importer is an ITA member and the exporter is a WTO member; this measures the trade creation effect of the ITA.
- The second variable is one if the importer is a WTO member but not an ITA member and the exporter is a WTO member; this measures the trade diversion of the ITA within the WTO. In other words, if an importer is a WTO member but not an ITA member, it will see its imports fall as exporters choose to allocate their exports to ITA members.
- The third variable is for all of the scenarios when one of the two countries is not a WTO member. As long as one of the countries is not in the WTO, its trade in either direction cannot benefit from the ITA. To be parsimonious, we do not distinguish between these different subcategories. This measure captures the trade diversion of the GATT/WTO.
- The last variable is one if neither country is a WTO member; this measures the baseline category in the analyses.

The dependent variable (M_{ijt}) is the c.i.f. import of country i from country j in year t taken from COMTRADE.[19] Besides the above dummy variables for ITA and WTO membership, the regression includes other standard control variables: the real GDP and GDP per capita of both countries; the great circle distance between countries; land contingency dummy; the geographic area of both countries; the number of island nations in a pair (0, 1, or 2); the number of landlocked nations in a pair (0, 1, or 2); common language dummy; colonial relationship; the military conflict intensity between countries; remoteness, measuring the

[19] Bora and Liu use import flows for trade data, rather than the sum of imports and exports for the following reasons. First, import data are usually regarded as more reliable than export data because customs are more interested in tracking imports than exports for tariff revenue reasons. Second, country or country pairs' characteristics usually affect imports and exports differently. With directional import data, they can avoid mixing the effects on imports and exports. Finally, most gravity models offer predictions for imports rather than the total trade.

Import data are from the UNCTAD COMTRADE database, aggregated over all ITA products as listed in Appendix 1 of Bora and Liu (2006). The import of country i from country j is filled by the export of j to i when the former is missing and the latter is available. A 10 percent c.i.f. is assumed when using the mirrored data. In the log-linear gravity regressions, the dependent variable $ln(M_{ijt})$ is substituted by $ln(M_{ijt}+1)$ to keep the zero trade values after taking logarithms. The measurement error created is small because trade data are converted into dollars (rather than millions or billions of dollars) before the one dollar is added.

distance of a country pair from the rest of the world weighted by all the other countries' GDPs in a year;[20] formal alliance dummy; generalized system of preferences (GSP) relationship; currency union dummy; regional trade agreement (RTA) dummy; year dummies and country pair dummies. For more explicit discussion of the data and sources, see Bora and Liu (2006). The panel dataset used in this chapter includes 217 countries over the years 1988–2003 and includes trade in IT products yielding about 135,000 observations.

This section presents the gravity regression results in Tables 5.3 and 5.4. We start with pooled OLS (ordinary least squares) with only year dummies. The ITA is very effective with large trade creation and trade diversion effects. This regression uses both within- and between-country pair variations. The between variations, however, often suffered from an endogeneity problem (i.e. reverse causation): the more a country trades in ITA products, the more likely it will be to join the ITA. Therefore the preferred regressions include country pair fixed effects.[21]

Fixed effects regressions use only the within variations. The country pair fixed effects control for the unobserved characteristics for each country pair; this partially fixes the endogeneity problem. Results from the fixed effects regression show that the coefficients on other covariates generally have expected signs. GSP, RTA, and alliance significantly increase bilateral ITA trade. "Remoteness" positively affects bilateral trade, as expected. Currency union, however, is insignificant.[22]

Fixed effects regressions respond to the following question: do two countries trade more in ITA products after one or both of them join the ITA, compared with their trade before joining the agreement?

- In this specification, a country will import 7 percent more ITA products if it is an ITA member and the exporter is a WTO member, compared with the baseline case of neither being a WTO member. If importer and exporter are both WTO members but the importer is

---

[20] This remoteness variable serves as a proxy for the "index of multilateral resistance" (Anderson and Wincoop, 2003). Bora and Liu expect that the "remoteness" variable will positively affect bilateral trade because two countries will trade more with each other, ceteris paribus, if they are remote from the rest of the world, e.g. Australia and New Zealand.

[21] The random effects model is based on a more stringent condition: that is, the error term must be uncorrelated with country pair dummies. The Hausman test rejects this condition, so we take the fixed effects regression as our preferred specification.

[22] It becomes significant when we restrict the sample to large traders only (i.e. import > $100,000 at 1995 prices).

Table 5.3. *Regression results*

	(1) Pooled OLS full sample		(2) Fixed effects full sample		(3) Random effects full sample		(4) Fixed effects large traders	
	coef.	z	coef.	z	coef.	z	coef.	z
*ita*wto	0.42***	10.50	0.07**	2.29	0.15***	5.31	0.11***	4.79
_*itawto*wto	−0.27***	−7.47	−0.06**	−2.07	−0.12***	−4.45	−0.01	−0.48
onewto	−0.37***	−10.45	−0.16***	−5.11	−0.20***	−7.03	−0.12***	−4.78
log(GDPi)	0.79***	115.9	−0.86***	−6.79	0.68***	46.80	−0.82***	−8.74
log(GDPj)	1.20***	178.6	0.20	1.51	1.00***	70.04	0.91***	7.80
log(GDPPCi)	0.38***	34.6	1.96***	15.54	0.29***	13.18	1.92***	20.17
log(GDPPCj)	0.93***	79.3	1.16***	8.35	0.73***	32.32	0.48***	3.74
log(Distance)	−0.82***	−64.1			−0.73***	−28.9		
Land adjacency	0.97***	20.6			1.12***	9.28		
log(AREAi)	−0.05***	−9.45			−0.04***	−3.25		
log(AREAj)	−0.28***	−52.9			−0.23***	−18.7		
Island	0.23***	12.6			0.28***	6.81		
Landlocked	−0.13***	−7.99			−0.17***	−4.98		
ComLang	0.21***	6.41			0.14**	2.00		
Ever Colony	1.76***	39.3			2.18***	15.2		
Com Colony	0.52***	18.3			0.38***	6.10		
Hostility	−0.66***	−12.3			−0.45***	−3.66		
Alliance	0.14***	4.69	0.25***	3.18	0.17***	3.20	0.47***	9.79
Remoteness	1.60***	6.62	0.65	1.21	0.88**	2.33	2.66***	6.44

Table 5.3. (cont.)

	(1) Pooled OLS full sample		(2) Fixed effects full sample		(3) Random effects full sample		(4) Fixed effects large traders	
	coef.	z	coef.	z	coef.	z	coef.	z
GSPij	−0.39***	−14.38	0.22***	3.78	−0.03	−0.84	0.34***	8.40
GSPji	0.28***	12.76	0.22***	4.51	0.44***	12.1	0.07**	2.38
FTA	0.22***	10.05	0.42***	10.88	0.39***	12.7	0.30***	11.66
CU	0.64***	11.67	0.48	0.59	0.37***	2.87	0.97*	1.75
Year dummy	Yes		Yes		Yes		Yes	
R2	0.51		0.82		0.50		0.88	
No. of observations	133,352		133,352		133,352		64,078	

Notes:
[1] Dependent variable is the logarithm of the real import of country A from country B.
[2] All continuous variables are in logarithms.
[3] ***, **, and * denote the significance levels at 1 percent, 5 percent, and 10 percent respectively.
[4] Regression (1) is OLS with year dummies and robust standard errors.
[5] Regression (2) has both year dummies and country pair fixed effects.
[6] Regression (3) has both year dummies and country pair random effects.
[7] Regression (4) has both year dummies and country pair fixed effects (real import>$10,000).
[8] The R2 for random effect regression is the overall R2.
[9] The R2 for fixed effect regression is the adjusted R2 recovered from country pair dummy variable least square regression (DVLS), which is not comparable with the R2 in the random effect regression.

Table 5.4. Fixed effects regression results, developing vs. developed countries

	(1) Full sample		(2) Large traders		(3) Full sample		(4) Large traders	
	coef.	z	coef.	z	coef.	z	coef.	z
ditawto	0.01	0.29	0.01	0.57				
uscaipitawto					0.11*	1.81	0.06	1.44
aunzitawto					0.28***	3.60	0.05	0.79
deuitawto					−0.05	−1.36	0.00	−0.09
dgitawto	0.12***	3.55	0.18***	7.34	0.12***	3.55	0.18***	7.34
_itawtowto	−0.07**	−2.24	−0.02	−0.81	−0.06**	−2.19	−0.02	−0.78
onewto	−0.16***	−5.03	−0.11***	−4.53	−0.16***	−5.01	−0.11***	−4.52
log(GDPi)	−0.93***	−7.27	−0.55***	−9.93	−0.98***	−7.65	−0.96***	−10.01
log(GDPj)	0.23*	1.72	0.57***	8.24	0.26*	1.88	0.97***	8.29
log(GDPPCi)	2.02***	15.86	2.03***	21.06	2.07***	16.19	2.04***	21.11
log(GDPPCj)	1.12***	8.08	0.41***	3.23	1.10***	7.92	0.40***	3.17
Alliance	0.26***	3.18	0.47***	9.83	0.26***	3.24	0.47***	9.85
Remoteness	0.63	1.18	2.59***	6.28	0.71	1.33	2.61***	6.32
GSPij	0.20***	3.53	0.32***	7.85	0.22***	3.89	0.32***	7.84
GSPji	0.23***	4.63	0.09***	2.77	0.22***	4.60	0.09***	2.76
FTA	0.41***	10.80	0.30***	11.49	0.42***	11.05	0.30***	11.58

Table 5.4. (*cont*.)

	(1) Full sample		(2) Large traders		(3) Full sample		(4) Large traders	
	coef.	z	coef.	z	coef.	z	coef.	z
CU	0.48	0.60	0.98*	1.78	0.48	0.60	0.99*	1.79
Year dummy	Yes		Yes		Yes		Yes	
R2	0.82		0.88		0.82		0.88	
No. of observations	133,352		64,078		133,352		64,078	

Notes:

[1] Dependent variable is the logarithm of the real import of country *i* from country *j*.

[2] All continuous variables are in logarithms.

[3] ***, **, and * denote the significance levels at 1 percent, 5 percent, and 10 percent respectively.

[4] All regressions have year dummies and country pair fixed effects.

[5] Regressions (1) and (3) use the full sample.

[6] Regressions (2) and (4) restrict the data to only bigger traders (real import > $10,000).

[7] R2 is the adjusted R2 recovered from country pair dummy variable least square regression (DVLS).

[8] *ditawto* is 1 if importer is a developed ITA member and exporter is in the WTO, and 0 otherwise.

[9] *uscajpitawto* is 1 if importer is US/Canada/Japan and exporter is in the WTO, and 0 otherwise.

[10] *aunzitawto* is 1 if importer is Australia/New Zealand and exporter is in the WTO, and 0 otherwise.

[11] *deuitawto* is 1 if importer is a member of both the EU and the ITA and exporter is in the WTO, and 0 otherwise.

[12] *dgitawto* is 1 if importer is *developing* ITA member and exporter is in the WTO, and 0 otherwise.

not an ITA member, the importer will, on average, import 6 percent less than the baseline case. This effect is economically significant given the fact that the ITA has been implemented for less than ten years and most developed countries already had low tariffs on ITA imports before joining the ITA.

- The trade creation effects of becoming an ITA member are large. Regression results suggest that a non-ITA WTO member would import 14 percent ($= e^{(0.06+0.07)}$) more from WTO members if it joins the ITA, ceteris paribus.

- The trade diversion effects of non-GATT/WTO membership are even stronger ($e^{0.16} = 17\%$). Imports would be 17 percent less if only one country is in the GATT/WTO, compared with the baseline case. These results imply that being a WTO member helps to avoid very large trade diversion even if the country does not sign the ITA.

- Robustness checks reveal that the trade creation effect of the ITA is even stronger (12 percent vs. 7 percent) for large traders (i.e. imports > $100,000, at 1995 prices).

- The ITA should have a larger impact for the developing world since high trade barriers in these countries (0–50 percent) should have fallen the most along with the implementation of the ITA.[23] The results confirm that the trade creation effect of the ITA is insignificant for developed countries, while much stronger for developing countries (13 percent).

- The extent of the liberalization of trade in ITA products may be different for different developed countries. The results show that the trade creation effect of the ITA is the largest for Australia and New Zealand, followed by the United States, Canada, and Japan. The European countries did much worse (negative although insignificant trade creation effects).[24] It is the European countries that drive the trade creation effects of developed ITA membership into insignificance.[25]

Recent developments in the theoretical foundation of a gravity specification suggest that time-varying country fixed effects can fully absorb

---

[23] The developed countries include Australia, Austria, Belgium, Canada, Denmark, Finland, France, Germany, Greece, Iceland, Ireland, Italy, Japan, Luxembourg, Netherlands, New Zealand, Norway, Portugal, Spain, Sweden, Switzerland, the UK and the USA; and they are now all ITA members.

[24] The developed European countries include Austria, Belgium, Denmark, Finland, France, Germany, Greece, Iceland, Ireland, Italy, Luxembourg, Netherlands, Norway, Portugal, Spain, Sweden, Switzerland, and the UK.

[25] Iceland is more protected than other developed European countries, but dropping Iceland from the dataset does not change our results much.

the "multilateral resistance" effects in a panel data gravity regression (see Baldwin and Taglioni, 2006). This method, however, is computationally cumbersome due to the very large number of interaction terms in regressions. To reduce the number of dummies for the year and importer/exporter interactions, we take two consecutive years as one period and then use the new period dummy to interact with importers and exporters. We expect that this new period variable will capture most of the variations over time. The coefficients on the key variables of our interests are even larger in absolute values. The result shows that a country will import 68 percent more ITA products if it is an ITA member and the exporter is a WTO member, compared with the baseline case of neither being a WTO member. If both importer and exporter are WTO members but the importer is not an ITA member, it will on average import 20 percent less than the baseline case. The trade diversion effects of the GATT/WTO are also stronger than those in the previous results (−55 percent).

There is a second significant caveat for the estimation is the "zero-trade data problem." Unfortunately, a significant problem with the COMTRADE data is that it includes data when trade takes place. Liu (2006, 2007), Felbermayr and Kohler (2006) and Helpman, Melitz, and Rubinstein (2006) show the extent to which results on the impact of trade agreements can be overturned when zero-trade data are included in the analysis.

Implications for ITA as a stepping stone

Overall, the results indicate that participation in the ITA increases bilateral trade, and being a WTO member can avoid large trade diversion effects. The analysis yielded a number of observations about the ITA that could be useful for the future round of negotiations and trade policy in general. Sectoral trade-offs are usually an essential ingredient for success in the GATT/WTO negotiations. The success of the ITA as a stand-alone sectoral agreement is a new approach. As noted by Hoda (2002), and discussed above, this is attributed to some unique features of the IT sectors. For example, the IT industry is highly globalized and there is keen competition to attract foreign direct investment in the industry. The duty-free treatment of inputs makes host countries attractive for foreign investors. Therefore, most governments were attracted to a worldwide agreement for the elimination of tariffs on IT products, even outside the framework of global negotiations on tariffs.

The same gravity regression analysis can be applied to other sectoral agreements under the GATT/WTO, such as the Uruguay Round zero-for-zero agreements, chemical harmonization, and the agreements on civil aircraft. We leave this for future research.

The gravity approach captures a variety of influences on trade beyond specific parameters. Since the ITA requires ITA tariffs to be bound at zero, the gravity approach captures the institutional effect of being a member of the WTO and a participant in the ITA. While the results of the regression analysis send a positive signal to WTO members as they debate the overall value of a sectoral approach, it is important to recognize the specific nature of the ITA and the mechanisms by which it can affect trade. The gravity equation approach is an ex post analysis that seeks to explain past trade patterns and values. The actual trade values that may arise from liberalizing ITA tariffs will depend upon a number of parameters, such as the value of trade, the values of elasticities, and other structural variables such as geography. This type of ex ante analysis might provide useful information, but differs from the type of analysis undertaken in this section.

6   Current challenges

Progress on ITA II

Negotiations on ITA II began almost as soon as the ink was dry on the ITA in 1997. Progress on extending the ITA has run into difficulties on four interrelated fronts: coverage, convergence, commitments, and non-tariff measures.

On coverage, the ITA does not cover certain IT products that some participants wanted to include at the time of the negotiations, such as consumer electronics. The second issue is convergence: the ITA does not cover some products that have both IT and non-IT uses, such as TVs for multimedia applications, cameras and speakers for video teleconferencing, or other appliances used increasingly in computing and internet applications. Keeping the spirit of ITA coverage alive is tough because technology convergence is merging the "third-rail" culture issue into the technology domain.

The convergence issue is related to the third key concern of commitments. In ITA I, the methodology for scheduling commitments does not accommodate the rapid evolution of IT products, even though the language of the agreement was supposed to bind the signatories to such an evolution.[26] For example, suppose the technological capability of a product currently scheduled changes to allow a wider range of functions: for example, set-top boxes that now have a communications function, but did not when duty-free treatment was scheduled. Does the duty-free commitment apply to the scheduled product or to the scheduled product with its now greater functionality, which may not have been scheduled to receive duty-free treatment? Thus technological convergence and coverage are merging to impact commitments.

Could differing views on this essential point of technological evolution precipitate a call for consultations under the WTO dispute settlement system? The United States and Japan have expressed concern about proposals by at least one ITA participant that would no longer provide or guarantee duty-free treatment for the technologically enhanced versions of ITA-covered products.

A subset of ITA participants, including the United States; Japan; Singapore; Hong Kong, China; Chinese Taipei; Malaysia; Canada; and the Philippines, have proposed that the Committee of Participants on the Expansion of Trade in Information Technology Products engage in informal consultations with the objective of reaching a consensus on how to ensure that duty-free treatment for such products will be maintained.

Finally, participants have been focusing on non-tariff issues that have come to reduce the benefits of the ITA tariff cuts, including, for example, different national safety standards and import licensing requirements.[27] The Committee of Participants on the Expansion of Trade in Information Technology Products agreed to proceed with a work program on NTMs on ITA products, on the following basis:[28]

• Phase I: identify NTMs that are impediments to trade in ITA products;
• Phase II: examine the economic and developmental impact of such measures on trade in ITA products and the benefits which would accrue to participants from addressing their undue trade-distorting effects;
• Phase III: the formal consideration by the Committee of the outcomes of Phases I and II.

---

[26] See e.g. www.petersoninstitute.org/publications/papers/wunsch1104.pdf.
[27] From the website of WTO: www.wto.org/english/thewto_e/minist_e/min99_e/english/book_e/12ita_e.htm, August 17, 2007.
[28] WTO, Non-Tariff Measure Work Program, G/L/756, November 13, 2000.

Here is an example of how a particular NTM issue is playing out:

> [The electromagnetic compatibility/electromagnetic interference (EMC/
> EMI)] workshop would be a forum for regulators responsible for EMC/
> EMI measures and trade policy representatives to discuss the survey
> results and consider what could be the next steps in this exercise. This
> would include where appropriate: identifying next steps, examining ways
> to harmonize the conformity assessment for ITA products on EMC/EMI,
> and examining other means to facilitate the market access of ITA
> products. The pilot project could ultimately contribute to how countries
> can choose to facilitate market access of ITA products.[29]

This level of detailed analysis runs the risk of dampening momentum
to extend the achievement of tariff reduction to moderate NTMs to
attain the objective of broad-based and liberalized trade.

Bringing non-signatories into the ITA

The previous empirical results show the value to trade flows of being a
signatory. The discussion of the economic potency of IT remarked on its
ability to raise economic well-being through investment and productivity
growth. Are there institutional incentives for non-signatories to accede to
the ITA? As noted, the United States, in its bilateral agreements, includes a
proviso that the partners accede to the ITA. But what about those countries not negotiating with the United States? Where is the opportunity to
engage those countries that did not accede to the ITA commitments?

On the one hand, these countries could accede to the ITA and then
engage in discussions on ITA II. Joining the ITA at this point would
represent a unilateral commitment, outside the request/offer standard
approach. But once "inside the tent" they could then participate in ITA II.
However, if a country has not acceded to the ITA, it is probably because it
is not a large exporter, and for whatever reason does not see the economic
benefit of liberalized imports of ITA-covered products. Therefore, it would
be unlikely to see the purpose in engaging in ITA II discussions.

Conclusion – *sui generis* or model stepping stone?

Factors that suggest that the ITA is *sui generis* include:

- IT elasticities and contribution to productivity growth make it a
  unique product.

---

[29] WTO, EMC/EMI Workshop.

- The hype of the 1990s made countries want to get on board, either as national export champions or to get domestic productivity benefits, which created a rare combination of interests.

Factors that suggest that the ITA can be a model stepping stone include:

- Outlines of initial agreement could be replicated, and are not unique to IT per se. Product coverage was broad (not request/offer) and MFN. The initial timetable and schedule were agreed to and generally have not been abrogated.
- Template bilaterals that use these principles can be stepping stones by creating a common set of rules and obligations that could then be made MFN. Once countries have already agreed to principles in the context of a bilateral agreement, they may be more willing to multilateralize the commitments.

Challenges of ITA II point to the difficulties of making the ITA a model stepping stone, including:

- the difficulties of extending coverage to new products;
- potential disputes over extending commitments to products with technologically enhanced functionality;
- no momentum for non-signatories to join.

The balance of evidence suggests that the ITA was *sui generis* – a product of the technology and the time. And the fact that coverage, commitments, and NTMs are contentious in ITA II does not bode well for its broadening to a wider group of products or countries. However, key elements of the ITA negotiations – enthusiasm for broad-based coverage rather than request/offer and MFN treatment – would be a good legacy of the agreement for future WTO negotiations.

References

Aggarwal, V. K. and Ravenhill, J. (2001) "Undermining the WTO: The Case Against 'Open Sectoralism'," analysis from the East–West Center, No. 50.

Anderson, J. and Wincoop, E. van (2003) "Gravity with Gravitas: A Solution of the Land Adjacency Puzzle," *American Economic Review* 93 (1): 170–92.

Baldwin, R. (1990) "The US Japan Semiconductor Agreement," CEPR Discussion Paper No. 387, London: Centre for Economic Policy Research.

(2006) "Multilateralising Regionalism," summary of "Multilateralising Regionalism: Spaghetti Bowls as Building Blocks on the Path to Global

Free Trade," available at: http://hei.unige.ch/~baldwin/PapersBooks/Multi
lateralise percent20Regionalism_Full_18Jul06.pdf.

Baldwin, R. and Taglioni, D. (2006) "Gravity for Dummies and Dummies for
Gravity Equations," Working Paper, Geneva: Graduate Institute of International Studies (HEI).

Barshefsky, C. (2001) "Trade Policy for a Networked World," *Foreign Affairs*,
March/April: 134–46.

Bayoumi, T. and Haacker, M. (2002) "It's Not What You Make, It's How You Use
IT: Measuring the Welfare Benefits of the IT Revolution Across Countries,"
IMF Working Paper 02/117, Washington DC: International Monetary Fund.

Bora, B. and Liu, X. (2006) "Evaluating the Impact of the WTO Information
Technology Agreement," draft.

Felbermayr, G. J. and Kohler, W. (2006) "Exploring the Intensive and Extensive
Margins of World Trade," *Review of World Economics* 142 (4): 642–74.

Finger, K. M. (2007) "An Overview of Tariff Liberalization and World Trade for
ITA Products, 1996–2005," WTO ITA Symposium, March 28–29.

Flamm, K. (1997) "More for Less: The Economic Impact of Semiconductors. In
Celebration of the 50th Anniversary of the Invention of the Transistor",
Semiconductor Industry Association, photocopy.

Fleiss, B. and Sauvé, P. (1997) "Of Chips, Floppy Disks, and Great Timing:
Assessing the Information Technology Agreement," paper prepared for
the International Food Policy Research Institute and Tokyo Club
Foundation.

Helpman, E., Melitz, M., and Rubinstein, Y. (2006) "Trading Partners and Trading
Volumes," mimeo, Cambridge, MA: Harvard Institute of Economic
Research.

Hoda, A. (2002) *Tariff Negotiation and Renegotiation under the GATT and the
WTO*, Cambridge: Cambridge University Press.

Johnson, B. T. (1991) "The U.S.–Japan Semiconductor Agreement: Keeping Up
the Managed Trade Agenda," Backgrounder No. 805, Washington DC:
Heritage Foundation.

Joseph, K. J. and Parayil, G. (2006) "Trade Liberalization and Digital Divide: An
Analysis of Information Technology Agreement of WTO," Working Paper
No. 381, Centre for Development Studies.

Kimura, F. (2006) "International Production and Distribution Networks in East
Asia: Eighteen Facts, Mechanics, and Policy Implication," *Asian Economic
Policy Review* 1 (2): 326–44.

Kimura, F. and Ando, M. (2005) "Two-dimensional Fragmentation in East Asia:
Conceptual Framework and Empirics," *International Review of Economics
and Finance* 14: 317–48.

Liu, X. (2006) "GATT/WTO Promotes Trade Strongly: Sample Selection and
Model Specification," draft.

(2007) "Membership has its Privileges: The Impact of GATT on International Trade: A Comment," draft.

Ludema, R. (2007) "Allies and Friends: The Trade Policy Review of the United States, 2006," *The World Economy* 30 (8): 1209–21.

Mann, C. L. (1994) "U.S. External Balance in 1993," *Federal Reserve Bulletin* 80 (May): 382–93.

(1997) "Computers and Semiconductors in the United States: Linking the World in Global Trade," in *Korea's Economy 1997*, Washington DC: Korea Economic Institute.

(2006) (assisted by J. F. Kirkegaard) "Accelerating the Globalisation of America: The Role for Information Technology," Washington DC: Peterson Institute for International Economics.

WTO (2007) *World Trade Report 2007*, Geneva: WTO.

Wunsch-Vincent, S. (2006) "Trade Rules for the Digital Age," paper for the Institute for International Economics, November, available at: www.iie.com/publications/papers/wunsch1106.pdf (accessed October 30, 2007).

~

Comment

A L E J A N D R O   J A R A

In order to fully appraise the feasibility of using the ITA as a model to seek liberalization that multilateralizes regionalism, it would be appropriate to recall what made this agreement possible and a success story.

In this context the negotiations towards the North America Free Trade Agreement (NAFTA) are a relevant point of departure. Article 308 and Annex 308.1 of NAFTA establish a common external tariff for a list of products described as 'certain automatic data processing goods and their parts'. While this list does not fully coincide with the products covered by the ITA, there is considerable overlap. It was further provided that, should one party agree to a lower duty in the Uruguay Round, this rate was to become the new NAFTA MFN tariff. Many of the products covered had the MFN rate set at duty-free, while for other items it ranged between 3.7 and 3.9 per cent. What made this outcome possible or even necessary?

Central to this was the realization on the part of the NAFTA negotiators that it is very difficult, if not impossible or foolish, to attempt to define a reasonable and workable rule of origin for those products. The centrepiece of a computer – the motherboard – is made up of hundreds of pieces that are manufactured in several countries. These pieces – chips and others – are soldered to the board in country X, and perhaps shipped to a different country where the final assembly takes place. How is it possible to determine the origin of a computer?

One of the most attractive features of the Asia Pacific Economic Cooperation (APEC) forum is the annual meeting of the 'Leaders'. Throughout the year, ministers and officials make sure that there will be 'deliverables' for the Leaders to show off. Based on the liberalization of IT products under NAFTA and the results of the Uruguay Round, it was a very attractive idea and a substantial deliverable to get APEC economies to endorse an initiative to pursue IT product liberalization in the WTO. After securing consensus in APEC[1] the action moved to Geneva.[2]

In the numerous FTAs negotiated, there is no evidence that other products or sectors have had similar problems in defining the rule of origin. From this perspective it seems that it is difficult to replicate in other sectors the rationale that made the ITA technically plausible and politically feasible.

Second, to liberalize one or more sectors but not others will have an impact on the allocation of resources that should be carefully considered and measured on a case-by-case basis.

Last, there is a political economy consideration. An approach by a critical mass of economies to liberalize on a sectoral basis will probably be possible only in some sectors, presumably those that are less sensitive. Once liberalization is secured, the industries concerned lose their appetite for seeking market openness. When a government attempts to liberalize sectors that enjoy high levels of protection and are more sensitive, there will be no trade-offs or support from sectors already liberalized. This greatly increases the political cost to open markets for sectors such as textiles, clothing, footwear, steel, etc. Again, this calls for multilateral liberalization across the board.

---

[1] Chile, an APEC member, did not join the consensus because sectoral liberalization was a departure from its single or flat tariff policy (FTAs notwithstanding), which at times was 11 per cent across the board. Later, in 1997, in the Chile–Canada FTA, the same approach as that of NAFTA was used.

[2] Interestingly one NAFTA partner – Mexico – did not subscribe to the ITA, presumably because it considered that 'critical mass' was absent without Brazil's participation.

PART III

Multilateralization: Sectors and Themes

6

Services provisions in regional trade agreements: stumbling blocks or building blocks for multilateral liberalization?

CARSTEN FINK AND MARION JANSEN[1]

1 Introduction

A remarkable feature of the recent wave of regional trade agreements (RTAs) is the inclusion of a trade in services component in many agreements. At the end of 2006, the WTO counted fifty-four such service accords, of which only five predate the conclusion of the Uruguay Round.[2] The rising interest in service trade agreements reflects a number of developments. First, as tariffs have come down, policymakers have turned their attention to other barriers restricting international commerce. Second, the growth of world trade in goods and the emergence of international production networks have highlighted the importance of an efficient services infrastructure — whether in telecommunications, finance, logistics or legal advice. Market openings in services offer the prospect of performance improvements in services, and allow goods producers to draw on multinational service networks in organizing their business.

Third, technological progress has vastly expanded the range of services that can be traded cross-border. The well-known outsourcing phenomenon has led to the emergence of new dynamic export industries in services, which hold significant potential for low-wage developing countries. Finally, many governments have transferred the provision of infrastructure services to the private sector, expanding the scope for foreign participation in services. Indeed, services FDI has grown faster

[1] The views expressed in this chapter are the authors' own and cannot be attributed to the World Bank, the WTO Secretariat, or WTO members. The authors wish to thank Rudolf Adlung, Richard Baldwin, Antonia Carzaniga, Dale Honeck, Patrick Low and Juan Marchetti for helpful comments and suggestions.
[2] See the WTO's website, www.wto.org/english/tratop_e/region_e/regfac_e.htm.

than total FDI in recent years, as service providers from high- and middle-income countries seek out new commercial opportunities in foreign countries.

Economists have long worried about the systemic consequences of RTAs. Will these agreements undermine the multilateral trading system – one of the cornerstones of the post-war growth in world trade and the rise in economic prosperity? Or will they actually be helpful for stimulating further multilateral integration? This so-called 'building blocks versus stumbling blocks' debate has so far been mainly confined to the liberalization of the trade in goods. However, the different nature of the trade in services warrants separate thinking, which is the objective of this chapter. To preview our conclusion, we find that overall we can be more optimistic about the building block properties of services RTAs than in the case of goods. However, certain forms of regional integration raise concerns about their discriminatory impact, suggesting a disciplining role for the WTO.

The chapter is structured as follows. After a brief introduction into the nature of the trade in services, we will review the main features and liberalization accomplishments of recent RTAs in services. With these considerations in mind, we will explore whether services RTAs are more likely to be building blocks or stumbling blocks for the multilateral cause. We then discuss whether the WTO can play a constructive role in promoting multilateral-friendly RTAs. Our final section offers brief concluding remarks.

2   What is unique about the trade in services?

Services are often seen as intangible, invisible and perishable, requiring simultaneous production and consumption. It is because of the latter characteristic that the trade in services often requires producers and consumers to be in the same place.[3] Think, for instance, of dental treatments and hotel services. For services that require personal contact between customers and clients, trade is possible only if either the customer or the producer travels across borders. This explains why, in the case of services, the concept of trade is broadened to include movements of investment and labour.

Another particularity of the trade in services is the role of regulation. Many service sectors are characterized by market failures and these tend

---

[3] Mattoo, Stern and Zanini (2007).

to differ across service sectors. As in the case of goods, the liberalization of the trade in services leads to questions regarding the role of domestic regulation and its effect on trade. But in the case of services, regulatory issues are arguably more sector-specific. It may therefore turn out to be difficult, if not impossible, to find answers to regulatory issues for service industries as a whole, and it may be useful to think along sectoral lines.

As in the case of trade in goods, the regulation of domestic services can represent a barrier to trade. Indeed, regulatory measures tend to represent the most frequent barrier, and price-related border measures, such as tariffs, are rarely used in services. This implies that the welfare analysis of the liberalization of regional services should focus on the reduction of non-tariff barriers, not on the reduction of tariff barriers, as in the standard analytical framework for the regional liberalization of goods trade.

Four modes of trade in services

The importance of personal contact between producer and client is reflected in the wide definition of the trade in services adopted by the General Agreement on Trade in Services (GATS). In particular, the Agreement distinguishes among the following four modes of supply:

- Mode 1, or 'cross-border', trade refers to services supplied from the territory of one country into the territory of another. Examples include financial transactions conducted over the phone, and software services supplied through the mail by a supplier in one country to consumers in another country.
- Mode 2, or 'consumption abroad', refers to services supplied in the territory of one country to the consumers of another. Examples are where the consumer moves to consume tourism, education or medical services in another country.
- Mode 3, or 'commercial presence', refers to services supplied through any type of business or professional establishment of one country in the territory of another. One example is an insurance company owned by citizens of one country establishing a subsidiary or branch in another country.
- Mode 4, or 'presence of natural persons', refers to services supplied by nationals of one country in the territory of another. This mode includes both independent service suppliers and employees of the

service supplier of another country. Examples are a doctor of one country providing treatment to a patient in another country by moving (temporarily) to the patient's country, or the foreign employees of a foreign bank.

Modes 3 and 4 thus refer to foreign direct investment and to labour movements but they clearly restrict this to the supply of services. Numerous RTAs follow the GATS approach but many others feature horizontal disciplines on investment and the movement of natural persons instead. This explains why relevant preferential agreements on investment or movement of labour play an important role in this chapter.

Services represent around two-thirds of global GDP, and the share of services value-added in GDP tends to rise with countries' level of income. The share of the trade in services in total global cross-border trade is around 20 per cent, a number that has been relatively stable in recent years. The discrepancy between the important role of services within national economies and their role in international trade reflects, inter alia, the difficulties of trading services across borders.

Measuring the trade in services is not straightforward with existing statistical databases, and things become more complex when trying to distinguish different types of trade in services, like the four modes of trade. Recent estimates by the WTO Secretariat underline the important role of mode 3 for the trade in services.[4] Figure 6.1 indicates that trade through commercial presence represents 50 per cent of the total trade in services and cross-border supplies 35 per cent. The role of the other two modes of trade is much smaller: 10 to 15 per cent for consumption abroad and only 1 to 2 per cent for the presence of natural persons. In other words, 'trade' in services is to a large extent about foreign investment, which is one reason why the perceived wisdom about regional integration coming from the traditional trade literature may not apply to regional agreements in services.

Services regulation at the domestic and international level

Many service sectors are characterized by regulatory intervention by the government. When those sectors are opened up to foreign competition, questions of a regulatory nature therefore automatically arise: do foreign services or service suppliers have to stick to domestic regulation; should

---

[4] WTO (2005).

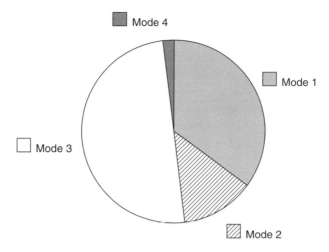

Figure 6.1 The relative importance of the four modes of services trade
Source: WTO (2005).

trading partners seek to harmonize regulation, or simply recognize each other's approach? The answers to these questions are not necessarily straightforward and probably differ across service sectors.

Table 6.1 gives an overview of the most relevant regulatory concerns in the main sectors negotiated under the GATS. The order of sectors in the table reflects an attempt to group sectors according to relevant regulatory objectives. The table indicates that concerns about the quality of services or service providers are an important reason for regulatory intervention in at least five service sectors: business and professional services, construction services, financial services, educational services, and health and social services. With respect to education and health, governments in many countries also aim to guarantee access to a minimum quality of service to everybody, no matter what their income or where they live within the country. Guaranteeing access to services in remote locations is also an important concern when it comes to communication services, like postal or telecommunication services. Besides, the telecommunication subsector is characterized by significant economies of scale. This is also the case for certain transport services and for energy services. One particularity about air transport services is that some countries are concerned about the liberalization of ownership and control provisions for airlines, partly because they fear that the country as a whole – because of its position or size – would not be adequately

Table 6.1 *Regulatory objectives and settings across services sectors*

Sectors as defined in GATS	Possible market failures and distributional concerns	Objective of regulatory intervention	Regulatory settings at 'global' level: examples
Business and professional services			
Accountancy services	Information asymmetry	Ensure quality	WTO Disciplines on Domestic Regulation in the Accountancy Sector
Architectural and engineering services	Information asymmetry	Ensure quality	
Legal services	Information asymmetry	Ensure quality	
Construction and related services	Information asymmetry	Ensure quality	
Financial services	Information asymmetry	Ensure quality of providers and stability of financial system	Basel Committee on Banking Supervision
Educational services	Information asymmetry; distributional (income) concerns	Ensure quality; universal and equal quality for all	
Health and social services	Information asymmetry; distributional (income) concerns	Ensure quality; universal access, equal quality for all	

Table 6.1 (*cont.*)

Sectors as defined in GATS	Possible market failures and distributional concerns	Objective of regulatory intervention	Regulatory settings at 'global' level: examples
Communication services			
Audiovisual services	Economies of scale combined with product differentiation	Ensure provision of sufficient variety	
Postal and courier, express, mail services	Distributional (geographical) concerns; natural monopoly	Universal access	
Telecommunications	Distributional (geographical) concerns; natural monopoly; network externalities	Prevent anti-competitive behaviour; universal access; ensure compatibility	WTO Reference Paper on Telecommunications; International Telecommunication Union
Transport services			
Transport of goods and people	Economies of scale and scope; distributional concerns (across countries)	Prevent anti-competitive behaviour; ensure access of all countries to international network	
Port services	Natural monopoly	Prevent anti-competitive behaviour	
Energy services	Natural monopoly	Prevent anti-competitive behaviour	
Environmental services	Positive consumption externalities	Encourage consumption	
Distribution services	Negative production externalities (environment)	Ensure that effects on environment are internalized	
Tourism services	Negative production externalities (environment)	Ensure that effects on environment are internalized	

served by international airlines. Environmental concerns with respect to tourism or distribution services may be behind zoning regulations in some countries.

Regulatory intervention for any of the reasons indicated in Table 6.1 may result in a barrier to trade if it is difficult for foreigners to obtain information about relevant regulations, or if domestic regulators apply regulations in an arbitrary way, maybe even discriminating against foreign suppliers. Such hurdles to trade can be reduced by increased transparency for domestic regulation and by commitments by regulators to apply rules in a consistent and non-arbitrary way. The WTO Reference Paper on Telecommunications and the WTO Disciplines on Domestic Regulation in the Accountancy Sector represent achievements that have been reached in this direction at the multilateral level.

Regulation that aims to set quality standards for services bears the potential for costs additional to the ones mentioned above. Foreign suppliers may have to incur costs to meet quality standards in the exporting country, as well as costs to prove that they are abiding by the relevant standard. Approaches towards reducing such costs include the harmonization of standards and the mutual recognition of standards and related certification procedures. An example of quality standards for services at the international level are the prudential standards set for banking services by the Basel Committee on Banking Supervision. The International Telecommunications Union also sets international standards for the telecommunications sector, many of which aim to solve problems of network externalities rather than quality concerns.

Incentives to harmonize standards at the global level are rare with respect to the accreditation of individual service providers in professional services or in the field of education or health, but they do exist.[5] Some observers are sceptical about the possibility of harmonizing such standards at the global level and argue in favour of regional initiatives in this respect (Stephenson, 2005).

The economic effects of services RTAs[6]

Expected effects

Mattoo and Fink (2004) have analysed the economic effects of preferential versus MFN-based liberalization of trade in services. They draw

---

[5] The International Union of Architects has, for instance, taken initiatives in this direction.
[6] This section draws on Fink and Molinuevo (2007).

three main conclusions from the viewpoint of a country that engages in liberalization. First, relative to the status quo, preferential liberalization in services brings about static welfare gains. This finding differs from the more ambiguous conclusion drawn in the goods case. The key difference is that protection of services tends to take the form of non-tariff barriers. Protection therefore does not generate fiscal revenue, as do tariffs on imported goods. In the case of goods, if preferential access is given to high-cost suppliers, the importing country has some gains from increased trade with the high-cost supplier but loses the tariff revenue from the low-cost supplier. Overall the nation may therefore lose from preferential liberalization. Services RTAs typically imply that a non-tariff barrier is no longer imposed on suppliers in the partner country. Because of the absence of this barrier, suppliers in the partner country may become competitive even if they produce at higher costs than third-country suppliers. Trade is then diverted away from low-cost to high-cost suppliers, but overall trade increases without any tariff losses for the importing country. Static welfare gains are therefore positive.

Second, unilateral MFN liberalization generally yields greater welfare gains than unilateral preferential liberalization.[7] Non-discriminatory market opening does not favour competition from abroad and therefore promotes entry of the most efficient service providers. Additional gains from trade, associated with greater economies of scale and knowledge spillovers, are also likely to be greater if liberalization proceeds on an MFN basis. There is one exception to this conclusion. If 'learning-by-doing' effects are important, preferential liberalization may enable domestic service suppliers from member countries to become more efficient, as they face some competition from within the FTA territory, but are not yet exposed to global competition. In theory, preferential liberalization can thus prepare infant domestic suppliers for competition at the global level. This 'learning-by-doing' rationale would apply mainly to agreements among developing countries, where firms operate below best-practice productivity levels.[8]

---

[7] Possible gains from better market access in partner countries are ignored here. Those gains will be discussed in more detail further on in this section.

[8] However, this variation of the infant industry argument relies on the strong assumptions that competition from FTA service suppliers is sufficiently mild to favour learning by doing, and that governments are in a position to correctly predict the extent of learning by doing in different service industries. In addition, even if these assumptions were to hold, non-discriminatory liberalization combined with subsidies to the infant firms may be a better policy instrument to address the underlying market failure.

Third, there is a special long-term trade diversion effect to worry about. High location-specific sunk costs and network externalities can give first movers a durable advantage in service markets. Preferential liberalization may thus lead to the entry of second-best service providers that will not be replaced by first-best providers from outside the RTA when trade is eventually liberalized on an MFN basis. Thus, even if preferences are temporary, they may have long-term implications for a country's ability to attract the world's most efficient service providers.

Rules of origin and the level of discrimination introduced by services RTAs

The degree of trade preferences – and thus the potential for trade diversion effects – depends critically on the rules of origin adopted by an RTA. In the case of trade in goods, rules of origin typically lay down in a detailed way which level of transformation a good needs to undergo in the partner country in order for it to be exported to another FTA partner at a preferential tariff. This level of transformation is typically spelled out in terms of the percentage of final product value that has been added in the partner country, changes in tariff headings, or through specific requirements concerning production processes used by exporting firms.

In the case of services FTAs rules of origin based on any of these criteria are not used. This may be because the concepts of imported service inputs and domestic transformation are conceptually and statistically not well developed in the case of the trade in services.[9] In fact, it is not clear whether a transformation rule could be meaningfully applied in this area. In the case of modes 1 and 2, rather than using a transformation criterion, services RTAs merely stipulate that liberalization measures apply to services that are supplied from or in the territory of another party. It is not clear from this definition to what extent services relying on imported service inputs would be eligible for trade preferences. In the case of modes 3 and 4, RTAs do not provide for any rule of origin for services.

Instead of focusing on the origin of services, RTA provisions have mainly sought to delineate the origin of service *providers* (see Table 6.2). Indeed, the need for physical proximity between service suppliers and consumers implies a strong link between the service and its supplier, whether in the form of a juridical or a natural person.

---

[9] Indeed tax authorities often face similar problems in measuring value-added for services.

Table 6.2 *Origin rules in service RTAs*

	Rules of origin for services	Rules of origin for service suppliers
Mode 1 Mode 2	Concept of territoriality	Main criteria: • Establishment
Mode 3	*None*	• Substantive business operations • Ownership and control
Mode 4	*None*	Main criteria: • Nationality • Permanent residency

In services RTAs rules of origin with respect to service suppliers typically take one or several of the following forms:

- criteria concerning the jurisdiction to which an entity belongs; in particular, FTAs often require that enterprises eligible for privileges are incorporated under the laws of one of the partner countries, and that eligible individuals ('natural persons') be citizens or residents of one of the countries;
- criteria concerning the location of services suppliers' economic activities; in particular, enterprises may be required to have 'substantive business activities' within the region and individuals are expected to have their 'centre of economic interest' there;
- criteria concerning 'ownership and control' of enterprises.

Under restrictive rules of origin, the set of service suppliers eligible for trade preferences is small and the scope for trade diversion effects will be more pronounced. Under liberal rules of origin, the set of eligible service suppliers is large, though much depends on circumstances. Among other things, the level of discrimination in this case will depend on the following factors: (i) the openness of RTA parties to foreign investment by non-parties; (ii) whether non-party service suppliers would do business in an RTA party anyhow; and (iii) the tax and business transaction costs associated with departures from a service supplier's preferred international corporate structure.

Additional considerations

Additional considerations apply from the viewpoint of a country that would see an expansion in service exports as a result of market opening in an RTA partner country. What may be considered as trade diversion from a global perspective amounts to an export opportunity from the perspective of the country benefiting from preferential market access abroad. For developing countries, such export opportunities may also underpin the 'learning-by-doing' effects mentioned above. In addition, preferential access to foreign markets may attract export-oriented investment from abroad. Indeed, a country with liberal entry conditions for suppliers from outside the RTA area can become a hub for companies wishing to access markets within this area.[10] The benefits from export-oriented foreign investment depend on the nature of the services supplied, but can include short-term employment gains, increased tax revenues, and the transfer of knowledge and managerial skills.

Again, the rules of origin adopted in an RTA are critical in shaping the eventual economic outcome. If they are restrictive, the benefits of preferential access would mostly be captured by 'indigenous' firms and the learning-by-doing rationale would be strengthened. If they are liberal, so that it is easy for service suppliers from outside the RTA area to become eligible for trade preferences, incentives for export-oriented foreign investment would be strengthened.

In sum, the welfare implications of preferential versus MFN-based liberalization differ for the preference-granting and preference-receiving countries and depend on a number of complementary factors, such as the rules of origin adopted and the significance of learning-by-doing effects. Unfortunately, the economic literature provides little empirical guidance on what type of economy would gain or lose under which circumstances.[11]

Measuring the economic effects of RTAs

It is difficult to determine the economic effects of regional services trade agreements because of insufficient data. In principle, balance of payments data would allow us to analyse the effect of such agreements on mode 1 trade and Foreign Affiliate Trade Statistics (FATS) would allow

---

[10] The government of Botswana, for instance, has chosen to focus on financial services as an area of growth in the economy. Although the domestic market is small, the government is trying to attract investment in an International Financial Services Centre (IFSC) to act as a conduit for funds from South Africa and the rest of the world into other parts of Africa (EIU, 2004).

[11] Mattoo and Fink (2004) review available evidence from the EU's Single Market Programme. However, they note that this evidence remains difficult to interpret in welfare terms.

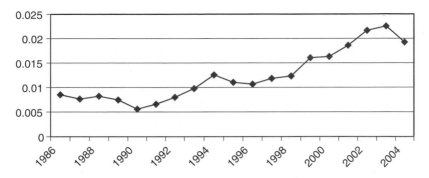

Figure 6.2 US service exports to Mexico, share of total exports

us to analyse the effects on mode 3 trade. However, relevant bilateral data are available only for selected, mostly developed, countries. In addition, most services RTAs are quite recent and not enough time has passed to allow us to analyse their effect on firms' behaviour.

As an illustration, consider the North American Free Trade Agreement (NAFTA), which was ratified in 1994. Figure 6.2 shows the evolution of Mexico's share in total US mode 3 service exports over time.[12] A simple look at the figure does not allow for the conclusion that NAFTA has had a significant impact on mode 3 exports from the US to Mexico. Even though sales of US service affiliates in Mexico have increased significantly, they started to increase a number of years before the ratification of NAFTA. A more thorough analysis, using econometric techniques, would be necessary in order to determine the real impact of the regional trade agreement. However, such an analysis is precluded by too few observations on relevant service trade flows.

3   Ongoing liberalization in the context of preferential trade agreements

In this section we will attempt to draw an overview of the extent and nature of service liberalization entailed in RTAs. We divide our discussion into explicit liberalization efforts (i.e. the removal of trade

---

[12] The US–Israel FTA was ratified in 1985, but the data on trade in services do not go far enough back to compare 'before' and 'after' FTA. US–Jordan was ratified in 2001, but no bilateral data are available for Jordan. The other bilateral agreements involving the US were ratified in 2004 or later and data are only available until 2005.

barriers) and regulatory cooperation agreements that seek to pro-actively open markets. To some extent this distinction is artificial, but it will be of relevance when discussing policy options for making services RTAs more WTO-friendly – as will be discussed in later sections of this chapter. The final part of this section considers a special feature of services RTA: non-party most favoured nation clauses (MFN).

How much explicit liberalization has taken place?

For RTAs to be meaningful, they have to offer something beyond countries' liberalization undertakings under the GATS. Two questions arise in this context: first, how 'deep' is the value-added offered by RTA commitments and, second, to what extent are non-parties to RTAs discriminated against.

Fink (2007) proposes a categorization of RTA commitments that attempts to address these two questions (see Table 6.3). The first cat-egory describes RTA commitments that merely replicate existing GATS undertakings. Clearly, such commitments do not offer any market opening and do not discriminate in the application of actual service policies against non-parties. Their sole benefit to parties is the possibility of invoking the RTAs dispute settlement mechanism(s) to enforce trade commitments made at the RTA level. This option is arguably of minor value in the case of state-to-state disputes, as the WTO already offers a credible mechanism for this form of arbitration. However, it could be important in case RTAs provide for investor-to-state dispute settle-ment, for which no alternative exists at the multilateral level. This form of dispute settlement is narrower in scope, as its reach only extends to investment in services (mode 3).[13] Governments willing to accept investor-to-state dispute settlement may be able to strengthen the credibility of their investment regime, even though economists dis-agree about the role of this feature in attracting larger flows of inward foreign direct investment.[14]

---

[13] In addition, some agreements remove key liberalization obligations (e.g. national treat-ment) from the scope of investor-to-state dispute settlement. See Fink and Molinuevo (2007).

[14] In a seminal study, Hallward-Driemeier (2003) found no or only a weak empirical relationship between the existence of a bilateral investment treaty and inflows of foreign investment. More recently, however, Neumayer and Spess (2005), using a different estimation sample, found a strong positive relationship.

Table 6.3 *Trade preferences created by services RTAs*

	Type of commitment	Nature of preference	Example	Degree of discrimination
1	RTA commitment reproduces GATS commitment	Parties can invoke dispute settlement mechanisms of RTA to enforce trade commitment	Cambodia's and Viet Nam's commitment under the ASEAN–China Agreement on Trade in Services	None
2	RTA commitment goes beyond GATS commitment, but does not imply actual liberalization	Reduced risk of policy reversal for service suppliers from parties	Indonesia's commitments under the ASEAN Framework Agreement on Services	None
3	RTA commitment implies actual liberalization, which is implemented in a non-discriminatory way	Reduced risk of policy reversal for service suppliers from parties	Chile's commitment to permit insurance branches under the Chile–US FTA	None
4	RTA commitment implies actual liberalization, rules of origin are liberal	Service suppliers from parties benefit from improved market access, set of eligible service suppliers is wide	China's commitments under the Mainland–Hong Kong Closer Economic Partnership Agreement	Weak, though it depends
5	RTA commitment implies actual liberalization, rules of origin are restrictive	Service suppliers from parties benefit from improved market access, set of eligible service suppliers is narrow	Thailand's elimination of a foreign equity limitation for construction and distribution services under the Thailand–Australia FTA	Strong

Source: Fink (2007).

The second category describes RTA commitments that are more liberal than corresponding GATS undertakings, but that do not imply any new liberalization and thus no actual discrimination. In other words, such commitments only reduce or eliminate the 'water' between bound and applied policies. They reduce the risk of policy reversals, as a party's non-compliance with its openness promise can be challenged by other parties through (an) RTA dispute settlement mechanism(s). An assurance of this type may be especially relevant where investors incur large up-front investments, of which the amortization depends critically on the stability of the policy regime. In addition, Mattoo and Wunsch-Vincent (2004) point out that policy bindings for mode 1 may help pre-empt protectionist pressures for electronically traded services, for which most countries' policies are still largely liberal.

Commitments in the third category imply new market opening, but the resulting liberalization measures are implemented in a non-discriminatory way. The main benefit of such a commitment to RTA parties is again a reduced risk of policy reversals. Why would countries choose to apply a preferential promise non-preferentially? The most likely explanation relates to the regulatory nature of trade barriers for services. Unlike tariffs, discriminatory application of measures affecting the trade in services may not always be feasible, or at least practicable. In addition, once a government has taken the decision to liberalize, it may seek to avoid the economic distortions associated with discriminatory treatment – such as the entry of second-best service providers. This motivation may be especially relevant when governments seek to enhance the performance of infrastructure services as part of a strategy to improve the competitiveness of goods exporters.[15] Finally, from a political economy perspective, the extension of liberalization measures to non-parties may face little remaining domestic opposition, once a government has taken the first step towards liberalization – e.g. the break-up of a monopoly.

Finally, the fourth and fifth categories describe commitments that lead to *de novo* liberalization and which are implemented in a discriminatory way. The difference between these two categories is the rule of origin associated with RTA benefits. In the former category, rules of origin are liberal in the sense that RTAs do not per se discriminate

[15] A third explanation may be that governments are bound by non-party most favoured nation clauses in other RTAs or bilateral investment agreements. See the discussion later in this section.

against the nationality of service suppliers. Indeed, the great majority of existing RTAs adopt liberal origin rules as they pertain to companies: preferential treatment is extended to all service suppliers that are established and have substantive business operations in at least one RTA party, regardless of who owns or controls them.

What explains the adoption of such liberal origin rules? To begin with, they are mandated by GATS Article V:6 as part of the WTO provision setting out a number of requirements for 'economic integration agreements' (EIAs) in services to constitute a lawful exception to the multilateral MFN discipline. However, this explanation is only partial. Why were countries willing to agree on the GATS Article V requirements in the first place? In addition, EIAs involving developing countries only are allowed to adopt a nationality criterion, yet most such agreements have still opted for the more liberal approach.

The most obvious explanation is that established non-party service suppliers are seen as part of the domestic economy. Just as in the case of trade in goods, they contribute to domestic employment and improved resource allocation, and pay taxes to local and federal governments. Countries may purposely offer RTA benefits to non-party service suppliers in order to attract greater inward foreign investment. That said, the economic benefits to the domestic economy of improved export performance depend crucially on the mode through which services are supplied. They are most apparent in the case of modes 1 and 2 – the modes most closely resembling trade in goods. However, for the commercially most significant mode 3, employment gains may well be limited and tax gains depend crucially on how companies transfer profits between different countries and on applicable tax treaties between nations.

The network characteristics of many services offer a second explanation for liberal company origin rules. Where economies of scale and scope are important, service providers can enhance their competitiveness by simultaneously supplying services in several countries. To maximize these benefits, service providers seek the maximum flexibility in designing their international corporate structures, with the freedom to choose from which location and through which mode to supply any given market. In other words, countries are collectively better off in an RTA landscape that offers liberal origin rules.[16]

---

[16] The political economy force behind this argument is similar to the 'spaghetti bowl as building block' force described by Baldwin (2006) in the case of trade in goods.

While these considerations go some way towards explaining why RTAs adopt liberal origin rules, they still leave some open questions. The choice of origin rule requires consent between all RTA parties. From the perspective of the 'importing' RTA party, liberal origin rules imply greater competition, which may not be in the (political) interest of that party. In addition, countries often pursue industrial policy objectives, in the form of promoting national champions or the development of an indigenous service industry.[17] Reflecting these and possibly other considerations, there are a number of bilateral RTAs that have adopted an ownership and control criterion in their company origin rules – notably, Australia–Thailand, India–Singapore, and Japan–Thailand. Relevant liberalization commitments under these agreements imply substantially stronger discrimination, associated with the fifth category in Table 6.3.[18] Similarly, RTA commitments that lead to the liberalization of 'mode 4' trade also lead to strong discrimination. Rules of origin for natural persons are usually based on nationality and/or residency criteria. In either case, the set of eligible service providers will be well circumscribed.

Having established the different categories of trade preferences in services and the extent of their discrimination, a natural question is how many RTA commitments fall into which categories. We can only answer this question partially. A number of recent studies have documented the extent to which RTA commitments add value to countries' GATS undertakings. For example, Roy, Marchetti and Lim (2007) review the commitments of thirty-six WTO members negotiated since 2000. Figure 6.3, taken from their study, graphically illustrates the share of RTA commitments for mode 3 that go further than the GATS. In virtually all cases, RTAs offer improvement over existing GATS commitments or undertakings in service sectors for which no GATS commitment previously existed. In many cases, the RTA value-added is substantial.[19] In other words, we can easily characterize category 1 as the exception

---

[17] Consistent with that view, groups in the United States and the European Union representing export interests in services do not appear to extend membership to service suppliers owned or controlled by non-nationals. See Fink (2007).

[18] Fink and Nikomborirak (2008) review a number of simulation studies undertaken for ASEAN countries which reveal that an ownership and control requirement can substantially reduce the set of service suppliers eligible for preferential treatment.

[19] Roy, Marchetti and Lim (2007) draw similar conclusions for RTA commitments on mode 1. Fink and Molinuevo (2007) and Stephenson (2005) offer additional evidence on the liberalization content of RTAs in the East Asia and Asia-Pacific regions, respectively.

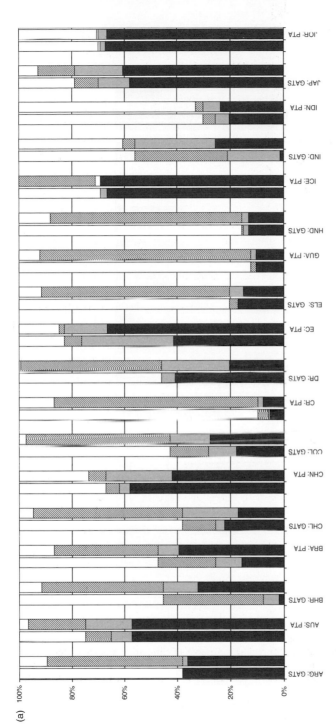

Figure 6.3 Proportion of subsectors with new and improved commitments under mode 3.

Note: For each country, the left-hand bar indicates the value-added of GATS Doha offers relative to existing GATS commitments, and the right-hand bar shows the value-added of PTA commitments relative to GATS Doha offers. 'Value-added' can take the form of either a new commitment in a sector previously unscheduled, or an improvement of a previously scheduled partial commitment. All bars are relative to the total number of subsectors identified under the GATS.

Source: Roy, Marchetti and Lim (2007).

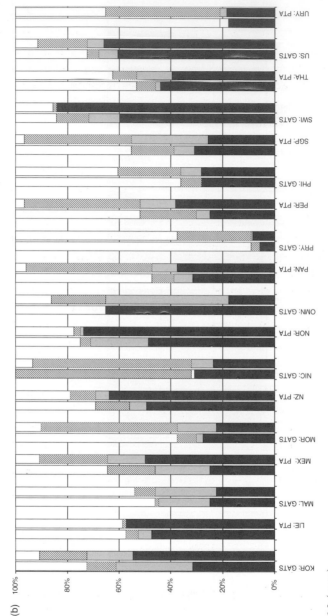

(b)

100% 80% 60% 40% 20% 0%

URY: PTA
US: GATS
THA: PTA
SWI: GATS
SGP: PTA
PHI: GATS
PER: PTA
PRY: GATS
PAN: PTA
OMN: GATS
NOR: PTA
NIC: GATS
NZ: PTA
MOR: GATS
MEX: PTA
MAL: GATS
LIE: PTA
KOR: GATS

Figure 6.3 (*cont.*)

to the rule – at least as far as overall schedules of commitments are concerned.

We also have some evidence that RTA commitments offer new market openings. Roy, Marchetti and Lim identify thirty-two instances of liberalization pre-commitments – promises to open up a particular service activity in the future. It is reasonable to assume that these promises imply *de novo* liberalization. However, we do not know whether these thirty-two cases are selected cases of actual market openings or just examples of a more general pattern. Just because other commitments are not phased in does not mean that they do not lead to new market openings. Unfortunately, there are no databases of service policies that would allow for a comparison of actual versus committed policies. As such, we do not precisely know how many commitments are implemented in a discriminatory as opposed to a non-discriminatory way. It is worth noting that there appear to be only two agreements – China's Closer Economic Partnership Agreements with Hong Kong, China and Macao, China – that have adopted a formal mechanism to verify the origin of service suppliers.[20] That said, discrimination can also be implemented through national laws or, even less transparently, through discretionary regulatory decisions, such as the allocation of licences.

Further, Fink and Molinuevo (2007) analyse the company rules of origin of twenty-five RTAs in the East Asia region and find only three agreements with an ownership and control criterion (see above). To the extent that their finding can be generalized, we can thus conclude that most commitments fall into categories 2, 3 and 4. The one exception to this conclusion is 'mode 4', given more restrictive rules of origin for natural persons. Indeed, Fink and Molinuevo (2007) find that many RTAs go beyond the GATS on mode 4, though their value-added often appears minor. RTA improvements often consist of minor expansions of the types of individual service suppliers covered. As under the GATS, most commitments are confined to highly skilled professionals and intra-corporate transferees. Japan, in its bilateral agreements with the Philippines and Thailand, seemingly offers deeper liberalization by permitting the entry of nurses and caregivers, provided they meet

---

[20] See Fink (2005) for a more detailed discussion of these trade agreements. In contrast to most other services RTAs, the rules of origin in these agreements set out a relatively large number of specific eligibility criteria. However, these criteria seek to define more closely the concept of substantive business operations. Importantly, the origin rules in China's two CEPAs do not feature an ownership and control test. See also Emch (2006).

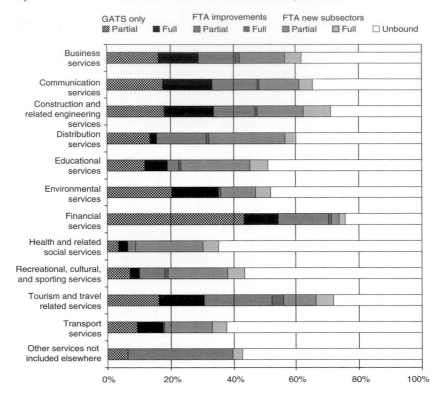

Figure 6.4 Liberalization content by sector.

Note: This figure shows the aggregate liberalization content of twenty-five East Asian RTAs, comprising forty-eight schedules of commitments for fourteen East Asian countries. The bars for the four liberalization categories are relative to the total number of subsectors and modes in a given sector.

Source: Fink and Molinuevo (2007).

certain qualification requirements.[21] In addition, Hoekman and Winters (Chapter 13 of this volume) point to a significant number of bilateral labour agreements outside the realm of RTAs that have liberalized temporary labour movements, even if in a managed way.

Finally, it is interesting to look at the sectoral distribution of RTA commitments. Are there sectors in which RTA commitments are more likely to make progress than others? Figure 6.4, taken from Fink and

---

[21] It is not clear whether Japan's commitments on nurses and caregivers fall within the definition of mode 4 under the GATS. If nurses are employed directly by public or private hospitals owned and controlled by Japanese persons, they would likely fall outside the scope of mode 4. See Chaudhuri, Mattoo and Self (2004) for further discussion.

Molinuevo's work on East Asia, depicts the share of RTA commitments that add value to the GATS for the twelve main service sectors identified under the GATS. Several patterns are worth pointing out. First, RTAs offer at least some value-added in all of the twelve main sectors. Second, sectors with few sensitivities towards foreign participation (e.g. business services) and which supply important inputs for firms in the economy (e.g. communications services) show the greatest liberalization ambitions in RTAs. By contrast, RTAs have not been able to progress much in sensitive sectors (especially transport, health, education and financial services), for which liberalization accomplishments at the multilateral level are equally limited.[22] In addition, a number of RTAs fully exclude certain sensitive service activities from the scope of all legal obligations, notably core air transport services (as under the GATS), financial services, and cabotage in maritime transport.

Removing implicit regulatory barriers

Barriers to the trade in services are not only created by explicit measures that are usually the subject of market opening commitments, but also by legitimate regulatory measures that address market failures or promote certain social objectives. The trade-restrictive effects of such regulatory measures are often incidental rather than intentional, though they may also be purposely abused for protectionist purposes.

Many RTAs discipline the use of regulatory barriers to trade by a provision that resembles GATS Article VI:4.[23] The NAFTA Agreement, for instance, stipulates that measures relating to the licensing or certification of nationals of another party should:

(a) be based on objective and transparent criteria, such as competence and the ability to provide a service;

(b) be not more burdensome than necessary to ensure the quality of a service; and

(c) not constitute a disguised restriction on the cross-border provision of a service.

Disciplines along these lines can help prevent the abuse of regulatory measures for protectionist purposes. However, the mere difference

---

[22] One exception to this pattern is financial services, for which the WTO registered some progress in the course of the post-Uruguay Round negotiations in 1997.

[23] For a more thorough discussion of GATS Article VI:4 and the necessity test included in it, see WTO Document S/WPDR/W/27.

between regulatory standards and practices can still create a prohibitive obstacle to trade. This possibility arises particularly in the case of licensing, certification and qualification requirements intended to resolve the information asymmetries commonly encountered in financial and professional services.

Consider, for example, a doctor facing different qualification requirements in a foreign country, which all serve to meet legitimate consumer and public health objectives. Requalification may take years and can be prohibitively expensive. The only way to overcome these types of barriers is through positive cooperation between the relevant regulatory authorities. Such cooperation can take the form of the harmonization of regulatory standards or the negotiation of recognition agreements. Indeed, the former is often a pre-requisite for the latter. Another example of trade-creating regulatory cooperation is the exchange of information between financial regulators on the soundness of financial institutions. In the area of mode 4 trade, governments often cooperate on matters such as pre-movement screening and selection, accepting and facilitating return, and combating illegal migration.

Regulatory cooperation, by nature, results in more favourable – i.e. discriminatory – treatment for service providers from certain countries. In terms of the classification proposed in Table 6.3, trade-creating regulatory cooperation falls into categories 4 and 5, depending on the rules of origin adopted. However, its long-term discriminatory impact is arguably more severe compared to unilateral liberalization measures, because differences in regulatory systems may not easily allow for an extension of negotiated trade preferences.

RTAs offer an obvious way to pursue regulatory cooperation, though it often takes place outside the realm of trade agreements. It is difficult to draw a complete picture of these types of regulatory cooperation initiatives, as they are often not exclusively designed to promote the trade in services. Still, some information is available on services-related mutual recognition agreements (MRAs). Mutual recognition in the context of services can in principle span a wide range of practices, including recognition of prudential measures under financial services (in order to facilitate mode 3),[24] recognition of educational qualifications with a view to enrolment in higher education or further training (to facilitate mode 2

---

[24] Approaches concerning financial services are typically dealt with in separate chapters on financial services rather than in MRAs.

consumption of education services), and the recognition of professional qualifications (to facilitate trade under mode 4).

OECD (2003) provides an overview of service-related MRAs that have been notified to the WTO. The overview indicates that many MRAs are undertaken by neighbouring countries or as part of broader regional cooperation or integration initiatives. Most MRAs are between developed countries, and even then seem to be largely based on a shared region or common cultural/historical ties (e.g. agreements within the EU or between Australia, Canada, Ireland, the UK, and the US). Agreements between non-OECD countries are largely limited to inter-Latin America agreements, with the exception of a number of agreements between Brazil and other non-OECD countries. Examples also exist of non-OECD Asian and African countries being included in recognition arrangements with OECD countries. China; Hong Kong, China; Malaysia; the Philippines; Singapore; and Viet Nam, for instance, all have some form of mutual exemption arrangement with the Engineering Institute of Australia. The South African Institute of Chartered Accountants is party to a bilateral agreement with the Institutions of Chartered Accountants in Australia. The latter example reflects the fact that a number of agreements are not government-to-government per se, but are managed and enforced by the responsible professional bodies. Even if MRAs are between governments, they often necessitate the involvement of these bodies. From a political economy perspective, their involvement may not always facilitate the conclusion of MRAs, as they may also represent the (protectionist) interests of domestic service suppliers.

OECD (2003) also reveals that, notwithstanding their titles, many of the MRAs covered in the Annexes do not provide for automatic recognition of qualifications. Some are far-reaching (e.g. within the EU), others provide merely for reduced requirements or procedures, provide a degree of facilitation, or are limited to broader types of cooperation or dialogue. While some agreements relate to specific sectors, other agreements are based on a general recognition of diplomas in partner countries. In the context of RTAs, most progress has been made in the case of specific sectors, notably those internationalized professions where most progress has also been made bilaterally or at the industry level: architecture, engineering and accountancy. Industry initiatives have also led to some progress in nursing, given the increasing international demand for this profession. Overall, OECD (2003) concludes that there has been limited progress on MRAs at the regional level and that even progress between similar countries has been modest.

This lack of progress in reducing implicit regulatory barriers to trade at the regional or bilateral level could indicate that the prospects for reducing such barriers at the multilateral level are rather bleak. On the other hand, in professions with great shortages in OECD countries, like medical and ICT professionals, workers are moving in large numbers via mode 4, even in the absence of extensive networks of MRAs. It could therefore be argued that, if real trade interests are present, solutions to recognition other than MRAs are being found (OECD, 2003).

Non-party most favoured nation treatment

A final important feature of many RTAs is the inclusion of clauses requiring the extension of trade preferences granted to non-parties – so-called non-party most favoured nation (MFN) clauses. For example, Article 76 of the Japan–Philippines Economic Partnership Agreement reads: 'Each Country shall accord to services and service suppliers of the other Country treatment no less favorable than that it accords, in like circumstances, to services and service suppliers of any non-Party.'

An MFN clause of this type should not be confused with the multi-lateral MFN discipline at the WTO. The latter ensures non-discrimination between members of the multilateral trade body. In the case of an MFN clause in a regional agreement, the promise of non-discriminatory treatment is a reciprocal trade preference between RTA partners. Unless otherwise specified, non-party MFN clauses apply to current and future preferences granted to third parties.[25]

What might motivate countries to incorporate such a provision in an RTA? From the perspective of an exporting country, a non-party MFN clause can only be beneficial, as it ensures the most liberal access conditions abroad. Country A may experience some erosion of trade preferences, if RTA partner B offers the same benefits in a future RTA to country C. However, preference erosion will be limited, to the extent that country B will never be able to offer country C better treatment than A. From the perspective of an importing country, the inclusion of a non-party MFN clause may lead to a weakened bargaining situation in future RTAs. If country C knows that any trade preference it negotiates

---

[25] Non-party MFN requirements are not an invention of services RTAs. The basic principle goes back to the nineteenth century. For example, the 1860 Cobden–Chevalier Treaty between Britain and France mandated non-party MFN treatment for tariffs.

Table 6.4 *Non-party MFN provisions in East Asian RTAs*

Agreement(s)	Type of MFN provision
EFTA–Rep. of Korea FTA, EFTA–Singapore FTA, Guatemala–Chinese Taipei FTA, Japan–Malaysia EPA, Japan–Mexico EPA, Japan–Philippines FTA, Nicaragua–Chinese Taipei FTA, Panama–Singapore FTA, Panama–Chinese Taipei FTA, Singapore–US FTA, Trans-Pacific EPA, Viet Nam–US BTA	Non-party MFN obligation subject to a negative list of reservations
Australia–Thailand FTA, India–Singapore ECA, Japan–Singapore EPA	Non-binding non-party MFN provision
AFAS, Australia–Singapore FTA, ASEAN–China TIS Agreement, Chile–Rep. of Korea FTA, Rep. of Korea–Singapore FTA, Lao PDR–US BTA, Mainland–Hong Kong CEPA, Mainland–Macao CEPA, Jordan–Singapore FTA, New Zealand–Singapore FTA	No MFN disciplines

Note: The type of MFN provision indicated here refers to FTAs' services chapters. Different types may prevail in the investment chapters of FTAs. The MFN obligations of the EFTA–Republic of Korea and EFTA–Singapore agreements do not apply to agreements concluded by one of the parties and notified under GATS Article V.

Source: Fink and Molinuevo (2007).

with B will be automatically extended to A, the value of preferences, and thereby the willingness of countries to strike reciprocal bargains, may be reduced.

It is unclear to what extent such strategic bargaining considerations are of much empirical relevance, especially in a world where RTAs proliferate rapidly and trade preferences may therefore be only transitory. Traditional arguments of protection may be more relevant in explaining the inclusion of non-party MFN clauses. Countries which maintain restrictive trade policies and a 'defensive' negotiating position in services are more likely to shun such a clause than countries with liberal service policies and 'offensive' interests. This prediction appears to be consistent with the incidence of non-party MFN clauses in existing agreements. Table 6.4, taken from Fink and Molinuevo's study of East Asian services RTAs, suggests that such clauses are more prevalent in agreements involving developed countries (though this rule does not always hold).

Notwithstanding the above considerations, it should be pointed out that the reach of non-party MFN clauses is often limited. Some RTAs exclude other trade agreements from the scope of the MFN discipline. Even where this is not the case, RTAs typically allow countries to lodge specific reservations to MFN treatment. These reservations can be quite broad and pertain to the exact measures for which they seek to discriminate.[26] It is therefore not straightforward to evaluate the precise reach of non-party MFN clauses. At the same time, in some cases they do bite. For example, Colombia is bound by such a clause under the Cartagena Accord of the Andean Community, and will therefore need to extend the liberalization measures in financial services under the Colombia–US FTA to fellow members of that Community.

4   Are service RTAs building blocks or stumbling blocks in multilateral services liberalization?

A useful first step in answering this question is to consider the political economy literature on the systemic impact of RTAs in the goods case. One of the most frequently made arguments why RTAs may be harmful to the multilateral trading system is that they generate vested interests that will tend to lose from non-discriminatory liberalization. Krishna (1998) develops a formal model in which he shows how inefficient firms benefiting from trade preferences will lobby against the multilateralization of these preferences. In principle, similar concerns apply in the case of the trade in services. Unless governments implement RTA market opening commitments in a non-discriminatory way, service providers from RTA parties will hold an advantage that they may be reluctant to give up.

At the same time, liberal origin rules may help to attenuate this 'stumbling block force'. RTAs that provide for such rules do not discriminate against the ownership of capital, as long as companies are established in the territory of the RTA party and have substantial business

---

[26] In addition to RTAs, bilateral investment treaties (BITs) often incorporate non-party MFN clauses. To the extent that such BITs cover investment in services, they may require the extension of RTA preferences negotiated under mode 3. That said, the reach of non-party MFN in BITs is equally limited by exclusions for other trade agreements and specific reservations lodged by BIT parties.

interests there. Thus, to the extent that third-party capital already benefits from trade preferences, opposition to further multilateral liberalization from domestic capital owners may be limited. That said, such an outcome is not guaranteed. It assumes that RTA parties are initially open to foreign investment from third parties, which may not always be the case. Even then, liberal origin rules may still imply substantial discrimination, especially against small and medium-sized enterprises that do not have a large international presence to begin with.

A related concern is that, in certain circumstances, RTAs may offer countries greater economic gains than multilateral trade openings. For example, a small economy is likely to be better off by having preferential market access to the otherwise protected market of a large economy, compared to the situation where the large economy is open to everyone. Levy (1997) formally shows that RTAs of this type again undermine political support for further multilateral liberalization. In theory, similar circumstances could exist in the services context, though liberal origin rules would again lower the attractiveness of RTAs. In addition, services market opening is not negotiated in isolation, but is typically part of a broader set of negotiations involving trade in goods, intellectual property rules, and other topics. In many recent North–South RTAs, developing countries' commitments in services are seen as the quid pro quo for improved access to developed countries' goods markets. To the extent that developing countries reap greater economic gains from striking this type of bargain in RTAs rather than at the WTO, they will be reluctant to engage in multilateral service negotiations.[27]

Turning to the building blocks forces, RTAs may strengthen the political support for further multilateral market opening in two ways. First, by accomplishing some liberalization, preferential market opening may weaken political opposition to foreign competition. As pointed out in the previous section, this effect may be particularly important when an RTA cracks a hard reform 'nut', such as the break-up of a monopoly.[28]

---

[27] Consistent with this notion, Roy, Marchetti and Lim (2007) find that countries' RTA commitments have typically been more ambitious than their offers tabled in the Doha services negotiations. However, this discrepancy is likely to reflect at least in part tactical behaviour, and final Doha commitments may well be more ambitious.

[28] This argument is similar to the one formally developed in Feeney and Hillman (2001). They argue that privatization of a home state-owned firm in any sector, and in any form that ultimately permits trade in equity of the firm, weakens pro-interventionist forces at home and creates a political climate that institutes free trade.

Second, RTAs may change the political economy equilibrium in countries excluded from their coverage. Fearing competitive disadvantages for their own exporters, governments in those countries may be more willing to strike a deal at the WTO. Alternatively, they may embark on RTA negotiations themselves. Over time, a domino effect may be triggered that may lead countries to enter into preferential arrangements with their major trading partners (Baldwin, 1995). In the case of the goods trade, such a situation is still not equivalent to multilateral free trade, as exporters still face origin rules that may restrict their use of intermediate imports.[29] By contrast, in services, widespread RTA liberalization may approximate multilateral liberalization more closely, because origin rules primarily deal with the origin of service *providers* rather than the origin of traded services.

Aside from these traditional political economy arguments, there are a number of other considerations that are relevant in assessing the systemic implications of services RTAs. First, the importance of economies of scale in many service sectors may have important implications for the sequence of market opening. For example, the conclusion of an RTA could allow regional service suppliers to reap economies of scale, allowing them to survive upon further multilateral market opening. Such dynamics may well have an effect on the political economy forces resisting or supporting multilateral services liberalization. It is difficult to predict, however, in which direction these forces will push for different countries at different stages of integration.

Second, the proliferation of such RTAs may undermine reciprocity at the WTO. In simple terms, the envisaged 'grand' bargain of the DDA involves developed countries committing to trade reforms in agriculture, and developing countries opening their markets for industrial goods and services. To the extent that the 'demandeurs' in services will be able to fulfil their 'offensive' interests through RTAs, their incentive to agree to ambitious trade reforms in agriculture is correspondingly reduced. While trade policies in agriculture and industrial goods can be equally negotiated in RTAs, the reduction of domestic support in agriculture, by nature, cannot be negotiated on a preferential basis, leaving the WTO as the only negotiating forum.

---

[29] Baldwin (2006) argues that increased production unbundling will ultimately lead firms operating international production networks to lobby for the multilateralization of preferential arrangements.

At the same time, we would argue that the current RTA landscape still leaves ample scope for bargaining at the WTO. There are still relatively few agreements between large economies. Only a few of the middle-income countries targeted most frequently in requests for market opening in services at the WTO have entered into RTAs with developed countries.[30] This situation may well change. The recent Republic of Korea–US agreement and several ongoing negotiations – for example, Australia–China, Australia–Japan, EC–ASEAN, EC–India, and EC–Republic of Korea – may herald a shift in the RTA landscape towards agreements between larger economies. However, such a shift is by no means certain – not least because countries with export interests in agriculture may want to preserve their negotiating coinage for negotiations at the WTO.

Third, the inclusion of non-party MFN clauses in RTAs may, on balance, weaken incentives to negotiate further trade liberalization through preferential agreements. A country bound by such clauses in agreements with its major trading partner will find itself in a situation where it cannot grant any real preferences to future RTA partners (or to current RTA partners in future negotiating rounds). To the extent that the value of non-preferential market opening is smaller, the willingness of RTA partners to 'pay' for a market opening commitment is reduced. In addition, a country may want to 'sell' its non-preferential market opening to the *whole* WTO membership and obtain market opening concessions from a larger set of countries. That said, the empirical relevance of this multilateralization force is not clear, not least because the precise reach of non-party MFN clauses remains uncertain.

Fourth, in light of the restrictive nature of origin rules for natural persons, 'stumbling block forces' may be stronger in the case of mode 4 trade. Greater discrimination makes it more likely that the beneficiaries of preferred access will lobby against the multilateralization of trade preferences at the WTO. At the same time, it remains uncertain how far the WTO will ever advance on mode 4, especially for low- and medium-skilled workers. Mattoo (2005) and Hoekman and Winters (Chapter 13 of this volume) argue that the movement of people differs in profound ways from the movement of goods and capital. Greater inward flows of foreign workers raises deeply rooted fears in societies, including loss of national identity and security, cultural erosion, loss of access

---

[30] The twelve most frequently targeted countries are Argentina, Brazil, China, Egypt, India, Indonesia, Malaysia, Pakistan, the Philippines, South Africa, Thailand and Turkey.

to local and national public goods, competition for jobs, and illegal immigration.

In principle, greater labour mobility promises substantial economic gains to low-wage developing countries. In addition, demographic shifts in developed countries have increased their demand for foreign workers, and this trend is likely to continue. However, preferential agreements may be better suited to accommodate the political sensitivities outlined above. In contrast to the GATS, they can expand flows of temporary workers in a managed way, taking into account cultural and other ties between countries. Admittedly, there will always be a role for the GATS in liberalizing the movement of highly skilled professionals and intra-corporate transferees. However, as far as low- and medium-skilled workers are concerned, discriminatory approaches may equip countries with the necessary flexibility to achieve at least *some* market opening.

Fifth, a similar argument applies to trade-creating regulatory cooperation between countries, whether it takes places in an RTA context or elsewhere. As discussed previously, such regulatory cooperation relates first and foremost to the harmonization of regulatory standards and the conclusion of recognition agreements, but also extends to information exchanges between regulators and cooperation on law enforcement activities. The exclusionary effects of regulatory deepening may unleash political economy forces, complicating further progress towards multilateral integration. However, as pointed out earlier in the chapter, regulatory cooperation may be neither feasible nor desirable among the 151 WTO members to begin with, due to differences in preferences, legal systems and levels of development. The ultimate impact of preferential regulatory cooperation will also depend on whether such arrangements are open for participation by initially excluded countries. As we will argue, the WTO can play a positive role in regulating cooperation agreements in this respect.

Sixth, there may be negotiating 'spillovers' between RTA and WTO negotiations, which can be positive or negative. On the one hand, RTA negotiations may compel countries to undertake a comprehensive stock-taking of their laws and regulations that may be subject to trade disciplines. Such a stock-taking can be resource-intensive, given the large size of the service sector and the broad reach of obligations established in trade agreements. Trade negotiators from developing countries often point to information gaps in explaining their reluctance to make binding market opening commitments at the WTO. To the extent that RTA negotiations can remedy such gaps, they may lead developing countries to be better prepared in multilateral service negotiations. On the other hand, RTA negotiations may divert scarce negotiating resources away from the WTO. Developing country governments can often draw on only a limited pool of informed negotiators and support staff. A country's involvement in several RTA negotiations may thus come at the expense of reduced engagement at the WTO.

In sum, only time will tell whether the current wave of RTAs proves to be helpful or harmful for the WTO. A multitude of political economy and negotiating forces are pushing in different directions. Compared to the goods trade, however, we would argue that the building block forces may be *relatively* stronger in the case of services. The main reason for such optimism lies in the adoption of liberal origin rules (where RTAs are implemented in a discriminatory way), which may prevent the emergence of vested interests resisting the multilateralization of RTA liberalization undertakings.

5 Facilitating the move from regional to multilateral services liberalization: is there scope for the WTO?

GATS rules on regional integration agreements

The MFN principle is fundamental to the multilateral trading system, and the existence of RTAs in fact sits oddly with this. Yet, the GATT has from its beginnings allowed for the existence of customs unions and free trade areas, and the GATS does the same. As already pointed out, GATS Article V stipulates under which conditions RTAs are not considered to be in conflict with WTO rules. GATS Article V:1 notably requires regional agreements to have 'substantial sectoral coverage' and elaborates in a footnote that this 'condition is understood in terms of number of sectors, volume of trade affected and modes of supply'. In addition, regional agreements are to do away with 'substantially all discrimination'.

The requirements in GATS Article V concerning the sectoral coverage and liberalization ambition of regional agreements are defined rather loosely. It is indeed difficult to see how these conditions can be effectively monitored with the data that are normally available on trade in services. Some observers (e.g. Feketekuty, 2000) have therefore asked for a redrafting of GATS Article V. The case for such an exercise is not entirely clear. Greater scrutiny may lead some WTO members to shun the formation of services RTAs, which may reduce negative welfare effects in countries excluded by them. However, it may also restrain the emergence of building block forces that could be supportive of multi-lateral liberalization in the longer term. More importantly, it appears unlikely that the same members concluding RTAs would have much appetite for more stringent disciplines.

The earlier discussion revealed that services RTAs involving developing countries have de facto embraced the liberal origin rules stipulated in GATS Article V:6, even though Article V:3 gives developing countries some flexibility in this respect. Given the WTO-friendliness of this rule, one could argue that developing countries might as well accept that Article V:6 disciplines should to be extended to them. An alternative would be for developing countries to sign up to a voluntary code pledging adherence to Article V:6. Yet both approaches would imply that developing countries forgo an aspect of 'special and differential treatment' accorded to them by the WTO membership, and it is questionable whether such a move would be politically feasible.

Roy, Marchetti and Lim (2007) make a less ambitious – and, correspondingly, politically less controversial – proposal. They call for strengthening WTO surveillance of RTAs, particularly with respect to the implementation of market opening commitments. For example, WTO members could be required to regularly report on changes in laws and regulations, as well as patterns of foreign participation, in the service sector. Such information would contribute to a better understanding of the extent of discrimination emanating from preferential agreements. Consequently, WTO members could better assess the systemic consequences of services RTAs and develop negotiating proposals favouring the multilateralization of RTA liberalization undertakings. A precedent for greater surveillance along these lines already exists at the WTO in the form of the transitional review mechanism to which China agreed as part of its accession.

The WTO Secretariat and the research community at large could further assist WTO members in assessing the systemic consequences of services RTAs by enhancing our understanding of the actual relevance of location-specific sunk costs in service sectors like communications, transport or energy (see Table 6.1). As explained earlier, first mover advantages can have long-term trade diverting effects, and negotiators may want to take such effects into account when defining their negotiation position at the regional or multilateral level.

The WTO and implicit regulatory barriers

The GATS in its current form disciplines the use of regulatory measures, but the legal texts invite the Council for Trade in Services to elaborate on the existing disciplines. The outcome of the ongoing negotiations in this regard may affect the extent to which multilateral approaches towards the setting of service regulation are explicitly encouraged.

Mutual recognition agreements among subsets of the WTO membership are allowed under the GATS, and it may well be that one MRA unleashes others, ultimately leading to mutual recognition at a broader level. Yet the actual design of MRAs is likely to affect how multilateral-friendly they are, and the WTO may therefore consider providing guidance on this aspect.

GATs rules on domestic regulation

GATS Article VI provides for some discipline on the use of regulatory measures, but Paragraph 4 of that Article leaves room for further deepening those disciplines. It invites the Council for Trade in Services to develop (through any appropriate bodies it may establish) any disciplines relating to qualification requirements and procedures, technical standards and licensing requirements that may be necessary to ensure that such measures do not constitute unnecessary barriers to trade in services.

Pursuant to this mandate the so-called Working Party on Professional Services was created, and one of the outcomes of its work has been the 'Decision on Disciplines on Domestic Regulation in the Accountancy Sector' adopted in 1998.[31] These Disciplines only refer to the accountancy sector but may give some insights into the directions in which the Working Party may be going.

The Disciplines stipulate that, in the context of relevant technical standards, members should 'take account' of the internationally recognized standards of relevant international organizations. The language here is weaker than, for instance, in the TBT Agreement, that stipulates that members 'shall' use relevant international standards, and that they shall play a full part in the preparation of such standards by means of appropriate international standardizing bodies. The Disciplines for the Accountancy Sector so far also make no reference to possible international standards regarding licensing or qualification requirements.

---

[31] WTO Document S/WPPS/W/21.

Given that efforts to design such standards are ongoing in international professional bodies, it could be an option for WTO legal texts to encourage members to take account of such work. In other words, the WTO could play a constructive role in developing international standards – at least as far as their adoption is feasible and desirable among its membership. Such an effort may help prevent the unnecessary fragmentation of the trading system along regional groupings.

The WTO and pro-active regulatory cooperation

We have already discussed existing efforts to agree on common disciplines on the use of regulatory measures. These efforts have resulted in a number of MRAs. We argued that regulatory cooperation agreements can have long-term discriminatory effects. Since progress on MRAs at the regional level appears to have been slow, the severity of this concern is not entirely clear.

In principle, by extending trade benefits to one country (or a small group of countries), MRAs may depart from the MFN obligation under the GATS. However, GATS Article VII allows for such a departure, provided that the WTO member in question notifies the MRA, and affords adequate opportunity to other interested members to negotiate a comparable arrangement.[32] This obligation already promotes the 'WTO-friendliness' of such agreements. Nonetheless, there seems to be a loophole to this discipline. It is not clear whether MRAs concluded in the course of an RTA fall under the scope of Article VII or are covered under GATS Article V on economic integration agreements. Indeed, most WTO members seem to hold the latter view (see Adlung, 2006). According to this interpretation, relevant members would not be obliged to afford third countries an opportunity to negotiate participation. Clarification in this domain would be desirable. This could, for instance, be achieved by making explicit in Article VII that MRAs concluded within the context of a preferential trade agreement also need to be notified under Article VII, even if the RTA itself is notified under Article V.

Another multilateral-unfriendly aspect of some MRAs is that they limit eligible service suppliers to nationals of the signatory parties (i.e. they provide for restrictive origin rules).[33] Such 'exclusionary' MRAs

---

[32] The TBT Agreement that applies to technical measures in the goods trade goes further and 'encourages' the conclusion of MRAs dealing with conformity assessment.

[33] For example, NAFTA facilitates licensing requirements for nationals of other parties in the case of legal consultants and engineers, and the Caribbean Community and

create unnecessary discrimination.[34] It is difficult to see why the quality of service providers should differ according to nationality, once they have met domestic licensing or certification requirements. In addition, recognizing service providers of all nationalities licensed in an RTA partner country does not mean that a country needs to afford market access to all nationalities. For example, RTAs are still free to incorporate a nationality criterion in origin rules as they apply to mode 4 commitments. GATS Article VII does not impose any express discipline on the origin of beneficiaries of MRAs. In order to promote 'open' MRAs, GATS Article VII could be redrafted to require WTO members to extend the benefits of recognition agreements to any service supplier, regardless of nationality or residency status, that meets the recognized licensing or certification requirements.[35]

The previous literature has suggested additional ways in which the WTO's role with respect to MRAs could be strengthened. OECD (2003), for instance, suggests that the WTO Guidelines for Mutual Recognition Agreements or Arrangements in the Accountancy Sector could also be applied as a template for MRAs in other professions.[36] This could, according to Nicolaïdis and Trachtman (2000), lead to the creation of a more open and transparent system of MRAs.

The guidelines are voluntary and non-binding, and have been established to facilitate the negotiation of recognition agreements and the access of third parties to such agreements. The introduction to the guidelines develops the idea that one bilateral agreement may unleash others, ultimately leading to mutual recognition more broadly.

The guidelines suggest that an MRA should clearly specify the conditions to be met for recognition in the territories of each party and the level of equivalence between the parties. Qualification requirements in terms of a minimum level of education or experience should, for instance, be specified. The rules and procedures to be used to monitor and enforce the provisions of the agreement should also be clearly stipulated. In addition, any licensing requirements other than qualifications should be explained.

---

[34] Baldwin (2001) makes a similar distinction between 'exclusionary' and 'open' mutual recognition agreements in the context of trade in goods.

[35] One may argue that existing GATS disciplines (e.g. Article VI:1, Article VII:1 or Article XVII) could already be interpreted to this effect. However, such an interpretation is uncertain.

[36] WTO Document S/L/38.

Indeed, a system of MRAs based on a unique template following the example of the guidelines would contribute to the transparency of MRAs and likely represent a building block rather than a stumbling block for multilateral integration, as it would be easier to match the regulatory regimes of different regions if they are built according to the same template.

Finally, multilateral disciplines on mutual recognition could be extended to other forms of regulatory cooperation between countries, such as information exchanges or collaboration between law enforcement agencies. For example, Mattoo (2005) argues that WTO members could agree on templates for regulatory conditions necessary to engage in mode 4 market opening. While such templates could not alter countries' inclination for preferential liberalization based on cultural considerations, they would offer excluded countries an opportunity to demonstrate that they meet the regulatory conditions for sending workers abroad.

6   Conclusion

The arguments put forward in this chapter suggest that the building block forces of RTAs may, on balance, be relatively stronger in services than in the case of goods. The main cause for this optimism lies in the weakly discriminatory nature of these agreements – as reflected in the non-discriminatory implementation of trade commitments and liberal rules of origin. That said, only time will tell whether the recent wave of services RTAs will prove to be helpful or harmful to the multilateral cause.

Special concerns exist in at least two areas. First, RTAs liberalizing mode 4 trade may be associated with strong discrimination, due to more restrictive origin rules. Second, preferential regulatory cooperation, by its very nature, also leads to discernible discrimination. The latter often pertains to mode 4 trade, but is also relevant for the other forms of the trade in services. Arguably, RTA commitments on mode 4 and regulatory cooperation initiatives have not gone very far, although selected agreements have shown that deeper liberalization is possible.

Multilateral progress in these areas may not always be feasible and sometimes not even desirable, especially when it comes to the harmonization of regulatory regimes. In this view, the WTO should not stand in the way of countries wishing to go deeper. However, there is some scope for disciplines to promote the friendliness of regional initiatives within the multilateral trading system. The GATS already has sensible rules promoting such friendliness – notably Article V:6 mandating a liberal rule of origin for juridical persons, and Article VII requiring WTO members to afford adequate opportunity for the extension of MRAs. Arguably, there is additional room for the WTO to scrutinize regional regulatory initiatives. A number of possible steps in this direction have been suggested in this chapter. In particular, WTO members could:

- strengthen the surveillance of services RTAs, particularly with respect to the implementation of market opening commitments;
- encourage the WTO Secretariat and the research community to analyse the relevance of first mover advantages with long-term trade-diverting effects in individual service sectors;
- encourage the development of international regulatory standards, insofar as they are feasible and desirable;
- further promote the transparency of MRAs by an explicit requirement to also notify under GATS Article VII MRAs that are concluded in the context of RTAs;
- reduce the potential of MRAs to be trade-distorting by prohibiting the use of nationality requirements for the recognition of certificates or licences;
- encourage the use of templates in MRAs. Such templates could, for instance, follow as far as possible the guidelines of the adopted Disciplines for the Accountancy Sector; and
- develop rules for other forms of regulatory cooperation, such as information-sharing agreements or collaboration between law-enforcement agencies.

References

Adlung, R. (2006) 'Services Negotiations in the Doha Round: Lost in Flexibility?' *Journal of International Economic Law* 9 (4): 865–93.

Baldwin, R. E. (1995) 'A Domino Theory of Regionalism', in Richard E. Baldwin, Pertti Haaparanta and Jaakko Kiander (eds.), *Expanding European Regionalism: The EU's New Members*, Cambridge: Cambridge University Press.

(2001) 'Regulatory Protectionism, Developing Nations and a Two-Tier World Trading System', *Brookings Trade Forum* 3: 237–80.

(2006) 'Multilateralising Regionalism: Spaghetti Bowls as Building Blocks on the Path to Global Free Trade', *The World Economy* 29 (11): 1451–518.

Chaudhuri, S., Mattoo, A. and Self, R. (2004) 'Moving People to Deliver Services: How Can the WTO Help?', *Journal of World Trade* 38 (3): 363–93.

EIU (Economist Intelligence Unit) (2004) *Botswana Country Profile 2004*, London: The Economist.

Emch, A. (2006) 'Services Regionalism in the WTO: China's Trade Agreements with Hong Kong and Macao in the light of Article V(6) GATS', *Legal Issues of Economic Integration* 33 (4): 351–78.

Feeney, J.-A. and Hillman, A. L. (2001) 'Privatization and the Political Economy of Strategic Trade Policy', *International Economic Review* 42 (2): 535–56.

Feketekuty, G. (2000) 'Assessing and Improving the Architecture of GATS', in Pierre Sauvé and Robert M. Stern (eds.), *GATS 2000: New Directions in Services Trade Liberalization*, Washington DC: Brookings Institution.

Fink, C. (2005) 'A Macroeconomic Perspective on China's Liberalization of Trade in Services', in H. Gao and D. Lewis (eds.), *China's Participation in the WTO*, London: Cameron May.

(2007) 'Preferential Trade Agreements in Services: Friends or Foes of the WTO?', Discussion Paper, Groupe d'Économie Mondiale, Paris: Sciences Po.

Fink, C. and Molinuevo, M. (2007) 'East Asian Free Trade Agreements in Services: Roaring Tigers or Timid Pandas?', East Asia and Pacific Region, Report No. 40175, World Bank, available at: http://go.worldbank.org/5YFZ3TK4E0.

Fink, C. and Nikomborirak, D. (2008) 'Rules of Origin in Services: A Case Study of Five ASEAN Countries', in M. Panizzon, N. Pohl and P. Sauvé (eds.), *Trade in Services: New Perspectives on Liberalization, Regulation, and Development*, Cambridge: Cambridge University Press.

Hallward-Driemeier, M. (2003) 'Do Bilateral Investment Treaties Attract Foreign Direct Investment?', Policy Research Working Paper No. 3121, Washington DC: World Bank.

Krishna, P. (1998) 'Regionalism and Multilateralism: A Political Economy Approach', *Quarterly Journal of Economics* 113 (1): 227–50.

Levy, P. I. (1997) 'A Political-Economic Analysis of Free-Trade Agreements', *American Economic Review* 87 (4): 506–19.

Mattoo, A. (2005) 'Services in a Development Round: Three Goals and Three Proposals', *Journal of World Trade* 39 (6): 1223–38.

Mattoo, A. and Fink, C. (2004) 'Regional Agreements and Trade in Services: Policy Issues', *Journal of Economic Integration* 19 (4): 742–79.

Mattoo, A. and Wunsch-Vincent, S. (2004) 'Pre-Empting Protectionism in Services: The GATS and Outsourcing', *Journal of International Economic Law* 7 (4): 765–800.

Mattoo, A., Stern, R. and Zanini, G. (eds.) (2007) *A Handbook of International Trade in Services*, Oxford: Oxford University Press.

Neumayer, E. and Spess, L. (2005) 'Do Bilateral Investment Treaties Increase Foreign Direct Investment to Developing Countries?', *World Development* 33 (10): 1567–85.

Nicolaïdis, K. and Trachtman, J. P. (2000) 'Liberalization, Regulation, and Recognition for Services Trade', in Sherry M. Stephenson (ed.), *Services Trade in the Western Hemisphere: Liberalization, Integration and Reform*, Washington DC: Brookings Institution.

OECD (2003) 'Service Providers on the Move: Mutual Recognition Agreements', TD/TC/WP(2002)48/FINAL, Paris: OECD.

Roy, M., Marchetti, J. and Lim, A. H. (2007) 'Services Liberalization in the New Generation of Preferential Trade Agreements (PTAs): How Much Further than the GATS?', *World Trade Review* 6 (2): 155–92.

Stephenson, S. (2005) 'Examining APEC's Progress Towards Reaching the Bogor Goals for Services Liberalization', draft paper prepared for Pacific Economic Cooperation Council.

WTO (2005) *International Trade Statistics 2005*, Geneva: World Trade Organization.

WTO International Trade Statistics Section (2008) 'Measuring Trade in Services', in A. Mattoo, R. Stern and G. Zanini (eds.), *A Handbook of International Trade in Services*, Oxford: Oxford University Press.

7

Harmonizing preferential rules of origin regimes around the world

ANTONI ESTEVADEORDAL, JEREMY HARRIS
AND KATI SUOMINEN[1]

1 Introduction

The proliferation of regional trade agreements (RTAs) around the world has focused policy attention to preferential rules of origin (ROOs). The concerns voiced over ROOs are two-fold: restrictiveness and divergence. Restrictive ROOs can introduce undue barriers to trade between RTA members and non-members, thus dampening RTAs' trade-creating potential. Divergences in ROOs across regimes can increase the transaction costs for countries and companies dealing on two or more RTA fronts simultaneously, especially when they are unable to cumulate production and inputs across agreements. These two issues are intricately linked: divergence matters more when ROOs are binding – i.e. when restrictiveness is consequential for economic decisions and affects firms' production. Non-binding ROOs around the world would obliterate the importance of divergence.

The purpose of this chapter is to analyse the restrictiveness and divergence in ROOs around the world, and to propose concrete ways for reducing them. In particular, we (1) discuss the costs of restrictiveness and divergence on global trade and investment flows and companies' supply chain strategies; (2) strive to quantify the extent of restrictiveness in and divergences among some fifty-eight ROOs regimes around the world (which contain a total of seventy-four sets of product-specific rules, listed in Appendix A); and (3) put forth a number of policy

---

[1] The opinions expressed herein are those of the authors and do not necessarily reflect the official position of the Inter-American Development Bank (IDB) or its member countries. The authors wish to thank Olivier Cadot and Richard Baldwin for helpful discussion and comments, and Santiago Florez Gomez for outstanding and persistent research assistance and comments.

options – including multilateralizing ROOs at the global level, inducing convergence of ROO regimes in the main world regions, and some combination of the two – so as to facilitate trade and efficient production around the world.

We define 'multilateralizing' ROOs as the establishment of multilateral disciplines on preferential rules within the WTO framework that set guidelines to minimize the systemic harm that can be caused by the current uncoordinated approach. 'Convergence' here is a process of establishing a common ROO regime that covers a set of RTAs, and subsequently permits cumulation among the members of these RTAs. Conversely, 'divergence' here refers not only to the existence of different rules across agreements, but, in cases of overlapping agreements, also to the absence of cumulation of production across the agreements.

We reach three main conclusions:

- ROOs in some of the largest trade blocs and partners (the European Union's RTAs, the North American Free Trade Agreement, NAFTA, and some Japanese agreements) are among the most restrictive. Agricultural products and textiles and apparel are marked by particularly high restrictiveness scores across regimes. However, it is also the case that US agreements have become less restrictive over time. The more recent intra-Asian agreements tend to be less restrictive and complex than their counterparts in Europe and the Americas.
- There are marked divergences across ROO regimes around the world: on average about one-third of the rules of all agreements coincide on any given product. Nonetheless, there are clear ROO families centred around the United States, the EU and Mexico, in particular, which suggests the potential for some form of regional ROO convergence. Moreover, there are some signs of a de facto cross-regional stylistic harmonization of ROOs, as US-style agreements are spreading into Asia via the recent trans-Pacific agreements.
- The most ideal solution to the ROO tangle is a strategy of regional convergence governed by a multilateral agreement: putting in place some global guidelines for preferential ROOs that would serve to counteract the tendency of larger cumulation zones to erect higher barriers to extra-zone inputs, while also striving to establish common ROOs at mega-regional levels in order to promote cumulation of production across the existing RTAs. In simple terms, global 'capping' of ROOs is important so as not to 'converge' into trade-diverting mega-blocs.

The following section of this chapter discusses the political economy and economic effects of ROOs. The next section gives a descriptive overview of the general patterns in ROOs by region. Then we put forth various analytical measures of the degree of restrictiveness of product-specific ROOs and flexibility provided by regime-wide ROOs, and use these measures to draw comparisons within and across ROO regimes. The following section goes to the policy recommendations. The last section concludes.

2   What are ROOs and what do they do?

What are ROOs?

There are two types of rules of origin, non-preferential ROOs and preferential ROOs. Non-preferential ROOs are used to distinguish foreign from domestic products and to determine the 'official origin' for purposes of establishing anti-dumping and countervailing duties, safeguard measures, origin-marking requirements, and/or discriminatory quantitative restrictions or tariff quotas, as well as in the context of government procurement. Preferential ROOs, meanwhile, define the conditions under which the importing country will regard a product as originating in an exporting country that receives preferential treatment from the importing country. RTAs, in effect, employ ROOs to determine whether a good qualifies for preferential treatment when exported from one member state to another.

Both non-preferential and preferential ROO regimes have two dimensions: sectoral, product-specific ROOs and general, regime-wide ROOs. We discuss each in turn.

Product-specific ROOs

The Kyoto Convention recognizes two basic criteria to determine origin: wholly obtained or produced, and substantial transformation.[2] The wholly obtained or produced category applies only to one RTA member, and concerns whether the commodities and related products have been entirely grown, harvested or extracted from the soil in the territory of that member, or manufactured there from any of these products. The

---

[2] The Revised Kyoto Convention is an international instrument adopted by the World Customs Organization (WCO) to standardize and harmonize customs policies and procedures around the world. The WCO adopted the original Convention in 1974. The revised version was adopted in June 1999.

rule of origin is met through not using any second-country components or materials. Most countries apply this strict and precise definition.

The substantial transformation criterion is more complex, involving three main components that can be used alone or in combinations with each other. The precision with which these components define ROOs in RTAs today contrasts sharply with the vagueness of the substantial transformation criterion used by the United States from 1908 until the inception of the Canada–US Free Trade Agreement (COSTA) in 1989 and, subsequently, the North American Free Trade Agreement (NAFTA) in 1994 (Reyna, 1995: 7).[3]

The first component of the substantial transformation criterion is a change in tariff classification (CTC) between the manufactured good and its inputs from extra-RTA parties used in the production process. The CTC may require the product to alter its chapter (two digits under the harmonized system, HS), heading (four digits), subheading (six digits) or item (eight to ten digits) in the exporting RTA member. The CTC can be modified by exceptions (prohibitions of inputs that would have met the CTC requirement) or additions (permitting inputs that would have been proscribed by the CTC requirement).

The second criterion is value content (VC), which requires the product to acquire a certain minimum local value in the exporting country. The value content can be expressed in three main ways: as the minimum percentage of value that must have been added in the exporting country (domestic or regional value content, RVC); as the difference between the value of the final good and the costs of the imported inputs (import content, MC); or as the value of parts (VP), whereby originating status is granted to products meeting a minimum percentage of originating parts out of the total.

The third ROO component is a technical requirement (TECH), which requires the product to undergo certain manufacturing operations in the originating country. TECH essentially prescribes or prohibits the use of certain input(s) and/or the realization of certain process(es) in the production of the good.[4] It is a particularly prominent feature in ROOs governing textile products.

---

[3] The old criterion basically required the emergence of a 'new and different article' from the manufacturing process applied to the original article. It was, however, much criticized for allowing – and indeed requiring – subjective and case-by-case determinations of origin (Reyna, 1995: 7).

[4] TECH can be highly discretionary, given the lack of classification tools available objectively to guarantee sufficient transformation in the production of the good.

The change of heading requirement is the staple of RTAs. It is used either alone or in tandem with other ROO criteria. It is also frequently used are the import content (usually ranging from 30 to 60 per cent), value of parts, and technical requirements. Adding analytical complexity, albeit administrative flexibility, means that many ROO regimes provide two or more alternative ROOs for a given product, such as a change of chapter or a change of heading plus RVC.

Regime-wide ROOs

Besides product-specific ROOs, ROO regimes vary by the types of general ROOs they employ – including the degree of *de minimis*, cumulation and certification.

First, most RTAs contain a *de minimis* rule, which allows for a specified maximum percentage of non-originating materials to be used without affecting origin. *De minimis* essentially softens the rough edges of CTC-based rules of origin. CTC rules are a binary test, with non-originating inputs either meeting the criteria or not, regardless of their real significance in the context of the final product as a whole. *De minimis* provisions allow goods to qualify as originating despite having some minimal content of non-originating inputs that do not meet the CTC requirements.

Second, cumulation allows producers of one RTA member to use materials from another RTA member (or members) without losing the preferential status of the final product. For the purposes of the policy questions we wish to address in this chapter, we define a more simplified taxonomy of cumulation types than is generally used in the literature. Bilateral cumulation refers to provisions that permit goods that qualify as originating in any one signatory country to be considered as such when incorporated into a subsequent product in another signatory country.

For our purposes, bilateral cumulation can be based on either products or processes (full cumulation).[5] Extended cumulation allows some use of inputs from non-signatories. Extended cumulation is the mechanism by which the spaghetti bowl problem can begin to be ameliorated,[6] and includes diagonal cumulation as a special case.

---

[5] The distinction between cumulation based on products or processes is significant but not essential to our policy analysis.

[6] See also Cornejo and Harris (2007) for extended discussion of this idea. We discuss these implications in the multilateral context later in the chapter.

Another major regime-wide ROO is certification. The purpose of establishing origin certification procedures is to put in place a mechanism for ensuring that preferences are granted only to originating goods, and to establish a system of checks on the accuracy and veracity of claims for preferential treatment. The method of certifying origin is important insofar as it is effective in achieving these objectives at a minimum possible administrative cost. It varies across RTAs. Three fundamental systems can be identified. The first two can be seen as public certification involving an official certifying entity, which can be either an interested party or a third party. The third party can be the exporting country's government or a designated private entity. The third method requires certification by an interested private party, which may include the producer, exporter or importer (in many cases these three may be one and the same). A complex method of certifying the origin of goods – generally the public one – is viewed as potentially imposing high administrative costs on exporters.

Why are ROOs used? Protectionist content – and intent?

The economic justification for ROOs is to curb trade deflection – to avoid products from non-RTA members being transhipped through a low-tariff RTA partner to a high-tariff one. As such, ROOs are an inherent feature of free trade agreements (FTAs) where the member states' external tariffs differ, since the members wish to retain their individual tariff policies vis-à-vis the rest of the world (ROW). ROOs are also widely used in customs unions (CUs), either as a transitory tool in the process of moving toward a common external tariff (CET), or as a more permanent means of covering product categories where reaching agreement on a CET is difficult, for instance due to large tariff differentials between the member countries. Thus, basically all RTAs contain rules for establishing the origin of goods.

Since a failure to meet the ROOs disqualifies an exporter from the RTA-conferred preferential treatment, ROOs can and must be seen as a central market access instrument reigning over preferential trade. Notably, the relevance of ROOs as gatekeepers of commerce can become accentuated over time: ROOs remain in place even after preferential tariffs have been phased out. Thus, initially governing access to a small preference, ROOs have little capacity for distortion; however, as the tariffs are phased out, the distortionary potential of ROOs grows.[7]

---

[7] Throughout this chapter, we assume this latter scenario has unfolded.

What makes ROOs particularly relevant is that they are hardly a neutral instrument: given that ROOs can serve as an effective means to deter transhipment, they can tempt political economy uses well beyond the efforts to avert trade deflection. Indeed, ROOs are widely described as a trade policy instrument that can work to offset the benefits of tariff liberalization.[8] Often negotiated at up to the eight- or ten-digit level of disaggregation, ROOs, like the tariff, make a superbly targetable instrument. Most prominently, ROOs can be employed to favour intra-RTA industry linkages over those between the RTA and the ROW, and, as such, to indirectly protect RTA-based input producers vis-à-vis their extra-RTA rivals (Krueger, 1993; Krishna and Krueger, 1995). As such, ROOs are akin to a tariff on the intermediate product levied by the country importing the final good (Falvey and Reed, 2000), and can be used by one RTA member to secure its RTA partners' input markets for the exports of its own intermediate products (Krueger, 1993; Krishna and Krueger, 1995).[9]

Empirical studies provide grounds for believing that ROOs are indeed used for political economy purposes. Estevadeordal (2000) and Suominen (2004) focus on the political economy of ROOs in the North American Free Trade Agreement (NAFTA) and EU–Mexico RTA, respectively, finding that tariffs and the restrictiveness of ROOs are driven by the same political economy dynamics, and that ROOs play an independent role in arbitrating preferential tariff liberalization. Producers that lobby for the most demanding ROOs also lobby for, and obtain, the longest tariff phase-outs. Harris (2007) examines determinants of ROO restrictiveness in a panel of five RTAs in the Americas and finds that restrictiveness responds to the interests of both domestic producers seeking protection and exporters seeking access to protected markets.

The policy implication of these findings are clear: stringent ROOs plus long phase-outs are the price integrationist forces will need to pay not only for RTA formation, but for forgoing manifold exclusions and building a meaningful, comprehensive and liberalizing RTA. Furthermore, while ROOs may be a necessary hurdle to unfettered free

---

[8] For example, Hirsch (2002), Estevadeordal and Suominen (2008), Cadot, Estevadeordal and Suwa-Eisenmann (2006).

[9] Furthermore, given that ROOs hold the potential for increasing local sourcing, governments can use ROOs to encourage investment in sectors that provide high value-added and/or jobs (Jensen-Moran, 1996; Hirsch, 2002).

trade within RTAs, there is evidence that exporter interests also affect restrictiveness. Do ROOs, then, distort economic outcomes?

Carrère and de Melo (2006) examine the rates at which US imports from Mexico take advantage of the NAFTA preferences, finding that ROOs indeed stifle incentives to qualify for tariff preferences: preference margins of 10 per cent would be needed to compensate for the costs of complying with a typical RVC rule of origin. Cadot *et al.* (2002) disentangle NAFTA's non-ROOs and ROOs-related administrative costs, finding the latter to approximate 2 per cent of the value of Mexican exports to the US market. Manchin and Pelksman-Baloing (2007) examine the interplay of tariff preferences in a number of East Asian RTAs, finding that only quite notable preferential margins (of some 25 per cent) result in utilization of preferences.

Suominen (2004) and Estevadeordal and Suominen (2008) examine the trade effects of ROOs in some 100 RTAs, finding that restrictive and selective ROOs discourage trade flows. At the sectoral level, both restrictive ROOs and selectivity in ROOs in final goods encourage trade in intermediate goods – which can mean that restrictive ROOs engender trade diversion in inputs. However, some regime-wide ROOs – ROOs that apply similarly to all sectors in a given RTA yet vary across RTAs, such as cumulation and *de minimis* – allow for flexibility in the application of product-specific ROOs and thus facilitate trade. As such, various regime-wide ROO provisions can counteract restrictive product-specific ROOs' negative effects on trade.

Estevadeordal, López-Córdova and Suominen (2006) analyse the sectoral *investment* effects of NAFTA ROOs in Mexico, finding both that foreign direct investment in post-NAFTA Mexico has flowed in sectors with flexible ROOs, and that flexible ROOs in downstream industries encourage investment upstream. Both findings suggest that NAFTA-era investment in Mexican final and intermediate goods industries has been made by efficient, globally competitive firms thriving on flexible ROOs.

Augier, Gasiorek and Lai-Tong (2005) study the effects of expanding cumulation within a set of countries already linked by RTAs. They find that the inability to cumulate production across 'spoke' economies in a hub-and-spoke arrangement depresses trade among the spokes by 10 to 70 per cent. If extending cumulation has such an effect, then the rules were distorting trade after all. The policy implication is that broadening cumulation should be encouraged in further settings.

Less well understood than the trade and investment effects of a given ROOs regime or set of regimes are the effects of divergent ROOs *across* regimes. Hypothetically, if the various agreements carry widely distinct ROOs, they can impose undue transaction costs for traders, investors and governments dealing in several RTA markets simultaneously (as opposed to the counterfactual case where the rules of the various RTA are exactly the same). IDB (2007) is the first attempt to measure ROO divergence, and IDB (forthcoming) strives to understand the effects of ROO divergence for companies operating in multiple RTA theatres. The exercises above should provide a firmer grasp on ROO divergence – while still not measuring its economic impact.

3   Rules of origin around the world: a descriptive mapping

This section provides a useful prelude to analysing ROO restrictiveness and divergence by describing the types of preferential ROOs used in selected RTAs around the world. We subsequently discuss the structure of non-preferential ROOs.

Product-specific ROOs

Europe: the Paneuro system

The ROO regimes employed across the EU's RTAs are highly uniform. This is owing largely to the European Commission's drive in the 1990s to harmonize the EU's ROO protocols with the European Free Trade Association (EFTA) countries that dated from 1972 and 1973, as well as across the EU's RTAs forged in the early 1990s in the context of the European Agreements with Bulgaria, the Czech Republic, Estonia, Hungary, Latvia, Lithuania, Poland, Slovakia and Romania.[10] The harmonization work culminated in 1997 in the launch of the Paneuro system,[11] which established identical ROO protocols across the EU's existing RTAs, as well as for the RTAs among the EU's partners, providing for cumulation among the participating countries. The Commission's Regulation 46 of January 1999 reiterates the harmonized protocols, outlining the so-called Single List ROOs. These ROOs are highly complex, combining a change of tariff classification mainly at the heading level with exceptions, value content rules, and technical requirements, and varying markedly across products. However, the

[10]   See Driessen and Graafsma (1999) for a review.
[11]   The Paneuro rules are also known as the Pan-European Cumulation System (PECS) or the Paneuro-Med rules.

harmonized ROOs do not represent a dramatic break with those of the pre-1997 era.[12]

The Single List became incorporated in the Euro-Mediterranean Association Agreements between the EU and the various southern Mediterranean countries, and the system of cumulation operates among the regional countries that have signed bilateral agreements with each other. The so-called Paneuro-Med cumulation zone covers the twenty-seven EU members and is gradually incorporating seventeen other countries or territories.[13] While the object of this 'cumulation system' is to enable goods that fulfil the ROOs of one agreement to automatically qualify for other agreements within the system, this also requires that all the countries within the system have RTAs in force with all other countries in the system, which is not yet the case for some bilateral relationships.

The Paneuro ROO model is incorporated also in the EU's RTAs outside the cumulation zone, including the EU's Stabilization and Association Agreements with Albania, Bosnia and Herzegovina, Croatia, the former Yugoslav Republic of Macedonia and Serbia and Montenegro, and the EU's extra-regional RTAs with South Africa, Mexico, and Chile.[14] Also the ROOs of the EU's Generalized System of Preferences (GSP) and the 2000 Cotonou Agreement with the African, Caribbean and Pacific (ACP) developing countries are nearly identical to the Paneuro rules. The European Free Trade Association's (EFTA) recently concluded RTAs with Mexico and Singapore also follow the model,

---

[12] For example, the ROOs in nearly 75 per cent of the products (in terms of tariff sub-headings) in Paneuro and the original EU–Poland ROOs protocol published in 1993 are identical. Both the new and the old versions combine CTC with VC and/or TECH. Indeed, EU ROOs feature remarkable continuity: the ROOs of the European Community–Cyprus RTA formed in 1973 are strikingly similar to those used today. One notable difference between the older and the newer protocols is that the latter allow for an optional way of meeting the ROOs for about 25 per cent of the products, whereas the former specify mostly only one way of meeting the ROOs. The second option, alternative ROOs, much like the first option ROOs, combine different ROO criteria; however, the most frequently used alternative ROO is a stand-alone import-content criterion.

[13] The Paneuro-Med system of cumulation operates between the EU and the member States of the European Free Trade Association (Iceland, Liechtenstein, Norway and Switzerland) and Turkey, and countries which have signed the Barcelona Declaration, namely Algeria, Egypt, Israel, Jordan, Lebanon, Morocco, Syria, Tunisia and the Palestinian Authority of the West Bank and Gaza Strip. The Faroe Islands have been added to the system as well.

[14] See Estevadeordal and Suominen (2003).

albeit providing an additional alternative rule in selected sectors, such as plastics, rubber, textiles, iron and steel products, and some machinery products.

The Americas: ROO poles

There is more variation across ROO regimes in the Americas. Nevertheless, distinct ROO families can be identified.[15] One extreme is populated by the traditional trade agreements based on the Latin American Integration Association (LAIA), which uses a general rule applicable across the board for all tariff items (a change in tariff classification at the heading level or, alternatively, a regional value-added of at least 50 per cent of the (f.o.b.) export value of the final good) plus a handful of specific rules applicable to specific products. The LAIA model is the point of reference for ROOs used in the Andean Community (CAN) and MERCOSUR, as well as the agreements between them and with Chile. The CARICOM rules of origin are also based on a general change of heading requirement, though the exceptions to this general rule have a flavour more reminiscent of the Paneuro rules and their predecessors.

At the other extreme lie the so-called new-generation RTAs such as NAFTA, which is used as a reference point for subsequent US and Canadian agreements in the hemisphere (US–Chile, US–Colombia, US–Peru, Chile–Canada, Canada–Costa Rica RTAs and the US–Central America–Dominican Republic RTA, or CAFTA), as well as many of Mexico's agreements, including Mexico–Costa Rica, Mexico–Chile, Mexico–Bolivia, Mexico–Nicaragua, Mexico–Northern Triangle (El Salvador, Guatemala and Honduras), and Mexico–Colombia–Venezuela (or G-3). The ROO regimes in these agreements may require a change of chapter, heading, subheading or item, depending on the product in question. In addition, many products combine the change of tariff classification with an exception, regional value content, or technical requirement. All of these agreements permit cumulation among the members of each agreement.

The Central American Common Market's (CACM) ROO regime can be seen as located between those of MERCOSUR and NAFTA: it chiefly uses change in tariff classification only, but in more precise and diverse ways than MERCOSUR, due to requiring the change to take place at either the chapter, heading, or subheading level, depending on the

---

[15] See, for example, Garay and Cornejo (2002) and Estevadeordal and Suominen (2005).

product in question. CAFTA co-exists with the CACM's market access mechanisms under the so-called multilateralism principle, which allows Central American producers to choose between the CACM and CAFTA market access regimes when exporting to the other Isthmus markets. A third set of ROOs will exist as an option for trade between CACM countries and the Dominican Republic.

Notably, unlike the EU's pattern of following the Paneuro system even in extra-regional RTAs, US bilateral RTAs with extra-hemispheric partners – Jordan and Israel – diverge markedly from the NAFTA model, operating on VC alone. US agreements with Morocco, Bahrain and Oman also use VC almost exclusively, except for textile products where the tariff-shift NAFTA-style rules are applied.

Trans-Pacific agreements

RTAs of the Americas are shaping the ROO regimes negotiated between countries of the Americas and Asia. US agreements with Singapore, Australia and the Republic of Korea are complex and resemble the CAFTA ROOs; meanwhile, ROOs in the Chile–Republic of Korea RTA follow the model of US–Chile ROOs. However, these trans-Pacific agreements are less complex overall than their counterparts in the Americas, featuring a strong change of heading component. Peru's agreement with Thailand, and Chile's agreement with Japan and the P4 agreement (Brunei, Chile, New Zealand and Singapore), as well as Mexico's agreement with Japan, all follow the detailed, selective model inherited from their agreements with the United States. Chile's agreement with China stands in contrast to these, applying an across-the-board VC rule with a handful of exceptions where change of chapter or change of heading are applied.

Meanwhile, further European overtures to the Asian front, such as towards ASEAN and India, will likely bring the Paneuro model to accompany the US model in the region.

Asia: multiple influences

Some of the main integration schemes in Asia – the ASEAN Free Trade Area, the ASEAN–China and ASEAN–Republic of Korea agreements, the Bangkok Agreement, the Australia–Singapore Free Trade Agreement, and the South Pacific Regional Trade and Economic Cooperation in Asia-Pacific (SPARTECA) – carry an across-the-board VC rule with relatively few exceptions. However, the proliferation of RTAs in Asia has delivered complexity to the region's ROO theatre, especially as these countries have entered into agreements with extra-regional partners.

The ROOs of the Japan–Singapore Economic Partnership Agreement are complex, as evinced by the ROOs protocol of more than 200 pages. However, much like in the Chile–Republic of Korea RTA, many of the Japan–Singapore ROOs are based on a simple change in heading criterion, which makes the regime much less complex when contrasted with the Paneuro and NAFTA models. Furthermore, for many products the Japan–Singapore Economic Partnership Agreement (JSEPA) introduces an alternative, usually Paneuro-type, freestanding VC rule, which instils generality and flexibility into the agreement. Japan's agreements with Malaysia and Thailand, on the other hand, repeat the more complex set of rules seen in Japan's agreement with Mexico.

The Australia–New Zealand Closer Economic Relations Trade Agreement (ANZCERTA) recently replaced their across-the-board VC rule with a set of rules that are quite similar to those established in the US–Australia regime. Australia and New Zealand have also entered into separate agreements with Thailand that carry a similar variety of rules.

Africa and the Middle East

The relative complexity of ROOs in Europe, the Americas and, increasingly, Asia stands in contrast to the generality of ROOs in many African and Middle Eastern RTAs. The Economic Community of West African States (ECOWAS) and the Common Market for Eastern and Southern Africa (COMESA) in Africa, and the Gulf Cooperation Council (GCC) in the Middle East, are based on an across-the-board VC rule that, when defined as regional value content (RVC), ranges from 30 per cent (ECOWAS) to 40 per cent (COMESA).[16] Some of the agreements allow, or indeed require, ROOs to be calculated on the basis of import content. Most of these regimes also specify alternative ROOs based on the CTC criterion; most often the alternative involves a change in heading or, in the case of ECOWAS, which has a relatively low RVC requirement of 30 per cent, change in subheading.

However, the Southern African Development Community (SADC) ROOs approximate the Paneuro model both in *types* of sectoral ROOs and in sectoral selectivity. Moreover, there have been some initiatives to renegotiate COMESA ROOs; such attempts may well eventually lead to regimes of greater complexity.

---

[16] This is the general case, but for some products the rule is 35 per cent regional content measured at factory cost.

Non-preferential ROOs

Non-preferential ROOs are used for purposes distinct from those of preferential rules. Even if a country did not use preferential ROOs, it would still apply some type of non-preferential ROOs. Unlike preferential ROOs, which have so far escaped multilateral regulation, non-preferential ROOs have been under a process of harmonization since 1995, as mandated by the Uruguay Round's Agreement on Rules of Origin (ARO). Indeed, the rapid spread of preferential ROO schemes stands in contrast to the very slow progress of harmonizing non-preferential ROOs. The harmonization work, propelled precisely by growing concerns about the divergent national ROOs' effects on trade flows, has been carried out under the auspices of the Committee on Rules of Origin (CRO) of the WTO and the Technical Committee on Rules of Origin (TCRO) of the Brussels-based World Customs Organization. The latter has been responsible for the technical part of the work, including discussions on the ROO options for each product.

The harmonization drive was initially scheduled for completion by July 1998. However, the deadline has been extended several times since then. At the moment, the pending product-specific issues involve some thirty products. There are also two major issues that have yet to be resolved — use of the value-added vs. change in tariff classification principle in assembly activities in Harmonized System chapters 84–90, and implementation issues, particularly the use of the harmonized non-preferential ROOs in anti-dumping cases.[17]

While ARO is centred on non-preferential ROOs, its Common Declaration with Regard to Preferential Rules of Origin spells out a requirement for the members to keep the Secretariat informed about their preferential ROOs. In their current structure, the non-preferential ROOs approximate the Paneuro and NAFTA models in sectoral specificity, yet are less demanding than either of the two main ROO regimes. However, since the final agreement has yet to be reached, the ultimate

---

[17] ARO states that non-preferential rules are to be the basis for anti-dumping actions. However, some WTO members, such as the United States, the Republic of Korea and Japan, have argued that the calculation of the margin of dumping – the wedge between the price of the exported good and its value in the domestic market – is, per the Agreement on Anti-Dumping, based on the concept of exporting country and not country of origin. Many members also resist the application of harmonized ROOs in anti-dumping actions because of the changes and constraints this would impose on their respective domestic anti-dumping legislation.

degree of complexity and restrictiveness of the non-preferential ROOs remains to be gauged.

Depicting product-specific ROOs around the world

This part maps out ROOs regimes around the world by their various components discussed above. Figure 7.1 focuses on the first ROO component and a staple of most ROO regimes, the change in tariff classification criterion, in the ROO regimes of twenty-six selected RTAs, plus the current status of the non-preferential negotiations.[18]

There are some clear families. The Andean Community, as well as MERCOSUR and its agreements with other South American countries, make very extensive use of the change in heading criterion, whereas US, Mexican and most Chilean agreements use a mix of CTC criteria. ROOs built upon the NAFTA ROO regime are based on change of heading and change of chapter criteria in relatively even quantities. The US–Chile RTA and CAFTA stand somewhat apart from the NAFTA format for requiring only a change in subheading for a substantial number of tariff lines. Meanwhile, the Chile–CACM RTA diverges from the NAFTA model due to its marked change in heading component, as do the Japan–Singapore and Chile–Republic of Korea RTAs. In contrast, the change of heading criterion dominates EU ROOs.

The Japan–Singapore agreement relies on a default rule of 'wholly obtained' for products with no other rule specified in the agreement Annex, and then relies heavily on change of heading. In contrast, ASEAN uses CTC for a very small number of products, and in its agreements with China and the Republic of Korea not at all, as is the case in COMESA and ECOWAS. The regimes of SADC and the EU depend on a fairly even split between change of heading and non-CTC rules. Table 7.4B in Appendix B presents a highly disaggregated description of the different criteria combinations used.

Another notable difference between the various RTAs is that some, such as the Bangkok Agreement, employ the VC criterion across sectors, completely forgoing the use of the CTC criterion. The EU does this in about a quarter of its ROOs.[19] Table 7.1B in Appendix B centres on the

---

[18] The figure is based on the first ROO only when two or more possible ROOs are provided for a tariff subheading.

[19] The bulk (more than 80 per cent) of these ROOs are based on the wholly obtained criterion used particularly in agricultural products, or on the import content rule that

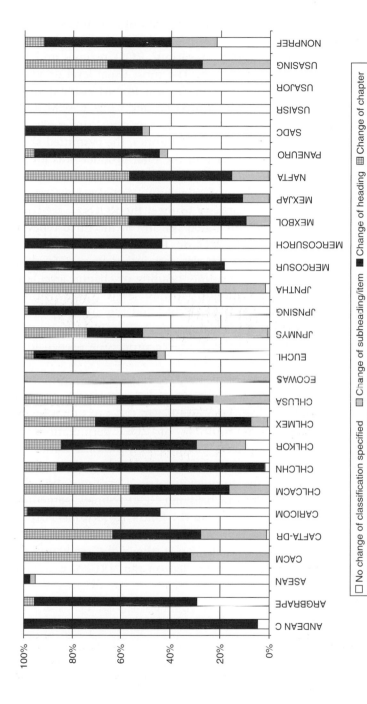

Figure 7.1. Distribution of CTC criteria by agreement, selected RTAs

Source: Authors' calculations on the basis of RTA texts.

level of the VC criterion in the tariff subheadings governed by VC (including combinations of VC with CTC, and VC when employed as an alternative to a CTC criterion) in various ROO regimes and the different calculation methods set forth. The most usual level of VC is 40–50 per cent, whether defined as maximum import content or as RVC. However, in the US–Chile RTA, CAFTA and Chile–CACM RTA, RVC is generally set at lower levels of 30–35 per cent; conversely, for some products in the Paneuro and SADC regimes, the permitted share of non-originating inputs in the price of the final product is as low as 15–30 per cent (roughly equivalent to a 70–85 per cent RVC requirement). Differences in the method of calculation can also have crucial implications for the exporters' capacity to meet the ROOs.

ROOs can specify requirements based on any of the three types of criteria mentioned earlier (CTC, VC or TECH) or a combination thereof. The CTC and VC criteria can also vary internally, as CTC rules can be specified at the item, subheading, heading or chapter level, and can include exceptions and/or additions at these levels as well. The VC criteria can specify different value thresholds, and can also vary in the required calculation method. A rule can thus combine these elements in different permutations to define the degree of processing needed for a product to qualify as originating.

The various ROOs employed in the seventy-four regimes around the world studied in this chapter use a total of 211 different combinations of ROO criteria. Figure 7.2 collapses the number of types of ROOs by the various regimes, analysing the number of ROO permutations by regime.[20] The detailed, descriptive typology – and the variation across ROO regimes – is a useful gateway to understanding the political economy of ROOs (and of the complexity of ROO regimes discussed below) as well as the difficulties of bridging ROO regimes, something we discuss with a more analytical eye in the following sections. NAFTA is the most complex of the agreements in the sample, followed by the two agreements most closely modelled on it, those of Canada and the US with Chile. Other agreements modelled on the NAFTA, as well as

---

imposes a ceiling of 40–50 per cent on non-originating components of the ex-works price of the final product. The stand-alone import content ROOs are used particularly frequently for optics, transportation equipment, and machinery and electrical equipment.

[20] Permutations are based on Harris's (2007) categorizations of change of classification, addition, exception, value test, technical requirement, and alternative criteria components (See Appendix C.2).

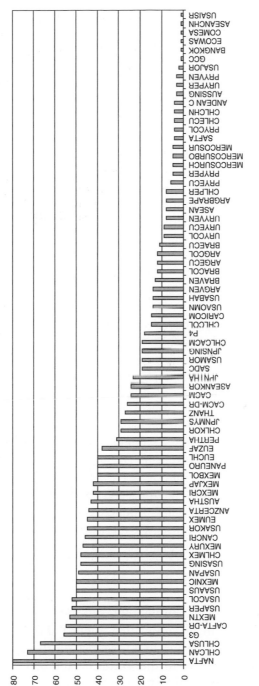

Figure 7.2 ROO permutations
Source: Authors' calculations on the basis of RTA texts.

the EU's agreements, are generally the most complex. Agreements within South America, Africa and Asia are generally the simplest.

Regime-wide ROOs

Besides product-level ROOs, the different ROO regimes can be compared by their general, regime-wide ROOs that apply similarly to nearly all goods with a regime. Table 7.2B in Appendix B contrasts the various ROO regimes by three key regime-wide ROOs – *de minimis*, cumulation and certification. While we do not analyse these ROOs in detail in this chapter, the point to keep in mind is that ROO regimes are immensely complex even beyond the product-specific ROOs. As such, measures of ROO types, as well as of restrictiveness of product-specific rules, should be used as but one indicator when analysing ROO regimes.

De minimis

EU ROO regimes feature a higher *de minimis* (at 10 per cent) than NAFTA and some other RTAs in the Americas; though most of the newer RTAs apply the higher level (US–Chile, CAFTA, US–Colombia, US–Peru), where the *de minimis* level is the same as in Paneuro. Meanwhile, there is no *de minimis* rule in MERCOSUR's RTAs or in most RTAs in Asia and Africa. However, the principle does have exceptions in most regimes: for example, the EU's *de minimis* does not apply to textiles and apparel, except for allowing an 8 per cent *de minimis* of the total weight of textile materials in mixed textile products. In the EU–South Africa RTA, *de minimis* is set at 15 per cent but excludes fish and crustaceans, tobacco products, and certain meat products and alcoholic beverages. NAFTA *de minimis* is also calculated based on weight rather than value for textiles and apparel, and does not extend to the production of dairy produce; edible products of animal origin; citrus fruit and juice; instant coffee; cocoa products; and some machinery and mechanical appliances, such as air conditioners and refrigerators (Reyna, 1995: 115–17). Many of these exceptions also appear in subsequent US, Canadian and Mexican RTAs.

Cumulation

The EU's Paneuro system of cumulation applied since 1997 draws a clear distinction between the EU ROO regimes on the one hand, and most ROO regimes elsewhere in the world, on the other. In concrete terms, the system enables producers to use components originating in any of the participating countries without losing the preferential status of the final product. This provision is only available, however, when these countries also have RTAs in force with each other, which is not yet true in many cases. The European Economic Association (EEA) agreement between the EU and EFTA also permits full cumulation.

The EU's extra-regional agreements do not form part of the Paneuro system, yet some cases allow for extended cumulation. The EU–South Africa RTA allows both parties to cumulate diagonally with the ACP states. In addition, it incorporates the 'single territory' concept, whereby South Africa can calculate working or processing carried out within the Southern Africa Customs Union (SACU) area as if these had been performed in South Africa (but not in the EU). The EU's agreements with Mexico and Chile, on the other hand, do not contain provisions for cumulation from any countries other than the direct signatories. The hypothetical reasons why these two agreements, despite lacking access to the Paneuro system of cumulation, still adopted the Paneuro ROOs include the EU's desire to minimize transaction costs for its customs and exporters operating in multiple RTA theatres at once, and/or the parties' hypothetical desire to ensure rapid accession to the Paneuro system of cumulation at a future date (as identical ROOs would be required for such an accession to occur).

There are various examples of extended cumulation that is not extensive enough to be properly considered diagonal. In the SPARTECA agreement, Australia and New Zealand allow members of the South Pacific Forum islands to cumulate among themselves and still receive preferential treatment. The Forum islands may not, however, cumulate inputs from New Zealand to export to Australia, or vice versa, as trade between Australia and New Zealand is governed by the ANZCERTA agreement (which does not provide for cumulation of Forum country originating inputs).[21]

For reasons probably more political than economic, cumulation in US agreements with Israel and Jordan is similarly tangled and limited. The US–Israel RTA permits cumulation of inputs from the West Bank and the Gaza Strip, but not Jordan. Prior to the negotiation of an RTA with Jordan, the US established a classification of qualifying industrial zones (QIZ) with Jordan and also with Egypt. This programme allowed for cumulation of inputs from Israel, the West Bank and Gaza, but not

---

[21] The ANZCERTA rules were completely renegotiated in 2006 with the new rules going into force in 2007.

between Jordan and Egypt. The subsequent RTA between Jordan and the US includes rules that permit cumulation only bilaterally, but the QIZ programme remains in effect, allowing continuation of the cumulation of inputs from Israel and the Palestinian territories. The QIZ, however, are still a unilateral concession of the US, not a bilateral treaty obligation like the RTA. The Canada–Israel RTA permits cumulation with the two countries' common RTA partners as of the agreement's entry into force – which, as it turns out, includes the United States and no other. Unlike the political issues that undoubtedly complicate the US agreements, this extension of cumulation most likely accommodates the existing integration of Canadian industry with US suppliers.

The DR–CAFTA agreement between the US, Central America and the Dominican Republic contains provisions for cumulation of inputs from Canada and Mexico in the production of garments of woven fabric (HS chapter 62). These provisions are subject to the negotiation of origin-verification protocols different from those in NAFTA, as well as adjustments to the rules in the agreements of the Central American countries with Mexico. Thus far, Mexico has participated actively in the negotiation and implementation of these changes, while Canada has shown less interest. This provision is available to the Dominican Republic for a transition period, by the end of which they must negotiate an RTA with Mexico in order for it to remain in effect.[22]

Elsewhere in Latin America, there are other attempts at extended cumulation. One case in point is the recent agreements between MERCOSUR and the Andean Community. While these agreements share a common origin text, including a provision for cumulation that includes all nine countries (including Bolivia), the product-level rules were negotiated bilaterally, resulting in sixteen full sets of rules. Because these rules are not uniform across bilateral relationships, there are many opportunities for 'triangulation' in which minor processes undertaken in one country can confer origin for purposes of export to a given partner, when those same processes would not confer origin for the same partner if undertaken in a third member of the group.[23] While there have been some initial attempts to mitigate this problem, no clear solution has yet been found.

Singapore has pursued innovative mechanisms in its RTAs that, while not extending cumulation properly speaking, do allow for greater participation of non-members in the production of originating goods. The

---

[22] The beginning of these negotiations has already been announced.
[23] See Table 8 of Cornejo and Harris (2007) for an analysis of the differences in the product-level rules of these agreements.

Table 7.1. *Operation of outward processing in Singapore's FTAs*

Stage 1	Stage 2	Stage 3

Singapore → Foreign country → Singapore → Exported
Conventional ROOs → Stage 3 = Local content
Recognition of OP → Stage 1+ Stage 3 = Local content

main idea is centred around adding flexibility to the calculation of the value content, in order to help the many Singaporean industries that have extensive outsourcing ties to qualify for the preferential treatment provided by its RTA partners. There are two main mechanisms: outward processing (OP) and integrated sourcing initiative (ISI). OP is recognized in all of Singapore's RTAs, while ISI is incorporated in the US–Singapore FTA. The concept of OP enables Singapore to outsource part of the manufacturing process, usually the lower value-added or labour-intensive activities, to neighbouring countries, yet to count the value of Singaporean production done prior to the outsourcing activity toward local, Singaporean content when meeting the ROOs required by the export market. Table 7.1 illustrates the process.

Although the OP concept applies only to products with a value-added rule, and the value added in the non member country is not counted towards the required originating content, it is credited with having encouraged higher-value activities to be retained in Singapore, while outsourcing labour-intensive and low-value processes. For its part, ISI operating in the US–Singapore RTA applies to non-sensitive, globalized sectors, such as information technologies. Under the scheme, certain IT components and medical devices are not subject to ROOs when shipped from either of the parties to the RTA.[24] The scheme is designed to reflect the economic realities of globally distributed production linkages, and to further encourage US multinationals to take advantage of ASEAN countries' respective comparative advantages.

Certification

EU ROO regimes employ the public certification method, requiring the use of a movement certificate that is issued by the exporting country

---

[24] Most of these products are subject to the Information Technology Agreement (ITA) and thus have zero MFN tariffs.

government once application has been made by the exporter or the exporter's competent agency. However, the EU regimes provide for an alternative method of certification by interested parties – the invoice declaration – for 'approved exporters' who make frequent shipments, and are authorized by the customs authorities of the exporting country to make invoice declarations. The fact that provision has been made for the authorization of interested party certification implies that there are recognized cost savings in avoiding the governmental certification process. The need to be authorized, however, may in some cases serve as something of a barrier to entry for new exporters.

Meanwhile, NAFTA and a number of other RTAs in the Americas, as well as the Chile–Republic of Korea RTA, rely on certification by interested parties, which entails that the exporter's signing of the certificate suffices as an affirmation that the items covered by it qualify as originating. In CAFTA, the importer claiming preferential tariff treatment, rather than the exporter, is the party ultimately responsible for declaring that the good is originating. While this system places the burden of proof on importers, and is thus the simplest and least costly for exporters, it opens the door to more potential abuse and fraud. As such, the cost to customs of establishing and operating an effective origin verification regime may be more significant.

Agreements based on the LAIA model, such as MERCOSUR, and the Andean Community, as well as CARICOM, ASEAN, ANZCERTA, SAFTA, the Bangkok Agreement, Japan–Singapore, and ECOWAS, require certification by a public body or a private umbrella entity approved as a certifying agency by the government. The exporter is required to furnish the certifying agency with a legal declaration of the origin of the product, which is then certified. This method has the advantages of review by a relatively disinterested third party, as well as the potential for certifying entities being more familiar with the production processes than government agents might be, but with similar costs to traders to the governmental certification method.

4   Restrictiveness and divergence: the scorecard

There are two main concerns voiced over ROOs: restrictiveness and divergence. Restrictive ROOs can introduce undue barriers to trade between RTA members and non-members. Divergence across ROO regimes can increase the transaction costs for countries and companies dealing on two or more RTA fronts simultaneously. These two concepts are linked: divergence matters more when ROOs are restrictive.

The manifold ROO combinations within and across ROO regimes present a challenge for cross-regime comparisons – that is, for observing restrictiveness and divergence. This section strives to overcome the complexity by quantifying ROO types and ROO restrictiveness. The first part discusses, and subsequently measures, restrictiveness and variation of restrictiveness across products *within* regimes, or complexity. The second part centres on discussing and measuring differences *across* ROO regimes.

Restrictiveness and complexity

The capacity of ROOs to affect economic decisions depends on the degree to which they restrict the options of economic actors and the size of the tariff preference to which compliance with these rules gives access. The degree to which ROOs restrict the options of producers/exporters is here called 'restrictiveness'. Two concepts are key for better understanding ROO restrictiveness – input pool and geographical pool.

In terms of input pool, ROOs establish for each product which of its inputs and/or what fraction of its inputs may be 'non-originating' in order for the product to retain access to the preferential tariff treatment established by the agreement. The fewer restrictions placed on the use of non-originating inputs, whether qualitative or quantitative, the more 'open' the preferential bloc is to the ROW. The more open the ROO regime, the bigger the input pool.

As for the geographical pool, any origin regime (implicitly or explicitly) establishes the list of countries whose originating products can be considered originating for purposes of the agreement (this might also be referred to as the 'cumulation zone'). In the case of most RTAs, this list is simply the set of direct signatories to the agreement. Some agreements, however, will also specify additional countries whose originating products may be used as inputs in one or more direct signatories, with these inputs being treated as originating in the latter. This is the case of the treatment of subregional integration groups in the EU's GSP scheme, and the bilateral agreements that make up the Paneuro cumulation system. The larger the list of countries whose products qualify as originating in the origin regime of a given RTA, the larger the implicit geographical pool. The longer the list of countries and the larger the countries are, the larger the geographical pool.

Rules of origin thus determine both the openness of a bloc and its size, which, in turn, play a role in defining restrictiveness. Increasing the openness or size – input or geographical pool – can be expected to reduce the distortions caused by the origin regime that governs a given bloc.

Measuring restrictiveness

How to measure restrictiveness? ROOs are more restrictive as they permit less use of inputs from outside the cumulation zone, where the zone is the set of countries whose products can be considered as originating when used as inputs in later production. This concept of restrictiveness is the most easily observed, as it is expressed in the text of the rules themselves.

There are two measures based on this idea. The first is Estevadeordal (2000), which constructs a categorical variable ranging from 1 (least restrictive) to 7 (most restrictive) on the basis of NAFTA ROOs. The index can be conceptualized as an indicator of how demanding given ROOs are for an exporter. The observation rule for the index is based on two assumptions: (1) change at the level of chapter is more restrictive than change at the level of heading, and change at the level of heading is more restrictive than change at the level of subheading, and so on; and (2) VC technical requirements (such as chemical transformations) attached to a given CTC add to the ROOs' restrictiveness. Several other studies have applied variations of Estevadeordal's index, such as Anson *et al.* (2003), Cadot *et al.* (2006), Suominen (2004) and Portugal-Perez (2006), based on the same underlying logic.

The second measure is Harris (2007). It presents a significant overhaul of Estevadeordal's methodology, applying similar logic but much more precisely capturing details of the variation across products and across agreements in the definition of the rules of origin.[25] Appendix C.2 gives a detailed explanation of the calculation of these indices.

Figure 7.3 reports the restrictiveness of ROOs as calculated at the six-digit level of disaggregation in selected RTAs using Harris's measure, while Figure 7.4 displays the 'selectivity' or 'complexity' (standard deviation in ROOs) of the ROO regimes by engaging the same

---

[25] Given that these measures of restrictiveness are a function of *ex ante* restrictiveness rather than the effective restrictiveness following the implementation of the ROOs, the methodology – much like that of Garay and Cornejo (2002) – is particularly useful for endogenizing and comparing ROO regimes. The methodology allows ROOs to be analysed in terms of their characteristics rather than their effects: that is, their observed rather than their effective restrictiveness.

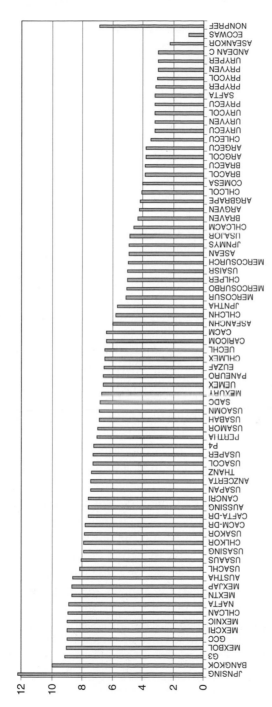

Figure 7.3 Restrictiveness of ROOs (Harris index)
Source: Authors' calculations on the basis of RTA texts.

measure. EU, Mexican, Chilean and US agreements are among the most restrictive. However, it is also the case that US agreements have become less restrictive over time: NAFTA is more restrictive than the US–Chile RTA of 2004, which is more restrictive than CAFTA of 2005, which is more restrictive than US–Peru and US–Colombia RTAs negotiated in 2006. Box 7.1 discusses these inter-temporal trends in detail.

Except for the Japan–Singapore RTA, where restrictiveness is caused by having set their default rule as wholly obtained (applicable when no rule is specified in the Annex), agreements in Asia are less restrictive, in part due to the tendency to set across-the-board VC rules.

Table 7.3B in Appendix B catalogues the sectoral restrictiveness by using Harris's measure. The data reveal that agricultural products, and textiles and apparel are marked by a particularly high restrictiveness score in each regime, which is consistent with the empirical results of Estevadeordal (2000), Suominen (2004), and Harris (2007) in that the restrictiveness of ROOs is driven by the same political economy variables that arbitrate the level of tariffs, particularly in the EU and the United States. Non-preferential ROOs exhibit similar patterns across sectors, communicating the operation of political economy dynamics also at the multilateral level. Suominen (2004) finds that weighting the sectoral restrictiveness values by trade produces very similar results – which may in and of itself be an indication that stringent ROOs stifle commerce.[26]

Complexity of regimes

As seen in Figure 7.2, ROO regimes can be immensely complex, containing numerous different ROOs and ROO types. Such complexity, also referred to as sectoral selectivity in ROOs, presents a further caveat for the analysis of restrictiveness and divergence, for a number of reasons. First, more complex ROO regimes will be more difficult to administer. If a country is party to several regimes that each feature across-the-board rules (zero complexity), there will never be a problem of confusion as to the rule applicable to a given product, or incentives to misclassify a product to take advantage of a different rule.

Compare this to a country party to one or, worse yet, several RTAs that each feature complex ROO regimes. An example might be NAFTA or the EU's ROO regimes, both among the most complex regimes in the world. Clearly, administering these rules of origin will require customs

---

[26] See Suominen (2004) for weighted ROOs.

BOX 7.1 GOOD NEWS ON ROOS IN THE AMERICAS

While ROO regimes may carry hidden protectionism, an examination of their evolution over the past few years in the Americas gives reason for optimism. First, NAFTA ROOs have been under a liberalization process.[27] The Working Group in charge of the rules of origin review process has completed two phases of ROO simplification, covering such sectors as alcoholic beverages, petroleum/topped crude, esters of glycerol, pearl jewellery, headphones with microphones, chassis fitted with engines, photocopiers, chemicals, pharmaceuticals, plastics and rubber, motor vehicles and their parts, footwear, and copper. The reforms, once complete, are estimated to extend to more than US$100 billion in trilateral trade.

Second, US ROO regimes have progressively evolved toward a more liberal framework from NAFTA to the US–Chile RTA, CAFTA, and on to US–Colombia and US–Peru RTAs. The latter three agreements incorporate simpler, more practical, and less restrictive product-specific rules of origin than NAFTA did.

Third, the various regimes designed after NAFTA are fairly similar, in both the types of rules of origin specified and their level of restrictiveness. This can alleviate any potential transaction costs for NAFTA-model adherents that export under preferential terms to two or more NAFTA-model RTAs.

Fourth, the NAFTA style regimes contain terms that alleviate the restrictiveness of product-specific ROOs. This helps alleviate the compliance costs of the product-specific rules of origin. Even more encouraging is the movement towards somewhat higher *de minimis* levels and the willingness to experiment with diagonal cumulation. CAFTA stipulates that the member countries can use materials for apparel (Chapter 62) from Mexico or Canada as if they were CAFTA-originating.

Fifth, the NAFTA model has now been adopted in numerous free trade agreements. The current adherents will thus find it fairly easy to negotiate, adopt and implement future free trade agreements. The costs of adjusting to ROOs should thus have been incrementally diminishing for a good part of the hemisphere.

Finally, negotiators on rules of origin throughout the Americas, and particularly in RTAs based on the NAFTA model, have proved their willingness to revise existing ROO regimes to make them more flexible. NAFTA's review of its rules of origin is the clearest example, demonstrating commitment to keeping North America's rules

---

[27] The initial set of revised NAFTA rules of origin took effect on 1 January 2003; see 'Regulations Amending the NAFTA Rule of Origin Regulations' (2003). In July 2004, the trade ministers of the NAFTA countries instructed the trilateral Working Group on Rules of Origin to extend the liberalization drive to all items with a zero most-favoured-nation tariff for all of the NAFTA members. The August 2007 joint declaration of the Montebello Summit from the three NAFTA countries' heads of state endorsed 'an analysis of the free trade agreements that each country has negotiated subsequent to the NAFTA, beginning with those in the western hemisphere, including opportunities for innovative provisions on rules of origin'.

BOX 7.1 (*cont.*)

of origin apace with changes in technology and the globalization of production, and potentially marking a growing role of export interests in setting trade policy.

More generally, the precision of the NAFTA-model rules of origin can be viewed as superior to the vaguely defined and subjective rules of origin of the past. Because the NAFTA regime is based on the change in tariff classification, it provides a fairer, more transparent and more easily verifiable ROO model than regimes based on value content, which paradoxically can be hard to meet in countries with low production costs and are difficult to implement in the face of fluctuations in exchange rates and changes in production costs. Precise rules of origin do not need to be restrictive; the NAFTA review process may well yield rules of origin that are both precise and flexible.

authorities to take much more care with identification of the correct rule and correct classification of the product.

When there are overlapping regimes that are complex, such as Chile's RTAs with the United States, the EU, the Republic of Korea and Mexico, the ROOs for any given product may vary across these regimes, increasing the likelihood that firms will be required to adjust their sourcing strategies to accommodate different export markets.[28] These costs could be significant.[29]

Figure 7.4 sets out to analyse the complexity of ROOs within various regimes. The MERCOSUR model pertinent to MERCOSUR–Chile and MERCOSUR–Bolivia RTAs is more general, yet still exhibits more cross-sectoral variation in the restrictiveness of ROOs than the LAIA model marked by the across-the-board change of heading ROOs. The generality of the LAIA model is replicated by most Asian and African ROO regimes. However, some newer RTAs – such as the Chile–Republic of Korea RTA and SADC – feature high levels of cross-sectoral variation in ROOs.

Two interesting points arise from a comparison of Figures 7.2 and 7.4. First, regarding US agreements, note that while NAFTA ranks first in Figure 7.2, based on the number of different combinations of qualification criteria, the more recent US agreements (with Panama, Australia, Singapore, Colombia, Peru, Central America and Chile) feature higher standard deviations of the restrictiveness index. This implies

---

[28] Most of Chile's exports consist of products that are wholly obtained in Chile and therefore will meet any origin requirement. The complexity of the origin regimes might, however, serve as an impediment to the diversification of Chile's exports.

[29] The IDB is currently undertaking a survey of firms in several countries in an attempt to begin to quantify these costs.

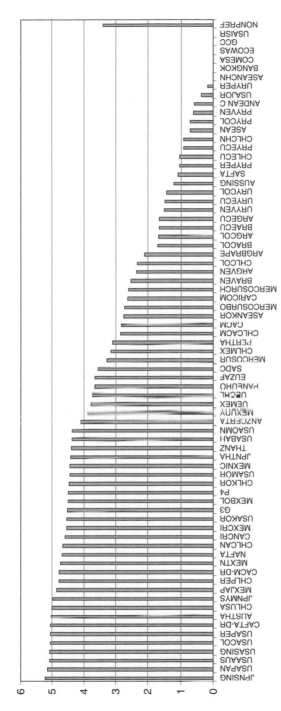

Figure 7.4 Complexity (standard deviation of ROOs) in selected RTAs
Source: Authors' calculations on the basis of RTA texts.

that NAFTA's eighty permutations all group tightly around a more restrictive mean, while subsequent agreements must feature a significant relaxing of the restrictiveness of many products, resulting in a lower average restrictiveness as well as a higher standard deviation.

Second, note that Japan–Singapore ranks first in standard deviation, but in the middle based on the number of rule combinations. This is due to that agreement's specification that all products for which no specific rule is specified in the Annex must be wholly obtained.

Caveats and stylized facts

There are some important real-life caveats to the above measures, and thus to the policy recommendations that can be fashioned on ROOs: the usefulness of distinguishing effective restrictiveness from observed restrictiveness, and understanding the complexity of ROOs as a function of the underlying complexity of the RTA trade among the member countries.

Observed vs. effective restrictiveness

It is important to note here that restrictiveness on paper is one thing: ROOs that are restrictive by the above measures may not be so when the 'real' input and geographical pools are taken into consideration. There are two key issues that qualify ROO restrictiveness, but that are not incorporated in the calculations above.

The first is the fact that ROO regimes employ several regime-wide mechanisms, such as *de minimis* and cumulation, that can add flexibility to the application of the product-specific ROOs and consequently attenuate the restrictiveness of ROOs – and even render them non-binding. Suominen (2004) and Estevadeordal and Suominen (2008) find that many such measures indeed alleviate the negative trade effects of restrictive product-specific ROOs. Several regimes have also experimented with innovative mechanisms to alleviate supply shortages and to help the developing member countries to comply with ROOs.[30]

Second, a ROO is 'effectively restrictive' to the extent that it limits both the input and geographical pools, thus *increasing the cost of production* by requiring firms to use higher-cost regional inputs. This concept of 'effective' restrictiveness is less observable, as it requires knowledge of the input–output structure of each product, as well as the scale and efficiency of production of the relevant inputs in each country

---

[30] See, for instance, Suominen (2004) or Estevadeordal and Suominen (2006) for details.

within the cumulation zone. However, this is the sense of restrictiveness that matters economically, both for the degree of liberalization achieved within an RTA and for the degree of impact on third parties. As such, it arbitrates the degree to which a producer can globalize production without forgoing the preferential access in an RTA.

Imagine trade in roasted ground coffee. In an agreement between the US and Canada, a rule that requires that all coffee products be derived from originating beans would be highly restrictive, effectively cancelling any preferential tariff treatment, as there is no significant production of coffee beans in either country. The same rule applied to trade between the US and Colombia, on the other hand, while still binding on producers of specialized blends of coffee, would be significantly less onerous, as Colombia is a major global producer of coffee.

As discussed above, 'real' or effective restrictiveness thus depends on the availability of efficient input supplies in the RTA member countries, which one would expect to be correlated with the size of the integrating economies. Larger economies are more likely to produce a greater variety of products on a larger scale, and thus with (probably) greater efficiency. This means that an RTA that covers a larger economic area (say, North America or Europe) is relatively less likely to exclude the global least-cost producer of any given intermediate than is an RTA that covers a smaller economic zone (say, Central America).

This issue of the size of the cumulation zone is of crucial importance when analysing the utility of connecting or multilateralizing ROO regimes. However, since effective restrictiveness is so difficult to observe, any broad analysis must move forward with measures of observed restrictiveness (that is, restrictiveness as inferred from the text of the rule alone) as a useful proxy, but bearing in mind that it is a proxy and not an ideal measure. Figure 7.5 illustrates the relationship between restrictiveness and the size of the cumulation zone, measured as combined GDP of the member countries.

A clear stylized fact is that observed restrictiveness is increasing in the size of the cumulation zone. There are two alternative conclusions that can be drawn from this. One is that large dominant partners such as the US and the EU tend to dictate more restrictive rules of origin in their RTAs, while developing countries tend to negotiate less restrictive regimes. This interpretation is perhaps the most popular,[31] and it is certainly not difficult to find anecdotal evidence to further support it.

---

[31] See, for instance, Cadot *et al.* (2006).

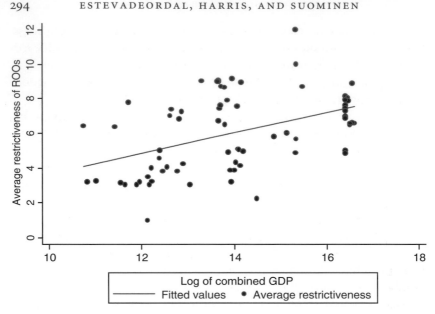

Figure 7.5 Restrictiveness vs. cumulation zone

However, this explanation ignores the fact that observed restrictiveness is not strictly linked to effective restrictiveness across agreements. A rule with high observed restrictiveness in an agreement with the US or Europe will still allow a firm to source inputs from the vast partner country in the cumulation zone, and the likelihood of that rule precluding the use of inputs from the global low-cost source is lower (though not necessarily zero) than in the case of a rule with the same observed restrictiveness in an RTA joining two small developing countries.

The alternative conclusion to be drawn is that average *effective* restrictiveness could have no relationship, or even a negative relationship, with the economic size of the cumulation zone. This is because the greater availability of inputs implied by the larger economy of the cumulation zone results in rules with greater *observed* restrictiveness in fact having lower *effective* restrictiveness.

Complexity of rules and of trade

The complexity of ROOs – product-by-product differentiation of ROOs within a regime – could be hypothesized to be directly related to the complexity of the bilateral trade relationship (Harris, 2007). It is broadly recognized that the level of restrictiveness of the rules of origin is affected by political economy variables. Regardless of the specific political economy model employed, the variables that will likely determine the rule of origin for a particular product will focus on the levels of its production in the participating countries, as well as the scale and efficiency of production of its inputs both within and outside the cumulation zone. Consequently, the number of products for which the political economy pressures reach some minimum threshold for influencing the negotiations of the product-specific rule will depend on the number of products actively traded among the participating countries.

The complexity of the origin regime (as measured by the standard deviation of ROO restrictiveness within an agreement[32]) is thus dependent on the complexity of the pattern of trade among the members of the RTA (as measured by the number of HS subheadings in which products are traded). For the purposes of the arguments presented here, the political economy forces that drive ROOs will apply to higher numbers of products when ROOs under negotiation govern the preferential trade of larger blocs (with consequently more complex trading relationships). This will hypothetically create a tendency to more complex origin regimes in RTAs, with more diversified sets of traded products. Figure 7.6 illustrates the degree to which this is observed in the data.

The strong outliers in this relationship are interesting cases. The points with low numbers of traded subheadings and high variation in rules of origin are most notably Mexico–Bolivia (85 products), US–Morocco (527 products), and Canada–Costa Rica (1,050 products). The first and third of these are agreements by NAFTA members that were negotiated shortly after the conclusion of the NAFTA negotiations, when those rules seemed the most appropriate (note that both feature net-cost-based VC rules, a calculation method that has largely fallen out of use in recent agreements except for automotive products). The US–Morocco agreement features an across-the-board VC requirement except for textiles and a small set of products that seem to have been of particular interest to Morocco (some fruits and vegetables, coffee, and some auto parts). This large difference in the restrictiveness of the general rule and those products identified for special treatment seems to be generating the especially high standard deviation figures.

---

[32] The same results obtain when complexity is measured by the number of different criteria combinations used in the set of product-level rules that we describe in Figure 7.2.

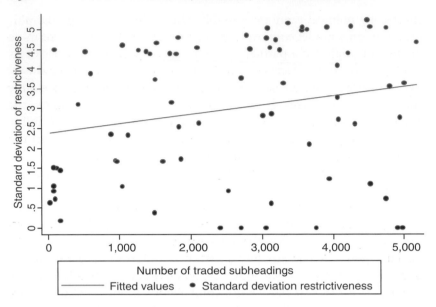

Figure 7.6 Complexity of ROOs and trade

In the opposite corner, the notable outliers are the larger Asian agreements (ASEAN, ASEAN–China, Bangkok Agreement) and the US–Israel agreement. All of these agreements feature across-the-board VC rules, except ASEAN, which has a relatively small number of specific rules for some products (primarily steel, textiles and wood). This choice of regime is a bit harder to explain. A possible reason might be that many of these countries maintain relatively low MFN tariffs or very limited preferential tariff liberalization, and so the levels of preference are quite low, necessitating only minimum rules.[33] This is backed up by anecdotal evidence of relatively low utilization rates in ASEAN.

We thus have a second stylized fact that the complexity of rules of origin is increasing in the diversity of products traded among RTA members. The more product-specific interests there are to satisfy in the origin negotiations, the more different outcomes we are likely to find.

Restrictiveness and complexity: the key policy issues

The main important point here, and key to capturing our policy recommendations, is that restrictiveness and complexity within regimes

---

[33] See, for example, Inama (2005).

imply that as regions of overlapping RTAs pursue convergence, forming groups with greater economic size and variety of traded goods, there could be a tendency towards greater observed restrictiveness and complexity. Both of these are potentially problematic for the international trading system. Greater observed restrictiveness, while not necessarily implying greater effective restrictiveness, still amounts to increasing barriers to trade between regions, a problem in terms of GATT Article XXIV, which precludes RTAs that raise barriers to third parties. Greater complexity of the origin regimes simultaneously implies increasing difficulty of administration and thus greater potential uncertainty, especially in developing countries.

To be sure, the caveats have their caveats. As noted above, the theory may not always play out in practice. The observed restrictiveness did not really change in the EU's ROO harmonization and pursuit of the Paneuro system, since the new ROOs were remarkably similar to the old ones. It may not necessarily occur in other regions, particularly if and when countries are already loosening their ROOs, as is the case of the United States. Moreover, economic dynamics, such as the expansion of global supply chains, can strengthen industry lobbies interested in ever looser ROOs.

Moreover, none of this is to say that the benefits of expanded cumulation (and the potential reduction in *effective* restrictiveness) within a convergence zone would not outweigh these potential problems. However, careful consideration of these problems ahead of time can lead to strategies for mitigating their effects.

Divergence

ROO restrictiveness can be consequential to, and even prohibitive of, trade in any one regime. However, ROOs also feature a systemic problem of divergence across regimes. To our knowledge, except for IDB (forthcoming) there are no empirical attempts to measure the costs of ROO divergence. Yet, besides the distortionary effects of ROOs in any given regime, the divergence can impart economic costs, at least in principle. The most acute costs of divergence are two-fold.

First, the proliferation of RTAs can 'balkanize' the global trading system. If the various agreements carry widely distinct ROOs, they can impose undue transaction costs on traders, investors and governments dealing in several RTA markets simultaneously (as opposed to the counterfactual case where the rules of the various RTAs are exactly the same).

Firms dealing on different RTA fronts may need to alter their production patterns to meet the idiosyncratic rules of origin and other requirements of each of the different RTAs; customs administering imports from numerous RTA partners may have to refer to multiple, divergent sets of rules instead of a single document applicable to all RTAs.

The administration costs for customs are also likely to be relevant for traders. For example, complications for customs can result in delays in shipments clearing customs, which increases the time to market for finished goods, and can increase inventory costs when the delayed shipments are intermediate goods. Also, complications in administration increase the likelihood of errors in the application of rules, and thus potential denial of preference for originating products, or uneven competition from firms that benefit from errors in the application of rules. In general, these problems can increase uncertainty for traders, depressing trade. All of these problems will likely hit traders in developing countries disproportionately, as theirs are the customs services more likely to be unprepared to handle the complicated administrative tasks.

Second, ROO divergence risks the rise of de facto hub-and-spoke systems centred around a few hub countries, where the potential cost savings from cumulation of production among the spokes remains untapped. While this arrangement may hold some benefits for the hub country, the spokes will be at an increasing disadvantage, as they will be unable to use inputs from other spokes when producing for the hub market. Even in cases where the hub-and-spoke pattern is less clear (i.e. where all bilateral pairs have RTAs, and there are multiple 'hubs'), the barriers to cumulation can generate significant inefficiencies and reduced trade. Indeed, except in the case of the EU, which has very little variation in rules across agreements, even the 'hubs', including the US, have generally negotiated significantly different rules of origin across their agreements. While these countries are expected to have customs administrations that can manage these variations, the differences could still cause difficulties for producers.

Again, both balkanization and hub-and-spoke problems are less relevant when ROOs are non-binding – non-restrictive or in the presence of zero MFN tariffs. They become increasingly relevant when ROOs are binding *and* when the various ROO regimes differ from each other.

Figures 7.7(a) and (b) illustrate these issues. Rules of origin effectively set up walls around RTA members that prevent the use of some inputs in each product. Multiple overlapping RTAs with divergent origin

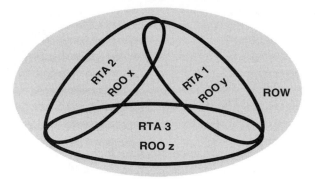

Figure 7.7(a) Divergence with high restrictiveness

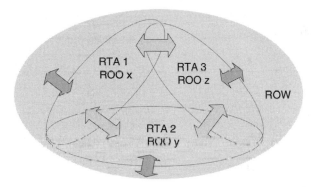

Figure 7.7(b) Divergence with low restrictiveness

regimes thus entail many such walls to free and efficient sourcing of inputs. When the rules are more restrictive, the walls are higher (as depicted by the heavier lines around each RTA in Figure 7.7(a)), and efficient allocation of resources is even more difficult. In this sense, then, more restrictive rules of origin will accentuate the divergence problem for countries that have entered into multiple RTAs, as both the number and height of the walls will be higher.

Figure 7.7(b), on the other hand, depicts the same set of RTAs but with lower restrictiveness. In this case the ROO barriers to trade are lower, both across RTAs and between members and ROW. Inputs can be sourced efficiently, raising the global gains from trade.

Measuring divergence

Divergence is due to the different needs of different producers in different cumulation zones, not carelessness in negotiation, but can also be expected to generate costs and uncertainty in practice. How divergent are agreements? We strive to answer this question by comparing ROO regimes to each other product-by-product by using Harris's (2007) restrictiveness index.

Figure 7.8 reports the frequency with which the most common rule, i.e. the 'mode rule', for each product within a 'family' of agreements is applied across those agreements. For example, if four out of five agreements within a family specify the same rule for product X, then that implies an 80 per cent similarity. The average of this measure across all products is reported in the figure.

In the Paneuro family of agreements, on average nearly all the agreements apply the same rule[34] for a given product. In the US family, on the other hand, just over half of the agreements will apply the same rule for any given product. In the African agreements, in fact, the 25 per cent outcome actually implies complete divergence, as there are only four agreements included in the analysis, and their rules never coincide.

On the other hand, the Americas–Asia family of transcontinental agreements, as well as the Mexico family, show significant similarities, with over half and nearly two-thirds of agreements coinciding on average, respectively. For the full global set of agreements, on average about one-third of agreements' rules will coincide on any given product.

It is fair to point out that for the countries around which these 'families' of RTAs are defined, some RTAs are more important than others. For Mexico, approximately two-thirds of imports are from the US and nearly 85 per cent of exports are destined for the US.[35] Thus the bulk of Mexico's trade is under a single origin regime. Nonetheless, there remains a third of imports and a sixth of exports that must be administered under MFN and a significant variety of differing origin regimes. Even among agreements with regimes modelled on NAFTA, there is a meaningful variation of rules. On average three of Mexico's

---

[34] By 'the same rule' we thus mean 'rules with the same level of restrictiveness', which is not necessarily the same thing. Containing twenty-eight different measures for ROO restrictiveness, and thus abstracting from the ROO typology (with 211 ROOs), the index provides a solid, and in our view sufficiently nuanced, basis for capturing cross-regime divergences. See Appendix I for a list of agreements included in each group.

[35] Based on 2004 IMF Direction of Trade (IMFDOT) figures.

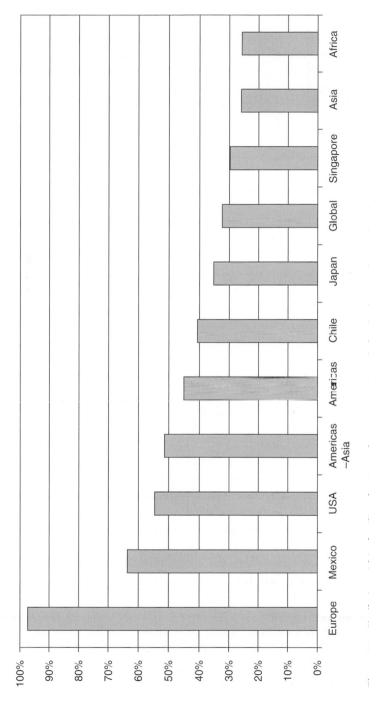

Figure 7.8. Similarity within families: fraction of agreements in each family sharing the mode rule
Source: Authors' calculations on the basis of RTA texts.

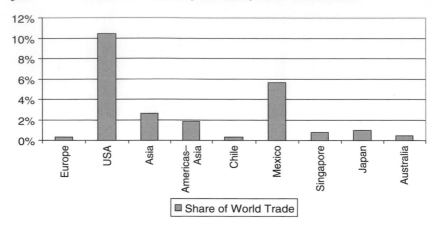

Figure 7.9 Share of world trade covered by agreements by family (2004 data)
Source: Authors' calculations based on IMFDOT.

nine agreements have rules that deviate from the 'mode' rule. Among the twelve US agreements this fraction is closer to a half. Even though some RTAs will be more important than others for a given country, except for the uniformity imposed by the EU, firms wishing to take advantage of multiple RTAs will most likely have to confront different rules.

Figure 7.9 shows the share of world trade covered by the agreements included in each family listed in Figure 7.8. Intra-European trade is not counted as part of the Europe family, as this trade is not subject to rules of origin in the customs union. The USA and Mexico families both include intra-NAFTA trade.

Table 7.2 furthers the analysis of rule of origin divergence by showing the number of agreements and the average frequency of the mode rules. It also displays the restrictiveness of the mode rules (a restrictiveness of 6 is equivalent to a change in heading rule or a VC requirement of 50 per cent), as well as characterizing the average deviations from the mode.

This average deviation from the mode gives an indication as to how these rules are negotiated. In the analysis of the complexity of ROOs, above, we showed that countries tend to have more selective rules when they trade more products, and hence have more product-specific interests to satisfy internally. Here, we can see whether satisfying these interests tends to lead to more or less restrictive rules on average.

Divergence from the mode rules within a family in the Chilean, Mexican and US cases is on average towards less restrictive rules. This is

Table 7.2. *Similarity of ROOs within families*

	Number of agreements	Average frequency of mode	Average restrictiveness of mode	Average deviation from mode
Africa	4	1.0	3.80	−0.02
America–Asia	7	3.6	7.48	−0.15
America	39	17.6	5.43	0.37
Asia	11	2.9	6.47	0.84
Chile	8	3.3	7.29	−0.72
Europe	4	3.9	6.92	0.00
Japan	4	1.4	7.10	0.58
Mexico	9	5.7	8.52	−0.48
Singapore	4	1.2	8.71	0.30
USA	12	6.5	7.63	−0.39
Global	69	22.4	6.27	−0.14

Source: Authors' calculations on the basis of RTA texts.

also true for trans-Pacific agreements and in the overall global case, though to a lesser degree. The opposite occurs in the Singapore, Japan, Asia and Americas families. In the case of the Asian, Japanese and Singaporean families, the relatively low frequency of the mode rules makes generalizations even more difficult. The tendency to deviate upwards here may be due to the fact that these countries often have origin regimes that consist of a fixed rule applying to all products which is generally fairly lax,[36] and apply exceptions to this rule only in cases where additional protection is desired.

While speculation on explanations for these results is likely to lead to some oversimplifications, it is worth offering an informed hypothesis. The US, Mexican and Chilean agreements generally follow a NAFTA-like model. Furthermore, negotiation of product-level rules in this model can be quite tedious, as anyone who has even tried to read them can imagine. Thus, when negotiating a new agreement, rules for products of no special interest to either party are likely to simply be copied from one or the other party's previous agreements. Deviations from the rules of previous agreements is likely to occur mainly in the

---

[36] Except Japan–Singapore, where the default rule is effectively a wholly obtained requirement except where otherwise stipulated.

cases of products that are of particular interest to one or the other party. What is interesting here is that these deviations are generally towards less restrictive rather than more restrictive rules. While this could be due to the fact that the 'default' rules tend to be sufficiently restrictive to begin with, so that no upward deviations are usually necessary, this probably also indicates that in these cases the task of negotiators is geared more to ensuring that their exporters will be able to meet the requirements than to seeking extra protection for domestic producers.

Divergence at the sectoral level

What sectors drive the average observed divergences and similarities in ROOs *within* families? This is a policy-relevant question: the sectors where divergence within the families is least should be the low-hanging fruit for negotiators in any attempts to bridge differences in ROOs across regimes.

Figure 7.10 shows the degree of similarity in ROOs within RTA families of the Americas, Asia, Europe and United States. The only divergence in the homogeneous European family arises from ROOs in plastics (section 7), textiles and footwear (sections 11 and 12) and machinery and equipment and transport equipment (sections 16–18). The 'new generation' (NG) US agreements (i.e. excluding those with Middle Eastern countries with across-the-board VC rules) are still quite diverse, with 80 per cent or more of the US agreements featuring the same ROOs in only eight of the twenty-one sectors. The Americas and Asia are even less homogeneous, rarely exceeding 50 per cent agreements coinciding on average. Table 7.1D in Appendix D details these patterns further.

Looking for similarities across families (see Appendix D), we find that generally textiles (section 11) have the most restrictive rules, though not so much in the case of the European rules, where agricultural products (sections 1–2) have more restrictive rules. Chilean and Japanese families also have restrictiveness peaks in agriculture. In most agreements, restrictiveness is lower in chemicals, plastics, and machinery and equipment.

Comparing US, EU and non-preferential ROOs

Given that the US and the EU are the two global poles in setting ROOs in preferential agreements, they would also hold the keys to any effective multilateral process to tackle ROOs. In principle, the more similar their ROO regimes are, the more likely would they be to find common ground in any ROO negotiation.

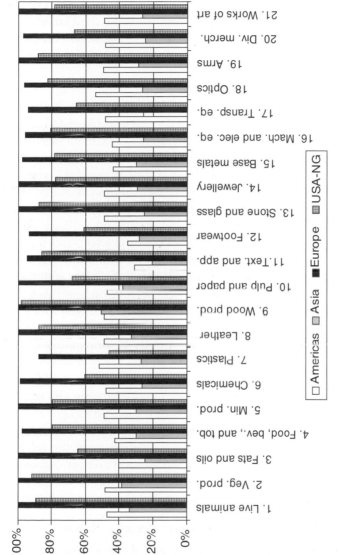

Figure 7.10 Similarity by HS section within RTA families of the Americas, Asia, Europe and the United States (percentage of agreements by family with the same ROO)

Source: Authors' calculations on the basis of RTA texts.

How divergent are US and EU ROOs? Figure 7.11 compares the most common rule for each product within the set of US agreements with the rule for that product in the Paneuro ROOs.

The overall average levels of restrictiveness of these two sets of rules are quite similar (a difference of less than 0.15 using the Harris (2007) scale). This overall average, however, masks some significant differences in certain sectors (indeed the standard deviation of the difference across all products is 5.5).

At the HS section level, the differences that stand out are in basic animal and vegetable products (1 and 2), animal and vegetable oils (3), chemical products (6), furs and hides (8), wood and paper (10), textile products (11), stone and its manufactures (13), common metals (15) and precision instruments (18).

The most dramatic of these differences in live animals (1), vegetable products (2), and textiles and apparel (11) are perhaps overstated by the comparison methodology, as the EU relies heavily in sections 1 and 2 on 'wholly obtained' criteria, while the US applies rules based on the change of classification criteria that in fact give a similar effect for these products. In textile products, the differences are somewhat overstated again, due to differences in approach to defining the rules, with the US again relying on CTC criteria and the EU relying on specifying production processes. In this case the differences boil down to the US requiring that material inputs be originating starting with yarn, whereas the EU generally requires that material inputs be originating starting with fabric.

Of the other HS sections, ten out of the twenty-one show a difference of less than one point (equivalent to the difference between an exception to a CTC of a heading and an exception of a subheading).

Despite recognizing that the differences in some sectors are somewhat overstated due to 'stylistic' differences in the definition of the rules, we must also emphasize the importance of stylistic differences. Agreement on the substance of a matter does not always lead easily to agreement on the particulars of implementation. The fact that the average difference in ten of the twenty-one HS sections is less than one point on the Harris scale, while encouraging in that differences may not be as large as one might think, does not imply that reaching an agreement would necessarily be simple. Recall, for example, Figure 7.1, which shows that the most recently approved US agreement (CAFTA) relies on criteria other than CTC for less than 3 per cent of products in its first rule, whereas the Paneuro rules eschew CTC for nearly 15 per cent of products. Even

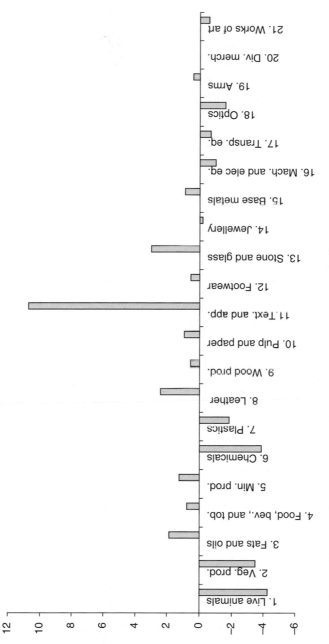

Figure 7.11 Comparing US and EU ROO section, average restrictiveness US–EU (Harris, 2007)

Source: Authors' calculations on the basis of RTA texts.

if the observed restrictiveness is quite similar in many cases, these stylistic differences, which derive from fundamentally different understandings of the best way to approach these issues, are significant.

Another potentially useful analysis is comparing the US and EU preferential ROO families to the non-preferential ROOs as they stand to date (See Figure 7.1D in Appendix D). While the non-preferential rules generally seem to be a compromise position between the US and EU standard preferential positions, there are several sections where this is not the case. There are seven sections where the non-preferential rules are more demanding than either the standard US or EU preferential rules, most notably food and beverages, mineral products, transportation equipment, and arms. There are also four sections where the non-preferential rules are less demanding than either of these, most meaningfully in plastics, jewellery, base metals, and machinery and equipment.

It is important to keep in mind that the ostensible[37] purpose of non-preferential rules is different from that of preferential rules. While preferential rules must simply allow a determination of whether a good is originating in an RTA member or not, the non-preferential rules must allow a determination of the 'official' originating country when this is not the country of export. These differing purposes may be the cause of the deviations noted above.

Beyond geographical families?

The above exercises studied ROO hubs and families defined *ex ante*. One could certainly ask whether there are sets of RTAs that frequently coincide in their origin requirements despite not falling into the same families – that is, whether there are families across the geographical families examined above. Such an exercise could help identify 'global ROO coalitions', or clusters of RTAs sporting common product-specific ROOs. In essence, it would help illustrate the divergence within the global bar in Figure 7.8. Figure 7.12 strives to get at such global families by looking at the frequency with which different numbers of agreements coincide across products.

Unsurprisingly, we find that there are no large unexpected coalitions. The peak at twenty-one coinciding agreements is due to the large group of agreements in South America that follow the LAIA model with a

---

[37] An important outstanding issue in the negotiations of harmonized non-preferential rules is the exact uses to which the agreed rules will be put.

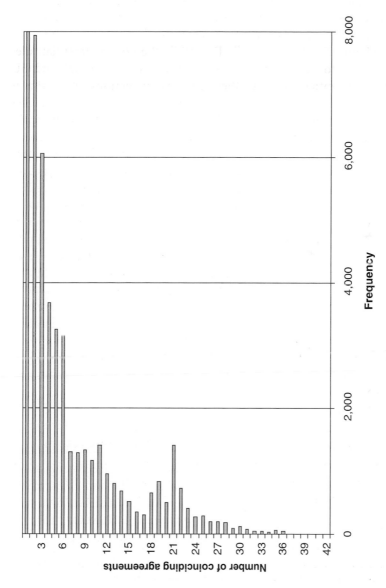

Figure 7.12. Frequencies of coinciding agreements
Source: Authors' calculations on the basis of RTA texts.

general rule that gives the alternative of a change in heading or a 50 per cent VC.

An alternative approach to this question is to look at which agreements coincide in each product and examine the frequency of these coincidences. Table 7.2D in Appendix D lists the 'revealed families' with frequencies in excess of 200 products. Again, there are no particular surprises. The most frequent outcome is for agreements to appear alone. Common groupings are of agreements with across-the-board low percentage VC requirements (for example, ASEAN, Chile–China, and US–Middle Eastern agreements). We also frequently see groupings within the families used above.

However, even if unexpected families were to emerge from this analysis, this exercise is likely to be of more academic than practical interest. For one, RTAs within a group with, say, 200 common ROOs may be fully divergent in the rest of the ROOs in the tariff universe – while, in addition, any one of them may coincide in a larger number of ROOs with an even larger number of RTAs. A second and a complementary issue is that if rules are a function of local political and economic factors, any of the members of RTAs in the global ROO clusters may have little motive to work together.[38]

Perhaps the most useful lesson of the exercise is that there are virtually no large global coalitions of RTAs outside the expected families. Nonetheless, in the presence of global 'ROO caps' that would limit the number of types of ROOs, the number of RTAs with common ROOs should expand.

Restrictiveness and divergence in sum

In sum, the above exercises have yielded three main observations:

- ROOs in EU, Mexican, Chilean, US and some Asian agreements, most notably the Japan–Singapore FTA, are among the most restrictive. Agricultural products and textiles and apparel are marked by a particularly high restrictiveness score across regimes. However, it is also the case that US agreements have become less restrictive over time.

---

[38] Furthermore, the exercise here employs not ROO typology but the restrictiveness index, which is an aggregation of the typology, and, as such, overlooks differences in ROO types falling into a particular restrictiveness code. For instance, a restrictiveness value of 10 carries fourteen different types of ROOs, and thus any one of the RTAs sharing a restrictiveness value of 10 in any one ROO may still have divergent ROO types.

The more recent intra-Asian agreements tend to be less restrictive and complex than their counterparts in Europe and the Americas.

- Real effective restrictiveness depends on factors beyond the ROO regime text, namely on the input pool and the geographical pool of supplies. The wider these are, the less the effective restrictiveness is likely to be.

- There are marked divergences across ROO regimes around the world: on average about one-third of all agreements' rules will coincide on any given product. Nonetheless, there are clear ROO families centred around the United States, the EU and Mexico, in particular, which suggests a potential for some form of regional ROO convergence. Moreover, there are some signs of a de facto cross-regional stylistic harmonization of ROOs, as US-style agreements are spreading towards Asia via the recent trans-Pacific agreements.

5   Multilateralization and convergence: where, when and how?

Rules of origin are a necessary element of any preferential trading scheme. Indeed, 'preferential' and 'ROOs' go hand-in-hand: by precluding free-riding, the latter enables the former. Taking as given that RTAs, either individually or collectively, can fuel and further the multilateral trading system, it must be recognized that they could not have been agreed to without origin regimes that to a certain degree limited the benefits of each agreement to its constituent members. As such, discussion of 'eliminating' rules of origin from preferential trading arrangements is nonsense.

Furthermore, if we accept the 'building block' hypothesis that successive and overlapping RTAs are the most viable path to global free trade, then the elimination of preferential origin regimes would itself be a stumbling block. After all, under the building block hypothesis, preferential origin regimes are *the* mechanisms that make RTAs viable by allowing the participating countries to focus on eliminating intra-regional trade barriers without concerns about inadvertently undertaking a broad unilateral liberalization.

We have shown that restrictive and divergent ROOs are facts in the RTA universe. We have also discussed the reasons why restrictiveness accentuates the importance of divergence, and described the potential transaction costs ensuing from the restrictiveness-divergence combination. While ROOs per se in any given agreement are not necessarily 'bad' for sound economic decisions, restrictive ROOs can be. This has been shown to hold empirically. Furthermore, at least in theory, differences *between* ROOs regimes can make a difference to the decisions of economic actors in favour of less efficient outsourcing and investment strategies, even in a simplified bi- or tripolar ROOs world. How, then, to tame the ROO tangle?

One way to relegate ROOs to irrelevance – and, indeed, to bring about the same effects as by multilateralizing regionalism – is by bringing MFN tariffs to zero globally. However, since this option is unlikely in the near future, there are four further options. The first is doing nothing: status quo RTA proliferation and a likely de facto bipolarization of the global ROOs world map into regimes following the US or EU ROO models – and with many countries sporting both, à la Chile and Mexico. This option does nothing to alleviate the problems with the ROOs discussed thus far. The second and third options are multilateralization and convergence. A fourth option is a combination of these two. We discuss the latter three options in turn.

Multilateralizing preferential rules of origin

Full harmonization of preferential ROOs would be as politically unfeasible as it would be technically unpalatable to producers around the world. While the technical process of harmonization could be hampered by the often marked differences in ROOs across regimes, even the more subtle differences could be difficult to overcome, due to political resistance by sectors benefiting from the status quo. Meanwhile, it is unlikely that an industry lobby would materialize to voice demands for harmonization. Perhaps most importantly, both the EU and the United States would likely be reluctant to adopt each other's ROOs. Both would likely also be concerned by the other's striving for ROOs that would allow it to tranship via the parties' common RTA partners, such as Mexico.

Moreover, harmonization could be harmful in that it could accentuate restrictiveness, and thus force rules on RTAs that prohibit the use of non-originating materials that do not exist within the RTA cumulation zone. This would effectively cancel liberalization of the affected products in that RTA since effective restrictiveness depends not only on observed restrictiveness but also on the size of the cumulation zone. In short, harmonization can be like being put in a straitjacket.

A better option than harmonizing is, then, multilateralizing preferential ROOs. Multilateralizing is different from harmonizing, and here it refers to the establishment of multilateral disciplines on preferential rules within the WTO framework that will set some limits on the restrictiveness and complexity of rules of origin in preferential agreements. Such a 'ROO cap', perhaps best conceived of as a limited range of potential ROO options (which would truncate the existing vast repertoire of ROO combinations displayed in Figure 7.2), would ensure that at least the qualifying production methods in a given sector remained relatively similar across export markets. While such a cap would likely have to be set relatively high in order to accommodate the various pre-set ROOs in RTAs, it could serve as a useful reference point in the same way as the benchmark rules discussed below.

A complementary approach could be for RTAs to agree to 'bind' their rules of origin at existing levels of restrictiveness and then negotiate reductions of these 'bindings' under future negotiations. Importantly, this kind of capping process ought to be couched in a principle of 'common flexibility': the multilateralization of ROOs, like that of other disciplines, should not result in the increased restrictiveness of ROOs – thus potentially harming trade as well as violating GATT Article XXIV – but preferably drive towards loosening both the observable and, by extension, the effective restrictiveness of ROOs.

There are various ways to conceive of the technical process of multilateralizing ROOs. For example, once agreement is reached on harmonization of the non-preferential rules of origin, these could be taken as a benchmark. Then some mechanism could be employed for quantifying the net deviation of each agreement's preferential rules of origin from this benchmark, perhaps using some variant of the indices employed in this chapter.

RTA member countries would then be assigned the task of ensuring that their rules of origin produced a net deviation from the non-preferential benchmark or cap by an agreed amount. Having established this target reduction of net deviation, the member countries of each agreement would be free to negotiate modifications to their rules of origin, to meet the target in a way that is mutually acceptable and that respects the availability of inputs within their respective cumulation zones. Note again that this mechanism does not aim to harmonize rules per se, but rather to reduce the restrictiveness of the rules of origin relative to a fixed benchmark, thus achieving the greater openness of each bloc towards the rest of the world. As blocs became more open to inputs from ROW, the distortionary effects of the ROOs would be reduced.

By using the net deviation, agreements could compensate for rules that are more restrictive than the benchmark on some products with rules that are less restrictive than the benchmark on others (note that the concept here is the observed restrictiveness, not the effective restrictiveness). It would also make sense, perhaps, to weigh deviations from the benchmark by the average external tariff of the countries party to the agreement, as more restrictive rules distort more in more protected sectors.

A further technical fix might be to attack the general ROOs instead of the product-specific ROOs: for instance, increasing *de minimis* and/or creating innovative cumulation-like methods in RTAs around the world, as is done in Singapore's FTAs. These methods could make ROOs non-binding (non-restrictive), thus obliterating the relevance of divergence as well.

Besides the technical 'what' of multilateralization, there are the political 'hows' and 'whos' of the process toward multilateralization. The first step might be the launching of a global mechanism – perhaps a technical group of ROO experts – that monitors and catalogues preferential ROOs and reports to WTO members on the existing rules. Alternatively, the task could be accomplished by an existing WTO body, such as under the auspices of the Committee on Regional Trade Agreements, although this might be more time-consuming. The technical group could also serve as a forum for consultations where countries and/or companies could communicate their concerns about being excessively restricted by ROOs, and/or excluded from markets by ROOs. As a starting point, this could bring increased transparency to ROOs by giving countries excluded from RTAs a (non-binding) voice on the issue, while also helping to gauge the relevance of multilateralizing ROOs to companies and the potential designs of such multilateralized ROOs.

Another potential institutional mechanism for addressing ROOs would be through the Transparency Mechanism on RTAs approved by the WTO General Council in December 2006, which mandates that the 'WTO Secretariat, on its own responsibility and in full consultation with the parties, shall prepare a factual presentation of the [notified] RTA'.[39] The mechanism entails that RTAs be subject to similar, albeit much lighter, examination by the WTO, as national trade policies are in the context of the Trade Policy Review Mechanism (TPRM). While this function of the WTO has no enforcement capacity, a rigorous and

---

[39] See http://docsonline.wto.org/DDFDocuments/t/WT/L/671.doc.

objective review of preferential ROOs in the factual presentation of the RTA would bring added transparency to these policies.

Who should join the multilateralization process? RTAs have evolved from intra-regionalism to transcontinentalism, engaging some rather unlikely partners such as Chile and the Republic of Korea, or Mexico and Israel. This trend is far from abating; given that RTAs are increasingly transcontinental in nature, and that all countries but one, Mongolia, are RTA members, effective multilateralization would seem to require all WTO members to step up to the plate and on equal terms: everyone should play and with a level playing field. Indeed, the drive toward less restrictive ROOs inherent in multilateralization should be acceptable to developing countries: various ROO regimes provide developing countries with more flexibility to fulfil their ROO requirements than is afforded to the more developed country members.[40] Developing countries are thus likely to gain from these regulations, as any of the above mechanisms would likely have relatively little effect on their ROOs, whereas reductions in the restrictiveness of developed country RTA rules would provide openings to their products. Moreover, it would also be immensely useful to include ROO end-users, that is, private sector actors, in the process from the beginning, perhaps as a consultative committee. Indeed, if globalized industries bought into the idea, they would help build political support for the negotiation and implementation of any outcome.

Getting the process moving toward actual multilateralization as understood here is a broader challenge. One major challenge is that the train has left the station. Revising the manifold existing ROO regimes would generally require re-submitting RTAs for legislative approval, which would be politically unpalatable in many capitals. One way to overcome the need to reopen product-specific ROOs could thus be a variable geometry approach – a simple capping process, such as a commitment to increase *de minimis*, in the existing regimes, accompanied by a cap for the product-specific ROOs in the forthcoming RTAs. An alternative (or complementary) mechanism might be to adopt two optional (capped) ROOs for any given product, as is done in EU, US and several other countries' ROO regimes. This would help accommodate the entrenched ROO regimes and help push the process forward.

To be sure, one facilitator of multilateralization could be an external shock, such as a push toward ROO convergence in a major world

[40] See Suominen (2004).

region such as Asia or the Americas, as this might hasten non-regional parties to the multilateralization table. Overall, the process should be much more streamlined than that of harmonizing non-preferential ROOs, which has dragged on for more than a dozen years.

What would multilateralizing mean to Article XXIV? As formulated here, multilateralization does not appear to necessitate a revision of the Article, but rather some independent agreement among WTO members. Regardless of the method, the process of multilateralizing ROOs could have positive externalities at the bilateral and national levels. Rules of origin are not regularly renegotiated for a variety of good reasons (predictability and stability of the trading rules) and bad reasons (inertia, negotiation costs, externalities, information gaps and asymmetries). One benefit of establishing negotiations to govern preferential rules is that it would generate an opportunity to open such negotiations, thus overcoming the negotiation inertia, and creating technical awareness of the negative aspects of restrictive ROOs. This objective could be made explicit by establishing mandatory review mechanisms whereby RTAs would have to revisit their ROOs every five to ten years. In the context of Baldwin's (2006) 'juggernaut effect', such a renegotiation is likely to result in falling levels of protection – in this case, less restrictive rules of origin in regional trade agreements.

Convergence

The second path to taming the ROO tangle is convergence. Before entering into what is implied by convergence, it is helpful to first discuss what it is not. Simply harmonizing rules of origin across RTAs is not 'convergence', and in fact would not even necessarily be particularly helpful. Recalling that ROOs are in part determined by the availability of inputs within the relevant cumulation zone, the imposition of a standardized set of rules would likely result in *increasing* the restrictiveness, both observed and effective, of some rules in some RTAs – which would be counter-productive.

Furthermore, having similar rules would not, of itself, actually result in more openness, except where the harmonization process resulted in rules moving to lower observed restrictiveness. This is because without changing the borders of the cumulation zone(s), there would be little gain in market access.

What convergence would have to mean, then, is the unification of multiple overlapping existing RTAs into a single cumulation zone, with

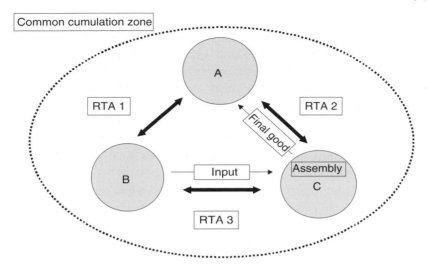

Figure 7.13. Three-RTA cumulation zone

a new, single list of rules of origin.[41] One such process was the creation of the Paneuro system in Europe; however, as noted above, the process involved harmonizing and connecting ROO regimes that were already very similar, if not fully alike in many instances. In a more diverse context, convergence would require multi-party negotiation of a new list, as well as negotiation of tariff elimination for any bilateral relationship where it had not been established by an existing RTA. The latter is important, as cumulation would not be viable if there were residual tariffs on either the final good or the inputs to be cumulated in any of the countries in which these originated: such differences could lead to distortions of trade and production patterns, with trade likely flowing through the lowest-tariff channels and production agglomerating in the hub country that faces the lowest tariffs in the other participating countries. In a simple example in Figure 7.13, then, convergence would enable C to import inputs free of duty from B under the B–C RTA and use the inputs for final goods destined to A's market under the A–C RTA, all governed by the new, mutually agreed, single list of ROOs.

When seeking to encourage harmonization (or, for that matter, multilateralization) of ROOs, it is important to be aware that a rule that establishes the exact same requirement in two different RTAs can have

---

[41] See Cornejo and Harris (2007) and IDB (2007) for a detailed treatment.

dramatically different effects on firms' cost structures in different contexts, given the differences in scale and efficiency of production of
inputs within the geographical and input pools. As such, while the
analysis of ROO divergence is important, in that it highlights the degree
to which any kind of coordination is absent from the development of
this discipline, the fact that rules differ across RTAs does not mean that
they are necessarily suboptimal in any particular case.

In practice, initial interest in expanded cumulation is implicit in
recent US agreements (chapter 62 provisions in CAFTA, for example).
Though their agenda is still vague, the Pacific Basin Forum of eleven
countries in Latin America has formed a work agenda to study, among
other things, trade convergence and integration.[42] The EU's new RTAs
will likely carry the Paneuro rules, expanding the uniformity conducive
to expanded cumulation. Finally, the growing discussion on a Free Trade
Area of the Asia-Pacific (FTAAP) might entail some form of convergence
rather than a full-blown mega-regional negotiation. However, bridging
ROO regimes is bound to be complex and would require at least five
considerations.

First, what should be the country and sectoral coverage of a negotiation aimed at a common regime? Obviously, for any one country, the
decision to join such a negotiation is ultimately a political one, but a
number of factors can make such a negotiation more useful. These
include an existing set of RTAs that cover the majority of the bilateral
relationships within a given group of countries, and a similar trade
policy strategy among these countries. To be sure, there can be a tipping
point effect produced either by a major economy joining or launching
such a process or by a sheer cascading in numbers of participants, when
the pay-offs of remaining outside could turn very negative.[43]

Second, and fundamentally important: what exact format should the
common ROO regime take so as to be agreeable to all countries, *and* not
to jeopardize the existing degree of liberalization in a region?[44] While we
do not address questions of whether CTC rules are preferable to VC

---

[42] See www.rree.gob.pe/portal/enlaces.nsf/3f08cf720c1dbf4805256de20052913d/e0380a5ecc8
2f6800525733f0077e87e/$FILE/Declaracion_de_Lima.pdf and www.rree.gob.pe/portal/enl
aces.nsf/3f08cf720c1dbf4805256de20052913d/608d2fa8bc449f260525733f007806df/$FILE/
Programa_Trabajo.pdf.

[43] I.e. the 'domino effect' of Baldwin (2006).

[44] Restrictive and complex ROO regimes have been shown to undercut RTAs' liberalizing
potential. See Suominen (2004), Estevadeordal and Suominen (2006), and Cadot and de
Melo (2007).

rules in this chapter, or whether self-certification is preferable to public certification, these questions remain important, and worthy of further study, especially at the empirical level, before any new regional (or global) standard is set.[45]

Third, how would a new common origin regime relate to the existing bi- and plurilateral regimes? Would it replace the existing origin regimes altogether, or would it co-exist with them? Under the former model, traders would be able to use the common regime only; under the latter, they could choose between the common regime (and reap the benefits of cumulation) or the existing bi- or plurilateral ROOs (and forgo cumulation). In the pasta metaphor, the individual spaghetti strands of the RTAs would continue to exist, but would be covered by the large flat piece of lasagne of the convergent origin regime.

Fourth, and critically, how would a common regime interface with extra-regional RTAs? A rapidly growing share of the RTAs formed by countries is with extra-regional partners. Most countries should thus have an interest in a common regime that is both compatible with the extra-regional RTAs, and amenable to trading with extra-regional partners, rather than sealing them off from a given region.[46] And surely all extra-regional players have an interest in continuing to see their market access expand rather than be cut off in these new overarching agreements. This situation would be helped by globally agreed guidelines for preferential ROOs.

Fifth, who would do the talking? While governments are necessary for forming and redefining international agreements, considerations of cumulation, like those of multilateralizing, call for private sector participation, not least given that they are the end users of RTAs and thus

---

[45] Gasiorek, Augier and Lai-Tong (Chapter 4 of this volume) propose a reform mechanism composed of value-added tariffs, VC ROOs, and full cumulation that would allow for better access for developing country exports to developed countries. The value-added tariff here is the key, as it levies the tariff only on the non-originating components of the final good. These ideas are very useful, especially for GSP-type preferences where the primary objective is to encourage development of export industries in the developing country. This mechanism could also serve as an add-on to the more standard determination of origin, which is binary. Generally, when a good is found to be non-originating there is no preference granted at all, regardless of the fact that there may be significant originating content, though insufficient for the rule. The proposed mechanism would then allow a sliding scale of preference that would allow some but not full tariff elimination for such goods, thus promoting the development of production capacity in these countries.

[46] For a mapping of ROOs in RTAs around the world, see Estevadeordal and Suominen (2006).

hold the best information about their operation and the relevance of the hypothetical problems posed by the RTA spaghetti bowl. Indeed, these are the actors responsible for the unbundling of production that leads to the political feasibility of such endeavours in the first place. As such, any process aimed at bridging RTAs should inherently involve public–private sector partnerships.

Sixth, what is the role of the multilateral trading system (and WTO) in such a process? One of a dispassionate or impotent observer, or a player in the process? This is a question we turn to next.

Multilateralism-cum-convergence: a 'cap-con' strategy

The issue of sequencing multilateralization and convergence is crucial, should the two concepts mean what they refer to in this chapter – 'capping' ROOs at the multilateral level while establishing single ROO regimes at the regional (or some other group/family) level to permit the formation of larger cumulation zones. Recall that Figure 7.5 illustrates the natural theoretical tendency for larger cumulation zones to negotiate rules of origin with more highly observed restrictiveness. Granted, any expansion of the US or EU zones would imply only marginal proportional increases in the size of the cumulation zones,[47] and thus in the degree to which the rules are likely to become more restrictive. However other regions, such as groupings within Latin America (Pacific Basin Forum), Asia (ASEAN+6) or Africa, should they follow convergence paths, would be well advised to take care to resist pressures to establish more restrictive rules than those prevailing in their existing regimes. Although any multilateral 'cap' is unlikely to bind on such arrangements, as it would have to be agreed by the larger players as well, the existence of such a reference point could aid in efforts to restrain protectionist tendencies in the negotiation of the new origin regime.

Moreover, the argument assumes away (1) ongoing MFN tariff liberalization among the members; (2) potential ROO loosening by some members or a major member (as per the NAFTA relaxation of ROOs); and (3) and related, the rise of an export lobby amid a convergence process to push for decreasingly restrictive ROOs. Indeed, that such a process could be launched at all would likely suggest the consolidation

---

[47] Adding all of South America to North America, or all of Africa to the EU, would not represent a very large shift to the right in Figure 7.4.

of the globalized industry lobbies (and the weakening of the import-protecting industries) – while of course not precluding increased efforts by protectionist lobbies aiming to expand rent-seeking opportunities in the convergence talks.

In any case, expansion of the ROO zone could lead to greater complexity. Moreover, to the extent that countries wish to pursue convergence that also leads to more liberal global trade, it could be important first, at the minimum, and as an insurance policy against the theoretical rise in restrictiveness, to have in place some global guidelines for (the convergent) preferential ROOs. Such guidelines would simply serve to counteract the theoretical tendency of larger cumulation zones to create complex ROOs and to erect higher barriers to extra-zone inputs, and thus entail simultaneous global capping and regional convergence processes.[48] This could be termed a 'cap-and-con strategy'. The strategy is based on a notion that global 'capping' of ROOs is useful so as not to 'converge' into trade-diverting mega-blocs.

The proposed optimal outcome is shown in Figure 7.14. The countries party to a group of overlapping RTAs decide to establish a convergent origin regime that will allow cumulation among all of them under a newly negotiated set of rules of origin. This new origin regime risks moving them up line A, following the natural tendency for larger grouping towards more complex and restrictive regimes. In the presence of multilaterally agreed guidelines (a cap), this movement would be counteracted with a move down line B.

Whether the guidelines would serve to promote one type of criterion over another (CTC over VC or vice versa, for example) is a question distinct from whether such guidelines function to limit the erection of new barriers to global trade. As discussed above, it is preferable that the limitations be imposed on some aggregate calculus and not product by product, as flexibility at this level would be indispensable for political economy reasons within each convergent group.

The important danger to keep in mind when establishing global caps, however, is that they must be set in such a way as to avoid reducing the incentive for convergence. Bringing groups of countries with multiple,

---

[48] Note that the argument presented earlier, that the effective restrictiveness of such rules is lower in larger blocs, applies to the effects that rules have on the production costs of members, as the globally low-cost producer is more likely to be included within the cumulation zone as it becomes larger. This attenuating effect is of no help to suppliers left outside the expanded cumulation zone, and it is this distortion that we seek to minimize through multilateral rules governing preferential origin regimes.

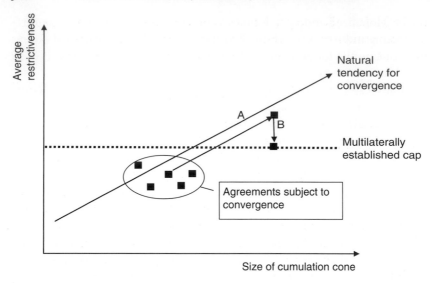

Figure 7.14. Effects of 'cap-and-con'

overlapping RTAs into a single cumulation zone has the potential to greatly increase trade, especially among those that might be considered spokes, as well as to create trade, as long as the zone in question was grounded on open regionalism. As such, convergence of the right, non-restrictive kind should be encouraged, not stifled. The wrong type of convergence – one that produces trade-diverting mega-blocs that would silo global commerce, and something that cap-and-con is meant to pre-empt – should be opposed with the most stringent of terms.[49] While the reduction of the restrictiveness of these rules may have minimal effect on intra-RTA trade, the lowering of barriers could increase openness to producers of intermediates in excluded countries.

While some global capping would optimally happen before the convergence processes began, that horse seems to have already left the stable, as evinced by the current policy debates on some regional bridging of RTAs in the Americas and Asia, and the EU's entrenched Paneuro regime. The Paneuro architecture implies that all the EU's new RTAs will have the potential to continue the expansion of that cumulation zone, though at

---

[49] Krugman (1993) finds that the globally most suboptimal trade bloc formation would be the rise of three mega-blocs. That extreme scenario is not likely in its theoretical form, as there are already many trans-bloc RTAs that would make Krugman's mega-blocs quite 'leaky'.

least in that case the prospect of the increasing restrictiveness of the rules is reduced as these agreements tend to carry identical rules to the previous agreements.

Where are we headed?

Having described what we consider to be the optimal path for both regional and multilateral treatment of rules of origin, let us step back and re-engage with reality. Optimal is one thing, but what is likely? We see five potential scenarios, summarized in Table 7.3.

The first potential scenario is one where nothing changes. Countries continue to negotiate RTAs bilaterally or in small groups, with no convergence of origin regimes and no rules established at a global level to regulate the origin regimes of current or future RTAs. This is a 'worst case scenario', where many small, overlapping RTAs channel preferential trade in narrow paths that prevent many producers from sourcing inputs efficiently, and prevent others from producing at all, as no cumulable inputs are available.

The second possible scenario is one where the multilateralization of preferential rules occurs, but there is little convergence of existing regimes. This is somewhat better than the 'worst case scenario' above, but would still exclude the gains to be had from expanding cumulation.

The third possible scenario is one of convergence, whereby groups of countries with overlapping RTAs begin to negotiate convergent origin regimes, but without any multilateral guidelines that would limit the theoretical natural tendency of larger cumulation zones to apply more restrictive rules. The gains to be had from allowing expanded cumulation within these groups of countries are likely to be quite significant.[50] However, these groupings could, at least in theory, accentuate the observed restrictiveness, hurting suppliers in excluded countries.

The fourth potential scenario to consider is the 'cap-and-con' outcome we describe in the previous section, where regional convergence is accompanied by multilateral limitations on rules of origin. This would capture the benefits of both expanded cumulation and relatively less restrictive ROOs.

The final relevant scenario is where there is successful multilateral tariff liberalization. The conclusion of a round of tariff reductions that

---

[50] Gasiorek, Augier and Lai-Tong (chapter 4 of this volume) estimate the implementation of the PECS increased spoke–spoke trade at between 14 and 72 per cent.

Table 7.3. *Potential scenarios for the ROO world*

Option	Main players	Pros and cons	Current likelihood
Nothing changes	Everybody	Pros (or cons?): no negotiation costs beyond those of RTAs; potential de facto broad global bipolar convergence under US and EU ROO models Con: potential exacerbation of the spaghetti bowl problem	Medium
Multilateralization	Global ROO hubs (US, EU, Mexico, Australia, Japan, Chile), plus spokes	Pro: spaghetti problem is attenuated by global limits on ROOs Cons: Negotiation is a time-consuming and costly global contest involving cycling; potential straitjacket ROOs resulting	Low
Convergence	Each family hub and its spokes	Pros: creation of lasagne from spaghetti; regional cumulation bowls Cons: Negotiation is a time-consuming and costly regional contest in the absence of a ROO hegemon; opens potential for trade-diverting plates and variety of lasagne	Highest
Cap-and-con	Main regional ROO hubs	Pros: flexibility-cum-openness at the regional level; simpler lasagne plates Con: potential straitjacket cap ROOs that discourage convergence	Low
Complete MFN liberalization (global free trade)	All WTO member countries	Pro: maximum efficiency Con: Politically improbable in the foreseeable future	Lowest

results in the binding of MFN tariffs at zero or very low levels for nearly all products would make all preferential origin regimes irrelevant, as there would be no meaningful tariff preferences to qualify for. That said, there seems to be little likelihood of such significant tariff reductions in the current round.

Of these five scenarios, the second is probably the most likely. Initial movements towards convergence are already visible, as described above. Most of the significant bilateral relationships in world trade are already subject to RTAs (certainly among countries prone to liberalization) and the unbundling of production within these RTAs is leading the 'juggernaut' forces for liberalization, currently frustrated at the multilateral level, to push on regional levers.

This is not the worst case scenario, but it is not optimal either. The outcome is likely to involve multiple overlapping 'lasagne plates', the largest of which would be centred on the US and Europe, with additional Latin American and Asian pieces. A bipolar ROO world is likely welfare-superior to a fully balkanized ROO world, as larger cumulation zones increase trade, especially among the current spoke countries. But it is not too difficult to imagine that such zones could end up with highly restrictive rules of origin that would serve to isolate production within each zone, with attendant losses for global efficiency. Some mechanism is needed to limit the degree to which these blocs are closed to outside trade.

6 Conclusion

The path to global free trade could proceed on several fronts: first, the standard front of multilateral tariff reductions; second, the gradual opening of preferential blocs via a reduction in the restrictiveness of preferential rules of origin. This can occur either via regulation at the global level or via autonomous reform. Third, a path may be found through the expansion of the cumulation zones of the preferential blocs in ways that at the same time promote further bloc-to-bloc liberalization. Finally, we may see some combination of the three mechanisms.

This chapter has analysed the feasibility, utility and mechanics of such paths, focusing in particular on RTA rules of origin. We have described ROO regimes around the world, detailed the degree of restrictiveness within them and divergence across them, and elaborated why these two dimensions matter for economic outcomes. We have subsequently discussed policy options for reducing restrictiveness and divergence around the world, and found that such a reduction might be most likely at the regional level. Nonetheless, in our view, such processes should be complemented by a multilateral process of ROO capping, though it is important that such caps do not discourage regional convergence.

In more specific terms, we suggest the following:

- At the multilateral level, there should be a process toward capping ROOs – an effort to establish a common and limited set of ROOs that can be employed in forthcoming, and perhaps also in currently existing, RTAs.
- At the regional level, groups of countries with multiple, overlapping RTAs should pursue avenues to establish inclusive origin regimes that permit cumulation in larger zones to promote trade among spokes – yet do so in order to further open regionalism.
- At the level of individual RTAs, the appropriateness of the ROOs should be re-evaluated on a regular basis, with an eye to reducing the barriers to the use of third-country inputs in the production of originating goods.

To be sure, opening a full renegotiation of an origin regime – or worse, regimes for several RTAs at once – and reconciling differences across regimes at either the regional or the global levels, certainly feels like opening a Pandora's box of endless troubles. Nonetheless, the prospect of incorporating lessons learned over the past decade or more concerning the operation of so many RTAs, and bringing the regimes up to date with the commercial and technological realities of the twenty-first century, certainly makes such an effort seem worthwhile. The way these issues are addressed, both regionally and globally, will determine how, when and if we arrive at global free trade.

References

Anson, J., Cadot, O., Estevadeordal, A., de Melo, J., Suwa-Eisenmann, A. and Tumurchudur, B. (2003) 'Rules of Origin in North–South Preferential Trading Arrangements with an Application to NAFTA', mimeo, University of Lausanne.

Augier, P., Gasiorek, M. and Lai-Tong, C. (2005) 'The Impact of Rules of Origin on Trade Flows', *Economic Policy* 20 (43): 567–624.

Baldwin, R. (2006) 'Multilateralising Regionalism: Spaghetti Bowls as Building Blocks on the Path to Global Free Trade', *The World Economy* 29 (11): 1451–518.

Cadot, O. and de Melo, J. (2008) 'Why OECD Countries Should Reform Rules of Origin', *World Bank Research Observer* 23 (1): 77–105.

Cadot, O., de Melo, J., Estevadeordal, A., Suwa-Eisenmann, A. and Tumurchudur, B. (2002) 'Assessing the Effect of NAFTA's Rules of Origin', mimeo.

Cadot, O., Estevadeordal, A. Suwa-Eisenmann, A. and Verdier, T. (eds.) (2006) *The Origin of Goods*, Oxford: Oxford University Press.

Carrère, C. and de Melo, J. (2006) 'Are Rules of Origin Equally Costly? Estimates from NAFTA' in O. Cadot, A. Estevadeordal, A. Suwa-Eisenmann and T. Verdier (eds.), *The Origin of Goods*, Oxford: Oxford University Press.

Cornejo, R. and Harris, J. (2007) 'Convergence in the Rules of Origin Spaghetti Bowl: A Methodological Proposal', IDB/INTAL Working Paper, available at: www.iadb.org/intal/aplicaciones/uploads/publicaciones/i_INTALITD_WP_34_2007_CornejoHarris.pdf.

Driessen, B. and Graafsma, F. (1999) 'The EC's Wonderland: An Overview of the Pan-European Harmonised Origin Protocols', *Journal of World Trade* 33 (4): 19–45.

Estevadeordal, A. (2000) 'Negotiating Preferential Market Access: The Case of the North American Free Trade Agreement', *Journal of World Trade* 34 (1): 141–66.

Estevadeordal, A. and Suominen, K. (2003) 'Rules of Origin in FTAs in Europe and in the Americas: Issues and Implications for the EU-MERCOSUR Inter-Regional Association Agreement', in A. G. A. Valladão and R. Bouzas (eds.), *Market Access for Goods and Services in the EU–MERCOSUR Negotiations*, Paris: Chaire MERCOSUR de Sciences Po.

(2005) 'Rules of Origin in Preferential Trading Agreements: Is All Well with the FTA Spaghetti Bowl in the Americas?', *Economia* 5 (2): 63–103.

(2006) 'Rules of Origin: A World Map', in O. Cadot, A. Estevadeordal, A. Suwa-Eisenmann and T. Verdier, eds., *The Origin of Goods*, Oxford: Oxford University Press.

(2008) *Gatekeepers of Global Commerce: Rules of Origin and International Economic Integration*, Washington DC: IDB.

Estevadeordal, A., López-Córdova, E. and Suominen, K. (2006) 'How Do Rules of Origin Affect Investment Flows? Some Hypotheses and the Case of Mexico', INTAL-ITD Working Paper 22. Buenos Aires: INTAL.

Falvey, R. and Reed, G. (2000) 'Rules of Origin as Commercial Policy Instruments', Research Paper No. 2000/18, Centre for Research on Globalization and Labour Markets, University of Nottingham.

Garay, L. J. and Cornejo, R. (2002) 'Metodología para el Análisis de Régimenes de Origen: Aplicación en el Caso de las Américas', INTAL-ITD-STA Working Paper, Washington DC: Inter-American Development Bank.

Harris, J. (2007) 'Measurement and Determinants of Rules of Origin in Preferential Trade Agreements', Ph.D. dissertation, University of Maryland.

Hirsch, M. (2002) 'International Trade Law: Political Economy and Rules of Origin', *Journal of World Trade* 36 (2): 171–89.

IDB (Inter-American Development Bank) (2007) 'Bridging RTAs in the Americas', Policy Report.

IDB (forthcoming) 'Using Trade Rules: Trade Integration Agreements and Private Sector Strategies in the Americas', report forthcoming 2009.

Inama, S. (2005) 'The Association of South East Asian Nations – People's Republic of China Free Trade Area: Negotiating Beyond Eternity with Little Trade Liberalization?' *Journal of World Trade* 39 (3): 559–79.

Jensen-Moran, J. (1996) 'Trade Battles as Investment Wars: The Coming Rules of Origin Debate', *Washington Quarterly* 19 (1): 239–53.

Krishna, K. and Krueger, A. O. (1995) 'Implementing Free Trade Areas: Rules of Origin and Hidden Protection', in A. Deardorff, J. Levinsohn and R. Stern (eds.), *New Directions in Trade Theory*, Ann Arbor: University of Michigan Press.

Krueger, A. O. (1993) '*Free Trade Agreements as Protectionist Devices: Rules of Origin*', NBER Working Paper No. 4352, Cambridge, MA: National Bureau of Economic Research.

Manchin, M. and Pelksman-Baloing, A. O. (2007) '*Rules of Origin and the Web of East Asian Free Trade Agreements*', World Bank Policy Research Working Paper No. 4273, Washington DC: World Bank.

Portugal-Perez, A. (2006) 'Disentangling the Determinants of Rules of Origin in North–South Preferential Trade Agreements: Evidence for NAFTA', mimeo, University of Geneva.

'Regulations Amending the NAFTA Rule of Origin Regulations' (2003) *Canada Gazette*, 1 January, available at: canadagazette.gc.ca/partII/2003/20030115/html/sor24-e.html.

Reyna, J. V. (1995) *Passport to North American Trade: Rules of Origin and Customs Procedures under NAFTA*, Colorado Springs, CO: Shepard's/McGraw-Hill.

Suominen, K. (2004) '*Rules of Origin in Global Commerce*', Ph.D. dissertation, University of California, San Diego.

Appendix A: RTAs considered in the study

Table 7.1A

Agreement	Family assignment											
	Europe	Americas	USA	USANG	Asia	Africa	Americas–Asia	Chile	Mexico	Singapore	Japan	Australia
Paneuro	x											
EU–Chile (EUCHL)	x							x				
EU–Mexico (EUMEX)	x								x			
EU–South Africa (EUZAF)	x											
Chile–USA (CHLUSA)		x	x	x				x				
NAFTA		x	x	x					x			
USA–Colombia (USACOL)		x	x	x								
USA–Panama (USAPAN)		x	x	x								
USA–Peru (USAPER)		x	x	x								
Argentina–Brazil–Peru (ARGBRAPER)		x										
Paraguay–Peru (PRYPER)		x										
Uruguay–Peru (URYPER)		x										
Argentina–Colombia (ARGCOL)		x										

Table 7.1A (*cont.*)

Agreement	Family assignment														
	Europe	Americas	USA	USANG	Asia	Africa	Americas–Asia	Chile	Mexico	Singapore	Japan	Australia
Argentina–Ecuador (ARGECU)		x										
Argentina–Venezuela (ARGVEN)		x										
Brazil–Colombia (BRACOL)		x										
Brazil–Ecuador (BRAECU)		x										
Brazil–Venezuela (BRAVEN)		x										
Paraguay–Colombia (PRYCOL)		x										
Paraguay–Ecuador (PRYECU)		x										
Paraguay–Venezuela (PRYVEN)		x										
Uruguay–Colombia (URYCOL)		x										
Uruguay–Ecuador (URYECU)		x										
Uruguay–Venezuela (URYVEN)		x										
CACM		x										
CACM–Dominican Republic (CACM-DR)		x										
CAFTA–Dominican Republic (CAFTA–RD)		x										
Canada–Costa Rica (CANCRI)		x										

Table 7.1A (cont.)

Agreement	Family assignment											
	Europe	Americas	USA	USANG	Asia	Africa	Americas – Asia	Chile	Mexico	Singapore	Japan	Australia
Andean Community (CANDINA)		x										
CARICOM		x										
Chile–Canada (CHLCAN)		x						x				
Chile–CACM (CHLCACM)		x						x				
Chile–Mexico (CHLMEX)		x						x	x			
Chile–Peru (CHLPER)		x						x				
G3		x										
MERCOSUR		x										
MERCOSUR–Bolivia (MERCOSURBOL)		x										
MERCOSUR–Chile (MERCOSURCHL)		x										
Mexico–Bolivia (MEXBOL)		x							x			
Mexico–Costa Rica (MEXCRI)		x							x			
Mexico–Nicaragua (MEXNIC)		x							x			
Mexico–Northern Triangle (MEXNT)		x							x			
Mexico–Uruguay (MEXURY)		x							x			

Table 7.1A (cont.)

Agreement	Family assignment											
	Europe	Americas	USA	USANG	Asia	Africa	Americas–Asia	Chile	Mexico	Singapore	Japan	Australia
Chile–Colombia (CHLCOL)		x										
Chile–Ecuador (CHLECU)		x										
USA–Australia (USAAUS)			x	x			x					x
USA–Bahrain (USABAH)			x									
USA–Israel (USAISR)			x									
USA–Jordan (USAJOR)			x									
USA–Republic of Korea (USAKOR)			x	x			x					
USA–Morocco (USAMOR)			x									
USA–Singapore (USASING)			x	x			x			x		
USA–Oman (USAOMN)			x									
ASEAN					x							
ASEAN–China (ASEANCHN)					x							
ASEAN–Republic of Korea (ASEANKOR)					x							
Australia–New Zealand (AUSNZ)					x							x
Australia–Singapore (AUSSING)					x					x		x

Table 7.1A (*cont.*)

Agreement	Family assignment											
	Europe	Americas	USA	USANG	Asia	Africa	Americas–Asia	Chile	Mexico	Singapore	Japan	Australia
Australia–Thailand (AUSTHA)					x							x
Bangkok					x							
Chile–China (CHLCHN)							x	x				
Chile–Republic of Korea (CHLKOR)							x	x				
COMESA						x						
ECOWAS						x						
Japan–Malaysia (JPNMYS)					x						x	
Japan–Singapore (JPNSING)					x					x	x	
Japan–Thailand (JPNTHA)					x						x	
Mexico–Japan (MEXJAP)							x		x		x	
P4							x			x		
SADC						x						
SAFTA						x						
Thailand–New Zealand (THANZ)					x							
Peru–Thailand (PERTHA)							x					
GCC												

Appendix B: Comparative statistics of rules of origin

Table 7.1B *VC criteria by agreement* (%)

	Regional value content/build-up	Build-down	Maximum imported content	Factory cost	Net cost
Andean Community			50–55		
Argentina–Brazil–Peru			50		
Argentina–Colombia			40–55		
Argentina–Ecuador			40–55		
Argentina–Venezuela			40–55		
ASEAN	40				
ASEAN–China	40		60		
ASEAN–Republic of Korea	35–70	40			
Australia–New Zealand	35–55	30–45		45–60	
Australia–Singapore	30–50				
Australia–Thailand	40–55				45
Bangkok			50		
Brazil–Colombia			40–55		
Brazil–Ecuador			40–55		
Brazil–Venezuela	55		40–50		
CAFTA–Dominican Republic	30–65	25–55			35
Canada–Costa Rica	30–60				20–30
CARICOM			30–65		
Chile–Canada	30–65				20–55

Table 7.1B (*cont.*)

	Regional value content/		Maximum imported content	Factory cost	Net cost
	build-up	Build-down			
Chile–China	40–50				
Chile–Ecuador			50		
Chile–Republic of Korea	45–80	30			
Chile–CACM	20–30				
Chile–Mexico	32–50				26–40
Chile–Peru	40–65	50	50		
USA–Chile	40–65	30–55			
Chile–Colombia	30–70				
COMESA			60	35	
ECOWAS				30	
EU–Chile				20–50	
EU–Mexico				20–60	
G–3	35–60				
Japan–Malaysia	40–60				
Japan–Singapore	40–60				
Japan–Thailand	40				
MERCOSUR	60		40		
MERCOSUR–Bolivia	60	40	40		
MERCOSUR –Chile	60	40			
Mexico–Bolivia	50				40–60
Mexico–Costa Rica	50				40–60

Table 7.1B (*cont.*)

	Regional value content/ build-up	Build-down	Maximum imported content	Factory cost	Net cost
Mexico–Japan	50–90				
Mexico–Nicaragua	50				40–
					41.66
Mexico–Northern Triangle	50				
Mexico–Uruguay	50–55		50		40–50
NAFTA	30–80				25–70
P4	45–50				
Peru–Thailand	35–60				
Paraguay–Colombia			50		
Paraguay–Ecuador			50–60		
Paraguay–Peru			50		
Paraguay–Venezuela			50		
SADC	40–65				30–65
SAFTA	25–60		60		
Thailand–India	20–40				
Thailand–New Zealand	50				
Uruguay–Colombia			50		
Uruguay–Ecuador			50		
Uruguay–Peru			50		
Uruguay–Venezuela			50		
USA–Australia	45–65	35–50			50

Table 7.1B (*cont.*)

| | Regional value content/ | | Maximum imported content | |
	build-up	Build-down	Factory cost	Net cost
USA–Bahrain	35			
USA–Colombia	35–65	20–65		35
USA–Israel	35			
USA–Jordan	35–60			
USA–Republic of Korea	30–60	30–55		35
USA–Morocco	35			
USA–Panama	30–65	20–55		35
USA–Peru	30–65	20–65		35
USA–Singapore	40–65	30–55		

Source: Authors' calculations on the basis of RTA texts.

Table 7.2B *Regime-wide ROOs in selected RTAs*

RTA	De minimis	Extended cumulation	Certification method
Andean Community	None	No	Public (or delegated to a private entity)
ANZCERTA	10%	No	Public (or delegated to a private entity)
ASEAN	None	No	Public (or delegated to a private entity)
ASEAN–China	None	No	Public (or delegated to a private entity)
ASEAN–Republic of Korea	10% (10% of weight in chs. 50–63)	No	Public (or delegated to a private entity)
Australia–Thailand	10%	No	Public (or delegated to a private entity)
Bangkok	None	No	Public (or delegated to a private entity)
CACM	10% (10% of weight in chs. 50–63)	No	Self-certification
CACM–Chile	8% (not chs. 1–27 unless CS)	No	Self-certification
CAFTA–Dominican Republic	10% (Not chs. 4 and 15)	Possibly ch. 62 (with Canada and Mexico)	Self-certification
Canada–Costa Rica	10% (except in chs. 10 to 24; 10% of weight in chs. 50–63)	No	Self-certification
Canada–Chile	9% (except in agriculture and industrial products; 9% of weight in chs. 50–63)	No	Self-certification

Table 7.2B (*cont.*)

RTA	De minimis	Extended cumulation	Certification method
Canada–Israel	10% (except in agriculture and industrial products; 7% of weight in chs. 50–63)	Yes (with USA)	Self-certification
CARICOM	None	No	Public (or delegated to a private entity)
Chile–China	8%	No	Public (or delegated to a private entity)
Chile–Colombia	10% (except in agriculture and processed agriculture products; 10% of weight in textile)	No	Public; limited self-certification
Chile–Ecuador	None	No	Public; limited self-certification
Chile–Republic of Korea	8% (not chs. 1–24 unless C5; 8% of weight in chs. 50–63)	No	Self-certification
Chile–Peru	None	No	Public; limited self-certification
COMESA	2%	No	Two-step private and public
ECOWAS	None	No	Public (or delegated to a private entity)
EU–Chile	10% (except chs. 50–63)	No	Public; limited self-certification
EU–Mexico	10% (except chs. 50–63)	No	Public; limited self-certification

Table 7.2B (*cont.*)

RTA	De minimis	Extended cumulation	Certification method
EU–South Africa	15% (10% for chs. 3 and 24) (not chs. 50–63)	Yes with ACP (full with SACU)	Public; limited self-certification
G3	7% (7% of weight in chs. 50–63)	No	Two-step private and public
Gulf CC	None	No	Public (or delegated to a private entity
Japan–Malaysia	To be determined	Limited products from ASEAN	Public (or delegated to a private entity)
Japan–Thailand	To be determined	Limited products from ASEAN	Public (or delegated to a private entity)
Japan–Singapore	To be determined	No	Public (or delegated to a private entity)
MERCOSUR	None	No	Public (or delegated to a private entity)
MERCOSUR–Bolivia	None	Yes (Bolivia may cumulate from LAIA)	Public (or delegated to a private entity)
MERCOSUR–Chile	None	No	Public (or delegated to a private entity)
MERCOSUR–Colombia–Ecuador–Venezuela	None	Yes (within MERCOSUR and Andean Community)	Public (or delegated to a private entity)
MERCOSUR–Peru	None	Yes (within MERCOSUR and Andean Community)	Public (or delegated to a private entity)
Mexico–Nicaragua	7% (except chs. 1–27 and 50–63)	No	Self-certification
Mexico–Northern Triangle	7% (except chs. 1–27 and 50–63)	No	Self-certification

Table 7.2B (*cont.*)

RTA	De minimis	Extended cumulation	Certification method
Mexico–Uruguay	8% (except chs. 1–27 and 50–63)	No	Self-certification
Mexico–Bolivia	7% (not chs. 1–27 unless 05; not chs. 50–63)	No	Self-certification
Mexico–Chile	8% (except in agriculture and industrial products; 9% of weight in chs. 50–63)	No	Self-certification
Mexico–Costa Rica	7% (except in chs. 4–15 and headings 0901, 1701, 2105, 2202)	No	Self-certification
NAFTA	7% (exceptions in agriculture and industrial products; 7% of weight in chs. 50–63)	No	Self-certification
P4	10%	No	Self-certification
Paneuro	10% (8–10% of weight in textiles)	Yes (full in EEA)	Public; limited self-certification
Peru–Thailand	10%	No	Public (or delegated to a private entity)
SAFTA	None	No	Public (or delegated to a private entity)
SADC	10% (not chs. 50–63, 37, 98)	No	Two-step private and public
Singapore–Australia	2%	No	Public (or delegated to a private entity)
Thailand–New Zealand	10%	No	Self-certification
USA–Republic of Korea	10% (by weight in textiles; except in agriculture and processed agriculture products)	No	Self-certification

Table 7.2B (*cont.*)

RTA	De minimis	Extended cumulation	Certification method
USA–Panama	10% (by weight in textiles; except in agriculture and processed agriculture products)	Possibly for chs. 61 or 62	Self-certification
USA–Colombia	10% (by weight in textiles; except in agriculture and processed agriculture products)	Possibly with Peru	Self-certification
USA–Peru	10% (by weight in textiles; except in agriculture and processed agriculture products)	Possibly with Colombia	Self-certification
USA–Australia	10% (except in agriculture and processed agriculture products)	No	Self-certification
USA–Bahrain	None	Possibly with regional countries	Self-certification
USA–Chile	10% (by weight in textiles; except in agriculture and processed agriculture products)	No	Self-certification
USA–Israel	None	Yes (West Bank and Gaza)	Self-certification
USA–Jordan	None	QIZ cumulation from Israel	Self-certification
USA–Singapore	10% (except in various agriculture products; 7% of weight in chs. 50–63)	ISI*	Self-certification

*Integrated sourcing initiative. Primarily ICT products need not meet any rule of origin if shipped directly between the signatories.
Source: Authors' calculations on the basis of RTA texts.

Table 7.3B *Average restrictiveness by HS section for selected agreements*

Section	Andean Community	Argent.-Brazil-Peru	ASEAN	Australia-Singapore	CACM	CAFTA-DR	CARICOM	Chile-China	Chile-Rep. of Korea	Chile-Mexico	Chile-USA	ECOWAS	EU-Chile	Japan-Malaysia	Japan-Singapore	Japan-Thailand	MERCOSUR	MERCOSUR-Chile	Mexico-Bolivia	Mexico-Japan	NAFTA	PANEURO	SADC	USA-Israel	USA-Jordan	USA-Singapore	Non-preferential
1. Live animals	3.0	3.0	5.0	7.0	9.2	9.0	13.6	8.0	10.5	8.4	8.7	1.0	13.6	13.6	16.0	9.8	3.2	3.1	8.8	9.9	8.5	13.6	16.0	5.0	5.0	8.6	11.9
2. Vegetable products	3.0	3.0	5.0	7.0	8.4	7.8	10.2	8.0	8.4	8.0	8.2	1.0	11.1	8.0	16.0	7.8	3.0	3.0	8.0	8.0	7.8	11.1	12.7	5.0	5.0	7.9	14.2
3. Fats and oils	3.0	8.3	5.0	7.0	9.0	8.0	4.7	8.0	11.0	8.1	13.6	1.0	5.0	7.8	16.0	8.1	6.9	4.2	13.9	8.5	13.6	5.0	5.5	5.0	5.0	13.6	6
4. Food, beverages and tobacco	3.0	7.8	5.0	7.0	8.0	8.6	6.0	6.5	8.2	8.5	9.3	1.0	7.0	10.7	15.6	10.5	4.7	4.4	10.4	11.3	8.4	7.3	5.6	5.0	5.0	8.5	7.5
5. Mineral products	3.0	3.0	5.0	7.0	7.6	6.2	5.9	5.7	7.5	8.6	5.5	1.0	5.1	2.8	14.0	6.4	3.1	3.0	8.6	8.7	8.6	5.1	6.0	5.0	5.0	5.4	10.4
6. Chemicals	3.0	4.5	5.0	7.0	5.3	3.1	5.2	5.6	4.0	5.0	3.2	1.0	6.7	2.3	10.3	2.6	7.6	3.7	6.1	5.3	5.8	6.7	6.0	5.0	5.0	3.1	4.8
7. Plastics	3.0	3.0	5.0	7.4	6.7	4.5	4.8	5.6	4.1	8.7	6.5	1.0	5.2	3.0	11.0	3.1	3.0	4.1	8.8	10.1	10.2	5.2	10.7	5.0	5.0	3.6	6.2
8. Leather goods	3.0	3.0	4.9	9.1	5.6	6.6	6.2	5.0	6.9	9.9	7.9	1.0	6.0	10.8	15.3	9.7	3.0	3.0	8.8	5.0	7.2	4.5	5.8	5.0	4.9	7.5	5.9
9. Wood products	3.0	3.0	4.1	7.0	5.8	6.1	7.4	5.9	6.1	7.0	6.0	1.0	5.4	6.0	14.6	6.6	3.0	3.0	6.7	7.1	6.5	5.4	6.1	5.0	5.0	6.1	5.3
10. Pulp and paper	3.0	3.0	5.0	7.0	5.3	8.5	6.0	5.9	6.4	7.6	8.6	1.0	6.2	1.0	7.7	5.3	3.7	4.3	8.0	8.0	9.5	6.2	6.1	5.0	5.0	6.2	6.1
11. Textiles and apparel	3.0	4.5	4.0	9.9	8.0	16.0	6.1	6.0	14.9	3.0	16.1	1.0	4.0	12.9	13.1	12.4	7.4	7.8	16.0	16.0	16.1	4.0	2.9	5.0	4.0	16.3	6.9
12. Footwear	3.0	3.5	4.8	9.2	10.0	8.6	8.6	5.5	12.0	12.3	11.2	1.0	6.8	8.1	13.1	8.7	3.7	5.9	12.3	14.2	14.4	6.8	6.9	5.0	4.8	9.7	6.8

Table 7.3B (cont.)

Section	Andean Community	Argent.–Brazil–Peru	ASEAN	Australia–Singapore	CACM	CAFTA–DR	CARICOM	Chile–China	Chile–Rep. of Korea	Chile–Mexico	Chile–USA	ECOWAS	EU–Chile	Japan–Malaysia	Japan–Singapore	Japan–Thailand	MERCOSUR	MERCOSUR–Chile	Mexico–Bolivia	Mexico–Japan	NAFTA	PANEURO	SADC	USA–Israel	USA–Jordan	USA–Singapore	Non-preferential
13. Stone and glass	3.0	3.0	5.0	7.1	6.7	9.2	5.6	5.3	10.0	10.0	9.1	1.0	5.1	3.3	12.6	3.5	3.1	3.3	9.8	9.9	9.7	5.1	5.6	5.0	4.9	9.3	5.6
14. Jewellery	3.0	3.0	5.0	7.6	6.5	7.5	5.8	5.0	9.4	9.4	9.0	1.0	5.7	4.0	14.0	5.5	3.0	3.0	10.6	9.4	9.2	5.7	5.8	5.0	5.0	9.0	6.7
15. Base metals	3.0	3.3	5.6	7.1	6.3	7.0	6.0	5.3	8.0	9.1	8.4	1.0	5.4	1.1	11.6	3.8	3.3	4.0	9.7	8.7	9.2	5.5	5.2	5.0	5.0	7.6	6.0
16. Machinery and electrical equipment	3.0	4.7	5.0	7.1	4.6	5.5	6.0	5.2	6.1	5.8	6.0	1.0	6.8	1.0	16.0	2.1	5.2	6.3	5.9	5.0	6.0	6.9	6.9	5.0	5.0	5.9	5.8
17. Transportation equipment	3.9	5.3	5.0	7.6	7.1	4.7	6.0	5.2	4.2	4.7	6.0	1.0	3.7	2.3	15.9	3.4	4.9	6.9	7.1	7.9	7.5	5.6	6.8	5.0	5.0	6.4	7.3
18. Optics	2.8	3.2	5.0	7.1	5.0	4.1	6.0	5.0	5.1	6.4	4.8	1.0	6.2	1.1	15.8	2.3	4.4	5.3	6.2	4.9	5.4	6.2	6.7	5.0	5.0	5.3	6.6
19. Arms and ammunition	3.0	3.0	5.0	7.0	6.0	6.1	6.0	6.0	5.6	6.3	6.1	1.0	6.0	1.0	6.5	3.0	3.0	3.0	6.3	6.1	6.1	6.0	5.0	5.0	5.0	6.5	7.2
20. Diversified merchandise	3.1	3.0	4.8	7.2	5.0	5.8	5.9	5.5	6.0	6.7	6.5	1.0	5.5	1.5	12.0	3.1	3.1	5.2	6.9	6.9	6.4	5.5	5.5	5.0	5.0	6.6	6.3
21. Works of art	3.0	3.0	5.0	7.0	4.0	5.4	6.0	5.0	6.0	8.0	4.0	1.0	6.0	1.0	16.0	3.0	3.0	3.0	8.0	8.0	8.0	6.0	6.0	5.0	5.0	5.4	6.1

Source: Authors' calculations on the basis of RTAs.

Table 7.4B ROO combinations around the world, by regime (%)

	Andean Community	ANZCERTA	Argentina–Brazil–Peru	Argentina–Venezuela	Argentina–Colombia	Argentina–Ecuador	ASEAN	ASEAN–China	ASEAN–Korea	Australia–Singapore	Australia–Thailand	Bangkok	Brazil–Colomba	Brazil–Ecuador	Brazil–Venezuela
NC + TECH	2.0	0.0	18.1	12.0	14.0	14.6	16.0		8.2		0.1		17.1	17.6	12.1
NC + VC	1.4	0.1	11.1	13.3	13.9	13.6	79.4		76.3		0.0		14.1	14.2	14.2
NC + VC + TECH								100.0	0.1	100.0		100.0			
Wholly obtained							0.0		0.5		0.2				
Subtotal	**3.3**	**0.1**	**29.2**	**25.2**	**27.8**	**28.3**	**95.4**	**100.0**	**85.1**	**100.0**	**0.4**	**100.0**	**31.2**	**31.8**	**26.3**
CI		0.0													
CI + TECH											0.0				
CI + VC															
CI + VC + TECH															
CI + ECTC															
CI + ECTC + TECH															
Subtotal	**0.0**	**0.0**	**0.0**	**0.0**	**0.0**	**0.0**	**0.0**	**0.0**	**0.0**	**0.0**	**0.0**	**0.0**	**0.0**	**0.0**	**0.0**
CS	0.0	25.1					1.9	0.0	1.1		22.4	0.0			
CS + TECH		0.3									0.2				

Table 7.4B (*cont.*)

	Andean Community	ANZCERTA	Argentina–Brazil–Peru	Argentina–Venezuela	Argentina–Colombia	Argentina–Ecuador	ASEAN	ASEAN–China	ASEAN–Korea	Australia–Singapore	Australia–Thailand	Bangkok	Brazil–Colomba	Brazil–Ecuador	Brazil–Venezuela
CS + VC		0.2									0.2				
CS + VC + TECH															
CS + ECTC		5.1									5.9				
CS + ECTC + TECH															
CS + ECTC + VC															
Subtotal	**0.0**	**30.7**	**0.0**	**0.0**	**0.0**	**0.0**	**1.9**	**0.0**	**1.1**	**0.0**	**28.8**	**0.0**	**0.0**	**0.0**	**0.0**
CH	96.7	31.8	59.8	65.6	68.6	68.3	2.0		2.4		29.5		65.2	64.9	64.6
CH + TECH		0.0	6.8						0.3		1.5				
CH + VC		6.8		5.7					0.1		4.1		0.2		5.7
CH + VC + TECH															
CH + ECTC		7.1		0.6	0.6	0.6	0.5		0.4		5.3		0.6	0.6	0.6
CH + ECTC + TECH															
CH + ECTC + VC		3.6									6.2				
Subtotal	**96.7**	**49.4**	**66.6**	**72.0**	**69.3**	**68.9**	**2.5**	**0.0**	**3.2**	**0.0**	**46.7**	**0.0**	**66.1**	**65.5**	**70.9**

Table 7.4B (cont.)

	Andean Community	ANZCERTA	Argentina-Brazil-Peru	Argentina-Venezuela	Argentina-Colombia	Argentina-Ecuador	ASEAN	ASEAN-China	ASEAN-Korea	Australia-Singapore	Australia-Thailand	Bangkok	Brazil-Colomba	Brazil-Ecuador	Brazil-Venezuela
CC		14.7	2.4	1.9	2.0	2.0	0.2		4.7		12.8		1.9	1.9	1.9
CC + TECH		2.0							4.7						
CC + VC		0.2		0.1	0.1	0.1			0.0		3.7		0.1	0.1	0.1
CC + VC + TECH		2.6									5.6				
CC + ECTC		0.2	1.8	0.8	0.8	0.7					2.0		0.7	0.7	0.8
CC + ECTC – TECH									1.1						
CC + ECTC + VC															
Subtotal	**0.0**	**19.7**	**4.3**	**2.8**	**2.9**	**2.8**	**0.2**	**0.0**	**0.5**	**0.0**	**24.1**	**0.0**	**2.7**	**2.7**	**2.8**
TOTAL	**100.0**	**100.0**	**100.0**	**100.0**	**100.0**	**100.0**	**100.0**	**100.0**	**100.0**	**100.0**	**100.0**	**100.0**	**100.0**	**100.0**	**100.0**

Table 7.4B (*cont.*)

	CACM	CACM–DR	CAFTA–DR	Canada–Costa Rica	CARICOM	Chile–CACM	Chile–Canada	Chile–China	Chile–Colombia	Chile–Ecuador	Chile–Rep. of Korea	Chile–Mexico	Chile–Peru	Chile–USA	COMESA
NC + TECH	0.0	0.3	0.5		12.4	8.2	0.0		1.3	9.3		0.1	0.3		
NC + VC			0.6		25.9	0.1		88.0	0.2		0.6	0.6	0.6		100.0
NC + VC + TECH										0.0					
Wholly obtained		11.4			5.6	1.7	0.0							0.0	
Subtotal	**0.0**	**11.6**	**1.1**	**0.0**	**43.9**	**10.0**	**0.0**	**88.0**	**1.5**	**9.4**	**0.6**	**0.6**	**0.9**	**0.0**	**100.0**
CI	0.2	0.1	0.1	5.0			1.0					0.4		0.0	
CI + TECH				0.1			0.0								
CI + VC				0.5											
CI + VC + TECH				0.0											
CI + ECTC			0.0	0.4			0.2					0.3			
CI + ECTC + TECH			0.1	0.0	0.1										
Subtotal	**0.2**	**0.1**	**0.2**	**6.2**	**0.1**	**0.0**	**1.2**	**0.0**	**0.0**	**0.0**	**0.0**	**0.8**	**0.0**	**0.0**	**0.0**
CS	30.2	13.7	19.9	13.6		19.1	10.3		0.3		1.6	3.0	0.0	15.8	
CS + TECH	0.9%	0.4%	0.2%				0.1%							0.2%	
CS + VC			0.2%			0.0%	0.1%		0.1%		2.0%	0.8%		0.3%	
CS + VC + TECH				0.0											
CS + ECTC	0.2	0.6	6.1	1.0		0.5	4.4				0.3	2.3		6.3	
CS + ECTC + TECH							0.0							0.1	
CS + ECTC + VC							0.0				0.2			0.0	

Table 7.4B (*cont.*)

	CACM	CACM-DR	CAFTA-DR	Canada–Costa Rica	CARICOM	Chile–CACM	Chile Canada	Chile–China	Chile–Colombia	Chile–Ecuador	Chile–Rep. of Korea	Chile–Mexico	Chile–Peru	Chile–USA	COMESA
Subtotal	**31.3**	**14.6**	**26.3**	**14.7**	**(0.0)**	**19.6**	**15.0**	**0.0**	**0.4**	**0.0**	**4.0**	**6.1**	**0.0**	**22.8**	**0.0**
CH	37.5	52.0	24.3	37.6	53.0	54.3	17.5	0.9	83.9	90.6	44.4	46.2	82.9	24.1	
CH + TECH	0.5	0.9	1.3	0.0	0.2	0.6	0.2		0.0			0.0		1.3	
CH + VC			1.2	2.8			3.4				4.6	0.3		2.0	
CH + VC + TECH				0.1											
CH + ECTC	6.7	6.7	8.7	10.1	1.5	0.3	18.5		0.7		10.8	16.0	5.8	11.2	
CH + ECTC + TECH							0.1							0.1	
CH + ECTC + VC			0.2				0.5		0.0		0.5	0.5		0.4	
Subtotal	**44.8**	**59.6**	**35.7**	**50.6**	**54.6**	**55.2**	**40.3**	**0.9**	**84.6**	**90.6**	**60.2**	**63.0**	**88.7**	**39.1**	**0.0**
CC	21.1	6.3	22.3	16.8	1.4	15.2	28.3	11.2	11.7		22.9	28.2	1.9	23.0	
CC + TECH		0.0	0.5	0.1			0.1				0.0	0.0		0.8	
CC + VC			0.1						0.1		1.7	0.6		0.0	
CC + VC + TECH															
CC + ECTC	2.6	7.7	8.2	5.9			9.5		1.7		4.9	0.6	2.7	8.5	
CC + ECTC + TECH			5.7	5.8			5.6				5.7		5.8	5.9	
CC + ECTC + VC															
Subtotal	**23.7**	**14.1**	**36.7**	**28.6**	**1.4**	**15.2**	**43.5**	**11.2**	**13.5**	**0.0**	**35.2**	**29.5**	**10.4**	**38.1**	**0.0**
TOTAL	100.0	100.0	100.0	100.0	100.0	100.0	100.0	100.0	100.0	100.0	100.0	100.0	100.0	100.0	100.0

Table 7.4B (cont.)

	ECOWAS	EU–Chile	EU–Mexico	EU–S. Africa	G3	GCC	Japan–Malaysia	Japan–Singapore	Japan–Thailand	MERCOSUR	MERCOSUR–Bolivia	MERCOSUR–Chile	Mexico–Bolivia	Mexico–Costa Rica	Mexico–Japan
NC + TECH	0.0	19.0	19.3	18.9	0.1		0.2	13.0	1.2	4.8	21.9	21.2		0.0	0.2
NC + VC		11.7	11.0	11.1	0.4		0.6		0.4	13.7	20.2	22.3	0.0	0.0	0.2
NC + VC + TECH		4.3	3.8	4.2											
Wholly obtained		7.5	7.1	7.4		100.0		61.7							
Subtotal	**0.0**	**42.4**	**41.2**	**41.5**	**0.5**	**100.0**	**0.8**	**74.7**	**1.7**	**18.5**	**42.1**	**43.5**	**0.0**	**0.1**	**0.5**
CI		0.3	0.3	0.3	0.1								0.4		
CI + TECH		1.6	1.4	1.6											
CI + VC					0.5%										
CI + VC + TECH															
CI + ECTC		1.0	0.6	1.0	0.3			0.0					0.3	0.0	0.0
CI + ECTC + TECH		0.3	0.4	0.3											
Subtotal	**0.0**	**3.3**	**2.7**	**3.2**	**0.9**	**0.0**	**0.0**	**0.0**	**0.0**	**0.0**	**0.0**	**0.0**	**0.7**	**0.0**	**0.0**
CS	100.0				1.7		50.2		19.1				2.9	2.9	8.5
CS + TECH					0.1									0.0	
CS + VC					4.7		0.2						4.2	4.3	0.1
CS + VC + TECH															
CS + ECTC					1.5			0.0	0.1				2.0	1.7	2.0
CS + ECTC + TECH															
CS + ECTC + VC					0.2										0.0

Table 7.4B (*cont.*)

	ECOWAS	EU–Chile	EU–Mexico	EU–S. Africa	(G-3)	GCC	Japan–Malaysia	Japan–Singapore	Japan–Thailand	MERCOSUR	MERCOSUR–Bolivia	MERCOSUR–Chile	Mexico–Bolivia	Mexico–Costa Rica	Mexico–Japan
Subtotal	**100.0**	**0.0**	**0.0**	**0.0**	**3.2**	**0.0**	**50.4**	**0.0**	**19.2**	**0.0**	**0.0**	**0.0**	**9.1**	**8.9**	**10.7**
CH		21.8	21.1	21.2	26.0		14.3	18.6	39.1	63.8	45.1	45.8	25.1	24.8	25.4
CH + TECH		14.0	13.7	14.8	0.1		0.2	0.2	0.1	9.5			0.0	0.0	0.1
CH + VC		13.0	12.4	13.3	2.2		0.4	0.0	0.2	8.1	12.7	10.7	2.7	2.8	3.2
CH + VC + TECH		0.3	0.4	0.5											
CH + ECTC		1.0	2.1	1.3	8.3		2.5	5.2	7.6				18.6	19.1	13.3
CH + ECTC + TECH		0.1	0.5	0.1			5.5		0.2				0.3	0.3	
CH + ECTC + VC			0.4		0.5			0.0					0.5	0.5	0.5
Subtotal	**0.0**	**50.2**	**50.6**	**51.2**	**47.1**	**0.0**	**23.0**	**24.0**	**47.2**	**81.5**	**57.9**	**56.5**	**47.2**	**47.5**	**42.5**
CC		4.2	4.2	4.1	29.3		13.7		19.8				29.5	31.6	30.3
CC + TECH			1.3		0.0		8.0		5.2				0.0		0.1
CC + VC					0.2								0.4	0.3	
CC + VC + TECH															
CC + ECTC			0.0		8.0		3.7	1.3	5.8				7.2	5.7	10.0
CC + ECTC + TECH					5.9		0.4		1.1				5.7	5.9	5.9
CC + ECTC + VC													0.1		
Subtotal	**0.0**	**4.2**	**5.5**	**4.1**	**43.3**	**0.0**	**25.8**	**1.3**	**32.0**	**0.0**	**0.0**	**0.0**	**42.9**	**43.5**	**46.3**
TOTAL	**100.0**	**100.0**	**100.0**	**100.0**	**100.0**	**100.0**	**100.0**	**100.0**	**100.0**	**100.0**	**100.0**	**100.0**	**100.0**	**100.0**	**100.0**

Table 7.4B (cont.)

	Mexico–N. Triangle	Mexico–Nicaragua	Mexico–Uruguay	NAFTA	P4	PANEURO	Paraguay–Colombia	Paraguay–Ecuador	Paraguay–Peru	Paraguay–Venezuela	Peru–Thailand	SADC	SAFTA	Thailand–N. Zealand	Uruguay–Colombia
NC + TECH	0.0	0.0	0.1	0.4		18.8		8.4	5.5	0.5	0.6	15.2		3.9	0.5
NC + VC		0.0	0.2			11.1		0.0				23.8			
NC + VC + TECH						4.3					3.3	0.8			
Wholly obtained				0.0		7.4						8.9			
Subtotal	**0.0**	**0.0**	**0.3**	**0.4**	**0.0**	**41.5**	**0.0**	**8.4**	**5.5**	**0.5**	**3.9**	**48.6**	**0.0**	**3.9**	**0.5**
CI	0.6	0.4	0.9	0.8		0.3						1.9		0.2	
CI + TECH				0.0		1.6					0.1				
CI + VC															
CI + VC + TECH															
CI + ECTC	0.4	0.3	0.3	0.4		1.1						0.5			
CI − ECTC + TECH						0.3									
Subtotal	**1.0**	**0.7**	**1.2**	**1.1**	**0.0**	**3.2**	**0.0**	**0.0**	**0.0**	**0.0**	**0.1**	**2.4**	**0.0**	**0.2**	**0.5**
CS	9.1	2.8	7.4	9.4	20.3						25.5	0.8		24.8	
CS + TECH				0.1							0.3				
CS + VC	0.2	4.1	0.2	0.1	0.0						0.3		3.4		
CS + VC + TECH															
CS + ECTC	3.5	2.5	3.2	4.3	0.5						1.2			0.2	
CS + ECTC + TECH				0.0										0.0	
CS + ECTC + VC		0.2		0.0											
Subtotal							**0.0**	**0.0**	**0.0**	**0.0**			**0.0**		**0.0**

Table 7.4B (cont.)

	Mexico–N. Triangle	Mexico–Nicaragua	Mexico–Uruguay	NAFTA	P4	PANEURO	Paraguay–Colombia	Paraguay–Ecuador	Paraguay–Peru	Paraguay–Venezuela	Peru–Thailand	SADC	SAFTA	Thailand–N. Zealand	Uruguay–Colombia
Subtotal	**12.8**	**9.6**	**10.7**	**14.0**	**20.8**	**0.0**	**0.0**	**0.0**	**0.0**	**0.0**	**27.3**	**0.8**	**3.4**	**25.0**	**0.0**
CH	23.6	24.6	40.6	18.0	44.8	21.2	99.6	89.5	93.6	99.2	36.2	44.5	96.6	40.8	97.2
CH + TECH	0.1	0.0	0.0	0.2		14.7					1.3	1.8		0.3	
CH + VC	0.8	2.7	0.1	3.7	4.2	13.3					0.8	0.1		1.6	
CH + VC + TECH						0.6						1.3			
CH + ECTC	17.8	19.1	16.0	18.4	1.4	1.3	0.0				8.1			0.2	0.6
CH + ECTC + TECH	0.1	0.5	0.5	0.4		0.1									
CH + ECTC + VC	0.3			0.6	4.2									5.4	
Subtotal	**42.7**	**46.9**	**57.3**	**41.2**	**54.5**	**51.2**	**99.6**	**89.5**	**93.6**	**99.2**	**46.4**	**47.7**	**96.6**	**48.2**	**97.8**
CC	28.8	29.8	24.7	28.0	16.7	4.1		1.8	0.1		21.2	0.5		13.3	0.6
CC + TECH		0.0	0.4	0.1							0.1			1.1	
CC + VC	0.0	0.3			2.4									3.3	
CC + VC + TECH					5.6									4.7	
CC + ECTC	9.2	6.8	5.4	9.6	0.1		0.4	0.2	0.7	0.3	1.1			0.2	1.0
CC + ECTC + TECH	5.7	5.6		5.6							0.0				
CC + ECTC + VC		0.1%													
Subtotal	**43.6**	**42.7**	**30.5**	**43.3**	**24.7**	**4.1**	**0.4**	**2.1**	**0.8**	**0.3**	**22.4**	**0.5**	**0.0**	**22.6**	**1.6**
TOTAL	100.0	100.0	100.0	100.0	100.0	100.0	100.0	100.0	100.0	100.0	100.0	100.0	100.0	100.0	100.0

Appendix C: Methodologies for measuring restrictiveness of ROOs

C.1   Estevadeordal (2000)

The observation rule yields a ROO index as follows:

$$
\begin{aligned}
y &= 1 && \text{if } y^* \leqslant \text{CI} \\
y &= 2 && \text{if CI} < y^* \leqslant \text{CS} \\
y &= 3 && \text{if CS} < y^* \leqslant \text{CS and VC} \\
y &= 4 && \text{if CS and VC} < y^* \leqslant \text{CH} \\
y &= 5 && \text{if CH} < y^* \leqslant \text{CH and VC} \\
y &= 6 && \text{if CH and VC} < y^* \leqslant \text{CC} \\
y &= 7 && \text{if CC} < y^* \leqslant \text{CC and TECH}
\end{aligned}
$$

where y^* is the latent level of restrictiveness of ROOs (rather than the observed level of restrictiveness); CI is the change of tariff classification at the level of tariff item (eight to ten digits), CS is the change at the level of subheading (six-digit HS), CH is the change at the level of heading (four digits), CC is the change at the level of chapter (two-digit HS); VC is a value content criterion; and TECH is a technical requirement.

Suominen (2004) makes three modifications to the observation rule in the case of ROOs for which no CTC is specified, in order to allow for coding of such ROOs in the Paneuro, SADC and other regimes where not all ROOs feature a CTC component. First, ROOs based on the import content rule are equated to a change in heading (value 4) if the content requirement allows up to 50 per cent of non-originating inputs of the ex-works price of the product. Value 5 is assigned when the share of permitted non-originating inputs is below 50 per cent, as well as when the import content criterion is combined with a technical requirement. Second, ROOs featuring one exception alone are assigned the value of 1 if the exception concerns a heading or a number of headings, and 2 if the exception concerns a chapter or a number of chapters. Third, ROOs based on the wholly obtained criterion are assigned value 7.

C.2   Harris (2007)

This index is based on a points system that adds or subtracts points, based on different elements used in the definition of the rule of origin. The change of classification points are based on the magnitude of the required change, as are exception points and the addition points.

(Additions are like negative exceptions, where non-originating inputs that would otherwise be prohibited by the change of classification are permitted.) Value test points are based on the magnitude of the required value content, with adjustments that depend on the method of calculation. The point values were calibrated by observing the relative frequencies of alternative rule combinations in a sample of thirteen RTAs in the Americas.

Restrictiveness points

Change of classification points

ΔI	+2
ΔS	+4
ΔH	+6
ΔC	+8

Exception points

exI	+4
> exI and ⩽ exS	+5
> cxS and ⩽ exII	+6
> exH and ⩽ exC	׀7
> exC	+8

Addition points

addI	−5
> addI and ⩽ addS	−6
> addS and ⩽ addH	−7
> addH and < addC	−8
add without CC[51]	+8

Value test points

> 0% and ⩽ 40%	+5
> 40% and ⩽ 50%	+6
> 50% and ⩽ 60%	+7
> 60%	+8
Net cost	+1
Technical requirement points	+4
Alternative rule points	−3
Wholly obtained	+16

Appendix D: Sectoral ROO restrictiveness in main ROO families

Table 7.1D *Similarity of rules in selected families (% of agreements coinciding at the product level)*

Section	Africa	Americas—Asia	Americas	Asia	Chile	Europe	Japan	Mexico	Singapore	USA	USA–NG	Global
1. Live animals	25	67	47	34	56	100	74	69	39	55	90	31
2. Vegetable products	27	77	48	39	61	100	61	81	40	58	92	34
3. Fats and oils	27	61	40	25	26	100	66	45	26	39	65	26
4. Food, beverages and tobacco	31	36	43	30	43	98	55	56	29	51	79	28
5. Mineral products	25	55	49	29	43	100	35	88	40	49	80	29
6. Chemicals	25	29	48	26	29	99	47	49	27	41	61	32
7. Plastics	25	30	52	27	29	88	45	46	30	32	46	35
8. Leather goods	25	54	49	32	37	100	54	46	32	56	88	30
9. Wood products	25	84	49	51	59	100	67	75	48	60	98	37
10. Pulp and paper	25	59	47	38	48	100	29	68	42	43	68	30
11. Textile and apparel	29	57	31	20	43	95	36	60	25	67	86	27
12. Footwear	25	45	35	28	42	94	39	71	33	42	61	25

Table 7.1D (*cont.*)

Section	Africa	Americas–Asia	Americas	Asia	Chile	Europe	Japan	Mexico	Singapore	USA	USA–NG	Global
13. Stone and glass	25	57	49	25	48	100	27	88	35	53	88	31
14. Jewellery	25	60	49	29	47	100	42	74	31	45	78	30
15. Base metals	26	46	44	50	45	98	27	69	35	49	79	29
16. Machinery and electrical equipment	25	42	44	26	43	96	30	74	31	49	81	31
17. Transportation equipment	25	41	48	26	40	94	28	64	27	52	66	34
18. Optics	25	50	54	26	53	96	31	69	30	56	83	37
19. Arms and ammunition	25	47	50	28	58	100	26	76	50	67	88	34
20. Diversified merchandise	26	42	48	25	42	97	29	81	29	55	67	32
21. Works of art, miscellaneous	25	46	49	26	25	100	25	89	25	48	79	30

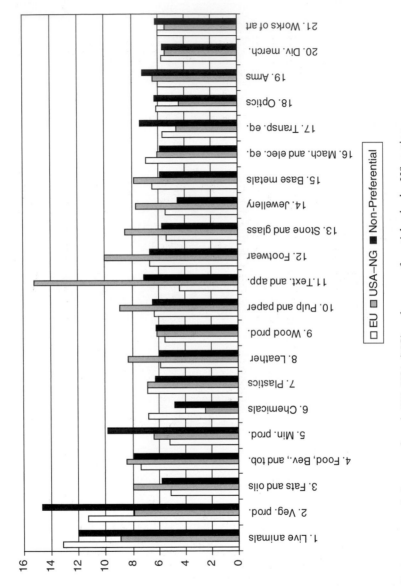

Figure 7.1D Average restrictiveness of mode EU, USA (NG) and non-preferential rules by HS section

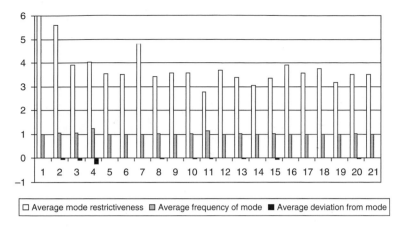

Figure 7.2D Africa (four agreements)

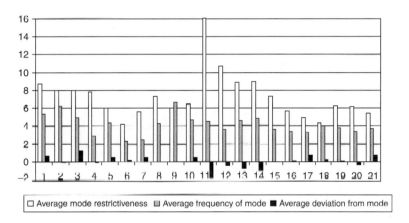

Figure 7.3D Americas–Asia (seven agreements)

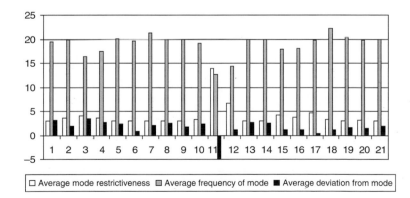

Figure 7.4D Americas (thirty-nine agreements)

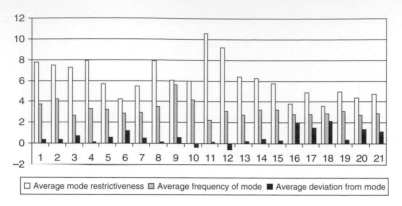

Figure 7.5D Asia (eleven agreements)

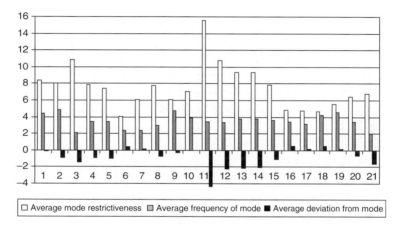

Figure 7.6D Chile (eight agreements)

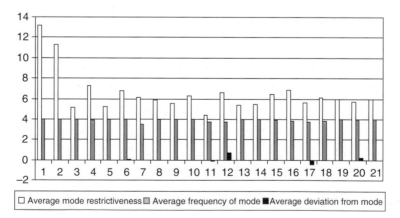

Figure 7.7D Europe (four agreements)

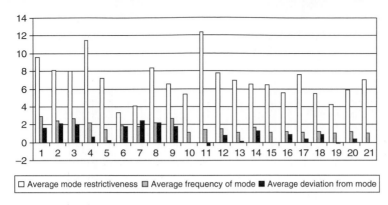

Figure 7.8D Japan (four agreements)

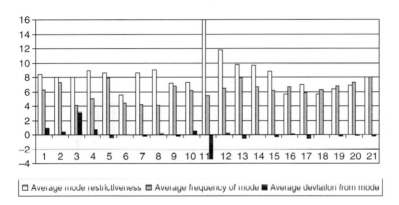

Figure 7.9D Mexico (nine agreements)

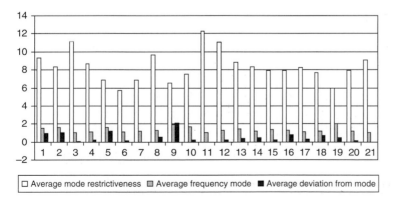

Figure 7.10D Singapore (four agreements)

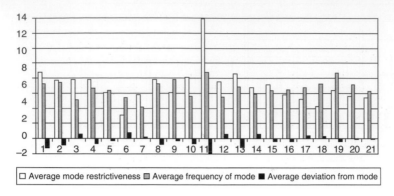

□ Average mode restrictiveness ▨ Average frequency of mode ■ Average deviation from mode

Figure 7.11D USA (thirteen agreements)

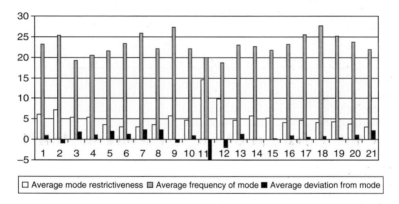

□ Average mode restrictiveness ▨ Average frequency of mode ■ Average deviation from mode

Figure 7.12D Global (sixty-nine agreements)

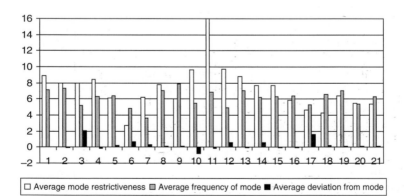

□ Average mode restrictiveness ▨ Average frequency of mode ■ Average deviation from mode

Figure 7.13D USA–NG (ten agreements)

Table 7.2D *Revealed families (occurring in more than 200 products)*

Revealed family	Frequency
Bangkok	2,227
JPNSING	1,822
AUSSING	1,650
ASEANKOR, ECOWAS, JPNMYS	1,148
ASEAN, CHLCHN, USABAH, USAISR, USAJOR, USAMOR	1,028
ASEAN, USABAH, USAISR, USAJOR, USAMOR	952
COMESA	828
ASEANKOR, ECOWAS	741
ARGBRAPER, PRYPER, URYPER, ARGCOL, ARGECU, ARGVEN, BRACOL, BRAECU, BRAVEN, PRYCOL, PRYECU, PRYVEN, URYCOL, URYECU, URYVEN, CANDINA, CHLPER, MERCOSUR, MERCOSURBOL, MERCOSURCHL, SAFTA	708
ECOWAS	708
AUSSING, Bangkok	574
USAISR	547
ASEANKOR, ECOWAS, JPNMYS, JPNTHA	458
MERCOSURBOL, MERCOSURCHL	409
AUSTHA	401
PANEURO, EUCHL, EUMEX, EUZAF	383
PRYPER	346
ASEANCHN, CARICOM, CHLCHN	334
AUSSING, MERCOSUR, MERCOSURBOL, MERCOSURCHL, SADC	307
P4, THANZ	294
AUSSING, PANEURO, EUCHL, EUMEX, EUZAF	276
CACM-RD	275
ARGBRAPER, PRYPER, URYPER, ARGCOL, ARGECU, ARGVEN, BRACOL, BRAECU, BRAVEN, PRYCOL, PRYECU, PRYVEN, URYCOL, URYECU, URYVEN, CANDINA, CHLPER, JPNTHA, MERCOSUR, MERCOSURBOL, MERCOSURCHL, SAFTA	272
AUSTHA, USACOL, USAPER	259
Bangkok, MERCOSUR	242
CHLKOR	236
ASEANKOR	233
ARGVEN	229
CHLMCCA, ECOWAS	218
AUSNZ, P4, THANZ	211
JPNMYS	202

Comment

OLIVIER CADOT

This is a very interesting chapter that breaks new empirical ground in the study of rules of origin through the sheer exhaustiveness of the authors' data analysis. The literature on rules of origin (ROOs) so far has been long on the cost of ROO restrictiveness and heterogeneity across products, but short on heterogeneity across RTAs. This is the first work — to my knowledge — to address the second, very important issue.

The chapter presents a remarkable snapshot of the current heterogeneity of ROOs in RTAs around world, the aim being to assess hurdles to convergence and harmonization. But before we talk about harmonization, let us step back a little and revisit the usual justifications for ROOs. As Michael Gasiorek and his colleagues remarked in Chapter 4, every paper on ROOs opens by stating that they are needed to avoid trade deflection. But in North–South regional trade arrangements (RTAs), ROOs are largely dictated by Northern partners, who have the lowest tariffs. If there was trade deflection, it would not go through Southern ports; so if trade deflection was the problem, the Northern countries' insistence on restrictive ROOs would be odd indeed. One may say, the question is not one of tariffs but of customs monitoring capabilities; a sort of weak-link argument. Fine, but if all EU-bound HDTV sets were ever to transit through Douala and sneak in under a 'made in Senegal' label, a more direct remedy would be capacity-building assistance for customs. Let us face reality: trade deflection is a fig leaf. ROOs are there to limit the capacity of Southern producers to compete in final-good markets and — more importantly — to create rents for Northern producers of intermediate goods.

Going back one more step, what are the key motivations of North–South RTAs? First, as explained in Ethier's 1998 paper, they are vehicles to encourage trade reforms in the South and lock them in. Trade preferences in intermediate products induce multinationals to channel FDI to the Southern partner, which is supported by empirical evidence. The FDI rewards the reform and makes it politically viable in the South.

In a frictionless world with 'symmetric' developing countries, marginal preferences can do the job; in reality, some market access improvement is needed. If ROOs nullify that improvement, the FDI will not take place.

Alternatively, North–South RTAs with ROOs can be used to create 'mini-worlds' where Heckscher–Ohlin trade can take place (capital-intensive intermediates being produced in the North and assembled with cheap labour in the South). Without this arrangement — say, if shirts were made from yarn to button-sewing at EU labour costs — the whole industry would have to move offshore. Thus, North–South RTAs can have the (intentional) effect of preserving the viability of vertical clusters for the benefit of upstream intermediate goods producers, at an acceptable welfare cost.

Why does this all matter? 'Multilateralizing RTAs' means making it easier for companies to set up regional production networks — what Richard Baldwin called 'unbundling'. The first of the two RTA aims identified above (the developmental one) is consistent with this, because unbundling means relocating labour-intensive activities to low-income countries. Thus, in practice if we want, say, Lesotho to grow a viable garment industry, what is needed is Asian FDI and relatively free use of Asian intermediates, implying flexible and mutually compatible ROOs for which Estevadeordal, Harris and Suominen have charted a course.

If, by contrast, the dominant objective is protectionist (preserving the viability of North–South clusters) then allowing free use of Chinese intermediates is precisely what we do not want. In that case, there will simply be no will for harmonization or convergence. Moreover, larger 'mini-worlds', being more self-sufficient, can impose restrictive ROOs at lesser welfare costs — which may help explain the authors' observation that size correlates with average restrictiveness.

Let us assume that intentions are good, so the issue is to make ROOs more compatible across RTAs. The chapter takes two approaches to measuring current divergence: in instrument use and in restrictiveness levels.

Start with the first. Although the authors take it for granted, it is not obvious what the business cost involved is if a maker of, say, fabric sells to a buyer in a zone with a 40 per cent local content and to another with a 60 per cent local content. What is more obvious is that when divergence in instrument use prevents cumulation, then we know that trade is depressed, so there must be a cost. But why would cumulation be impossible with different ROOs? Again, the authors take for granted that if two overlapping RTAs had cumulation and the same external tariffs, but different ROOs – say, different local value contents – evil things would happen. They do not explain, however, what those evil things would be. We need more work to establish what is the real cost to companies from facing different ROOs, and whether divergence in ROOs really jeopardizes prospects for cumulation.

As for divergence in restrictiveness levels, we know from Esteva-deordal's pioneering work how to go about it using an observational rule, but we are interested in what the authors call 'effective restrict-iveness', which depends not just on the ROOs on the books, but on industry input–output structures, about which we do not know much. To see what the problem is, consider the 'wholly obtained' criterion. Taken at face value, it looks very restrictive (zero per cent foreign content) but in practice, given that it is mostly applied to agriculture, it is unlikely to bind. The authors' choice in this regard is to go for a coding of ROOs that is more detailed than Estevadeordal's original coding, but that comes at the cost of a higher risk of misclassification, and what is needed is arguably not to go into more detail but to base the coding on a stronger theoretical basis.

The last part of the chapter develops the idea that the ultimate objective of the multilateralization of RTAs could be achieved by the merger of RTAs into a single cumulation zone with a single list of ROOs – a sort of 'global Paneuro'. As the authors themselves admit, the multilateral route based on their 'cap-and-con' principle (putting limits on the restrictiveness of ROOs and then negotiating them down multi-laterally) is 'unlikely to work' given the very slow pace of non-preferential ROO negotiation, where the stakes are lower.

I would suggest an alternative approach based on the 'competition of systems', because the EU's current approach to reforming ROOs has the potential to set a standard. The EU transformed its preferential ROO regime in two steps: by going from different ROO lists across RTAs to a single list in 1997, and by going from the single-list system to a single instrument today. Why a single instrument? Essentially, the benefit is in the transparency. Eliminating the most opaque and discretionary instruments (like technical requirements which act much like technical barriers to trade, TBTs) would make it easier to compare system re-strictiveness. So the argument in favour of a single instrument is much like that in favour of tariffication of NTBs.

Which single instrument? There are essentially two candidates. A change of tariff classification (CTC) across the board would be simple to use, but the problem is that it would have to be based on the harmonized system, which was not designed for that. A change of heading can mean very different things in textiles where headings are narrow, or in machinery where they are very wide. But reducing differences in effective CTC restrictiveness would mean varying requirements across products – re-opening the Pandora's box. By contrast, a regional value content (RVC) is conceptually clearer and logical. The problem is that it may not necessarily be easy to use for small companies. Be that as it may, this is the route that the EU has decided on. Once the instrument is chosen, the real difficulty is the conversion itself. One approach is to use preference utilization rates as the yardstick, to regress them on ROOs, and then to invert the equation to find the 'neutral' RVC that would give the same utilization rate. Doing this has the benefit of highlighting the 'revealed-preference' restrictiveness of current systems. Once this conversion is done, the next step would be to reduce cross-product variance in RVCs so as to strive for a uniform rate. That uniform rate could then be negotiated down much more easily than the current array of complex and opaque rules.

Would competition of systems work? Is there any competition between systems? The authors remark that there is a general trend towards less restrictive ROOs in the Americas, so in a way the Commission's proposed reform goes in a direction that is 'in the air', and the adoption of a single RVC instrument would make Paneuro more similar to ASEAN and could then facilitate the emergence of a global model of preferential ROOs.

References

Ethier, W. (1998) 'The New Regionalism', *Economic Journal* 108 (449): 1149–61.

8

Legal avenues to 'multilateralizing regionalism': beyond Article XXIV[1]

JOOST PAUWELYN

1 Introduction

A core feature of regional trade agreements (RTAs) is that they offer, or are supposed to offer, WTO-plus liberalization. The question that this book examines is how these WTO-plus elements could be 'multilateralized'. To give teeth to WTO-plus benefits in RTAs, most RTAs include regional dispute settlement. This chapter analyses how these regional dispute settlement systems, and the legal disciplines they enforce, interact with multilateral dispute settlement at the WTO. Failure to give effect to regional dispute settlement may endanger WTO-plus liberalization; finding a legal balance and mutual support between RTAs and the WTO can be one of the ways to 'multilateralize regionalism'.

Most legal analyses of the WTO and regionalism focus on GATT Article XXIV.[2] This Article (like GATS Article V) explains when the WTO permits the creation of inherently discriminatory customs unions (CUs) and free trade agreements (FTAs). A focus on Article XXIV puts the WTO and its rules at the centre of the universe. It presumes that the WTO effectively decides on when and how regional agreements are concluded.

This chapter takes a different approach. It is grounded in general international law. Its starting point is that Article XXIV is inoperative as a discipline or brake on the creation and continued existence of regional agreements: politically, WTO members consistently fail to check regional

---

[1] This chapter has been financed by the State Secretariat for Economic Affairs (SECO). The views expressed in the chapter are the views of its author and do not necessarily reflect the views or positions of SECO and Switzerland.
[2] For recent examples see the chapters in Bartels and Ortino (2006). For a notable exception in that volume, see Van Damme (2006).

agreements[3]; in dispute settlement, WTO members shy away from challenging regional agreements[4] and where Article XXIV is raised as a defence, panels and the Appellate Body do everything to avoid it.[5] The political *and* legal reality is, therefore, that regional agreements are here to stay, whether or not they comply with WTO rules. Rather than lament their inconsistency with WTO principles, or be exasperated by the 'spaghetti bowl' of overlapping agreements that results, it may be more fruitful to think of how the web of WTO and co-existing regional agreements can be untangled so as to give maximum effect to both.

Consequently, the central question that this chapter addresses is this: given that Article XXIV is inoperative and, as a result, regional agreements continue to exist and proliferate (whether or not they comply with Article XXIV), how do WTO rules and regional agreements interact and what happens in the event of overlap or conflict? How can negotiators regulate this overlap and what should adjudicators do when they face it?

The 'maze of regulatory regimes' (Fiorentino, Verdeja and Toqueboeuf, 2006: 26) or 'continued splintering of trading arrangements' ('Multilateralizing Regionalism', 2007: 1) that result from the proliferation of regional agreements is often referred to as one of the principal drawbacks of regionalism. Any progress towards untangling this maze – the principal objective of this chapter – has multiple benefits: it would

---

[3] The only exception being the Czech Republic–Slovakia customs union. See Fiorentino, Verdeja and Toqueboeuf (2006: 27).

[4] See Mavroidis (2006: 187) ('WTO Members have only on very few occasions challenged the consistency of a PTA with the multilateral rules before a panel.'). Three possible reasons for why WTO members refrain from challenging regional agreements before a panel are: (i) all WTO members (except Mongolia) have now concluded regional agreements and no one has an interest in clarifying or tightening the rules under Article XXIV as this might work against members' own regional programmes; (ii) WTO members may not trust panels to make binding decisions on the economically complex question of Article XXIV compliance; (iii) if a regional agreement does not liberalize 'substantially all the trade' within the region, and thereby violates Article XXIV, third parties may not have an incentive to challenge this inconsistency, as the most logical result would be more discrimination (i.e. more regional liberalization and preferences) rather than less discrimination.

[5] See, for example, the Panel and Appellate Body in *Turkey – Textiles* which simply presumed (without further analysis) that the EC–Turkey customs union meets GATT Article XXIV. See also WTO case law under the Safeguards Agreement where panels and the Appellate Body have managed to avoid any ruling under Article XXIV on the question of non-application of a safeguard to imports from within a regional arrangement (discussed in Pauwelyn, 2004a). Most recently, the panel in *Brazil – Tyres* equally avoided any examination of an exclusion for MERCOSUR imports under GATT Article XXIV.

reduce the cost of business, facilitate the work of policymakers and adjudicators and, most importantly, unlock the welfare benefits of trade liberalization in both the WTO and regional agreements.[6]

To shift the focus from the WTO's (unsuccessful) claim to hierarchy and supremacy over regional agreements (e.g. in Article XXIV), to a situation of mutual recognition, accommodation and respect, this chapter advocates in particular:

(1) that the WTO stop focusing on regional agreements, which it ought to control, as its nemesis (e.g. pursuant to Article XXIV) and instead integrate regional developments into WTO activities by, for example, allowing WTO dispute settlement panels to interpret and apply WTO rules with reference to regional arrangements agreed to by both parties ('multilateralize regionalism' at the WTO); and

(2) instead of relying solely on Article XXIV as an interface, that negotiators of regional agreements themselves carefully regulate interactions with WTO agreements so as to preserve the integrity of both systems ('multilateralize regionalism' in regional agreements).

From this perspective, untangling the maze of WTO and regional agreements so as to enhance mutual recognition and respect at both levels is but one legal avenue for 'multilateralizing regionalism' (the WTO considers regional developments; regional fora consider the WTO).

The chapter proceeds as follows. First, we set out the different scenarios of overlap between WTO and regional agreements so as to facilitate and sharpen the analysis. Second, the chapter describes the basic rules on overlap and conflict of multiple agreements under general international law. Third, the chapter applies these basic rules to specific questions of overlap/conflict under recently concluded FTAs (such as the TRIPS-plus debate and competing dispute settlement procedures). The chapter focuses in particular on how FTAs recently concluded by the US and the EC regulate overlap, and the lessons that can be drawn from these FTAs for other WTO members when they negotiate or litigate regional agreements. Finally, the chapter concludes with a number of policy guidelines on how to facilitate the interaction between WTO and regional agreements.

---

[6] A more cynical view is that one should not untangle the maze or spaghetti bowl of WTO and regional agreements, but rather let it fester in the hope that 'the political and economic costs of increasing fragmentation [will] lead to a reversal of regionalism' ('Multilateralizing Regionalism', 2007: 1).

2 Different scenarios

To start our analysis of how the WTO and regional agreements interact outside the existential limits of Article XXIV, let us first lay out a number of scenarios where such interactions can occur. At least four distinctions with important legal consequences can be made, as follows.

Overlaps of substantive trade rules versus overlaps in dispute settlement procedures

A procedural overlap arises, for example, where a country challenges another country first under a regional agreement (such as MERCOSUR or NAFTA) and, thereafter, the dispute is sent a second time before the WTO (*Argentina – Poultry* and *Mexico – Soft Drinks* offer related examples).[7] One of the case studies in the section below focuses on this type of overlap. In contrast, a substantive overlap arises, for example, when the WTO permits a safeguard or health measure but a regional agreement prohibits such measure within the region (see *US – Steel* and *Brazil – Tyres* for related examples).

Importantly, an overlap of substantive rules can occur in a specific dispute settlement procedure (e.g. before a NAFTA or WTO panel) where special rules on applicable law and conflict may exist,[8] or in the abstract, that is outside any dispute settlement mechanism (e.g. where governments or businesses ask which rule prevails under public international law outside a specific dispute).

Overlaps between WTO and regional agreements versus overlaps amongst different regional agreements

In most debates the question is how, for example, WTO rules on the tariffication of agricultural quotas relate to NAFTA rules on a tariff

---

[7] Although generally about the same 'measure' or 'subject matter', one 'dispute' before NAFTA or MERCOSUR and another 'dispute' before the WTO may, however, have crucial differences. For example, anti-dumping and countervailing duties can be challenged under NAFTA Chapter 19 before bi-national panels; they can also be challenged directly at the WTO. Yet NAFTA proceedings check the duties against the domestic law of the defending country; the WTO proceedings check the duties against the international rules of the WTO. Similarly, a dispute before MERCOSUR, by definition, challenges the measure under MERCOSUR rules (say, MERCOSUR rules on non-tariff barriers as in *Argentina – Poultry*), whereas the dispute before the WTO, by definition, challenges the measure under WTO rules (say, the Anti-dumping Agreement as in *Argentina – Poultry*).

[8] See rule 8 below.

standstill (see the NAFTA dispute on *Canada – Agricultural Products*). In other situations, however, different regional agreements may overlap: for example, how do the US–Chile and the EC–Chile FTAs interact; how does SACU affect US–South Africa FTA negotiations; how does the EC–Turkey customs union interact with FTAs concluded by the EC and third parties such as Mexico or the Republic of Korea; or how would NAFTA interact with a future FTA? In Section 4 we address some of these overlaps.

Overlaps where the rules are complementary versus equivalent versus contradictory

In overlap situations where the FTA simply adds new obligations (on, for example, competition, investment or labour), none of which were previously covered by the WTO, no genuine problems arise. In that scenario, complaints under those chapters can obviously only be brought under the FTA. In other overlap scenarios, however, the two regimes impose substantially equivalent rules. One example is national treatment under the WTO and NAFTA, or sanitary and phyto-sanitary measures (SPS) disciplines under the WTO and US FTAs. In such cases one of the core questions is where a dispute under such substantially equivalent rules can or should be brought (the WTO, NAFTA or potentially both).[9] This scenario is complicated by the fact that, for example, national treatment can be committed under the WTO and NAFTA or FTA provisions on both trade and investment. In *Mexico – Soft Drinks*, for example, the US brought a national treatment claim to the WTO. At the same time, US investors in Mexico brought a similar investment claim before a NAFTA Chapter 11 tribunal.

In a third scenario the overlapping rules are neither complementary nor substantively equivalent, but rather potentially contradictory. Here one can distinguish between two types of cases:

(1) A regional agreement may prevent or excuse what would otherwise be a breach of WTO law. In *Mexico – Soft Drinks*, for example, Mexico tried (unsuccessfully) to excuse its breach of WTO national treatment with reference to NAFTA. In *Brazil – Tyres*, Brazil referred to a MERCOSUR ruling to excuse an exclusion for MERCOSUR imports which the EC claimed to be inconsistent with GATT.

---

[9] Discussed in Section 4 below.

(2) A WTO rule may prevent or excuse what would otherwise be a breach of a regional agreement. In *Canada – Agricultural Products* (a NAFTA Chapter 20 panel) Canada successfully justified new tariffs that were on the face of it inconsistent with a NAFTA standstill clause with reference to Canada's WTO tariffication obligations under the WTO Agreement on Agriculture. A similar question may arise in the context of the TRIPS and public health debate: could WTO decisions offering flexibility on compulsory licensing be used to overcome claims of intellectual property (IP) violations under a regional (TRIPS-plus) agreement?[10]

Overlaps where the two agreements are binding on both parties versus overlaps that involve an agreement that is binding on only one of the parties

An overlap situation must always be judged as between two specific countries. In most cases, the overlapping agreements will be binding on both countries. This is the case, for example, when in a dispute between the US and Mexico, WTO rules and NAFTA rules overlap. WTO and NAFTA rules are binding on both the US and Mexico, but in other situations one of the overlapping agreements may be binding on only one of the two countries. In *EC – Bananas*, for example, there were overlaps between WTO rules and the Lomé Convention, to which the US was not a party. Similarly, in *Brazil – Tyres*, where there were overlaps between WTO and MERCOSUR rules, the EC was obviously not bound by MERCOSUR.

3 Basic rules

With the above scenarios of overlap in mind, we can now turn to some of the basic rules of international law that apply to overlapping or conflicting agreements. This section develops eight such rules.[11]

Rule 1: All treaties are, in principle, of equal value

Unlike domestic law where there is a hierarchy between, for example, the constitution, statutes and communal decrees, in international law

---

[10] Discussed in Section 4 below.   [11] For a full discussion see Pauwelyn (2003a).

there is no inherent hierarchy.[12] Unless otherwise provided, all treaties are, in principle, created equal.

Thus, the fact that, for example, the WTO has 151 members and NAFTA only 3, or that the WTO is a multilateral treaty and an FTA is a bilateral treaty, does not mean that the WTO by definition prevails over other trade agreements. Both the WTO and NAFTA are treaties and, as such, they have in principle the same legal value. If there is to be a hierarchy between treaties it is, as explained below, to be found in either (1) specific treaty provisions which put one treaty above the other (rules 4 and 5), or (2) general principles such as the later-in-time rule (rule 6) or the rule that a more specific treaty prevails over a more general one (rule 7).

Rule 2: A treaty can only affect those countries that agreed to it

A treaty is binding upon the parties to it (Vienna Convention on the Law of Treaties, Article 26). If parties that are bound by two treaties that are contradictory (say, the WTO and NAFTA between the US and Canada), that is the rule that creates the legal situation of conflict. At the same time, a treaty 'does not create either obligations or rights for a third State without its consent' (Vienna Convention on the Law of Treaties, Article 34). In other words, NAFTA cannot create obligations or rights for Australia, nor can MERCOSUR affect the WTO rights of the EC.[13]

Thus, in one of the scenarios described earlier – namely, overlaps that involve an agreement that is binding on only one of the parties – the solution is simple: the agreement that binds both parties prevails.[14] In other words, in *EC – Bananas*, when the Lomé Convention was binding only on the EC (and not the US) the WTO agreement prevailed. It was

---

[12] The only exception are so-called peremptory norms or rules that have the status of *jus cogens*. According to the Vienna Convention on the Law of Treaties any treaty that violates *jus cogens* is or becomes void (Vienna Convention on the Law of Treaties, Articles 53 and 64).

[13] Article 41.1(b)(i) of the Vienna Convention on the Law of Treaties prohibits any bilateral or regional contracting-out from a multilateral agreement if it 'affect[s] the enjoyment by the other parties of their rights under the treaty or the performance of their obligations'.

[14] See Article 30 of the Vienna Convention on the Law of Treaties entitled 'Application of successive treaties relating to the same subject matter': 'as between a State party to both treaties and a State party to only one of the treaties, the treaty to which both States are parties governs their mutual rights and obligations'.

only because WTO members (including the US) granted a waiver to give effect to the Lomé Convention, notwithstanding GATT Article I, that some of the US claims were rejected. Similarly, in *Brazil – Tyres*, when Brazil tried to justify certain GATT violations with reference to MERCOSUR, WTO rules prevailed, as the claimant in the dispute (the EC) did not agree to MERCOSUR. Only WTO rules themselves (such as GATT Article XXIV or XX) can then justify Brazil's breach of the WTO treaty, not MERCOSUR.[15] Finally, where questions of overlap between, for example, the US–Chile and EC–Chile FTA arise, for the US only the US–Chile agreement applies; for the EC only the EC–Chile agreement applies. The US cannot see its rights affected by the EC–Chile FTA; nor can the EC see its rights affected by the US–Chile FTA.

Rule 3: Where treaties overlap there is a presumption against conflict

Treaties are an expression of state consent. Where a state expresses its consent through different treaties, the starting point is that these different treaties confirm or supplement each other. A contradiction or conflict should only be found in case it is impossible to interpret the two treaties in a harmonious fashion. This presumption against conflict – or principle of 'systemic integration' – is confirmed, for example, in Article 31.3(c) of the Vienna Convention on the Law of Treaties. This Article instructs that a treaty must be interpreted in a way that takes account of 'any relevant rules of international law applicable in the relations between the parties'. Article 31.3(c) can be seen as the 'gene therapy' against excessive fragmentation of international law (e.g. between the WTO and regional agreements) and promotes a coherent view of international arrangements (ILC, 2006).

Rule 4: One treaty can provide that it is subject to,
or prevails over, another treaty

Although there is no inherent hierarchy between treaties (rule 1), one treaty can prohibit the conclusion of another, e.g. a multilateral

---

[15] Whereas the Panel in *Brazil – Tyres* accepted MERCOSUR as a justification for the differential treatment under the *chapeau* of GATT Article XX, the Appellate Body rejected the MERCOSUR excuse. Yet the Appellate Body did not go further, and failed to examine whether GATT Article XXIV could have justified Brazil's exclusion for MERCOSUR imports from Brazil's general import ban on retreaded tyres.

agreement can prohibit the conclusion of subsequent regional agreements (discussed in rule 5 below). In addition, one treaty can provide that in the event of conflict (i.e. in case 'systemic integration' is impossible pursuant to rule 3) the treaty is subject to, or prevails over, another. NAFTA Article 103.2, for example, states that, unless otherwise provided, NAFTA prevails over the GATT.[16] Conversely, Article 1.2.2 of the US–Republic of Korea FTA provides that the FTA remains subject to 'any international legal obligation between the Parties that provides for more favorable treatment ... than that provided for under this Agreement'.

Rule 5: A treaty is valid and legal unless it is declared otherwise

A multilateral treaty can provide that bilateral or regional contracting-out by some of the parties is, in certain conditions, prohibited.[17] That is what, for example, GATT Article XXIV does (albeit only indirectly). Note, indeed, that GATT Article XXIV does not legally prohibit any FTAs, not even those that fail the Article XXIV test. Instead, GATT Article XXIV obliges WTO members who concluded FTAs inconsistent with Article XXIV to either expand all FTA benefits to all other WTO members to make the FTA comply with Article XXIV, or to get rid of the FTA. Put differently, GATT Article XXIV excuses some FTAs from the MFN principle (those that meet the Article XXIV test) and subjects all others to MFN (it does not as such prohibit FTAs). Crucially, even where 'illegal' contracting-out occurs (i.e. FTAs are concluded contrary to Article XXIV), it will be presumed 'legal' (i.e. consistent with the multilateral treaty) unless it is decided otherwise.

In other words, GATT Article XXIV – in combination with the WTO's MFN principle – prohibits the conclusion of discriminatory CUs or FTAs that do not meet the conditions in GATT Article XXIV. Yet even if such 'illegal' CUs or FTAs are concluded, international law

---

[16] NAFTA Article 103.2: 'In the event of any inconsistency between the provisions of this Agreement [NAFTA] and such other agreements [e.g. GATT], the provisions of this Agreement shall prevail to the extent of the inconsistency, except as otherwise provided in this Agreement.'

[17] See Article 41.1 of the Vienna Convention on the Law of Treaties: 'Two or more of the parties to a multilateral treaty may conclude an agreement to modify the treaty as between themselves alone if: (a) the possibility of such a modification is provided for by the treaty; or (b) the modification in question is not prohibited by the treaty and: (i) does not affect the enjoyment by the other parties of their rights under the treaty or the performance of their obligations; (ii) does not relate to a provision, derogation from which is incompatible with the effective execution of the object and purpose of the treaty as a whole.'

presumes that they are 'legal' (i.e. consistent with Article XXIV), unless WTO members or a WTO panel or Appellate Body declare otherwise. Given the absence (explained above) of either political or judicial rulings on the consistency of regional agreements with Article XXIV, all regional agreements are, therefore, presumed to be WTO-consistent and continue to operate, even those that are not consistent with Article XXIV.

This legal reality is crucial, as it means that even if the critics are right and many regional agreements violate Article XXIV, these agreements remain legal and continue to affect trade flows. Dispute settlement panels are also likely to accept or at least presume the legality of such regional agreements whenever they are raised in a trade dispute (unless the dispute is one on the very question of legality of the agreement under GATT Article XXIV). This principle obviously means that the possibility for overlaps increases, as even regional agreements that are inconsistent with Article XXIV can continue to affect the outcome of trade flows and trade disputes.

Rule 6: Unless otherwise provided, a later treaty prevails over an earlier one

Subject to the rule that an earlier multilateral treaty may prohibit the conclusion of a later regional agreement (see rule 5), if overlapping agreements are silent on what to do in the event of conflict (see rule 4), the fall-back rule is that the most recent treaty prevails.[18] The reason for this 'later-in-time' rule is that all treaties are based on state consent. It is this state consent that gives treaties their binding value. As a result, a later expression of state consent must be presumed to prevail over an earlier expression of state consent. Thus, in the event of conflict between a treaty concluded by two states in 1947 and a treaty concluded by the same states in 1990, the 1990 treaty prevails (unless, of course, the 1990 treaty explicitly states that it remains subject to the 1947 treaty).

Rule 7: A specific treaty provision normally prevails over a more general treaty provision

According to the so-called *lex specialis* principle, a more specific treaty rule prevails over a more general one. This rule is, once again, based on

---

[18] Article 30 of the Vienna Convention on the Law of Treaties provides that 'as between States Parties to both treaties', 'the earlier treaty applies only to the extent that its provisions are compatible with those of the later treaty'.

the principle of state consent: a more specific expression of state consent must be presumed to prevail over a more general expression of state consent.

The *lex specialis* principle can operate to resolve overlaps between provisions within the same treaty (say, two GATT provisions) or between different treaties that were concluded at the same time (say, between two WTO agreements, all of which were concluded on the same date, in April 1994). In both situations we are not dealing with successive treaties (but rather with simultaneous treaties) and, as a result, the 'later-in-time' rule (rule 6) does not apply.

Yet what to do in the event of successive treaties where the earlier treaty provision is more specific than the later one? In other words, what to do if rule 6 (later-in-time rule prevails) conflicts with rule 7 (more specific rule prevails)? International law does not offer a clear response to this question. One way to deal with it is to find that there is no genuine conflict between two rules in case the (later) general rule does not specifically address the (earlier) specific rule.[19] In *US – Cotton*, for example, the Appellate Body found that the specific prohibition in the Subsidies Agreement for subsidies contingent on domestic inputs does not conflict with the general permission in the Agreement on Agriculture to provide domestic support up to each country's agreed aggregate level of support. According to the Appellate Body, the Agreement on Agriculture does not specifically address the question of subsidies contingent on domestic inputs. Therefore, there is no conflict and the more specific rule (here, the prohibition in the Subsidies Agreement) prevails.

Another way to give preference to a more specific rule, even if it is earlier in time, is to revert to the principle of state consent and ask the question: which of the two rules most accurately expresses the current state consent of the two parties? If the earlier treaty is a bilateral treaty that specifically deals with the subject matter at hand (such as the 1992 EC–US agreement on aircraft subsidies), one could argue that it remains the most accurate expression of state consent, even if there is a later multilateral treaty that includes more general rules that seem to contradict the earlier bilateral agreement (such as the 1994 WTO agreement on subsidies generally, not specific to the aircraft industry). The argument could then go as follows: as the later multilateral agreement was

---

[19] Article 30 of the Vienna Convention on the Law of Treaties, which sets out the later-in-time rule, is specifically limited to successive treaties on 'the same subject matter'.

negotiated between over 100 parties, addressing the much broader subject matter of subsidies in all possible sectors, that was not the place to either confirm or overrule the earlier bilaterally agreed, specific rule on aircraft subsidies. This very issue is currently being debated before the ongoing panel on *EC – Aircraft Subsidies.*

In sum, any conflict between rule 6 (later-in-time rule) and rule 7 (*lex specialis*) will need to be decided on a case-by-case basis. The fact that regional agreements regulate the more specific trade relations between two countries is, however, an argument in support of giving preference to regional agreements over WTO rules, irrespective of the timing of the two treaties (unless, of course, either treaty explicitly provides that the WTO treaty prevails). Indeed, applied to the trade relations between, for example, France and Belgium, would it not be odd to find that from 1947 to 1994, the later EC treaties (concluded in the 1950s) prevailed over the earlier (1947) GATT agreement, whereas, from 1994 onwards, the WTO agreements prevailed, and when the later Treaty of Amsterdam (1997) was concluded, EC treaties once again prevailed? In this context, one could find that EC treaties, as the more specific rules in the relations between France and Belgium, prevail over the more general GATT/WTO rules, irrespective of timing.

Rule 8: Dispute panels can only find violations under their respective treaties, but that does not mean that other treaties are irrelevant

WTO panels can only find violations under WTO-covered agreements (Dispute Settlement Understanding (DSU), Article 1). That is their restricted mandate or jurisdiction. Yet the fact that they are only asked to decide on claims of WTO violation does not mean that in their examination of these WTO claims they must restrict themselves to the four corners of the WTO treaties. In international law, this is known as the distinction between 'jurisdiction' (which claims can be brought) and 'applicable law' or 'relevant law' (what law can be referred to in the examination of WTO claims).

When interpreting and applying WTO treaties so as to come to a conclusion on whether or not there is WTO breach, panels should, in certain circumstances, refer to non-WTO treaties, including regional agreements (see rule 3 above and the principle of 'systemic integration' confirmed in Article 31.3(c) of the Vienna Convention). This is one of the major proposals of this chapter, a proposal that would 'multi-lateralize regionalism' by elevating regional agreements to the attention of WTO panels.[20] Such elevation or multilateralization is a core element in achieving mutual recognition and respect between the WTO and regional agreements. As one prominent observer (and adjudicator) of WTO–NAFTA relations stated: 'there is a serious anomaly resulting from the fact that WTO law is central to the interpretation of an FTA, while the WTO dispute settlement procedure is blind to the fact of an increasing body of FTA law and practice around the world' (De Mestral, 2006: 366).

At the same time, there are some positive developments in WTO case law. In *Mexico – Soft Drinks*, for example, the Appellate Body refused to make findings on claims of violation of NAFTA (as those claims were rightly decided to be outside the panel's jurisdiction), but it left the door open for NAFTA to be referred to so as to interpret WTO provisions, or as a defence against WTO breach, between NAFTA parties. In *Brazil – Tyres* the panel referred to a MERCOSUR ruling in support of its finding that Brazil's exclusion for MERCOSUR imports is not 'arbitrary' in the sense of the *chapeau* of GATT Article XX (this ruling was subsequently reversed, however, by the Appellate Body[21]).

Yet those WTO developments remain a far cry from, for example, NAFTA dispute settlement where, as one author put it, 'NAFTA arbitrators ... have made a strong case for accommodation or, at least, [for] the awareness of accommodation, because of their concern with normative coherence and system integrity' (Tiny, 2005: 1).[22] In *Canada – Agricultural Products*, for example, a NAFTA Chapter 20 panel extensively referred to WTO agreements in its interpretation and application of NAFTA provisions between Canada and the US. The panel essentially internalized the underlying WTO logic of preference of tariffs over non-tariff barriers into the NAFTA legal system, and rejected a US claim that new tariffs imposed by Canada as a result of its WTO obligations under the Agreement on Agriculture violated Canada's early obligations under the NAFTA tariff standstill clause.

---

[20] For further elaboration see Pauwelyn (2003b).

[21] See note 15 above. The Appellate Body found that differential treatment under the *chapeau* of GATT Article XX(b) can only be justified on health or environmental grounds, not with reference to a MERCOSUR ruling that was unrelated to any of these legitimate objectives. Yet, as noted in note 15, the question remains whether Brazil's exclusion in favour of MERCOSUR imports from its general import ban on retreaded tyres could have been justified under GATT Article XXIV, a question the Appellate Body did not examine.

[22] Tiny refers, in contrast, to the Appellate Body decision in *Turkey – Textiles* as 'a strong claim made by the Appellate Body in favour of normative supremacy of the world trading system over regional trade systems' (2005: 1).

What this chapter proposes – reference to regional agreements by WTO panels and vice versa – is not generally accepted. Based on present WTO rules some authors are in favour,[23] others against.[24] If not only the 'jurisdiction' but also the 'relevant law' were limited to the specific treaty of the adjudicating forum (say, in the WTO, only WTO law; in NAFTA, only NAFTA law) questions of overlap would be easily resolved: the law of the forum prevails as it is the only relevant one. Yet such a solution is far from satisfactory and would obviously increase the fragmentation between different trade arrangements: in the WTO, a dispute could be decided one way under WTO law only; at the NAFTA, the same dispute could be decided another way under NAFTA law only. Thus, in the end, there would still be overlap or even conflict. A better solution, that integrates different trading arrangements, is for both WTO and regional dispute panels to recognize each other's rules and rulings. As Isabelle Van Damme points out: 'The recognition by panels and the Appellate Body of the relevance of these regional agreements for the interpretation of WTO law is only one means to counter the problems arising from the proliferation of RTAs for the "security and predictability of the multilateral trading system"' (Van Damme, 2006: 567). Such mutual recognition and respect must, however, be subject to certain limits, in particular:

(1) only WTO panels can find violations of WTO law, and only FTA panels can find violations of FTA law (the question of 'jurisdiction', to be distinguished from 'relevant law'); and
(2) no WTO member can be held to an FTA – or an interpretation or application of WTO rules with reference to an FTA – to which it does not agree (rule 2 above).

The WTO treaty does not include an explicit provision on applicable or relevant law (although it refers to the rules of interpretation of the Vienna Convention which, in turn, refer to non-WTO treaties: see rule 3). The same is true under NAFTA's trade chapters.[25] One way to improve the integration between WTO and regional agreements would

---

[23] See, for example, Van Damme (2006) and, in terms of FTAs referring to WTO law, Garcia Bercero (2006: 402) ('bilateral panels should always be able to use WTO law as a tool to interpret FTA provisions').
[24] Kwak and Marceau (2006: 484).
[25] Yet, as De Mestral points out, 'Virtually every chapter of NAFTA asserts the compatibility of the agreement with the law of the WTO. In the same vein, NAFTA is replete with interpretative provisions requiring interpretations of words and concepts in a

be to explicitly expand the 'applicable law' before both WTO and FTA panels to all relevant international law consented to by the disputing parties (with the caveat, of course, that panels cannot decide on claims of violation under outside agreements, i.e. that 'jurisdiction' remains limited to the forum's treaty only).

A good example in this direction is NAFTA Chapter 11 on investment protection. Articles 1116 and 1117 restrict the jurisdiction of NAFTA investment arbitration panels to certain claims of violation of NAFTA Chapter 11 only. Yet, NAFTA Article 1130, entitled 'governing law', provides that: 'A Tribunal established under this Subchapter shall decide the issues in dispute in accordance with this Agreement [NAFTA] and applicable rules of international law.' In other words, the 'jurisdiction' of NAFTA Chapter 11 tribunals is limited to certain claims under NAFTA Chapter 11 only; the 'governing law' to resolve those claims includes the whole of NAFTA and all other applicable rules of international law. A similar provision was included in the EFTA–Bulgaria FTA of 1993: 'The arbitral tribunal shall settle the dispute in accordance with the provisions of this Agreement and applicable rules and principles of international law.'

4   Case studies

Let us now apply the eight rules set out in Section 3 to a number of specific overlaps between WTO and regional agreements. Obviously, many more overlaps exist, as the different scenarios set out in Section 2 illustrate.

The TRIPS Agreement versus TRIPS-plus FTAs

The TRIPS-plus debate is a perfect example of how the interaction between the WTO and regional agreements goes beyond Article XXIV. Unlike GATT and GATS, the TRIPS Agreement does not include an exception for regional arrangements. As a result, when WTO members commit to higher (IP) standards in regional agreements (so-called TRIPS-plus agreements), the MFN principle in the TRIPS Agreement (Article 4) continues to apply. Thus, any IP benefit conferred regionally between, for example, the US and Chile, must be extended automatically

---

manner compatible with the law of the GATT 1947 and successor agreements, unless the contrary is required' (2006: 376).

to all WTO members (Mercurio, 2006). In other words, regionalism in IP is automatically 'multilateralized' and the core problem of how to 'multilateralize regionalism' is resolved.

Another consequence of the absence of an Article XXIV-type provision in TRIPS is that the regionalism debate in the field of IP has nothing to do with regional deals *discriminating against third parties* (the main objection against regional liberalization in goods and services). Critics of IP regionalism do not fear that regional partners will increase IP protection only between themselves; rather, they fear that TRIPS-plus agreements impose IP standards *between the regional partners* that are too high and/or undo flexibilities guaranteed under TRIPS. Put differently, whereas in goods and services regionalism focuses on third parties and discrimination, in IP regionalism focuses on the regional parties themselves and whether they (in particular, developing countries) went too far with IP protection (Maine, 2005).

This is obviously not the place to discuss the optimal protection of IP rights in developing countries. However, the peculiarity of the regionalism debate as it concerns IP has important legal consequences under the rules developed in Section 3:

(1) If, for example, Panama or the Republic of Korea agree in an FTA with the US to increase IP protection, such an agreement is, in principle, of equal value to the TRIPS agreement (rule 1).

(2) Given the consent rule in international law, once Panama or the Republic of Korea freely agree to such an FTA, the higher IP protection agreed therein is binding upon them, although, of course, not binding on other WTO members that did not agree to the FTA (rule 2). Given the MFN rule that continues to operate under TRIPS, no one is being discriminated against. The only question is: should Panama or the Republic of Korea have agreed to higher IP protection in the FTA (e.g. are developing countries pushed into higher IP standards because of unequal bargaining power in FTA negotiations; or, rather, are they making a deliberate choice, accepting, for example, stronger copyright protection, which they see as almost costless, in exchange for valuable market access to, say, the lucrative US or EC markets)?

(3) Pursuant to rule 3 – the presumption against conflict and the principle of 'systemic integration' – any TRIPS-plus FTA must be read together, and to the furthest extent possible harmoniously, with TRIPS including TRIPS flexibilities for public health. When an

FTA panel is asked, for example, to examine whether a compulsory licence issued by an FTA partner violates the FTA, the panel must interpret and apply FTA rules on IP in a way that takes account of the TRIPS flexibilities confirmed in the Doha Declaration on TRIPS and public health and subsequent instruments (see rule 8). Given this principle of 'systemic integration', fears that US FTAs take away TRIPS flexibility are often exaggerated.[26]

(4) In case there is nonetheless a genuine conflict between the FTA and TRIPS (e.g. the FTA explicitly excludes compulsory licensing where TRIPS permits it), in the absence of specific treaty provisions, the FTA is likely to prevail either as the later in time (rule 6) or as the more specific provision (rule 7). Even so, only an FTA panel would then have 'jurisdiction' to find the compulsory licence in violation of the FTA; a WTO panel does not have jurisdiction to enforce the stricter FTA rule (rule 8). To protect TRIPS, however, many FTAs explicitly provide that the FTA leaves intact, or is subject to, TRIPS flexibilities offered for the protection of public health and access to essential medicines (pursuant to rule 4).[27] Such explicit provision putting TRIPS above the FTA ought to be respected before both WTO and FTA panels (see rule 8).

WTO dispute settlement versus dispute settlement under FTAs

When it comes to the overlap of dispute settlement procedures in the WTO and FTAs, two core questions arise (Kwak and Marceau, 2006; Pauwelyn, 2004b):

(1) First, if a measure can be challenged under either procedure – albeit, of course, under WTO rules before the WTO, and under FTA rules before the FTA – where should it be brought? This is the so-called 'choice of forum' question.

(2) Second, can a measure be challenged first under an FTA and then a second time before the WTO, or vice versa? This raises the question of whether there should be a so-called 'forum exclusion' clause.

---

[26] Mercurio (2006: 226, 229), for example, is of the view that rules on market approval and data exclusivity in US FTAs would effectively prevent the use of compulsory licences. All of these FTA rules must, however, be interpreted with reference to TRIPS flexibilities.

[27] See, for example, Article 18.11 of the US–Republic of Korea FTA entitled 'Understanding regarding certain public health measures'.

It is important that both questions be explicitly addressed when drafting FTAs (as permitted under rule 4). Just as importantly, if, for example, Mexico and the US agree in NAFTA that a dispute must be sent to NAFTA (and not the WTO), a WTO panel must give effect to this Mexico–US agreement (see rule 8). Similarly, if Mexico and the US agreed that once a dispute was brought to NAFTA, it could not be brought a second time to the WTO, a WTO panel should be given the authority to refer to this NAFTA provision and decline jurisdiction. For WTO panels to turn a blind eye on FTA forum provisions (and vice versa) would seriously endanger the project of coordination and coherence between the WTO and regional agreements, and thereby obstruct the goal of 'multilateralizing regionalism'.

As regards 'forum exclusion clauses', there is no doubt that they are generally desirable.[28] Especially for developing countries with scarce legal resources, it would be very hard to first defend a measure in one forum, only to find out later that the case was to be brought a second time to another forum. As Peter Drahos has pointed out: 'The most obvious consequence of a trade regime that has many trade courts is that it will favour states that have the capacity to analyze its complex pathways and pick those that best suit their purposes' (Drahos, 2007: 199).

Forum exclusion clauses also limit the scope of conflicting rulings and thereby facilitate mutual integration of WTO and regional agreements. Most FTAs have therefore included a provision stating that once dispute settlement procedures have been initiated in one forum, it shall be to the exclusion of the other. Article 2005.6 of NAFTA provides, for example, that: '[o]nce dispute settlement procedures have been initiated under [NAFTA] Article 2007 … the forum selected shall be used to the exclusion of the other [e.g. the WTO]'.[29]

---

[28] In the absence of an explicit 'forum exclusion clause', the fall-back principle of *res judicata* (according to which the same dispute cannot be tried twice) is, indeed, unlikely to apply. *Res judicata* only stops the second proceedings if the first proceedings were (1) regarding the same matter, (2) between the same parties, and (3) regarding the same legal claims. Since, in our situation, the first proceedings under an FTA would deal with different claims from those brought in the second, WTO proceedings (FTA claims versus WTO claims), the principle of *res judicata* is unlikely to apply.

[29] This has obviously not prevented overlapping dispute settlement procedures between the WTO and NAFTA. Article 2005.6 only applies in respect of NAFTA Chapter 20 trade disputes. NAFTA Chapter 19 anti-dumping or countervailing duties disputes have, in practice, overlapped with WTO procedures (see, for example, *US – Softwood Lumber* disputes, discussed in Pauwelyn, 2006). The same is true for NAFTA Chapter 11 investment disputes.

We now turn to the logically preceding question of 'choice of forum' (i.e. where to file proceedings the first time around), which FTAs can regulate in three ways, as follows.

Leave the choice of forum up to the complainant

This is what most US FTAs provide for, as well as, for example, Article 1(2) of the Olivos Protocol in respect of WTO–MERCOSUR dispute settlement proceedings.[30] The advantage of this option is that it allows the complainant to choose what it regards as the most appropriate and probably most beneficial forum for its case. Some have argued against this solution, as in their view it is likely to attract almost all cases to the WTO (Garcia Bercero, 2006: 403). This is, of course, a good thing if one is trying to 'multilateralize regionalism'.

Others have criticized the solution of leaving the choice of forum up to the complainant because it allows the more powerful FTA partner (e.g. the US) to bring cases under the FTA where it has more political clout, instead of at the WTO where 'the third party procedures of the DSU create the possibility of coalition building by a weak actor involved in a dispute with a strong actor' (Drahos, 2007: 201). For that reason, especially developing countries in their FTAs with, for example, the EC or the US, may want to exclude FTA procedures for certain matters in favour of the WTO (as discussed below).

Oblige the complainant to submit the dispute to the WTO

Such preference for WTO dispute settlement is, of course, in line with the objective of 'multilateralizing regionalism' (or at least avoids FTA dispute settlement attracting disputes that would otherwise be sent to the WTO). It can be obtained in several ways.

First, some FTAs include a chapter on SPS disciplines or anti-dumping which largely confirms WTO rules, and at the end of that chapter state that disputes under this specific chapter cannot be brought before the dispute settlement procedures of the FTA. Articles 8.4 and 10.7.2 of the Republic of Korea–US FTA offer examples. As a result, SPS,

---

[30] NAFTA Article 2005.1, for example, states that 'disputes regarding any matter arising under both [NAFTA] and [GATT/WTO], may be settled in either forum at the discretion of the complaining party'. See also, most recently, Article 22.6 of the Republic of Korea–US FTA.

anti-dumping and countervailing duties disputes between the Republic of Korea and the US must be brought to the WTO, and cannot be brought under the FTA.

A second way to give preference to WTO dispute settlement can be found in the EC–Chile FTA. Article 189.4(c) provides that '[u]nless the Parties otherwise agree, when a Party seeks redress of a violation of an obligation under this Part of the Agreement which is *equivalent in substance* to an obligation under the WTO, it shall have recourse to . . . the WTO Agreement'. In other words, if Chile, for example, wants to challenge an EC measure for violation of national treatment, Chile must bring its case to the WTO, not the FTA (as the national treatment obligation in the FTA is equivalent in substance to that in the WTO). Given the uncertainty as to when an obligation is 'equivalent in substance', Ignacio Garcia Bercero (a European Commission official) has stated that 'the consequence is likely to be a much greater reluctance by the parties to have recourse to bilateral dispute settlement' (Garcia Bercero, 2006: 403).

In certain instances it may, indeed, be useful to exclude FTA dispute settlement for example, for matters where the FTA does not really add to the WTO or, more generally, for weaker FTA partners who may favour the multilateral setting of the WTO over settlement in an FTA with asymmetric power relations (Drahos, 2007). In the IP context, Drahos submits that '[o]ne priority that developing countries should be thinking about is to argue for provisions in . . . [FTA] dispute settlement chapters that require the parties in the case of double breach to take the matter to the WTO' (Drahos, 2007: 209). As noted earlier, that is exactly what was done in the EC–Chile FTA.

At the same time, in most cases where WTO and FTA rules are broadly equivalent, the advantages of WTO dispute settlement (even for the more powerful countries) are likely to push the dispute to the WTO anyway. As advantages of WTO dispute settlement, William Davey points to (i) the expertise of the WTO Secretariat support staff (most RTA panels, including NAFTA panels, in contrast, are not supported by a permanent secretariat); (ii) more effective enforcement through greater informal (multilateral) pressures to comply in the WTO compared to bilateral FTAs; and, most importantly, (iii) the fact that WTO decisions are viewed as more legitimate (WTO panellists are not appointed by the parties, nor are they normally nationals of the disputing parties; there is the possibility of appeal; and the WTO system is generally less power-based than bilateral FTAs, especially those with asymmetric power relations) (Davey, 2006).

Davey goes as far as stating that the WTO dispute settlement mechanism alone will ensure the survival of the multilateral trading system: 'the apparent superiority of the WTO dispute settlement system is a significant reason why regional trade agreements do not ultimately threaten to supplant or even burden the operation of the WTO system' (Davey, 2006: 344).[31] In other words, one of the main engines for 'multilateralizing regionalism' may well be the WTO dispute settlement system. This is confirmed in Davey's statistics, which demonstrate that WTO dispute settlement is used much more frequently than FTA dispute settlement, where in many cases only a few disputes (such as under NAFTA Chapter 20) have been filed, and sometimes not a single dispute (such as in most EC FTAs).

That said, where an FTA offers WTO-plus liberalization, this can obviously only be enforced in FTA dispute settlement. For such WTO-plus disputes, the claimant cannot go to the WTO dispute settlement, whatever its advantages. In that scenario, the top priority is to improve FTA dispute settlement rules and procedures (e.g. Chapter 20 of NAFTA and the ongoing problem faced there with the selection of panel members).

Oblige the complainant to submit the dispute under the FTA

A third option for 'choice of forum' clauses in respect of WTO and FTA procedures is to give preference to FTA procedures. These will automatically be relied on to enforce FTA obligations that are WTO-plus, as such WTO-plus obligations cannot possibly be enforced before a WTO panel. Yet, as Garcia Bercero (2006) has pointed out in respect of WTO-plus disputes before FTAs, even there, 'in order to enhance the predictability and coherence of international trade law, it would be highly desirable if bilateral [FTA] panels were to consider relevant WTO rulings'.

As Mexico experienced in its sugar dispute with the US, for such WTO-plus obligations to stick, it is crucially important to have a

---

[31] Similarly, De Mestral (2006: 381): 'can an FTA prevail over the multilateral rules and thus undermine the global system? Here the experience of NAFTA may suggest that the multilateral trade system is more resilient than many have thought. Experience of the various NAFTA dispute settlement procedures seems to point squarely to the paramountcy of the multilateral order'.

workable FTA dispute settlement mechanism; if not, WTO-plus elements cannot be enforced.[32]

Where a dispute could genuinely be brought before either the WTO or the FTA (because both treaties cover the matter), the FTA can specify that the dispute must be brought under the FTA (not the WTO). NAFTA Article 2005.4 provides, for example, that where a dispute relates to SPS or standards, the respondent has a right to insist that the dispute be brought under NAFTA (as it was apparently considered that NAFTA rules might be more lenient for the defendant than WTO rules). Article 292 of the EC Treaty reserves more generally any 'dispute concerning the interpretation or application of this Treaty' to the exclusive jurisdiction of EC courts. Article 42.1 of the Cartagena Agreement Creating the Court of Justice of the Andean Community sets out a similar exclusive jurisdiction clause.

If, notwithstanding such an exclusive jurisdiction clause, the complainant submitted the dispute to the WTO anyway, a WTO panel should, in my view, give effect to the 'choice of forum' clause (be it in NAFTA, the EC Treaty or the Cartagena Agreement) and decline jurisdiction in favour of the regional agreement (rule 8 above).

To reserve exclusive jurisdiction under the regional agreement is most appropriate for closely integrated regional arrangements such as customs unions and common markets. That is also where one finds such exclusive jurisdiction clauses.[33] In those settings the argument can be made that trade disputes are best and most appropriately settled within the integrated, regional community. In most FTA settings, however, the presumption should be against exclusive jurisdiction under the FTA. As pointed out earlier, in particular for FTAs with asymmetric power relations, it may be more appropriate to direct cases where WTO and FTA rules are substantially equivalent to the WTO. Moreover, where the FTA includes WTO-plus elements, disputes

---

[32] In the US–Mexico sugar dispute, Mexico attempted to enforce certain WTO-plus quota rights it had negotiated under NAFTA, but failed, essentially because the US refused to agree on a roster of NAFTA Chapter 20 panellists. If NAFTA had included a procedure where panellists were automatically appointed in the absence of a roster, the subsequent *Mexico – Soft Drinks* dispute before the WTO could have been avoided. In that case, the US successfully challenged, at the WTO this time, a Mexican tax on sweeteners which Mexico had enacted when it realized that its request for a NAFTA panel was not going anywhere. See Pauwelyn (2006).

[33] For an overview, see Pauwelyn (2004b: 285).

under those elements can only be brought to the FTA. As a result, there is no need to make the FTA jurisdiction exclusive.

WTO safeguards versus regional safeguards

Another area of overlap that FTA negotiators must keep in mind is safeguards. Whereas WTO anti-dumping and countervailing duty rules are normally left untouched in regional agreements, many regional agreements do provide for 'safeguards' – that is, the reintroduction of trade barriers against regional partners in special emergency situations. Such regional safeguards (often with special mechanisms for agriculture and/or textiles)[34] can obviously overlap with multilateral WTO safeguards.

To limit such overlaps, the US–Republic of Korea FTA provides, for example, that no FTA safeguard (be it a general one under Chapter 10 or a special one for agriculture or textiles) can be combined, for the same good, with a WTO safeguard.[35] Neither can FTA safeguards lead to customs duties on regional imports that exceed the most-favoured-nation (MFN) applied rate on the good in question (thereby protecting FTA partners against higher duties than those that other WTO members face under MFN).[36] Many US FTAs also provide that FTA partners 'may' exclude each other from a global WTO safeguard in case 'imports [from the FTA partner] are not a *substantial cause* of serious injury or threat thereof'.[37]

Where FTA partners do exclude one another from a WTO safeguard (say, the US excludes the Republic of Korea from a global safeguard on

---

[34] The EC–Chile FTA only provides for a special safeguard for agriculture (Article 73). It does not have a bilateral safeguard mechanism in place for other products. Instead, the FTA confirms the continued application, between the EC and Chile, of WTO safeguard rules, with some additional guarantees in case the affected FTA party has 'a substantial interest as exporter of the product concerned' (Article 92).

[35] See Article 3.3.4 (Agricultural Safeguard Measures) and Article 10.5.2 (Trade Remedies). The EC–Chile FTA, in contrast, does not exclude the combination of an FTA safeguard with a WTO safeguard. For FTA agricultural safeguards the EC–Chile FTA may even permit safeguards more easily compared to the special safeguard mechanism under Article 5 of the Agreement on Agriculture. Article 73 of the EC–Chile FTA provides that its emergency clause for agricultural products is '[n]otwithstanding . . . Article 5 of the WTO Agreement on Agriculture'.

[36] See Article 10.1(b)(i) of the Republic of Korea–US FTA.

[37] Article 10.5.1 of the Republic of Korea–US FTA. The EC–Chile FTA does not refer to any bilateral exclusion from WTO safeguards. Instead, it confirms WTO safeguard rules and offers additional guarantees in the context of WTO safeguards to the FTA partner whenever it has 'a substantial interest as an exporter of the product concerned' (Article 92).

semiconductors), obviously no intra-FTA dispute will arise. What may happen, however, is that another WTO member (say the EC, which is not a party to the FTA) complains about the FTA exclusion as a violation of the WTO Safeguards Agreement which provides that WTO safeguards must, in principle, apply to all countries. Pursuant to rule 2 above, the EC cannot, in our example, be held by the US–Republic of Korea FTA rule that permits the US exclusion of Korean imports (the EC never agreed to this rule). Yet, before a WTO panel, the US may be able to justify Korea's exclusion from the safeguard based on GATT Article XXIV.[38]

Subsequent changes to the WTO and how they affect pre-existing regional agreements

Where a regional agreement refers to or incorporates WTO rules, is this reference or incorporation static or dynamic? In other words, is it limited to WTO rules as they existed at the time of the conclusion of the regional agreement, or does it include subsequent changes to the WTO? This is another question of interaction and overlap that FTA negotiators are strongly advised to regulate explicitly.

An example of dynamic incorporation can be found in NAFTA, as interpreted by the panel in *Canada – Agricultural Products*. In that case, the panel interpreted NAFTA rules on a tariff standstill with reference to post-NAFTA rules agreed to in the new WTO agreement on agriculture that permitted Canada to transpose agricultural quotas into new tariffs. An example of static incorporation is the Republic of Korea–US FTA.[39]

The *disadvantage* of dynamic incorporation is that FTA parties lose control over which WTO changes they want to incorporate into the FTA. The *advantage* of dynamic incorporation is that there is no need to update regional agreements every time the WTO treaty changes. In addition, if references to WTO rules in FTAs are different from current, updated WTO rules, the process of coordination and mutual recognition between WTO and regional agreements can be seriously undermined. As FTA partners anyhow retain a veto power in the WTO to

---

[38] For a full discussion in support of such exclusions pursuant to GATT Article XXIV, see Pauwelyn (2004a).

[39] Article 24.3: 'If any provision of the WTO Agreement that the Parties have incorporated into this Agreement is amended, the Parties shall consult to consider amending the relevant provision of this Agreement, as appropriate.'

block WTO amendments, there should be a presumption in favour of dynamic incorporation (only, of course, if both FTA parties have agreed and ratified the WTO amendment). At the very least, when WTO jurisprudence evolves subsequent to the conclusion of an FTA, such new jurisprudence should be allowed to influence and permeate the interpretation of WTO rules as referred to or incorporated in the earlier FTA.

In closely integrated customs unions like the EU, where certain incorporated rules can be directly relied on by private parties before domestic courts, dynamic incorporation may pose greater problems. There, incorporation of new WTO rules (and even new WTO jurisprudence under existing rules) into the regional (EU) system could also give rights to private parties. This, of course, does change the depth of a WTO member's commitment to new WTO rules. Sara Dillon has pointed out, for example, that the core reason for the EC courts' scepticism towards WTO law, and their refusal to give 'direct effect' to WTO obligations, is the 'unpredictable outcomes' of the GATT/WTO legal system and the 'unexpected ways' in which the WTO can challenge EC law and measures (Dillon, 2002: 384). These considerations should, however, not affect the presumption in favour of dynamic incorporation of WTO rules into FTAs where, in the majority of cases, FTA rules remain purely state-to-state and cannot be relied on directly by private parties.

How do new regional agreements interact with pre-existing regional agreements?

As discussed under rule 2 above, overlapping agreements must always be evaluated between two countries. If one of the countries is not bound by one of the overlapping agreements, it cannot be held by that agreement. Take the EC and Chile as an example. They have concluded an FTA. Yet, before that, the EC concluded a customs union with Turkey. When it comes to the overlap of the FTA (with Chile) and the CU (with Turkey), only the EC is bound by both agreements, against different parties. Thus any inconsistencies between the FTA and the CU are the EC's problem alone. Turkey cannot be held by the FTA; Chile cannot be held by the CU.

All the same, the EC can, of course, give certain directions to, for example, Chile, so as to make it easier for the EC to comply with both the FTA and the CU. In an EC Declaration attached to the Chile–EC FTA, the EC did 'invite Chile to enter into negotiations with Turkey as soon as possible', given that, pursuant to the EC–Turkey CU, all members of the CU must have substantially the same external trade policies.[40] Indeed, this obligation makes negotiating an FTA with only one member of a CU most difficult. It explains why, for example, the US insisted on expanding FTA negotiations with South Africa to include all members of the Southern African Customs Union (SACU).[41]

A different problem is this: what happens if an FTA partner confers even more preferential treatment to a third party in a subsequent FTA? For example, Chile gives a better deal to the US in the US–Chile FTA compared to the earlier EC–Chile FTA. Can the EC in these circumstances claim the more favourable treatment? The answer would be yes if the EC–Chile FTA were to include an unconditional MFN obligation: in that case, any benefit subsequently conferred by either party to any other country (here the US) would automatically also be granted to the FTA counterpart (here the EC). Yet FTAs normally do *not* include such MFN obligation,[42] and the EC–Chile FTA is no exception to this rule.[43] The reason for doing so is obviously to tailor FTA concessions according to what the counterpart is willing to reciprocate in turn. If a later FTA partner is willing to 'give more', it may 'get more', but that does not

---

[40] In the EC–Turkey CU, the EC foresaw this problem and included an obligation on Turkey 'to align itself on the Common Customs Tariff and, progressively, with the preferential customs regime of the Community'. Turkey thereby agreed to conduct its own negotiations each time the EC concluded an FTA with a third party.

[41] Conversely, the EC–Chile FTA also includes a provision relating to MERCOSUR, to which only Chile is an associate member. Article 49 'Regional cooperation and regional integration': 'Both Parties should use all existing cooperation instruments to promote activities aimed at developing an active and reciprocal cooperation between the Parties and the Mercado Comun del Sur (Mercosur) as a whole.'

[42] See, on the other hand, Article 2.3.3 of the US–Colombia FTA: 'For greater certainty, paragraph 2 [on progressive tariff elimination] shall not prevent Colombia from granting identical or more favorable tariff treatment to a good as provided for under the legal instruments of the Andean integration.'

[43] The Chile–EC FTA does not include an MFN clause and, on the contrary, states in Article 56 'Customs unions and free trade areas': 'Nothing in this Agreement shall preclude the maintenance or establishment of customs unions, free trade areas or other arrangements between either of the Parties and third countries, insofar as they do not alter the rights and obligations provided for in this Agreement.' The Chile–EC FTA does, however, include one specific MFN obligation imposed on Chile, namely in Article 61.2, which obliges Chile to ensure that its price band system for certain imports 'does not afford more favourable treatment to imports of any third country, including countries with which Chile has concluded or will conclude in the future an agreement notified under Article XXIV of the GATT 1994'. Thus any benefit Chile would give to third parties (e.g. the US or MERCOSUR members) under its price band system must, pursuant to this MFN clause, automatically be extended also to the EC.

mean that an earlier FTA partner now gets the same deal. For that, new reciprocal negotiations would have to start.

The absence of an MFN clause in FTAs means that FTA concessions remain within the FTA, and are not multilateralized to other previous or later FTA partners. To include such MFN obligations in FTAs would, of course, be a major boost to 'multilateralizing regionalism': it would multilateralize any new FTA concessions to all other FTA partners of the country concerned, and thereby dramatically simplify FTA relations, as every given country would only have one preferential FTA standard, namely the most beneficial treatment it has ever awarded in any FTA.

The absence of an MFN clause in FTAs stands in contrast to the traditional MFN clause that is normally included in bilateral investment agreements or the investment chapter of FTAs.[44] Pursuant to this MFN clause for investment, if, for example, Chile offers better investment protection to any other country, this higher level of protection must automatically be extended also to the US (the same is true pursuant to MFN under TRIPS which, as discussed earlier, continues to apply to FTAs). Negotiators might want to consider including an MFN clause in FTAs, albeit one limited to trade concessions under other FTAs (and excluding preferential treatment under CUs and unilateral concessions to developing countries).

Would trade sanctions authorized by the WTO violate an FTA and vice versa?

Imagine that the Republic of Korea wins a WTO dispute against the US. The US fails to implement the WTO ruling and Korea obtains WTO authorization to suspend concessions, e.g. to introduce 100 per cent tariffs on US semiconductor exports to Korea. Are such sanctions permitted under the bilateral Republic of Korea–US FTA? Article 2.3.4(b) of the Republic of Korea–US FTA answers in the affirmative. In the FTA's section on 'Elimination of Customs Duties', it states that: 'For greater certainty, a Party may ... (b) maintain or increase a customs duty as authorized by the Dispute Settlement Body of the WTO'.

Pursuant to Rule 4 above, an FTA can indeed give preference to certain action under the WTO treaty (here WTO retaliation). However,

---

[44] See, for example, Article 10.3 'Most-Favored-Nation Treatment' of the US–Chile FTA: '1. Each Party shall accord to investors of the other Party treatment no less favorable than that it accords, in like circumstances, to investors of any non-Party.'

even without such explicit provision, a WTO authorization to impose sanctions should anyhow prevail over an earlier FTA: (i) because the WTO authorization, pursuant to a system that both the Republic of Korea and the US agreed to, is later in time (rule 6); (ii) because the WTO authorization is arguably also the more specific rule (rule 7).

The same would be true if bilateral sanctions were authorized under the FTA (e.g. because the US failed to implement an FTA ruling), as under the later in time rule, and arguably the more specific rule, such FTA authorization should prevail over any WTO obligation that the Republic of Korea, the FTA retaliator, may have. Crucially, if the US were nonetheless to challenge Korea's FTA retaliation before a WTO panel, the panel should give effect to the FTA authorization to retaliate and recognize it as a defence that the Republic of Korea can rely on against the US claim of WTO breach.

Equally, any WTO authorization to retaliate by suspending IP protections under TRIPS may contradict the retaliator's obligations under WIPO conventions outside the WTO. Yet, in this scenario as well, the WTO authorization should prevail over WIPO under both the later in time rule and the more specific rule.

5   Policy conclusions

The ultimate goal of this chapter is to shift the debate on regionalism from one that focuses on hierarchy and the supremacy of the WTO (through, in particular, GATT Article XXIV) to a debate that centres on mutual recognition, accommodation and respect between the WTO and regional agreements.

Law and legal analyses, in and of themselves, will not resolve the problems of regionalism or how to 'multilateralize' it. Yet, at the edges, legal provisions and legal rules on overlap and conflict (as developed in the eight rules set out in Section 3) offer tools to untangle the maze of WTO and regional agreements. By doing so, law and lawyers can contribute to the process of 'multilateralizing regionalism'.

The policy proposals that can be deduced from this chapter are:

1. The WTO must embrace regional agreements in its research and negotiating activities and, in particular, in WTO dispute settlement. Interaction and dialogue are more likely to untangle the 'spaghetti bowl' of WTO and regional agreements than unilateral claims to hierarchy and supremacy. *Reference by the WTO to regional agreements*

is but one form of 'multilateralizing regionalism'. One specific way to improve the integration between WTO and regional agreements would be to explicitly expand the 'applicable' or 'relevant law' before both WTO and FTA panels to all relevant international law consented to by the disputing parties. This does not mean that WTO panels must enforce WTO-plus concessions. It only means that WTO claims must be read and applied in the context of what the parties themselves (and only those parties) agreed to elsewhere (e.g. forum exclusion clauses in an FTA; retaliation or safeguards approved by an FTA).

2. From their side, negotiators of regional agreements must be aware of overlaps with the WTO and other regional agreements. To avoid conflicts, they must explicitly regulate questions of overlap. Specific areas of concern are: TRIPS-plus and the WTO decisions on access to medicines, overlapping dispute settlement procedures, WTO versus regional safeguards, the impact of changes at the WTO on pre-existing FTAs, and the relationship between different regional agreements. If FTA negotiators do not regulate these overlaps, FTA and WTO dispute settlement panels will do it for them (pursuant to the eight rules developed in Section 3), with possibly surprising results. *Reference by FTA negotiators and FTA dispute panels to WTO provisions and jurisprudence* (e.g. when it comes to an FTA dispute over TRIPS-plus provisions) is just another form of 'multilateralizing regionalism'.

3. To avoid repeat proceedings and protect scarce resources, especially of developing countries, regional agreements should include a 'forum exclusion clause' which states that once a matter is brought to the WTO or to an FTA panel, the same matter cannot be litigated a second time in the other forum.

4. To avoid conflicts and protect weaker parties in particular, where FTA and WTO provisions are substantially equivalent (say, in respect of national treatment or where the FTA does not provide WTO-plus liberalization), regional agreements should direct complainants to bring the dispute to the WTO (not the FTA).

5. Only in deeply integrated customs unions should there be exclusive jurisdiction for the regional courts. That said, WTO-plus obligations will obviously need to be enforced before an FTA panel as, in that case, there is no overlap with the WTO.

6. For the enforcement of WTO-plus concessions in FTAs it is crucially important that FTA dispute settlement mechanisms are carefully designed and work automatically (unlike Chapter 20 of NAFTA, as Mexico experienced in its sweeteners dispute with the US). Improving

FTA dispute settlement rules and procedures so that WTO-plus liberalization actually materializes must be a top priority.

7. WTO members must carefully guard the success of the WTO dispute settlement mechanism. As others have pointed out, one of the features that regional agreements are unlikely to match is the effectiveness and legitimacy of WTO dispute settlement. That mechanism alone is likely to preserve the survival of the multilateral trading system.

8. To enhance consistency between regimes, cross-references in regional agreements to WTO rules must be presumed to be dynamic – that is, automatically include WTO updates – unless otherwise provided.

9. FTA negotiators should consider including an MFN clause in FTAs that would automatically extend any subsequent FTA concessions to all previous and future FTA partners. Such an MFN clause would be an important step towards 'multilateralizing regionalism' and could be limited to FTAs only (and exclude, for example, preferential treatment under CUs and unilateral concessions to developing countries).

References

Bartels, L. and Ortino, F. (2006) *Regional Trade Agreements and the WTO Legal System*, Oxford: Oxford University Press.

Davey, W. (2006) 'Dispute Settlement in the WTO and RTAs: A Comment', in L. Bartels and F. Ortino (eds.), *Regional Trade Agreements and the WTO Legal System*, Oxford: Oxford University Press, pp. 343–57.

De Mestral, A. (2006) 'NAFTA Dispute Settlement: Creative Experiment or Confusion?', in L. Bartels and F. Ortino (eds.), *Regional Trade Agreements and the WTO Legal System*, Oxford: Oxford University Press, pp. 359–82.

Dillon, S. (2002) *International Trade and Economic Law and the European Union*, Oxford: Hart Publishing.

Drahos, P. (2007) 'Weaving Webs of Influence: The United States, Free Trade Agreements and Dispute Resolution', *Journal of World Trade* 41: 191–210.

Fiorentino, R., Verdeja, L. and Toqueboeuf, C. (2006) 'The Changing Landscape of Regional Trade Agreements: 2006 Update', Regional Trade Agreements Section, Discussion paper No. 12, available at: www.wto.org/english/res_e/booksp_e/discussion_papers12a_e.pdf (accessed 16 October 2007).

Garcia Bercero, I. (2006) 'Dispute Settlement in the European Union and FTAs: Lessons Learned?', in L. Bartels and F. Ortino (eds.), *Regional Trade Agreements and the WTO Legal System*, Oxford: Oxford University Press, pp. 383–406.

ILC (United Nations International Law Commission) (2006) 'Report of the Study Group on Fragmentation of International Law: Difficulties Arising from the Diversification and Expansion of International Law', 29 July 2006, UN Document A/CN.4/L.676.

Kwak, K. and Marceau, G. (2006) 'Overlaps and Conflicts of Jurisdiction between the WTO and RTAs', in L. Bartels and F. Ortino (eds.), *Regional Trade Agreements and the WTO Legal System*, Oxford: Oxford University Press, pp. 465–524.

Mavroidis, P. (2006) 'If I Don't Do It, Somebody Else Will (or Won't): Testing the Compliance of Preferential Trade Agreements with the Multilateral Rules', *Journal of World Trade* 40: 187–214.

Mayne, R. (2005) 'Regionalism, Bilateralism, and "TRIPS Plus" Agreements: The Threat to Developing Countries', UNDP Human Development Report Office, Occasional Paper 18, available at: http://hdr.undp.org/docs/publicat ions/background_papers/2005/HDR2005_Mayne_Ruth_18.pdf (accessed 16 October 2007).

Mercurio, B. (2006) 'TRIPS-Plus Provisions in FTAs: Recent Trends', in L. Bartels and F. Ortino (eds.), *Regional Trade Agreements and the WTO Legal System*, Oxford: Oxford University Press, pp. 215–38.

'Multilateralizing Regionalism' (2007), World Trade Organization and Graduate Institute of International Studies conference, Geneva, 10–12 September 2007; programme available at: www.wto.org/english/tratop_e/region_e/ conference_sept07_e.htm (accessed 16 October 2007).

Pauwelyn, J. (2003a) *Conflict of Norms in Public International Law – How WTO Law Relates to Other Rules of International Law*, New York: Cambridge University Press.

(2003b) 'How to Win a WTO Dispute Based on Non-WTO Law: Questions of Jurisdiction and Merits', *Journal of World Trade* 37: 997–1030.

(2004a) 'The Puzzle of WTO Safeguards and Regional Trade Agreements', *Journal of International Economic Law* 7: 109–42.

(2004b) 'Going Global, Regional or Both? Dispute Settlement in the Southern African Development Community (SADC) and Overlaps with the WTO and Other Jurisdictions', *Minnesota Journal of Global Trade* 13: 231–304.

(2006) 'Adding Sweeteners to Softwood Lumber: The WTO–NAFTA "Spaghetti Bowl" Is Cooking', *Journal of International Economic Law* 9: 1–10.

Tiny, N. (2005) 'Judicial Accommodation: NAFTA, the EU, and the WTO', New York University Jean Monnet Working Paper, April.

Van Damme, I. (2006) 'What Role is there for Regional International Law in the Interpretation of the WTO Agreements?', in L. Bartels and F. Ortino (eds.), *Regional Trade Agreements and the WTO Legal System*, Oxford: Oxford University Press, pp. 553–76.

List of cases

Argentina – Poultry. Argentina – Definitive Anti-Dumping Duties on Poultry from Brazil, WT/DS241/R, adopted 19 May 2003, DSR 2003:V, 1727.

Brazil – Tyres. Brazil – Retreaded Tyres, WT/DS332/R, circulated 12 June 2007.

Canada – Agricultural Products. Tariffs Applied by Canada to Certain US-Origin Agricultural Products, Final Report of the Panel Established Pursuant to NAFTA Article 2008, CDA-95-2008-01, 2 December 1996.

EC – Aircraft Subsidies. European Communities – Measures Affecting Trade in Large Civil Aircraft, WT/DS316.

EC – Bananas. European Communities – Regime for the Importation, Sale and Distribution of Bananas, WT/DS27/AB/R, WT/DS27/R/USA, Complaint by the United States, adopted 25 September 1997, DSR 1997:II, 591.

Mexico – Soft Drinks. Mexico – Tax Measures on Soft Drinks and Other Beverages, WT/DS308/AB/R, WT/DS308/R, adopted 24 March 2006.

Turkey – Textiles. Turkey – Restrictions on Imports of Textile and Clothing Products, WT/DS34/AB/R, WT/DS34/R, adopted 19 November 1999, DSR 1999:VI, 2345.

US – Steel. United States – Definitive Safeguard Measures on Imports of Certain Steel Products, WT/DS248/AB/R, WT/DS249/AB/R, WT/DS251/AB/R, WT/DS252/AB/R, WT/DS253/AB/R, WT/DS254/AB/R, WT/DS258/AB/R, WT/DS259/AB/R, WT/DS248/R, WT/DS249/R, WT/DS251/R, WT/DS252/R, WT/DS253/R, WT/DS254/R, WT/DS258/R, WT/DS259/R, and Corr.1 adopted 10 December 2003, DSR 2003:VII, 3117.

PART IV

Multilateralization: Regional Perspectives

9

Multilateralizing regionalism: case study of African regionalism

PETER DRAPER AND MZUKISI QOBO

1 Introduction

Regionalism emerged as a global policy concern during the Uruguay Round of multilateral trade negotiations, towards the end of the 1980s. Before then it had comfortably co-existed alongside the multilateral trading system. The stability of the system hinged strongly on the leadership that the US had provided since the early days of the GATT until the late 1980s. It was only when the US turned to regionalism that the edifice of the multilateral system began to experience tremors, and regionalism started becoming a threat to the functioning and credibility of the multilateral trading system. The stumbling block/building block metaphor widely credited to the Columbia University scholar, Jagdish Bhagwati, reflected the anxiety that the rapid spread of regionalism caused.

In the Sutherland Commission report for the World Trade Organization (WTO), the relationship between Regional Trade Agreements (RTAs) and the multilateral trading system is discussed extensively, although it has very little to say about those involving developing countries. The report is extremely cautionary about RTAs, suggesting that some of their agendas 'might lead the WTO to a wrong direction' (WTO 2004, 19). It further argues that the administration of these schemes is complicated by their preferential rules of origin and with particularly onerous costs for small corporations and traders, and hence for developing countries.[1] Despite these misgivings, it is now widely accepted that RTAs are here to stay and will continue to exist alongside the multilateral trading system.

---

[1] Alec Erwin, quoted WTO (2004, 22).

Of particular importance is how the two processes – regional and multilateral – co-exist in a manner that facilitates global trade liberalization. In this respect 'multilateralizing regionalism' is proffered as a possible path by Baldwin (2006) in his recent paper on the subject.[3] But what are the prospects for and pitfalls of this path for developing countries?

The positioning of developing countries in the global economy has led them, generally, to resist at a political level the regulatory convergence imperative or 'standards harmonization' agenda emanating from the industrialized world. Yet African countries in particular, with the notable exception of South Africa, are largely takers rather than shapers of international economic institutions, including regulations. This is also the case with respect to their relationship to changes in the structures of global production and services which increasingly shape the agenda of regional trade integration. This resultant sense of vulnerability is playing out in the Doha Round and in Economic Partnership Agreement (EPA) negotiations with the European Union (EU). From this standpoint it is difficult to see how African countries can constructively contribute to the 'multilateralizing regionalism' agenda. In fact the reverse is likely to be the case.

This chapter begins with an assessment of the key ideas underlying the 'multilateralizing regionalism' concept. The focus then moves to the enormous development challenges confronting African countries, rooted in chronic institutional weaknesses best considered a generalized crisis of the state. We show how these deeply entrenched challenges require Africa to engage more deeply with the developed world by adopting its standards as far as possible, in the hope of better plugging African economies into the globalization mainstream. This points to the centrality of the North–South axis; but that runs counter to the political impulse to resist economic dependence on the developed world.

We also show how regional economic integration in Africa is often poorly conceived and in some regions suffers from chronic duplication, while the economic and political bases for it are often woefully lacking. Furthermore, regional economic integration on the continent is often externally driven and characterized by donor-dependence. These channels of Western influence are reproduced in EPA negotiations. Hence if, as seems likely, the European Union successfully links its aid to the implementation of EU standards and insists on convergence to its regulatory standards, it is likely that African countries would, as Baldwin's domino theory (outlined below) predicts, ultimately fall into line.[2] The key question then is whether an appropriate balance can be found between African countries' legitimate needs for policy space, the pressing need for them to upgrade their regulatory capacities, and the needs of the multilateral trading system. We conclude by illustrating these points via a brief case study of the Southern African Development Community (SADC), and its fraught EPA negotiations with the EU.

2 Reflections on 'multilateralizing' regionalism

There are various reasons why countries join RTAs. Some of these are political and relate to factors such as geographic proximity, cultural affinity, shared political objectives, economic ties, and shared historical bonds.[3] For some countries this is to do with collective action problems linked to security or economic development. In some cases building a collective bargaining capacity to negotiate effectively at the World Trade Organization is an important consideration for participating in regional integration mechanisms, although this can hardly be a stand-alone justification. More concretely, creating economies of scale and providing an opportunity for learning-by-doing to foster competitiveness is a common thread that runs through almost all RTA arrangements (see UNCTAD, 2007).

The scope of obligations in many developing country regional trade agreements is limited to a subset of tariffs, and covers goods only, while in some it is broader and goes beyond border measures to cover regulatory issues (Crawford and Fiorentino, 2005). That there is no standard pattern followed by countries in pursuing regionalism is a function of a number of factors. Countries' priorities and expectations with regard to trade integration are different. There are also different standards that countries use to calculate the costs and benefits of participating in regional and multilateral trade negotiations, as well as with regard to their judgement on their rights and obligations. Some of the difficulties that developing countries face, for example fiscal adjustments or poor institutional environments, are less of a challenge for developed economies that may find it fairly straightforward to create more outward-

---

[2] This is what Jagdish Bhagwati refers to as the 'outside of trade reciprocity' which, because of the quid pro quo arrangement may encourage liberalization in return for financial assistance. See Bhagwati (2001).

[3] Mansfield and Milner (1999). Jeffrey Frankel also identifies some of these factors, especially cultural ties or language, as having some importance in encouraging trading relations between different countries. See Frankel (1997).

oriented regional initiatives. These difficulties are also expressed in the recent UNCTAD Trade and Development Report (2007), and suggest that a mix of both trade liberalization and cooperation in regional arrangements could help in simultaneously addressing collective action problems and facilitating trade liberalization (UNCTAD, 2007).

The essence of Baldwin's domino theory is that forces of regionalism, initially working independently of each other, will at a certain point trigger a multiplier effect that would knock down protective barriers like a row of dominoes, and open a path to regional and possibly global trade liberalization (Baldwin, 1997). Trade and investment diversion, resulting from the formation or deepening of preferential trade arrangements, trigger other countries to join existing regional integration arrangements, or to form their own, to tilt the scales of commercial flows in their favour. As Baldwin argues, this happens through the emergence of new political economy forces in non-participating (or excluded) countries, which pressure governments to join integration schemes or form their own. The impulse for regional integration originates largely from exporters who are a powerful political voice for regional integration.

Being excluded is very costly: firms from excluded countries have high import tariffs slapped on them while their home countries miss out on efficiency-seeking foreign direct investment. Avoiding losses incurred as a result of exclusion puts pressure on firms to lobby their governments to conclude trade deals, so as to create new market access opportunities. In Baldwin's formulation the key organizing principle for these trade agreements is reciprocity, which in turn unleashes a 'juggernaut' effect once export interests outweigh import-competing ones (Baldwin, 2006). Bhagwati makes a similar point when he argues that '[i]n a pluralistic system, [reciprocity] may help a government mobilize export-oriented lobbies who would profit from expanding foreign markets to countervail the import-competing lobbies that profit instead from reducing trade (Bhagwati, 2001).' Indeed, reciprocity creates new political economy forces where export interests become advocates for trade liberalization; in the long run this is good for freer trade.

Regional trade agreements offer short-term gains (they facilitate competitive liberalization) for export interests in advanced countries, whereas the multilateral trading system can become a less useful instrument for exporters, especially if agreements are based on the lowest common denominator and far below their targeted commercial access. Baldwin suggests that regionalism, when viewed in this manner (i.e. seeking to advance liberalization in areas where multilateral trade negotiations may have reached a point of exhaustion), may well become a stepping stone for global trade liberalization (Baldwin, 1997). In other words, this would facilitate scaling up the level of commitments above the multilateral ceiling. Where does this leave unilateral liberalization? This can play a powerful role in inducing what Bhagwati characterizes as 'sequential reciprocity', where countries that have demonstrable success through unilateral liberalization encourage other countries to follow suit (the so-called China effect) (Baldwin, 1997). Of course, this takes full effect where there is a pairing of mutual concessions.

Baldwin's domino view also fits neatly with the notion of WTO-plus credited to the former Treasury Under-Secretary in President Clinton's administration, Lawrence Summers. He argued that whatever form trade liberalization takes, be it unilateral, bilateral, plurilateral, or multilateral does not matter since all forms lead to the same objective.[4]

Import-competing interests resist the liberalization of, primarily, labour-intensive sectors. In the face of these political voices, politicians often find it difficult to justify liberalization, especially in the absence of strong and powerful export sectors that could immediately reap benefits in external markets, and be a new coalition group for trade reform. Export firms in developed countries may view the current agenda of the WTO as representing partial multilateral trade liberalization which, as Robert Lawrence points out, is second-best to a complete preferential trade liberalization (Lawrence, 2003).

The attraction of intra-regional liberalization is that, politically, it may be more palatable for governments to liberalize with respect to their neighbours than to do so multilaterally (Lawrence, 2003). Because unilateral import liberalization is generally difficult for reasons mainly to do with politics or policy concerns, a piecemeal approach undertaken via regional agreements could, in principle, serve multilateral trade liberalization better. This is especially so, given the fact that at the multilateral level there are many players, all with different expectations, needs, agendas and capacities, who are part of the multilateral trading system, making decisions difficult to arrive at. The downside to the regional approach is, of course, the proliferation of regulations or 'spaghetti'.

---

[4] See Bhagwati (1995) and Frankel (1997). Frankel points out that the US views all the 'lateralisms' as having an equal and benign weight; and this is a strategy that defines the US approach to global trade engagements. Frankel attributes this strategy to US concern with its declining political and economic hegemony, a point which Baldwin disputes, instead placing emphasis on the impulse of export-oriented sectors.

Baldwin's arguments are forcefully restated in his recent work (Baldwin, 2006). In tracing the history of the juggernaut effect and the domino theory to the Kennedy Round, a force that continued through the successive rounds until the Uruguay Round, he suggests a strong linkage between reciprocal concessions on industrial tariffs and the pro-liberalization forces that took shape in developed countries that made commitments during these rounds.

To align political economy forces in support of liberalization (a coalition for trade reform) in developed economies, there had to be market access opportunities for export interests, especially in the areas of services, technical barriers to trade and investment guarantees (Baldwin, 2006). According to Subramanian, 'industrial countries have less need and hence enthusiasm for the multilateral trade system as a means of achieving market access objectives' (Subramanian, 2007). He concludes that there is a lack of serious private sector interest in the Doha Round because it does not offer prospects for expanded commercial opportunities.

As Krugman (1993, 69) suggests, the bargaining process in trade negotiations reflects 'linkage both across industries and between the trade policies of different nations'. In other words, there has to be a pairing of mutual concessions and complementarity of interest for trade liberalization to gain political credibility. In a context where there does not seem to be much trade policy shift in areas such as services in developing countries, there will hardly be any interest for developed economies to make further liberalization concessions in key areas where developing countries could reap benefits. In this schema, the orthodox logic becomes inverted: multilateral trade setting becomes 'second-best' for pursuance of market access opportunities, and regional trade agreements naturally emerge as a 'first-best option'.

This is also observed by Baldwin, as he suggests, for example, that wide-ranging FTAs could harvest real liberalization outcomes – more than could be achieved through unilateral or multilateral trade processes (Krugman, 1993, 1485). He argues that, in the earlier period of Europe's internal liberalization, the political economy logic was manifest in the teaming up of the spaghetti bowl syndrome with the unbundling of manufacturing processes, in part responding to competitive pressures (cost structure and productivity factors) and new market opportunities offshore (mainly in former Eastern European countries), and this repositioned the formerly import-competing sectors to become new advocates for liberalization.

The unbundling (or offshoring) process pulled the plug on protective cover offered under the regional trade mechanism, making EU firms victims of the spaghetti bowl rules (for example, complex rules of origin, ROOs), and this acted as a stepping stone to creating a coherent EU free-trade zone. The demand for ROO/cumulation protection was weakened by manufacturing unbundling as the size of import-competing industries shrank (unbundled), and labour-intensive processes went offshore to cheaper locations (Baldwin, 2006). Production unbundling has a natural propensity to increase trade, with intermediate inputs crossing borders several times during the manufacturing process (Feenstra, 1998).

In this environment, 'industrialized countries' trade is already largely duty-free, especially because much of their trade was liberalized in successive GATT rounds until the Uruguay Round. Intra-OECD trade is fairly open and tariffs are of lesser value compared to services and regulatory issues. Therefore, a limited agenda on industrial products and services in the current round will not be sufficient to appeal to political economy forces in the developed economies. They would have to look elsewhere – to regional trade deals – for new commercial opportunities (or competitive liberalization).

But, as Baldwin suggests, the 'special and differential treatment' that is sought by developing countries in both regional and multilateral trade negotiations is incompatible with a liberalizing agenda. It places limits on the extent to which countries can be expected to liberalize their trade, and frees countries of the obligation to fully reciprocate, something which is a cardinal principle of the multilateral trading system, and of trade negotiations more broadly. Indeed, 'free-riding' has been the hallmark of the participation of developing countries in the multilateral trading system until the Uruguay Round (1986–93), and as a result their economies are still characterized by substantial protective barriers (Hoekman, 2002). This, and the continued misgivings about the benefits of the multilateral trade negotiations, has left domestic political economy forces relatively intact in many developing countries.[5]

In the current Doha negotiations, developing countries have objected to more substantive requirements that emphasize quantitative

---

[5] Of course there is a track record of unilateral trade reforms in developing countries, as well as structural adjustment in the case of LDCs. These processes must have impacted on domestic political economy forces – perhaps strengthening the hand of import-replacement interests.

(statistical) benchmarks as well as measures to broaden the coverage of regional trading arrangements to fulfil the 'substantially all trade' criterion. This tendency could significantly weaken the juggernaut, especially where it manifests in systemically significant developing countries such as Brazil, India and China.

It is based upon concerns that overambitious FTAs may inhibit their utility as developmental devices, and could become burdensome for countries that have limited institutional capacity. Maintaining special and differential treatment provisions in regional trade agreements figures quite prominently in the position of developing countries. Most of the regional trade arrangements established by developing countries were notified under the Article V Enabling Clause, and this exempts them from the more rigorous tests associated with Article XXIV's 'substantially all trade' requirement. Baldwin views this as 'disabling' rather than 'enabling' for developing countries, as they miss out on deep tariff cuts and the allocative efficiencies that this could generate in their economies. Such efficiencies would be generated as import-competing firms are rolled over by the withering force of external competition.

For different reasons, sub-Saharan countries' reluctance to engage in far-reaching reforms is also evident in the current Doha Round. They view the round as about rebalancing the global trading system in their favour – or to support development objectives. Developing countries in general, and those in sub-Saharan Africa in particular, believed that the concessions made at the Uruguay Round in new areas such as intellectual property, TRIMs, and services were not matched by significant concessions by developed countries on agriculture and textiles (Finger and Nogues, 2002). Indeed, as Baldwin (2004) has suggested, the gains made by developing countries in these two sectors were not comparable to those made by developed countries in trade in services and the TRIPS agreements.

In this respect, the current round is viewed in some developing countries less through commercial lenses than through 'development' imperatives. This reflects the obvious reality that in many developing countries, especially those containing the 'bottom billion' (Collier, 2007) of the world's population, there are no domestic export juggernauts to speak of. Indeed, many of these countries barely have functioning states, and hence are not capable of organizing export interests or sometimes providing functional domestic regulatory frameworks. In these countries regulatory upgrading is imperative, if very difficult to achieve in the context of chronically weak and sometimes failing domestic institutions.

The pertinent question is whether the multilateralizing regionalism agenda can be harnessed for this purpose.

In this perspective if multilateral trade negotiations and regional trade agreements with Northern countries (especially in the context of EPAs with the European Union) are to be politically marketable in sub-Saharan Africa, then they should be seen to support interests identified by developing countries. This would require balancing 'commercial imperatives' and developmental concerns, where acquiescing to 'new-generation' issues is paired with development assistance, either in the form of compensatory funds or targeted assistance *à la* 'aid for trade' aimed at building relevant institutions, including upgrading standards and regulatory capabilities, enhancing production diversification and encouraging export competitiveness.

This could also help to improve the investment climate and induce the activity of export interests which could respond to new incentives and act as a voice for liberalization. We explore this assertion with respect to the African case in the following section.

3 Political economy realities of sub-Saharan Africa

The political economy dynamics in sub-Saharan Africa are different to those sketched out by Baldwin. Chabal and Daloz (2000) argue that the nature of politics in 'black Africa' needs to be understood on its own terms, rather than through the prism of Western modernization theories, within which development is seen as a largely linear process of advancement along Western lines. As the title of their intriguing book suggests, their thesis is that African politics tends towards disorder and the undermining of state institutions, largely owing to the prevalence of patrimonial politics across the subcontinent, impelling political elites or 'big men' to prioritize their networks of influence over national development priorities. They conclude that this political dynamic is inimical to development.

This resonates with Herbst's scheme, in which African state apparatuses barely control national borders, never mind a concerted development process (Herbst, 2000). He argues persuasively that Africa's crisis is best understood as a generalized crisis of the state. In his view this arises from a context where African states are geographically large, while populations are predominantly rural and dispersed, and institutions are characterized by pervasive weakness. This confluence renders internal political control tenuous; hence rulers are primarily concerned with maintaining that control. This naturally limits the extent to which they are prepared to cede control to others, internal or external; while in some cases old-fashioned authoritarian instincts compound this dynamic. And, as Chabal and Daloz argue, the edifice of political control is in any event built on patrimonial foundations.

These dynamics inevitably result in chronic problems in managing trade flows, as reflected, for example, in deficient border administrations. It is difficult to see how states constructed on such weak foundations could engage with the regulation-intensive 'new-generation' trade issues. They have enough difficulties dealing with the standard goods agenda. In our view this points to the imperative of building trade-management institutions slowly, while prioritizing basic trade facilitation in its broadest sense over regulation-intensive policy areas. Such an agenda would be of particular utility to the substantial number of landlocked countries on the continent, to which the formal mechanisms of regional economic integration are not of much use if their goods cannot make their way cheaply to ports. External actors could play critical roles in this regard by providing technical assistance and targeted aid for trade.

Furthermore, the relationship of African states to the global economy is fundamentally different from that of their developed country peers. The subcontinent is by and large incorporated into the global economy as an exporter of commodities based substantially on preferential access to developed country markets, primarily the European Union via the Cotonou Partnership Agreement (CPA), and an importer of manufactures and services.[6] This reflects both colonial histories and comparative advantages.

While preferences in principle ensure market access for products from sub-Saharan Africa on more favourable terms than for their developing country competitors, they are probably not sustainable in the long term. In the specific case of trade with Europe, which accounts for the bulk of African exports (see Table 9.1 for a breakdown of southern and eastern African export destinations), this is most certainly a problem, given that the CPA's commodity protocols expire at the end of 2007.[7]

In a recent paper, Paul Collier and Anthony Venables revisit this issue of preferences and suggest that these be reoriented towards clusters in

---

[6] Of course this aggregate picture requires some nuancing. For example, Kenya is emerging as a regional manufacturing hub for East Africa, exporting increasingly substantial quantities of manufactures to its neighbours. South Africa does not readily fit the bill either.

[7] For an extended discussion of the political economy of economic partnership agreement negotiations between the EU and sub-Saharan African groupings, see Draper (2007).

Table 9.1. *Eastern and Southern Africa's world trade by major market (2003–2005 average) (US$ 000)*

Reporting country	Imports by 'world'	Share attributable to (%)						Country total
		EU	NAFTA	China	Japan	SA		
1 Lesotho	496,371	5.1	94.4	0.0	0.1	0.0		99.7
2 Congo, Dem. Rep.	1,268,471	71.8	16.1	8.4	0.7	0.4		97.4
3 Mauritius	1,735,850	74.0	16.3	0.3	0.6	1.1		92.3
4 Madagascar	1,179,459	52.1	36.1	1.0	2.7	0.2		92.0
5 Namibia	1,432,826	65.6	16.2	4.2	1.7	3.4		91.2
6 Botswana	3,215,510	83.1	3.5	0.1	0.9	3.6		91.2
7 Angola	16,043,695	11.9	43.6	32.6	0.3	1.4		89.7
8 Sudan	4,296,273	4.5	1.3	51.4	32.4	0.0		89.6
9 Libya	22,022,940	83.2	3.5	2.4	0.0	0.0		89.2
10 Seychelles	362,333	72.8	3.2	0.0	8.7	0.9		85.7
11 Mozambique	1,503,422	76.4	0.8	3.6	1.2	2.4		84.5
12 Comoros	29,926	51.2	24.0	0.0	6.0	0.4		81.6
13 Ethiopia (excludes Eritrea)	544,484	49.7	10.4	6.9	12.6	0.4		80.0
14 Burundi	51,653	66.1	9.9	1.6	0.6	0.7		78.9
15 Uganda	431,907	62.3	7.8	2.6	2.0	1.2		75.9
16 Zimbabwe	1,657,471	28.0	4.8	9.1	7.8	24.7		74.4
17 Malawi	479,018	37.3	18.7	0.1	4.9	12.6		73.7
18 South Africa	44,986,439	40.0	14.6	6.4	10.7	0.0		71.7
19 Egypt, Arab Rep.	9,587,412	48.8	19.2	2.0	0.9	0.3		71.2
20 Tanzania	992,929	36.2	8.3	9.4	9.0	3.1		66.0

Table 9.1. (*cont.*)

Reporting country	Imports by 'world'	Share attributable to (%)					
		EU	NAFTA	China	Japan	SA	Country total
21 Eritrea	12,508	50.6	6.3	4.1	2.9	0.7	64.6
22 Kenya	2,351,014	39.2	14.5	0.6	1.3	1.4	57.0
23 Swaziland	753,298	20.1	30.2	2.5	0.9	0.0	53.8
24 Zambia	1,289,278	16.5	2.4	14.2	6.8	13.1	52.9
25 Rwanda	212,291	16.1	2.9	6.5	0.1	0.2	25.8
26 Djibouti	25,754	12.0	2.4	0.9	0.2	0.2	15.7
Group total	**116,962,532**	**46.1**	**16.1**	**9.8**	**6.0**	**1.3**	**79.2**

Note: Generating an accurate figure for the whole world's imports from the countries in Table 9.2 in a way that is consistent across all of them (i.e. from the same reporting data source), is difficult. The following caveats must therefore be borne in mind when interpreting the figures. First, the aggregate figure for 'world' imports from these countries is almost certainly lower than the real figure. Cross-checking with alternative sources for South Africa's total exports to the world, for example, confirms this. The principal reason for this under-reporting is poorly recorded imports by many other developing countries, including those in Africa. The data for these African countries' exports is no more reliable, but imports recorded by the EU, NAFTA, China, and Japan, are. As such, their shares in total world imports from these African countries are overstated, implying higher geographical concentration than is actually the case. However, this problem applies to all countries in the table, as the same source and methods were used for all of them. Thus the overall pattern or profile is broadly representative.

key African cities where (North–South) input–output linkages could be developed, thereby encouraging the development of new (but narrow) export sectors, building on nascent comparative advantage, that could be scaled up and inserted into global production networks (Collier and Venables, 2007). Rules of origin, as Collier and Venables assert, would have to be liberal, while at the same time appropriately structured to prevent transhipment or trade deflection. This fits with the basic trade facilitation agenda outlined above.

One of the limitations of Collier and Venables' approach is that it does not clearly specify the threshold criteria for developing globally competitive clusters that could benefit from trade preferences. Furthermore, it runs the risk of creating dual economies – as seems to have been the case in Mexico – where the input–output linkages do not go deep enough to integrate endogenous capital, but only benefit a fraction that is active in the clusters. The extent of technological spillovers and know-how might also be constrained by the fact that such activities are most likely to be of the assembly type.[8] Collier and Venables' approach may be over-optimistic with regard to the development of productive capacities that could be fast-tracked to globally competitive production networks, and ignores the glaring lack of infrastructure, logistics capabilities, and technical know-how, as well as poor human capital. Indeed, as indigenous export interests are very weak, they are not well placed to respond to new supply incentives in international markets. Yet this is important for the juggernaut to take off in sub-Saharan Africa. Unsurprisingly, the majority of producers in the region are predominantly import-competing and may mobilize against outward-oriented regionalism which could expose them to the vagaries of international competition. This also coincides with the preoccupation of state actors with preserving policy space and flexibility for nurturing and promoting infant industries. The underlying objective here is to replace imported inputs into export products with domestic inputs. Hence import-substitution industrialization has a strong appeal and takes on a nuanced shape in intra-regional trade agreements. While it may be possible to construct region-wide import-substitution industrialization as a short-term measure, as some regional integration schemes seek to do in sub-Saharan Africa, these would remain inefficient and uncompetitive in international markets.

---

[8] See UNCTAD, for an extensive critique of the Mexico case in NAFTA's preferential trade arrangements.

So it will be hard for sub-Saharan Africa to evolve an export trajectory on the back of import-substitution industrialization in the way Asia did in the 1960s, due to a lack of the requisite infrastructure, skills, cost-effectiveness and productivity of factors of production. The continent is deficient in capital, skills and population, which makes it difficult for manufacturing to take off, despite several attempts in the past to kick-start it by import-substitution industrialization.

Hence the foreign direct investment (FDI) likely to be attracted is either of the tariff-jumping type to take advantage of high tariffs, or resource-seeking, rather than market-seeking or efficiency-seeking. Sub-Saharan Africa does not provide an attractive export base for foreign capital, which inhibits the development of indigenous capital that could benefit from supply-chain linkages.

The imperative of production-unbundling in bringing about the liberalization of spaghetti bowl proliferation is thus unlikely to have resonance for sub-Saharan Africa. However, in the long run, intra-regional cross-border investment emanating from growing regional poles such as South Africa, Mauritius and Kenya, associated with joint ventures and strategic alliances with private sector agents from these countries, may provide sufficient stimulus. Furthermore, with the anticipated growth in manufacturing productivity of China in the long run, Africa may potentially become the next base for manufacturing offshore (see below).

Although sub-Saharan Africa possesses some advantages vis-à-vis Asia, for example with respect to lower income levels, there are serious problems with institutional capacity, policy environment, infrastructure, and the lack of competitive real exchange rates, which strongly militate against attracting productive investment (Collier, 2000). Furthermore, as Paul Collier notes, 'the wage in African manufacturing may be higher relative to the returns to labour in the economy as a whole than in Asia. This might reflect labour market policies, such as minimum wages, or the greater power of African labour to extract rent-sharing wage levels.' With lower total factor productivity and weak logistics, attracting export-oriented manufacturers would not be possible.

However, Collier is more optimistic about Africa's manufacturing potential, especially if it can address the policy environment, as well as correct its institutional and infrastructural bottlenecks (Collier, 2000). Indeed, breaking into manufacturing is not completely impossible, but in the short run the continent would be well served by exploiting its comparative advantages in commodities to earn foreign exchange that could in the long run be utilized for importing intermediate inputs and diversifying into manufacturing. Horizontal diversification into services may hold greater prospects for countries in sub-Saharan Africa in the short to medium term than manufacturing. This would require breaking the stranglehold of monopolies in key network service sectors such as utilities, transport and telecommunications. This in turn points to the importance of FDI and the associated need for regulatory upgrading, and the potential utility of the multilateralizing regionalism agenda as one tool towards achieving these objectives.

If export markets cannot provide the stimulus required to generate sustainable growth, what about domestic markets? In sub-Saharan Africa, even in the so-called 'big states',[9] with the significant exception of South Africa, domestic markets remain small, dispersed and primarily subsistence-based, and this is likely to change relatively slowly over time. Unlike in the case of Mexico in the NAFTA arrangement, lucrative markets are located some distance away from sub-Saharan Africa. This reality will undermine any potential competitiveness, even with a much better infrastructure, as envisaged by Collier and Venables.

It may be more fruitful for countries in sub-Saharan Africa to expand regional markets by deeper integration with relatively advanced economies within the region. The candidates for this would be South Africa (in the SACU/SADC region), Kenya (in the EAC and COMESA region), and Nigeria in ECOWAS. Indeed, conventional wisdom, and much of 'progressive civil society', aver that building regional markets through regional economic communities (RECs) offers a solution. This seems to be partly rooted in the notion that regional economic integration will promote economies of scale amongst tiny markets, and as such could be considered an extension of the infant industry argument. The notion of building institutional strength in negotiations with external actors is also important, and resonates with deep-seated notions of African solidarity, lending integration processes political support that is often not grounded in substance.

However, proponents of the 'new economic geography' advance strong arguments against promoting South–South economic integration schemes among poor developing countries.[10] The theory predicts that, while all countries in such schemes have a comparative disadvantage in manufacturing relative to the global economy, there will be one with less

---

[9] For an interesting political perspective on why big African states tend to fail, see Ottaway *et al.* (2004)

[10] For an exposition of this logic see World Bank (2000).

of a disadvantage than the others. In this sense, industrial activity will tend to relocate to the relatively advantaged country at the expense of the others. This effect will be aggravated by agglomeration economics, which promote industrial concentration in the relatively advantaged country (consider South Africa and Kenya in southern and eastern Africa respectively).

Furthermore, as tariff levels decline overall within the REC, so those countries suffering from industrial relocation will also experience trade diversion effects – importing relatively expensive goods from the growing industrial centre rather than from more efficient global producers, thereby lowering their overall welfare. Meanwhile, the favoured country will gain as regional industry relocates to its soil and real wages will rise as a result. Clearly these effects would generate substantial political tensions over time[11] which in turn would undermine integration processes. These are serious considerations.

Yet considerable benefits may be derived from economic integration in so far as it promotes the building or upgrading of trade-supporting infrastructure across the region. Thus, on the trade facilitation front, deepened regional integration is critical for a highly fragmented continent like Africa, which has more landlocked countries than any other continent. This points to a more limited agenda, tailored to regional capacities. External actors have a critical role to play in supporting the development of institutions such as customs authorities and infrastructure systems through an 'aid for trade' agenda. These initiatives may have the added benefit of promoting regional value chains and integrated production, thereby developing economies of scale over time to compete globally. The downside, however, will be the agglomeration forces noted above. Furthermore, establishing regional production pipelines or value chains may not be easy, especially where clear comparative advantages have not been established. Input costs may well be higher than in the rest of the world, production inefficiencies might be generated, and the choice of consumers, including firms that rely on the importation of intermediate inputs, could be significantly constrained.

Yet the economic logic of North–South integration is much more compelling: it reinforces comparative advantages, promotes income

---

[11] This process was a substantial factor behind the unravelling of the original East African Community, as Kenya attracted manufacturing investment and relocation at the expense of Uganda and Tanzania. It also partly explains why South Africa continues to 'compensate' its customs union partners for their membership of SACU.

convergence, and over time should also promote knowledge transfers from developed to developing countries.[12] While it does not directly promote economic diversification in its own right, provided receipts from increased resource exports are appropriately reinvested – particularly in building Africa's productive capacities – in time this could support diversification. This is a strong theoretical argument in support of EPAs, but more broadly of integration into the global economy via the WTO plus unilateral measures.

Unfortunately it is not a popular political position, especially if there are no clear incentives in the form of development (aid) transfers to upgrade infrastructure and other trade-related capacity-building, and to support export competitiveness. Furthermore, it is questionable whether vulnerable economies could cope with the competition from efficient Northern producers if the agreements are not sensitive to development needs. And if they do not have appropriate institutions in place to manage the ensuing liberalization (a very likely scenario in sub-Saharan Africa) the ultimate effect could be further dislocation. Yet if liberalization is only partial, as seems probable in the case of EPAs, then it is unlikely that production shifts will actually occur. The end result therefore may be to increase profit margins for the more powerful actors in supply chains – most likely foreign companies – without the efficiency-enhancing effects associated with meaningful liberalization.

Furthermore, even though a number of African countries undertook structural reforms in the 1980s and 1990s, when the ideological climate in Africa shifted in favour of neo-classical policies,[13] their record is mixed. This was mainly intended to improve the investment climate. Externally imposed stabilization programmes have a far smaller chance of success – however excellent they may be – than those that are endogenously driven.

Moreover, the transmission mechanisms (institutions) for such reforms are generally too weak to sustain them into the future. This is confirmed by the recent World Bank Independent Evaluation Group Report. Of critical importance in this report is emphasis on the importance of institutions and complementary policies to support trade

---

[12] The accession of relatively poor countries into the European Union in various waves provides strong evidence of such convergence effects.

[13] These policy positions were reflected in various World Bank reports, principally the Elliot Berg Report in 1981, as well as the subsequent stabilization programmes. Africa's Priority Programme for Economic Reform, implemented between 1986 and 1990, signalled the end of the Lagos Plan era.

reform measures, and especially to focus on poverty reduction and distributional outcomes. (World Bank, 2006). In essence, the international financial institutions overestimated the impact of reforms in countries that had weak institutional mechanisms for their implementation. These, coupled with weak political administration, poor design of structural adjustment programmes, intolerant political cultures in recipient countries, and poor sequencing of the reforms, are some of the reasons cited for the lack of positive results. Issues related to geography (notably the landlocked nature of some of the countries) and institutions were not given proper attention during this phase of reform. Yet, along with political governance issues, these are important determinants of success.

This attests to the importance of domestically driven reform processes rather than those imposed by external agents. Ideally it is on the basis of domestic successes that regional integration schemes can be sustained: in Oyejide's view, 'regional integration schemes should constitute an extension of the domestic reforms of member countries rather than act as a force to engineer them' (Oyejide, 2000). Yet this would require countries to have in place a strong governance culture and financial infrastructure that include viable public service institutions, macro-economic stability and the capacity for a competitive domestic economy through the development of the private sector. Furthermore, inculcating an entrepreneurial spirit, creating a supportive climate for a viable and independent private sector, and nurturing a coalition for reform (on the basis of clear market access advantages abroad) could lend significant weight in promoting trade openness in sub-Saharan Africa.

However, as argued at the beginning of this section, the prevailing political dynamic in sub-Saharan Africa does not seem favourable to this outcome. Indeed, the first generation of post-colonial leaders opted for state-led import-substitution industrialization, thereby suffocating entrepreneurship and the development of an active private sector (Ndulu and O'Connell, 1999). A number of countries are still struggling to completely shed this political culture and fully embrace economic reforms.

Concerning the politics of building African RECs, the most important issue to confront is that of deepening political commitment to regional economic integration. In light of the relative 'youth' of states in the region, it is perhaps not surprising to find that leaders in many countries are reluctant to yield their prerogatives. After all, regional integration involves pooling sovereignty – in Africa's case it is newly acquired.[14] Part of this political commitment should involve rationalizing the RECs, given the well-known problem of overlapping membership (see Table 9.2) and conflicting integration processes (see Draper *et al.*, 2007). These are problems peculiar to Africa, requiring Africans to resolve them. Unfortunately the necessary leadership seems to be in short supply.

Confusingly, EPA negotiation configurations, at least in southern and eastern Africa, are not coterminous with existing RECs (see Table 9.2). This places further stress on a delicate situation in which institutional capacities are already overstretched, and consequently threaten to divide the region even further. It also makes it difficult for constituent countries to agree on common negotiating positions, given that their tariff schedules and domestic regulations are generally not harmonized.[15] And it raises substantial legal uncertainties as the negotiating groupings do not have formal legal status, unlike the RECs that constitute them. So it is not clear who exactly the EC will sign agreements with, and how they would be administered. All of this highlights the fragile nature of African RECs.

Aggravating this situation is the fact that European Development Funds (EDF 10 specifically) will apparently not be allocated to RECs in the next five-year tranche (2008–13), but rather to groupings negotiating EPAs. In the case of southern and eastern Africa, as Table 9.2 shows, this places considerable pressure on countries to consolidate their membership if they are to access those regional resources; it also places pressure on the Secretariats to justify their existence, given that they may not be the ones to allocate funding. While it is always a good thing for organizations to justify their existence, especially in a region as confused as southern and eastern Africa, this nonetheless raises questions about who exactly is driving the regional agenda. In this light there are persistent concerns that the EU, in promoting the regional economic integration agenda, has its own model in mind for Africa.[16] While this may be a useful long-term aspiration, its current practical utility to a continent facing so many development challenges and a generalized crisis of the state is, at the very least, questionable.

---

[14] For an exposition of this argument see Mbeki, (2004).

[15] Although COMESA does seem to be converging with the EAC in respect of common tariff bands.

[16] The EC's Director-General for Development, Stefano Manservisi, stated at a round table hosted by SAIIA that the EU is 'consciously projecting' its model, but not exporting it. It is not clear to us what the difference may be.

Table 9.2. *Membership of regional organizations in Southern and Eastern Africa*

	ESA–EU EPA	SADC–EU EPA	SADC	COMESA	IOC	EAC	IGAD	SACU
Angola		X	X					
Botswana		X	X					X
Burundi	X			X FTA		X		
Comoros	X			X	X			
Djibouti	X			X FTA			X	
DRC	X		X	X				
Egypt				X FTA				
Eritrea	X			X			X	
Ethiopia	X			X			X	
Kenya	X			X FTA		X	X	
Lesotho		X	X					X
Madagascar	X		X	X FTA	X			
Malawi	X		X	X FTA				
Mauritius	X		X	X FTA	X			
Mozambique		X	X					
Namibia		X	X					X
Rwanda	X			X FTA		X		
Seychelles	X			X	X			
South Africa			X					X
Sudan	X			X FTA			X	
Swaziland		X	X	X				X
Tanzania		X	X			X		
Uganda	X			X		X	X	
Zambia	X		X	X FTA				
Zimbabwe	X		X	X FTA				
Aim	EPA 2008	EPA 2008	CU 2010	CU 2008		CU 2004		

4   Can the multilateralizing regionalism agenda work for Africa?

Notwithstanding the myriad political economy constraints outlined above, the multilateralizing regionalism agenda could be of some benefit to sub-Saharan Africa. The case for this rests on the fact that, if Africa is to participate effectively in the global economy, countries will have to undergo regulatory upgrading, in the context of an international trading environment that, from the regulatory standpoint, is easier to access. While this may appear paradoxical (one thrust promotes more regulations, the other requires fewer) we believe it is not.

On the one hand, effective regulatory environments in the context of functioning states are indispensable to promoting manufacturing and services FDI of the type that contributes to long-term development. This means adopting regulatory standards consistent with what international investors require, albeit at a pace that fits African capacities to manage these frameworks. High on our list are services regulations conducive to FDI in network infrastructure industries, and competition policy to manage the potentially anti-competitive results of foreign investors moving into small markets. The former will bolster fragile national reform efforts, whereas the latter could be adopted regionally in order to attain economies of scale in an institutional sense. In both cases the politics of implementing these regulations and establishing the necessary institutions will be difficult. Furthermore, it is very difficult to conceive of such processes working without sustained international assistance in the form of 'aid for trade'.

On the other hand, minimizing external spaghetti, such as conflicting systems of rules of origin in GSP, contributes to a more liberal export environment, which in turn also encourages the 'beneficial' kind of FDI needed in Africa. To the extent that sub-Saharan Africa is able to attract efficiency-seeking FDI, and therefore participate in global value chains, the extension of more liberal rules of origin to preference schemes in which they participate is essential. One danger with this path, though, is the potential for export enclaves to develop. But then, as the famous Cambridge economist, Joan Robinson is reputed to have said: 'the only thing worse than being exploited is not being exploited'. It seems to us that the choices many African countries face are not enviable.

Can the WTO play a role in helping African states to manage the multilateralizing regionalism agenda? One clear role it can play, and already does, is to pursue the 'aid for trade' process. Within this the WTO Secretariat's core competency is assistance with regulatory management and upgrading, or 'technical assistance'. Here the integrated framework for the LDCs seems to have established a good track record and could serve as the basis for an expanded programme focused on regulatory upgrading.

Furthermore, the WTO Secretariat could assist national governments and/or regional institutions to refine their trade facilitation instruments and institutions. While there are already a number of international institutions providing this kind of support (the World Bank, World Customs Organization, UNCTAD, etc.), none has the analytical and empirical focus on trade policy that the WTO Secretariat, through its system of trade policy reviews, possesses. From this perspective the WTO Secretariat could play an effective coordination role, with particular emphasis on the imperative of trade facilitation.

5   Concluding remarks

Clearly the politics of negotiation do not lend themselves (currently) to an easy extension of the domino effect to southern Africa, and sub-Saharan Africa more broadly. Similar dynamics are at play in the Doha Round, where the Africa group has actively resisted the developed world's regulatory agenda, while pushing for continued carve-outs in the form of preference erosion mitigation and 'aid for trade'. And as outlined in the discussion of African political economy dynamics, the continent is primarily a recipient, not a shaper, of globalization. Taken together, it is not surprising that the continent's trade diplomacy is basically defensive, actively resisting falling dominos where possible. The absence of a domestic juggernaut effect in sub-Saharan Africa reinforces this perspective, and also substantially explains why regional integration arrangements do not work optimally.

Notwithstanding this situation, however, it is probably the case that, at the level of technical or regulatory detail, the situation is quite different. For example, several key South African government agencies, notably customs and standards administration, take their cue from the relevant multilateral institutions (the World Customs and International Standards Organizations respectively) within which developed countries play dominant roles. Furthermore, across Africa regulatory and legislative frameworks have been inherited from an assortment of colonial powers, to which African states frequently turn for aid to assist in building their institutional and regulatory capacities, thereby entrenching their status as recipients of imported frameworks. By and large, despite the political economy of trade negotiations and the emergence of new competitors on the African scene (especially China), SADC, and sub-Saharan Africa more broadly, remain locked into the European orbit.

Thus the politics of dependency rooted in colonial inheritances clashes with the need for African states to leverage their economic and political relations with the West, and Europe in particular, for their own development. In the end, while many African elites find the domino effect politically unpalatable, they are nonetheless subject to its inexorable force.

References

Baldwin, R. E. (1997) 'The Causes of Regionalism', *The World Economy* 20 (7): 865–88.

(2004) 'Key Challenges Facing the WTO', in Mike Moore (ed.), *Doha and Beyond: The Future of the Multilateral Trading System*. Cambridge: Cambridge University Press.

(2006) 'Multilateralising Regionalism: Spaghetti Bowls as Building Blocks on the Path to Global Free Trade', *The World Economy* 29 (11): 1451–1518.

Bhagwati, J. (1995) 'U.S. Trade Policy: The Infatuation with Free Trade Areas', in J. Bhagwati and A. O. Krueger (eds.), *The Dangerous Drift to Preferential Trade Agreements*. Washington DC: American Enterprise Institute for Public Policy Research.

(2001) 'Introduction: The Unilateral Freeing of Trade versus Reciprocity', in J. Bhagwati (ed.), *Going Alone: The Case for Relaxed Reciprocity in Freeing Trade*. Cambridge, MA: MIT Press, pp. 10–13.

Chabal, P. and Daloz, J. (2001) *Africa Works: Disorder as Political Instrument*. Oxford: International African Institute and James Currey.

Collier, P. (2000) 'Africa's Comparative Advantage', in Hossein Jalilian, Michael Tribe and John Weiss (eds.), *Industrial Development and Policy in Africa*. Cheltenham: Edward Elgar.

(2007) *The Bottom Billion: Why the Poorest Countries Are Failing and What Can Be Done about it*. Oxford: Oxford University Press.

Collier, P. and Venables, A. J. (2007) 'Re-thinking Trade Preferences to Help Diversify African Exports', Center for Economic Policy Research, Policy Insight no. 2.

Crawford, J.-A. and Fiorentino, R. (2005) 'Changing Landscape of Regional Trade Agreements', World Trade Organization Working Paper. Geneva: WTO.

Draper, P. (2007) 'EU-Africa Trade Relations: The Political Economy of Economic Partnership Agreements', Jan Tumlir Policy Essay2. European Centre for International Political Economy, Available at: www.ecipe.org.

Draper, P., Halleson, D. and Alves, P. (2007) 'SACU, Regional Integration, and the Overlap Issue in Southern Africa: From Spaghetti to Cannelloni?', SAIIA Trade Policy Report 15, February.

Feenstra, R. C. (1998) 'Integration of Trade and Disintegration of Production in the Global Economy', *Journal of Economic Perspective* 12 (4): 31–50.

Finger, M. J. and Nogues, J. (2002) 'Unbalanced Uruguay Outcome: The New Areas in Future WTO Negotiations', *The World Economy* 25 (3): 321–40.

Frankel, J. A. (1997) *Regional Trading Blocs in the World Economic System.* Washington DC: Institute for International Economics.

Herbst, J. (2000) *States and Power in Africa: Comparative Lessons in Authority and Control.* Princeton, NJ: Princeton University Press.

Hoekman, B. (2002) 'Developing Countries and the Political Economy of the Trading System', World Institute for Development Economic Research (WIDER) Publication, Discussion Paper no. 2002/126. United Nations University.

Krugman, P. (1993) 'Regionalism versus Multilateralism: Analytical Notes', in J. de Melo and A. Panagariya (eds.), *New Dimensions in Regional Integration.* Cambridge: Cambridge University Press.

Lawrence, R. Z. (2003) 'Regionalism, Multilateralism, and Deeper Integration: Changing Paradigms for Developing Countries', in C. Roe, C. P. Goddard and C. D. Kishore (eds.), *International Political Economy: State-Market Relations in a Changing Global Order.* Basingstoke: Palgrave Macmillan.

Mansfield, E. and Milner, H. V. (1999) 'The New Wave of Regionalism', *International Organization* 53 (3): 589–627.

Mbeki, M. (2004) 'Regionalization and the Search for Africa's Economic Renewal', *eAfrica*, vol. 2, available at: www. saiia.wits.org.za.

Ndulu, B. J. and O'Connell, S. A. (1999) 'Governance and Growth in Africa', *Journal of Economic Perspectives*, 13(3): 41–66.

Ottaway, M., Herbst, J. and Mills, G. (2004) 'Africa's Big States: Toward a New Realism', Policy Outlook, Carnegie Endowment for International Peace, February.

Oyejide, T. A. (2000) 'Regional Economic Integration in Africa', Economic Research Papers no. 2. Abidjan: African Development Bank.

Subramanian, A. (2007) 'Doha, RIP', *Business Standard*, 10 July.

UNCTAD (2007) *Regional Cooperation for Developement*, Trade and Development Report. Geneva: UNCTAD.

World Bank (2000) *Tade Blocs*, Policy Research Report. Oxford: Oxford University Press, pp. 51–61.

(2006) *Assessing World Bank Support for Trade, 1987–2004: An IEG Evaluation*, World Bank Independent Evaluation Group. Washington, DC: World Bank.

World Trade Organization (WTO) (2004) *The Future of the WTO*, report by the Consultative Board to the Director-General Supachai Panitchpakadi. Geneva: WTO.

10

Multilateralizing RTAs in the Americas: state of play and ways forward[1]

ANTONI ESTEVADEORDAL, MATTHEW
SHEARER AND KATI SUOMINEN

1 Introduction

The countries of the Americas[2] have been key drivers of the now global spree of regional trade agreements (RTAs). Collectively, the regional economies have notified three dozen intra- and extra-regional RTAs to the World Trade Organization (WTO) (Figure 10.1), and are negotiating several further agreements. Major contributors to the global spaghetti bowl of RTAs, and the source of nearly a fifth of global trade, the countries of the region can also play a major role, if not serve as the focal point, in the search for options for multilateralizing RTAs – for arriving at global free trade by way of regionalism.

Conceptually, multilateralization can be accomplished through two alternative (yet also complementary) measures: (1) deepening tariff liberalization by RTA members vis-à-vis each other, while also reducing discrimination toward non-members until it becomes inconsequential; and/or (2) incorporating non-members to an RTA until all countries are members. The latter measure in particular would, by default, eradicate one of the key potential problems of the RTA spaghetti bowl of overlapping agreements, namely differences in rules between the various RTAs. Simply put, multilateralization would 'flatten' and expand RTAs; this would also tame the RTA rule tangle.

[1] The authors wish to thank Marcelo Olarreaga for comments and Naoko Uchiyama, Santiago Florez Gomez, Maria Jose Casanovas for research assistance and Sara Marzal Yetano for an outstanding analysis of services and investment provisions. The opinions expressed here are those of the authors and do not necessarily reflect the views of the Inter-American Development Bank or its member countries.

[2] Due to methodological issues, 'Americas' and 'hemispheric' refer in this chapter to a group composed of Canada, the Dominican Republic, Mexico, Central and South America, and the United States.

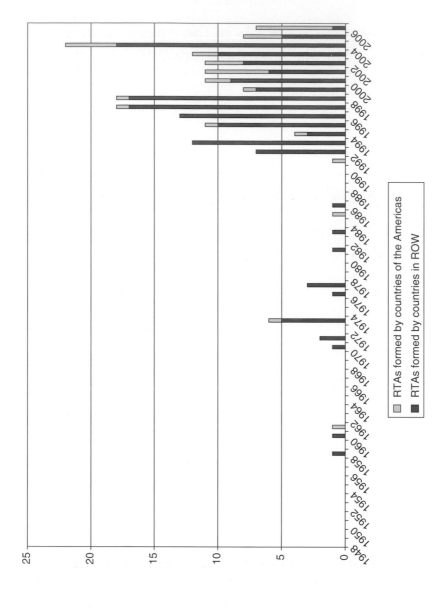

Figure 10.1 RTAs notified to the WTO in the Americas and around the world, 2007

The purpose of this chapter is to examine the extent of liberalization in RTAs in the Americas in comparison to agreements in other world regions, and to put forth policy recommendations for multilateralizing the regional RTAs. While primarily focusing on market access in goods – and tariff liberalization schedules, in particular – we also explore the regional RTAs' employment of rules of origin, investment and services provisions. While the analysis centres on the depth of liberalization accomplished by the region's RTAs, we preliminarily investigate the extent to which the regional RTAs feature 'open regionalism' – i.e. liberalization vis-à-vis third parties.

Our main finding is that the Americas comprise a notably liberalized region in terms of the maturity, geographical coverage and depth of its RTAs. Rather than the pursuit of new negotiations, the region's main challenge today is further synergies between the existing agreements, all the while forging extra-regional ties with Europe and countries of Asia, and deepening liberalization vis-à-vis third parties.

The following section takes stock of the advance of regional integration in the Americas, and details the 'liberalization state of play' in the RTAs formed by the countries of the Americas. The third section surveys the extent of open regionalism in the Americas. Section 4 examines investment and services provisions. The fifth section puts forth policy proposals for further multilateralizing RTAs formed by countries of the Americas; section 6 concludes.

2   Liberalization in RTAs in the Americas

This section focuses on the comparative depth of liberalization in RTAs formed by the countries of the Americas over the past decade and into the next twenty years. The first part describes the advance of integration in the regional economies' trade policy portfolios. The second part centres on the liberalization statistics.

RTA pathways in the Americas: from intra-regionalism to trans-continentalism

Countries in different regions of the world have had distinct RTA paths over the past two decades between four main 'stations': intra-regional blocs, intra-regional bilateral RTAs, continental mega-blocs, and trans-continental RTAs. In the Americas, the common path has been from intra-regional blocs to an attempted mega-bloc, accompanied and followed by intra-regional bilateral agreements, and subsequently trans-continental RTAs.

The first RTAs were intra-regional customs unions formed (or reformed) in the early 1990s – the Andean Community, the Caribbean Community (CARICOM), the Central American Common Market (CACM), and the Southern Common Market (MERCOSUR). The North American Free Trade Agreement (NAFTA) launched in 1994 connected Canada, Mexico and the United States. The same year, the first Summit of the Americas launched the thirty-four-country negoti-ations for the Free Trade Area of the Americas (FTAA), which was to merge the aspiring customs unions and NAFTA under a single umbrella. The FTAA process was paralleled by bilateral agreements, particularly between Mexico and Chile, on the one hand, and numerous other countries of the region, on the other. The stagnation of the FTAA talks in 2003 furthered and 'regionalized' the quest for bilateral intra-regional FTAs. Among the most recent highlights are the MERCOSUR–Andean Community FTA of 2004, the US–Central America–Dominican Republic FTA (DR–CAFTA) of 2005, and the culmination of the US–Colombia, US–Peru, US–Panama, Chile–Peru, and Chile–Colombia FTA negotiations last year.

Intra-regionalism is today yielding to trans-continentalism. Many regional countries have sought to establish an early foothold in Asia's fast-growing RTA panorama. In 2003 Chile and the Republic of Korea signed the Asian country's first comprehensive bilateral FTA, and in 2005 Chile concluded negotiations for a four-party FTA (P-4) with Brunei Darussalam, New Zealand and Singapore. An FTA between Chile and China – the East Asian economy's first extra-regional FTA – came into effect in October 2006, and in November 2006 Chile became the second country of the Americas to reach an FTA with Japan. In 2003 the United States and Singapore reached one of the first agreements of Singapore's now extensive network of RTAs, and the US–Australia agreement came into force in 2005. The Mexico–Japan Economic Partnership Agreement, Japan's first extra-regional free trade agreement, also took effect in 2005. The same year, Peru and Thailand signed a bilateral FTA, while FTAs between Taipei, China and Panama and Guatemala took effect in 2004 and 2006, respectively. Panama also concluded FTA negotiations with Singapore in 2006.

Trans-Pacific agreements are set to proliferate further: for instance, the United States has concluded negotiations with the Republic of Korea, and Chile has launched talks with Malaysia. Furthermore, five countries of the Americas – Canada, Chile, Mexico, Peru and the United States – are pursuing closer ties with Asia in the context of the Asia-Pacific Economic Cooperation (APEC) forum founded in 1989.

Countries of the Americas have also been reaching across the Atlantic for agreements with the European Union (EU). Mexico launched an FTA with the EU in 2000, as did Chile in 2003. In May 2006, the EU and CACM countries announced the launch of comprehensive Association Agreement negotiations, while the EU–CARICOM talks have entered the final phase. The EU and the Andean Community have explored the opening of Association Agreement negotiations. Furthermore, in addition to the trans-Pacific and trans-Atlantic fronts, MERCOSUR has concluded an agreement with India, and the United States is building a network of agreements with selected Middle Eastern countries.

The geographic composition of the trade flows of the countries of the Americas appears to have followed the advance of regionalism (see Tables 10.1(a) and (b)). The most notable change in the Latin American and Caribbean (LAC) export profile is the decline of the importance of trade with Europe and the rise in the importance of the intra-hemispheric market, as well as a moderate increase in the share of Asia Pacific as an export destination. To be sure, there are wide intra-regional differences; countries such as Argentina, Brazil, Chile and Peru have seen their commodity exports to China surge markedly in their export profiles.

Western hemisphere exports, which include those of the United States and Canada, have grown, particularly in the North American market. On the import side, however, Asia has penetrated the LAC market forcefully, accounting for roughly a fifth of the region's imports. This appears to have come at the expense of Europe, whose import share in LAC has been eclipsed to some 14 per cent of the region's total imports.

While trade per se has surged in importance in regional output in the past two decades, so has the relevance of RTAs in governing the regional economies' trade. For instance, the share of imports with RTA partners of total imports was 85 per cent for Chile, 74 per cent for Mexico, 45 per cent for Argentina, and more than 30 per cent for the United States in 2006 (Figure 10.2). Of the total intra-Americas trade, the share of trade among countries with a common RTA is today above 90 per cent of total intra-regional trade; the level is still three-quarters of all trade when NAFTA is not taken into account. While these figures do not capture the level of trade that comes under the RTA regime (as opposed to MFN or other regimes), they indicate that a sizeable share of the

Table 10.1(a). *Destination of western hemisphere exports, 1990–2006*

	Millions of US$					% of exports to world				
	1990	1995	2000	2005	2006	1990	1995	2000	2005	2006
Destination of LAC exports										
World	125,193	226,084	362,706	572,324	768,258	100	100	100	100	100
LAC	16,882	43,562	56,227	92,577	115,719	13	19	16	16	15
Canada–US	51,081	104,817	214,681	302,298	330,020	41	46	59	53	43
European Union	31,179	37,604	41,042	71,155	94,396	25	17	11	12	12
Asia-Pacific	11,908	19,740	18,108	46,757	68,389	10	9	5	8	9
Rest of world	14,144	20,361	32,647	59,536	159,735	11	9	9	10	21
Destination of western hemisphere exports										
World	644,746	999,817	1,410,014	1,836,066	2,194,816	100	100	100	100	100
LAC	71,266	141,579	225,704	287,502	342,788	11	14	16	16	16
Canada–US	229,429	383,737	629,942	816,269	880,679	36	38	45	44	40
European Union	146,466	175,373	221,816	278,569	333,273	23	18	16	15	15
Asia-Pacific	127,851	204,383	214,613	276,862	335,551	20	20	15	15	15
Rest of world	69,734	94,744	117,939	176,863	302,525	11	9	8	10	14

Table 10.1(b). *Origin of western hemisphere exports, 1990–2006*

	Millions of US$					% of imports from world				
	1990	1995	2000	2005	2006	1990	1995	2000	2005	2006
Origin of LAC imports										
World	108,498	244,043	397,873	539,378	627,505	100	100	100	100	100
LAC	17,683	43,971	60,933	103,185	129,576	16	18	15	19	21
Canada–US	45,609	109,683	205,136	211,726	246,157	42	45	52	39	39
European Union	22,461	43,500	55,795	75,929	87,434	21	18	14	14	14
Asia-Pacific	10,016	26,743	43,398	100,701	110,622	9	11	11	19	18
Rest of world	12,730	20,147	34,612	47,838	53,716	12	8	9	9	9
Origin of western hemisphere imports										
World	757,160	1,194,759	1,898,889	2,616,267	2,930,318	100	100	100	100	100
LAC	88,539	158,283	282,245	424,958	493,455	12	13	15	16	17
Canada–US	222,167	377,873	603,395	698,821	765,227	29	32	32	27	26
European Union	143,526	201,767	312,709	437,146	476,347	19	17	16	17	16
Asia-Pacific	200,242	330,947	435,972	727,732	818,643	26	28	26	28	28
Rest of world	102,687	125,890	214,569	327,611	376,647	14	11	11	13	13

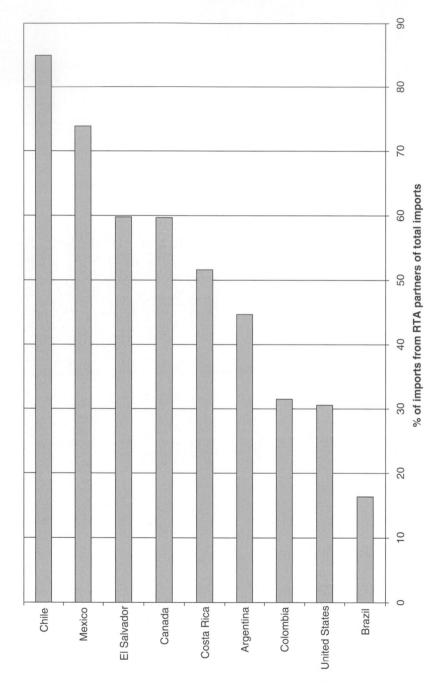

Figure 10.2 Trade with RTA partners total trade in 2006, selected countries

hemispheric economies' trade is with their RTA partners, and that countries of the region have forged ties with some of their leading trade partners.

State of integration in the Americas in a comparative perspective

This section strives to break new ground in dissecting the state of play of liberalization in RTAs in the Americas. We focus on the tariff liberalization schedules of seventy-six parties in thirty-eight RTAs (see Appendix A, Table 10.1A).[3] Much of the data here is drawn from IDB (forthcoming).[4] The first part of this section surveys the overall approach of the tariff liberalization regimes in the thirty-eight RTAs.[5] The second part analyses tariff-line data from the RTA parties' tariff liberalization schedules, and also tariff rate quotas and exceptions and exclusions. The third part explores alternative measurements – the share of liberalized tariff lines trade-weighted by Harmonized System chapters, and the share of trade that is liberalized from the RTA partner in a given year – in sub-samples of twenty-seven and twenty-three RTAs, respectively. We examine three sets of agreements – those formed in the Americas (here, 'intra-regional'), those formed between a country of the Americas and a partner in another region ('inter-regional' or 'Americas as Partner'), and agreements not involving any countries of the Americas ('extra-regional').

---

[3] The tariff liberalization schedules were obtained from the Foreign Trade Information System at www.sice.oas.org/ and some national sources, including websites. Some tariff data were obtained from TRAINS. The study also maps out the coverage in RTAs of four trade disciplines besides tariffs, including non-tariff measures, rules of origin, special regimes and customs procedures.

[4] There are a handful of other studies on tariff liberalization in RTAs. The World Trade Organization (2002) carries out an extensive inventory of the coverage and liberalization of tariff concessions in 47 RTAs of a total of 107 parties. The data cover the tariff treatment of imports into parties to selected RTAs, tariff-line treatment as obtained from individual countries' tariff schedules, and tariff dispersion for a number of countries. Scollay (2005) performs a similarly rigorous analysis of tariff concessions in a sample of eighteen RTAs. IDB (2002) presents an exhaustive survey of market access commitments of RTAs in the Americas, while the World Bank (2005) carries out a more general mapping of the various disciplines in RTAs around the world.

[5] Various prior studies characterize tariff elimination carried out on the basis of a positive or a negative list, or based on a certain formula. This study strives to abstract from these characteristics and classify liberalization programmes by their categorization of goods into distinct paths of liberalization. To be sure, some of the categories are more aligned with a positive list approach, while others lend themselves to a negative list approach.

Empirical survey: tariff liberalization regime models

Tariff liberalization could be classified along the lines of three different regimes, divided here into basket, sectoral and preferential tariff approaches. The basket approach assigns all products to a set of distinct categories in the tariff elimination programme, each providing a time frame and trajectory towards the complete elimination of tariffs. Also included are any Tariff Rate Quotas (TRQs), typically with a reference to an appendix with the quantities, as well as exceptions to preferential treatment (that are typically entered into a basket of continued MFN treatment).[6] Many of the agreements in this study, such as those signed by the US, tend to follow the basket approach. This generally subjects nearly the entire tariff universe to eventual full tariff elimination, with some of the less visible 'action' in the US agreements taking place within the framework of TRQs.[7]

The sector approach, typically reflected in the EU and European Free Trade Association (EFTA) agreements, subjects all industrial products to a general tariff elimination schedule.[8] A separate list for exceptions and separate annexes or protocols govern the treatment of such products as agriculture, fish and processed agricultural goods. The protocols tend to be quite complex and feature various regimes, such as end-point preference margins or residual preferential tariffs, TRQs, reference quantities, and a phased reduction of tariffs to a final level (which can be non-zero).[9]

---

[6] Thailand–Australia and Thailand–New Zealand FTAs defy easy categorization, as they do not use any clearly defined baskets, but rather implement staging simply by cross-tabbed reduced tariff rates. This lends itself mostly to the basket approach, due to the use of comprehensive schedules. However, there are a large number of case-by-case trajectories, which suggests a preferential tariff approach as well.

[7] It should be noted that the in-quota quantities (and even the existence of in-quota treatment) in these agreements differ greatly within CAFTA. Although the United States has given the same schedule with the same baskets to the other countries, the treatment within these baskets differs greatly between countries. So although the statistics will reflect the identical treatment of all Central American countries, this will not be the case, especially when considering that a number of the products subject to TRQs are those in which Central America will have a strong comparative advantage (such as sugar).

[8] In this chapter, the data on tariff elimination in the EFTA–Mexico FTA are based on Switzerland's tariff schedules.

[9] The recent EU–Chile FTA that came into effect in 2003 diverged from the EU's standard practice of dividing tariff elimination into separate venues by establishing a single schedule for each party that contains all products. In its category column, the schedule includes various measures that will be maintained, such as TRQs, the elimination of only the ad valorem component of a mixed duty (including cases where the non-ad valorem component is linked to an entry price), products subjected to a tariff concession of 50 per cent

Some agreements, including many of those forged under the Latin American Integration Association (LAIA) framework, involve a preferential tariff approach, focusing on the end-point preferential tariff or margin of preference. The Bangkok Agreement also focuses on the end-point preferences, with additional concessions provided to less-developed RTA members. These models take a positive list approach to the concessions, whereby the schedules contain the products to which the market access provisions of the RTA apply, rather than a negative list approach, and lend themselves more to partial scope agreements.

This chapter generally focuses on relatively comprehensive agreements, and is thus mainly geared towards those in the first two categories. In the next section, a more nuanced approach to tariff liberalization is used that focuses on the trajectories of individual tariff concession schedules.

Tariff liberalization statistics

This part turns to analysing tariff-line data developed on the basis of the tariff liberalization schedules of seventy-six parties in thirty-eight RTAs. An introductory set of general indicators strives to capture the share of each individual RTA party's tariff lines that are accorded some tariff reductions, and the share of lines that are duty-free by certain benchmark years (generally year 1, year 5, year 10, and year 15 or 20) after the launching of the RTA.[10] Year 1 refers here to the year of entry into force.

---

of the basic customs duty, and cases where no liberalization takes place, for instance due to 'protected denominations'.

[10] Dummies are assigned according to when a product becomes duty-free (whether in year 1, 5, 10 or 15). The dummies are subsequently multiplied by the number of lines with that treatment, and then divided by the total number of lines to obtain the percentage incidence. The total number of lines includes all tariff lines, regardless of whether that line was duty-free prior to the entry into force of the agreement. 'Split products' or products partially covered by an agreement, are, as a general rule, accorded tariff reduction on the first date at which any of the various baskets accord a reduction. Owing to the aggregation method employed here, these products are here considered to have undergone tariff elimination only after the entire product (rather than the 'split' tariff line) has been fully liberalized. In other words, a tariff line on which tariffs are eliminated in a given year is treated as not having been fully liberalized until the entire product that the line forms part of is liberalized. In the case of split products, duty-free treatment must cover a product in its entirety before any one part of the split product is considered to be liberalized. The analysis includes lines subject to TRQs, based on when out-of-quota tariff rates are reduced or phased out. For example, where tariff eliminations are made on in-quota tariff rates, the product in question is treated as not receiving full tariff elimination. Products subject to entry prices are, when relevant, counted as receiving tariff reduction, but not as having tariffs eliminated.

Figure 10.3 provides an overview of the share of tariff lines liberalized by the partners in the thirty-eight RTAs by mapping out the shares of national tariff lines that become duty-free in year 1, years 2–5, years 6–10, years 11–20, and more than 20 years into the RTA. The three-letter International Standards Organization code of each country giving the concession (i.e. the importing country) precedes the arrow, while the code of the partner country follows the arrow.

Agreements formed in the Americas, and particularly those signed by the NAFTA members, generally liberalize trade relatively fast, with some 75 per cent or more lines freed in the first year of the agreement. On the other hand, some of MERCOSUR's agreements have somewhat more backloaded liberalization, with a large share of lines being liberalized between years 6 and 10 into the agreements. Asia-Pacific RTAs stand out for being particularly frontloaded: they liberalize the bulk of the tariff universe in the first year of the RTA; this is in good part due to Singapore's according duty-free treatment to all products upon the entry into force of its agreements.

Figures 10.4(a) and (b) assess the extent of tariff elimination reciprocity between parties to an RTA by years 5 and 10. They are sorted in descending order from the least reciprocal to the most reciprocal. Two patterns emerge. First, while the parties' respective product coverage often diverges markedly in year 5, with some partners (such as the Republic of Korea) liberalizing up to twice as many lines as their partners (such as Chile) are freeing, the differences shrink considerably by year 10. Second, agreements formed in the Americas tend to be more reciprocal than agreements formed with extra-regional partners. This is owing to the North–South differences in liberalization – a pattern that is evident throughout the sample. Nonetheless, while the countries of the Americas have wide variations in their liberalization trajectories, most liberalize more than 90 per cent of lines by the tenth year into the agreement.

Safeguards are not taken into account here (i.e. as interfering with tariff elimination). Other sidenotes are dealt on an ad hoc basis. Any TRQ, regardless of whether reductions occur on the in-quota or out-of-quota tariff rate, are counted in the TRQ incidence measure. Note that for the CAFTA agreement, indicators for the Dominican Republic and each of the five Central American countries were calculated individually and then averaged together to create a single, indicative partner to the United States. Similarly, for NAFTA, Canadian and US concessions to Mexico are averaged together to make a single US–Canada partner to Mexico, and Mexico's concessions to the two countries are averaged together to make a single representative concession to the US–Canada. Where possible, similar averaging is performed for other agreements with more than two signatories.

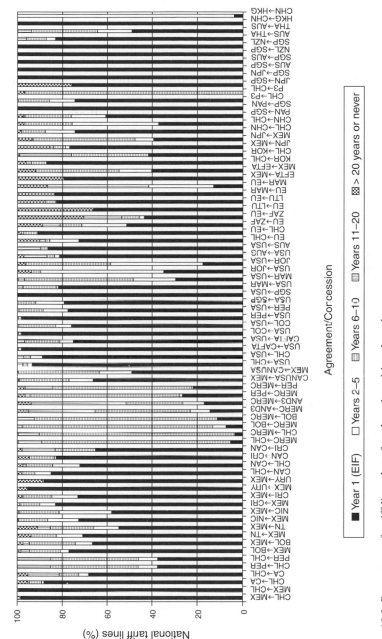

Figure 10.3 Percentage of tariff lines duty-free, by selected benchmark years

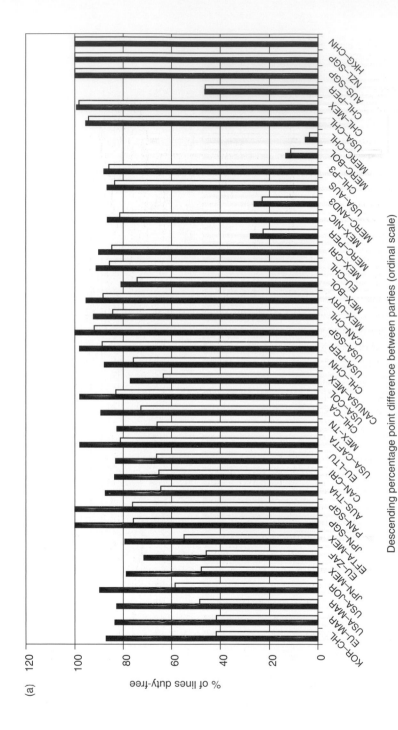

Figure 10.4(a) Reciprocity of concessions, year 5

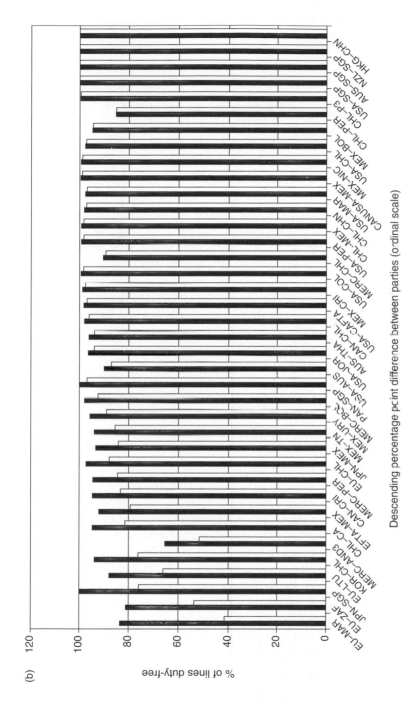

Figure 10.4(b) Reciprocity of concessions, year 10

Figure 10.5 disaggregates the liberalization schedules between three sets of RTAs: those signed in the Americas, those between countries of the Americas and extra-regional partners, and extra-regional agreements. The 90 per cent threshold, which is often used as a benchmark for 'substantially all trade', is marked with a horizontal line.

The figure echoes the prior findings in two ways. First, it shows that while some countries, such as the original NAFTA partners, employ a 'stair-step' approach to tariff liberalization (stemming from the use of various gradual baskets), others have a constant percentage coverage of tariff lines in what could be characterized as a 'now-or-never' approach. Examples of this include Singapore, which liberalizes basically 100 per cent of tariff lines in year 1 of the agreement, as well as the EU in some agreements, albeit at a level below 100 per cent. Still others – often developing countries in Asia and Latin America – start from a low coverage, proceeding through one or two jumps to a near-100 per cent coverage.

Second, the averages of the three samples (in bold) reveal differences. Intra-regional agreements start from a relatively low level of liberalization, but accelerate in the fourth year, surpassing the liberalization in extra-regional agreements by year 9. The inter-regional agreements also start off more boldly, but are met by the intra-regional agreements in year 10.

On average, a substantial part of liberalization in the intra-hemispheric agreements takes place in the interim period following entry into force (especially in years 5–10) as opposed to up-front. This is due not only to a greater use of the stair-step approach, but also to the heterogeneity of the sample. Agreements between Central America, Mexico and the United States tend to be characterized by a large number of small steps, as are US agreements with Peru and Colombia. However, Mexico's agreements with Chile and Uruguay frontload concessions. The Chile–Central America FTA and Canada's agreements with Chile and Costa Rica fall somewhere between the two poles.

The Southern Cone's approach is different still. ACE 58 and ACE 59, the agreements between MERCOSUR and the Andean Community, start at a very low share of duty-free lines, and then increase substantially, with a small number of large jumps after year 5. This is most pronounced in MERCOSUR's earlier agreements with Bolivia and Chile, where duty-free coverage is minimal to around year 8, and then quickly jumps to around 90 per cent or more, followed by an eventual progression towards nearly 100 per cent coverage over time.

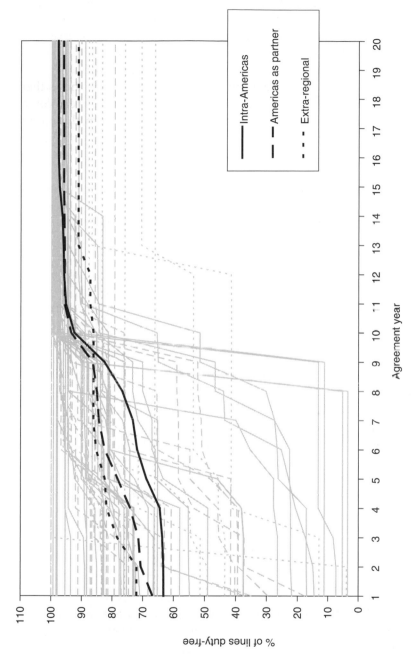

Figure 10.5 Evolution of duty-free treatment in selected RTAs

Most of the inter-regional agreements follow the stair-step model. In agreements involving a Northern and a Southern party, the latter generally starts at a lower initial point and takes larger steps than the Northern counterpart. This is particularly clear in the Republic of Korea–Chile FTA (with the Republic of Korea classified as North), and US agreements with Jordan and Morocco. However, there are exceptions. Concessions are much more even in the EU–Chile agreement; in the EFTA–Mexico FTA, Mexico's schedule starts at around 40 per cent of lines duty-free and surpasses the 90 per cent threshold well before year 10 by means of a few jumps, at the same time overtaking Switzerland's constant coverage of slightly less than 80 per cent of lines.

Extra-regional agreements exhibit a greater variation in tariff lowering. This can be explained in part by two counter-balancing forces. For one, the sample includes a number of agreements involving Singapore, where Singapore gives duty-free access to 100 per cent of lines from the entry into force of the agreement.[11] However, the countervailing force consists of agreements with low initial coverage and large jumps; once again these tend to be caused by the Southern parties in North–South agreements. China's concession to Hong Kong, China is one such case, with duty-free coverage starting at around 4 per cent and then jumping to 100 per cent in year 3. Accentuating the flatness of the extra-regional average are Japan's schedule for Singapore, and the EU's concessions to Morocco and Lithuania. Since the 'flat' schedules in these agreements entail coverage well below 100 per cent, they serve to moderate the behaviour of the overall extra-regional average as well.

Table 10.2 presents the same information in a 'real-time state of play' matrix. Grey boxes indicate FTAs; the numbers therein denote the share of liberalized tariff lines between the countries in 2007.[12] Boxes in grey without numbers are FTAs for which liberalization statistics are currently lacking in the study. The black boxes indicate common customs unions; liberalization in these agreements can be seen as nearly full and complete. Within the Americas, 57 per cent of the total possible 380 pairs of

---

[11] In the case of Australia and New Zealand's agreements with Singapore, both parties provide immediate duty-free access to 100 per cent of tariff lines.

[12] Importantly, the matrix is not intended to present the state of play of FTAs worldwide. The primary focus of this study is the western hemisphere; thus the matrix contains the countries of the Americas and those countries with which the Americas have signed an agreement, plus a few countries that are party to a small number of select agreements outside the hemisphere. Thus the matrix is not representative of the scope of involvement of extra-regional countries in FTAs in the sense that it is not fully 'Copernican'.

Table 10.2 *Trade agreements involving selected countries: state of play, 2007*

Country giving preference	Country receiving preference										
	ARG	BOL	BRA	CAN	CHL	COL	CRI	DOM	ECU	GTM	HND
Argentina	X	97.9			98.0	12.2			15.9		
Bolivia	92.4	X	92.4								
Brazil		97.9	X		98.0	33.9			28.3		
Canada				X	97.9		83.6				
Chile	97.7		97.7	97.3	X	96.8	94.9		96.7		
Colombia	10.9		25.6		95.7	X					
Costa Rica				65.2	82.5		X	98.0			
Dominican Republic							98.3	X		98.3	98.3
Ecuador	21.6		22.0		91.6				X		
Guatemala								98.0		X	
Honduras								98.0			X
Mexico		97.7		99.3	99.3	95.8	98.8			93.9	83.3
Nicaragua								97.5			
Panama											
Peru	10.4		9.8		85.1						
Paraguay		97.9			96.3	14.8			15.0		
El Salvador					79.1			98.0			
Uruguay		97.9			98.0	12.1			11.4		
United States				98.0	95.5	98.0*	97.9	97.9		97.9	97.9
Venezuela	8.7	n.a.	10.9			n.a.			n.a.		
Australia											
Brunei					68.9						
China					62.9						
EFTA (Switzerland)					n.a.						
EU					85.7						
Hong Kong, China											
Japan											
Jordan											
Korea, Rep. of					87.1						
Lithuania											
Morocco											
New Zealand					82.4						
Singapore					n.a.						
South Africa											
Thailand											

Table 10.2 (*cont.*)

Country giving preference	Country receiving preference										
	MEX	NIC	PAN	PER	PRY	SLV	URY	USA	VEN	AUS	BRN
Argentina				4.7					12.3		
Bolivia	96.7				92.4		92.4		n.a.		
Brazil				20.2					27.4		
Canada	99.0							98.8			
Chile	98.3			85.2	96.1	94.1	97.7	94.3			74.6
Colombia	90.7				21.0		25.0	76.0	n.a.		
Costa Rica	97.6							71.7			
Dominican Republic		98.3					98.3	76.5			
Ecuador					19.4		21.2		n.a.		
Guatemala	76.0							79.7			
Honduras	63.0							74.4			
Mexico	X	99.4				93.6	95.4	99.8			
Nicaragua	98.8	X						71.5			
Panama			X					n.a.*			
Peru				X	9.1		59.4	77.6	n.a.		
Paraguay				15.5	X				14.9		
El Salvador	76.1					X		77.8			
Uruguay	88.4			65.3			X		10.7		
United States	98.8	97.9	n.a.*	98.0*		97.9		X		81.3	
Venezuela				n.a.	10.0		9.0		X		
Australia								86.7		X	
Brunei											X
China											
EFTA (Switzerland)	79.3										
EU	n.a.										
Hong Kong, China											
Japan	77.1										
Jordan								58.5			
Korea, Rep. of											n.a.
Lithuania											
Morocco								39.2			
New Zealand										n.a.	82.4
Singapore			100					100		100	100
South Africa											
Thailand										54.4	n.a.

Note: includes only customs unions (black cells) and free trade agreements (grey cells), not unilateral preferences. Numbers in cells show percentage of total national tariff lines duty-free in 2007.

Table 10.2 (*cont.*)

Country receiving preference												
CHN	EFTA	EU	HKG	JPN	JOR	KOR	LTU	MAR	NZL	SGP	ZAF	THA
74.6	n.a.	91.2				41.6			74.6	74.6		
	91.3	n.a.		39.4								
										60.7		
					89.8			81.8		92.0		
									n.a.	100		83.2
						n.a.			68.9	68.9		n.a.
X		100				n.a.						
	X	n.a.			n.a.	n.a.	n.a.	n.a.		n.a.		
	n.a.	X			n.a.		66.2	83.4			81.1	
100			X									
				X						75.9		
	n.a.	n.a.			X			n.a.		n.a.		
n.a.	n.a.					X				n.a.		
	n.a.	87.8					X					
	n.a.	41.6			n.a.			X				
									X	100		n.a.
	n.a.			100	n.a.	n.a.			100	X		n.a.
		53.7									X	
									n.a.	n.a.		X

n.a. = not available at this time.

* Signed but not yet entered into force as of 31 July 2007. Assuming entry into force in 2007.

countries have no comprehensive RTA,[13] a third of all pairs feature a comprehensive FTA, while 12 per cent of pairs share a customs union.

The main finding is the extent of deep liberalization throughout the FTAs in the Americas: most members have liberalized more than four-fifths of the tariff items to their intra-regional partners. To be sure, liberalization in the 2004 MERCOSUR–Andean agreement, which is an amalgam of bilateral agreements among the groups' members, is only incipient. Meanwhile, Chile, Mexico and the United States are the main drivers of the inter-regional agreements formed by the countries of the Americas. The liberalization in these agreements is generally somewhat lower than in the intra-regional RTAs.[14]

Figure 10.6 goes beyond the 2007 snapshot to explore the entire period of 1994–2026. The bold line maps out the simple average for the intra-regional sample from 2007 onward (i.e. the period during which all agreements considered here are expected to have come into effect). The main finding is the extent of deep liberalization throughout the Americas: as of today, most RTA members have liberalized more than four-fifths of the tariff items to their partners; some of the newer FTAs will attain this level by 2010. Liberalization in the recent MERCOSUR–Andean agreements is more limited, reaching about a fifth or a quarter of tariff lines by 2010.

Overall, the figure conveys the maturity of liberalization in intra-regional agreements in the Americas: even with the slower pace of the MERCOSUR–Andean agreements, the regional agreements will have freed more than 95 per cent of lines by 2015. Moreover, the ongoing proliferation of FTAs in Asia could affect the extra-regional average if the newer agreements were included. In contrast, the Americas is a rather saturated region in terms of intra-regional agreements, which means that the figure provides a particularly accurate reflection of the progression of future liberalization in the case of intra-regional agreements.

Laggards and leaders in liberalization

The aggregate tariff reduction statistics disguise what could be expected to be an important variation in the speed of liberalization across

---

[13] i.e. an RTA that liberalizes more than 4,000 tariff lines.

[14] The apparent clustering in the south-east corner of the matrix is of interest as well. This clustering is particularly pronounced for a subset of the Asia-Pacific countries in the sample, both in terms of the prevalence of agreements (proximity of grey cells), as well as the depth of the agreements (statistics within cells).

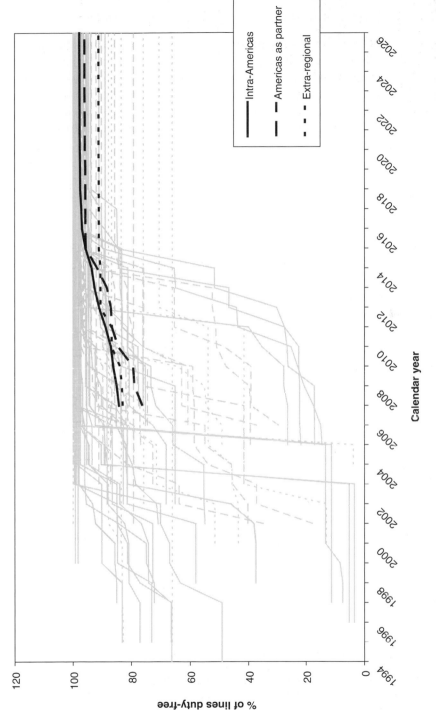

Figure 10.6 Evolution of duty-free treatment in RTAs signed between countries in the Americas: calendar years by region

product categories.[15] Which products are the laggards and which the leaders in liberalization?

Figures 10.7(a) and (b) take the first stab at revealing cross-sectoral patterns by displaying the degree of liberalization in the ninety-seven Harmonized System chapters within the liberalization schedules of sixty-four RTA parties. Parties in the south-east corner feature deep liberalization across the board. Meanwhile, those in the north-west corner are marked by limited liberalization and a high dispersion of liberalization across chapters. Black diamonds indicate RTAs formed by countries of the Americas, while triangles represent agreements where a country of the Americas is a partner, and white squares are extra-regional agreements. The bulk of countries approach across-the-board liberalization by year 10.

Overall, intra-regional agreements feature not only the deepest liberalization, but also the least dispersion across chapters in tariffs, particularly by year 10 – which means that even sectors that have yet to be freed of duties have rather low tariffs.[16] Even for those schedules that exhibit a substantial share of lines that are not fully liberalized, the standard deviation tends to be below those agreements involving extra-regional parties with similar shares. However, outlier sectors persist in many extra-regional agreements. The most marked dispersion occurs in Morocco's and South Africa's schedules in their FTAs with the EU, a pattern that reflects sensitivities in the agricultural and textile sectors.[17]

---

[15] Viewing the percentages of lines that are duty-free by a certain benchmark year (e.g. year 10) disaggregated by two-digit HS chapters may be ideal, given that the level of disaggregation is detailed enough to provide distinct product categories. Furthermore, two-digit chapters tend to be more stable across time, i.e. between various versions of the HS. A four-digit approach may be useful as well, but can be excessively complex and disguise the more general trends. The best method could be to identify some two-digit chapters that have the least comprehensive tariff elimination, and then use these as the rationale for conducting four- or six-digit analysis within these chapters.

[16] Of course, an average liberalization level of 1 (100 per cent coverage) will necessarily be accompanied by a standard deviation of zero, but there are cases where one chapter may exhibit a higher standard deviation (dispersion among agreements) than another for a given level of liberalization, or vice versa.

[17] Note, however, the outlier behaviour exhibited by MERCOSUR–Bolivia and MERCOSUR–Chile at the five-year benchmark, with a uniformly low duty-free statistic. However, these four dots have moved to the south-east corner by year 10. This raises an important point regarding the sample set. Mapping out the myriad relationships entailed within the MERCOSUR–Andean agreements was not feasible at this stage. However, from the aggregate numbers we can deduce that the average chapter coverage would be low, mitigating to some degree the findings that the intra-regional agreements were more liberalized.

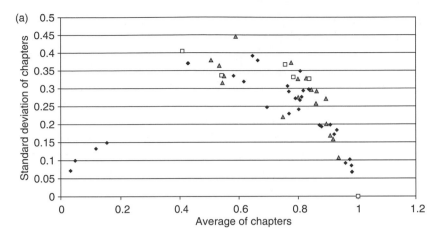

Figure 10.7(a) Distribution of liberalization of chapters in RTA parties' schedules, year 5

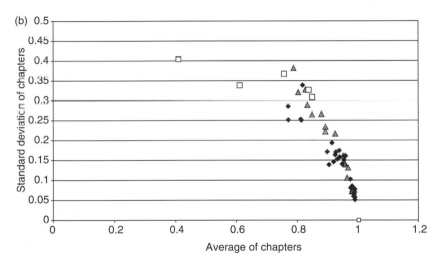

Figure 10.7(b) Distribution of liberalization of chapters in RTA parties' schedules, year 10

Agriculture is one of the main laggards in liberalization. Figure 10.8 maps out the evolution of duty-free treatment for agricultural and industrial products (as grouped by the WTO) by three main regional samples. As expected, in each region agricultural products are protected longer and more strongly than industrial products are. On average, for

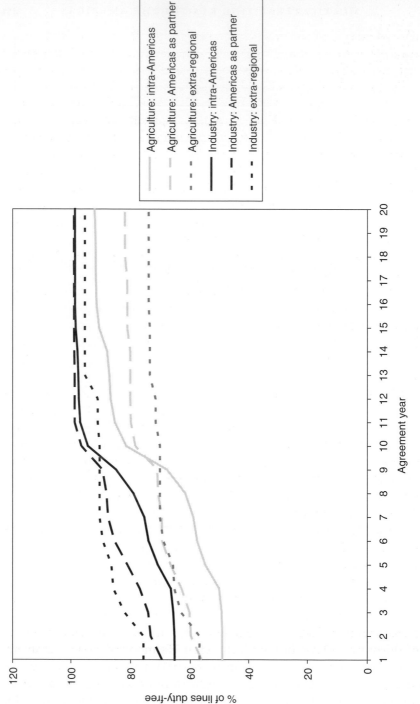

Figure 10.8 Evolution of sectoral duty-free treatment in selected RTAs.

Legend:
- Agriculture: intra-Americas
- Agriculture: Americas as partner
- Agriculture: extra-regional
- Industry: intra-Americas
- Industry: Americas as partner
- Industry: extra-regional

% of lines duty-free

Agreement year

the full sample of all agreements together, the RTAs explored here liberalize only 61 per cent of tariff lines in agriculture by year 5 and 78 per cent by year 10, while reaching duty-free treatment for 77 and 94 per cent of industrial goods by the same points in time.

However, notably, intra-regional FTAs in the Americas take off in agricultural liberalization in year 10, surpassing the other regional groups. This is largely due to very large jumps (in the order of 60 percentage points or more) in agricultural duty-free coverage in the MERCOSUR–Bolivia and MERCOSUR–Chile agreements, as well as smaller increases in coverage in the Mexico–Nicaragua and Mexico–Costa Rica FTAs and the representative average Central American countries' schedule in CAFTA vis-à-vis the United States. Peru's agricultural concession to MERCOSUR also increases substantially in year 10.

The inter-regional average also sees a meaningful, though smaller, jump in year 10. This is due primarily to increases in coverage in that year by Jordan and Morocco in their agreements with the United States, China's concession to Chile, and Panama's to Singapore. Extra-regionally, the jump is less substantial and comes earlier, driven mainly by increases in coverage in the China Hong Kong, China schedule in year 3, and Morocco–EU, South Africa–EU, and EU–South Africa schedules in year 4.

In industrial goods, both intra-regional agreements and FTAs with a country of the Americas as a partner feature progressively deeper liberalization, with the take-off again occurring in year 10. In fact, the trajectories of agricultural versus industrial goods for the three subsets of agreements almost appear as parallel lines, with industry simply starting at a higher intercept on the vertical axis. In the intra-regional sphere, the jump in year 10 is in part due to Mexico's industrial coverage rising from 72 to 100 per cent that year. In 'America as partner', there is a very large jump in Mexico's coverage of Japan's industrial products that year. The patterns driving the extra-regional average still hold, with the exception that South Africa's industrial concession to the EU does not change to the same extent in the early years as in agriculture.

Figures 10.9(a) and (b) provide further nuance by measuring the average liberalization (x-axis) and dispersion of liberalization (y-axis) across the liberalization schedules of sixty-four RTA partners (in a total of thirty-two RTAs) in the ninety-seven Harmonized System chapters. The black diamonds indicate chapters generally consisting of agricultural products, while white squares refer to chapters consisting of mostly

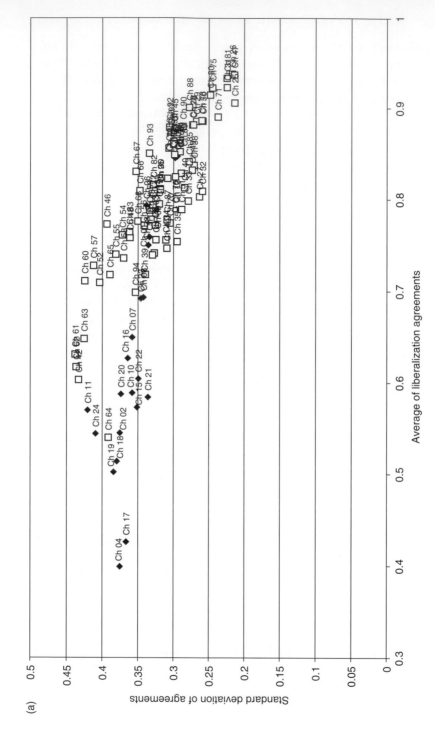

Figure 10.9(a) Distribution of liberalization by RTA parties in chapters, year 5

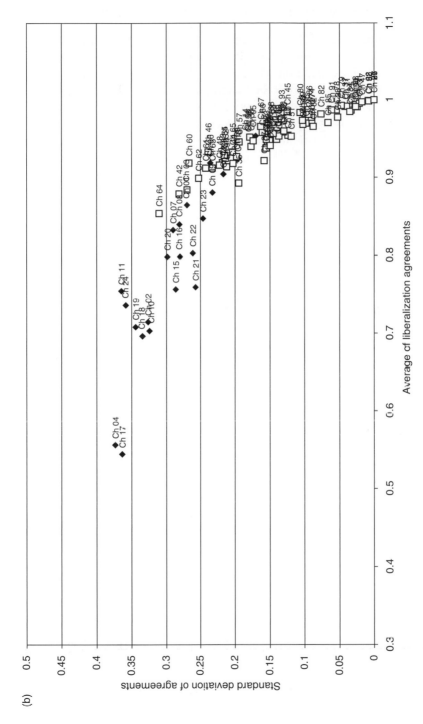

Figure 10.9(b) Distribution of liberalization by RTA parties in chapters, year 10.

industrial products.[18] The chapters in the south-east corner are those in which all RTAs analysed here feature deep liberalization, with negligible dispersion values resulting. Chapters in the north-west corner indicate limited liberalization across RTAs and particularly shallow liberalization in some RTAs, with high dispersion resulting.

The pattern is clear: agricultural chapters in RTAs feature the least liberalization and also the highest dispersion of liberalization across RTAs, indicating that these chapters are particularly protected in some RTA parties' schedules. The figures also show the relatively slow pace of liberalization: on average, RTA parties liberalize well below 50 per cent of tariff lines in the most sensitive chapters – dairy products (Chapter 04) and sugars (Chapter 17) – by the fifth year of the agreement, and less than 55 per cent in several others, including meat, cocoa, prepared cereals and baked goods, tobacco, and footwear (Chapters 02, 17, 18, 24, and 64, respectively), while sugar and dairy products still remain below 60 per cent at year 10.

When the figures are analysed at the intra-regional level (not shown here), a very distinct picture emerges. For one, it is intra-regional agreements that are driving much of the overall protectionism in dairy products, sugar and footwear.[19] Moreover, there is great variation in the treatment of chapters at the intra-regional level – even in the case of chapters that are relatively liberalized. Meanwhile, the extra-regional sample even at the five-year benchmark resembles the overall findings at year 10: there is a crescent of points stretching from the highly liberalized south-east to the more protected north-west. The inter-regional sample falls somewhere in between. Agreements involving Singapore tend to increase the averages of all chapters in the extra-regional sample, and to a lesser extent in the inter-regional sample.

Encouragingly, however, RTA parties on average liberalize more than 75 per cent of tariff lines in the bulk of chapters by year 5 and more than 90 per cent of tariff lines in most chapters by year 10. The fastest and deepest liberalization is effected in such non-sensitive products as ores (Chapter 26), fertilisers (Chapter 31), wood pulp (Chapter 47), and some base metals (Chapter 81); perhaps one of the reasons is that these

---

[18] For ease of presentation, in these figures Chapters 1–24 (excluding Chapter 3) are highlighted as agriculture. However, in the analyses of tariff liberalization statistics, agricultural and industrial products are defined at the six-digit HS level.

[19] Notably, dairy products have the lowest standard deviation of all of the chapters, showing that the low duty-free share of products in this chapter is relatively common across agreements in the Americas.

are intermediate inputs into other products. There is, however, a notable variation across countries of the Americas in these goods as well as in leather (Chapter 42). However, overall, the intra-regional set now resembles the ten-year figure for the full sample.

Notably, there is significant movement in the textile chapters between the five and ten-year benchmarks; by the same measure, dairy products and sugar show little additional liberalization. The persistent variation in agriculture is owing largely to the EU's agreements, where liberalization tends to be postponed – at times in perpetuity, as is the case, for example, of certain live animals, fish, meat, dairy products, grains, and sugar products originating in South Africa in the EU–South Africa RTA.

Trade-weighted tariff liberalization

Simply measuring the share of liberalized tariff lines fails to capture the full effects stemming from the exclusion of sensitive products from RTAs if those products are covered in a very small number of tariff lines. Does the picture of integration in the Americas change with alternative measurements?

We strive to shed light on this question by combining the data on liberalization as a share of tariff lines with data on trade flows. In particular, we introduce two alternative methods of exploring the depth and speed of liberalization in RTAs: liberalization statistics examined above as weighted by trade at the HS chapter level, and the actual percentage of total trade (imports) from the RTA partner that is liberalized.[20]

Figure 10.10 examines the evolution of duty-free treatment as a trade-weighted share of tariff lines. There are general similarities with the unweighted data in Figure 10.5; however, it is notable that the initial point at year 1 is higher in the trade-weighted dataset than in the unweighted tariff lines. This is hardly surprising: most trade occurs in sectors that are opened up rapidly, while sectors with backloaded liberalization tend to have very little trade (precisely because they are protected). To be sure, while the averages in bold in the two figures are also similar, they are not immediately comparable due to different numbers of observations – thirty-eight versus twenty-seven RTAs.

In the intra-regional sample, one of the most striking results is the high degree of liberalization in the early years (as opposed to the finding

---

[20] The calculations are based on data from United Nations Comtrade database, United Nations Department of Economic and Social Affairs/UN Statistics Division.

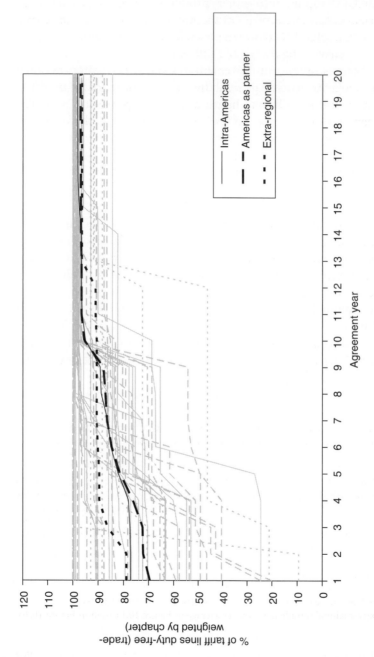

Figure 10.10 Evolution of duty-free treatment as trade-weighted percentage of tariff lines

in Figure 10.5). However, this is mainly due to methodological reasons: the more backloaded agreements involving MERCOSUR were excluded from the sample, which flattens the average.[21]

Figure 10.11 measures the evolution of duty-free treatment as a share of imports from the partner that are liberalized. By this measure, RTA partners in all regions on average reach the 90 per cent mark at year 10.[22] Moreover, and importantly, the figure does not capture the potential trade between the RTA partners. This is due in part to the endogeneity of trade flows: even if the share of actual trade excluded from an RTA were very small, the potential trade could be very significant in the absence of policy barriers.[23]

TRQs and exceptions

While RTAs around the world are encompassing and liberalizing, it is also the case that they carry provisions that could potentially be classified as 'other restrictive regulations of commerce' under Article XXIV, such as TRQs, exceptions, and demanding rules of origin (ROOs). Such provisions can qualify the market access provided for in the tariff-lowering schedules, and, as such, affect the degree of liberalization conferred by RTAs.

TRQs in RTAs are usually additional to TRQ entitlements under the WTO Agreement on Agriculture, so that the RTA parties' existing

---

[21] For the extra-regional case, the average is higher here than in the non-weighted case. There are two reasons for this. The most obvious is that EU–Lithuania and Thailand–Australia RTAs were excluded from the sample, and thus the agreements involving Singapore, where one or both countries provided immediate duty-free access, became more highly weighted. Second, all of the remaining schedules left in the trade-weighted sample exhibited higher duty-free statistics (or the same when they reached 100 per cent coverage) than in the unweighted sample where only tariff lines were analysed. This was especially true of the EU–South Africa agreement, where both schedules returned a positive difference of around 20 percentage points in the first three years, while South Africa's schedule maintained this difference throughout the twenty-year period under study.

[22] Ideally, imports were averaged over a three-year period immediately prior to the entry into force of the agreement. However, due to data availability constraints, as well as to ensure consistency between versions of the Harmonized System, the number of years taken, as well as the years themselves, varied somewhat from party to party.

[23] That the extra-regional sample has a higher average in Figure 10.11 than in Figure 10.10 is partially due to the sample set: here the EU–Morocco agreement was additionally excluded from this sample, increasing the average somewhat. The change in measurement method also had a strong positive effect on coverage in the two early years of the China–Hong Kong, China concession, flattening the initial part of the curve.

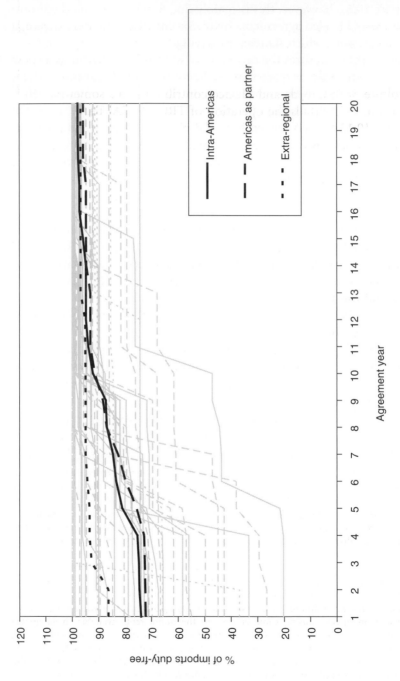

Figure 10.11 Evolution of duty-free treatment as percentage of imports

entitlements are not affected.[24] Figure 10.12 maps out the use of TRQs in the three sets of data. Countries of the Americas, like extra-regional agreements, are frequent TRQ users, particularly in agriculture, and also employ TRQs in textiles (where extra-regional agreements do not apply them). In the Americas, US agreements drive the TRQ incidence in agriculture, with Canada and Mexico contributing to a somewhat lesser extent. Box 10.1 details the operation of TRQs in CAFTA.

Figure 10.13 turns to exceptions, defining the share of product categories in which at least one of the parties to an RTA has placed an exception (i.e. never brings the tariff on the product to zero) or an exclusion (i.e. has exempted a product from the RTA concessions altogether). Exceptions in most RTAs fall on the most protected sectors – agricultural products, food preparation, chemicals, and textiles and apparel. In the Americas, Mexico's agreements are the main drivers of exceptions in agriculture. Mexico–Northern Triangle, Chile–Central America and Canada–Costa Rica FTAs contribute to the count in a broad number of sections. On the extra-regional front, the EU agreements and the Japan–Singapore FTA drive the figures.

In sum, the analysis of liberalization in RTAs yields three main results. RTAs formed by the countries of the Americas are unique in three ways in comparison to other regions: they are mature; most of them are encompassing, liberalizing all or nearly all products of the tariff universe; and RTAs signed by the original NAFTA members in particular free most products rapidly (usually some 70 per cent in the first year), while the South American FTAs are somewhat more backloaded. In contrast, agreements in Asia are rather young, less encompassing, and, like European agreements, more backloaded. Singapore is a clear exception; it liberalizes basically all goods in the first year.

---

[24] GATT Article I establishes disciplines on general most favoured nation treatment and for preferential margins in arrangements that are mentioned in the article. The Appellate Body in the dispute *Turkey – Restrictions on Imports of Textile and Clothing Products* found that a dispensation could be available in cases where it could be shown that the proposed measure was essential to the formation of the PTA, but did not set the criteria by which this condition could be fulfilled in practice. Nevertheless, in quota-controlled markets, where the Agreement on Agriculture allocates quotas to several supplying countries, the expansion of the quota of one supplying RTA partner will put downward pressure on prices, causing some erosion in the quota rents available to all quota-holders, while only the RTA partner is compensated by increased market access. Given the possible negative impact on other quota-holders, it is not clear that TRQs in RTAs are consistent with the WTO rules on quotas. It is also unclear whether Article XXIV provides a dispensation from those rules – or from GATT Article I.

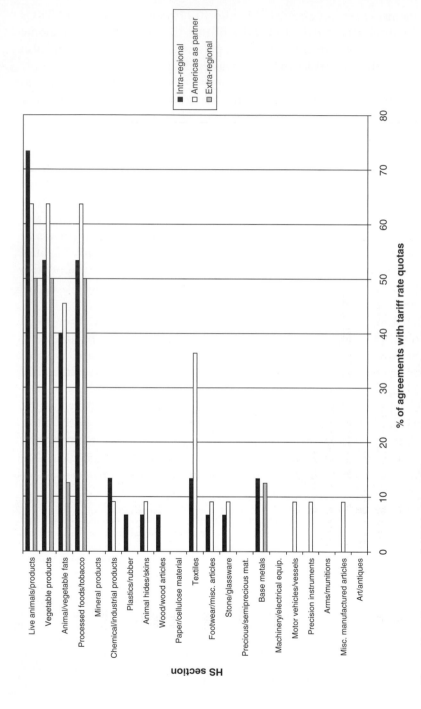

Figure 10.12 Percentage of RTAs with tariff rate quotas, by region and HS section

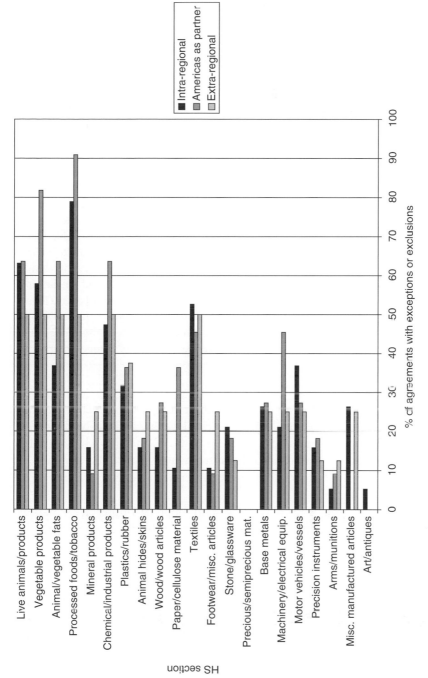

Figure 10.13 Percentage of RTAs with exceptions or exclusions, by region and HS section

---

BOX 10.1 TARIFF RATE QUOTAS IN CAFTA

The United States presented a single schedule of tariff concessions to the Central American countries and the Dominican Republic in CAFTA. However, there are some differences in the actual concessions to each Latin American party. The differences in treatment arise from the granting of immediate elimination of duties for finite quantities of some goods by means of a tariff rate quota. While some of the parties receive duty-free access under a quota, others do not, and while the products subject to quotas are similar across the parties, the quantities vary widely among them (Table 10.3).[25] The differences can have substantial implications, as the products in question are among the most sensitive, and as the tariff reduction takes a long time and may be subject to periods of grace before actual reductions begin.

Each of the Central American parties and the Dominican Republic have their individual schedules on products entering from the United States. The concessions are similar for the various product categories between these countries. Table 10.4 displays the TRQs by the Central American countries and the Dominican Republic on the United States.[26] Indeed, while there are some differences in the tariff elimination treatment within Central America for individual products and for the in-quota quantities, the products on which the Central American parties open TRQs tend to be very similar. The Dominican Republic has a slightly different list of products from those of the Central American parties; however, the differences can in part be explained by the aggregation of the TRQ in terms of product coverage.

There are similarities between the Americas and the extra-regional sample. Most extra-regional agreements, like those formed by countries of the Americas, liberalize 90 per cent of tariff lines (as well as trade-weighted lines) by year 10 into the agreement. As such, the coverage of products in all RTAs tends to become rather homogeneous by the end of the first decade.

All three regional samples carry a number of outlier RTA parties (often Southern parties) and product categories (particularly in sensitive

---

[25] Tables 10.3 and 10.4 are summary versions of those used in the Comparative Guide to the Chile–United States Free Trade Agreement and the Dominican Republic–Central America–United States Free Trade Agreement, a joint project of the Tripartite Committee (Inter-American Development Bank (IDB), Organization of American States (OAS) and Economic Commission for Latin America and the Caribbean (ECLAC)). The categories in the US–Chile table are in order of appearance in the US General Notes, while those for the Central America/Dominican Republic table are an alphabetized common set.

[26] TRQs between the Dominican Republic and Costa Rica and Nicaragua are also part of the agreement, but are not shown in these tables.

Table 10.3. *Products subject to tariff rate quotas in CAFTA: US tariff quotas on products entering from Central American and the Dominican Republic*

| Product category | Out-of-quota tariff elimination treatment[1] | Initial quantity[2] | | | | | | Unit |
		CRI	DOM	SLV	GTM	HND	NIC	
Beef	15-year	10,536	1,320	105	*	525	10,500	Metric tons
Sugar[3]	Continued MFN	11,000	10,000	24,000	32,000	8,000	22,000	Metric tons
Sugar (organic)[3],[4]	Continued MFN	2,000[2]	*	*	*	*	*	Metric tons
Peanuts	15-year, non-linear, 6-year grace period	*	*	500	*	*	10,000	Metric tons
Peanut butter	15-year	*	*	*	*	*	280	Metric tons
Cheese	20-year, 10-year grace period	300	413	450	500	350	625 (250[5])	Metric tons
Milk powder	20-year, 10-year grace period	50	*	*	*	*	*	Metric tons
Butter	20-year, 10-year grace period	50	*	60	*	100	*	Metric tons
Other dairy products	20-year, 10-year grace period	150	110 (220[6])	120	250	*	100	Metric tons
Ice cream	20-year, 10-year grace period	97,087	166,194	77,670	194,174	48,544	266,989	Litres

Table 10.3. (*cont.*)

Product category	Out-of-quota tariff elimination treatment[1]	Initial quantity[2]							Unit
		CRI	DOM	SLV	GTM	HND	NIC		
Fluid fresh milk and cream, and sour cream	20-year, 10-year grace period	407,461	*	366,715	305,596	560,259	254,663		Litres
Ethyl alcohol (Central America originating)	Immediate	Unlimited	Unlimited	Unlimited	Unlimited	Unlimited	Unlimited		Gallons
Ethyl alcohol (non-Central America originating)	Most favoured nation	31,000,000[2]	*	6,604,322[7]	*	*	*		Gallons

[1] In-quota imports shall be free of duty as of entry.

[2] With the exceptions of imports of 'Sugar (organic)' and 'ethyl alcohol (non-Central America originating)' from Costa Rica, which remain fixed, access quantities will be subject to growth over time.

[3] TRQ access based on trade surplus condition.

[4] A fixed 2,000 MT TRQ was allocated by the US to Costa Rica for organic sugar under the US specialty sugar TRQ, and applies to tariff lines AG17011110, AG17011210, AG17019110, AG17019910, AG17029010 and AG21069044.

[5] In the case of Nicaragua, an additional initial quantity of 250 metric tons applies to five tariff lines of the fifty-two total tariff lines making up the entire Cheese TRQ.

[6] In the case of the Dominican Republic, an additional initial quantity of 220 metric tons applies to four tariff lines of the forty-six total tariff lines making up the entire 'Other dairy products' TRQ.

[7] Or 10 per cent of the base quantity of dehydrated alcohol and mixtures established under Section 423, whichever is the smaller.

* No TRQ.

Source: Adapted from Tripartite Committee, *Comparative Guide to the Chile–United States Free Trade Agreement and the Dominican Republic–Central America–United States Free Trade Agreement*, based on TRQ Annexes to CAFTA Agreement.

Table 10.4. *Products subject to tariff rate quotas in CAFTA: Central American and DR tariff quotas on products entering from the United States*

Product category	Out-of-quota tariff elimination treatment[1]						Initial quantity in metric tons[2]					
	CRI	DOM	SLV	GTM	HND	NIC	CRI	DOM	SLV	GTM	HND	NIC
Bacon	*	10-year	*	*	*	*	*	220	*	*	*	*
Beans	*	15-year	*	*	*	*	*	8,560	*	*	*	*
Beef	*	*	15-year, NL, Special[3]	10-year	*	*	*	*	105	1,060	*	*
Beef, prime and choice	*	15-year	*	*	*	*	*	1,100	*	*	*	*
Beef, trimmings	*	15-year	*	*	*	*	*	220	*	*	*	*
Butter	20-year, 10-year GP	10-year	20-year, 10-year GP	20-year, 10-year GP	20-year, 10-year GP	20-year, 10-year GP	150	220	100	100	100	150
Buttermilk, curdled cream and yogurt	*	*	20-year, 10-year GP	*	*	*	*	*	10	*	*	*
Cheese	20-year, 10-year GP	*	20-year, 10-year GP	20-year, 10-year GP	20-year, 10-year GP	20-year, 10-year GP	410	*	410	450	410	575
Cheese, cheddar	*	15-year	*	*	*	*	*	138	*	*	*	*
Cheese, mozzarella	*	20-year, NL, 10-year GP	*	*	*	*	*	138	*	*	*	*
Cheeses, other	*	10-year	*	*	*	*	*	138	*	*	*	*
Chicken meat, mechanically de-boned	*	10-year	*	*	*	*	*	440	*	*	*	*
Chicken leg quarters	17-year, NL, 10-year GP	20-year, NL, 10-year GP	18-year, NL, 10-year GP	18-year, NL, 10-year GP	18-year, NL, 10-year GP	18-year, NL, 10-year GP	330	550	0	21,810[2]	0	0
Corn, white	*	*	Con't MFN[c]	Con't MFN	Con't MFN	Con't MFN	*	*	35,700	20,400	23,460	5,100

Table 10.4. (*cont.*)

Product category	Out-of-quota tariff elimination treatment[1]						Initial quantity in metric tons[2]					
	CRI	DOM	SLV	GTM	HND	NIC	CRI	DOM	SLV	GTM	HND	NIC
Corn, yellow	*	*	15-year, NL, 6-year GP[4]	10-year	15-year, NL, 6-year GP	15-year, NL, 6-year GP	*	*	367,500	525,000	190,509	68,250
Fresh onions	Con't MFN	*	*	*	*	*	300	*	*	*	*	*
Fresh potatoes	Con't MFN	*	*	*	*	*	300	*	*	*	*	*
Frozen french fries	5-year	12-year	*	*	*	*	2,631	*	*	*	*	*
Glucose	*	12-year					*	1,320				
Ice cream	20-year, 10-year GP	12-year	20-year, 10-year GP	20-year, 1 0-year GP	20-year, 10-year GP	20-year, 10-year GP	150	165	120	160	100	72,815[6]
Liquid dairy	*	*	20-year, 10-year GP	0-year GP	*	*	*	*	10	*	*	*
Liquid milk	*	10-year	*	*	*	*	*	220	*	*	*	*
Milk powder	20-year, 10-year GP	20-year, 10-year GP	20-year, 10-year GP	20-year, 10-year GP	20-year, 10-year GP	20-year, 10-year GP	200	2,970	300	400	300	650
Other dairy products	20-year, 10-year GP	*	20-year, 10-year GP	10-year	20-year, 10-year GP	20-year, 10-year GP	140	*	120	182	140	50
Pig fat	*	12-year	*	*	*	*	*	550	*	*	*	*
Pork	15-year, 6-year GP	*	15-year, NL, 6-year GP[4]	15-year	15-year, NL, 6-year GP	15-year	1,100	*	1,650	4,148	2,150	1,100
Pork cuts	*	15-year, NL, 6-year GP[4]	*	*	*	*	*	3,465	*	*	*	*
Rice, brown	*	20-year, NL, 10-year GP	*	*	*	*	*	2,140	*	*	*	*

Table 10.4. (cont.)

Product category	Out-of-quota tariff elimination treatment[1]						Initial quantity in metric tons[2]					
	CRI	DOM	SLV	GTM	HND	NIC	CRI	DOM	SLV	GTM	HND	NIC
Rice, milled	20-year, NL, 10-year GP[4]	20-year, NL, 10-year GP	18-year, NL, 10-year GP	18-year, NL, 10-year GP	18-year, NL, 10-year GP	18-year, NL, 10-year GP	5,250	8,560	5,625	10,500	8,925	13,650
Rice, rough	20-year, NL, 10-year GP[4]	*	18-year, NL, 10-year GP[4,5]	18-year, NL, 10-year GP[4]	18-year, NL, 10-year GP[4]	18-year, NL, 10-year GP[4]	51,000	*	62,220	54,600	91,800	92,700
Sorghum	*	*	15-year	*	*	*	*	*	263	*	*	*
Turkey meat	*	12-year	*	*	*	*	*	3,850	*	*	*	*
Yogurt	*	20-year, 10-year GP	*	*	*	*	*	110	*	*	*	*

GP = grace period; NL = non-linear.

[1] With the exception of 'Milk powder' in the Dominican Republic, in-quota imports shall be free of duty as of entry into force of the Agreement.

[2] With the exception of imports of 'Chicken leg quarters' by Guatemala from the United States, where there are reductions in the duty-free quantity in several years, followed by unlimited access in year 18; access quantities will be subject to growth over time.

[3] Duties in this category shall be reduced to 15 per cent in year 1.

[4] May be subject to performance requirements.

[5] The aggregate quantity of goods entering El Salvador from the United States under SAC provision 1006 shall be free of duty in any calendar year specified, 'and shall not exceed 3,000 MT for "parboiled rough" rice or its equivalent "parboiled milled" rice quantity in any such year. Parboiled milled equivalency shall be calculated according to a 0.7 conversion factor, where 1 MT of parboiled rough rice is equivalent to 0.7 MT of parboiled milled rice.'

[6] Quantities are measured in litres for the Nicaragua Ice Cream TRQ.

* No TRQ.

Source: Adapted from: Tripartite Committee, Comparative Guide to the Chile–United States Free Trade Agreement and the Dominican Republic–Central America–United States Free Trade Agreement, based on TRQ Annexes to CAFTA Agreement.

sectors – agricultural products, food preparation, textiles and apparel, and footwear) that trail the overall trend of liberalization. Many agreements in the Americas also carry provisions that could potentially be classified as 'other restrictive regulations of commerce', such as tariff rate quotas and exceptions. Such instruments appear to capture the price the region's integrationist interests are willing to pay for the liberalizing and encompassing RTAs. They could certainly also be interpreted as a challenge to multilateralizing RTAs, or at least as an issue that prolongs moves towards multilateralization. Indeed, some analysts see RTAs as useful vehicles for protectionist lobbies to lock in protection and capture rents in the RTA region.[27] However, and more positively, the fact that RTAs in most instances and in the Americas in particular, do eventually drive protectionism down in virtually all of the products in these sectors augurs well for multilateralization: RTAs could be seen as *the* instruments to start overcoming protectionism.

3   Open regionalism in the Americas?

The Americas is one of the most integrated regions in the world. Liberalization within the regional RTAs is deep, and many countries of the Americas are connected to most others in the region. But how discriminatory are agreements formed by countries in the Americas? Are RTAs in the region based on 'open regionalism' – i.e. has regional liberalization been paralleled by multilateral liberalization – and have the region's RTAs created, rather than diverted, trade? The first part of this section examines this question in a preliminary fashion by addressing applied external tariffs and rules of origin. The second part discusses some recent empirical findings on the trade effects of RTAs in the Americas and beyond.

Multilateral tariffs in the Americas

In the 1990s, MFN liberalization in the Americas proceeded in step with RTA liberalization, with preferential margins remaining for the most part unchanged during the period. Indeed, in the late 1980s, many countries of Latin America started MFN liberalization from average levels as high as 40 per cent or more. However, the more recent period has seen fewer changes in the western hemisphere countries' external

---

[27] See, for example, Krueger (1995).

tariffs: the proliferation of RTAs has been accompanied by little additional downward movement on external tariffs.

Appendix A, Figures 10.1B and 10.2B take a snapshot of the applied tariff profiles of regional economies and those of China, the EU, India and Japan, and the tariffs applied by these countries in the various HS chapters. The median chapter average of applied external tariffs in Latin America ranges from around 14 per cent (Colombia) to 6 per cent (Chile). The regional median is not very different from that of China; however, all Latin American countries have a lower median than is applied by India. US and Canadian tariffs are 2.8 per cent and 3.5 per cent, respectively.[28] Tariff dispersion in the region is moderate, barring extreme outliers, particularly in Mexico (meat, cereals and tobacco), and Costa Rica and Panama (dairy products). As for dispersion across countries by chapter (see Figure 10.15(b)), the dispersion is moderate across the tariff universe; yet outliers persist in textiles (Mexico) and agriculture (India, the EU, Mexico and the United States, among others). Averages are also higher in these sectors.

Whether the Americas features less or more discrimination than in the late 1990s requires a more detailed analysis than is performed here. It is the case that the advance of RTA liberalization has been accompanied by a more modest liberalization of external tariffs in the past few years than was the case in the 1990s. In general, however, it can also be said that the region's most liberalized countries in the RTA sphere also have the lowest MFN tariffs and least MFN tariff dispersion. Moreover, the formation of new RTAs has alleviated discrimination vis-à-vis the new partners (while also accentuating the disadvantages of remaining outside the RTA spaghetti bowl).

Rules of origin

Rules of origin arbitrate the discriminatory impact and trade-creating potential of RTAs. Since a failure to meet the ROOs disqualifies an exporter from the RTA-conferred preferential treatment, ROOs can and must be seen as a central market access instrument reigning over

---

[28] It should be noted that non-ad valorem tariffs are not included in the averages (i.e. calculations do not include ad valorem equivalents). Since non-ad valorem tariffs are generally more highly protective, the actual level of protection applied by the US and Canada would be slightly higher. Mexico, the EU and Japan also apply non ad valorem tariffs to some degree.

preferential trade. The potential effects of ROOs are accentuated over time: ROOs remain in place even after preferential tariffs have been phased out.

ROOs are widely considered to be a trade policy instrument that can work to offset the benefits of tariff liberalization in RTAs.[29] ROOs in effect set up walls around RTA members that prevent them from using some inputs in each final product. This can limit the access of member country producers to inputs from the rest of the world, as well as input providers' sales to the RTA region. When rules are more restrictive, the walls are higher, and efficient allocation of resources is even more difficult. Moreover, multiple overlapping RTAs with divergent origin regimes entail many such walls to free and efficient sourcing of inputs. The multiple criss-crossing RTAs in the Americas make ROOs of particular importance in the region.

Particularly agreements forged by the original NAFTA partners carry some of the most complex and restrictive rules of origin (Figure 10.14).[30] Encouragingly, however, unlike the straitjacket ROO model that the EU uses in all its RTAs, agreements in the Americas are marked by diversity in ROOs that suggests not only political economy forces but also accommodation of RTA-specific idiosyncrasies. The regional countries have also employed such measures as short supply clauses to help producers adjust to shocks in availability of intra-regional inputs.

Furthermore, developments over time are marked by a trend towards market-friendly rules of origin, particularly in North America. US ROO regimes have evolved towards a more liberal framework from NAFTA to the US–Chile FTA, CAFTA, and US–Colombia and US–Peru FTAs; in the meantime, the NAFTA ROO regime itself has been under a liberalization process, with more flexible ROOs being adopted in sectors as varied as alcoholic beverages, petroleum, chassis fitted with engines, photocopiers, chemicals, pharmaceuticals, plastics and rubber, motor vehicles and their parts, footwear, copper, and others.

---

[29] Most prominently, ROOs can be employed to favour intra-RTA industry linkages over those between the RTA and the rest of the world, and, as such, to indirectly protect RTA-based input producers vis-à-vis their extra-RTA rivals (Krueger, 1993; Krishna and Krueger, 1995). As such, ROOs are akin to a tariff on the intermediate product levied by the country importing the final good (Falvey and Reed, 2002; Lloyd, 2001).

[30] See Suominen (2004), Estevadeordal and Suominen (2006a), and Estevadeordal, Harris and Suominen (2007).

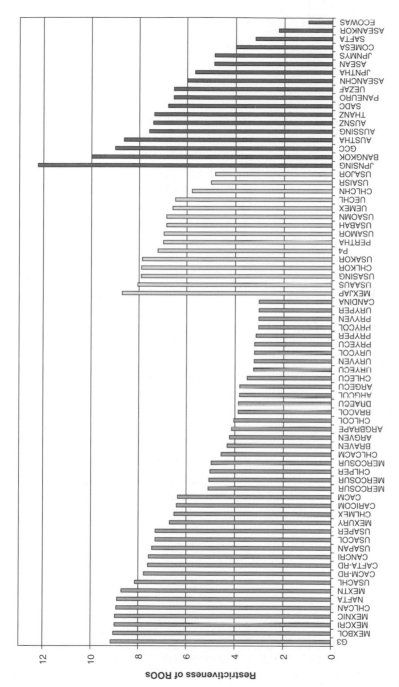

Figure 10.14 Restrictiveness of rules of origin in RTAs, by region

Economic effects of RTAs in the Americas: trade creation or trade diversion?

The academic literature remains divided as to whether RTAs are ultimately trade-creating or trade-diverting, and whether RTAs are a stepping stone or a stumbling block to global free trade.[31] Deardorff and Stern (1994), Baldwin (1993, 2006), Wei and Frankel (1995), Bergsten (1995), Frankel, Stein and Wei (1997), Ethier (1998), Cadot, de Melo and Olarreaga (2001), Freund (2000) and Ornelas (2005), and, on the political science side, Oye (1992) and Kahler (1995), provide grounds for believing that RTAs can be ever-expanding and propel strategic interactions conducive to global free trade. In contrast, Bhagwati (1993) argues that reduced protection between RTA members will be accompanied by increased protection vis-à-vis outsiders, with RTAs ultimately undermining multilateral liberalization.

For many authors, such as Van der Mensbrugghe, Newfarmer and Pierola (2005) and Schott (2004), much depends on the exact characteristics of RTAs. Aghion, Antràs and Helpman (2006) arrive at two equilibria: one in which global free trade is attained only when preferential trade agreements are permitted to form (a building block effect), and another in which global free trade is attained only when preferential trade agreements are forbidden (a stumbling block effect). To be sure, while seeing RTAs as the second-best option to multilateral free trade, most analysts view them as superior to not liberalizing at all.

There are few studies that engage tariff concessions. Limão (2006), examining concessions, finds that the United States and the EU have limited their multilateral tariff liberalization in goods traded with RTA partners. Limão and Olarreaga (2006) make a similar finding in the case of import subsidies afforded to RTA partners by the United States, the EU and Japan.

However, Estevadeordal and Robertson (2004) and Estevadeordal, Freund and Ornelas (2005), operationalizing tariff liberalization in a number of western hemisphere RTAs, find that RTAs in the Americas have not only been liberalizing and conducive to trade in the region, but

---

[31] For early works on the welfare effects of RTAs, and customs unions in particular, see Viner (1950), Meade (1955), Lipsey (1960), Johnson (1965), Mundell (1964), Corden (1972), and Kemp and Wan (1976). Richardson (1994) and Panagariya and Findlay (1996) extend the political economy analysis of PTA formation to look at the welfare implications of endogenously determined RTAs.

have helped further multilateral liberalization. Estevadeordal, Freund and Ornelas (2005) examine the effects of RTAs on external trade liberalization, using industry-level data on applied MFN tariffs and bilateral preferences for ten Latin American countries from 1989 to 2001. The results show that the greater the tariff preference that a country gives to its RTA partners in a given product, the more that country tends to reduce its MFN tariff in that product. The authors conclude that RTAs can further open regionalism and set in motion a dynamic that attenuates their potential trade diversionary effects.

Suominen (2004) and Estevadeordal and Suominen (2006b) find that, while RTAs help create trade, restrictive ROOs embedded in them dampen their trade-creating potential. Meanwhile, restrictive ROOs in final goods encourage trade in intermediate goods, and can thus entail trade diversion in inputs. Estevadeordal, López-Córdova and Suominen (2006) extend the analysis of the effects of ROOs to investment flows in manufacturing industries in Mexico, finding that investment in Mexico during the NAFTA era has been attracted to sectors with flexible ROOs – ROOs that allow industries to establish production and supply networks of global reach, and thus also import supplies from around the world (rather than from the NAFTA market alone, as they would have to do in the presence of restrictive ROOs).

Overall, the empirical evidence of RTAs' trade-creating effects remains mixed. Much appears to depend on the instrument (tariffs, ROOs, etc.), time period, and set of countries and product categories that are analysed. Nonetheless, the continued drive toward RTAs even among distant partners should help ensure, barring the implications of ROOs, that blocs become increasingly connected to the rest of the world, if not by multilateralism then by way of regionalism, evolving to an increasingly 'fuzzy' and 'leaky' format (Baldwin, 2006).

4 Beyond market access: services and investment

Analysing tariffs and other instruments governing trade in goods provides at best a limited view of the anatomy and effects of RTAs. RTAs formed by countries in the Americas, much like RTAs around the world, contain a host of disciplines beyond tariffs, ranging from investment to competition policy; from labour issues to dispute settlement; from standards to government procurement and transportation. These can provide for important complementarities, such as between tariff, services and investment liberalization.

This section strives to supplement the tariff liberalization statistics by providing a brief comparative analysis of the coverage (rather than depth of liberalization) of investment and services provisions (listed in Appendix A) in agreements formed by countries in the Americas in a comparative context, as well as vis-à-vis multilateral agreements such as the General Agreement on Trade in Services (GATS) and the Agreement on Trade-Related Investment Measures (TRIMs). The main question examined here is not the extent of liberalization by RTAs, but rather the extent of their comprehensiveness. As such, this analysis can also help elucidate the extent to which RTAs are 'WTO-plus' in terms of incorporating a larger number of specific provisions than are present in the multilateral regime.

Services

Services chapters in RTAs usually only cover modes 1 and 2, and are therefore separate from RTA chapters on investment and temporary entry of business persons. RTAs generally cover a large number of services provisions, particularly most favoured nation treatment, national treatment, market access, local presence, domestic regulation, recognition of qualifications, transparency, restriction of transfers and denial of benefits. Many RTAs also contain (whether in different chapters or in annexes to the services chapters) specific provisions for telecommunications and financial services.

Intra-hemispheric RTAs are particularly comprehensive and often go well beyond GATS provisions (Figures 10.15 and 10.16). Older agreements such as NAFTA, the first agreement to cover services in an exhaustive manner, cover MFN treatment, national treatment, market access, local presence, domestic regulation, recognition of qualifications, transparency, restriction of transfers and denial of benefits, as well as certain provisions for telecommunications and financial services. The coverage of services in these two sectors has increased in recent US agreements with Chile, Peru, Colombia and Panama, and, on the inter-regional front, with Australia, Singapore, and Morocco. By contrast, most South American agreements do not have specific services provisions.

Overall, this means that more than 60 per cent of inter- and intra-regional agreements cover MFN treatment, national treatment, market access and unnecessary barriers to trade, and prohibit discriminatory treatment – all areas addressed by fewer extra-regional agreements,

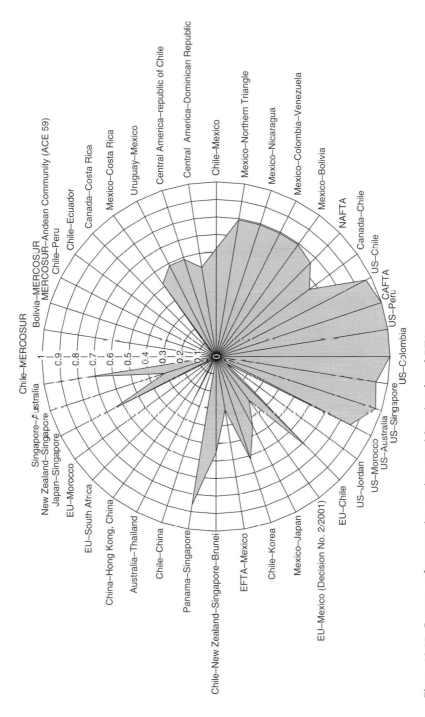

Figure 10.15 Coverage of twenty-nine services provisions in selected RTAs

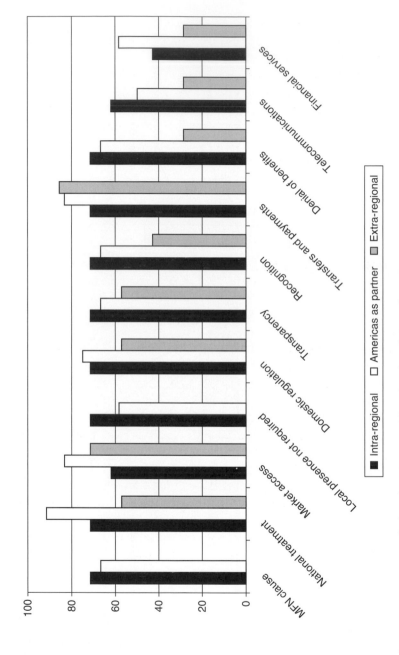

Figure 10.16 Coverage of selected services provisions in selected RTAs, by region

which are in general much thinner, with the exception of the Japan–Singapore FTA, which covers national treatment, market access, domestic regulation, recognition of qualifications, transparency and restriction of transfers, as well as certain provisions on telecommunications and financial services.

Mexico and Chile's agreements with the EU differ. The EU–Chile FTA covers national treatment, market access, domestic regulations, recognition of qualifications, transparency and restrictions of transfers, and also contains a thorough regulation of telecommunications and financial services. The EU–Mexico FTA covers only MFN treatment, national treatment, market access, restrictions of transfers, and denial of benefits, while having no provisions on telecommunications, and covering financial services only rather marginally.

Investment

As in services, the latest RTAs' investment chapters tend to be encompassing, extending to such areas as MFN treatment, national treatment, transparency, denial of benefits and restriction of transfers, nationality of management and boards of directors, performance requirements, expropriation, and investor–state disputes.

It is intra-hemispheric RTAs, and US RTAs in particular, that are comprehensive – and often extend well beyond GATS and TRIMs (Figure 10.17).[32] Indeed, all RTAs forged in the Americas apply the four modalities of investment – establishment, acquisition, post-establishment operations and resale – and also cover such disciplines as MFN treatment, national treatment, and dispute settlement (Figure 10.18). Eighty per cent or more also cover transparency, denial of benefits and restriction of transfers, nationality of management and board of directors, performance requirements and expropriation. In inter-regional agreements, the coverage is somewhat lower, due to the limited coverage of disciplines in the EU–Mexico and EU–Chile agreements, as well as in the Chile–China FTA, P-4, and the US–Jordan FTA. On the extra-regional front, Singapore and Australia's agreements are more encompassing, but other agreements have scant coverage.

---

[32] An FTA's investment provisions are coded when there is an investment chapter in an RTA or when the RTA refers to a bilateral investment treaty as the agreement applicable to the RTA. When no such mention is made, a zero value is assigned (even if the RTA partners are connected via a bilateral investment treaty (BIT)).

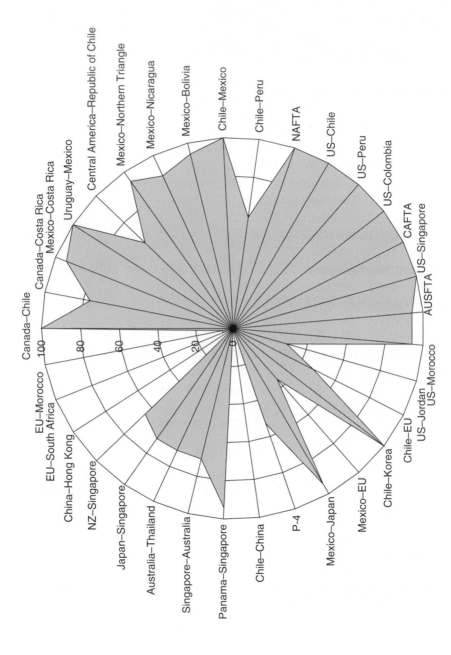

Figure 10.17 Coverage of investment provisions in selected RTAs

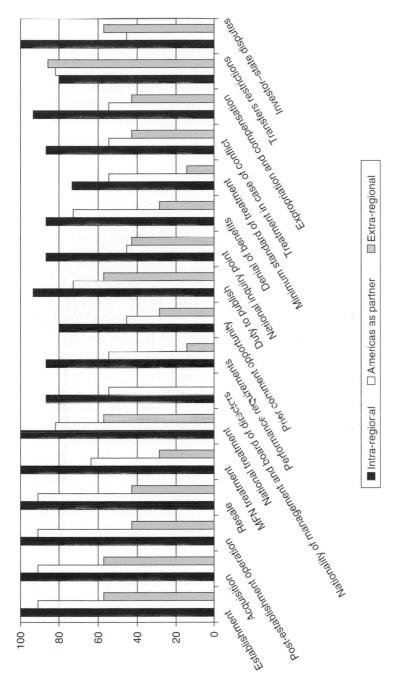

Figure 10.18 Coverage of selected investment provisions in selected RTAs, by region

Legend: ■ Intra-regional □ Americas as partner ▨ Extra-regional

In sum, there is a marked variation across RTAs in the coverage of services and investment provisions. Yet the analysis also shows the clustering of RTAs by main world regions – Asia, Europe, North America and South America. A closer inspection of the data also suggests the exportation of RTA models from one region to the next through trans-continental RTAs, such as 'borrowing' some of the US–Chile RTA's market access provisions in the Chile–Republic of Korea RTA. Many US RTAs in particular could be viewed as WTO-plus in terms of incorporating a larger number of specific provisions than are carved out in the multilateral regime. This indicates the perceived usefulness of rule-making in the RTA context, perhaps both as a means of overcoming slow multilateral negotiations, and as a way to deepen and appropriately mould provisions that are particularly pertinent to the RTA relationship – as well as being a tool to attain greater synergies across the various RTA disciplines.

5   Furthering multilateralization in the Americas

Countries of the Americas are at a crossroads: their intra-regional integration is increasingly complete and mature, and many regional countries have already established ties with numerous extra-regional partners. As such, the key challenge for many countries of the region is not so much the negotiation of new agreements but optimizing the benefits of their existing RTA portfolios. One key measure for achieving this is to address the domestic supply-side constraints to trade. Another has to do with the external environment, where one policy option is multilateralizing the regional RTAs.

Conceptually, multilateralization can be achieved through pulling three alternative (yet complementary) levers: multilateral, regional and two-way. The multilateral lever could entail changing and/or making more precise the multilateral rules governing RTAs, particularly the rather vague requirement of the GATT Article XXIV that RTAs liberalize 'substantially all trade' among the partners and eradicate 'restrictive regulations on commerce' within a 'reasonable length of time', and not raise new barriers to trade vis-à-vis non-members. For transparency purposes, the multilateral path could also entail strengthening the notification of RTAs to the WTO and deepening the incipient multilateral examinations of RTAs' compliance with Article XXIV.

The regional lever could be applied within each individual RTA or among groups of RTAs. The former would mean driving down intra-RTA barriers and lowering discrimination toward non-members (or incorporating new members). The latter would entail convergence – merging RTAs together into broader cumulation zones through the adoption of common rules and regulations – while driving external protection to the lowest common denominator.

The two-way lever would entail using what is 'regional' to shape what is 'multilateral', and vice versa. For instance, it could mean using the empirical measures of liberalization and external discrimination in RTAs – something this chapter has sought to establish – as a revealed regional preference and reality check in multilateral rule-making on RTAs, and as an agreed-upon benchmark for new RTAs to aspire to. It could also mean employing tried and tested trade-related disciplines in RTAs that currently go beyond multilateral rules in coverage and/or precision in crafting new multilateral trade rules.

Conversely, the two-way lever could be pulled to incorporate new multilateral rules governing RTAs in the texts of new RTAs, and even involve some mechanisms to enforce compliance with multilateral mandates at the regional level. It could also bring some multilateral rules to govern regional convergence processes to ensure that expanded RTA zones would not result in discrimination vis-à-vis non-members, or in systemically problematic scenarios along the lines of Krugman's (1991) three-bloc world.

Besides the political opposition to multilateralization, however accomplished, the risk to be managed in any of these processes would be one of the incentives. Stronger multilateral monitoring of RTAs could turn countries away from regionalism, and also do little to guarantee that they would turn their energies to multilateralism. Regional convergence among RTAs risks yielding trade-diverting mega-blocs if the regional countries decide not to continue tariff elimination vis-à-vis non-members. Pulling the two-way lever risks putting regions in a straitjacket, with unsuitable one-size-fits-all multilateral rules and, conversely, succumbing to the political economy of RTAs at the multilateral level.

More concretely, what might be some of the regional levers countries of the Americas could pull (a process over which countries of the region have control) as opposed to the multilateral levers (which they do not fully control)?

The first alternative is an 'all countries, all disciplines' approach: pursuit of a broad integration scheme in the Americas that would open all regional trade channel, and streamline the regional trade architecture, essentially superseding the RTAs crisscrossing the region. Traders, investors and customs authorities would need to refer only to one single agreement on such issues as market access and rules of origin, services and investment regulations, standards, dispute settlement, and so on. Akin to the FTAA, a region-wide RTA would also help circumvent the rise of intra-regional RTA-induced hub-and-spoke systems – and further trade creation when based on open regionalism (external tariff-lowering by the members, and ROOs that result in lower effective restrictiveness than those of the existing regional RTAs).

The second and seemingly more feasible alternative would be a 'selected countries, selected disciplines' convergence approach. This would at first mean knitting subsets of the existing RTAs together and allowing for cumulation among them. The initial focus of such a convergence could be market access provisions and rules of origin; again, the drive should be towards the least restrictive ROOs.[33] The convergence package could be gradually expanded to incorporate further disciplines and/or further countries (i.e. move towards an 'all countries, all disciplines' model), perhaps with some form of variable geometry. While differing in process from that aiming for a mega-regional agreement, convergence would have similar effects to those of a single integration agreement among the set of RTAs pursuing it – opening the current non-RTA channels and simplifying the whole of the regional RTA network – and this would also likely be greater in terms of the economic impact than the sum of the parts. Some of this thinking is taking hold in the Americas, perhaps most concretely among the Pacific Basin Forum of eleven countries in Latin America, which has formed a working agenda to study, among other things, trade convergence and integration.

The third and again more feasible alternative would be a 'case-by-case' approach: accelerating liberalization within each individual RTA (as well as vis-à-vis non-members), for instance by reducing the restrictiveness of rules of origin, as has been pursued in the NAFTA context since 2003.

---

[33] See Estevadeordal, Harris and Suominen (2007) for details.

There are other, shorter-term, more piecemeal tactical measures that could be taken. One possibility would be to liberalize goods (both in RTAs and vis-à-vis third parties) in product categories that countries in the region have already liberalized to major exporters in or outside the region, so that the marginal pain of liberalization in these sectors would be small if not non-existent. For example, in CAFTA, Central American countries freed photographic or cinematographic goods (HS Chapter 37) and fruit and nuts (Chapter 08) to imports from the United States, the key source of their imports in the two sectors, yet they also maintain positive applied MFN rates in these sectors. Another example is wood pulp (Chapter 47) for Chile in the Chile–US FTA.

6 Conclusion

The underlying notion of this chapter is that there are no clear and simple answers to whether RTAs are 'multilateralized' or 'multi-lateralizable': much depends on the RTA, RTA partners, and product categories under analysis. We have found that RTAs in the Americas are among the most mature and liberalized in the world. However, as in other regions, in the Americas there are some outlier RTA parties and product categories that remain closed for extended periods of time. RTAs formed by the countries of the Americas also carry a number of trade policy instruments, such as TRQs and exclusions, which can curb liberalization between the parties, or restrictive rules of origin, which can undermine trade between RTA members and non-members (as well as between RTAs).

Overall, however, the findings of this chapter are encouraging, particularly that the manifold RTAs formed by the original NAFTA partners liberalize the bulk of goods, and do so rapidly. Furthermore, the region's integration was, especially in its early days, accompanied by forceful multilateral tariff liberalization – the slowing of which may today be in part compensated by the regional economies' seemingly incessant RTA spree with partners around the world. Countries of the Americas, and the United States in particular, have also pushed the frontiers of such RTA disciplines as services and investment. Today's challenge for the region is managing the risks of the regional lever: pursuing a path that is good both for the regional countries and for the multilateral trading system.

References

Aghion, P., Antràs, P. and Helpman, E. (2006) 'Negotiating Free Trade', mimeo, Harvard University.

Baldwin, R. (1993) 'A Domino Theory of Regionalism', NBER Working Paper No. W4465, Cambridge, MA: National Bureau of Economic Research.

(2006) 'Multilateralising Regionalism: Spaghetti Bowls as Building Blocks on the Path to Global Free Trade', *The World Economy* 29 (11): 1451–518.

Bergsten, C. Fred (1995) 'APEC: The Bogor Declaration and the Path Ahead', APEC Working Paper Series 95–1, Washington DC: Institute for International Economics.

Bhagwati, J. (1993) 'Regionalism and Multilateralism: An Overview', in J. de Melo and A. Panagariya (eds.), *New Dimensions in Regional Integration*, New York: Cambridge University Press.

Cadot, O., de Melo, J. and Olarreaga, M. (2001) 'Can Regionalism Ease the Pain of Multilateral Trade Liberalization?', *European Economic Review* 45: 27–44.

Corden, W. M. (1972) 'Economies of Scale and Customs Union Theory', *Journal of Political Economy* 80 (3): 465–75.

Deardorff, A. and Stern, R. (1994) 'Multilateral Trade Negotiations and Preferential Trading Arrangements', in A. Deardorff and R. Stern (eds.), *Analytical and Negotiating Issues in the Global Trading System*, Ann Arbor: University of Michigan Press.

Estevadeordal, A. and Robertson, R. (2004) 'From Distant Neighbors to Close Partners: FTAA and the Pattern of Trade', in A. Estevadeordal, D. Rodrik, A. M. Taylor and A. Velasco (eds.), *Integrating the Americas: FTAA and Beyond*, Cambridge, MA: Harvard University Press.

Estevadeordal, A. and Suominen, K. (2006a) 'Mapping and Measuring Rules of Origin around the World', in O. Cadot, A. Estevadeordal, A. Suwa-Eisenmann and T. Verdier (eds.), *The Origin of Goods*, Oxford: Oxford University Press.

(2006b) 'Trade Effects of Rules of Origin', Mimeo, Washington DC: Inter-American Development Bank.

Estevadeordal, A., Freund, C. and Ornelas, E. (2005) 'Does Regionalism Help or Hinder Multilateralism? An Empirical Evaluation', paper presented at the conference on 'The Sequencing of Regional Economic Integration: Issues in the Breadth and Depth of Economic Integration in the Americas', Kellogg Institute for International Studies, University of Notre Dame, IN, 9–10 September 2005.

Estevadeordal, A., Harris, J. and Suominen, K. (2007) *Multilateralizing Preferential Rules of Origin around the World*, Washington DC: Inter-American Development Bank.

Estevadeordal, A., López-Córdova, J. E. and Suominen, K. (2006) 'How Do Rules of Origin Affect Investment Flows? Some Hypotheses and the Case of

Mexico', Institute for the Integration of Latin America and the Caribbean/ Integration, Trade and Hemispheric Issues Division Working Paper 22, Washington DC: Inter-American Development Bank.

Ethier, W. J. (1998) 'Regionalism in a Multilateral World', *Journal of Political Economy* 106 (6): 1214–45.

Falvey, R. and Reed, G. (2002) 'Rules of Origin as Commercial Policy Instruments', *International Economic Review* 43: 393–407.

Frankel, J. A., Stein, E. and Wei, S. (1997) *Regional Trading Blocs in the World Economic System*, Washington DC: Institute for International Economics.

Freund, C. (2000) 'Multilateralism and the Endogenous Formation of Preferential Trade Agreements', *Journal of International Economics* 52 (2): 359–76.

Inter-American Development Bank (IDB) (2002) 'Beyond Borders: The New Regionalism in Latin America', in *Economic and Social Progress in Latin America, 2002 Report*, Washington, DC: IDB.

IDB (forthcoming) 'Market Access Provisions in Regional Trade Agreements', presented at the IDB/WTO conference on 'Regional Rules in the Global Trading System', 26–27 July 2006, Washington, DC.

Johnson, H. (1965) 'An Economic Theory of Protectionism, Tariff Bargaining, and the Formation of Customs Unions', *Journal of Political Economy* 73: 256–83.

Kahler, M. (1995) *International Institutions and the Political Economy of Integration*, Washington DC: Brookings Institution.

Kemp, M. C. and Wan, H. Y. Jr. (1976) 'An Elementary Proposition Concerning the Formation of Customs Unions', *Journal of International Economics* 6: 95–8.

Krishna, K. and Krueger, A. O. (1995) 'Implementing Free Trade Areas: Rules of Origin and Hidden Protection', in A. Deardorff, J. Levinsohn and R. Stern (eds.), *New Directions in Trade Theory*, Ann Arbor: University of Michigan Press.

Krueger, A. O. (1993) 'Free Trade Agreements as Protectionist Devices: Rules of Origin', NBER Working Paper No. 4352. Cambridge, MA: National Bureau for Economic Research.

—— (1995) 'Free Trade Agreements versus Customs Unions', NBER Working Paper No. 5084. Cambridge, MA: National Bureau for Economic Research.

Krugman, P. (1991) 'The Move Toward Free Trade Zones', in *Policy Implications of Trade and Currency Zones*, Jackson Hole, WY: Federal Reserve Bank of Kansas City.

Limão, N. (2006) 'Preferential Trade Agreements as Stumbling Blocks for Multilateral Trade Liberalization: Evidence for the US', *American Economic Review* 96 (3): 896–914.

Limão, N. and Olarreaga, M. (2006) 'Trade Preferences to Small Developing Countries and the Welfare Costs of Lost Multilateral Liberalization', *World Bank Economic Review* 20 (2): 217–40.

Lipsey, R. G. (1960) 'The Theory of Customs Unions: A General Survey', *Economic Journal* 70: 498–513.

Lloyd, P. J. (2001) 'Rules of Origin and Fragmentation of Trade', in L. K. Cheng and H. Kierzkowski (eds.), *Global Production and Trade in East Asia*, Boston, MA: Kluwer Academic Publishers.

Meade, J. (1955) *The Theory of Customs Unions*, Amsterdam: North Holland.

Mundell, R. A. (1964) 'Tariff Preferences and the Terms of Trade', *Manchester School of Economic and Social Studies* 32: 1–13.

Ornelas, E. (2005) 'Trade Creating Free Trade Areas and the Undermining of Multilateralism', *European Economic Review* 49 (7): 1717–35.

Oye, K. (1992) *Economic Discrimination and Political Exchange: World Political Economy in the 1930s and 1980s*, Princeton, NJ: Princeton University Press.

Panagariya, A. and Findlay, R. (1996) 'A Political-Economy Analysis of Free-Trade Areas and Customs Unions', in *The Political Economy of Trade Reform: Essays in Honor of Jagdish Bhagwati*, Cambridge, MA: MIT Press.

Richardson, M. (1994) 'Why a Free Trade Area? The Tariff Also Rises', *Economics and Politics* 6 (1): 79–96.

Schott, J. J. (2004) *Free Trade Agreements: US Strategies and Priorities*, Washington DC: Institute for International Economics.

Scollay, R. (2005) '"Substantially All Trade." Which Definitions Are Fulfilled in Practice? An Empirical Investigation', report prepared for the Commonwealth Secretariat, APEC Study Centre, University of Auckland.

Suominen, K. (2004) 'Rules of Origin in Global Commerce', PhD dissertation, University of California, San Diego.

Van der Mensbrugghe, D., Newfarmer, R. and Pierola, D. (2005) 'Regionalism vs. Multilateralism', in R. Newfarmer (ed.), *Trade, Doha and Development: A Window into the Issues*, Washington DC: World Bank.

Viner, J. (1950) *The Customs Union Issue*, New York: Carnegie Endowment for International Peace.

Wei, S. and Frankel, J. A. (1995) *European Integration and the Regionalization of World Trade and Currencies: The Economics and the Politics*, Berkeley, CA: University of California.

World Bank (2005) *Global Economic Prospects*, Washington DC: World Bank.

Appendix A

Table 10.1A *Tariff liberalization schedules of seventy-six in thirty-eight RTAs*

Agreement	Year of entry into effect	Tariff line schedules	Services	Investment
Australia–New Zealand	28/03/1983	✓	✓	✓
Australia–Thailand	01/01/2005	✓	✓	✓
CAFTA	17/12/04 (SV), 03/03/2005 (HO), 10/03/05 (GU), 11/10/C5 (NI), 27/07/05 (US)*	✓	✓	✓
Canada–Chile	05/07/1997	✓	✓	✓
Canada–Costa Rica	11/01/2002	✓	✓	✓
Canada–Israel	01/01/1997	✓	✓	✓
Central America–DR	07/03/2002 (CR), 04/10/2001 (SV), 03/10/2001(GJ), 19/12/2001 (HO)	✓	✓	✓
Chile–Central America	15/02/2002 (CR), 03/06/2002 (SV)	✓	✓	✓
Chile–Korea, Rep. of	01/04/2004	✓	✓	✓
Chile–Mexico	01/08/1999	✓	✓	✓
Chile–New Zealand–Singapore–Brunei	3/6/2005 8/11/2006 (CHL), June 2006 (NZL, SGP, BRN)	✓	✓	✓
China–Hong Kong, China	01/01/2004	✓	✓	✓
COMESA	08/12/1994	✓	✓	✓
EC–South Africa	01/01/2000	✓	✓	✓
EC–Chile	01/02/2003	✓	✓	✓
EC–Lithuania	01/01/1995	✓		
EC–Mexico	01/07/2001	✓	✓	✓

Table 10.1A (*cont.*)

Agreement	Year of entry into effect	Tariff line schedules	Services	Investment
EC–Morocco	01/03/2000	✓	✓	✓
EC–Romania	01/02/1995	✓	✓	✓
EFTA–Mexico	01/07/2001	✓	✓	
EFTA–Singapore	01/01/2003	✓	✓	✓
Japan–Singapore	30/11/2002	✓	✓	✓
Mexico–Bolivia	01/01/1995	✓	✓	✓
Mexico–Colombia–Venezuela	01/01/1995	✓	✓	✓
Mexico–Costa Rica	01/01/2005	✓	✓	✓
Mexico–Israel	01/07/2000	✓	✓	✓
Mexico–Japan	01/04/2005	✓	✓	✓
Mexico–Nicaragua	01/07/1998	✓	✓	
Mexico–Northern Triangle	15/03/2001 (SV, GU), 01/06/2001 (HO), 14/03/2001 (MEX)	✓	✓	
Mexico–Uruguay	15/07/2004	✓		
NAFTA	01/04/1994	✓		
New Zealand–Singapore	01/01/2001	✓	✓	✓
Singapore–Australia	28/07/2003	✓	✓	✓
United States–Australia	01/01/2005	✓	✓	✓
United States–Chile	01/01/2004	✓	✓	✓
United States–Jordan	17/12/2001	✓	✓	✓
United States–Morocco	01/01/2006	✓	✓	✓
United States–Singapore	01/01/2004	✓	✓	✓

* = Ratification dates.

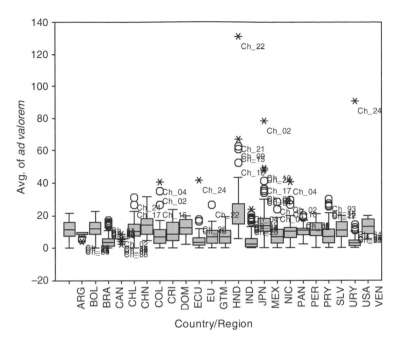

Figure 10.1B Boxplots by country (chapter distributions).
Source: INT calculations based on UNCTAD TRAINS data.

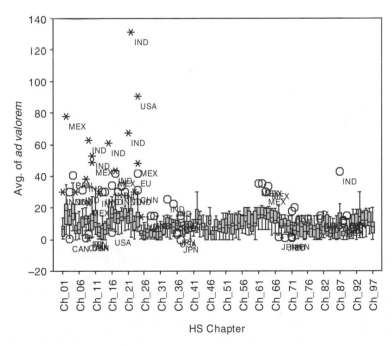

Figure 10.2B Boxplots by HS chapter (country distributions)
Source: INT calculations based on UNCTAD TRAINS data.

~

Comment

MARCELO OLARREAGA

This is another impressive data collection task undertaken by the Integration and Trade Sector of the Inter-American Development Bank (IDB). Their consistent effort in collecting detailed trade policy data has now spanned a decade and has allowed us to better understand the functioning and consequences of different, and often obscure, trade policy instruments, such as rules of origin. The profession has clearly benefited from their work.

Because my role as a discussant is to uncover areas for improvement, it is worth mentioning that on the data dissemination front the Integration and Trade Sector have been lagging behind. A publicly accessible website with the series of datasets collected over the last decade would be welcomed by researchers and policymakers in the Americas and elsewhere, as there is much to be learnt from the experiences in the region. Clearly, the social returns of their efforts would be much larger, as different authors would be able to study these important problems, and compare their results to existing evidence. But the private returns to the IDB will also be much larger, as these researchers and users of their datasets would be able to provide feedback on their data and their various construction methods and analytical methodologies. Unfortunately, transparency in data collection tends to be under-rated. Let us hope it changes.

This is a very good chapter and I agree with most of its analyses. Given the space constraint, I will focus my comments on three areas where I disagree. The first one is one important conclusion of the chapter. The two others are marginal byproducts.

First, I do not share the assessment that "the Americas comprise a highly liberalized region in terms of the maturity, geographical coverage and depths of its RTAs." Other authors using similar data, but different techniques, have reached very different conclusions. To make their claim, Estevadeordal, Shearer and Suominen show that by 2020 almost 100 percent of intra-Americas trade will be duty-free. Vaillant (2007) disagrees. He argues that using the share of duty-free tariff lines is misleading, as a single line can have a very large economic importance. Instead Vaillant uses the share of exports to the world, weighted by the importer's MFN tariffs on those items that are subject to intra-regional duty-free treatment, to capture the economic importance of the preference, which will depend on both the extent of tariff preference and the potential level of exports. He finds that in only 60 percent of bilateral agreements there will be more than 90 percent of the potential trade that will be subject to free trade by 2018 (Figure A1 of Vaillant, 2007). The economic importance of preferences granted by Andean countries to MERCOSUR countries is on average below 10 percent (third panel of Table A9 in Vaillant, 2007) – a very different picture from the one reached by Estevadeordal, Shearer and Suominen. Perhaps more importantly, the two largest economies of Latin America (Mexico and Brazil), representing almost 70 percent of the region's GDP, have not yet signed a regional trade agreement.

Vaillant also argues that, as tariff reductions have been implemented within regional trade agreements, we have witnessed the emergence of non tariff barriers on intra-regional trade. This goes well beyond the agricultural tariff quotas studied in the chapter. A recent study (Kee, Nicita, and Olarreaga, 2008) has shown that non-tariff barriers are on average much more restrictive than tariffs, so this can, in principle, erode most if not all of the granted tariff preferences. The emergence of non-tariff barriers has put a lot of pressure on the credibility of regional agreements, their goals and institutions. An extreme and sad example is that over the last two years Argentina has had several bridges over the Uruguay River closed to traffic over an environmental dispute with Uruguay.[1] I am sure many Uruguayan exporters would be happy to pay the most favored nation tariff if the bridges over the river were to be re-opened. Thus it seems that at least in South America there is a lot of room for improvement, and hopefully maturity has not yet been reached.

My second disagreement relates to the idea that, in order to "multilateralize" the Americas, it is necessary to merge "RTAs together into broader cumulation zones through the adoption of *common* rules and regulations" (emphasis added). I have difficulty understanding why there is a need for common rules. Assume that within LAIA Colombia grants duty-free access to textiles originating in Brazil. Assume also that Colombia grants duty-free access to shirts originating in Argentina.

---

[1] For a legal perspective on the dispute, see Del Cerro (2007).

It makes perfect sense that, through diagonal cumulation (which is rare in the region), Argentina imports textiles from Brazil, processes them into shirts and exports them duty-free to Colombia. Otherwise, Colombia could nullify the preferences that it has given either to Brazil or Argentina. Note that, in this example, there is no need for the adoption of common rules. We actually never specified what the rules were in the two preferential agreements (Colombia–Argentina and Colombia–Brazil). While allowing that cumulation will not be a panacea for multilateralizing regionalism, it can help without necessarily requiring common rules.

Finally, I am probably a bit more pessimistic regarding the presence in the region of a "juggernaut" effect, as defined by Baldwin (2006). I believe that part of the reason why we have not seen much external liberalization or "open regionalism" in South America has to do with the fact that the composition of intra-regional exports is often very different from the composition of extra-regional exports, and this is particularly true for the larger countries, such as Brazil. If exporters to the region are not the same as exporters to the world, the multi-lateralization of regionalism through the "juggernaut" effect is unlikely. This is probably very different from what we observe in other regions such as East Asia.

References

Baldwin, R. (2006) "Multilateralising Regionalism: Spaghetti Bowls as Building Blocks on the Path to Global Free Trade," *The World Economy* 29 (11): 1451–518.

Del Cerro, M. A. (2007) "Paper Battle on the Uruguay River: The International Dispute Surrounding the Construction of Pulp Mills on the River Uruguay," mimeo, available at: http://works.bepress.com/cgi/viewcontent. cgi?article=1000&context=maria_del_cerro.

Kee, H. L., Nicita, A. and Olarreaga, M. (2008) "Estimating Trade Restrictiveness Indices," *Economic Journal*.

Vaillant, M. (2007) "Convergencias y divergencias en la integración sudamericana," Commission économique pour l'Amérique latine, Serie Comercio Internacional 83.

11

Multilateralizing regional trade arrangements in Asia[1]

MASAHIRO KAWAI AND GANESHAN WIGNARAJA

1 Introduction: key issues

East Asian economies have grown rapidly over the last four decades, driven by the expansion of international trade and foreign direct investment (FDI). They have now moved toward formal economic integration through bilateral and plurilateral free trade agreements (FTAs). The Association of Southeast Asian Nations (ASEAN) is emerging as the integration hub for FTAs in East Asia, while the People's Republic of China, Japan, and the Republic of Korea also have formal economic ties with ASEAN, and India, Australia and New Zealand are joining the bandwagon. How can East Asia ensure that the region's noodle bowl of FTAs can be consolidated into a single East Asian FTA – a stepping stone toward global integration?[2]

This chapter analyses this question and its ramifications. Section 2 highlights the progress of market-driven regional economic integration

---

[1] Earlier versions of this chapter were presented at "Ten Years after the Crisis: Evolving East Asian Financial System and Challenges," organized by the Policy Research Institute of Japan's Ministry of Finance and the Asian Development Bank Institute, Tokyo, June 12, 2007; and the Latin American/Caribbean and Asia-Pacific Economics and Business Association (LAEBA) panel for the Consejo de Estudios Latinoamericanos de Asia y de Oceanía (CELAO, Latin American Studies Council of Asia and Oceania) conference, organized by the Latin American Studies Association of Korea, Seoul, June 21–23, 2007. The authors are grateful for comments made by Prema-chandra Athukorala, Richard Baldwin, Giovanni Capannelli, Inkyo Cheong, Patrick Low, Peter Petri, Shujiro Urata, Tran Van Tho, and other conference participants. Thanks are also due to Dorothea Lazaro and Rosechin Olfindo for efficient research assistance and to Patricia Decker for editorial assistance. The findings, interpretations, and conclusions expressed in the chapter are entirely those of the authors and do not necessarily represent the views of the Asian Development Bank, its Institute, its executive directors, or the countries they represent.

[2] For pioneering work on spaghetti bowls as building blocks on the path to global free trade, and a possible new role for the WTO, see Baldwin (2006 and 2007).

in East Asia through trade and FDI. Section 3 summarizes some salient characteristics of East Asian FTAs. Section 4 tackles policy issues for helping to multilateralize East Asian FTAs at the regional level, so that this effort can become a stepping stone, rather than a stumbling block, to global economic integration. Section 5 concludes by focusing on how East Asia should strengthen trade and FDI ties with North America and Europe. The Appendix examines the economic impact of various types of FTAs in East Asia (among them, ASEAN+1, ASEAN+3, and ASEAN +6) using a computable general equilibrium (CGE) model.

2   Economic integration and FTA initiatives in East Asia

Market-driven economic integration in East Asia

Economic integration through trade and FDI

East Asia has long enjoyed a market-driven expansion of trade and FDI. The region's exports rose from 14 percent of world total exports in 1980 to 27 percent in 2006, while its imports expanded from 15 percent to 24 percent during 1980–2006.[3] FDI inflows into East Asia (including Japan) more than tripled from 5 percent of the world total in 1980, to 14 percent in 2006, while East Asian FDI outflows increased from 5 to 11 percent of the world total over the same period. This has also been accompanied by rising intra-regional concentration of trade and FDI activities.

Table 11.1 summarizes changes in the share of intra-regional trade for various groupings in the world over 1980–2006. It shows that intra-regional trade as a share of East Asia's total trade has risen from 37 percent in 1980 to 55 percent in 2006 (including Japan) or from 23 to 46 percent over the same period (excluding Japan). Intra-regional trade within East Asia remains below that of the European Union-15 (which peaked at 66 percent in 1990), but exceeds that of the North American Free Trade Area (which peaked at 49 percent in 2001).

FDI inflows into emerging East Asia have contributed to regional economic integration. Table 11.2 summarizes the source regions/ countries of emerging East Asian FDI inflows (cumulative figures) for

---

[3] Here, East Asia includes the ten ASEAN members (Brunei Darussalam, Cambodia, Indonesia, Lao People's Democratic Republic, Malaysia, Myanmar, Philippines, Singapore, Thailand, and Viet Nam); China; Hong Kong, China; Japan; Republic of Korea; and Chinese Taipei.

Table 11.1 *Intra-regional trade share, 1980–2006 (%)[a]*

Region	1980	1985	1990	1995	2000	2001	2002	2003	2004	2005	2006
NIEs (4)[b]	8.6	9.2	11.9	15.5	15.5	15.3	15.8	15.2	14.6	13.9	13.6
ASEAN (10)[c]	17.9	20.3	18.8	24.0	24.7	24.1	24.4	26.6	26.7	27.2	27.2
ASEAN+China+Rep. of Korea+Hong Kong, China+Chinese Taipei (14)	22.7	27.2	33.0	39.1	40.6	41.1	43.4	44.7	45.2	45.5	45.8
ASEAN+3 (13)[d]	30.2	30.2	29.4	37.6	37.3	37.1	37.9	39.0	39.2	38.9	38.3
ASEAN+3+Hong Kong, China+Chinese Taipei (15)	36.8	39.0	43.1	51.9	52.1	51.9	53.8	55.4	55.9	55.4	54.5
ASEAN+6 (16)[e]	34.6	34.8	33.7	40.8	40.5	40.6	41.3	42.4	43.0	43.1	42.6
ASEAN+6+Hong Kong, China+Chinese Taipei (18)	40.5	42.7	46.3	54.5	54.6	54.5	56.3	57.7	58.5	58.4	57.6
NAFTA (3)	33.8	38.7	37.9	43.1	48.8	49.1	48.4	47.4	46.4	46.1	44.3
MERCOSUR	11.1	7.2	10.9	19.2	20.3	17.9	13.6	14.7	15.2	15.5	15.7
Old EU (15)	60.7	59.8	66.2	64.2	62.3	62.2	62.5	63.0	62.2	60.4	59.5
New EU (27)	61.5	60.0	66.8	66.9	66.3	66.7	67.4	68.1	67.6	66.2	65.8

Notes: [a] Intra-regional trade share is computed as $X_{ii} / [(X_{iw} + X_{wi}) / 2]$, where X_{ii} is the value of intra-regional exports, X_{iw} is the value of total exports of the region to the world, and X_{wi} is the value of total exports of the world to the region.
[b] NIEs = Hong Kong, China; China; Republic of Korea; Singapore; and Chinese Taipei.
[c] ASEAN = Brunei Darussalam, Cambodia, Indonesia, Lao PDR, Malaysia, Myanmar, the Philippines, Singapore, Thailand, and Viet Nam.
[d] ASEAN+3 = ten ASEAN countries, China, Japan, and the Republic of Korea.
[e] ASEAN+6 = thirteen ASEAN+3 countries, Australia, New Zealand, and India.

Sources: IMF Direction of Trade Statistics CD-ROM June 2007). Data for Chinese Taipei from 1989–2006 sourced from the Bureau of Foreign Trade website, and 1980–8 from the *Statistical Yearbook* published by the Directorate-General of Budget, Accounting and Statistics.

Table 11.2 *Emerging East Asia's FDI inflows, 1995–2005 (%)*

| | Source regions/countries of FDI inflows to emerging East Asia | | | | | | |
FDI inflows to:	United States (%)	European Union (%)	Japan (%)	Asian NIEs (%)	ASEAN-9 (%)	Total (%)	(US$ millions)
Asian NIEs	16.8	15.8	8.1	5.2	3.9	100.0	(437,999)
Hong Kong, China	5.1	7.4	5.7	5.3	1.8	100.0	(215,999)
Republic of Korea	22.4	40.1	13.3	4.1	7.4	100.0	(55,975)
Singapore	31.7	19.3	8.5	4.0	5.8	100.0	(142,748)
Chinese Taipei	19.9	13.1	15.5	14.2	2.5	100.0	(23,277)
ASEAN-9	18.4	29.1	19.1	29.2	4.2	100.0	(116,413)
Indonesia	5.7	50.9	3.3	15.0	9.3	100.0	(11,839)
Malaysia	27.4	23.4	13.6	22.0	2.1	100.0	(44,651)
Philippines	23.4	10.3	23.1	16.9	1.1	100.0	(13,709)
Thailand	10.5	10.5	25.1	27.6	0.9	100.0	(37,428)
Viet Nam	4.8	19.1	14.4	39.2	6.6	100.0	(18,225)
China	8.1	8.1	8.6	54.0	1.6	100.0	(537,163)
Total	13.9	14.7	10.5	34.9	3.1	100.0	(992,516)

Note: FDI recipient data compiled by Institute for International Trade and Investment (IITI) are adjusted so that they are consistent with balance of payments figures.

Sources: UNCTAD, *World Investment Report 2006*; IMF, *International Financial Statistics*; ASEAN Secretariat for Singapore and ASEAN9 data; *China Statistical Yearbook* for China data; OECD data for Republic of Korea data; IITI for Hong Kong, China and Chinese Taipei data.

1995–2005. Firms from major industrialized countries, as well as those from within emerging East Asia are the main investors. Indeed, multinational corporations from the European Union (EU), the United States (US), and Japan account for 15 percent, 14 percent, and 11 percent, respectively, of cumulative FDI inflows over the period. More specifically, the largest investors in Asia's newly industrializing economies (NIEs), particularly Singapore and Chinese Taipei, come from the US. In contrast, the EU is the largest developed country investor in ASEAN-9 (which excludes Singapore), particularly in Indonesia and Viet Nam, while Japan is the largest developed country investor in Thailand. However, in Thailand and Viet Nam, Asian NIE firms are the most dominant investors. In the case of China, Hong Kong, China is by far the largest investor.[4] Notable is the rising importance of FDI by Asian NIEs, which accounts for 29 percent of total FDI inflows to ASEAN-9 and 54 percent of total inflows to China. More recently firms from middle-income ASEAN countries, such as Malaysia and Thailand, have also begun to invest in other ASEAN countries and China. Emerging East Asia itself – in addition to the EU, the US, and Japan – has become a very important foreign direct investor in emerging East Asia.[5]

Factors behind trade and FDI integration

There are several factors behind the expansion of trade and FDI and the resulting economic integration of East Asian economies. First, East Asian economies have pursued trade and investment liberalization as part of outward-oriented trade and FDI policies within the multilateral framework under the General Agreement on Tariffs and Trade (GATT)/ World Trade Organization (WTO) and open regionalism through the Asia-Pacific Economic Cooperation (APEC). A key feature is that the region has avoided discriminatory trade practices, and has adopted complementary domestic reforms.

Second, through FDI, global multinational corporations (MNCs), and later local East Asian firms, have formed production networks and supply chains throughout East Asia. This has promoted the dynamic evolution of the intra-regional division of labor and has led to the rise of

---

[4] The large volume of Hong Kong China's FDI flows to China, however, may contain "round-tripping" from China, which aims to take tax and other favorable advantages provided to "foreign" direct investment by China authorities.

[5] If data for the early 1990s and 1980s are included, Japan is seen as a major investor in ASEAN.

vertical intra-industry trade in parts, components, and semi-finished and finished manufactured products.[6] The large inflows of FDI have stimulated the region's use of trade in a way that reflects the individual economies' stages of industrial development. Asian NIEs were the first to join such networks, followed by middle-income ASEAN countries, and later by China and Viet Nam.

Third, improved investment in physical and digital infrastructure has reduced trade and logistics costs, and thus encouraged trade and investment. This has helped the emergence of spatially concentrated clusters of manufacturing firms and supplier networks within East Asia.

Fourth, the rapid growth of the largest emerging market economy, China, has contributed to closer economic linkages within East Asia. China now plays a major role in production networks and supply chains, as its expanding exports require intermediate product imports from its neighbors. India's robust economic growth is also expected to further strengthen regional economic linkages.

All of these factors have led to East Asia's greater economic openness and globalization, which in turn has created a natural (de facto) regional concentration of trade and FDI activities in East Asia. North America and Europe remain important markets for East Asia's finished manufactured products, but with the growth of regional markets, the relative importance of these outside markets has been declining over time.

FTA initiatives in East Asia

Proliferation of FTAs in East Asia

East Asia is a latecomer in the move towards FTAs compared with the Americas, Europe, and Africa, but has seen an unprecedented increase in total FTA activity since the 1990s.[7] Multilateralism through the WTO framework, and open regionalism centered on APEC, were the bedrock of the region's approach to international trade for several decades. Recently, many governments in East Asia have embarked on bilateral

---

[6] See Kawai (1997, 2005b), Kawai and Urata (1998, 2004), Urata (2001), Athukorala (2003), and Fukao et al. (2003).

[7] According to Estevadeordal, Shearer, and Suominen (Chapter 10 of this volume) the first FTAs in Latin America and the Caribbean were several intra-regional customs unions (e.g. the Andean Community, the Central American Common Market, the Caribbean Community and Southern Common Market) formed in the early 1990s. There has been a notable increase in agreements, and three dozen intra-regional FTAs had been notified to the WTO by 2006 (see Fiorentino, Crawford, and Toqueboeuf, Chapter 2 of this volume).

and plurilateral trade arrangements. Notably, Japan has implemented bilateral economic partnership agreements (EPAs) with Singapore, Mexico, Malaysia, Chile, and Thailand; has signed EPAs with the Philippines, Brunei Darussalam, and Indonesia; has reached an agreement in principle with ASEAN; and is negotiating agreements with the Republic of Korea, Viet Nam, India, and Australia.[8] China has implemented an FTA on goods with ASEAN and is now negotiating on agreements on services and investment. The Republic of Korea has also implemented an FTA with Chile and an FTA on goods with ASEAN, and has reached an agreement on an FTA with the US. ASEAN is even more aggressive in pursuing FTAs. While enacting FTAs with China and the Republic of Korea, ASEAN is negotiating with Australia–New Zealand and India, and considering negotiating with the EU. Some ASEAN members, such as Singapore and Thailand, are actively pursuing bilateral FTAs. In this sense, there have been bandwagon effects among the East Asian economies in their drive for FTAs/EPAs. Recently, Australia, New Zealand and India have joined this wave. The timeframe of liberalization schedules of East Asian economies indicates that most of the liberalization measures will have been fully implemented by 2020 (Table 11.3).

China has proposed a Northeast Asian FTA among China, Japan, and the Republic of Korea,[9] as well as an East Asia-wide FTA for ASEAN+3 (ASEAN plus China, Japan, and the Republic of Korea). Japan has also proposed an even bigger regional EPA for ASEAN+6 countries (ASEAN+3 plus Australia, New Zealand, and India). Official studies have been conducted or initiated on the feasibility and desirability of these two East Asian FTAs. However, no timeframe has been proposed for negotiations.

---

[8] The Japanese government promotes EPAs that include, but go beyond, elements of FTAs (elimination/reduction of tariffs and liberalization of services trade). Essentially EPAs (i) ensure free movement of goods, services, and people (mutual abolition of tariffs; development of logistics systems, infrastructure, and simpler customs clearance; services deregulation; and movement of skilled temporary workers and provision of training programs); (ii) facilitate intraregional economic activities (standardization of investment rules and dispute settlements; and harmonization of intellectual property systems, certification systems, and competition laws); and (iii) promote economic cooperation (economic/social infrastructure and cooperation in human resource development, industrial policy, environment, and energy conservation).

[9] Japan is cautious about such an arrangement with China at this point. Its official view is that, before negotiating an FTA/EPA, China must clearly demonstrate compliance with all the commitments made in WTO accession negotiations.

Table 11.3. *Liberalization timeframe for major economic groups in East Asia*

Group/FTA (Year full negotiation complete)	For developed countries	For developing countries	
		For advanced six ASEAN members	For other four ASEAN members
APEC (voluntary and unilateral)	By 2010	By 2020	By 2020
ASEAN (1992)	–	By 2002 (0 percent tariff by 2010) ASEAN Economic Community to be launched by 2015	By 2007 (0 percent tariff by 2015)
ASEAN+China (2010)	–	By 2010	By 2015
ASEAN+Rep. of Korea (2008)	–	By 2009 (excluding Thailand)	By 2015 (flexibility allowed)
ASEAN+Japan (2007)	By 2010	By 2012	By 2017
ASEAN+India (2011)	–	By 2011 (excluding Philippines)	By 2016 (including Philippines)
ASEAN+CER (Australia and New Zealand) (2009)	By 2010	By 2017	By 2017

Source: authors' compilation.

For Northeast Asian economies, these FTA initiatives symbolize a change in their long-standing policy of pursuing trade liberalization only in a multilateral framework based on the WTO and APEC. They decided to pursue trade policy using a three-track approach based on global (WTO-based) cum trans-regional (APEC-based), regional (ASEAN+3 or ASEAN+6), and bilateral liberalization. Regional and bilateral liberalization could achieve deeper integration with trading partners on a formal basis, going beyond reductions in border restrictions – pursuing investment liberalization, promoting greater competition in the domestic market, and harmonizing standards and procedures. The challenge is

Table 11.4. *Growth of FTAs in East Asia, 1976–2008 (cumulative number of FTAs)*

| Year | Number of FTAs | Status of FTAs[a] | | |
		Concluded	Under negotiation	Proposed
1976	1	1	0	0
1986	1	1	0	0
1996	4	3	0	1
2000	7	3	1	3
2001	10	5	2	3
2002	14	6	4	4
2003	23	9	5	9
2004	42	14	16	12
2005	67	21	30	16
2006	96	31	42	23
2007[b]	106	38	40	28

Notes:

[a] Concluded FTAs include those signed and/or under implementation; FTAs under negotiation cover those with or without a signed Framework Agreement; and proposed FTAs include official pronouncements of parties' intentions to negotiate an FTA or actually conduct a feasibility study.

[b] Data as of January 31, 2008.

Source: Compiled from ADB FTA database, Asia Regional Integration Center (www.aric.adb.org).

to maintain an appropriate balance between the regional and bilateral approach and the WTO liberalization framework, which remains an important element of the region's trade policy.

Table 11.4 identifies three types of FTA activity in East Asia by status, during 1976–2008: (i) concluded FTAs (those signed or under implementation); (ii) FTAs under negotiation (those being officially negotiated, with or without a framework agreement being signed); and (iii) proposed FTAs (where parties issued joint statements with the intention of negotiating an FTA, established a joint study group, or conducted a joint feasibility study to determine the desirability of establishing an FTA). By 2000, only three FTAs had been concluded, one was under negotiation, and another three had been proposed.[10] Within seven years, there was a ten-fold increase in FTAs concluded in East Asia and a larger increase in those under negotiation. By the end of January 2008, there were thirty-eight FTAs concluded, forty under negotiation, and twenty-eight proposed. Today, East Asia is at the forefront of FTA activity in Asia, with a total of 106 FTA initiatives at various stages – equivalent to about half of Asia's total FTA initiatives.[11] East Asia makes up two-thirds of FTAs under negotiation in Asia.

Factors underlying FTA initiatives

There are basically three factors behind recent FTA initiatives in East Asia: (i) the deepening of market-driven economic integration; (ii) the progress of European and North American economic integration; and (iii) the Asian financial crisis.[12] First, the most fundamental factor behind the emergence of recent initiatives for FTAs is the progress of regional economic linkages and interdependence. Market-driven economic integration eventually requires policy measures to support and further it – i.e. harmonization of policies, rules, and standards governing trade and FDI. Policymakers in East Asia are increasingly of the view that FTAs, if designed widely in terms of scope, can support expanding trade and FDI activities through further elimination of cross-border impediments, facilitation of trade and FDI, and harmonization of various rules, standards, and procedures. In this way, FTAs can be regarded as part of a supporting policy framework for the deepening production networks and supply chains formed by global MNCs and emerging East Asian firms.

Second, economic regionalism in Europe and North America – including the successful launch of an economic and monetary union by the euro-area countries and the expansion of the EU to its eastern neighbors, as well as the success of NAFTA and its incipient move to the Free Trade Area of the Americas (FTAA) in North, Central, and South America – has motivated the East Asian economies to pursue regional trade arrangements. Governments in East Asia fear that the two giant blocs – the European Union and the United States – might dominate

---

[10] Prior to 2000, the concluded FTAs had been the Bangkok Treaty (1976) which is now known as the Asia-Pacific Trade Agreement (APTA), the Lao PDR–Thailand PTA (1991), and the ASEAN FTA (1992).

[11] As of June 2007, there were 198 FTAs at various stages in Asia. Of these, 90 were concluded, 61 were under negotiation, and 47 were proposed.

[12] More complete explanations can be found in Kawai (2005a).

rule-setting in the global trading system, while marginalizing the role and weight of Asia in global competition and multilateral negotiations. They have increasingly realized the importance of stepping up their own process of integration and uniting to strengthen their bargaining power in the global arena, and raise the region's voice in, and for, global trade issues. In addition, facing the slow progress of the WTO/Doha negotiation process and the perceived loss of steam in the APEC process, FTAs can be considered as an insurance policy against the periodic difficulties with multilateral trade liberalization.

Third, the Asian financial crisis of 1997–8 has taught the important lesson that East Asia needs to strengthen economic cooperation in order to sustain economic growth and stability. The global initiative to strengthen the international economic system in this regard has been unsatisfactory, while the national efforts to strengthen individual economic fundamentals take time to bear fruit. Hence, the general sentiment in Asia has been that the region must establish its own "self-help" mechanism for economic management. The 1997–8 Asian financial crisis nurtured the sense of a "region" with a common set of challenges.

Evolving economic architecture in East Asia

East Asia has seen the development of several key groupings over the last fifteen years, including ASEAN, ASEAN | 3, East Asia Summit (ASEAN+6), APEC, and Asia–Europe Meeting (ASEM).

ASEAN

Until recently, the Association of Southeast Asian Nations (ASEAN), established in August 1967, had been the only formal organization that pursued regional economic integration in East Asia. The ASEAN Declaration stated that it aimed to accelerate economic growth, social progress, and cultural development in the region and promote regional peace and stability. The association has embarked on several economic integration initiatives, including the ASEAN Free Trade Agreement (AFTA), the ASEAN Framework Agreement on Services (AFAS), and the ASEAN Investment Area (AIA). In December 1997, the ASEAN leaders adopted the ASEAN Vision 2020, which envisioned ASEAN as outward-looking, living in peace, stability, and prosperity, and bonded together in partnership in dynamic development in a community of caring societies. In October 2003, the ASEAN leaders adopted the Declaration of ASEAN Concord II (Bali Concord II), whereby they agreed on the establishment by 2020 of an ASEAN Community comprising three pillars, namely, the ASEAN Security Community, the ASEAN Economic Community, and the ASEAN Socio-cultural Community.

The lynchpin of the ASEAN economic integration initiative is AFTA, introduced in January 1992, which aimed to establish an ASEAN Free Trade Area within fifteen years. The Common Effective Preferential Tariff (CEPT) Scheme was introduced as the main mechanism for lowering intra-ASEAN tariffs to the 0–5 percent range.[13] Despite the slow pace of trade liberalization, AFTA has been in effect between the first six signatories – Brunei Darussalam, Indonesia, Malaysia, Singapore, Thailand, and the Philippines – since January 2002 and has successfully reduced tariffs on almost all products in the Inclusion List to the 0–5 percent range. Implementation has been delayed for newer members – for Viet Nam in 2006, Lao PDR and Myanmar in 2008, and Cambodia in 2010. The six original signatories are expected to eliminate tariffs altogether by 2010 and the four latecomers by 2015. By then ASEAN as a whole will become a tariff-free FTA.

The AFAS, signed in December 1995, aims to substantially eliminate restrictions to trade in services among ASEAN members – by progressively improving market access and ensuring equal national treatment – and improve the efficiency and competitiveness of ASEAN services suppliers. The AFAS was amended in September 2003 to allow for the application of the "ASEAN minus x" formula in the implementation of services commitments. Under this formula, member countries that are ready to liberalize a certain service sector may proceed to do so without having to extend the concessions to non-participating countries. The AIA, adopted in October 1998, aims to make ASEAN a more competitive and freer investment area through liberalizing investment rules and policies in protected sectors, and promoting greater flows of capital, skilled labor, professional expertise and technology within the region. The AIA agreement has expanded to cover manufacturing, agriculture, mining, forestry and fishery sectors, and services incidental to these sectors.

The ASEAN Economic Community (AEC), one of the three pillars of the ASEAN Community, is considered to be the realization of the

---

[13] For products not covered by the CEPT Scheme, the ASEAN Preferential Trading Arrangements could be used. The ASEAN Industrial Cooperation Scheme (AICO), introduced in April 1996, applies the CEPT rate of tariffs (0 to 5 percent) on approved AICO products to strengthen industrial cooperation among ASEAN-based companies.

end-goal of economic integration, as outlined in the ASEAN Vision 2020. ASEAN is expected to become a single market and production base by 2020, with a free flow of goods, services and investment, a freer flow of capital, equitable economic development, and reduced poverty and socio-economic disparities.[14] In moving in this direction, new mechanisms and measures are expected to be introduced to: strengthen the implementation of its existing economic initiatives, including the AFTA, AFAS, and AIA; accelerate regional integration in the priority sectors; facilitate movement of business persons, skilled labor and talents; and improve the existing ASEAN Dispute Settlement Mechanism. At the Cebu Summit in January 2007, ASEAN leaders decided to bring the timeframe of the ASEAN Community, including AEC, forward to 2015.

ASEAN+

The leaders of Japan, China and the Republic of Korea were invited to the informal ASEAN leaders' meeting in December 1997, in the midst of the Asian financial crisis, which de facto initiated the ASEAN+3 process. There are many ministerial processes within the ASEAN+3 framework: for foreign affairs, economy and trade, macro-economic issues and finance, environment, energy, health, labor, science and technology, and social welfare, among others. In addition to economic ministers, finance ministers have been particularly active in regional financial cooperation, including the launch of the regional liquidity support arrangement (Chiang Mai Initiative), the regional economic surveillance process, and the Asian bond market development. China regards ASEAN+3 as a natural grouping for East Asia's trade and investment cooperation.

In November 2004 the ASEAN+3 leaders agreed to the establishment of an "East Asian Community" as a long-term objective, and affirmed the role of ASEAN+3 as the main vehicle for this. The idea of creating an "East Asian Community" had been proposed by the East Asia Vision Group (2001).[15] The community's principal aims, relating

---

[14] See Hew and Soesastro (2003) and Hew (2007) for a number of ideas on deepening ASEAN economic integration.

[15] The East Asia Vision Group was established in 1999 under the leadership of Korean President Kim Dae Jung, and the group recommended: (a) economic cooperation, (b) financial cooperation, (c) political and security cooperation, (d) environmental cooperation, (e) social and cultural cooperation, and (f) institutional cooperation.

to economic, trade, and investment integration, can be summarized as follows:

- the establishment of an East Asian Free Trade Area (EAFTA), and liberalization of trade well ahead of the APEC Bogor Goal;
- the expansion of the Framework Agreement on an ASEAN Investment Area (AIA) to all of East Asia;
- the promotion of development and technological cooperation among regional countries, to provide assistance to less-developed countries; and
- the realization of a knowledge-based economy and the establishment of a future-oriented economic structure.

The group had envisioned the progressive integration of the East Asian economies, ultimately leading to an "East Asian economic community." Once a region-wide FTA is formed, covering both trade and investment, and institutions for other types of regional cooperation are established, the basic foundation for an East Asian economic community will have been prepared. In 2002 the ASEAN+3 leaders received the final report of the East Asia Study Group (EASG), which was essentially government officials' responses to the Vision Group's recommendations, and identified seventeen concrete short-term measures and nine medium- to long-term measures to move East Asian cooperation forward. In 2003 the leaders endorsed the implementation of the short-term measures – to be completed by 2007 – and in 2004 encouraged a speedy implementation of the short- and long-term measures of the EASG.

East Asia Summit (ASEAN+6)

One recent, significant development is the November 2004 agreement by ASEAN leaders in Vientiane to convene an East Asian Summit (EAS). The creation of this new forum had been suggested by the East Asia Vision/Study Group, but without a clear view of which countries should be members. The first EAS meeting was held in Kuala Lumpur in December 2005, and the second one in Cebu in January 2007, with the participation of thirteen ASEAN+3 members, as well as Australia, India, and New Zealand. This wider group focuses on issues common to the wider participants, including avian flu, education, energy, finance, and natural disasters. Japan regards ASEAN+6 as an appropriate group for East Asia's trade and investment cooperation.

Future economic cooperation in East Asia, leading to an East Asian economic community, is likely to evolve around the multiple agreements under the ASEAN, ASEAN+1, ASEAN+3 and East Asia Summit (EAS, or ASEAN+6) processes.[16] It is likely that the "ASEAN Economic Community," to be created by 2015, will be the center of East Asian economic cooperation. It is now understood that the core of East Asian cooperation lies in ASEAN as the "driving force," with ASEAN+3 as the "main vehicle" for the realization of an eventual East Asian economic community, with the EAS as "an integral part of the overall evolving regional architecture."

APEC and ASEM as trans-regional forums

APEC, established in 1989, has played a useful role in encouraging trade and investment liberalization in a voluntary and unilateral fashion within an Asia-Pacific context, and includes as members the United States, Canada, and Australia, among others. Australia played a major role in promoting APEC as a trans-regional forum with the basic principle of "open regionalism." One of its most important achievements was to induce the unilateral, voluntary trade liberalization of non-WTO members such as China and Chinese Taipei. In addition, the Bogor Declaration of 1994 set the goal of zero tariffs by 2010 for developed countries, and by 2020 for developing countries. The modality of achieving the Bogor goals was clarified in the so-called Osaka Action Agenda. Nonetheless, APEC's prominence appears to have declined since the Asian financial crisis because of its inability to effectively respond to the crisis, and the recent proliferation of bilateral and sub-regional FTAs pursued by member economies. But the basic principle of "open regionalism," set out by APEC, may remain important if APEC members take APEC – and WTO – principles as a liberalization infrastructure for their FTAs, and attempt to go beyond such basic principles.[17]

The Asia–Europe Meeting (ASEM) was created in 1996 as a forum for Asia–European Union economic cooperation. Its membership initially covered five of the original ASEAN members, plus China, Japan, the Republic of Korea and the EU, but was later expanded to include all ASEAN members, and more recently key South Asian countries such as India and Pakistan. ASEM has not been active as a forum for trade and investment liberalization, as is the case with APEC.

---

[16] The ASEAN+1 processes include ASEAN+China, ASEAN+Japan, ASEAN+Republic of Korea, ASEAN+India, and ASEAN+CER mainly in the form of FTAs or EPAs.

[17] In response to the proliferation of various FTAs in the Asia-Pacific region, APEC agreed to encourage its members to pursue the best-practice model of an FTA.

3   Salient characteristics of East Asian FTAs

There is a dearth of studies which have tried to systematically map the trends and characteristics of East Asian FTAs.[18] This gap in the literature may be due to the recent origin of many East Asian agreements, and the lack of comprehensive regional databases.[19] As part of the international effort to promote the transparency of FTAs in the Asia-Pacific region, the Asian Development Bank (ADB) recently launched the Asia Regional Integration Center (ARIC) FTA database.[20] This section provides an analysis of the trends and characteristics of East Asian FTAs, drawing on information from this database. The following are mapped below: coverage of trade, configuration, geographical orientation, WTO notification, scope (in terms of "WTO-plus" issues), and rules of origin.

The role of larger, richer economies

The recent increase in FTAs has been driven by five of the region's larger and richer economies – Singapore, Japan, the Republic of Korea, China, and Thailand – suggesting a link between FTA growth and economic prosperity. For instance, these five economies were parties to 84 percent of the concluded FTAs in East Asia by the end of January 2008.

Singapore is the most active East Asian economy and has the broadest geographical coverage of agreements. It is a member of AFTA and has implemented or concluded agreements with the largest economies in East Asia (China [through ASEAN], Japan and the Republic of Korea) as well as outside (including the US, India, and Australia). Japan has implemented or concluded agreements with six East Asian countries

---

[18] Recent studies include Bonapace (2005), Feridhanusetyawan (2005), and Chia (2007).

[19] FTA databases which cover East Asian economies include the WTO RTA Gateway (www.wto.org) and the UNESCAP Asia-Pacific Trade and Investment Agreements Database (www.unescap.org/tid/aptiad). Although covering FTA activity throughout the world, the WTO database only provides information on East Asian FTAs notified to the WTO. Concluded agreements not notified to the WTO, and those under negotiation or proposed, are excluded. The UNESCAP database provides summaries of FTAs undertaken by UNESCAP members including some in East Asia.

[20] Launched in October 2006 by ADB, the FTA database (www.aric.adb.org) provides three types of information: (i) statistical tables on the status of FTAs in Asia; (ii) available information on each FTA (i.e. legal documents, official summaries, studies, news, opinions, FTA membership, and an external link to the UNESCAP database); and (iii) a comparative FTA toolkit which enables the comparison of chapters/provisions of concluded Asian FTAs. The information is gathered from official sources, research sites, and online news items.

(Brunei Darussalam, Malaysia, Singapore, the Philippines, Thailand, and Indonesia) and two outside (Mexico and Chile). The Republic of Korea has agreements with APTA, ASEAN, and Singapore within East Asia, and outside with Chile and European Free Trade Agreement (EFTA) countries. It also signed the region's biggest agreement with the US in June 2007. Within East Asia, China has agreements with ASEAN; Hong Kong, China; Thailand (through ASEAN); APTA; and Macao, China; and outside with Chile and Pakistan. Thailand is also a member of AFTA and has agreements with China (through ASEAN), Japan, Lao PDR, Australia, and New Zealand.

With some exceptions, the region's poorer economies (notably, Cambodia, Lao PDR, Viet Nam, the Philippines, and Indonesia) have tended to rely on ASEAN for concluding FTAs with the region's larger economies. This may reflect weak institutional capacity and insufficient resources to undertake FTA negotiations in poorer economies. The ASEAN framework offers the possibility of pooling scarce capacity and resources.

FTA coverage of trade

It is informative to get an idea of how much of a country's trade is covered by FTA provisions.[21] This is difficult to measure accurately because of the exceptions and exclusions contained in many agreements. Furthermore, data on the utilization rates of FTA preferences are hard to come by, and data on the direction of services trade do not exist. Nevertheless, by making the bold assumption that all goods trade is covered by concluded FTAs, estimates can be obtained. Figure 11.1 shows the ratio of a country's bilateral trade with its FTA partners to the country's total trade with the world for 2006. In general, ASEAN members have higher shares than the region's larger economies, indicating a greater reliance on FTAs. Within ASEAN, four countries (Lao PDR, Brunei, Singapore, and Myanmar) have shares in excess of 65 percent while the others have shares in the range of 35 percent to 52 percent. The shares of East Asia's large economies are: the Republic of Korea (46 percent), China (29 percent) and Japan (14 percent). Meanwhile, the share of Hong Kong, China is 46 percent while that of Chinese Taipei is only 0.1 percent. By comparison, others, such as Australia, New Zealand, and India, have shares of under 28 percent.

---

[21] See Fiorentino *et al.* (2007) on this point.

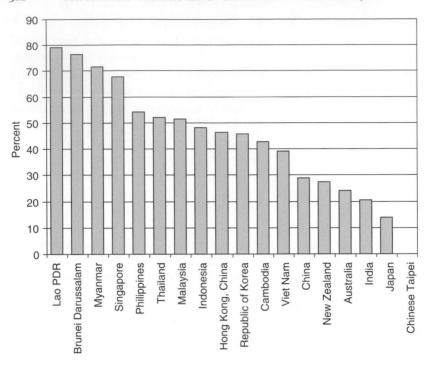

Figure 11.1 Share of an economy's trade with its FTA partners,* relative to the economy's total trade with the world (%), 2006
* Covers concluded FTAs only.

Configuration: bilateral versus plurilateral FTAs

The configuration of FTAs in East Asia can be divided into bilateral and plurilateral, as in Table 11.5. Bilateral FTAs refer to agreements between two countries. Plurilateral FTAs include several forms – agreements involving more than two countries, one country (or countries) and a trading bloc (such as ASEAN), or two trading blocs (e.g. ASEAN–EU).[22]

---

[22] An issue may arise when a trading bloc with a single authority (such as the EU) forms an FTA with a particular country. Though such an FTA may be considered as bilateral, it is plurilateral in our definition, as in the case of the Singapore–EU or Republic of Korea–EFTA FTAs. Other definitions of bilateral and plurilateral FTAs exist in the literature. For instance, Crawford and Fiorentino (2005) define a bilateral agreement as one which may include more than two countries where one of them is a trading bloc itself (e.g. the ASEAN–China FTA) while a plurilateral agreement refers to an FTA in which the

Table 11.5 *Number of FTAs in East Asia, 2008*

FTAs by status[a]	Number of FTAs	By configuration[b]		By geographical orientation[c]	
		Bilateral	Plurilateral	Intra-East Asia	Extra-East Asia
Concluded	38	29	9	13	25
Under negotiation	40	30	10	4	36
Proposed	28	19	9	4	24
Total	106	28	28	21	85

Notes:

[a] See Table 11.4 for definitions.

[b] Bilateral FTAs involve only two parties, while plurilateral FTAs involve more than two parties (e.g. ASEAN).

[c] Intra-East Asia FTAs are those among East Asian economies only, while extra-East Asian FTAs are those between at least one East Asian economy and a partner (or partners) from outside East Asia.

Source: Compiled from ADB FTA database; as of January 31, 2008.

On the whole, countries are opting for simple bilateral FTA configurations rather than the more complex plurilateral ones, as they may be easier to negotiate. As of January 2008, there were twenty-nine bilateral FTAs (i.e. 76 percent of the total) and nine plurilateral FTAs[23] (24 percent of the total) among the thirty-eight concluded FTAs. Bilateral FTAs also dominate FTAs that are yet to be concluded, making up 75 percent of those under negotiation and 68 percent of those proposed.

Among the nine concluded plurilateral agreements, AFTA stands out for its economic importance in the region, and as a natural hub for East Asia's FTA activities. ASEAN has also become a focal point for the emergence of a new category of trading-bloc-to-trading-bloc agreements (e.g. the ASEAN–EU Free Trade Agreement and the ASEAN–Australia

number of FTA partners exceeds two. If we reclassify our data according to this definition, there would be even more bilateral FTAs in East Asia (ninety-two bilateral agreements and eleven plurilateral agreements).

23 They are: APTA; AFTA; the Preferential Trade Agreement–Group of Eight Developing Countries; the Trans-Pacific Strategic Economic Partnership Agreement; the ASEAN–China FTA; the ASEAN–Republic of Korea FTA; the Republic of Korea–EFTA FTA; the Singapore–EFTA FTA; and the Chinese Taipei–El Salvador–Honduras FTA.

and New Zealand Free Trade Agreement). The other concluded plurilateral agreements connect various East Asian countries with others
outside the region. For instance, APTA covers East Asia (China, the
Republic of Korea, and Lao PDR) and South Asia (Bangladesh, India, and
Sri Lanka). There are also ten plurilateral agreements under negotiation
and another eight have been proposed.

Geographical orientation: intra-regional versus extra-regional FTAs

Table 11.5 also shows the geographical orientation of East Asian FTAs
with countries/groups within the region and those outside. The high
degree of extra-regional orientation of East Asian FTAs is striking – in
January 2008, twenty-five out of the thirty-eight concluded FTAs (65
percent of the total) were with countries or groups outside East Asia.
The extra-regional orientation of the East Asian FTAs under negotiation
or proposed is even higher, at 90 percent and 86 percent, respectively.

Both bilateral and plurilateral FTAs exhibit high degrees of extra-
regionalism in a sample of 103 FTAs (including both concluded and
non-concluded FTAs) – twenty-two of the plurilateral agreements and
sixty-three of the bilateral agreements are with countries/groups outside
East Asia. ASEAN as a group is considering negotiations with the
European Union, and has commenced negotiations with India, Australia,
and New Zealand. Singapore has concluded eight extra-regional agreements, with a wide geographical spread from Latin America to the
Pacific. The Republic of Korea, Thailand, China, and Japan have
concluded FTAs with Latin American countries. China has concluded
FTAs with Pakistan and Chile, and is negotiating FTAs with Australia,
New Zealand, the Gulf Cooperation Council, and Iceland. Thus East
Asian economies have a strong preference for maintaining open trading
relations with the rest of the world rather than becoming inward-looking
(Kawai, 2005a).

WTO notification

A breakdown of the 378 concluded East Asian FTAs by WTO notification status shows that 55 percent of concluded FTAs (twenty-one) had
been notified to the WTO by February 2008. This figure is set to rise, as
eleven of the seventeen FTAs not yet notified to the WTO were only
concluded in 2006–7. These findings indicate a significant adherence to
WTO rules and procedures on FTAs in East Asia. In addition, with a

growing tendency to notify East Asian FTAs under the GATT/GATS framework (sixteen concluded), notifications under the Enabling Clause have remained static (five concluded).[24] All fifteen concluded FTAs notified under GATT Article XXIV are also notified under GATS Article V. One interpretation is that East Asian FTAs are getting more comprehensive in scope over time, and extending beyond tariff preferences for some goods into services and regulatory issues.

Scope: "WTO-plus" elements

Studies of FTAs conducted outside East Asia report two interesting findings on their scope (e.g. Crawford and Fiorentino, 2005; World Bank, 2005; Fiorentino et al., 2007): (i) many recent agreements frequently go beyond the WTO regulatory framework to include provisions on a host of issues (trade facilitation, investment, government procurement, competition, intellectual property, environment, and labor, among others); and (ii) FTAs between developed and developing countries often include such provisions, which may reflect the emphasis that developed economies give to these issues. The four "Singapore issues" (trade facilitation, investment, government procurement, and competition policy) were conditionally included in the work program for the Doha Round in November 2001, but were subsequently dropped at the WTO Ministerial Conference in Cancun in 2004. Accordingly, agreements containing such provisions are sometimes referred to in the literature as "WTO-plus" agreements. How prevalent are "WTO-plus" FTAs in East Asia?

Table 11.6 classifies thirty-six concluded FTAs in East Asia into four types according to increasing scope: (i) goods only; (ii) goods and services; (iii) goods, services, and Singapore issues; and (iv) goods, services, Singapore issues, and cooperation enhancement.[25] Cooperation enhancement refers to additional WTO-plus provisions (such as labor standards, IT cooperation, SMEs, and the environment) which are

---

[24] The 1979 Enabling Clause provides for the mutual reduction in tariffs on trade in goods among developing countries. It also allows for developed countries to give a reduction in tariffs to developing countries, but not necessarily on a reciprocal basis. Article XXIV of GATT sets rules for FTAs in the area of goods and Article V of GATS in the area of services.

[25] As of January 2008, there were thirty-eight concluded FTAs in East Asia. However, the Chinese Taipei–Nicaragua FTA and the Chinese Taipei–El Salvador–Honduras FTA could not be included in Table 11.6, as the texts were not available.

Table 11.6 *Scope of concluded FTAs in East Asia, 2001 and 2008*

Scope of FTAs[a]	No. of concluded FTAs		By configuration[b] (January 2008)	
	December 2001	January 2008	Bilateral	Plurilateral
Goods	3	8[f]	4	4
Goods and services	0	3[g]	2	1
Goods, services, and Singapore issues[c]	2	9[h]	7	2
Goods, services, Singapore issues, and cooperation enhancement[d]	0	16[i]	15	1
Total	5	36[e]	28[e]	8

Notes:

[a] Refers to FTA provisions.

[b] Bilateral FTAs involve only two parties, while plurilateral FTAs involve more than two parties (e.g. ASEAN).

[c] Singapore issues include trade facilitation, investment, government procurement, and competition policy.

[d] Cooperation enhancement includes provisions on environment, e-commerce, information exchange, SMEs, and labor standards.

[e] Does not include Chinese Taipei–Nicaragua FTA and Chinese Taipei–El Salvador–Honduras FTA, due to difficulty in accessing the official text of agreements.

[f] Asia-Pacific Trade Agreement (1976), Lao PDR–Thailand Preferential Trading Arrangement (1991), ASEAN Free Trade Agreement (1993), China–Thailand Free Trade Agreement (2003), ASEAN–Republic of Korea Free Trade Agreement (2006), China–Chile Free Trade Agreement (2006), China–Pakistan Free Trade Agreement (2006), and Preferential Tariff Arrangement Group of Eight Developing Countries (2006).

[g] China–Hong Kong, China Closer Economic Partnership Arrangement (2004), China–Macao, China Closer Economic Partnership Arrangement (2004), and ASEAN–China Free Trade Agreement (2005).

[h] Singapore–European Free Trade Association (EFTA) Free Trade Agreement (2001), Singapore–New Zealand Closer Economic Partnership Agreement (2001), Republic of Korea–Chile Free Trade Agreement (2004), Chinese Taipei–Panama Free Trade Agreement (2004), Republic of Korea–European Free Trade Association (EFTA) Free Trade Agreement (2005), Singapore–India Comprehensive Economic Cooperation Agreement (2005), Japan–Malaysia Economic Partnership Agreement (2006), Chinese Taipei–Guatemala Free Trade Agreement (2006), and Japan–Chile Strategic Economic Partnership Agreement (2007).

[i] Japan–Singapore Economic Agreement for a New-Age Partnership (2002), Singapore–Australia Free Trade Agreement (2003), Singapore–United States Free Trade Agreement (2004), Japan–Mexico Economic Partnership Agreement (2005), Singapore–Jordan Free Trade Agreement (2005), Thailand–Australia Free Trade Agreement (2005), Thailand–New Zealand Closer Economic Partnership Agreement (2005), Japan–Philippines Economic Partnership Agreement (2006), Republic of Korea–Singapore Free Trade Agreement (2006), Singapore–Panama Free Trade Agreement (2006), Trans-Pacific Strategic Economic Partnership Agreement (2006), Japan–Brunei Economic Partnership Agreement (2007), Republic of Korea–United States Free Trade Agreement (2007), Japan–Indonesia Economic Partnership Agreement (2007), and Malaysia–Pakistan Free Trade Agreement (2008).

Table 11.7 Coverage of selected 'WTO-plus' East Asian FTAs, 2007

Provisions	Agreement	Japan–Singapore EPA (2002)	Japan–Mexico EPA (2005)	Japan–Philippines EPA (2006)	Japan–Thailand EPA (2007)	Japan–Brunei Darussalam EPA (2007)	Japan–Indonesia EPA (2007)	Rep. of Korea–US FTA (2007)	US–Singapore FTA (2004)	Singapore–Australia FTA (2003)	Thailand–Australia CER FTA (2005)	Thailand–New Zealand CEPA (2005)	Rep. of Korea–Singapore FTA (2006)	Singapore–Jordan FTA (2005)	Singapore–Panama FTA (2006)	Transpacific Strategic EPA (2006)
(A) Goods	**Goods**															
Tariff elimination		■	■	■	■	■	■	■	■	■	■	■	■	■	■	■
ROO		■	■	■	■	■	■	■	■	■	■	■	■	■	■	■
Trade remedies – anti-dumping			■		■	■	■	■			■	■	■	■	■	■
Trade remedies – subsidies and countervailing		■	■	■	■	■	■	■	■		■		■	■	■	■
Trade remedies – bilateral safeguards		■	■	■	■	■	■	■	■	■	■	■	■	■	■	■
Tariff rate quotas			■	■			■		■							
Early harvest program			■				■	■	■							■
Agriculture covered			■	■	■	■	■	■				■	■		■	■
Textiles and apparel			■		■	■	■	■	■							

- Quarantine and SPS measures
- Other NTBs
- Technical barriers to trade
- Standards and conformance, mutual recognition
- Customs administration and procedures
- Paperless trading

(B) Services

Services

- Telecommunications
- Financial services
- Professional services
- Labor mobility/temporary entry of business persons

(C) Singapore issues

Singapore issues

- Trade facilitation
- Investment
- Government procurement
- Competition policy

Table 11.7 (cont.)

Provisions	Japan–Singapore EPA (2002)	Japan–Mexico EPA (2005)	Japan–Philippines EPA (2006)	Japan–Thailand EPA (2007)	Japan–Brunei Darussalam EPA (2007)	Japan–Indonesia EPA (2007)	Rep. of Korea–US FTA (2007)	US–Singapore FTA (2004)	Singapore–Australia FTA (2003)	Thailand–Australia CER FTA (2005)	Thailand–New Zealand CEPA (2005)	Rep. of Korea–Singapore FTA (2006)	Singapore–Jordan FTA (2005)	Singapore–Panama FTA (2006)	Transpacific Strategic EPA (2006)
(D) Cooperation enhancement															
Intellectual property	■	■	■	■	■	■	■	■	■	■	■	■	■		
E-commerce			■	■	■	■	■	■	■	■				■	■
Labor standards/movement of natural persons	■	■	■	■	■	■	■	■		■					■
Environment			■	■	■				■			■		■	■
ECOTECH	■	■	■	■	■				■					■	■
Strategic partnership						■									■
Capacity-building				■		■									
Information exchange				■		■									
Energy						■						■			

	1	2	3	4	5	6	7	8	9	10	11	12	13	14	15
Transport and communications	■	■			■			■				■	■	■	
Construction	■	■											■		
SME	■		■	■											
Trade and investment promotion			■	■	■		■					■	■	■	
Transparency				■	■	■	■	■	■	■	■		■		■
State trading enterprises															
Education				■			■								
(E) Dispute settlement	■	■	■				■	■	■	■	■		■		■
Percentage of goods and services provisions covered (A+B)	68	53	68	79	68	68	89	53	47	53	37	74	42	74	68
Percentage of WTO-plus provisions covered (C+D)	50	45	55	75	75	60	55	45	40	30	40	60	15	45	50

Source: Compiled from ADB FTA database and official documents; data as of October 31, 2007.

included in some agreements along with the Singapore issues. It is noteworthy that the majority of concluded East Asian FTAs in 2008 – twenty-five, or 69 percent of the total – had "WTO-plus" provisions in addition to goods and services provisions. Of these, nine had the Singapore issues only, while another sixteen were even more comprehensive in scope (with both the Singapore issues and cooperation enhancement provisions). This indicates that East Asian economies typically favor comprehensive "WTO-plus" agreements rather than agreements in trade in goods and services only.[26]

Nonetheless, even the most comprehensive East Asian FTAs vary in their coverage of "WTO-plus" provisions, reflecting economic interests, bargaining power, and negotiating capacity. Table 11.7 maps the provisions relating to the four Singapore issues and sixteen categories of cooperation enhancement in fifteen such agreements. With the exception of the Singapore–Jordan FTA, most of these FTAs provide for universal or near-universal coverage of the Singapore issues. The coverage of cooperation enhancement is patchier, but sensitive new issues are reasonably well covered. For instance, intellectual property is included in thirteen FTAs, the environment in ten FTAs, labor standards in nine FTAs and e-commerce in seven FTAs. As a crude summary measure of FTA comprehensiveness, the last row of Table 11.7 also provides the ratio of a given FTA's "WTO-plus" provisions to the total possible "WTO-plus" provisions in the most comprehensive agreement. With ratios in excess of 55 percent, the Japan–Thailand EPA, the Japan–Brunei Darussalam EPA, the Republic of Korea–Singapore FTA, the Japan–Philippines EPA, the Japan–Indonesia EPA, and the Republic of Korea–US FTA have the highest coverage of "WTO-plus" provisions. Meanwhile, the Singapore–Jordan FTA has the lowest. In between (with ratios of 30–50 percent) come the remaining FTAs. Thus international trends towards the expanding scope of FTAs are broadly confirmed in East Asia, but there is still further room to expand "WTO-plus" provisions in existing and new FTAs.

In general, developed countries (Japan, the US, Australia, and New Zealand) seem to prefer a "WTO-plus" format of agreement with

---

[26] Our findings on the comprehensive WTO-plus scope of East Asian FTAs thus confirm those of Banda et al. (2005) for FTAs involving more developed ASEAN members (e.g. Singapore, Thailand, and Malaysia). They observe that FTAs concluded by these countries go beyond WTO disciplines, and deal with competition policy, mutual recognition, movement of persons, investment, and cooperation in specific areas.

developing countries in the region, and sixteen of the "WTO-plus" agreements involve developed and developing countries (see Table 11.6). Many of the FTAs that contain only goods and services trade provisions are basically between developing countries (and the Republic of Korea and Singapore behave much like developing countries when they act together with ASEAN members). Otherwise, the Republic of Korea and Singapore tend to act like developed countries – i.e. they form FTAs with "WTO-plus" elements – when their partners are developing countries.

Multiple rules of origin

Rules of origin (ROOs), which exist to determine which goods will enjoy preferential bilateral tariffs and thus prevent trade deflection among FTA members, are a particularly interesting aspect of East Asian FTAs. For manufactured goods, ROOs may be of three types: (i) a change in tariff classification (CTC) rule defined at a detailed Harmonized System (HS) level; (ii) a regional (or local) value content (VC) rule which means that a product must satisfy a minimum regional (or local) value in the country or region of an FTA; and (iii) a specific process (SP) rule which requires a specific production process for an item.

Table 11.8 provides an overview of the main ROOs adopted by thirty-one concluded FTAs in East Asia.[27] Strikingly, the majority of FTAs in East Asia (twenty-one) have adopted a combination of the three ROOs rather than applying a single rule. Of the remaining FTAs, three use the value-added rule only, another three use the value-added and/or CTC rule, and another four use the value-added and/or SP rule. The simplest ROOs can be found in the AFTA and the ASEAN–China FTA, which specify a 40 percent regional value content across all tariffs. Meanwhile many agreements involving Japan, the Republic of Korea, and Singapore tend to use a combination of ROOs. The latter introduces complexity and additional costs for business.

Further insights are provided by looking at the ROOs applied to the major auto and auto parts products in eleven major concluded FTAs (see Table 11.9). ASEAN's FTAs vary somewhat in their ROOs. For instance, the 40 percent value content rules apply for AFTA and the ASEAN–China FTA, but more stringent ROOs for some products

---

[27] For six of the thirty-seven concluded FTAs, the FTA texts (and hence ROO provisions) were not available.

Table 11.8 *Rules of origin of selected concluded FTAs in East Asia, 2007*

Agreement	Notes	Compared with AFTA (40 percent) VA rule
Value-added rule (VA) only (three FTAs)		
1 Singapore–New Zealand Closer Economic Partnership Agreement (2001)	At least **40 percent** of the cost is of New Zealand or Singapore origin, and the last place of manufacture is in New Zealand or Singapore.	Consistent
2 Singapore–Australia Free Trade Agreement (2003)	For manufactured products: (a) local value-added (VA) content of **50 percent** or (b) VA content of **30 percent** for 114 tariff subheadings. These include electrical and electronic equipment and precision instruments.	Some products more/ less restrictive
3 Singapore–Jordan Free Trade Agreement (2005)	All products, *with the exception of textiles and apparel, goods*, need only fulfill a general rule of origin of a relatively low threshold of **35 percent** local VA content. For textiles and apparel, specific process rules apply.	Less restrictive
VA and/or change of tariff classification (CTC) rules (three FTAs)		
1 Chinese Taipei–Panama Free Trade Agreement (2004)	Regional VA content requirement: **35 percent, 40 percent, 45 percent.**	Some products more/ less restrictive

2 Thailand–New Zealand Closer Economic Partnership Agreement (2005)	Regional VA content requirement: **50 percent.**	More restrictive
3 China–Chile Free Trade Agreement (2006)	Regional VA content requirement: **40** or **50 percent.**	Some products more restrictive
VA and/or specific product rules (four FTAs)		
1 Asia–Pacific Trade Agreement (1976)	Regional VA content requirement: **45 percent** for most products. *Special criteria percentage:* products originating in Least Developed Participating States can be allowed a favorable 10 percentage points applied to the percentages established in rules 3 and 4 of APTA.	More restrictive
2 ASEAN Free Trade Agreement (1993)	Local or regional VA content of **40 percent** or product-specific rule for the following sectors: (a) process criterion for textiles and textile products; (b) change in chapter rule for wheat flour; (c) CTC for wood-based products; (d) CTC for certain aluminum and articles thereof.	Consistent
3 ASEAN–China Free Trade Agreement (2005)	Regional or local VA content of **40 percent** or product-specific rule. Process criterion required for textiles and textile products.	Consistent
4 China–Pakistan Free Trade Agreement (2006)	Regional VA content requirement: **40 percent.**	Consistent

Table 11.8 (*cont.*)

Agreement	Notes	Compared with AFTA (40 percent) VA rule
Combination of all rules (VA, CTC, SP, others) (twenty-one FTAs – selected examples shown)		
1 Japan–Singapore Economic Agreement for a New-Age Partnership (2002)	For manufactured products, change in tariff heading (CTH) for all imported inputs used in the manufacture of the product; Singapore must be the place where the last substantial manufacture takes place. Additional flexibility for 264 products; CTH or local value-added content (VA) of **60 percent.**	More restrictive
2 Singapore–United States Free Trade Agreement (2004)	For manufactured products, (a) CTC for all imported inputs used in the manufacture of the product; Singapore must be the place where the last substantial manufacture takes place; (b) regional value-added content (VA) of **35–60 percent** (applies mainly to electronic products); (c) process rule (applies mainly to chemicals and petrochemicals).	some products more/ less restrictive
3 Rep. of Korea–European Free Trade Association (EFTA) Free Trade Agreement (2005)	Regional VA content requirement: **25 percent, 30 percent, 45 percent, 50 percent, or 60 percent.**	Some products more/ less restrictive

No.	Agreement	Rule of origin	Assessment
4	Singapore–India Comprehensive Economic Cooperation Agreement (2005)	Local VA content requirement: **40 percent.**	Consistent
5	Japan–Mexico Economic Partnership Agreement (2005)	Regional or local VA content requirement: **50 percent, 65 percent,** or **70 percent.**	More restrictive
6	Thailand–Australia Free Trade Agreement (2005)	Regional VA content requirement: **40–45** or **55 percent.**	Some products more restrictive
7	ASEAN–Rep. of Korea Free Trade Agreement (2006)	Regional VA content requirement: **40 percent, 50 percent,** or **60 percent.** Specific manufacturing process for textiles and garments.	Some products more restrictive
8	Trans-Pacific Strategic Economic Partnership Agreement (2006)	A product will qualify for preferential treatment if (a) it meets the specific rule of origin applicable to it (in many cases, this is a liberal CTH rule); or (b) where so stipulated, if at least **45 percent** of the cost originates from the party.	More restrictive
9	Rep. of Korea–Singapore Free Trade Agreement (2006)	Regional VA content requirement: **55 percent.**	More restrictive
10	Japan–Thailand Economic Partnership Agreement (2007)	Regional VA content requirement: **40 percent.**	Consistent
11	Rep. of Korea–United States Free Trade Agreement (2007)	Regional VA content requirement: **35/45 percent; 40/50 percent; 55 percent** (build-up/build-down method).	Some products more/ less restrictive

Table 11.9 *Rules of origin for major auto and auto parts products in selected East Asian FTAs*

FTA	JAPAN			KOREA	CHINA	ASEAN			SINGAPORE		THAILAND
HS Code	Japan–Malaysia EPA (2006)	Japan–Singapore EPA (2002)	Japan–Thailand EPA (2007)	Rep. of Korea–Singapore FTA (2006)	China–Pakistan FTA (2006)	ASEAN Free Trade Area (1993)	ASEAN–China FTA (2005)	ASEAN–Rep. of Korea FTA (2006)	Singapore–Australia FTA (2003)	United States–Singapore FTA (2004)	Thailand–Australia FTA (2005)
Product description											
87.01 Tractors (other than works, warehouse equipment)	CTH (6-digit) or RVC of 40%	CTH; last substantial manufacture	CTH or RVC of 40%	CTH plus RVC of 55%	RVC of not less than 40%	RVC of not less than 40%	RVC of not less than 40%	RVC of not less than 40% or a CTH (4-digits)	VC of not less than 50%	CTH plus RVC of at least 30% (build-up)	CTH plus RVC of 40%
87.03 Motor vehicles for transport of persons (except buses)	CTH or RVC of 60%	CTH; last substantial manufacture	CTH or RVC of 40%	CTH plus RVC of 55%	RVC of not less than 40%	RVC of not less than 40%	RVC of not less than 40%	RVC of 45%	Last process of manufacture within territory of the party	CTH plus RVC of at least 30% (build-up)	CTH plus RVC of 40%
87.04 Motor vehicles for the transport of goods	CTH or RVC of 50%	CTH; last substantial manufacture	CTH or RVC of 40%	CTH plus RVC of 55%	RVC of not less than 40%	RVC of not less than 40%	RVC of not less than 40%	RVC of 45%	VC of not less than 50%	CTH plus RVC of at least 30% (build-up)	CTH plus RVC of 40%

HS	Product											
87.08	Parts and accessories for motor vehicles		CTH; last substantial manufacture	CTH or RVC of 40%	CTH plus RVC of 50; 55%	RVC of not less than 40%	RVC of not less than 40%	RVC of not less than 40%	RVC of 45%	Last process of manufacture within territory of the party	CTH (6-digit) or CTH plus RVC of at least 30% (build-up)	CTH (6-digit) plus RVC of 40%
87.11	Motorcycles, bicycles, etc. with auxiliary motor	CTH or RVC of 60%	CTH; last substantial manufacture	CTH or RVC of 40%	CTH plus RVC of 55%	RVC of not less than 40%	RVC of not less than 40%	RVC of not less than 40%	RVC of not less than 40% or a CTH (4-digit)	VC of not less than 50%	CTH (4-digit) or CTH plus RVC of at least 30% (build-up)	CTH (6-digit) and/or RVC of 40%
87.14	Parts and accessories of bicycles, motorcycles, etc.	CTH or RVC of 40%	CTH; last substantial manufacture	CTH or RVC of 40%	CTC (4-digit)	RVC of not less than 40%	RVC of not less than 40%	RVC of not less than 40%	RVC of not less than 40% or a CTH (4-digit)	VC of not less than 50%	CTH (6-digit) or CTH plus RVC of at least 30% (build-up)	CTH (6-digit)

Notes: The general rules of origin of the FTA are adopted when there is no specific product (SP) rule provided. CTH = change of tariff headings; RVC = regional value content; VC = value content.

Source: Authors' compilation.

(e.g. 45 percent value content for HS 8703, 8704, and 8708) are found in the ASEAN–Republic of Korea FTA. Furthermore, the ROOs for the same products are different in bilateral FTAs involving the same major economy. In the Japan–Malaysia FTA, the value content requirement for HS 8703 and 8711 is 60 percent, while in the Japan–Thailand FTA it is 40 percent for the same two products. Similar instances can be found in the case of the Singapore–Australia FTA and the Thailand–Australia FTA.

Studies of ROOs in East Asia indicate that complex ROOs are associated with increased transaction costs to businesses, and that multiple ROOs in overlapping FTAs are particularly burdensome, giving rise to the famous "noodle bowl" effect.[28] The textile and garment sector is particularly affected by stringent and restrictive ROOs. Precise quantitative estimates of the magnitude of the costs of multiple ROOs (e.g. as a percentage of export sales) are hard to come by. Using a gravity model, Manchin and Pelkmans-Balaoing (2007) obtain results that suggest that the administrative costs of obtaining CEPT status within AFTA might be in the range of 10–25 percent, and that such costs are not much reduced even when an alternative rule for origin determination is provided. One of the implications is that the presence of multiple ROOs may further increase administrative costs.

Results of firm surveys

Firm surveys are useful for highlighting the business impact of multiple ROOs in East Asia. Insights at a regional level are provided by a JETRO survey of Japanese MNCs, which are a major driver of production networks and intra-regional trade (see Table 11.2). Of ninety-seven Japanese MNCs using (or planning to use) FTA preferences in East Asia in 2006, about 30 percent felt that the existence of multiple ROOs leads to increased export costs – either through dealing with complicated procedures to prove country of origin, or because of changes to production processes (JETRO, 2007). Another 33 percent of Japanese MNCs thought that proliferating FTAs and ROOs would lead to increased export costs in the future. Finally, a majority of Japanese MNCs (64 percent) were in favor of the harmonization of East Asia's ROOs, with the largest number (24.7 percent) wanting to be able to choose either the value content rule or the change in tariff classification as the common rule.

---

[28] See, for instance, Cheong and Cho (2007), James (2006) and Lee et al. (2006).

Additional evidence from Thailand (which is at the center of production networks in automobiles and electronics, and has five major FTAs in effect[29]) is available from a 2007 ADB survey of 118 MNCs and domestic firms (Wignaraja *et al.*, 2007). Tariff preference utilization rates in Thai FTAs seem quite high, with about 60 percent of the sample firms using or planning to use preferences. The challenge of dealing with multiple ROOs is apparent, with 22 percent of firms reporting that ROOs in Thailand's FTAs were an obstacle to using FTA preferences, while another 23 percent said ROOs may be a future obstacle. On average, the firms estimated that the business costs (e.g. hiring ROO specialists, or changing production processes) arising from multiple ROOs were less than 1 percent of export sales, which could be significant in highly cost-competitive exports. Interestingly, Thai domestic enterprises (particularly SMEs) seemed more concerned than MNCs about the costs of dealing with multiple ROOs, underlining the MNCs superior access to technical know-how in dealing with ROOs. Accordingly, domestic Thai enterprises argued for enhanced information, training, and technical support from the government and business associations. Finally, firms said that FTAs had an impact on their business plans, with 58 percent reporting that they had changed, or were planning to change, business plans in response to FTAs.

The available evidence suggests that multiple ROOs are beginning to manifest themselves as a problem in East Asia (with a disproportionate effect on domestic firms) and that additional policy and institutional support may be required for enterprise adjustment. There is a need for annual firm-level surveys in East Asia to monitor the business impacts of multiple ROOs and to further the business case for harmonization of ROOs in East Asian FTAs.

4   Policy issues and implications

Maximizing the benefits and minimizing the costs of FTAs

There are both benefits and costs associated with the formation of FTAs. Given that almost all East Asian economies are currently pursuing FTAs, a realistic approach would be to encourage them to design FTAs in such a way as to maximize benefits and minimize potential costs. This

---

[29] These are: the ASEAN FTA, the ASEAN–China FTA, the Thailand–Australia FTA, the Thailand–New Zealand Closer Economic Partnership Agreement, and the India–Thailand FTA (early harvest).

requires FTAs to induce domestic structural reforms and be made consistent with WTO rules.

Benefits and costs of FTA

FTAs, if designed properly, can achieve dynamic gains by generating greater trade and FDI among the members, through the liberalization of trade in goods and services, and the facilitation of trade and FDI market access. FTAs can help achieve deeper economic integration through the "WTO-plus" agreements, including many areas not covered by the WTO negotiations, and areas in which it is difficult to make substantial progress in a multilateral framework (OECD, 2003) – investment provisions, intellectual property rights, labor mobility, environmental issues, and regulatory harmonization. FTAs between FDI source and recipient economies would allow the latter to obtain advanced technologies, connect with external markets, and promote trade, industrialization, employment, and economic growth. These dynamic gains can generate trade and FDI with non-members, as the members grow faster as a result of FTAs. These benefits are great if FTAs can induce difficult domestic structural reforms. Once such structural reforms are pursued, it is much easier for the country to provide greater market access to non-members through WTO or other FTAs.

One of the most serious costs of FTAs is that they discriminate against non-members, particularly small, poor, developing economies which cannot join FTAs because they do not have much to offer, and hence cannot attract the interest of others. The costs of FTA negotiations could also be high for small, poor economies with limited negotiation capacity – such as the CLMV countries (Cambodia, Lao PDR, Myanmar, and Viet Nam) – particularly when gains from FTAs are unevenly distributed across the various participating countries. The proliferation of many overlapping FTAs with different rules of origin and standards can create the risk of Asian "noodle bowls," thereby reducing incentives for businesses to utilize the intended freer trade arrangements. This may in particular, be the case for SMEs, which may face higher administrative and business costs, as their capacity to deal with them is limited.

With or without the success of the WTO Doha Round, trends for more FTAs will continue. This is a reality. Hence, there is an even more urgent need to make FTAs a stepping stone toward the greater liberalization of trade and FDI, and toward further regional, and ultimately global, integration. For this purpose, East Asia needs to design best-practice FTAs so that their benefits can be maximized and their costs minimized. The region must also manage the proliferation of FTAs, so that they function as a means for reducing domestic protection and expanding trade and FDI. For this purpose, FTAs must enforce substantial domestic structural reforms to allow domestic industries to cope with greater competition from abroad.

WTO consistency, breadth, and depth

In addition to domestic structural reforms, each FTA can be made more multilateral-friendly and consistent with GATT Article XXIV and GATS Article V through adopting the lowest tariff rates among members; a wide membership; a comprehensive coverage of liberalization measures (goods, services, investment, and beyond); the elimination of exclusions; simple and non-restrictive rules of origin; and harmonized regulatory and institutional frameworks. In this regard, actions like the APEC Best-Practice Guidelines for FTAs, the various trade and investment harmonization initiatives of ASEAN (e.g. the ASEAN Investment Area), and periodic meetings of ASEAN with outsiders (e.g. the EU and the US) are steps in the right direction toward multilateralizing East Asian FTAs.

One point is worth noting: the larger the number of participating countries in an FTA, and the wider the coverage of liberalization measures and policy issues addressed, the more benefits there are for an FTA. Hence there is a need to broaden FTAs in terms of country coverage, and to do this, aiming for an ASEAN+3 or an ASEAN+6 FTA is proposed. There is also a need to deepen FTAs in terms of liberalization measures and policy issues, and, from this perspective, inclusion of a wide range of trade in goods (both manufactured and agricultural) and services, as well as "WTO-plus" issues – i.e. investment, labor migration, intellectual property rights, competition policy, non-restrictive rules of origin, and dispute settlement – would be preferable.

There usually exists a trade-off between the size and depth of an FTA: that is, as the number of countries participating in an FTA rises, the scope of measures and issues to be addressed in the FTA may be limited. In other words, an FTA with a limited number of countries can relatively easily achieve deep economic integration, while an FTA with a large number of countries may have to compromise on depth. Therefore a good balance must be sought between breadth (the number of participating countries) and depth (the measures to be addressed) in an FTA.

Consolidation into an ASEAN+3 or ASEAN+6 FTA?

The coordination of rules of origin and the harmonization of standards at the global level would be most desirable, and it would be better for all FTAs to be consolidated into a single world-wide FTA to reduce business costs. But given the politically difficult task of global (WTO) trade liberalization, consolidation into a single East Asia-wide FTA could make a significant positive contribution. Then the question is: what is the natural group for East Asian FTA consolidation?

ASEAN is clearly a natural "hub" for the creation of an East Asian FTA, as key production networks are rooted in ASEAN and major economies are linked to ASEAN via ASEAN+1 FTAs. The timeline for the ASEAN Economic Community has also been brought forward from 2020 to 2015. An East Asian FTA could be built upon ASEAN+1 FTAs, and FTAs among subsets of non-ASEAN countries (i.e. Australia, India, Japan, the Republic of Korea, New Zealand, and China) would also be useful in forming a single East Asian FTA with ASEAN as its core.

Our computable general equilibrium (CGE) model results indicate a large income gain from an ASEAN+3 FTA and an even larger gain from an ASEAN+6 (East Asia Summit) FTA – the former yields a gain in world income of US $214 billion compared with US $260 billion for the latter (see Appendix for details). Hence East Asia is recommended to aim for an ASEAN+6 FTA. However, one of the challenges of this approach is likely to be the differing levels of openness and market-orientation of the larger membership. Table 11.10 provides three proxy indicators (average import tariffs, time for import, and time to start a business) to represent openness and market-orientation of the member countries. India is a relative latecomer to economic reforms, which began in the 1990s (see Panagariya, 2004; WTO, 2007) and, as a result, has relatively high import tariffs (15.7 percent) and a longer time is required for importing to take place (forty-one days) than the averages for ASEAN (9.5 percent and thirty-two days, respectively), Northeast Asian economies, or Australia–New Zealand. The time taken to start a business in India (thirty-five days) is also higher than for more developed economies in the region (e.g. Singapore, Japan, the Republic of Korea, Australia, and New Zealand). Accordingly, differences in openness and market-orientation between India and other ASEAN+6 FTA partners could prolong negotiations, and reduce the scope of FTA coverage/liberalization. Further structural reforms in India will be

Table 11.10 *Indicators of openness and market orientation of ASEAN+6 countries, 2005*

Country	Average import tariff rates[a] (manufactures, in %)	Time for import (no. of days)	Time to start a business (no. of days)
Japan	3.49	11	23
Republic of Korea	7.23	12	22
China	10.36	22	35
India	15.67	41	35
Australia	4.20	12	2
New Zealand	4.22	13	12
Brunei Darassalam	5.42	–	–
Cambodia	17.11	45	86
Indonesia	10.10	30	97
Lao PDR	9.88	78	163
Malaysia	11.53	22	30
Myanmar	5.64	–	–
Philippines	7.10	20	48
Singapore	0.00	3	6
Thailand	10.59	22	33
Viet Nam	17.92	36	50
Average for ASEAN	9.53	32	64[b]

Notes:
[a] MFN rate; data as of 2005, except for Republic of Korea (2004) and Cambodia (2003).
[b] Average for ASEAN excluding Lao PDR is 50.
Sources: Compiled from UNCTAD and World Bank data.

required before it can initiate formal ASEAN+6 FTA negotiations. Hence the appropriate sequencing could be to start with an ASEAN+3 FTA and then move to an ASEAN+6 FTA as conditions are created for ensuring sufficient depth of integration within ASEAN+6 countries.

The CGE computation also indicates the negative impact of an ASEAN+3 or ASEAN+6 FTA on the US which, though small, needs to be addressed by maintaining openness. After the completion of an ASEAN+3 or ASEAN+6 FTA, East Asia may be ready to connect itself with North America (as well as with Europe).

Providing complementary support

The ambitious economic integration initiative among ASEAN nations – through the acceleration of the AFTA process and the creation of the ASEAN Economic Community – and the formation of various ASEAN+1 FTAs, and a future ASEAN+3 or ASEAN+6 FTA, would increase the efficiency and competitiveness of ASEAN as a whole, because these arrangements provide the benefit of economies of scale and dynamic efficiency. To be successful, individual ASEAN members need to create favorable climates for competitive, private firms to prosper, while allowing weak, inefficient firms to exit through pro-competition policies, effective insolvency procedures, and a reduction in structural rigidities in their economies. Domestic industrial restructuring is surely needed to enable them to climb up the value-added product ladder. A shift to a knowledge-based economy is crucial for Malaysia and Thailand, and institutional and governance reforms and the restoration of a good investment climate should be priorities for Indonesia and the Philippines.

Low-income ASEAN countries (CLMV; Cambodia, Lao PDR, Myanmar, and Viet Nam) must strengthen the structural, institutional foundations of their economic systems – through building both hard infrastructure, such as transportation and telecommunications facilities, and soft infrastructure, such as legal, judicial, and governance systems – and develop skilled human resources. With its open FDI trade regime, Viet Nam has been following China's development path while still in need of improved governance, rule of law, and institutions for a well-functioning market economy. Though Cambodia is beginning to participate in the regional and global production networks – particularly in textiles and apparel – it must strengthen the fundamental underpinnings of the economy, particularly its legal institutions and public sector, to benefit from WTO entry. Lao PDR faces similar, perhaps more demanding, challenges. Myanmar clearly needs to improve its governance regime.

The international community is encouraged to provide various types of financial and technical support to enable ASEAN countries to cope with such demanding challenges. Many economies need trade-related infrastructure (national or cross-border transport, logistics, etc., for trade expansion); support for trade facilitation and customs modernization, and for enhancing SME trade and finance; and support for capacity-building on trade policymaking, reform, and negotiation. They also need technical support for improving information transparency, and educating businesses and the public about the potential benefits of trade and FDI openness, including through FTAs. The greatest challenge is to narrow the development gaps within ASEAN between its advanced members and its less advanced members (CLMV), so that ASEAN can accelerate its own economic integration process – to forge the ASEAN economic community and deepen its economic relationships with the +3 or +6 countries.

5   Conclusion: challenges ahead

Economic regionalism is taking root in East Asia. The region is becoming highly integrated through market-driven trade and FDI activities, and at the same time FTAs are proliferating. This chapter has argued that consolidation of multiple and overlapping FTAs into a single East Asian FTA can help mitigate the harmful "noodle bowl" effects of different ROOs and standards. This move will encourage the participation of low-income countries in freer trade arrangements, reduce trade-related business costs particularly for SMEs, and promote trade and investment.

The chapter has also suggested that WTO-plus elements need to be further expanded, and that consolidation at the ASEAN+6 level would yield the largest gains to East Asia among plausible regional trade arrangements – while the losses to non-members would be relatively small. For such consolidation to occur, ASEAN must act as the regional "hub" by further deepening ASEAN economic integration; the +3 countries (China, Japan, and the Republic of Korea) need to collaborate more closely; and India needs to pursue further structural reforms. Furthermore, substantial international support is required to strengthen the supply-side capacity of poorer ASEAN countries – including the building of trade-supporting infrastructure (transport, energy, and tele-communications) – so that they can take advantage of integrated regional markets and narrow development gaps within ASEAN.

Relationships with the US (and the EU) are important for the region. For many East Asian economies, the US is the crucial ally from a security perspective, particularly given the geopolitical concerns in the Korean Peninsula. APEC remains important for East Asia and the US because it is the only multilateral economic forum that connects the US with East Asia. A natural approach for East Asia is to strengthen economic ties with the US through the formation of an East Asia–North

America Free Trade Area FTA (or an APEC FTA). While several East Asian countries have agreed bilateral FTAs with the US, some have reservations about a comprehensive agreement with the US. Deeper questions also remain as to whether the US is ready to agree an FTA with East Asia – including China – and whether the US trade promotion authority (which expired in June 2007) will be extended.

While the consolidation of FTAs within East Asia is clearly desirable, and its eventual connection with the US (and Europe) will be on the next agenda, it is important for the East Asian economies to make their bilateral and plurilateral FTAs more multilateral-friendly. They can do so by further pursuing some of the positive practices they have taken over the years and adopting some innovative measures:

- the unilateral reduction of MFN tariffs (such as through APEC);
- the coordination of dates of completion of various FTAs in the region, with phased elimination of exclusions, particularly in small, poor countries;
- the inclusion of as many WTO-plus elements as possible in FTAs, with the formation of a wider investment area;
- the adoption of simpler ROOs (such as a 40 percent regional VC rule);
- periodic consultation of the plurilateral group with outsiders to coordinate on trade and FDI issues; and
- allowing cumulation of VC requirements across countries that conclude FTAs with each other.

References

Athukorala, P.-C. (2003) "Product Fragmentation and Trade Patterns in East Asia," Working Paper No. 2003/21 (October), Canberra: Division of Economics, Research School of Pacific and Asian Studies, Australian National University.

Baldwin, R. (2006) 'Multilateralising Regionalism: Spaghetti Bowls as Building Blocks on the Path to Global Free Trade', *The World Economy* 29 (11): 1451–518.

    (2007) "Managing the Noodle Bowl: The Fragility of East Asian Regionalism," ADB Working Paper Series on Regional Economic Integration No. 7, Manila: Office of Regional Economic Integration, Asian Development Bank.

Banda, O., Dayaranta, G. and Whalley, J. (2005) "Beyond Goods and Services: Competition Policy, Investment, Mutual Recognition, Movement of Persons, and Broader Cooperation Provisions of Recent FTAs involving

ASEAN Countries," NBER Working Paper Series 11232 (March), Cambridge, MA: National Bureau of Economic Research.

Bchir, M. H. and Fouquin, M. (2006) "Economic Integration in Asia: Bilateral Free Trade Agreements Versus Asian Single Market," CEPII Discussion Papers No. 15 (October), Paris: Centre d'Études prospectives et d'Informations internationales.

Bonapace, T. (2005) "Free Trade Areas in the ESCAP Region: Progress, Challenges and Prospects," in Asian Development Bank (ed.), *Asian Economic Cooperation and Integration: Progress, Prospects, and Challenges*, Manila: Asian Development Bank, pp. 95–122.

Cheong, I. (2005) "Estimation of Economic Effects of FTAs in East Asia – CGE Approach," in Choong, Yong Ahn, R. Baldwin, and I. Cheong (eds.), *East Asian Economic Regionalism: Feasibilities and Challenges*, Dordrecht: Springer, pp. 139–55.

Cheong, I. and Cho, J. (2007) "Market Access in FTAs: Assessment Based on Rules of Origin and Agricultural Trade Liberalization," RIETI Discussion Paper Series 07-E-016 (March), Tokyo: Research Institute of Economy, Trade and Industry.

Chia, Siow Yue (2007) "Whither East Asian Regionalism? An ASEAN Perspective," mimeo (April), Singapore: Singapore Institute of International Affairs.

Crawford, J.-A. and Fiorentino, R. (2005) "The Changing Landscape of Regional Trade Agreements," WTO Discussion Paper 8 (May), Geneva: World Trade Organization.

East Asia Study Group (2002) "Final Report of the East Asia Study Group," ASEAN+3 Summit (November 4), Phnom Penh, Cambodia.

East Asia Vision Group (2001) "Toward an East Asian Community: Region of Peace, Prosperity and Progress," East Asia Vision Group Report.

Feridhanusetyawan, T. (2005) "Preferential Trade Agreements in the Asia-Pacific Region," IMF Working Paper WP/05/149 (July), Washington, DC: International Monetary Fund.

Fiorentino, R. V., Verdeja, L., and Toqueboeuf, C. (2007) "The Changing Landscape of Regional Trade Agreements: 2006 Update," WTO Discussion Paper 12 (May), Geneva: World Trade Organization.

Francois, J. F. and Wignaraja, G. (2007) "Pan-Asian Integration: Economic Implications of Integration Scenarios," mimeo, Manila: Office of Regional Economic Integration, Asian Development Bank.

Francois, J. F., McQueen, M., and Wignaraja, G. (2005) "European Union–Developing Country FTAs: Overview and Analysis," World Development 33 (10): 33–10.

Fukao, K., Hikari Ishido, and Keiko Ito (2003) "Vertical Intra-industry Trade and Foreign Direct Investment in East Asia," *Journal of the Japanese and International Economies* 17(4): 468–506.

Gilbert, J., Scollay, R., and Bora, B. (2004) "New Regional Trading Developments in the Asia-Pacific Region," in Shahid Yusuf, M. Anjum Altaf and Kaoru Nabeshima (eds.), *Global Change and East Asian Policy Initiatives*, Washington, DC: World Bank, pp. 121–90.

Hew, D. (ed.) (2007) *Brick by Brick: The Building of an ASEAN Economic Community*, Singapore: Institute of Southeast Asian Studies.

Hew, D. and Soesastro, H. (2003) "Realizing the ASEAN Economic Community by 2020 – ISEAS and ASEAN-ISIS Approaches," *ASEAN Economic Bulletin*, 20 (3): 292–6.

James, W. E. (2006) "Rules of Origin in Emerging Asia-Pacific Preferential Trade Agreements: Will PTAs Promote Trade and Development?," ARTNeT Working Paper Series, No. 19 (August), Bangkok: Asia-Pacific Research and Training Network on Trade, UNESCAP.

Japan External Trade Organization (JETRO) (2007) *FY2006 Survey of Japanese Firms' International Operations*, Tokyo: JETRO.

Joint Export Group (JEG) (2006) "Towards an East Asia FTA: Modality and Road Map," a report by Joint Expert Group for Feasibility Study on EAFTA, Jakarta: ASEAN.

Kawai, M. (1997) "Japan's Trade and Investment in East Asia," in D. Robertson (ed.), *East Asian Trade after the Uruguay Round*, Cambridge: Cambridge University Press, pp. 209–26.

(2005a) "East Asian Economic Regionalism: Progress and Challenges," *Journal of Asian Economics* 16 (1): 29–55.

(2005b) "Trade and Investment Integration and Cooperation in East Asia: Empirical Evidence and Issues," in Asian Development Bank (ed.), *Asian Economic Cooperation and Integration: Progress, Prospects, and Challenges*, Manila: Asian Development Bank, pp. 161–93.

Kawai, M. and Urata, S. (1998) "Are Trade and Direct Investment Substitutes or Complements? An Empirical Analysis of Japanese Manufacturing Industries," in Hiro Lee and David W. Roland-Holst (eds.), *Economic Development and Cooperation in the Pacific Basin: Trade, Investment, and Environmental Issues*, Cambridge: Cambridge University Press, pp. 251–93.

(2004) "Trade and Foreign Direct Investment in East Asia," in Gordon de Brouwer and Masahiro Kawai (eds.), *Economic Linkages and Implications for Exchange Rate Regimes in East Asia*, London: Routledge Curzon, pp. 15–102.

Kawai, M. and Wignaraja, G. (2007) "ASEAN+3 or ASEAN+6: Which Way Forward?," ADB Institute Discussion Paper No. 77, Tokyo: Asian Development Bank Institute.

Lee, C. J., Hyung-Gon Jeong, HanSung Kim, and Ho Kyung Bang (2006) "From East Asian FTAs to an EAFTA: Typology of East Asian FTAs and Implications for an EAFTA," Policy Analyses 06-01 (December), Seoul: Korea Institute for International Economic Policy.

Lee, J. W. and Park, I. (2005) "Free Trade Areas in East Asia: Discriminatory or Non-Discriminatory?," *World Economy* 28 (1): 21–48.

Manchin, M. and Pelkmans-Balaoing, A. O. (2007) "Rules of Origin and the Web of East Asian Free Trade Agreements," World Bank Policy Research Working Paper 4273 (July), Washington, DC: World Bank.

Mohanty, S. K., Sanjib Pohit, and Saikat Sinha Roy (2004) "Towards Formation of Close Economic Cooperation among Asian Countries," RIS Discussion Papers 78 (September), Delhi: Research and Information Systems for the Non-Allied and Other Developing Countries.

Organization for Economic Co-operation and Development (OECD) (2003) *Regionalism and Multilateral Trading System*, Paris: OECD.

Panagariya, A. (2004) "India in the 1980s and 1990s: A Triumph of Reforms," IMF Working Paper WP/04/43, Washington, DC: International Monetary Fund.

Piermartini, R. and Teh, R. (2005) "Demystifying Modelling Methods for Trade Policy," WTO Discussion Paper 10 (September), Geneva: World Trade Organization.

Plummer, M. G. and Wignaraja, G. (2006) "The Post-Crisis Sequencing of Economic Integration in Asia: Trade as a Complement to a Monetary Future," *Économie Internationale* 107, pp. 59–85.

Urata, S. (2001) "Emergence of an FDI-Trade Nexus and Economic Growth in East Asia," in J. Stiglitz and S. Yusuf (eds.), *Rethinking the East Asian Miracle*, New York: Oxford University Press, pp. 407–59.

Urata, S. and Kiyota, K. (2003) "Impacts of an East Asian FTA on Foreign Trade in East Asia," NBER Working Paper Series 10173 (December), Cambridge: National Bureau of Economic Research.

Wignaraja, G. (2003) "Competitiveness Analysis and Strategy," in G. Wignaraja (ed.), *Competitiveness Strategy in Developing Countries*, London: Routledge, pp. 15–60.

Wignaraja, G., Rosechin Olfindo, Wisarn Pupphavesa, Jirawat Panpiemras, and Sumet Ongkittikul (2007) "Impact of Free Trade Agreements on Business Activity: Thailand Country Study," Manila: Asian Development Bank.

World Bank (2005) *Global Economic Prospects 2005: Trade, Regionalism and Development*, Washington, DC: World Bank.

World Trade Organization (WTO) (2007) *Trade Policy Review – India. Report by the Secretariat*, Geneva: World Trade Organization.

Appendix: CGE analysis of East Asian FTA scenarios

A growing body of empirical literature has been developed on the impact of prospective FTAs on East Asian economies using computable general equilibrium (CGE) models in response to advances in CGE models and policy interest in alternative FTA arrangements. This literature includes contributions by Urata and Kiyota (2003); Mohanty *et al.* (2004), Gilbert *et al.* (2004), Cheong (2005), Bchir and Fouquin (2006), Plummer and Wignaraja (2006) and Zhang *et al.* (2006). These studies commonly use the Global Trade Analysis Project (GTAP) database, but vary in the underlying model and behavior of agents, the policy scenarios analyzed and the version of the database used.[30] While there has been some CGE work on an ASEAN+3 FTA and other alternatives, only limited work is available on the effects of an ASEAN+6 FTA, or a comparison between an ASEAN+3 and an ASEAN+6 FTA. Furthermore, such work tends to focus narrowly on an FTA involving goods only, while other aspects of the coverage of East Asian FTAs (e.g. services and trade costs) are excluded. There is a need for a more comprehensive set of CGE estimates on East Asian FTAs to fill these gaps. Accordingly, a CGE exercise was undertaken by ADB, using a variant of the GTAP model.[31] The model is characterized by an input–output structure (based on regional and national input–output tables) that explicitly links industries in a value-added chain from primary goods, over continuously higher stages of intermediate processing, to the final assembling of goods and services for consumption. Inter-sectoral linkages are both direct, such as the input of steel in the production of transport equipment, and indirect, via intermediate use in other sectors. The model captures these linkages by modeling the use made by firms of factors and intermediate inputs. The key aspects of the model are as follows: (i) it covers world trade and production; (ii) it includes intermediate linkages between sectors; and (iii) it allows for trade to affect capital stocks through investment activities. The final point means that medium- to long-run investment effects are captured in the model.

The main database used is the GTAP dataset version 6.3, which included detailed national input–output, trade, and final demand structures. This database was projected through to 2017 trade and production patterns to represent a post-Uruguay Round world. The coverage of FTA provisions is a stylized FTA that includes goods, services, and some aspects of trade cost reduction. Hence the analysis

---

[30] For a review of East Asian FTA studies, see Kawai and Wignaraja (2007).

[31] The CGE estimates for the ASEAN+3 FTA scenario reported in this chapter draw on a modeling exercise for an ADB project "Study on Economic Cooperation between East Asia and South Asia." The ASEAN+6 sccnario was specifically computed for this chapter. For more details of the CGE model used, see Francois and Wignaraja (2007).

includes the impact of regional tariff elimination for goods, the liberalization of services trade, and trade facilitation, including improved trade-related infrastructure. Forward projection of the database, and extending the coverage of FTAs beyond goods, are recent developments in the CGE FTA studies.

Based on this CGE framework, five East Asian FTA scenarios are considered:

1. an ASEAN+China FTA: free trade among the ten ASEAN members and China;
2. an ASEAN+Republic of Korea FTA: free trade among the ten ASEAN members and Republic of Korea;
3. an ASEAN+Japan FTA: free trade among the ten ASEAN members and Japan;
4. an ASEAN+3 FTA scenario: free trade among the ten ASEAN members, Japan, and Republic of Korea;
5. an ASEAN+6 FTA scenario: free trade among the ten ASEAN members, China, Japan, Republic of Korea, India, Australia, and New Zealand.

The five scenarios selected represent a range of FTA possibilities in East Asia. Scenarios 1–3 are FTAs between ASEAN and each of the Northeast Asian countries. Scenarios 1 and 2 have been concluded, while scenario 3 is under negotiation (see Table 11.A2). Scenarios 4 and 5 represent ongoing discussions among policymakers on region-wide FTAs. Based on bridging ASEAN and the region's Northeast Asian neighbors, scenario 4 was an early attempt at an East Asia-wide FTA. Scenario 5 has emerged with the realization that the synergies could be gained by linking Australia–New Zealand and India with ASEAN+3.

Table 11.1A shows the estimated impacts on national income of the FTA scenarios. The two East Asia-wide FTA scenarios – ASEAN+3 FTA and ASEAN+6 FTA – offer larger gains to world income than any of the three ASEAN+1 FTA scenarios. The ASEAN+6 FTA scenario – which is broader in terms of country coverage – offers the larger gains to world income (US$260 billion, measured in constant 2001 prices) than the ASEAN+3 FTA scenario (US$214 billion). Looking separately at the ASEAN+1 scenarios, the ASEAN+China FTA scenario indicates larger gains (US$82 billion) to world income than the other two ASEAN+1 scenarios.

A breakdown of the world income figure for the ASEAN+6 FTA scenario indicates that the gains to members of the FTAs are significant

(US$285 billion), while the losses to non-members are relatively small (US$25 billion). Similarly, in the ASEAN+3 scenario, the gains for members are large, at US$228 billion, while losses to non-members are only US$14 billion. Hence, insiders gain and outsiders lose relatively little from the formation of an ASEAN+3 or an ASEAN+6 FTA.

The ASEAN+3 and ASEAN+6 FTA scenarios have different impacts on regions and countries. The three Northeast Asian economies (members of all proposed FTAs) are expected to see the largest gains under the ASEAN+3 FTA (US$166 billion) and the ASEAN+6 FTA (US$172 billion).[32] The ASEAN economies (also members of the proposed FTAs) experience the largest gains from the ASEAN+China FTA (US$44 billion) among the three ASEAN+1 FTAs, and obtain further gains from the ASEAN+3 FTA (US$62 billion) and the ASEAN+6 FTA (US$67 billion). The projected gains for ASEAN members as a percentage change from a 2017 baseline income are substantial under the ASEAN+6 scenario – Thailand 12.8 percent; Viet Nam 7.6 percent; Malaysia 6.3 percent; and Singapore 5.4 percent. Among the Northeast Asian countries, Republic of Korea (6.4 percent) experiences larger gains than Japan or China.

India, Australia, and New Zealand experience either gains or losses, depending on whether an ASEAN+3 FTA or an ASEAN+6 FTA is formed. They experience losses in the ASEAN+3 scenario and gains in the ASEAN+6 scenario. Under the ASEAN+6 scenario, the projected gains as a percentage change from a 2017 baseline income are 2.4 percent for India, 3.9 percent for Australia, and 5.2 percent for New Zealand.

The impact of the ASEAN+3 or ASEAN+6 FTAs on third parties is limited, with a few exceptions (such as Chinese Taipei). There are small losses (typically less than 1 percent change from a 2017 baseline income) for the rest of South Asia, the rest of Oceania, Central Asia, and the US and Russia. Meanwhile, there are small gains for the EU, Canada, Mexico, and sub-Saharan Africa.

The estimated wage effects for unskilled workers (see Table 11.2A) are a rough measure of the distributional impact of the FTA scenarios.

---

[32] Our findings confirm those of previous CGE studies that, under an ASEAN+3 scenario, Northeast Asian economies and ASEAN gain significantly. For instance, Zhang et al. (2006) report gains of US$67 billion for Japan, Republic of Korea, and China and US$38 billion for ASEAN economies. Cheong (2005) finds gains of US$42 billion for the three Northeast Asian economies and US$20 billion for ASEAN.

These are to some degree related to the income gains for members under the alternative scenarios. In the ASEAN+6 scenario, Thailand, Republic of Korea, Viet Nam, Singapore, and Malaysia – with relatively large income effects – experience relatively large unskilled wage increases (between 5 and 12 percent). Several other countries (e.g. Japan, China, Indonesia, the Philippines, and India) – with relatively smaller income effects – witness unskilled wage increases of under 2 percent. Unexpectedly, however, Cambodia, Australia, and New Zealand see small declines in unskilled wages. Outsiders to the agreements also experience small declines in unskilled wages.

CGE simulation studies are useful in quantifying the income effects of eliminating import tariffs on trade in goods and liberalizing cross-border trade in services through the formation of an FTA. As they are unable to incorporate rules of origin and non-tariff measures (e.g. TBT) which may afford more protection for domestic industries than tariffs, CGE studies are best when combined with an analysis of the complex structure of FTAs and enterprise perception studies of the benefits of FTAs.[33]

---

[33] See François *et al.* (2005) and Piermartini and Teh (2005).

Table 11.1A Income effects of alternative scenarios compared to 2017 baseline (at constant 2001 dollars)

	ASEAN+China FTA		ASEAN+Japan FTA		ASEAN+Rep. of Korea FTA		ASEAN+3 FTA[a]		ASEAN+6 FTA[b]	
	Value ($ millions)	Percentage change	Value ($ millions)	Percentage change	Value ($ millions)	Percentage change	Value ($ millions)	Percentage change	Value ($ millions)	Percentage change
Northeast Asia	**9,756**	**0.11**	**18,624**	**0.21**	**7,256**	**0.08**	**165,720**	**1.85**	**172,087**	**1.93**
Japan	−3,965	−0.08	24,943	0.51	−1,308	−0.03	74,825	1.54	77,137	1.59
Republic of Korea	−5,382	−0.67	−1,844	−0.23	10,916	1.37	49,393	6.19	51,351	6.43
China	19,103	0.58	−4,475	−0.14	−2,351	−0.07	41,502	1.26	43,598	1.33
ASEAN	**44,211**	**3.72**	**28,831**	**2.43**	**8,088**	**0.68**	**62,186**	**5.23**	**67,206**	**5.66**
Cambodia	68	0.75	30	0.33	15	0.16	107	1.20	109	1.21
Indonesia	6,924	2.30	2,834	0.94	1,475	0.49	7,884	2.62	8,588	2.86
Malaysia	7,551	4.02	4,453	2.37	1,339	0.71	10,391	5.54	11,869	6.33
Philippines	2,556	2.13	1,915	1.59	630	0.52	3,177	2.64	3,431	2.85
Singapore	6,854	4.13	3,171	1.91	793	0.48	7,943	4.79	9,002	5.43
Thailand	16,324	7.39	14,107	6.39	2,640	1.20	26,728	12.10	28,346	12.84
Viet Nam	3,371	4.68	2,119	2.94	1,136	1.58	5,293	7.35	5,490	7.63
Others	563	0.50	203	0.18	60	0.05	661	0.59	370	0.33

Other East Asia	**−2,676**	**−0.30**	**−1,124**	**−0.13**	**−528**	**−0.06**	**−11,649**	**−1.32**	**−13,530**	**−1.54**
Hong Kong, China	−112	−0.03	−68	−0.02	−73	−0.02	−1,051	−0.33	−1,900	−0.59
Chinese Taipei	−2,519	−0.49	−1,093	−0.21	−443	−0.09	−10,493	−2.03	−11,527	−2.23
Others	−44	−0.11	38	0.0⊓	−12	−0.03	−105	−0.25	−102	−0.24
South Asia	**−1,059**	**−0.09**	**−823**	**−0.07**	**−530**	**−0.05**	**−3,620**	**−0.32**	**17,193**	**1.52**
Bangladesh	−85	−0.08	−62	−0.06	−47	−0.04	−297	−0.26	−418	−0.37
India	−809	−0.10	−658	−0.08	−370	−0.05	−2,371	−0.30	19,270	2.42
Pakistan	−162	−0.11	−83	−0.06	−86	−0.06	−824	−0.55	−1,179	−0.79
Sri Lanka	−21	−0.07	−15	−0.05	−22	−0.07	−117	−0.38	−209	−0.67
Others	19	0.05	−4	−0.0⊓	−5	−0.01	−12	−0.03	−271	−0.73
Oceania	**1,326**	**0.20**	**−1,272**	**−0.19**	**−26**	**0.00**	**−2,600**	**−0.38**	**26,385**	**3.88**
Australia	1,046	0.18	−1,204	−0.2⊓	−9	0.00	−2,376	−0.41	22,546	3.91
New Zealand	166	0.21	−73	−0.09	12	0.02	−216	−0.27	4,136	5.24
Others	114	0.48	5	0.02	−28	−0.12	−8	−0.03	−296	−1.25
Central Asia	**70**	**0.04**	**−41**	**−0.02**	**−26**	**−0.01**	**−159**	**−0.09**	**−205**	**−0.11**
NAFTA	**9,985**	**0.06**	**−214**	**0.0⊓**	**273**	**0.00**	**−235**	**0.00**	**−4,474**	**−0.03**
Canada	1,211	0.12	363	0.04	155	0.02	1,796	0.18	1,546	0.15
United States	7,713	0.05	−782	−0.01	287	0.00	−4,966	−0.03	−8,917	−0.06
Mexico	1,062	0.11	205	0.02	−169	−0.02	2,935	0.31	2,897	0.30
Latin America	**2,667**	**0.13**	**−109**	**−0.01**	**−303**	**−0.01**	**−2,082**	**−0.10**	**−2,958**	**−0.14**

Table 11.1A (*cont.*)

	ASEAN+China FTA		ASEAN+Japan FTA		ASEAN+Rep. of Korea FTA		ASEAN+3 FTA[a]		ASEAN+6 FTA[b]	
	Value ($ millions)	Percentage change	Value ($ millions)	Percentage change	Value ($ millions)	Percentage change	Value ($ millions)	Percentage change	Value ($ millions)	Percentage change
EU27	12,921	0.11	867	0.01	253	0.00	6,786	0.06	1,806	0.02
Sub-Saharan Africa	604	0.15	68	0.02	8	0.00	396	0.10	457	0.12
Rest of the world	4,193	0.13	326	0.01	−292	−0.01	−824	−0.03	−4,130	−0.13
EFTA	874	0.17	193	0.04	94	0.02	1,089	0.21	1,074	0.21
Turkey	−17	−0.01	−90	−0.03	−143	−0.05	−538	−0.19	−713	−0.25
Russia	438	0.09	135	0.03	75	0.01	−197	−0.04	−333	−0.07
Other Europe	−36	−0.04	−19	−0.02	−21	−0.02	−52	−0.06	−85	−0.10
North Africa and Middle East	2,761	0.17	119	0.01	−299	−0.02	−1,083	−0.07	−3,549	−0.22
South Africa	172	0.10	−13	−0.01	1	0.00	−44	−0.03	−524	−0.32
World	**81,998**	**0.17**	**45,134**	**0.09**	**14,173**	**0.03**	**213,919**	**0.45**	**259,837**	**0.54**

Notes: [a] ASEAN+3 includes the ten ASEAN members (Brunei Darussalam, Cambodia, Indonesia, Lao PDR, Malaysia, Myanmar, Philippines, Singapore, Thailand, and Viet Nam) and China, Japan, and the Republic of Korea.
[b] ASEAN+6 includes ASEAN+3 countries, +Australia, India, and New Zealand.
Source: ADB estimates.

Table 11.2A *Unskilled workers' wage effects of FTA scenarios, percentage change compared to 2017 baseline (at constant 2001 dollars)*

	ASEAN+3 FTA[a]	ASEAN+6 FTA[b]
Northeast Asia		
Japan	1.79	1.77
Republic of Korea	9.33	9.26
China	1.83	1.80
ASEAN		
Cambodia	−1.07	−1.14
Indonesia	1.67	1.53
Malaysia	4.91	5.00
Philippines	0.65	0.69
Singapore	4.64	5.58
Thailand	11.07	11.95
Viet Nam	7.96	8.24
Others	−0.53	−1.41
Other East Asia		
Hong Kong, China	−0.62	−0.64
Chinese Taipei	−1.97	−2.02
Others	−0.44	−0.46
South Asia		
Bangladesh	0.44	0.97
India	−0.19	1.66
Pakistan	−0.15	−0.25
Sri Lanka	−0.26	0.52
Others	0.00	−2.47
Oceania		
Australia	−0.69	−0.74
New Zealand	−0.60	−0.60
Others	−0.49	−0.50

Notes:

[a] ASEAN+3 includes ASEAN members, China, Japan, and Republic of Korea.

[b] ASEAN+6 includes ASEAN+3 countries, Australia, India, and New Zealand.

Source: ADB estimates.

Comment

INKYO CHEONG

Overlapping FTAs in East Asia and estimation
of an East Asian FTA

According to Kawai and Wignaraja (Chapter 11), as of June 2007 a total
of 102 bilateral FTAs were being promoted, of which 36 were already
concluded (implemented), 41 were still under negotiation and 25 were
under discussion. The growing adoption of FTAs is a global trend and
East Asian countries have been the most active in this respect for the
past several years. Prior to the year 2000, however, the development of
regionalism in East Asia was slow.

An accurate estimation of the economic effects of East Asian FTAs
requires that the major FTAs are reflected in the calculations. A com-
putational general equilibrium (CGE) model is generally used in the
estimation of the economic effect of FTAs. The various FTAs concluded
in East Asia overlap with one another. Bilateral FTAs concluded between
the ASEAN and China, Japan and the Republic of Korea after 2004 had a
considerable impact on the overall economic effect of the East Asian
FTAs. As pointed out in Cheong (2007), in estimating the economic
effect, most studies assume that EAFTA is to be the first FTA in the
region. The Kawai and Wignaraja study may overestimate the effects of
an EAFTA.

Which country will lead economic integration in East Asia?

Only in terms of economic power can it be accepted that Japan plays the
natural role of the hub of East Asia. East Asian countries have relied on
the Japanese market, but recently their reliance on the Chinese market
has been growing. Baldwin (2003) focuses on ASEAN countries' high
reliance on Japan for their exports. However, most ASEAN countries'
exports to Japan are not accounted for by native companies, but by
Japan-based companies' exports to their own country (i.e. intra-company

trade). Also, Japan has the lowest tariff level in the world for manufacturing goods, but it cannot actively push for an FTA because of its agricultural protection policy. Although Japan is a major economic power and an advanced country, it is passive in reform and liberalization, and has been left behind by China and the Republic of Korea in pursuing FTAs. Regarding this point, Fukagawa (2007) states that, 'After [Japan's] economic recovery, complacency prevails to allow traditional protectionism to survive in Japan.'

As discussed above, the entire size of the ASEAN economy is relatively small in East Asia and its internal consolidating power is weak, making it hardly fit to be an FTA hub, and currently China and the Republic of Korea also have weaknesses that prevent them from becoming a hub. However, China, which is expected to surpass Japan and have an economy similar in size to that of the United States in the next twenty years, has the potential to develop into an FTA hub. A country that has expanded its economy, encouraged a market system, and undertaken many other economic reforms can truly become the hub.

Although no particular country in East Asia currently plays the role of an FTA hub, the region is not necessarily unfavourably placed to build an East Asian FTA. In case any particular country becomes the hub, that country could reinforce diplomatic trade efforts to perpetuate a hub–spoke system and to maintain profits as the hub. However, if the three countries of Northeast Asia, namely China, Japan and the Republic of Korea, which account for 90 percent of the East Asian economy, should conclude an FTA, or if two of them form a bilateral FTA, then they could jointly become the FTA hub.

ASEAN+3 versus ASEAN+6

With regard to pushing forward with the creation of an East Asian FTA, one of the newly debated issues is the range of member countries. Traditionally, ASEAN+3 countries have held a regular summit meeting, but since 2003 Japan has been proposing that the US, Canada, India, Australia, New Zealand, and others should also be included. Also, some countries among these non-East Asian countries have wished to participate in the meeting on East Asian economic cooperation. Australia, New Zealand and India participated in the East Asian summit for the first time at the meeting held in 2006.

Scholars may define the East Asian region in different ways, but it is generally defined as thirteen countries, that is, the ASEAN 10 countries and China, Japan and the Republic of Korea. These countries have discussed East Asian economic cooperation since 1997. Whether or not Chinese Taipei and Hong Kong, China have been included can be seen as a reflection of China's position.

Also, in the East Asian FTA expert conference in 2005–6, the issue of ASEAN+3 versus ASEAN+6 was debated. Japanese scholars proposed ASEAN+6, which was seriously criticized by experts from several countries. The Japanese proposal was not accommodated, but since then Japan has been studying East Asian economic integration in the form of ASEAN+6. One of Japan's arguments for the proposal of the ASEAN+6 is that Australia, New Zealand and India are closely connected with the East Asian economy. Kawai and Wignaraja present quantitative estimates including these countries in an East Asian FTA. They contended that ASEAN+6 would be economically more favourable for integration in East Asia than ASEAN+3.

If East Asian FTA member countries are selected based on economic linkages, the US, rather than these countries, should be included. Also, if the number of member countries increases, or the range of FTA member countries is expanded, it is natural that the economic effects will also become bigger. Larger economic effects could be expected from the inclusion of the US rather than the three countries mentioned above. Some have suggested that East Asian countries, which depend heavily on the US, can hardly conclude any EAFTA while excluding the US. Li (2007) states that 'the US has not participated in the East Asian regional economic cooperation, but East Asia is of strategic importance to the US and it can't afford doing nothing in the process'. As Singapore's former Prime Minister Goh Chok Tong mentioned in a speech in 2003, 'Without the US, East Asian regionalism will, over time, be dominated by one player' and 'Embedding the US in East Asian regionalism is a strategic as well as economic imperative.'

The increase in the number of member countries would not only make decision-making more complex, but also trigger competition for the FTA hub. It is not desirable that the number of member countries should increase when an EAFTA has not yet been fully formed. It would be more realistic to recommend that these countries join after arrangements for pushing forward an EAFTA have been determined, and the proposed hub has been formed.

In this regard, during the drive for the creation of the EAFTA, it can also be considered whether all the ASEAN+3 countries should join from the beginning. As East Asian countries differ in many respects, a gradual expansion strategy should be adopted after an FTA among some of these countries has been concluded. In this process, doors will be open to Australia, New Zealand and India as well, and for additional economic effects, the US can be included among the member countries.

References

Baldwin, R. E. (2003) 'Asian Regionalism: Promises and Pitfalls', Geneva: Graduate Institute of International Economics.

Bhagwati, J. (1992) 'Regionalism versus Multilateralism', *The World Economy* 15 (5): 535–56.

Cheong, I. (2005) 'The FTA Approach towards East Asian Economic Integration: Progress and Challenges', in Vo Dai Luc and Do Hoai Nam (eds.), *Towards East Asian Economic Community*, Hanoi: The Gioi Publisher.

(2007) 'Two Bloc Hubs vs. a Super Bloc Hub in East Asia: Qualitative and Quantitative Assessment', presentation to the third Conference of East Asian Institutes Forum on 'East Asian Economic Integration: Recent Development and Key Agenda' organized by the KIEP, 29 October 2007/ COEX, Seoul, Republic of Korea.

Fukagawa, Y. (2007) 'Regional Integration and Next Step of KORUS FTA: Japan's View', Eighth World Knowledge Forum, Seoul, October.

Kimura, F. (2007) 'Production Networks and De Facto Integration in East Asia', presented at KIET Symposium on 'Change in East Asian Production Network and the Future of Korea Manufacturing Industries', 1 July.

Li, W. (2007) 'China in the World's Regional Economic Cooperation Trend', Eighth World Knowledge Forum, Seoul, October.

Yu, S.-L. and Jeong, S.-T. (2007) 'An Analysis on the ASEAN–Korea, China, Japan FTA Effects in Korea Steel Industry', *Journal of Korea Research Society for Customs* 8 (3): 247–63 (in Korean).

12

Fitting Asia-Pacific agreements into the WTO system

GARY HUFBAUER AND JEFFREY SCHOTT[1]

1 Introduction and overview

It is commonplace to note the proliferation of customs unions (CUs), free trade agreements (FTAs) and kindred arrangements, often collectively called preferential trade agreements (PTAs). In fact, the number of agreements concluded between 2000 and 2007 (185) is just under half the number of agreements concluded during the twentieth century (374).[2] These figures can be found in Table 12.1. In addition to being a chronological summary, this table provides a breakdown of PTAs by region. Countries in Europe (not including the Former Soviet Union) have concluded the most agreements (232) to date. Countries in the Americas have concluded the second most agreements (166). If we consider the Asia-Pacific region (Americas, East and South Asia, and Oceania) as a unit, the total number of concluded agreements (234) matches that of Europe.

Figure 12.1 shows the web of PTAs in force and proposed in the Asia-Pacific region. The figure distinguishes between agreements that are already in place (solid lines) or under consideration (dashed lines), and names the member countries in each arrangement. As Figure 12.1 illustrates, many of the existing and proposed agreements overlap. In the

---

[1] Jisun Kim and Matthew Adler, both research assistants at the Peterson Institute, made extensive and valuable contributions to this chapter. Dean A. DeRosa carried out the gravity model analysis reported in the second section. This chapter has been financed by the State Secretariat for Economic Affairs (SECO). The views expressed in the chapter are the opinions of its authors and do not necessarily reflect the views or positions of SECO and Switzerland, nor the views of the Peterson Institute or its staff.

[2] See Table 12.1. This figure of 374 PTAs includes agreements that have either lapsed or have been superseded. Moreover, the figure includes agreements that both have and have not been notified to the World Trade Organization. Much of our analysis here focuses on agreements that have been (or presumably will be, if enacted) notified to the WTO.

Table 12.1 *Concluded bilateral and plurilateral trade agreements*[a]

	Africa[b]	Americas	East and South Asia	Oceania	Europe	Former Soviet Union	Mideast[b]	World
Twentieth century	**52**	**111**	**17**	**8**	**156**	**95**	**54**	**374**
1913–54	4	2	0	0	3	0	1	10
1955–74	19	16	3	3	29	1	9	57
1975–89	14	45	7	4	21	1	12	78
1990–9	15	48	7	1	103	93	32	229
Twenty-first century								
2000–7	24	55	37	6	76	24	38	185
Memorandum								
Total	76	166	54	14	232	119	92	559

[a] Agreements are classified into regions of its parties. Agreements involving parties from different regions are recorded for each region. The world total figure corrects the double counting implicit in the regional values. Reshaped agreements are counted as new agreements.
[b] Agreements of North African countries from Morocco to Egypt are counted in both regions.
Source: The underlying data is available from the World Trade Institute, Bern, Switzerland.

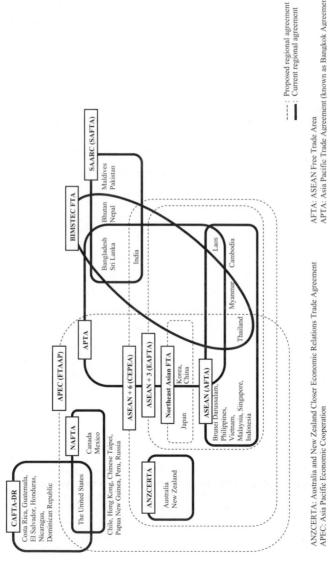

ANZCERTA: Australia and New Zealand Closer Economic Relations Trade Agreement
APEC: Asia Pacific Economic Cooperation
ASEAN: Association of Southeast Asian Nations
CAFTA-DR: Central America Free Trade Agreement and the Dominican Republic
EAFTA: East Asia Free Trade Area
NAFTA: North American Free Trade Agreement
SAFTA: South Asian Free Trade Area

AFTA: ASEAN Free Trade Area
APTA: Asia Pacific Trade Agreement (known as Bangkok Agreement)
BIMSTEC: Bay of Bengal Initiative for Multi-Sectoral Technical and Economic Cooperation
CEPEA: Comprehensive Economic Partnership in East Asia
FTAAP: Free Trade Area of the Asia-Pacific
SAARC: South Asian Association for Regional Cooperation

Figure 12.1 Current and proposed regional agreements in the Asia-Pacific region

extreme case, the United States and other members of the Asia Pacific Economic Cooperation (APEC) forum have vetted a Free Trade Area of the Asia Pacific or FTAAP that would cover all APEC members but not South Asian countries (notably India, Pakistan, Bangladesh, and Sri Lanka).

To keep the picture manageable, Figure 12.1 omits relatively small regional agreements in the Asia-Pacific region, such as the Melanesian Spearhead Group (MSG) and the Pacific Islands Countries Trade Agreement (PICTA). Moreover, the size of each "box" has nothing to do with the collective commercial importance of the countries. For example, NAFTA is the largest existing Asia-Pacific arrangement in terms of trade volume and GDP, but it is represented by a small box in Figure 12.1.

The following sections examine the extent of trade and investment under PTAs for selected countries and regions within the Asia-Pacific region.[3] The data underlying this discussion are provided in Appendix Tables 12.1A and 12.2A.[4] For easy reading, Tables 12.2 and 12.3 summarize the appendix tables. We conclude this overview with a summary of APEC initiatives on FTAs.

The US hub

NAFTA, which entered into force in 1994, is by far the largest free trade agreement in the Asia-Pacific region. In 2005, NAFTA covered about 30 percent of total US merchandise trade (imports plus exports) and about 70 percent of total Canadian and Mexican merchandise trade. About 14 percent of inward and outward US FDI stocks are covered by NAFTA and over 60 percent of FDI stocks based in Canada and Mexico. To this day, NAFTA serves as the reference point and basic template for US free trade agreements.

---

[3] A detailed gravity model analysis of the effects of FTAs on trade and investment in the Asia-Pacific region is provided later in this chapter.

[4] These tables do not include smaller FTAs (e.g. the agreement between China and Macao, China). Also, to organize our discussion of trade agreements in the Asia-Pacific area, we distinguish between larger countries – which we label "dominant partners," with apologies to the ode of political correctness – and their trade agreement partners. Our tables enumerate six dominant countries: the United States, China, Japan, ASEAN, Republic of Korea, and India. For this purpose, ASEAN is treated as if it were a single country; thus trade between ASEAN member states is ignored. In addition, the FTAs between dominant partners are covered in the entries for both dominant partners in Appendix Table 12.1A.

Table 12.2 *Percentage of two-way merchandise trade covered by FTAs under various scenarios*[a]

| Dominant country | Scenario 1 Covered by FTAs in force | | Scenario 2 Covered by FTAs in force, signed and under negotiation | | Scenario 3 Covered by FTAs in force, signed, under negotiation and under consideration[b] | | |
| | | | | | | Partner countries | |
	Dominant country	Partner countries	Dominant country	Partner countries	Dominant country	Only with dominant country	With all parties in the FTAAP
United States	32.9	46.7	39.4	35.0	61.9	45.2	84.4
China	19.3	17.9	21.4	16.8	62.5	17.8	60.8
Japan	6.1	5.7	21.8	11.1	66.1	13.9	57.0
ASEAN[c]	19.0	8.4	41.4	10.7	67.0	11.6	60.5
Korea, Rep. of	10.4	6.0	40.1	3.6	64.8	6.1	51.6
India	6.3	3.1	11.3	1.2	40.1	1.5	49.7

Notes:
[a] Based on Appendix Table 12.1A. When a dominant country has an FTA with a partner country both bilaterally and plurilaterally, the trade share of a partner country is taken into account only once.
[b] We include a possible FTAAP. We consider the FTAAP not as an independent partner, but as a group of plurilateral partners. In the denominator, total FTAAP trade with the world includes intra-FTAAP trade among partner countries.
[c] We consider ASEAN as one dominant partner, and do not include intra-ASEAN trade in total ASEAN trade with the world.

Table 12.3 *Percentage of two-way FDI stocks covered by agreements under various scenarios*[a]

Dominant country	Scenario 1 Covered by FTAs in force		Scenario 2 Covered by FTAs in force, signed and under negotiation		Scenario 3 Covered by FTAs in force, signed, under negotiation and under consideration[b]	
	Dominant country	Partner countries	Dominant country	Partner countries	Dominant country	Partner countries
United States	20.0	57.0	22.2	53.6	31.3	39.0
China	53.5	23.1	53.6	19.1	73.5	6.9
Japan	5.0	7.1	11.7	11.0	69.5	6.7
ASEAN[c]	15.8	7.1	32.6	6.5	85.1	4.2
Korea, Rep. of	5.6	1.6	50.3	0.9	68.0	1.7
India	6.4	0.4	22.3	0.4	81.5	0.2

Notes:

[a] Based on Appendix Table 12.2A. When a dominant country has an FTA with a partner country both bilaterally and plurilaterally, the FDI stock of a partner country is taken into account only once.

[b] We include a possible FTAAP.

[c] We consider ASEAN as one dominant partner and do not include intra-ASEAN FDI stocks.

Stimulated by NAFTA, leaders throughout the western hemisphere met in Miami in December 2004 to launch work on a Free Trade Area of the Americas (FTAA). They promised to complete FTAA negotiations by 2005, but that date has come and gone. The FTAA fell victim both to the widespread backlash against globalization and to the fundamentally different perspectives in Brazil and the United States.

Meanwhile, the United States has pursued other dimensions of its free trade strategy. In 1993, President Clinton convened the thirteen APEC leaders to Blake Island, Seattle, for the first APEC economic leaders' meeting. This summit elevated the priority of US economic relations in the Asia-Pacific region. Since then, the United States has advanced various plans for promoting Asia-Pacific trade liberalization.

In 2002, the Bush administration narrowly secured Congressional approval of a "fast-track" negotiating authority, renamed Trade Promotion Authority (TPA).[5] Using TPA, the Bush administration signed free trade agreements with Chile (in force in 2004), Singapore (in force in 2004), Australia (in force in 2005), five Central American countries and the Dominican Republic (CAFTA–DR, with El Salvador, Honduras, Nicaragua, Guatemala, and the Dominican Republic in 2006, and ratified by Costa Rica in October 2007), Morocco (in force in 2006), Bahrain (in force in 2006) and Oman (approved by Congress in 2006, but not yet in force) and with Colombia, Peru, Panama and the Republic of Korea (all awaiting ratification). Considering each partner in these agreements, only the US–Republic of Korea FTA and the US–Singapore FTA individually cover more than 1 percent of US merchandise trade. Only the US–Singapore FTA and the US–Australia FTA cover more than 1 percent of total US FDI stocks. As a share of trade and investment, the agreements are of course far more important to the partner countries.

The central purpose of TPA was to conclude the Doha Round under the auspices of the World Trade Organization (WTO). However, the Doha talks have marked time, with little progress despite six years of negotiation. Meanwhile, the Bush administration views bilateral and regional FTAs as part of a "competitive liberalization" strategy – pushing

---

[5] This fast-track negotiating authority gives the president of the United States power to negotiate agreements that the Congress can only vote for or against without amendment. Fast-track provisions were included in the Trade Act of 1974 and subsequent legislation from 1975 to 1994, and were restored in 2002 by the Trade Act of 2002. The authority expired in June 2007.

reluctant countries either to join their own bilateral free trade arrangements, or commit to liberalization in the Doha Round.

The United States is the country most interested in advancing the Free Trade Area of the Asia-Pacific region (FTAAP). Within the United States, Peterson Institute Director C. Fred Bergsten is the most vocal proponent. Given the prospect for shallow WTO results, or a complete breakdown of WTO negotiations, Bergsten has argued that the world needs a "plan B" to revive the liberal trade agenda, and considers the FTAAP the best available alternative for this purpose (Bergsten, 2007). If created, the FTAAP would become the world's largest free trade area – covering about 60 percent of US two-way trade (Table 12.2) and roughly 30 percent of total US FDI stocks (Table 12.3).

The China hub

Since its WTO accession in 2001, China has concluded bilateral trade agreements with countries around the world. However, China sees these agreements more as a tool for building diplomatic relations than as a means of boosting commerce. This explains why Chinese FTAs are much less comprehensive than US FTAs and often exclude provisions on intellectual property, services, investment, and social issues (labor and environment).

China initially pursued FTAs with territories and countries that have strong political and geographical ties, namely Hong Kong, China; Macao, China; and ASEAN. China then expanded its list of potential partners to strengthen relations with natural resource suppliers (such as Chile) and to enhance its position in world affairs. China's potential FTA partners include: New Zealand, Australia, Singapore, Japan, Republic of Korea, India, Mexico, and Peru. China is considering the FTAAP, though not with the same level of interest as the United States. Not shown in Appendix Table 12.1A, China also has FTAs either under negotiation or under consideration with the Gulf Cooperation Council (GCC), Iceland, and South Africa, mainly to advance its goal of security of access to energy and natural resources.

The FTAAP would cover about 63 percent of Chinese two-way trade and about 74 percent of Chinese FDI stocks. With the exception of the Hong Kong, China agreement, other Chinese agreements cover no more than 10 percent of its trade or investment. The agreement with Hong Kong, China covers roughly 10 percent of China's two-way merchandise trade and roughly 46 percent of its FDI stocks. The agreements, in percentage terms, are more important for China's partners, with the qualified exception of Hong Kong, China. While the agreement is more important to Hong Kong, China than to China for merchandise trade, it covers roughly half of China's FDI stocks, but only about a quarter of Hong Kong, China's.

China's surge has increased competition both within East Asia and across the Asia-Pacific region. Other countries have altered their FTA policies accordingly. If the last decade was an era of proliferation of FTAs within the Asia-Pacific region, the next decade could become an era of triangular consolidation of spheres of influence, colored by competition between the three major powers, the United States, China, and Japan.

The Japan hub

Until very recently, the sole focus of Japan's external economic policy was the multilateral trading system, under the auspices of GATT and the WTO. The Asian financial crisis and the global proliferation of FTAs prompted Japan to alter its historic opposition to preferential trade agreements. Even so, Japan is joining the FTA race late compared to the European Union and the United States.[6] The Abe cabinet pushed for regional integration and the Economy and Fiscal Council launched a project team to accelerate the conclusion of FTAs. It remains to be seen whether Prime Minister Fukuda will continue these initiatives.

Japan has tilted its FTA policy by pursuing a high level of market opening in manufacturing, services, and investment, while resisting the liberalization of agriculture or fisheries. The balance between bilateral and multilateral negotiations continues to influence the timing and speed of Japan's FTA negotiations: Japan is anxious that FTA negotiations should not undercut the Doha Round.

Japan has four FTAs in force, with Singapore, Mexico, Malaysia, and Chile. Collectively they cover about 6 percent of Japan's total two-way trade and about 5 percent of its total FDI stocks. Japan has signed FTAs with Thailand, Indonesia and Brunei Darussalam (not in force as of October 2007). Japan is currently negotiating agreements with the Republic of Korea and ASEAN. These agreements would cover 6 percent

---

[6] Japan's first FTA, with Singapore in 2002, preceded China's first FTA, with Hong Kong, China, in 2004. Since then, however, China has embraced a more active FTA policy than Japan.

and 13 percent of Japanese trade, respectively, and 2 percent and 8 percent of Japanese investment, respectively. Japan is also considering a broader East Asian agreement among sixteen countries as a way-station to an Asia-Pacific pact. An FTAAP would cover 66 percent of Japanese trade and roughly 70 percent of Japanese investment.

From the beginning, Japan has given priority to the ASEAN region in its FTA policy; this reflects Japan's substantial investments in the region, and its reliance on ASEAN resources. Japan has used trade agreements to strengthen these ties, to further political security in Southeast Asia, and to forestall China from becoming the only serious commercial partner for the ASEAN group.

The ASEAN hub

ASEAN was created in 1967 with five members (Indonesia, Malaysia, the Philippines, Singapore, and Thailand). Subsequently, ASEAN has added five new members (Brunei Darussalam, Viet Nam, Lao PDR, Myanmar and Cambodia), which has brought large disparities in economic development levels between the ten constituent countries, complicating the process of regional economic integration. In its early decades, the main purpose of ASEAN was to end guerilla wars between the founding members, and thereby enhance the security of Southeast Asia. Over the past decade, the members have put more emphasis on internal economic ties; moreover, since 2000, ASEAN has pursued FTAs with large trading partners, namely Japan, China, Republic of Korea, and Australia–New Zealand (CER). Individual ASEAN countries have also pursued agreements with the United States. While ASEAN's external FTA policy seeks to expand trade and investment, ASEAN has been very careful to ensure that its external FTAs do not undermine its internal integration efforts. In October 2003, the member states of ASEAN signed the Bali Concord II, which reiterates ASEAN's commitment to creating a stable, prosperous and highly competitive ASEAN economic region. In August 2007, the ASEAN ministers issued a declaration calling for the elimination, by 2015, of market access barriers on the establishment of a commercial presence in the service sector. When accomplished, this will greatly liberalize FDI in the service industries.

Currently, ASEAN has two FTAs in force, with China and the Republic of Korea (only for goods), which cover 13 percent and 6 percent of ASEAN's total external two-way trade respectively, and roughly 14 percent and 2 percent of its FDI stocks. ASEAN is considering arrangements that would expand the free trade zone to include the Republic of Korea (for services), and Japan (ASEAN+3). Under this scenario 37 percent of current ASEAN trade would be covered, along with 32 percent of ASEAN FDI stocks. ASEAN is also considering the FTAAP; if created, the FTAAP would cover 67 percent of ASEAN's external two-way trade and 85 percent of its FDI stocks. In geopolitical terms, ASEAN would benefit from an FTAAP, since the arrangement would, to some extent, balance the major powers (the United States, China, and Japan), and give ASEAN more scope for playing the role of "honest broker" between Asia-Pacific powers.

The Republic of Korea hub

Over the course of five decades, the tactics of Korean trade policy have changed significantly, but engagement with the world economy has always been the driving force in the Republic of Korea's economic ascent. During the post-Korean War period of the 1960s, the Republic of Korea adopted an outward-looking strategy focusing on export growth. This was a departure from the import-substitution strategies then popular among other developing countries.

Following its accession to the GATT in 1967, the Republic of Korea became a vocal supporter of the multilateral trading system. It has flirted with a bilateral US deal on several occasions over the past two decades, due to concerns about trade diversion resulting from the US–Canada FTA and the NAFTA. Each time preliminary consultations stalled over the inclusion of agriculture. By the late 1990s, however, the global proliferation of RTAs, coupled with the Asian financial crisis, shifted the focus of Korean policy toward regionalism.[7] FTA initiatives have now become a major pillar of the Republic of Korea's trade policy. The main objective of Korean FTA policy is to address the competitive challenges of China and India, and to counter the adverse demographic trends facing Korean society over the next generation (Schott, Bradford and Moll, 2006).

Currently the Republic of Korea has three FTAs in force – with Chile, Singapore, and ASEAN (for goods only). Together, these cover about 10 percent of the Republic of Korea's total two-way trade and roughly 6 percent of its FDI stocks. In June 2007, the Republic of Korea signed an FTA with the United States. If ratified, it will cover about 13 percent

---

[7] See WTO (2004).

of the Republic of Korea's total two-way trade and roughly 33 percent of its FDI stocks. If extended into an FTAAP, the resulting pact would cover about 65 percent of the Republic of Korea's total two-way trade and roughly 67 percent of its FDI stocks.

The Republic of Korea's roster of current and potential FTA partners spreads broadly across the world; it is negotiating FTAs with the European Union, Canada, and Japan and pursuing FTAs with the Persian Gulf countries and MERCOSUR to secure energy supplies.

The India hub

In the mid 1990s, after decades of mediocre performance, India began to reform its internal economic regulation and reduce its sky-high tariffs. At the same time, knowledge-based industries took off – especially information technology (IT) services and pharmaceuticals. India has now become the new emerging power in the world, gaining much attention in commercial and financial circles.

India's FTA policy historically emphasized the South Asia region, but, since the early 1990s, India has adopted a "Look East" policy, attempting to strengthen ties with East Asia. India has ten trade agreements in force, and several of them overlap in terms of partner countries: a non-reciprocal agreement with Nepal; a preferential trade agreement with Afghanistan; four FTAs with Singapore, Sri Lanka, Bhutan, and SAFTA;[8] and five "framework" agreements – those with BIMSTEC,[9] Thailand, ASEAN, Singapore, and Bangladesh. Except for the framework agreement with ASEAN, which accounts for 9 percent of India's two-way trade, the trade agreements with other partners cover small shares of India's two-way trade, ranging from zero to 4 percent.

---

[8] The South Asian Association for Regional Cooperation (SAARC) was established in 1985 with seven members (Bangladesh, Bhutan, India, the Maldives, Nepal, Pakistan, and Sri Lanka). The South Asian Free Trade Area (SAFTA) among SAARC members was launched in 2006. SAFTA is a traditional trade agreement, which covers tariffs, rules of origin, safeguards, institutional structure, and dispute settlement. So far the extent of liberalization within SAFTA is limited. For more details, see Appendix A in Hufbauer and Burki (2006).

[9] The Bay of Bengal Initiative for Multi-Sectoral Technical and Economic Cooperation (BIMSTEC) is a sub-regional grouping with seven members (Bangladesh, India, Myanmar, Sri Lanka, Thailand, Bhutan, and Nepal). It was created in June 1997, with four initial members: Bangladesh, India, Sri Lanka, and Thailand (BIST-EC or BIST-Economic Cooperation). After three new members (Myanmar, Nepal, and Bhutan) joined, its name was changed to BIMSTEC.

Moreover, these agreements are riddled with exceptions, so that trade between India, Pakistan, and Bangladesh is far more restricted by barriers than, for example, trade between India and Europe.

India is eager to join APEC, but existing members have their reservations; in any event, no new members will be considered until 2010 at the earliest. From a geopolitical standpoint, China would find it hard to put out the welcome mat; from an economic standpoint, the United States is not enthusiastic about a new APEC member that maintains some of the highest trade barriers in the world. Unless India dramatically changes its commercial policy, and reaches a geopolitical accommodation with China, India will not be invited to join APEC or the FTAAP. However, as an alternative to participation in a regional pact, India is pursuing bilateral FTAs with the Republic of Korea and Japan, and is considering an FTA with China. In addition, EU–India negotiations on an Economic Partnership Agreement began in 2007.

Regionalism scenarios

Tables 12.2 and 12.3 summarize the foregoing discussion. In these tables, current and prospective FTAs are classified under three different scenarios: agreements now in force (scenario 1); scenario 1 plus agreements signed and under negotiation (scenario 2); and scenario 2 plus agreements under consideration including, most importantly, a possible FTAAP (scenario 3).

In scenario 1, among dominant countries, the United States shows the largest coverage of two-way trade by FTAs now in force (33 percent). Partner countries generally conduct a larger fraction of their two-way trade with the dominant partner than vice versa. China shows the largest coverage of FDI by FTAs now in force (54 percent). The pattern for partner countries is similar for FDI stocks and for merchandise trade, but it is not as pronounced.

In scenario 2, FTAs (and other agreements) already signed and under negotiation are added to the FTAs already in force. In this scenario, the United States and China do not show much increase in their coverage of total two-way trade, by comparison with scenario 1, but both Japan and ASEAN make an impressive jump. Japanese two-way total trade coverage increases from 6 percent to 22 percent, mainly due to FTAs with ASEAN and the Republic of Korea, now under negotiation. The agreements signed and under negotiation by ASEAN with Japan, Republic of Korea, Australia, and New Zealand would raise ASEAN's coverage of total two-way trade from 19 percent to about 41 percent. A similar pattern exists for FDI stocks.

Scenario 3 in Tables 12.2 and 12.3 depicts the coverage of present and prospective Asia-Pacific FTAs, including, most importantly, a possible FTAAP. In this scenario, FTAs would cover more than 60 percent of total two-way trade of each dominant country except India (where the coverage is about 50 percent). Under scenario 3, FDI coverage would be similar in magnitude to trade coverage, except for the United States where only 30 percent of FDI stocks would be covered. Taking intra-FTAAP trade into account, scenario 3 also shows a large increase in the total two-way trade coverage of partner countries, expanding from about 50 to around 80 percent of their world commerce.[10] Since India is not a current member of APEC, in scenario 3, we put India in the FTAAP but *only* in calculating India's potential trade linkages. We do not include India in the FTAAP scenario for existing APEC members. If APEC members show genuine signs of creating an FTAAP, the prospect of being "left out" might prompt India to radically reorient its trade policy.

Table 12.4 shows a matrix of "overlapping trade" among dominant countries via FTAs already in force and potential FTAs. "Overlapping trade" is defined as occurring when two dominant countries have the same partner. The percentages in the table indicate the share of trade of the dominant country listed in the row that overlaps, via the common partner, with the dominant country listed in the column. The rationale for this concept is that intermediation through the common partner may provide a limited conduit for integration between two dominant partners. However, Table 12.4 indicates that the current extent of overlapping trade is quite low (and, in the case of India, non-existent). This reflects both the regional emphasis of each dominant country, and the limited reach of FTAs in force. Table 12.4 also indicates that the potential for overlapping trade would be quite high in an FTAAP scenario.

APEC initiatives

The Asia-Pacific Economic Cooperation (APEC) forum, established in 1989 with twelve founding members, has grown to become the leading

---

[10] Due to the substantial gaps in FDI data, we do not have intra-FTAAP FDI shares. Table 12.3 only provides the share of FDI stocks of all FTAAP partners specifically with the dominant country.

Table 12.4 *Comparison between current and potential overlapping agreements: dominant partner A's two-way merchandise trade with countries that currently or potentially have FTAs with dominant partner B*[a] *(percentage of overlapping trade)*

Dominant partner A \ Dominant partner B	US		China		Japan		ASEAN[b]		Republic of Korea		India	
	Current[c]	Potential[d]	Current[c]	Potential[d]	Current[c]	Potential[d]	Current[c]	Potential[d]	Current[c]	Potential[d]	Current[c]	Potential[d]
US			1.9	61.2	13.0	61.2	0.0	61.2	1.9	61.2	1.4	61.2
China	2.8	61.2			5.0	62.5	9.2	61.2	9.7	62.5	2.3	62.5
Japan	3.6	66.1	5.3	66.7			0.0	66.1	5.3	66.7	2.3	66.7
ASEAN[b]	0.0	67.0	13.0	67.0	0.0	67.0			6.0	67.0	0.0	67.0
Korea, Rep. of	2.9	64.8	10.4	66.0	3.0	66.0	9.8	64.8			2.3	66.0
India	3.6	37.3	3.6	37.3	3.6	37.3	0.0	37.3	3.6	37.3		

Notes:

[a] Based on Appendix Table 12.1A. Overlapping agreements include agreements between dominant partners themselves.

[b] We consider ASEAN as one dominant partner, and do not include the intra-ASEAN trade share.

[c] *Current* indicates percentage of overlapped trade via FTAs currently in force.

[d] *Potential* indicates percentage of overlapped trade via FTAs in force, signed, under negotiation and under consideration (including a possible FTAAP).

regional grouping in the Asia-Pacific with twenty-one member economies.[11]

In November 1994, leaders of the APEC nations gathered in Bogor, Indonesia, and declared common goals (known as the Bogor Goals), including free trade and investment in the region by 2010 for industrialized economies, and by 2020 for developing economies. To advance the Bogor Goals, APEC has adopted a series of interim strategies, but none of them has proved highly successful. The absence of binding commitments as a negotiating principle may have slowed progress in achieving the Bogor vision.

In 1995, APEC adopted the Osaka Action Agenda, which established a framework for reaching the Bogor Goals through unilateral trade and investment liberalization, business facilitation, and economic and technical cooperation (known together as the three pillars). Unilateral steps were modest, and in 1997, at their fifth meeting in Canada, the APEC trade ministers endorsed another proposal, labeled Early Voluntary Sectoral Liberalization (EVSL). The EVSL initiative identified fifteen sectors in which members agreed to strive for liberalization. Again, achievements were modest.

Subsequent meetings of the APEC ministers were less noteworthy. According to Bergsten (2001), the Kuala Lumpur summit in 1998 broke the momentum of trade liberalization by terminating the effort to open additional sectors. At the Auckland summit in 1999, APEC members were in disarray over the merits and content of a new WTO trade round. The Seattle debacle ensued three months later.[12]

Government leaders left the next few APEC meetings empty-handed. However, in response to the proliferation of regional trade agreements, APEC ministers, meeting in Santiago in 2004, endorsed a call for high-level standards for free trade agreements (FTAs) and regional trading agreements (RTAs). At the meeting in Busan, Republic of Korea, in 2005, APEC leaders adopted "the Busan Roadmap towards the Bogor Goals." The Roadmap endorses specific strategies, such as a strong multilateral trading system, high-quality FTAs and RTAs, and measures to promote sustainable development. At the APEC trade ministers

---

[11] The current membership of APEC consists of twenty-one countries and territories: Australia; Brunei Darussalam; Canada; Chile; China; Chinese Taipei; Hong Kong, China; Indonesia; Japan; Republic of Korea; Malaysia; Mexico; New Zealand; Papua New Guinea; Peru; the Philippines; Russia; Singapore; Thailand; the United States; and Viet Nam.

[12] For more details, see Bergsten (2001).

meeting in Jeju, Republic of Korea, in 2005, the ministers endorsed a ministerial statement which expressed APEC support for the WTO Doha Development Agenda and a breakthrough for Non-Agricultural Market Access (NAMA) negotiations. The meeting of APEC economic leaders, held in Vietnam in 2006, reaffirmed strong support for the Doha Round and announced the Hanoi action plan, designed to implement the Busan Roadmap.

In 2005, the Center for International Economics (CIE) evaluated APEC's achievements and concluded that both tariff and non-tariff barriers have been reduced to a great extent. Applied tariff barriers in the APEC region have fallen from an average of about 16 percent in 1988 to about 6 percent in 2004; many non-tariff barriers have been either removed or converted to tariffs or (in the case of agriculture) to tariff-rate quotas. The CIE also found that linkages among APEC members and with the rest of world, in terms of trade and investment flows, have been strengthened. Importantly, the economies of lower-income members have grown at particularly rapid rates.[13]

These beneficial outcomes largely reflect forces other than APEC. Foremost, led by China, Asia has become a pole for rapid economic growth. APEC embraces the United States and Canada as well, and North America has enjoyed enormous productivity gains since the early 1990s. Moreover, the Asia-Pacific region is the locus of vigorous liberalization initiatives through bilateral and regional trade agreements: NAFTA, ANZCERTA, and ASEAN (already in place) and ASEAN + 3, ASEAN + 6 and a possible Northeast Asian FTA (under study).[14]

Whatever its accomplishments in the trade and investment field, APEC provides a unique forum for bringing together top leaders for dialogue on political and economic issues. The newest initiative, still in an exploratory phase, is a possible FTAAP that would embrace all APEC members. This initiative has been actively promoted by the APEC Business Advisory Council (ABAC) since 2004. The FTAAP has been discussed among APEC members as a catalyst to spur the revival of the Doha Round, or as "plan B" to restart the process of liberalization if the WTO negotiations falter.[15]

---

[13] For more details, see CIE (2005).

[14] For a descriptive picture, see Figure 12.1.

[15] For more details, see Bergsten (2007). At the summit meeting in Sydney in September 2007, the APEC leaders endorsed steps to enhance the coordination of free trade agreements and to explore an FTAAP with further studies, even though Japan and China

2   Gravity model estimates[16]

Model mechanics

With the proliferation of preferential trading arrangements, the gravity model has been widely used to analyze their consequences.[17] The basic gravity model evaluates thousands of one-way or two-way bilateral merchandise trade flows, measured in a common currency (and adjusted for inflation), against the gravitational "mass" of core explanatory variables, such as distance and combined GDP. Additional explanatory variables are specified as well, and these are of greatest interest. The additional variables show how much one-way or two-way trade is enlarged or reduced from the quantity predicted by the basic core variables on account of institutional or policy features of the partners. For instance, trading partners that share a common language or currency, or have a free trade agreement, typically enjoy greater mutual trade.

To analyze customs unions and free trade agreements, a dichotomous (0, 1) explanatory variable – often called a "dummy" or indicator variable – is introduced on the right-hand side of the regression equation to represent a preferential agreement. If the coefficient on the dummy variable is positive and significant, then the agreement is judged to expand two-way trade between the agreement members. Additional dummy variables are introduced to assess the effect of the agreement on a member country's imports from, and exports to, a non-member country.[18]

---

seemed skeptical of the FTAAP concept. For details, see *Inside US Trade*, September 14, 2007.

[16] The gravity model analysis was carried out by Dean A. DeRosa.

[17] For an introduction to gravity models applied to trade agreements see Greenaway and Milner (2002), Rose (2004), and Baldwin and Taglioni (2006). Our method follows the approach of Frankel (1997) and Choi and Schott (2001), using the general framework of the Rose (2004) gravity model with extensions from Rieder (2006) to assess the impact of a trade agreement on non-member countries.

[18] The extent of trade expansion is usually measured in percentage terms. Given the log-linear specification of dummy variables in a gravity model regression equation, the impact of a free trade agreement on bilateral trade can be computed in percentage terms as $100^*[\exp(b_{fta}) - 1.00]$. In this expression, b_{fta} is the estimated coefficient for the dummy variable representing the presence of a free trade agreement, and $\exp(b_{fta})$ is the value of the natural number e raised to the exponent b_{fta}. For example, if the coefficient b_{fta} is 0.33, then the value of $\exp(b_{fta})$ is 1.39, and the percentage expansion in trade is estimated as $100^*[1.39 - 1.00]$, which equals 39 percent.

Analytical framework

Our gravity model results are initially used to summarize the effects of existing trade agreements within the Asia-Pacific region. Following this, the results are used to extrapolate the future effects of possible new agreements within the region.[19]

Dataset

Our econometric results are based on bilateral trade flows worldwide from 1976 to 2005, at the 1-digit Standard International Trade Classification (SITC) level. This data set was compiled by DeRosa (2007) from the UN Comtrade database (using the World Integrated Trade Solution of the World Bank). Bilateral trade flows (either one-way or two-way), the dependent variable, are paired with several explanatory variables, as shown in Table 12.16. Year and country specific data for the core gravity variables, such as joint GDP and distance, and secondary gravity variables, such as common language and common border, are taken from an extensive data set compiled by Rose (2004). Data for free trade agreements are based on historical notifications of the date the agreements entered into force and their contemporary participants.[20] Following Rieder (2006), among others, we include "not in agreement" indicator variables alongside the "in agreement" indicator variables to determine the amount of trade diversion (if any) resulting from an agreement.

We round out our dataset with information on FDI stocks compiled by DeRosa (2007) from data underlying the UNCTAD *World Investment Report* (2006). FDI stock figures are considerably sparser than bilateral trade data, resulting in a much smaller dataset; about 325,000 observations over thirty years rather than nearly two million observations for bilateral trade. FDI stock data are typically missing from smaller and less developed countries. Narrowing the dataset in this way means that the resulting coefficients emphasize trade relations between larger and more advanced countries. However, there are payoffs: we can investigate the effect of FDI stocks on bilateral trade, and we can also investigate the effect of a trade agreement on bilateral FDI stocks.

---

[19] "Future agreements" includes signed agreements which have not been ratified, agreements under negotiation, major agreements under consideration, and a possible FTAAP.

[20] To illustrate, the NAFTA dummy for US–Mexico trade would not have a value of 1 until 1994.

Calculation scheme

Gravity model studies often aggregate customs unions (CUs) and free trade agreements (FTAs) into one, two, or three types of agreements to assess the impact of different degrees of preference on bilateral trade.[21] However we go further and use individual dummy variables for nine prominent CUs and FTAs (or FTA types), both to identify differences between them and to better predict the effect of potential future FTAs based on the experience of existing FTAs. For example, we assume that the effect of a potential Japan–Republic of Korea trade deal is better predicted by using ASEAN Free Trade Area (AFTA) coefficients than by using a generic FTA coefficient that also reflects the experience of NAFTA and the EU. As mentioned, we distinguish nine prominent CUs and FTAs (or FTA types) in our regression analysis.[22] This provides coefficients for an analysis of current and future trade agreements in the Asia-Pacific region and insight into actual and potential trade diversion effects.

Table 12.5 summarizes our organization of actual and potential trade agreements in the Asia-Pacific region. We differentiate between "prime partners" – larger countries – and their associates. FTAs are separated into agreements currently in force, signed but not ratified, under negotiation, major agreements under consideration, and a possible FTAAP. The last column indicates which coefficient from our regression analysis was used to calculate the effect of the FTA in a given row. The results are discussed in the next section.

Results for bilateral trade

We use our gravity model coefficient estimates (discussed later in this section) and our calculation scheme to estimate the impact on two-way trade of existing and potential FTAs. Another way of making such estimates is to use a computable general equilibrium (CGE) model. CGE

---

[21] See Hufbauer and Baldwin (2006) and Hufbauer and Burki (2006).

[22] The distinct trade agreements are: the European Union (EU), the European Free Trade Area (EFTA), EU bilateral free trade agreements (EU FTAs), the North American Free Trade Area (NAFTA), the Southern Common Market (MERCOSUR), Chile, Mexico, Australia, and Singapore bilateral free trade agreements (CMAS FTAs – separately distinguished because these are truly free trade countries), the ASEAN Free Trade Area (AFTA), the South Asia Free Trade Agreement (SAFTA), and all other customs unions and free trade agreements.

Table 12.5 *Scheme for trade impact calculations for Asia-Pacific FTAs in force, signed, and under negotiation versus major FTAs under consideration and a possible FTAAP*

Prime partner	Status	Year	Partner	FTA name	Gravity coefficients assumed
Australia	In force	1977	PNG	PATCRA	CMAS
Australia	In force	1983	New Zealand	ANZCERTA	CMAS
ASEAN	In force	1992	ASEAN	AFTA	AFTA
US	In force	1994	NAFTA	NAFTA	NAFTA
Chile	In force	1998	Peru	Chile–Peru	CMAS
Chile	In force	1999	Mexico	Chile–Mexico	CMAS
Mexico	In force	1995	Peru	Mexico–Peru	CMAS
Canada	In force	1997	Chile	Canada–Chile	CMAS
New Zealand	In force	2001	Singapore	NZ–Singapore	CMAS
Australia	In force	2002	Singapore	Australia–Singapore	CMAS
Chile	In force	2004	Korea, Rep. of	Chile–Korea	CMAS
Australia	In force	2005	Thailand	Australia–Thailand	CMAS
New Zealand	In force	2005	Thailand	NZ–Thailand	CMAS
Korea, Rep. of	In force	2006	Singapore	Korea–Singapore	CMAS
US	In force	2004	Singapore	US–Singapore	NAFTA
US	In force	2004	Chile	US–Chile	NAFTA
US	In force	2005	Australia	US–Australia	NAFTA
China	In force	2004	Hong Kong, China	China–Hong Kong	AFTA

China	In force	2005	ASEAN	China–ASEAN	AFTA
China	In force	2006	Chile	China–Chile	CMAS
Japan	In force	2002	Singapore	Japan–Singapore	CMAS
Japan	In force	2005	Mexico	Japan–Mexico	CMAS
Japan	In force	2006	Malaysia	Japan–Malaysia	AFTA
Japan	In force	2006	Chile	Japan–Chile	CMAS
US	Signed	2006	Peru	US–Peru	NAFTA
US	Signed	2006	Colombia	US–Colombia	NAFTA
US	Signed	2006	Panama	US–Panama	NAFTA
US	Signed	2006	Korea, Rep. of	US–Korea, Rep. of	NAFTA
Japan	Signed	2005	Thailand	Japan–Thailand	AFTA
Japan	Signed	2007	Indonesia	Japan–Indonesia	AFTA
US	Under negotiation	2004	Thailand	US–Thailand	NAFTA
US	Under negotiation	2006	Malaysia	US–Malaysia	NAFTA
China	Under negotiation	2004	Australia–NZ	China–CER	AFTA
China	Under negotiation	2006	Singapore	China–Singapore	AFTA
Japan	Under negotiation	2003	Korea, Rep. of	Japan–Korea, Rep. of	AFTA
Japan	Under negotiation	2006	ASEAN	Japan–ASEAN	AFTA
Japan	Under negotiation	2007	India	Japan–India	AFTA
ASEAN	Under negotiation	2004	CER	ASEAN–CER	AFTA
ASEAN	Under negotiation	2004	Korea, Rep. of	ASEAN–Korea, Rep. of	AFTA

Table 12.5 (*cont.*)

Prime partner	Status	Year	Partner	FTA name	Gravity coefficients assumed
US	Major under consideration	–	ASEAN	US–ASEAN	NAFTA
US	Major under consideration	–	Japan	US–Japan	NAFTA
ASEAN	Major under consideration	–	ASEAN+3	ASEAN+3	AFTA
FTAAP	Possible	–	FTAAP	FTAAP	NAFTA

models have the great advantage of being built on consistent structural equations that describe economic activity in each economy. But CGE models are considerably more costly to construct and maintain than gravity models.[23] Moreover "plain vanilla" CGE models usually generate very modest trade impact estimates, since they ignore monopolistic competition, economies of scale, and any inducement to investment flowing from trade liberalization. When resources permit, we prefer to use both CGE and gravity models to estimate trade impacts. However, in this chapter, we had resources only for gravity model analysis.

Table 12.6 shows average annual dollar trade over the period 2001–5 for selected Asian-Pacific countries and regions. These amounts serve as the base figures for calculating the percentage impacts displayed in Tables 12.8, 12.10, and 12.12. Table 12.7 presents the estimated dollar impact of the distinct FTAs on the total trade of major countries and regions in the Asia-Pacific. The first column of Table 12.7 (as in Tables 12.8 through 12.12) provides the estimated dollar or corresponding percentage impact to trade of agreements currently in force in a given country or region; the other six columns provide the predicted impacts of potential FTAs (based on the assumed correspondence between actual and potential FTAs provided in Table 12.5).[24] Predicted impacts shown in Table 12.7 are divided into aggregate trade between FTA partners (thus *excluding* any trade diversion effects),[25] exports to partners, and imports from partners.[26]

Implementing the FTAAP, according to these results, would augment trade for most countries by roughly 50 percent. This translates into an estimated increase in two-way merchandise trade for the United States of nearly US$1.2 trillion, an increase for China of nearly US$600 billion, and for Japan of nearly US$900 billion. This agreement would increase two-way merchandise trade in the region as a whole by US$4.8 trillion. Of the major countries, the impact on China would be the smallest in percentage terms and the impact on Japan would be the largest.

---

[23] The data set and statistical analysis underlying the gravity models results reported here cost approximately $25,000. Constructing and maintaining a CGE model covering the same ground could cost $200,000.

[24] The Japan–Chile FTA went into force on September 3, 2007. Table 12.5 reflects this fact but Tables 12.7 through 12.16 do not.

[25] Trade diversion effects are discussed separately under the next subheading.

[26] The reader should be forewarned that a simple combination of the estimates in Table 12.16 and the scheme in Table 12.5 *cannot* be used to arrive at the impact calculations provided in Tables 12.7 through 12.15. Computing the impact calculations requires far more information and resources than could reasonably accompany this chapter.

Table 12.6 *Average levels of merchandise trade in the Asia-Pacific region by commodity category, 2001–2005 (billions of US dollars at 2005 prices)*

Region		All traded goods SITC 0 to 9	Food and agriculture SITC 0, 1	Raw materials SITC 2, 4	Fuels SITC 3	Manufactures SITC 5 to 8
				Exports + Imports		
Asia-Pacific	US	2,286	118	67	211	1,816
	China	1,111	28	53	50	974
	Japan	994	50	34	95	798
	Korea, Rep. of	432	12	15	55	344
	APEC	7,944	393	316	774	6,275
Asia	ASEAN	988	51	45	118	755
	CER	215	31	24	30	122
	SAFTA	204	15	18	14	148
	Other Asia	904	35	28	115	703
Pacific	NAFTA	3,244	174	108	306	2,550
	Other America	466	75	48	76	260
				Exports		
Asia-Pacific	US	842	57	40	22	709
	China	688	20	8	13	643
	Japan	567	3	6	3	548
	Korea, Rep. of	232	3	2	9	215
	APEC	3,934	188	160	284	3,212

Asia	ASEAN	535	30	31	60	403
	CER	105	25	22	21	32
	SAFTA	103	10	7	5	80
	Other Asia	432	9	15	88	305
Pacific	NAFTA	1,342	88	67	91	1,055
	Other America	268	60	41	52	110

Imports

Asia-Pacific	US	1,443	61	28	189	1,108
	China	423	8	45	37	332
	Japan	426	48	28	92	250
	Korea, Rep. of	200	9	12	46	129
	APEC	4,010	205	156	490	3,063
Asia	ASEAN	453	21	13	58	352
	CER	110	6	2	9	89
	SAFTA	101	4	11	9	68
	Other Asia	471	26	13	27	398
Pacific	NAFTA	1,902	86	41	215	1,495
	Other America	198	15	7	24	150

Source: Peterson Institute trade and investment gravity model dataset.

Table 12.7 *Average annual impacts of selected FTAs in the Asia-Pacific region on total merchandise trade (SITC 0 through 9) by region and selected countries, 2001–2005 (billions of US dollars at 2005 prices)*

Region		Selected Asia-Pacific FTAs combined			Major FTAs under consideration			Possible
		In force	Signed	Under negotiation	US–ASEAN	US–Japan	ASEAN+3	FTAAP
Exports + Imports								
Asia-Pacific	US	492	83	61	151	301	0	1,190
	China	147	0	19	0	0	174	598
	Japan	31	36	142	0	301	247	883
	Korea, Rep. of	2	71	63	0	0	94	245
	APEC	1,482	228	695	456	601	714	4,839
Asia	ASEAN	248	35	379	311	0	203	644
	CER	31	0	40	0	0	0	143
	SAFTA	0	0	5	0	0	0	0
	Other Asia	113	0	0	0	0	0	597
Pacific	NAFTA	906	83	61	151	301	0	1,698
	Other America	11	14	0	0	0	0	30
Exports								
Asia-Pacific	US	229	45	25	64	112	0	496
	China	121	0	13	0	0	95	377
	Japan	21	19	90	0	188	136	513
	Korea, Rep. of	1	36	30	0	0	45	132
	APEC	741	117	347	227	301	357	2,420

Asia	ASEAN	116	16	175	167	0	83	327
	CER	11	0	18	0	0	0	68
	SAFTA	0	0	3	0	0	0	0
	Other Asia	10	0	0	0	0	0	225
Pacific	NAFTA	458	45	25	64	112	0	763
	Other America	5	3	0	0	0	0	15
				Imports				
Asia-Pacific	US	262	38	35	87	188	0	694
	China	26	0	5	0	0	79	222
	Japan	10	17	52	0	112	111	371
	Korea, Rep. of	1	35	33	0	0	49	113
	APEC	742	11	349	229	301	357	2,420
Asia	ASEAN	132	19	203	144	0	120	317
	CER	20	0	22	0	0	0	75
	SAFTA	0	0	2	0	0	0	0
	Other Asia	102	0	0	0	0	0	372
Pacific	NAFTA	448	38	35	87	188	0	935
	Other America	6	10	0	0	0	0	15

Source: Calculated from regression estimates displayed in Table 12.16, and applied to all observations in the gravity model dataset on intra-bloc trade by 1-digit categories, 2001–5.

The Republic of Korea stands to gain significantly from bilateral FTAs even without the FTAAP. If the Republic of Korea–US FTA is ratified, it will increase global Korean two-way trade by an estimated US$70 billion (16 percent). The Republic of Korea would gain a similar amount (US$63 billion) if the Japan–Republic of Korea FTA and the Republic of Korea–ASEAN FTA are both agreed to. In percentage terms, the United States stands to gain far less than its proposed partners in future US–ASEAN and US–Japan agreements; not surprisingly, the smaller party shows larger gains in percentage terms. However, our model estimates that the US–Japan agreement would increase two-way trade between the countries by US$300 billion, and the US–ASEAN agreement would increase US two-way trade by US$150 billion and ASEAN two-way trade (calculated as the sum of its members) by US$310 billion.[27]

The one-way trade panels shown in Table 12.7 (and the corresponding percentage impacts in Table 12.8) indicate impacts of similar magnitude on total exports and on total imports for most of the countries and regions identified. The United States is the notable exception. Table 12.8 suggests that in every FTA classification the estimated percentage impact on US exports exceeds the estimated percentage impact on US imports. We point this out to ease fears – now widespread in the American political class – that the United States might create a web of FTAs that would asymmetrically increase US imports, more to the benefit of FTA partners than US producers.[28]

Tables 12.9 through 12.12 show the estimated impact of FTAs on members' agriculture and manufacturing trade – the two sectors which typically arouse the most political concern during the course of negotiations. According to these calculations, the FTAAP would increase agricultural trade by roughly 65 percent (US$260 billion) and manufacturing trade by roughly 85 percent (US$5.2 trillion).[29] In percentage

---

[27] The great difference between the two-way trade estimates for the US–ASEAN agreement (US$150 billion versus US$310 billion) is caused by the predicted increase in trade *among* ASEAN members as a result of the agreement.

[28] Our dollar estimates of the effect on one-way trade show a larger increase in imports, simply because the current US import base is much larger than the US export base.

[29] The estimated impact of the FTAAP on manufacturing trade is larger than the estimated impact on total trade because we use coefficient estimates from different regressions in our calculations. As will be discussed later in this section, we run separate gravity model regressions with total trade, trade in agriculture, and trade in manufacturing as our dependent variables. Separate regressions allow for analysis of the most politically sensitive sectors (agriculture and manufacturing), but lead to estimated sector impacts that differ from our estimates for total trade.

Table 12.8 *Average annual percentage impacts of selected FTAs in the Asia-Pacific region on total merchandise trade (SITC 0 through 9) by region and selected countries, 2001–2005 (per cent)*

Region		Selected Asia-Pacific FTAs combined			Major FTAs under consideration			Possible
		In force	Signed	Under negotiation	US–ASEAN	US–Japan	ASEAN+3	FTAAP
		Exports + Imports						
Asia-Pacific	US	21.5	3.6	2.7	6.6	13.2	0.0	52.1
	China	13.2	0.0	1.7	0.0	0.0	15.7	53.9
	Japan	3.1	3.6	14.3	0.0	30.3	24.8	88.9
	Korea, Rep. of	0.5	6.3	14.6	0.0	0.0	21.7	56.7
	APEC	18.7	2.9	8.8	5.7	7.6	9.0	60.9
Asia	ASEAN	25.1	3.5	38.4	31.5	0.0	20.5	65.2
	CER	14.2	0.0	18.5	0.0	0.0	0.0	66.5
	SAFTA	0.0	0.0	2.4	0.0	0.0	0.0	0.0
	Other Asia	12.5	0.0	0.0	0.0	0.0	0.0	66.1
Pacific	NAFTA	27.9	2.6	1.9	4.6	9.3	0.0	52.4
	Other America	2.4	2.9	0.0	0.0	0.0	0.0	6.5
		Exports						
Asia-Pacific	US	27.2	5.3	3.0	7.6	13.3	0.0	58.9
	China	17.6	0.0	1.9	0.0	0.0	13.9	54.8
	Japan	3.7	3.3	15.8	0.0	33.2	24.0	90.4
	Korea, Rep. of	0.4	15.5	12.7	0.0	0.0	19.3	57.1
	APEC	18.8	3.0	8.8	5.8	7.6	9.1	61.5

Table 12.8 (*cont.*)

Region		Selected Asia-Pacific FTAs combined			Major FTAs under consideration			Possible
		In force	Signed	Under negotiation	US–ASEAN	US–Japan	ASEAN+3	FTAAP
Asia	ASEAN	21.7	3.0	32.9	31.2	0.0	15.5	61.1
	CER	10.3	0.0	17.2	0.0	0.0	0.0	64.4
	SAFTA	0.0	0.0	2.5	0.0	0.0	0.0	0.0
	Other Asia	2.4	0.0	0.0	0.0	0.0	0.0	52.0
Pacific	NAFTA	34.2	3.3	1.9	4.8	8.4	0.0	56.9
	Other America	2.0	1.2	0.0	0.0	0.0	0.0	5.5
				Imports				
Asia-Pacific	US	18.2	2.6	2.5	6.0	13.1	0.0	48.1
	China	6.2	0.0	1.5	0.0	0.0	18.7	52.4
	Japan	2.3	4.0	12.2	0.0	26.3	26.0	87.0
	Korea, Rep. of	0.5	17.3	16.7	0.0	0.0	24.5	56.3
	APEC	18.5	2.8	8.7	5.7	7.5	8.9	60.3
Asia	ASEAN	29.1	4.1	44.9	31.9	0.0	26.4	70.0
	CER	18.0	0.0	19.7	0.0	0.0	0.0	68.5
	SAFTA	0.0	0.0	2.4	0.0	0.0	0.0	0.0
	Other Asia	21.7	0.0	0.0	0.0	0.0	0.0	79.0
Pacific	NAFTA	23.5	2.0	1.9	4.6	9.9	0.0	49.2
	Other America	2.9	5.2	0.0	0.0	0.0	0.0	7.7

Source: Percentage changes relative to the average levels of merchandise trade 2001–5 in Table 12.6.

Table 12.9 *Average annual impacts of selected FTAs in the Asia-Pacific region on trade in food and agriculture (SITC 0 and 1) by region and selected countries, 2001–2005 (billions of US dollar at 2005 prices)*

Region		Selected Asia-Pacific FTAs combined			Major FTAs under consideration			Possible
		In force	Signed	Under negotiation	US–ASEAN	US–Japan	ASEAN+3	FTAAP
		Exports + Imports						
Asia-Pacific	US	28	5	4	9	21	0	72
	China	6	0	2	0	0	14	20
	Japan	1	5	10	0	21	18	50
	Korea, Rep. of	0	3	3	0	0	5	8
	APEC	87	19	59	28	42	52	261
Asia	ASEAN	19	4	34	20	0	16	34
	CER	5	0	9	0	0	0	20
	SAFTA	0	0	1	0	0	0	0
	Other Asia	3	3	0	0	0	0	20
Pacific	NAFTA	50	5	4	9	21	0	102
	Other America	3	3	0	0	0	0	6
		Exports						
Asia-Pacific	US	10	4	1	3	20	0	43
	China	5	0	1	0	0	12	16
	Japan	0	0	1	0	1	1	3
	Korea, Rep. of	0	0	3	0	0	3	3
	APEC	43	10	29	14	21	26	130

Table 12.9 (cont.)

Region		Selected Asia-Pacific FTAs combined			Major FTAs under consideration			Possible
		In force	Signed	Under negotiation	US–ASEAN	US–Japan	ASEAN+3	FTAAP
Asia	ASEAN	9	4	19	11	0	10	20
	CER	4	0	5	0	0	0	16
	SAFTA	0	0	1	0	0	0	0
	Other Asia	0	0	0	0	0	0	6
Pacific	NAFTA	23	4	1	3	20	0	62
	Other America	3	2	0	0	0	0	5
				Imports				
Asia-Pacific	US	17	1	3	6	1	0	29
	China	1	0	0	0	0	1	4
	Japan	1	5	9	0	20	17	48
	Korea, Rep. of	0	3	0	0	0	2	5
	APEC	43	10	30	14	21	26	130
Asia	ASEAN	10	0	15	9	0	6	14
	CER	1	0	4	0	0	0	4
	SAFTA	0	0	0	0	0	0	0
	Other Asia	3	0	0	0	0	0	14
Pacific	NAFTA	27	1	3	6	1	0	40
	Other America	0	1	0	0	0	0	1

Source: Calculated from regression estimates displayed in Table 12.16, and applied to all observations in the gravity model dataset on intra-bloc trade by 1-digit categories, 2001–5.

Table 12.10 *Average annual percentage impacts of selected FTAs in the Asia-Pacific region on trade in food and agriculture (SITC 0 and 1) by region and selected countries, 2001–2005 (per cent)*

Region		Selected Asia-Pacific FTAs combined			Major FTAs under consideration			Possible
		In force	Signed	Under negotiation	US–ASEAN	US–Japan	ASEAN+3	FTAAP
		Exports + Imports						
Asia-Pacific	US	23.4	4.4	3.0	7.7	17.7	0.0	60.5
	China	22.5	0.0	5.5	0.0	0.0	49.6	72.8
	Japan	2.1	10.2	19.5	0.0	41.5	35.6	100.0
	Korea, Rep. of	0.9	27.3	25.3	0.0	0.0	41.0	68.4
	APEC	22.1	4.9	15.0	7.2	10.7	13.2	66.5
Asia	ASEAN	37.0	8.3	66.3	39.5	0.0	31.3	66.9
	CER	16.5	0.0	28.6	0.0	0.0	0.0	64.1
	SAFTA	0.0	0.0	6.0	0.0	0.0	0.0	0.0
	Other Asia	9.4	0.0	0.0	0.0	0.0	0.0	58.4
Pacific	NAFTA	28.7	3.0	2.0	5.2	12.0	0.0	58.6
	Other America	4.0	3.7	0.0	0.0	0.0	0.0	7.7
		Exports						
Asia-Pacific	US	18.3	7.0	1.7	5.7	35.4	0.0	75.6
	China	25.3	0.0	5.3	0.0	0.0	61.0	79.0
	Japan	6.9	6.1	28.6	0.0	29.5	40.3	110.8
	Korea, Rep. of	1.4	14.8	103.8	0.0	0.0	107.4	118.7
	APEC	23.0	5.1	15.4	7.5	11.2	13.8	69.6

Table 12.10 (cont.)

Region		Selected Asia-Pacific FTAs combined			Major FTAs under consideration			Possible
		In force	Signed	Under negotiation	US–ASEAN	US–Japan	ASEAN+3	FTAAP
Asia	ASEAN	28.4	13.6	63.6	37.9	0.0	33.7	66.5
	CER	15.2	0.0	20.8	0.0	0.0	0.0	61.9
	SAFTA	0.0	0.0	8.4	0.0	0.0	0.0	0.0
	Other Asia	0.5	0.0	0.0	0.0	0.0	0.0	71.0
Pacific	NAFTA	26.5	4.5	1.1	3.7	22.8	0.0	69.9
	Other America	4.5	2.8	0.0	0.0	0.0	0.0	7.8
				Imports				
Asia-Pacific	US	28.2	1.9	4.2	9.5	1.3	0.0	46.5
	China	15.0	0.0	6.1	0.0	0.0	19.1	56.3
	Japan	1.8	10.5	19.0	0.0	42.2	35.3	99.4
	Korea, Rep. of	0.7	30.7	3.8	0.0	0.0	22.8	54.6
	APEC	21.2	4.7	14.7	7.0	10.2	12.7	63.7
Asia	ASEAN	49.2	0.8	70.0	41.8	0.0	27.8	67.3
	CER	22.1	0.0	64.6	0.0	0.0	0.0	74.2
	SAFTA	0.0	0.0	0.0	0.0	0.0	0.0	0.0
	Other Asia	12.6	0.0	0.0	0.0	0.0	0.0	53.9
Pacific	NAFTA	31.0	1.4	3.0	6.8	0.9	0.0	46.9
	Other America	2.2	7.4	0.0	0.0	0.0	0.0	7.2

Source: Percentage changes relative to the average levels of merchandise trade 2001–5 in Table 12.6.

Table 12.11 *Average annual impacts of selected FTAs in the Asia-Pacific region on trade in manufactures (SITC 5 through 8) by region and selected countries, 2001–2005 (billions of US dollars at 2005 prices)*

Region		Selected Asia-Pacific FTAs combined			Major FTAs under consideration			Possible
		In force	Signed	Under negotiation	US–ASEAN	US–Japan	ASEAN+3	FTAAP
		Exports + Imports						
Asia-Pacific	US	494	91	82	189	338	0	1,310
	China	294	0	32	0	0	331	709
	Japan	33	51	254	0	338	464	938
	Korea, Rep. of	0	79	130	0	0	192	284
	APEC	1,838	274	1,118	573	675	1,304	5,327
Asia	ASEAN	354	50	589	402	0	328	730
	CER	24	0	58	0	0	0	118
	SAFTA	0	0	7	0	0	0	0
	Other Asia	243	0	0	0	0	0	715
Pacific	NAFTA	898	91	82	189	338	0	1,806
	Other America	8	12	0	0	0	0	26
		Exports						
Asia-Pacific	US	254	41	30	71	88	0	502
	China	256	0	26	0	0	176	456
	Japan	29	40	197	0	249	297	651
	Korea, Rep. of	0	48	57	0	0	91	163
	APEC	916	140	555	283	338	650	2,663

Table 12.11 (*cont.*)

Region		Selected Asia-Pacific FTAs combined			Major FTAs under consideration				Possible
		In force	Signed	Under negotiation	US–ASEAN	US–Japan	ASEAN+3	FTAAP	FTAAP
Asia	ASEAN	159	10	242	224	0	94	360	
	CER	4	0	23	0	0	0	30	
	SAFTA	0	0	3	0	0	0	0	
	Other Asia	22	0	0	0	0	0	270	
Pacific	NAFTA	456	41	30	71	88	0	725	
	Other America	2	1	0	0	0	0	8	
					Imports				
Asia-Pacific	US	240	49	52	117	249	0	808	
	China	39	0	6	0	0	156	253	
	Japan	5	10	57	0	88	167	287	
	Korea, Rep. of	0	31	73	0	0	101	121	
	APEC	922	134	562	290	338	654	2,663	
Asia	ASEAN	195	40	347	178	0	234	370	
	CER	20	0	36	0	0	0	88	
	SAFTA	0	0	5	0	0	0	0	
	Other Asia	221	0	0	0	0	0	444	
Pacific	NAFTA	442	49	52	117	249	0	1,081	
	Other America	6	10	0	0	0	0	18	

Source: Calculated from regression estimates displayed in Table 12.16, and applied to all observations in the gravity model dataset on intra-bloc trade by 1-digit categories, 2001–5.

Table 12.12 *Average annual percentage impacts of selected FTAs in the Asia-Pacific region on trade in manufacture (SITC 5 through 8) by region and selected countries, 2001–2005 (per cent)*

Region		Selected Asia-Pacific FTAs combined			Major FTAs under consideration			Possible
		In force	Signed	Under negotiation	US–ASEAN	US–Japan	ASEAN+3	FTAAP
Exports + Imports								
Asia-Pacific	US	27.2	5.0	4.5	10.4	18.6	0.0	72.1
	China	30.2	0.0	3.3	0.0	0.0	34.0	72.8
	Japan	4.2	6.3	31.8	0.0	42.3	58.1	117.6
	Korea, Rep. of	0.1	22.9	37.7	0.0	0.0	55.7	82.4
	APEC	29.3	4.4	17.8	9.1	10.8	20.8	84.9
Asia	ASEAN	46.9	6.7	78.0	53.2	0.0	43.4	96.7
	CER	20.1	0.0	48.0	0.0	0.0	0.0	97.3
	SAFTA	0.0	0.0	5.1	0.0	0.0	0.0	0.0
	Other Asia	34.6	0.0	0.0	0.0	0.0	0.0	101.7
Pacific	NAFTA	35.2	3.6	3.2	7.4	13.2	0.0	70.8
	Other America	3.1	4.5	0.0	0.0	0.0	0.0	10.0
Exports								
Asia-Pacific	US	35.8	5.9	4.2	10.1	12.5	0.0	70.8
	China	39.8	0.0	4.1	0.0	0.0	27.4	71.0
	Japan	5.2	7.3	36.0	0.0	45.5	54.2	118.8
	Korea, Rep. of	0.1	22.3	26.3	0.0	0.0	42.3	75.9
	APEC	28.5	4.4	17.3	8.8	10.5	20.2	82.9

Table 12.12 (*cont.*)

Region		Selected Asia-Pacific FTAs combined			Major FTAs under consideration			Possible
		In force	Signed	Under negotiation	US–ASEAN	US–Japan	ASEAN+3	FTAAP
Asia	ASEAN	39.4	2.6	59.9	55.5	0.0	23.4	89.3
	CER	12.9	0.0	69.8	0.0	0.0	0.0	93.2
	SAFTA	0.0	0.0	3.3	0.0	0.0	0.0	0.0
	Other Asia	7.2	0.0	0.0	0.0	0.0	0.0	88.7
Pacific	NAFTA	43.2	3.9	2.8	6.8	8.4	0.0	68.8
	Other America	2.1	1.2	0.0	0.0	0.0	0.0	7.3
				Imports				
Asia-Pacific	US	21.7	4.4	4.7	10.6	22.5	0.0	72.9
	China	11.7	0.0	1.8	0.0	0.0	46.9	76.3
	Japan	1.8	4.1	22.8	0.0	35.3	66.9	114.8
	Korea, Rep. of	0.2	24.1	56.5	0.0	0.0	78.0	93.3
	APEC	30.1	4.4	18.4	9.5	11.0	21.3	87.0
Asia	ASEAN	55.6	11.4	98.7	50.6	0.0	66.4	105.3
	CER	22.7	0.0	40.2	0.0	0.0	0.0	98.8
	SAFTA	0.0	0.0	7.2	0.0	0.0	0.0	0.0
	Other Asia	55.5	0.0	0.0	0.0	0.0	0.0	111.8
Pacific	NAFTA	29.6	3.3	3.5	7.8	16.7	0.0	72.3
	Other America	3.9	6.9	0.0	0.0	0.0	0.0	12.0

Source: Percentage changes relative to the average levels of merchandise trade 2001–5 in Table 12.6.

terms, the agreements currently in force are estimated to have increased manufacturing trade more than agricultural trade, but by no more than 10 percentage points in any one country or region. The same pattern prevails for potential future agreements, but with larger differences between the two sectors. Since manufacturing trade far exceeds agriculture trade in dollar value, a comparison of the effects of FTAs on the two sectors in dollar terms does not accurately reflect the exaggerated political sensitivity of agriculture. However, some of the more notable dollar effects in the sectors can be summarized as follows: a $30 billion increase in US agriculture trade due to agreements currently in force; a predicted US$50 billion increase in agriculture trade among the potential members if ASEAN+3 is enacted; a US$500 billion increase in US manufacturing trade due to agreements currently in force; and a US$1.3 trillion increase in manufacturing trade among the potential members if ASEAN+3 is enacted.

Expressed in both dollar and percentage terms, export and import effects are similar for manufacturing trade. But export and import effects are quite dissimilar in agriculture trade. For instance, the calculations suggest that a US–Japan agreement would increase US agriculture exports by roughly US$20 billion (35 percent) but US imports by only US$1 billion (1 percent).

Trade diversion estimates

Table 12.13 displays the estimated trade diversion effects on countries and regions by the various FTAs in our sample. Table 12.13 (along with Tables 12.14 and 12.15) is structured much like the tables discussed under the preceding subheading, but there is an important difference. For any country or region, the diversion effects displayed are those caused by *all* agreements under a column heading (e.g. "In force") to which the country or region is *not* a party.[30] Diversion effects are displayed both for one-way trade flows (exports and imports separately) and for two-way trade flows. Moreover, positive and negative diversion effects are displayed separately, as well as in a combined total of positive and negative effects.

---

[30] The FTAAP is not displayed in Tables 12.13 through 12.15 because almost all countries in these tables would be members. Hence, diversion from the group as a whole would be trivial. Moreover, our tables do not report trade diversion that might be experienced by countries *outside* the Asia-Pacific area, e.g. the European Union.

Table 12.13 Trade diversion – average annual impacts of selected FTAs in the Asia-Pacific region on total merchandise trade (SITC 0 through 9) of non-member countries, by region and selected countries, 2001–2005 (billions of US dollars at 2005 prices)

| | | Selected Asia-Pacific FTAs combined | | | | | | | | | Major FTAs under consideration | | | | | | | | |
| | | In force | | | Signed | | | Under negotiation | | | US–ASEAN | | | US–Japan | | | ASEAN+3 | | |
Region		Neg.	Pos.	Total	Neg.	Pos.	Total	Neg.	Pos.	Total	Neg.	Pos.	Total	Neg.	Pos.	Total	Neg.	Pos.	Total
								Non-member exports + imports											
Asia-Pacific	US	0	287	**287**	0	286	**286**	0	756	**756**	0	0	**0**	0	0	**0**	0	263	**263**
	China	0	105	**105**	0	146	**146**	0	255	**255**	−6	17	**11**	−10	28	**18**	0	0	**0**
	Japan	0	288	**288**	−49	146	**97**	0	303	**303**	−19	52	**33**	0	0	**0**	0	0	**0**
	Korea, Rep. of	0	83	**83**	0	62	**62**	0	105	**105**	−4	10	**6**	−8	11	**3**	0	3	**3**
	APEC	−30	1,258	**1,227**	−97	1,101	**1,004**	0	2,250	**2,250**	−62	145	**83**	−73	141	**67**	0	501	**501**
Asia	ASEAN	−10	116	**106**	0	124	**124**	0	174	**174**	0	0	**0**	−16	29	**13**	0	0	**0**
	CER	0	34	**34**	0	27	**27**	0	61	**61**	−3	4	**1**	−4	7	**3**	0	26	**26**
	SAPTA	0	26	**26**	0	14	**14**	0	40	**40**	−2	3	**1**	−1	3	**2**	0	13	**13**
	Other Asia	0	207	**207**	0	133	**132**	0	445	**445**	−9	19	**9**	−14	19	**5**	0	172	**172**
Pacific	NAFTA	−19	419	**400**	−47	459	**412**	0	898	**898**	−19	42	**23**	−21	45	**24**	0	299	**299**
	Other America	−21	56	**34**	−19	51	**32**	−2	50	**48**	−7	12	**4**	−8	13	**5**	0	14	**14**

Non-member exports

		Neg.	Pos.	Total	Neg.	Pos.	Total	Neg.	Pos.	Total	Neg.	Pos.	Total	Neg.	Pos.	Total	Neg.	Pos.	Total
Asia-Pacific	US	0	76	76	0	37	37	0	101	101	0	0	0	0	0	0	0	33	33
Asia	China	0	84	84	0	84	84	0	91	91	0	17	17	0	28	28	0	0	0
	Japan	0	217	217	0	146	146	0	143	143	0	52	52	0	0	0	0	0	0
	Korea, Rep. of	0	51	51	0	30	30	0	37	37	0	10	10	0	11	11	0	0	0
	APEC	0	773	773	0	641	641	0	630	630	0	145	145	0	141	141	0	64	64
	ASEAN	0	93	93	0	80	80	0	57	57	0	0	0	0	29	29	0	0	0
	CER	0	15	15	0	19	19	0	22	22	0	4	4	0	7	7	0	6	6
	SAPTA	0	14	14	0	12	12	0	10	10	0	3	3	0	3	3	0	2	2
	Other Asia	0	100	100	0	68	68	0	79	79	0	19	19	0	19	19	0	19	19
Pacific	NAFTA	0	208	208	0	210	210	0	197	197	0	42	42	0	45	45	0	38	38
	Other America	0	56	56	0	51	51	0	32	32	0	12	12	0	13	13	0	3	3

Non-member imports

		Neg.	Pos.	Total	Neg.	Pos.	Total	Neg.	Pos.	Total	Neg.	Pos.	Total	Neg.	Pos.	Total	Neg.	Pos.	Total
Asia-Pacific	US	0	211	211	0	249	249	0	655	655	0	0	0	0	0	0	0	230	230
	China	0	22	22	0	62	62	−6	164	164	−6	0	−6	−10	0	−10	0	0	0
	Japan	0	71	71	−49	0	−49	−19	160	160	−19	0	−19	0	0	0	0	0	0
	Korea, Rep. of	0	32	32	0	32	32	−4	68	68	−4	0	−4	−8	0	−8	0	0	0
	APEC	−30	485	455	−97	460	363	−62	1,620	1,620	−62	0	−62	−73	0	−73	0	436	436

Table 12.13 (cont.)

Region		Selected Asia-Pacific FTAs combined									Major FTAs under consideration								
		In force			Signed			Under negotiation			US–ASEAN			US–Japan			ASEAN+3		
								Non-member imports											
		Neg.	Pos.	Total	Neg.	Pos.	Total	Neg.	Pos.	Total	Neg.	Pos.	Total	Neg.	Pos.	Total	Neg.	Pos.	Total
Asia	ASEAN	−10	24	**13**	0	45	**45**	0	117	**117**	0	0	**0**	−16	0	**−16**	0	0	**0**
	CER	0	19	**19**	0	8	**8**	0	39	**39**	−3	0	**−3**	−4	0	**−4**	0	20	**20**
	SAPTA	0	12	**12**	0	2	**2**	0	30	**30**	−2	0	**−2**	−1	0	**−1**	0	12	**12**
	Other Asia	0	108	**108**	0	65	**65**	0	366	**366**	−9	0	**−9**	−14	0	**−14**	0	153	**153**
Pacific	NAFTA	−19	211	**192**	−47	249	**202**	0	701	**701**	−19	0	**−19**	−21	0	**−21**	0	261	**261**
	Other America	−21	0	**−21**	−19	0	**−19**	−2	18	**16**	−7	0	**−7**	−8	0	**−8**	0	10	**10**

Source: Calculations based on gravity model estimates of the impacts of major customs unions and free trade agreements on extra-bloc trade by 1-digit categories.

Table 12.13 shows that, in the aggregate, there is no decline in any non-member country's two-way merchandise trade on account of FTAs for which it is an "outsider." Negative trade diversion is present for several countries and regions, but is strongly outweighed by trade creation. Some of the notable estimates include a projected US$18 billion increase in Chinese two-way trade if a US–Japan FTA is enacted, and a projected US$260 billion increase in US two-way trade if ASEAN+3 is enacted.

We do not place a great deal of weight on the foregoing estimates, but we do believe that the available evidence refutes a common assumption that an FTA inevitably decreases trade between "outsiders" and "insiders." For selected PTAs and particular products (notably agriculture, and textiles and clothing), trade diversion no doubt occurs on a substantial scale. When it occurs, it should be compensated under WTO principles – though in practice that rarely happens. The overall pattern, however, is trade *creation* vis-à-vis "outsiders" rather than trade diversion.

Table 12.14 provides estimates of trade diversion in agriculture trade. According to these calculations, several Asia-Pacific countries and regions would be negatively impacted by FTAs with respect to their agricultural trade. Large differentials between preferential tariff rates and MFN rates, coupled with discriminatory favoritism of FTA partners with respect to other barriers (e.g. TRQs and TBTs), may explain these results. Surprisingly, the United States would appear to be unscathed in agricultural trade by other FTAs in agriculture trade. In fact, non-US agreements currently in force are estimated to increase US two-way agriculture trade by some US$8 billion. Moreover, the ASEAN+3 FTA is projected to increase US two-way agriculture trade by US$7 billion if enacted. Other countries and regions are not so fortunate. Japan, for example, is estimated to have lost US$9 billion in two-way agriculture trade, due to existing FTAs for which it is an "outsider," and the US–ASEAN FTA, if enacted, is projected to cost Japan another US$4 billion in two-way agriculture trade.

Table 12.15 displays the estimated impacts of FTAs on the manufacturing trade of non-members. The estimates are similar to those for total merchandise trade. This reflects the dominant role of manufactures in total merchandise trade. However, due to our separate analysis of total trade, agriculture trade, and manufacture trade, the magnitude of our estimates of the impact on non-FTA members' manufacturing trade does not "add up" to our estimates of the impact on total trade. In fact,

Table 12.14 Trade diversion – average annual impacts of selected FTAs in the Asia-Pacific region on trade in agriculture (SITC 0 and 1) of non-member countries by region and selected countries, 2001–2005 (billions of US dollars at 2005 prices)

Region		Selected Asia-Pacific FTAs combined									Major FTAs under consideration								
		In force			Signed			Under negotiation			US–ASEAN			US–Japan			ASEAN+3		
		Neg.	Pos.	Total	Neg.	Pos.	Total	Neg.	Pos.	Total	Neg.	Pos.	Total	Neg.	Pos.	Total	Neg.	Pos.	Total
								Non-member exports + imports											
Asia-Pacific	US	0	8	8	0	9	9	0	22	22	0	0	0	0	0	0	0	7	7
	China	−1	2	1	−1	3	2	0	7	7	−1	0	−1	−1	0	−1	0	0	0
	Japan	−9	0	−9	−12	0	−12	0	1	1	−4	0	−4	0	0	0	0	0	0
	Korea, Rep. of	−1	1	−1	−1	1	0	0	1	1	0	0	0	−1	0	−1	0	0	0
	APEC	−23	13	−10	−28	15	−13	−3	44	41	−10	0	−10	−9	0	−9	0	13	13
Asia	ASEAN	−3	0	−3	−2	0	−2	−1	3	2	0	0	0	−2	0	−2	0	0	0
	CER	0	1	1	−1	1	0	0	4	4	−1	0	−1	−1	0	−1	0	2	2
	SAPTA	0	0	0	0	0	0	0	1	1	0	0	0	0	0	0	0	0	0
	Other Asia	−2	1	−1	−3	1	−2	0	5	5	−1	0	−1	−1	0	−1	0	2	2
Pacific	NAFTA	−6	8	3	−8	9	1	−2	23	21	−3	0	−3	−3	0	−3	0	8	8
	Other America	−7	0	−7	−7	0	−7	−2	1	−1	−2	0	−2	−2	0	−2	0	1	1

Non-member exports

		Neg.	Pos.	Total	Neg.	Pos.	Total	Neg.	Pos.	Total	Neg.	Pos.	Total	Neg.	Pos.	Total	Neg.	Pos.	Total
Asia-Pacific	US	0	7	**7**	0	9	**9**	0	17	**17**	0	0	**0**	0	0	**0**	0	6	**6**
	China	0	2	**2**	0	3	**3**	0	7	**7**	0	0	**0**	−1	0	**−1**	0	0	**0**
	Japan	0	0	**0**	0	0	**0**	0	0	**0**	0	0	**0**	0	0	**0**	0	0	**0**
	Korea, Rep. of	0	1	**1**	0	1	**1**	0	1	**1**	0	0	**0**	0	0	**0**	0	0	**0**
	APEC	−4	11	**7**	−6	15	**9**	−1	36	**35**	−3	0	**−3**	−6	0	**−6**	0	10	**10**
Asia	ASEAN	−1	0	**−1**	−1	0	**−1**	0	2	**2**	0	0	**0**	−1	0	**−1**	0	0	**0**
	CER	0	1	**1**	0	1	**1**	0	4	**4**	−1	0	**−1**	−1	0	**−1**	0	2	**2**
	SAPTA	0	0	**0**	0	0	**0**	0	1	**1**	0	0	**0**	0	0	**0**	0	0	**0**
	Other Asia	0	1	**1**	0	1	**1**	0	3	**3**	0	0	**0**	0	0	**0**	0	1	**1**
Pacific	NAFTA	−2	7	**5**	−4	9	**5**	−1	18	**17**	−1	0	**−1**	−2	0	**−2**	0	7	**7**
	Other America	−4	0	**−4**	−4	0	**−4**	−1	1	**0**	−1	0	**−1**	−2	0	**−2**	0	1	**1**

Non-member imports

		Neg.	Pos.	Total	Neg.	Pos.	Total	Neg.	Pos.	Total	Neg.	Pos.	Total	Neg.	Pos.	Total	Neg.	Pos.	Total
Asia-Pacific	US	0	1	**1**	0	1	**1**	0	5	**5**	0	0	**0**	0	0	**0**	0	1	**1**
	China	−1	0	**−1**	−1	0	**−1**	0	0	**0**	0	0	**0**	0	0	**0**	0	0	**0**
	Japan	−9	0	**−9**	−12	0	**−12**	0	1	**1**	−4	0	**−4**	0	0	**0**	0	0	**0**
	Korea, Rep. of	−1	0	**−1**	−1	0	**−1**	0	0	**0**	0	0	**0**	0	0	**0**	0	0	**0**
	APEC	−19	1	**−18**	−23	1	**−22**	−3	9	**6**	−7	0	**−7**	−4	0	**−4**	0	3	**3**

Table 12.14 (*cont.*)

		Selected Asia-Pacific FTAs combined									Major FTAs under consideration								
		In force			Signed			Under negotiation			US–ASEAN			US–Japan			ASEAN+3		
Region		Neg.	Pos.	**Total**	Neg.	Pos.	**Total**	Neg.	Pos.	**Total**	Neg.	Pos.	**Total**	Neg.	Pos.	**Total**	Neg.	Pos.	**Total**
							Non-member exports + imports												
Asia	ASEAN	−2	0	**−2**	−2	0	**−2**	0	0	**0**	0	0	**0**	−1	0	**−1**	0	0	**0**
	CER	0	0	**0**	0	0	**0**	0	0	**0**	0	0	**0**	0	0	**0**	0	0	**0**
	SAPTA	0	0	**0**	0	0	**0**	0	0	**0**	0	0	**0**	0	0	**0**	0	0	**0**
	Other Asia	−2	0	**−2**	−3	0	**−3**	0	2	**2**	−1	0	**−1**	−1	0	**−1**	0	1	**1**
Pacific	NAFTA	−4	1	**−2**	−5	1	**−4**	−2	5	**4**	−1	0	**−1**	−1	0	**−1**	0	1	**1**
	Other America	−3	0	**−3**	−3	0	**−3**	−1	0	**−1**	−1	0	**−1**	−1	0	**−1**	0	0	**0**

Source: Calculations based on gravity model estimates of the impacts of major customs unions and free trade agreements on extra-bloc trade, by 1-digit categories.

Table 12.15 *Trade diversion – average annual impacts of selected FTAs in the Asia-Pacific region on trade in manufactures (SITC 5 through 8) of non-member countries by region and selected countries, 2001–2005 (billions of US dollars at 2005 prices)*

		Selected Asia-Pacific FTAs combined									Major FTAs under consideration								
		In force			Signed			Under negotiation			US–ASEAN			US–Japan			ASEAN+3		
Region		Neg.	Pos.	Total	Neg.	Pos.	Total	Neg.	Pos.	Total	Neg.	Pos.	Total	Neg.	Pos.	Total	Neg.	Pos.	Total
								Non-member exports + imports											
Asia-Pacific	US	0	731	731	0	723	723	0	1,777	1,777	0	0	0	0	0	0	0	640	640
	China	0	177	177	0	275	275	0	477	477	−1	20	19	−2	30	28	0	0	0
	Japan	0	463	463	−6	172	165	0	439	439	−2	59	57	0	0	0	0	0	0
	Korea, Rep. of	0	164	164	0	151	151	0	221	221	−1	12	11	−1	12	10	0	0	0
	APEC	0	2,460	2,460	−6	2,133	2,126	0	4,675	4,675	−10	147	138	−13	124	110	0	1,180	1,180
Asia	ASEAN	0	205	205	0	266	266	0	360	360	0	0	0	−3	27	24	0	0	0
	CER	0	65	65	0	51	51	0	114	114	−1	2	1	−1	2	1	0	50	50
	SAPTA	0	51	51	0	29	29	0	79	79	0	4	4	0	4	3	0	28	28
	Other Asia	0	456	456	0	295	255	0	959	999	−2	21	19	−3	20	18	0	400	400
Pacific	NAFTA	0	923	923	0	917	917	0	2,050	2,050	−3	33	29	−4	33	30	0	723	723
	Other America	0	49	49	0	48	48	0	59	99	−1	6	4	−1	6	4	0	30	30

Table 12.15 (*cont.*)

Region		Selected Asia-Pacific FTAs combined									Major FTAs under consideration								
		In force			Signed			Under negotiation			US–ASEAN			US–Japan			ASEAN+3		
		Neg.	Pos.	Total	Neg.	Pos.	Total	Neg.	Pos.	Total	Neg.	Pos.	Total	Neg.	Pos.	Total	Neg.	Pos.	Total
								Non-member exports											
Asia-Pacific	US	0	50	50	0	25	25	0	84	84	0	0	0	0	0	0	0	27	27
	China	0	86	86	0	90	90	0	87	87	0	20	20	0	30	30	0	0	0
	Japan	0	234	234	0	172	172	0	155	155	0	59	59	0	0	0	0	0	0
	Korea, Rep. of	0	54	54	0	31	31	0	38	38	0	12	12	0	12	12	0	0	0
	APEC	0	721	721	0	610	610	0	567	567	0	147	147	0	124	124	0	49	49
Asia	ASEAN	0	90	90	0	83	83	0	47	47	0	0	0	0	27	27	0	0	0
	CER	0	4	4	0	5	5	0	6	6	0	2	2	0	2	2	0	2	2
	SAPTA	0	17	17	0	14	14	0	12	12	0	4	4	0	4	4	0	2	2
	Other Asia	0	101	101	0	71	71	0	79	79	0	21	21	0	20	20	0	18	18
Pacific	NAFTA	0	150	150	0	157	157	0	155	155	0	33	33	0	33	33	0	29	29
	Other America	0	26	26	0	24	24	0	15	15	0	6	6	0	6	6	0	1	1

Non-member imports

Region	Economy	Neg.	Pos.	Total	Neg.	Pos.	Total	Neg.	Pos.	Total	Neg.	Pos.	Total	Neg.	Pos.	Total
Asia-Pacific	US	0	682	**682**	0	698	**698**	0	1,693	**1,693**	0	0	**0**	0	613	**613**
	China	0	90	**90**	0	186	**186**	−1	390	**390**	−2	0	**−2**	0	0	**0**
	Japan	0	229	**229**	−6	0	**−6**	−2	284	**284**	−2	0	**−2**	0	0	**0**
	Korea, Rep. of	0	111	**111**	0	120	**120**	−1	182	**182**	−1	0	**−1**	0	0	**0**
	APEC	0	1,739	**1,739**	−6	1,522	**1,516**	−10	4,108	**4,108**	−13	0	**−13**	0	1,131	**1,131**
Asia	ASEAN	0	115	**115**	0	183	**183**	0	313	**313**	−3	0	**−3**	0	0	**0**
	CER	0	61	**61**	0	46	**46**	−1	107	**107**	−1	0	**−1**	0	49	**49**
	SAPTA	0	35	**35**	0	15	**15**	0	57	**67**	0	0	**0**	0	26	**26**
	Other Asia	0	355	**355**	0	224	**224**	−2	920	**920**	−3	0	**−3**	0	382	**382**
Pacific	NAFTA	0	773	**773**	0	760	**760**	−3	1,896	**1,896**	−4	0	**−4**	0	694	**694**
	Other America	0	23	**23**	0	24	**24**	−1	84	**84**	−1	0	**−1**	0	28	**28**

Source: Calculations based on gravity model estimates of the impacts of major customs unions and free trade, agreements on extra-bloc trade by 1-digit categories.

the estimated impact on manufacturing trade often *exceeds* the estimated impact on total trade. That anomaly simply reflects differing datasets for estimating the coefficients. The more important point is that our estimates of "trade diversion" vis-à-vis outsiders, in the realm of manufacturing trade, all turn out to show either trade creation or very little impact.

Regression coefficients for bilateral trade

Table 12.16 presents the regression coefficients calculated with two-way bilateral trade as the dependent variable. The results are as expected for the core variables: for example, greater distance reduces bilateral trade, and a larger joint economy (joint GDP) enhances trade. Table 12.16 also presents regression coefficients for two-way bilateral agriculture and manufacturing trade taken separately as dependent variables. These estimates are included to provide insight into the most contentious areas of trade politics. Large countries generally prize self-sufficiency in agriculture, and this may explain the finding that larger joint GDP is associated with *less* bilateral agriculture trade. Other core coefficients mostly follow the sign and magnitude of coefficient estimates for total bilateral trade.[31]

We now turn to the coefficients that estimate the impact of FTAs on bilateral trade. The primary FTA coefficients for two-way bilateral trade in all commodities (first column in Table 12.16) generally indicate an increase (the exception is EFTA). MERCOSUR provides the largest estimated gain with a 120 percent increase, and NAFTA is close behind with a 117 percent increase.

The estimated increase in two-way bilateral agricultural trade (second column in Table 12.16) from participation in an FTA is substantial.[32] For example, the stimulus to agricultural trade from AFTA is estimated to exceed 125 percent. For the EU it is 65 percent, which is far beyond the percentage effect on total bilateral trade, estimated at 31 percent.

---

[31] A notable exception is found for the common country dummy variable. The model estimates that if two countries were formerly one, their bilateral manufacturing trade will be approximately 250 percent higher, while both their agricultural trade and total bilateral trade will be lower.

[32] The coefficient estimate for agricultural trade in SAFTA is negative in sign but not statistically different from zero. This reflects the tense relationship between Pakistan and India, the dominant economies in SAFTA. The effect of EFTA is also zero, probably reflecting the disjointed nature of membership in this arrangement.

Table 12.16 *Fixed-effect estimates for trade, by product categories specifying principal customs unions (CUs) and free trade agreements (FTAs), 1976–2005*

	SITC 0–9 (All merchandise)	SITC 0–1 (Agriculture)	SITC 5–8 (Manufactures)
Distance	−1.00 ***	−1.11 ***	−1.03 ***
Joint GDP	0.02 ***	−0.03 ***	0.04 ***
Joint GDP per capita	0.01 ***	0.02 ***	−0.03 ***
Common language	0.07 ***	0.25 ***	−0.05 ***
Common border	0.38 ***	−0.01	0.37 ***
Landlocked	−1.00 ***	−1.10 ***	−0.77 ***
Island	0.56 ***	0.60 ***	0.43 ***
Land area	0.24 ***	0.30 ***	0.20 ***
Common colonizer	−0.59 ***	−0.53 ***	−1.26 ***
Colony	0.58 ***	0.59 ***	0.55 ***
Ever a colony	1.13 ***	1.66 ***	1.12 ***
Common country	−0.20 *	−1.17 ***	1.26 ***
GSP	0.26 ***	0.12 ***	0.47 ***
Joint FDI stocks	0.10 ***	0.08 ***	0.14 ***
EU	0.27 ***	0.50 ***	0.06 ***
EU_x	0.03 ***	−0.13 ***	0.03 ***
EU_m	−0.02 **	−0.16 ***	0.04 ***
EFTA	0.00	0.00	0.00
EFTA_x	0.00	0.00	0.00
EFTA_m	−0.46 ***	−0.64 ***	−0.39 ***
EU FTAs	0.09 ***	0.08 ***	0.08 ***
EU FTAs_x	0.00	0.12 ***	0.07 ***
EU FTAs_m	0.00	−0.05 ***	0.09 ***
NAFTA	0.78 ***	0.71 ***	0.89 ***
NAFTA_x	−0.13 ***	−0.16 ***	−0.02 **
NAFTA_m	0.20 ***	−0.11 ***	0.21 ***
MERCOSUR	0.79 ***	1.01 ***	0.80 ***
MERCOSUR_x	0.16 ***	0.37 ***	0.06 ***
MERCOSUR_m	0.68 ***	0.65 ***	0.78 ***
CMAS FTAs	0.24 ***	0.63 ***	0.06 ***
CMAS FTAs_x	−0.07 ***	−0.02	−0.09 ***
CMAS FTAs_m	0.03 ***	0.01	0.01
AFTA	0.62 ***	0.82 ***	1.04 ***
AFTA_x	0.50 ***	0.18 ***	0.97 ***
AFTA_m	0.18 ***	0.23 ***	0.17 ***
SAFTA	0.16 ***	−0.07	0.41 ***

Table 12.16 (*cont.*)

	SITC 0–9 (All merchandise)	SITC 0–1 (Agriculture)	SITC 5–8 (Manufactures)
SAFTA_x	0.01	0.12 ***	0.26 ***
SAFTA_m	−0.01	−0.30 ***	−0.16 ***
Other CUs and FTAs	0.24 ***	0.26 ***	0.22 ***
Other CUs and FTAs_x	0.04 ***	−0.07 ***	0.13 ***
Other CUs and FTAs_m	0.12 ***	0.11 ***	0.16 ***
Constant	8.25 ***	9.29 ***	10.28 ***
R-squared	0.91	0.91	0.95
Observations (thousands)	325	65	140
Clusters (thousands)	35	7	15

Notes: Fixed-effects estimates are obtained by a method of vector decomposition, based on a three-step FE/OLS routine developed by Plumper and Troeger (2007). The dependent variable is log real trade. Distance, joint real GDP, joint real GDP per capita, joint land area, and joint real FDI stocks are measured in log terms. *,**,*** denote statistical significance at the 10, 5, and 1 percent levels.

Trade agreements represented by dummy variables are: European Union (EU), European Free Trade Area (EFTA), EU bilateral free trade agreements (EU FTAs), North American Free Trade Area (NAFTA), Southern Common Market (MERCOSUR), Chile, Mexico, Australia, and Singapore bilateral free trade agreements (CMAS FTAs), ASEAN Free Trade Area (AFTA), South Asia Free Trade Agreement (SAFTA), and all other customs unions and free trade agreements.

Observations are the number of individual country years of trade data.

Clusters are the number of export country–import country–SITC category combinations in the panel dataset underlying the fixed-effects estimation procedure.

The impact on manufacturing trade is small for the EU and the CMAS FTAs, but over 100 percent for NAFTA, MERCOSUR, and AFTA.[33]

Table 12.16 also displays coefficients that estimate the impact of each FTA (or FTA group) on "outsiders" – countries not members to the agreement. Two variables are used for this purpose, one showing the impact of exports from the FTA member to outsiders (FTA_x) and the other showing the impact on imports by the FTA member from

---

[33] As a reminder, the percentage impact of a dummy variable coefficient is found by ($e^{\wedge}$coefficient −1.00)*100.

outsiders (FTA_m).[34] Perhaps surprising to economists who have grown up on a diet of Vinerian trade diversion, or have spent long hours absorbing Bhagwati and Panagariya on the evils of FTAs,[35] the coefficients for only three agreements indicate diversion of total trade that is statistically different from zero at the 1 percent level.[36] The EFTA caused members' imports from non-member countries to fall by 37 percent, the NAFTA caused members' exports to non-member countries to fall by 12 percent, and the CMAS FTAs caused exports to non-members to fall by 7 percent.

Estimates of trade diversion for manufactures mimic the trade diversion effects for total trade. Only one agreement, SAPTA, shows significant trade diversion in manufactures that was not present for total trade.[37] On the other hand, estimates of trade diversion for agriculture are common: diversion appears in six of the nine FTA groupings. Only AFTA and MERCOSUR clearly show an absence of trade diversion in agriculture.[38] Trade diversion in agriculture is not surprising given the high degree of MFN protection prevalent in that sector. The largest estimate of agriculture trade diversion occurred in the EFTA, with an estimate of 50 percent fewer imports from "outsiders" than would have otherwise occurred. Again, this is not surprising, given the very high agricultural protection characteristic of EFTA members (Switzerland, Iceland, and Norway). Agricultural trade diversion effects associated with the EU and the NAFTA are remarkably similar. These agreements caused members to reduce their agriculture exports to, and imports from, "outside" countries by roughly 13 percent.

To conclude this section: trade diversion *is* important for agriculture, but it is *not* important for total trade. The likely explanation is that FTA liberalization reduces the cost of manufacturing components, and boosts the productivity of manufacturing firms, thereby stimulating both exports to, and imports from, non-members. We would expect the

---

[34] The coefficient estimates from these variables are the estimates used to make the trade diversion calculations discussed under the previous subheading.

[35] See Bhagwati and Panagariya (1996).

[36] The model estimates that EU membership caused external imports to decline by 2 percent; this effect is statistically different from zero with 95 percent confidence.

[37] The coefficient estimate of SAFTA member imports from non-members was negative, indicating trade diversion, but the effect was not statistically different from zero.

[38] The CMAS FTA_x variable indicates trade diversion, but the effect is not statistically different from zero.

same positive results in the trade in services, if sufficient bilateral data was available to estimate gravity model coefficients.

Table 12.16 also provides coefficients for joint FDI stocks as an explanatory variable. For this variable the coefficients represent implied elasticity values. According to the coefficients, a 1.0 percent increase in joint FDI stocks leads to an increase of 0.1 percent in two-way bilateral trade in all commodities. Differentiating by sector, the implied impact is an increase of 0.08 percent in agriculture trade and an increase of 0.14 percent in manufacturing trade. The greater sensitivity in manufacturing is unsurprising, given the importance of network investment and the cross-supply of components and finished goods by multinational enterprises.

The impact of FTAs on FDI

An important motivation for entering an FTA pact – particularly for the smaller and less developed member – is to attract foreign direct investment, not only from the larger partner but also from third countries. We have applied the gravity model framework to evaluate the success of this strategy.[39]

Table 12.17 shows the coefficient estimates for the core gravity variables, using the inward FDI stock from the bilateral partner (either an FTA member or an outsider) as the primary dependent variable. The sign and magnitude of the core coefficients are similar to estimates with bilateral trade as the dependent variable, with a few notable exceptions. If two countries were formerly one country, the inward FDI stock in each country is close to 800 percent higher than otherwise; by contrast, the trade model estimates that two-way trade would be 18 percent lower. A common language brings about 150 percent higher FDI stocks but only 7 percent more trade. Table 12.17 also provides estimates of the impact of total two-way trade and the existence of an FTA on FDI stocks. Those coefficients are of great interest.

The first point to note is that trade is the mother of inward direct investment, with an elasticity estimate of 0.52. In other words, when a country increases its trade with the world by 10 percent, its inward FDI stock also increases by 5 percent. Intuition might suggest that the

---

[39] As far as we are aware, the gravity model was first applied to evaluate the FDI attraction strategy in a study published by the Australian Productivity Commission by Adams *et al.* (2003). The method used here tracks the APC method.

Table 12.17 *Fixed-effect estimates for inward foreign direct investment stocks specifying principal customs unions (CUs) and free trade agreements (FTAs), 1976–2005.*

	Estimated coefficient	Implied percentage change %	Implied elasticity
Distance	−0.48 ***	n.a.	−0.48
Joint GDP	−0.10 ***	n.a.	−0.10
Joint GDP per capita	0.22 ***	n.a.	0.22
Common language	0.94 ***	156	n.a.
Common border	0.60 ***	83	n.a.
Landlocked	−0.30 ***	−26	n.a.
Island	0.58 ***	79	n.a.
Land area	0.16 ***	n.a.	0.16
Common colonizer	−0.41 ***	−34	n.a.
Colony	−0.43 *	−35	n.a.
Ever a colony	1.78 ***	495	n.a.
Common country	2.18 ***	784	n.a.
GSP	0.21 ***	24	n.a.
Joint trade with all partners	0.52 ***	n.a.	0.52
EU	0.49 ***	62	n.a.
EU_x	0.19 ***	21	n.a.
EU m	0.24 ***	27	n.a.
EFTA	0.00	0	n.a.
EFTA_x	−0.45 ***	−37	n.a.
EFTA_m	0.00	0	n.a.
EU FTAs	0.15 ***	16	n.a.
EU FTAs_x	−0.20 ***	−18	n.a.
EU FTAs_m	0.04 *	4	n.a.
Canada–US FTA (CUSFTA)	−0.83 ***	−56	n.a.
CUSFTA_x	−0.34 ***	−29	n.a.
CUSFTA_m	0.03	3	n.a.
US–Mexico FTA (USMXFTA)	−0.08	−8	n.a.
USMXFTA_x	−0.03	−3	n.a.
USMXFTA_m	0.26 ***	29	n.a.
Canada–Mexico FTA (CMXFTA)	0.35 *	42	n.a.
CMXFTA_x	0.22 ***	25	n.a.
CMXFTA_m	−0.11 *	−10	n.a.

Table 12.17 (*cont.*)

	Estimated coefficient	Implied percentage change %	Implied elasticity
MERCOSUR	1.27 ***	257	n.a.
MERCOSUR_x	−0.10 **	−10	n.a.
MERCOSUR_m	−0.16 ***	−15	n.a.
CMAS FTAs	0.50 ***	65	n.a.
CMAS FTAs_x	0.13 ***	14	n.a.
CMAS FTAs_m	0.11 ***	12	n.a.
AFTA	0.88 ***	142	n.a.
AFTA_x	0.35 ***	42	n.a.
AFTA_m	−0.15 ***	−14	n.a.
SAFTA	−0.99 ***	−63	n.a.
SAFTA_x	−0.25 ***	−22	n.a.
SAFTA_m	0.09 **	10	n.a.
Other CUs and FTAs	0.10 ***	10	n.a.
Other CUs and FTAs_x	−0.02	−2	n.a.
Other CUs and FTAs_m	0.13 ***	14	n.a.
Constant	−14.29 ***	n.a.	n.a.
R-squared	0.93		
Observations (thousands)	36		
Clusters (thousands)	4		

Notes:

The dependent variable is the inward stock of FDI in the subject country from its bilateral partner when estimating the primary coefficients (e.g. EU, EFTA, etc.) and the inward FDI diversion coefficients (e.g. (EU_m, EFTA_m, etc.). The dependent variable is the outward stock of FDI from the subject country to a partner country that is not a member of the CU or FTA in question when estimating the outward FDI diversion coefficients (e.g. EU_x EFTA_x, etc.).

In the case of CUSFTA and NAFTA members, the "entry dates" of the respective trade agreements are advanced by two years, on the argument that new flows of FDI anticipated the signing of the respective agreements.

The implied elasticity values apply to the non-dummy variables, since both the dependent variable (FDI stocks) and the independent variables are expressed in logarithmic terms. The elasticity value can be interpreted as the percentage impact on inward FDI stocks from a 1.00 percent increase in a given independent variable.

primary FTA coefficients would uniformly indicate larger FDI stocks from the bilateral partner when an FTA is in place. While this is true for several agreements (e.g. EU, MERCOSUR, and AFTA), surprisingly some FTA coefficients indicate a negative impact on the bilateral FDI stock. Most noteworthy, the CUSFTA coefficient suggests a sharp reduction in the bilateral FDI stock between Canada and the United States.[40] We attribute this to two factors. First, the growth of trade often leads the growth of FDI. As Table 12.17 shows, the elasticity of inward FDI stocks with respect to joint trade with all partners is very high, namely 0.52. A big FTA, such as CUSFTA, substantially and quickly increases the trade of each member. It may take a while for the inward FDI stock of each member to catch up. Hence the primary FDI coefficient may be negative, given the new and higher level of trade. Second, there could have been substantial investment in both directions between the two partners long before they formed an FTA, simply to "jump" the tariff wall. Very likely this was the case between the United States and Canada in the 1960s, 1970s, and 1980s. That particular motivation came to an end once the CUSFTA entered into force in 1989. Since the agreement assures firms based in either country that they will have unfettered access to markets across the border, CUSFTA may have led to disinvestment in small and inefficient "branch plants."

In the Mexican case, the NAFTA coefficient is also negative, but statistically insignificant.[41] Of more importance to Mexico, the FDI_m coefficient attached to NAFTA is strongly positive – reflecting the spur that NAFTA provided to European and Asian investment stakes in Mexico.

The gravity model can also be adapted to indicate the effect that an FTA has on a country's outward FDI to a non-member (FTA_x) simply by using outward investment to the partner country as the dependent variable. Combining the various results tabulated in Table 12.17, it appears that membership in the EU increases FDI stocks between two member countries by 62 percent, as shown by the primary EU variable. According to the same model, EU membership also increases inward FDI from non-members by 27 percent (the EU_m term). Finally,

---

[40] For a longer discussion of Canada's poor performance in attracting FDI, see Mintz and Tarasov (2007).

[41] The primary coefficient for SAFTA is also negative – attributable to strained relations between India and Pakistan. The primary coefficient for EFTA is zero – not surprising given the disjointed membership and that Switzerland has heavily invested in the European Union.

outward FDI from an EU member to non-members increases by 21 percent (the EU_x term).[42] Overall, some eighteen of the FTA_x and FTA_m coefficients are statistically significant (at the 90 percent or better level). Of these eight are negative. In some cases that might reflect the tendency of total trade to expand faster than FDI stocks in the wake of a substantial free trade agreement. Nevertheless, the negative coefficients point to possible investment diversion – a matter that deserves further investigation.[43]

3   Policy implications

The burst of activity detailed in the previous sections of this chapter will likely continue, and could well accelerate in the aftermath of meager results from the Doha Round. In this section, we examine how regional trade agreements in the Asia-Pacific could be better designed and implemented to complement the multilateral trading system. We start with basic observations on the diverse types of agreements already in force or under construction. We then examine options for "multilateralizing" Asia-Pacific regionalism, by both using WTO rules to shape or discipline RTAs, and constructing RTAs that limit discrimination and promote multilateral "building blocks."

Asian versus American regionalism

Before analyzing whether Asia-Pacific regionalism can be "multilateralized," it is important to note that there is no such thing as a single Asia-Pacific model of integration. How Asian countries "do" trade agreements is substantially different than the US or EU model, and attempts to harmonize them – primarily in the APEC context – have not progressed very far (as discussed later).

Compared to the self-professed "gold standard" FTA model pursued by the United States, intra-Asian pacts tend toward political commitments more than legal obligations, and foresee a longer time horizon for the integration process. East Asian trade pacts also differ markedly in

---

[42] None of these figures reflects the impetus given by the EU to FDI through the conduit of expanded trade, both internally and externally.

[43] Instrumental variable techniques might be used to sort out the causality from trade to inward FDI stock, and vice versa. We did not attempt such research for this chapter.

terms of coverage and participation. These temporal and substantive differences merit elaboration.

First, East Asian initiatives have an aspirational quality, and the time horizon is measured in decades – look at the drawn-out process of the ASEAN FTA (AFTA), or the "vision" of free trade projected in the Bogor Declaration of APEC; by contrast, US initiatives are more concrete and focus on near- to medium-term results. The "Asian" approach to integration is incrementalist: building consensus takes time; similarly, adjusting to new competition requires moderation to buffer political regimes from the backlash of those left behind. Asian-style regionalism *follows* the evolution of trade and investment in the marketplace, and *pauses* to accommodate political responses to the adjustment process. It reflects a historical perspective that twenty years is not particularly long. This measured tempo now clashes with the commercial reality of a rapidly growing China, and the near-term consequences for trade and investment in the region.

Second, compared to the comprehensive scope and legal detail of provisions contained in FTAs that the United States has negotiated, most of the Chinese and ASEAN pacts have much more limited coverage, and are full of exceptions. Japan's Economic Partnership Agreements (EPAs) cover a broader range of economic activities, but tread softly on agricultural reforms, on services, and on domestic regulatory issues. In large measure, East Asian pacts ratify the status quo, and in some sense codify the integrated production networks already operating in the region – networks that are linked by expanding flows of intra-regional trade and investment. In other words, regional integration is evident in the marketplace, and government pacts essentially represent a catch-up effort, both to acknowledge that fact and to facilitate its further evolution.

However, there is an important common thread to the fabric of Asia-Pacific regionalism. In all cases, the trade initiatives are driven by a combination of economic and political considerations, just as APEC was at its founding almost twenty years ago. In that era, as today, many countries pursued Asia-Pacific accords to keep the United States politically, economically, and militarily engaged in East Asia. That was the core objective of APEC in 1989; it is still central to the broader initiatives that are under discussion, including the long-term trade initiatives put forward at the APEC meeting in Australia in September 2007, ranging from ASEAN+ accords to the US trans-oceanic proposal for a Free Trade Area of the Asia Pacific (FTAAP). It is also a key reason why the

Bush administration has advocated an FTAAP, particularly at a time when the future trends of US trade policy are in doubt both because new leaders have taken control of Congress and because a new president will occupy the White House in January 2009.

Adapting Asia-Pacific RTAs to the WTO

Regional integration arrangements were born and raised in a multilateral world. Some of them have loosely complied with the lax disciplines of the GATT/WTO system; most are still in their formative years – seemingly obedient but potentially rebellious to multilateralism. This section examines incentives or disciplines that have been or could be incorporated into the WTO to reinforce the consistency and compatibility of RTAs with the WTO, and specific provisions that might "multilateralize" Asia-Pacific RTAs.[44]

We first examine what has been done to "enhance" the WTO requirements for an RTA to qualify for the WTO's special exemption from the most favored nation (MFN) principle. We then turn to proposals to "improve" the construction of RTAs so that they complement and reinforce the multilateral trading system.

Enhancing WTO requirements for RTAs

The WTO has flexible disciplines, contained in GATT Article XXIV and GATS Article V, that allow RTAs to derogate from the system's fundamental MFN principle. The language of those articles is vague, and their application has been prone to abuse. RTAs have included important sectoral exceptions (e.g. agriculture) and embody rules of origin that effectively discriminate against third-country trade and investment. Countries have consistently bent the multilateral disciplines without fear of significant GATT/WTO surveillance, much less enforcement via dispute settlement cases. Only one RTA has passed muster and has been affirmatively deemed to be GATT/WTO-consistent; none has been condemned as GATT/WTO-illegal. Most inhabit a legal limbo in which WTO member countries "reserve their rights" to

---

[44] Note that some of these provisions could involve the "harmonization" of RTA texts. Whether such harmonization promotes multilateralism will depend on the standard to which the texts converge.

return to the matter some time in the future – though no member has ever exercised that right.

A vast literature explores these problems and offers numerous creative but ultimately impractical ideas for fixing them. The definitions and standards by which RTAs are judged against WTO norms are deliberately fuzzy, and are likely to remain so. To date, efforts to negotiate new multilateral disciplines on RTAs have yielded modest and mostly hortatory results.

The Uruguay Round included an "Understanding on the Interpretation of Article XXIV of the General Agreement on Tariffs and Trade 1994" which attempted, inter alia, to clarify the key obligations regarding the transition period for phasing in RTA liberalization ("should exceed 10 years only in exceptional cases"), and the use of weighted average applied tariffs to determine whether the RTA raised barriers to third-country trade. In addition, the Uruguay Round created a new Trade Policy Review Mechanism (TPRM) to monitor the trade policies of member countries, including "their impact on the functioning of the multilateral trading system." However, with the exception of the world's largest RTA, the European Union, the policies and practices of RTAs generally have not been the subject of periodic TPRM reviews. In any event, WTO members firmly stated that the TPRM was not "intended to serve as a basis for the enforcement of specific obligations under the Agreements or for dispute settlement procedures, or to impose new policy commitments on Members" (Annex 3 of the Marrakesh Agreement).[45]

In the Doha Round, rules on RTAs have again been vetted, pursuant to Paragraph 29 of the Doha Ministerial Declaration of November 2001, with the aim of "clarifying and improving disciplines and procedures under existing WTO provisions applying to regional trade agreements." In this area, the Doha negotiations have surprisingly produced some results. In December 2006, the WTO General Council established a new "Transparency Mechanism for Regional Trade Agreements" that is being implemented on a provisional basis pending completion of the comprehensive Doha Round accords. This approach follows the precedent of the TPRM, which was authorized and applied provisionally after the Montreal mid-term review in 1988 until the Uruguay Round accords were signed in 1994.

Will the transparency mechanism help promote the consistency of future RTAs (and changes in existing RTAs) with the WTO disciplines

---

[45] For a detailed assessment of the TPRM, see Keesing (1998).

of GATT Article XXIV and GATS Article V? As drafted, the new obligations are constructive and marginally useful. Their main objective is to get countries to notify the WTO when they are negotiating RTAs, and then supplement that notice with details about the pact once it is signed (Para. 1). Article XXIV already obligates members to notify RTAs; the provisional accord seeks to speed up the process, and specifies that notifications generally should be made "no later than" the time of ratification and "before the application of preferential treatment between the parties" (Para. 3). Either the Committee on Regional Trade Agreements or the Committee on Trade and Development (for pacts between developing countries) will then review the submissions, based on a "factual presentation of the RTA" prepared by the WTO Secretariat, normally within one year of the notification date. However, the mechanism forbids the Secretariat report from making "any value judgment" and precludes the use of the report in any dispute settlement procedure (Paras. 9 and 10).

Importantly, the new mechanism also requires that members of existing RTAs notify "changes affecting the implementation of an RTA" as soon as possible after they occur, and submit a final report on completion of the implementation of the pact (Paras. 14 and 15). These submissions will alert WTO members when RTA preferences, or RTA provisions, such as rules of origin, are modified, and afford members the opportunity for additional consultations on the RTA (Para. 16).[46]

The biggest problem with the new mechanism is not the notification procedures, but rather the notification requirements. The data required relate primarily to tariffs on goods and other traditional border measures (including quotas and safeguard measures). For services, RTA members are supposed to submit general economic statistics; however, regulatory policies and practices that confer preferences on firms from RTA member countries are not included. "Relevant statistics on foreign direct investment (FDI)" are required only for services – odd, since many developing countries complain that a major problem caused by RTAs is investment diversion in manufacturing!

In sum, despite the new transparency mechanism, WTO members continue to favor their traditional "don't ask too much, don't tell too

---

[46] Schott (1996: 22) noted that WTO surveillance of RTAs fails "to track regional pacts after they are signed, when transition provisions or rule changes can significantly affect market access for third-country suppliers." New procedures should help remedy that problem.

much" policy toward RTAs. Moreover, they are adamant that Secretariat reports must not lay the groundwork for WTO disputes that would challenge RTA practices. These limits reflect in large measure the old "glass house syndrome": countries are reticent to "throw stones" at others, for fear that their own agreements will come under scrutiny. The malady is ubiquitous in the WTO, since almost every member belongs to one or several regional arrangements.

Making RTAs more WTO-friendly

Can incentives to reinforce multilateralism be built into Asia-Pacific pacts? To answer this question, we examine efforts to harmonize policies through the development of APEC guidelines on RTA "best practices." We then address rule-making provisions (e.g. accession clauses, rules of origin) that seek to broaden access to preferential treatment until the regional pact approximates the MFN principle of the multilateral trading system.

APEC guidelines for bilateral arrangements

The Asia-Pacific region is home to a large and growing number of RTAs. Almost all countries in the region are also members of the WTO, and thus are obligated to construct and implement their RTAs in compliance with WTO rules. Given the diverse nature of their pacts, APEC members have sought to develop guidelines for rights and obligations covered by RTAs that would encourage the harmonization of regional pacts to a high standard, and thus promote the achievement of the Bogor vision of free trade and investment in the Asia-Pacific region (Scollay, 2006).

At the APEC ministerial meeting in Santiago, Chile, in 2004, member countries agreed to develop a set of non-binding "best practices" guidelines for FTAs. The guidelines should contain the following characteristics (APEC, 2004):

- consistency with APEC principles
- consistency with WTO regulations
- exceed WTO commitments
- comprehensiveness (tariffs and non-tariffs)
- transparency
- trade facilitation (unified regulations)

- dispute settlement mechanism
- simple rules of origin
- cooperation (i.e. information sharing)
- sustainable development
- open to accession
- periodic reviews.

Despite concerns that such vague objectives would foster hortatory declarations, the APEC Committee on Trade and Investment (CTI), which is responsible for drafting the specific guidelines, has produced several model chapters (on trade in goods, technical barriers to trade, transparency, government procurement, cooperation, dispute settlement, trade facilitation, rules of origin, sanitary and phytosanitary standards, and e-commerce), and several more are being considered or drafted (CTI, 2006, 2007b). In many respects these guidelines follow precedents set in corresponding chapters of the US FTAs with Chile and Australia.

The best practices guidelines fall under an APEC mandate to create "high-quality RTAs." There is no agreed definition for high-quality RTAs, but it has been suggested that a high-quality RTA should exhibit the following qualities (Park, 2006):

- They should promote market access, and the economic development of members, without an adverse impact on non-members. In other words, they should be consistent with the objectives of GATT Article XXIV and GATS Article V.
- They should contain "WTO-plus" chapters, including, but not limited to, investment, labor, and environmental standards.
- They should provide for accession by future members.
- The time implementation should coincide with deadlines for the Bogor Goals.

A draft for a model FTA chapter on investment has already been circulated for review by APEC countries, and work on drafts for sensitive chapters covering the environment, competition policy, and temporary entry of business persons has already begun (CTI, 2007a). Unfortunately, the initial reactions to the investment draft echo the fractious debates that ended up in past failures to negotiate investment agreements, both in the OECD and the WTO.

To date, the guidelines have not had a perceptible impact on trade negotiations. National initiatives continue to follow national templates.

Attempts to harmonize existing pacts have failed to bridge the basic divide over the appropriate standard. APEC efforts to craft model provisions for WTO-plus issues have fallen foul of the same controversies that have limited progress within the WTO. The most positive impact may be educational: the "best practices" exercise may help government officials learn lessons from the experiences of other countries in their respective RTA ventures. But it remains an open question whether those lessons will support the process of multilateralizing regionalism.

Open-ended accession clauses

Following the NAFTA model established in the early 1990s, RTAs in the Asia-Pacific region have sometimes included accession clauses that supposedly afford other countries an opportunity to join the agreement. None of them has ever been utilized. Why?

From an academic perspective, the ability to expand the customs territory of an RTA by allowing new members to sign up to existing obligations seems desirable; the RTA rules would then cover a larger market and the implicit protection afforded by some RTA provisions, especially rules of origin, would be diluted. In practice, however, the process is far from automatic. Member countries almost always resist gratuitous entry by "outsiders," mainly because that would reduce the implicit protection provided by the original deal. The "guts" of any accession, whether to an RTA or to the WTO, is the negotiation of a national schedule for implementing reforms, coupled with specific and agreed exceptions to the liberalization timetable. No country has ever totally committed to free trade and investment in an RTA – not even Hong Kong, China, thanks to its restrictions on trade and investment in the service sector. So the concept of "open regionalism" – long bruited in the Asia-Pacific context – is really an ideal end point rather than a pathway toward achieving the Bogor Goal of free trade and investment. Strong resistance to adoption of the "cumulation" concept for meeting rules of origin tests in US FTAs illustrates the lack of political will to expand RTAs without mercantilist "payment" through reciprocal concessions.

Rules of origin

Rules of origin were aptly called "tools of discrimination" by a senior US Treasury official during the NAFTA negotiations. While necessary to determine which goods qualify for RTA preferences, they inherently limit the application of the preferences to a targeted class of products based on their specific requirements. To coin a phrase, "the devil *is* the details." The more complex and industry-specific the origin requirements, the more the rules will have a chilling effect on trade, in large part by raising the cost of compliance. Indeed, in the US–Canada context, some firms have decided that the additional transaction costs would be higher than the MFN tariff, and thus have not applied for the FTA preferences.

As we have argued elsewhere, the best solution to discriminatory origin rules on merchandise trade is to eliminate the source of the problem: the margin of preference between MFN tariffs and the RTA rate. Even though the United States initially proposed the elimination of industrial tariffs in the Doha Round, few countries were willing to accept the challenge (and US officials no longer revive that proposal). As a half-way measure to that desirable result, we have suggested in the NAFTA context that the North American partners should harmonize, over a short period of time, the tariffs that each member applies to third countries on an MFN basis. If that happens, then rules of origin are no longer necessary to avert "trade deflection."[47] The key to this approach, however, is that the standard of convergence should be the lowest rate applied by any of the RTA members. Such an approach might be achieved in the NAFTA context, and perhaps in other regional groupings as well. It could be a problem, however, in some APEC countries that have large gaps between their own WTO tariff bindings and their applied tariff rates on the one hand, and the WTO tariff bindings and applied rates of their RTA partners on the other.

Perhaps the best news on rules of origin is that, for most services (apart from mode 4 – movement of natural persons), the negotiated rules do *not* discriminate strongly against third country suppliers. Fink and Molinuevo (2007) provide a comprehensive account of East Asian trade agreements in services. The happy result just summarized flows from the general absence of tracing mechanisms that seek to identify the ultimate owners of service firms. Thus a service firm with "outside" equity participation, based in one RTA partner, generally enjoys

---

[47] To be sure, even with a harmonized external MFN tariff, member governments would be faced with pressure to maintain rules of origin, so as to discourage the purchase of inputs from "outside" suppliers. However, the call for maintaining rules of origin would then be exposed for what it is – not a legitimate response to trade deflection but rather pure protection.

preferential access to the scheduled service market of another RTA partner. Moreover, in many cases, RTA provisions contain an MFN clause for access to service markets. Thus if an RTA member subsequently concedes better access terms to a third country, the original RTA partner will enjoy the same concession. Since services represent a growing share of world trade, these provisions – which clearly facilitate multilateral trade and investment – will assume greater importance in the years ahead.

Asia-Pacific regionalism: prospects going forward

"Competitive liberalization" is thriving in East Asia, propelled by a strengthening of regional integration among the members of the Association of Southeast Asian Nations (ASEAN) and the new wave of Chinese initiatives with other Asian countries, following China's accession to the World Trade Organization (WTO) in 2001. China's trade talks with the ASEAN group and India have prompted Japan and the Republic of Korea to emulate the Chinese initiatives. Like Japan and the Republic of Korea, China has also concluded an FTA with Chile, and is pursuing trade initiatives (though not "free trade" agreements) in other regions. Its policies are designed to enhance security of access to raw materials and to diversify its rapidly growing export markets.

APEC is now considering broader integration initiatives, including the FTAAP. The September 2007 meeting of APEC leaders in Australia discussed what might be called competitive liberalization studies, assessing the political and economic merits of various trading agreements, ranging from ASEAN+3 to a possible FTAAP. The previous APEC meeting had already delivered a mandate to begin looking into these alternatives, and the process of research and development could well accelerate if the Doha Round talks stall or lead to shallow results.

The APEC study process will inevitably uncover widely differing ambitions and scope among the Asia-Pacific agreements profiled in Table 12.5. However, all the models suggested – ASEAN+1, ASEAN+3, ASEAN+6, or even FTAAP – have at their heart the ASEAN FTA.[48] Yet

---

[48] ASEAN+1 is really three individual ASEAN agreements with China, Japan, and Republic of Korea. ASEAN+3 is a possible free trade area encompassing ASEAN, China, Japan, and Republic of Korea. ASEAN+6 is a possible free trade area encompassing ASEAN, China, Japan, Republic of Korea, Australia, New Zealand, and India. FTAAP is a possible free trade area among all the current members of APEC.

even today AFTA is not an integrated unit. An inevitable conclusion is that further integration will take time, and market forces will more often lead policy initiatives than the other way around.

The evolution of integration in East Asia and the Asia-Pacific region will depend most importantly on what happens in the WTO and the outcome of the Doha Round. If the WTO process collapses, or delivers meager results, it will have important implications for regional economic integration. On balance, either a WTO collapse or a shallow outcome will likely spur the creation of new pacts in East Asia and the Asia-Pacific region.

The big question is whether the WTO outcome and the competitive liberalization spirit will spawn a trilateral deal between China, the Republic of Korea, and Japan. Such a pact is currently under study. Whether the results of that effort will pave the way to FTA negotiations remains to be seen. We are skeptical, since such studies are often commissioned simply to defer decisions on politically sensitive matters – much like the recent ASEAN decision with respect to the Japanese proposal for the ASEAN+6 initiative. But a Northeast Asian FTA would link three powerful manufacturing economies with substantial financial resources, and all but ensure eventual expansion to the "ASEAN+3" East Asian free trade zone, since each Northeast Asian country is conducting parallel negotiations with ASEAN members.

None of these agreements includes Chinese Taipei, and in fact they all discriminate against Chinese Taipei. The US–Republic of Korea FTA will likely cause significant trade diversion away from Chinese Taipei exports to both Korean and US exports. Future agreements that Japan might reach with the Republic of Korea and the United States will do the same. That may not be a big economic problem for everyone else, but does raise important political questions. The FTAAP is the only option vetted to date that could accommodate the intractable problem of Chinese Taipei.

Will all this bilateral activity lead to the fulfillment of the original APEC vision of free trade and investment by 2020, agreed at Bogor in 1994? The APEC Business Advisory Council is not so sure, and accordingly advocated a fresh look at the FTAAP option in a report to the APEC leaders when they met in Santiago, Chile, in November 2004. Not surprisingly, the official reaction was muted. No American or Japanese politician wants to talk about free trade with China – even as a long-term proposition. But events may propel reconsideration, particularly if the Doha Round goes into hibernation and subsequent efforts at trade liberalization are centered on bilateral FTAs. That outcome could easily create an atmosphere of commercial discrimination in the Asia-Pacific region, which would make an FTAAP look quite attractive.

4 Conclusions

The process of economic integration in the Asia-Pacific region will proceed in an incremental fashion, and will struggle with the task of melding trade arrangements that differ widely in terms of coverage and participation. Attempts to harmonize existing and prospective RTAs in the region risk a "least common denominator" approach that limits the scope of liberalization, weakens the force of rules, and harbors numerous sector-specific and product-specific exemptions.

We are skeptical that sufficiently forceful WTO obligations will be adopted to shape the evolving regional framework in a multilateral direction. The new RTA transparency mechanism, implemented on a provisional basis by WTO members in December 2006, represents a step forward, but ultimately will have minimal effect because of its weak notification requirements.

Will Asia-Pacific countries themselves adopt a set of rules that help make their RTAs more WTO-friendly? Judging by the evidence to date, such discipline is easier to discuss than to legislate. Model provisions designed to harmonize future RTA initiatives proffer detailed guidance concerning tertiary issues, but voice only vague exhortations on the key substantive issues. Accession clauses are rarely invoked because they do not meet the practical test of reciprocal bargaining. Cumulating content requirements across RTAs with a common hub run foul of political lobbies that insist on restrictive origin rules in each pact. Fortunately, however, RTA service provisions generally do not discriminate strongly against "outsiders," and in this sense the agreements contain a welcome "pro-multilateral" tilt. Perhaps the best solution for multilateralizing regionalism in the realm of merchandise trade still remains viable: to reduce substantially the margin of preference between the RTA tariff schedules and the most favored nation tariff rates. Harmonizing the MFN tariffs of each member down to the level of the lowest rate applied by any of the RTA members would make the RTA more WTO-friendly, eviscerate the "trade deflection" argument for restrictive rules of origin, and strengthen the drive toward multilateral trade liberalization.

Table 12.1A *FTAs, in the Asia-Pacific region, organized by dominant partner, GDP and trade flows*

Dominant partner	Status (as of Sep. 2007)	Year since	Counter-party	Dominant partner's GDP and two-way merchandise trade (2005)				Partner country's GDP and two-way merchandise trade (2005)			
						Trade with partner				Trade with dominant partner	
				GDP (billions)	Total trade (billions)	Dollar amount (billions)	Share of total trade (%)	GDP (billions)	Total trade (billions)	Dollar amount (billions)[a]	Share of Total trade (%)
United States	In force	1994	Canada/ Mexico (NAFTA)	12,456	2,636.8	795.0	30.2	1,901	1,155.1	795.9	68.9
		2004	Singapore			36.0	1.4	117	397.1	36.0	9.1
		2004	Chile			12.6	0.5	115	71.9	12.6	17.5
		2005	Australia			23.4	0.9	709	236.0	23.4	9.9
	Signed	2006	Peru			7.7	0.3	79	30.5	7.7	25.2
		2006	Colombia			14.8	0.6	122	42.4	14.8	34.9
		2006	Panama			2.5	0.1	16	5.1	2.5	49.0
		2007	Korea, Rep. of			73.2	2.8	788	545.5	73.2	13.4
	Under negotiation	2004	Thailand			28.3	1.1	173	228.3	28.3	12.4
	Under consideration	2006	Malaysia			45.1	1.7	131	254.6	45.1	17.7
			ASEAN			153.0	5.8	883	870.4	153.0	17.6
			Japan			197.4	7.5	4,567	1,110.1	197.4	17.8
			FTAAP[b]			1614.8	61.2	12,654	3,562.3	1,614.8	45.3

Country	Status	Year	Partner								
China	In force	2004	Hong Kong, China	2,234	1,422.6	136.7	9.6	178	589.5	136.7	23.2
		2005	ASEAN			130.5	9.2	883	870.4	130.5	15.0
		2006	Chile			7.1	0.5	115	71.9	7.1	9.9
	Under negotiation	2005	Australia–New Zealand			29.9	2.1	817	283.9	29.9	17.2
		2006	Singapore			33.2	2.3	117	397.1	33.2	8.4
	Under consideration		India			18.7	1.3	772	232.6	18.7	8.0
			FTAAP[b]			870.5	61.2	22,876	4,776.5	870.5	18.2
Japan	In force	2002	Singapore	4,567	1,110.1	25.2	2.3	117	397.1	25.2	6.3
		2005	Mexico			9.4	0.8	768	458.2	9.4	2.1
		2006	Malaysia			27.3	2.5	131	254.6	27.3	10.7
		2007	Chile			5.9	0.5	115	71.9	5.9	8.2
	Signed	2005	Thailand			38.1	3.4	173	228.3	38.1	16.7
		2006	Indonesia			30.1	2.7	281	143.3	30.1	21.0
	Under negotiation	2003	Korea, Rep. of			71.1	6.4	788	545.5	71.1	13.0
		2005	ASEAN			148.7	13.4	883	870.4	148.7	17.1
		2007	India			6.7	0.6	772	232.6	6.7	2.9
	Under consideration		FTAAP[b]			733.9	66.1	20,542	5,088.9	733.9	14.4
ASEAN	In force	2005	China	883	670.4	113.1	13.0	2,234	1,422.6	113.1	8.0
		2007	Korea, Rep. of (goods only)			52.2	6.0	788	545.5	52.2	9.6

Table 12.1A (*cont.*)

Dominant partner	Status (as of Sep. 2007)	Year since	Counter-party	Dominant partner's GDP and two-way merchandise trade (2005)		Trade with partner		Partner country's GDP and two-way merchandise trade (2005)		Trade with dominant partner	
				GDP (billions)	Total trade (billions)	Dollar amount (billions)	Share of total trade (%)	GDP (billions)	Total trade (billions)	Dollar amount (billions)[a]	Share of Total trade (%)
	Under negotiation	2004	CER			38.4	4.4	814	272.4	38.4	14.1
		2005	Japan			153.9	17.7	4,567	1,110.1	153.9	13.9
	Under consideration		ASEAN+3[e]			319.2	36.7	7,589	3,078.2	319.2	31.4
			FTAAP[b d]	788	545.5	582.9	67.0	24,249	5,010.4	582.9	11.6
Korea, Rep. of	In force	2004	Chile			3.4	0.6	115	71.9	3.4	4.7
		2006	Singapore			12.7	2.3	117	397.1	12.7	3.2
		2007	ASEAN goods			53.5	9.8	883	870.4	53.5	6.1
	Signed	2007	United States			72.3	13.3	12,456	2,636.8	72.3	2.7
	Under negotiation	2003	Japan			72.4	13.3	4,567	1,110.1	72.4	6.5
		2005	Canada			6.1	1.1	1,132	703.9	6.1	0.9
		2006	Mexico			4.2	0.8	768	451.2	4.2	0.9

Status	Year	Economy						
India	2006	India	772	232.6	6.7	6.7	1.2	2.9
Under consideration		FTAAP[b]	24,322	5,653.5	353.4	353.4	64.8	6.3
In force	2001	Sri Lanka	24	15.2	2.4	1.0	2.4	15.7
	2005	Singapore	117	397.1	8.3	3.6	8.3	2.1
	2006	Bhutan	1	n.a.	0.2	0.1	0.2	n.a.
	2006	SAFTA[c]	205	82.7	6.4	2.8	6.4	7.7
Under negotiation	2006	Korea, Rep. of	788	545.5	5.8	2.5	5.8	1.1
	2007	Japan	4,567	1,110.1	5.8	2.5	5.8	0.5
Under consideration		China	2,234	1,422.6	16.3	7.0	16.3	1.1
		FTAAP[b]	25,110	6,199.1	86.8	37.3	86.8	1.4

Notes: Chart does not include framework agreements, PTAs, or non-reciprocal agreements.

[a] Figures are based on two-way trade with a partner country, as reported by the dominant partner.

[b] Data for Chinese Taipei is not available. Dominant partner is not included in calculation of a possible FTAAP's total trade and GDP.

[c] India is not included in calculation of SAFTA's total trade and GDP.

[d] Dominant partner includes member countries of either APEC or ASEAN (for convenience, Laos, Cambodia and Myanmar, which are not APEC members, but are ASEAN members, are included). Partner country includes APEC member countries which are non-ASEAN member countries.

[e] Refers to an expansion of ASEAN to include China, Japan, and Republic of Korea.

Source: IMF World Economic Outlook Database, September 2006, IMF Direction of Trade Statistics, January 2007.

Table 12.2A *FTAs in the Asia-Pacific region, organized by dominant partner, FDI stocks, 2005*

Dominant partner	Status (as of Sep. 2007)	Year since	Counter-party	Dominant country's two-way (outward and inward) FDI stocks (2005)			Partner country's two-way (outward and inward) FDI stocks (2005)		
				Total FDI stocks (billions)	FDI stocks with partner		Total FDI stocks (billions)	FDI stocks with partner	
					Dollar amount (billions)	Share of total FDI stocks (%)		Dollar amount (billions)[a]	Share of total FDI stocks (%)
United States	In force	1994	Canada/Mexico (NAFTA)	3,613.8	498.5	13.8	829.6	498.5	60.1
		2004	Singapore		50.5	1.4	137.9	50.5	36.6
		2004	Chile		16.2	0.4	69.8	16.2	23.2
		2005	Australia		157.4	4.4	230.7	157.4	68.2
	Signed	2006	Peru		3.9	0.1	18.0	3.9	21.7
		2006	Colombia		3.4	0.1	5.8	3.4	58.6
		2006	Panama		16.6	0.5	22.6	16.6	73.5
		2006	Korea, Rep. of		30.3	0.8	93.1	30.3	32.5
	Under negotiation	2004	Thailand		8.7	0.2	35.3	8.7	24.6
	Under consideration	2006	Malaysia		16.1	0.4	53.3	16.1	30.2
			ASEAN		92.2	2.6	264.1	92.2	34.9
			Japan		225.0	6.2	506.0	225.0	44.5
			FTAAP[b]		1,110.9	30.7	2,869.7	1,110.9	38.7

Economy	Status	Year	Partner						
China	In force	2004	Hong Kong, China	492.5	227.1	46.1	806.8	227.1	28.1
		2005	ASEAN		36.4	7.4	264.1	36.4	13.8
		2006	Chile		0.0	0.0	69.8	0.0	0.0
	Under negotiation	2004	Australia/New Zealand		0.6	0.1	239.7	0.6	0.3
		2006	Singapore		28.1	5.7	137.9	28.1	20.4
	Under consideration		India		0.0	0.0	15.7	0.0	0.0
			FTAAP[b]		362.2	73.5	5,242.2	362.2	6.9
Japan	In force	2002	Singapore	506.0	13.9	2.7	137.9	13.9	10.1
		2005	Mexico		3.6	0.7	98.6	3.6	3.7
		2006	Malaysia		5.6	1.1	53.3	5.6	10.5
		2006	Chile		2.4	0.5	69.8	2.4	3.4
	Signed	2005	Thailand		11.7	2.3	35.3	11.7	33.1
		2006	Indonesia		7.7	1.5	30.1	7.7	25.6
	Under negotiation	2003	Korea		9.2	1.8	93.1	9.2	9.9
		2005	ASEAN		42.4	8.4	264.1	42.4	16.1
		2007	India		1.8	0.4	15.7	1.8	11.5
	Under consideration		FTAAP[b]		349.8	69.1	5,216.3	349.8	6.7
ASEAN	In force	2005	China	264._	36.4	13.8	492.5	36.4	7.4
		2007	Korea, Rep. of (goods only)		5.2	2.0	93.1	5.2	5.6
	Under negotiation	2004	CER		2.0	0.8	239.7	2.0	0.8

Table 12.2A (cont.)

Dominant partner	Status (as of Sep. 2007)	Year since	Counter-party	Dominant country's two-way (outward and inward) FDI stocks (2005)			Partner country's two-way (outward and inward) FDI stocks (2005)		
				Total FDI stocks (billions)	FDI stocks with partner		Total FDI stocks (billions)	FDI stocks with partner	
					Dollar amount (billions)	Share of total FDI stocks (%)		Dollar amount (billions)[a]	Share of total FDI stocks (%)
		2004	Japan		42.4	16.1	506.0	42.4	8.4
	Under consideration		ASEAN+3[e]		84.0	31.8	1,091.6	84.0	7.7
			FTAAP[b, d]		224.8	85.1	5,321.3	224.8	4.2
Korea, Rep. of	In force	2004	Chile	93.1	0.0	0.0	69.8	0.0	0.0
		2006	Singapore		0.7	0.8	137.9	0.7	0.5
		2007	ASEAN (goods)		5.2	5.6	251.9	5.2	2.1
	Signed	2007	United States		30.3	32.5	3,613.8	30.3	0.8
	Under negotiation	2003	Japan		9.2	9.9	506.0	9.2	1.8
		2005	Canada		1.1	1.2	733.9	1.1	0.1
		2006	Mexico		0.3	0.3	98.6	0.3	0.3
		2006	India		0.7	0.8	15.7	0.7	4.5
	Under consideration		FTAAP[b]		62.6	67.2	3,664.7	62.6	1.7

India	In force	1991	Sri Lanka	15.7	n.a.	n.a.	0.3	n.a.	n.a.
		2005	Singapore (2004 data)		1.0	6.4	258.8	1.0	0.4
		2006	Bhutan		n.a.	n.a.	0.0	n.a.	n.a.
		2006	SAFTA[c]		0.0	0.0	5.6	0.0	0.0
	Under negotiation	2006	Korea, Rep. of		0.7	4.5	93.1	0.7	0.8
		2007	Japan		1.8	11.5	506.0	1.8	0.4
	Under consideration		China		0.0	0.0	492.5	0.0	0.0
			FTAAP[b]		12.8	81.5	5,372.5	12.8	0.2

Notes: Table does not include framework agreements, PTAs, or non-reciprocal agreements.

[a] Figures are based on FDI stock with a partner country, as reported by the dominant partner.

[b] Data for Chinese Taipei is not available. Dominant partner is not included in calculation of a possible FTAAP's total FDI and GDP.

[c] India is not included in calculation of SAFTA's total FDI and GDP.

[d] Dominant partner includes member countries of either APEC or ASEAN (for convenience, Laos, Cambodia and Myanmar, which are not APEC members, but are ASEAN members, are included). Partner country includes APEC member countries which are non-ASEAN member countries.

[e] Refers to an expansion of ASEAN to include China, Japan, and Republic of Korea.

Source: Database constructed at the Peterson Institute.

Table 12.3A *Trade and FDI gravity model regression variables*

Variable	Description
Dependent variables	
Dependent variable (Table 12.16, trade regression)	Log value of bilateral trade by 1-digit SITC, real US dollars
Dependent variable (Table 12.17, FDI regression)	Log value of bilateral inward stock of FDI, real US dollars
Explanatory variables	
Distance	Log of distance between partners, expressed in kilometers by the great circle route
Joint GDP	Log of product of real GDP of the partners
Joint GDP per capita	Log of product of real GDP per capita of the partners
Common language	Common language dummy (0 or 1)
Common border	Common border dummy (0 or 1)
Landlocked	Number of countries in pair that are landlocked (0, 1 or 2)
Island	Number of island countries in the partner pair (0, 1 or 2)
Land area	Log of product of land areas of the partners (million square kilometers)
Common colonizer	Dummy for common colonizer, post-1945 (0 or 1)
Colony	Dummy for country pairs currently in colonial relationship (0 or 1)
Ever a colony	Dummy for country pairs ever in a colonial relationship (0 or 1)
Common country	Dummy for same nation or a continuing colony (0 or 1)
GSP	Dummy for country pairs using generalized system of preferences (GSP) between the partners (0 or 1)
Joint FDI stocks (Table 12.16 only)	Log of product of total inward FDI stock from the world of the partners, real US dollars
Joint trade with all partners (Table 12.17 only)	Log of product of total merchandise trade with the world of the partners, real US dollars
FTA variables	
FTA primary (e.g. EU)	Dummy variable indicating an FTA is in place for a country pair (0 or 1)

Table 12.3A (*cont.*)

Variable	Description
EU_m (e.g. EU_m)	Dummy variable (0 or 1) indicating that an FTA country is importing from a country other than its FTA partner (e.g. a value of 1 is given for the NAFTA_m variable for the US imports from Japan in 1999 because Japan is not a member of NAFTA).
FTA_x (e.g. EU_x)	Dummy variable (0 or 1) indicating that an FTA country is exporting to a country other than its FTA partner (e.g. a value of 1 is given for the NAFTA_x variable for the US exports to Japan in 1999 because Japan is not a member of NAFTA).
Fixed effects variables	
Ordered country pair dummy, by trade category (fixed-effect, not in tables)	Dummy for each exporting-to-importing country pair, by 1-digit SITC (e.g. US exports to Japan of chemical products, SITC 5)
Year dummy (fixed-effect, not in tables)	Dummy for a specific year (e.g. 1999)

References

Adams, R., Dee, P., Goli, J., and McGuire, G. (2003) "The Trade and Investment Effects of Preferential Trading Arrangements – Old and New Evidence," Staff Working Paper, Canberra: Australia Productivity Commission.

Asia-Pacific Economic Cooperation (APEC) (2004) "Best Practices for RTAs/FTAs in APEC," submitted by SOM Chair for consideration to the sixteenth APEC Ministerial Meeting in Santiago, Chile. Forum Doc. No. 2004/CSOM/028rev1. Doc. No. 2004/AMM/003, Agenda Item V.2.

Baldwin, R. E. and Taglioni, D. (2006) "Gravity for Dummies and Dummies for Gravity Equations," Discussion Paper Series No. 5850, London: Centre for Economic Policy Research.

Bhagwati, J. and Panagariya, A. (1996) "Preferential Trading Areas and Multilateralism – Strangers, Friends, or Foes?," in J. Bhagwati and A. Panagariya (eds.), *The Economics of Preferential Trade Agreements*, Washington DC: American Enterprise Institute.

Bergsten, C. Fred (2001) "Brunei: Turning Point for APEC," Policy Brief 01–1, Washington DC: Peterson Institute for International Economics.

(2007) "Toward a Free Trade Area of the Asia Pacific," Policy Brief 07–2, Washington, DC: Peterson Institute for International Economics.

Centre for International Economics (CIE) (2005) "Open Economies Delivering to People, 2005: Regional Integration and Outcomes in the APEC region," Canberra: CIE.

Choi, I. and Schott, J. (2001) *Free Trade between Korea and the United States?*, Washington DC: Institute for International Economics.

Committee on Trade and Investment, APEC (CTI) (2006) "Appendix 1 to Committee on Trade and Investment Report to Asia Pacific Economic Cooperation Ministers, CTI Agreed RTAs/FTAs Model Measures Texts," available at: www.apec.org/etc/medialib/ apec_media_library/downloads/committees/cti/pubs/2006.Par.0021.File.v1.1 (accessed August 16, 2007).

(2007a) "Achievements and Current Activities," available at: www.apecsec. org.sg/apec/apec_groups/committees/committee_on_trade.html. (accessed August 16, 2007).

(2007b) *Annual Report to Ministers.* Singapore: APEC Secretariat.

DeRosa, D. A. (2007) *International Trade and Investment Data Set by 1-Digit SITC, 1976–2005*, gravity model dataset on DVD developed for the Peterson Institute and the World Trade Institute, Washington: Peterson Institute for International Economics.

Fink, C. and Molinuevo, M. (2007) "East Asian Free Trade Agreements in Services: Roaring Tigers or Timid Pandas?," Washington DC: World Bank.

Frankel, J. A. (1997) *Regional Trading Blocs in the World Economic System*, Washington DC: Institute for International Economics.

Greenaway, D. and Milner, C. (2002) "Regionalism and Gravity," *Scottish Journal of Political Economy* 49: 574–85.

Hufbauer, G. C. and Baldwin, R. E. (2006) *The Shape of a Swiss–US Free Trade Agreement*, Washington DC: Peterson Institute for International Economics.

Hufbauer, G. C. and Burki, S. J. (2006) *Sustaining Reform with a US–Pakistan Free Trade Agreement*, Washington DC: Peterson Institute for International Economics.

Keesing, D. B. (1998) *Improving Trade Policy Reviews in the World Trade Organization*, Policy Analyses in International Economics, vol. LII, Washington: Institute for International Economics.

Mintz, J. M. and Tarasov, A. (2007) "Canada is Missing out on Global Capital Market Integration," e-brief, Toronto: C. D. Howe Institute.

Park, S.-H. (2006) "Sub-regionalism (FTAs/RTAs) in the APEC Region and the Road to the Bogor Goals," in *Broadening the Horizon for Pacific Economic Cooperation: Korean Perspective*, papers presented at the Korean National Committee for Pacific Economic Cooperation (KOPEC), Seoul.

Plumper, T. and Troeger, V. E. (2007) "Efficient Estimation of Time-Invariant and Rarely Changing Variables in Finite Sample Panel Analyses with Unit Fixed Effects," *Political Analysis* 15 (2): 124–39.

Rieder, R. (2006) "Playing Dominoes in Europe: An Empirical Analysis of the Domino Theory for the EU, 1962–2004," Institute for International and Development Studies (HEID) Working Paper No. 11/2006, Geneva: Graduate Institute of International Studies.

Rose, A. K. (2004) "Do We Really Know that the WTO Increases Trade?," *American Economic Review* 94 (1): 98–114.

Schott, J. J. (ed.) (1996) *The World Trading System: Challenges Ahead*, Washington DC: Institute for International Economics.

Schott, J., Bradford, S. C., and Moll, T. (2006) "Negotiating the Korea–United States Free Trade Agreement," Policy Briefs 06–4, Washington DC: Peterson Institute for International Economics.

Scollay, R. (2006) "WTO Rules on RTAs/FTAs from Perspective of Developing Economies. APEC," workshop on "Best Practices in Trade Policy for RTAs/FTAs: Practical Lessons and Experience for Developing Economies," Ha Noi, Viet Nam, Doc. No. 2006/SOM1/CTI/FTA-RTA/003.

UNCTAD (2006) *World Investment Report*, New York: United Nations.

WTO (2004) *Trade Policy Review: Republic of Korea*, Geneva: WTO.

13

Multilateralizing preferential trade agreements: a developing country perspective

BERNARD HOEKMAN AND L. ALAN WINTERS[1]

1 Introduction

Preferential trade agreements (PTAs) continue to proliferate. Always a central element of the trade policy strategy of European countries, 'regionalism' has now become the dominant form of international cooperation on trade policy for virtually all the members of the WTO, developed and developing. The proliferation of PTAs has been accompanied by steadily declining barriers to trade generally, and high growth rates in world trade. The uniform tariff equivalent of all applied most favoured nation tariffs of high-income OECD countries in 2005 was 4.8 per cent. Excluding agricultural products, the figure drops to 2.7 per cent (Kee, Nicita and Olarreaga, 2008). For the developing countries, the focus of this chapter, applied MFN tariffs have also fallen substantially; Kee *et al.* estimate that the median average overall trade restrictiveness index was 7.5 per cent for the fifty-seven countries for which data are available in 2005, compared with 12.3 per cent ten years earlier. This reduction in external MFN protection reflects mostly unilateral, autonomous actions by governments (Martin and Messerlin, 2007). While PTAs can be building blocks or stumbling blocks for multilateral liberalization, it is incontrovertible that the level of MFN trade barriers has been falling.

From a welfare perspective what matters is not only the applied MFN level of protection, however, but also the extent of discrimination in the treatment of alternative sources of supply of a given good or service. The lower MFN tariffs are *and* the less discrimination there is, the better

[1] We are grateful to Ivan Crowley for research assistance and to Richard Baldwin, Peter Holmes and Philip Levy for helpful comments. The views expressed are personal and should not be attributed to the World Bank.

off the world is as a whole. An important function of the WTO is to encourage members to reduce external levels of protection through recurring rounds of multilateral trade negotiations (MTNs), also reducing the discrimination that is entailed in PTAs in the process.[2]

In addition to MTNs, other forces may also 'multilateralize regionalism'. These are of interest as possible alternative routes through which the objective of a multilateral, non-discriminatory trade regime might emerge endogenously from a sequence that includes PTAs. The original conception in Baldwin (2006) was applied to straightforward border barriers to goods trade, emphasizing, in particular, the costs associated with the implementation of PTAs, especially rules of origin. Baldwin, Evenett and Low (Chapter 3 of this volume) extend the concept to a number of other policies that are the subject of PTA disciplines.

This chapter considers the prospects for – and implications of – 'multilateralizing' PTAs for developing countries – considering the implications for both member and non-member countries.[3] We deal with border measures such as tariffs and also at greater length with 'deep integration'– areas of domestic and regulatory policy (behind-the-border) where the objective is not (primarily) to discriminate against or between foreign suppliers of a good or service. To make this broad area more concrete and specific, we consider one aspect of deep integration in greater detail – the temporary mobility of labour, including through mode 4 of the GATS and its PTA equivalents. We discuss whether PTAs have so far shown signs of multilateralization, and what might be done to encourage greater 'multilateral' outcomes. Overall we do not find that PTAs have added much to the unilateral and multilateral approaches to liberalization, and are not very optimistic that they can generally do so.

So-called 'deep integration' has become an increasingly important feature of PTAs over the last decade and a half as border barriers decline, and it is increasingly appealed to as a justification for pursuing PTAs. It spans many aspects of product and market regulation, including product standards, government procurement, investment, competition policy, labour, environmental policies, and protection of intellectual

---

[2] Although the WTO has rules on the design and implementation of recent PTAs, these have never been enforced. In practice, MTNs are the primary mechanism through which WTO members address the trade-diverting effects of PTAs and push PTAs towards multilateralization.

[3] We do not employ the term regionalism in this chapter, as many PTAs are not regional in the sense of involving neighbouring countries.

property and other intangible and tangible assets. Such 'regulatory' policies are especially important for service industries, which have become
more prominent in PTA negotiations as a result of the increasing trad-
ability of services and the inclusion of investment policies in the set of
issues covered.

The prospects for the multilateralization of PTA commitments in these
areas may be greater than for goods and traditional trade barriers. In
many cases, regulation is quite naturally applied in a non-discriminatory
fashion, treating domestic and all overseas suppliers or firms equally –
where 'domesticity' is defined more frequently in terms of location of
production than ownership. This is quite different from tariffs and
NTBs affecting trade in goods, where domestic/foreign and intra-foreign
discrimination is the *objective*. From the perspective of achieving
regulatory objectives, nationality often will not (and should not) matter.
But even if regulation applies to all sources of supply, it can still have the
effect of segmenting markets and reducing competition. The multilateral challenge is to get members of PTAs to adopt regulations and
reforms that enhance the contestability of the relevant markets, independent of the nationality of producers and suppliers.

If liberalization – defined as taking actions to enhance the contestability
of a market – is more likely to be multilateral (non-discriminatory) for
regulations than for merchandise trade barriers, it is, equally, less likely
to come about at all. This is because it is inherently more far-reaching
and because it is simultaneously necessary and very difficult to distinguish between regulations that are genuinely needed for the achievement
of domestic objectives and those that are oriented towards segmenting
markets and protecting domestic incumbents. In practice it is certainly
not inevitable that regulations are applied on a nationality-blind basis –
insofar as protectionism is an objective of policymakers, regulation can
be (and is) used to achieve this. One reason is that the legitimate, non-
protectionist class of regulation frequently requires the acquiescence of
domestic firms if it is to be implemented effectively, and almost always
entails consulting those firms about any reforms. With the complex and
subtle nature of many regulations, incumbents (and national regulators)
will have a great deal of influence over regulatory structures and details,
and may well have veto power over policymakers.

For cooperation on product market regulation and domestic policies
in PTAs ('deep integration'), one can envisage three different processes
of multilateralization. First, *hegemonic multilateralization*. A hegemonic
economic power is essentially able to impose its own model (or at least a

model consistent with its own point of view) on its partners, not necessarily coercively but by the force of its market size. As different partners adopt the hegemon's approach over their own local one, a degree of multilateralism is achieved. And it is possible that, as the partners enter further bilateral or regional arrangements with other partners, the model is extended. Unlike in Baldwin's goods cases, the deep hegemonic route is generally implemented as the bilateral agreements are signed rather than afterwards. Although the accretion of users of a particular regulatory model may increase the chances of that model being adopted globally, we do not yet have any examples of such progress. Moreover, as Schiff and Winters (2003) observed, the accretion of two different groups of supporters around two different models – say a US and an EU model – could make the final multilateral step (harmonization or recognition of equivalence) less rather than more likely. Moreover, intuitively, it might not even be multilateralizing, in the sense of decreasing the average degree of discrimination or difference in treatment across the world.[4]

Hegemonic multilateralization refers not to discrimination across sources of supply by a single market, but to the degree of harmonization of standards and regulations across markets. If a high degree of similarity or consistency is achieved, goods and services designed for one market can be sold elsewhere, greatly increasing the contestability of markets. Examples of the hegemonic model abound in 'deep integration'. The US requires partners in bilateral investment treaties (BITs) to conform to an identical template, and imposes its own intellectual property right (IPR) protection provisions in its PTAs (World Bank, 2005). These rules are applied by partners to all sources of investment or intellectual property; they may have displaced discriminatory regimes, but even if they have not, their uniformity across countries eases the regulatory burden on firms looking to invest or use IPRs. Another example is the EU interest in extending its system of geographical indications through its PTAs.

The second route to multilateralism is a *convergence route*. This operates within a PTA where the erosion of barriers to trade increases the pressure to harmonize regulations because they start to have greater

---

[4] As Winters (1999) discusses, multilateralism is actually rather hard to define and measure precisely. A world divided into two very different camps may involve more friction and discrimination than one in which many standards are used, each slightly different from another.

impact on trade patterns, competitiveness and profitability. This is essentially the 'competition between rules' that featured in the EU's Single Market Programme, which applies equally to goods and services. It depended, in the case of goods, not only on the removal of traditional barriers to intra-EU trade (tariffs, quotas, etc.) but on the aggressive policy of the European Commission and the European Court of Justice towards other limitations on the freedom of movement of goods, such as product standards (where the principle of mutual recognition was applied). In services the political sensitivity of the convergence route is evident in the constrained liberalization of cross-border services espoused by the recent Services Directive in the EU and the difficulties that have affected efforts by the EU and the US to make progress in moving towards accepting each other's regulatory norms for specific services as being effectively 'equivalent'.[5] Note that the convergence route also spans a frequently mentioned rationale for PTA-based cooperation in 'non-WTO' areas: PTAs may be a useful forum for experimentation and learning. Successful examples of cooperation between members of a PTA may be adopted in other PTAs (or unilaterally), thus promoting multilateralization over time.

The third route to multilateralism is that identified by Baldwin (2006) for trade in goods – what we might term a *political evolution route* – whereby changes in the political weight of different parties, or in the relative importance of different costs, change the political economy so that groups that once sought to segment markets now seek to integrate them. This route is, of course, premised on policies being applied in a discriminatory manner vis-à-vis non-members of a PTA. One difference for deep integration is that, compared with restrictions on goods trade, regulations are complex and require greater complicity from the relevant industry. The strong position of incumbents may make liberalization more difficult; in particular, it is difficult to envisage incumbents in a sector seeking the liberalization of that sector. However, offsetting this is that downstream (using) sectors may have stronger incentives to oppose policies that raise the costs of services than is the case with goods.

The plan of the chapter is as follows. In Section 2 we summarize a few 'stylized facts' regarding the coverage, content and implementation of

---

[5] For example, the failure under the EU–US Transatlantic Economic Partnership to agree on the mutual recognition of professional qualifications and the 'equivalence' of regulatory standards for financial services providers.

developing countries' PTAs. We find little hard evidence that PTAs advance developing countries' deep integration much beyond what they are willing to undertake unilaterally or multilaterally. Section 3 interprets this experience with a view to understanding how discriminatory it might be and why it has come about. It also asks whether what deep integration PTAs might achieve is multilateralizable, and on the whole it is not very optimistic. Section 4 considers the temporary movement of labour – mode 4 of the GATS – and the forces affecting the prospects of multilateralization for existing bilateral arrangements. While there are some grounds for expecting that such trade will be liberalized eventually, we argue that the prospects for doing so multilaterally, rather than unilaterally or bilaterally, are limited. Section 5 discusses what might be done to encourage multilateralizing cooperation, so as to benefit developing countries both included and excluded from a PTA. Section 6 concludes.

2   Cooperation in PTAs: how much more and how discriminatory?

Although numerous pro-competitive reforms have been implemented by governments across the world, there is substantial evidence that barriers to trade and investment remain prevalent in many countries, and that there is substantial scope to reduce the trade-restricting and cost-raising effects of domestic regulation. The consensus view is that the tariff equivalents of the trade-restricting effects of domestic policies are a (large) multiple of the prevailing border tariffs today. Studies that use available information on prevailing policies conclude that further services liberalization would have much greater positive effects on national welfare than the removal of trade barriers – see, for example, Konan and Maskus (2006) on Tunisia and Jensen, Rutherford and Tarr (2007) on Russia. Instead of the 'standard' 1 per cent increase in welfare from goods liberalization, introducing greater competition in services markets raises the gains to the 5–10 per cent range or more. These large effects of services liberalization reflect both the importance of services in the economy, and the extent to which many sectors continue to be protected.[6]

---

[6] While the potential gains may be greatest in developing countries, they can also be significant for high-income economies. Kox and Lejour (2006) conclude that the cost-raising effects of policy heterogeneity within the EU reduces intra-EU services trade by

While there are potentially large gains from reducing the prevalence and costs of differences in regulation, as well as policies that simply prevent access to specific markets, a key question is whether progress on liberalization can be (and is) facilitated *through PTAs*. Whether PTA-based cooperation will promote or result in a 'multilateral' outcome – i.e. a non-discriminatory and reasonably uniform one – is only an interesting question if PTAs actually result in cooperation that changes domestic policy.

The need for PTAs as a driver of regulatory reforms is not obvious. Because inefficient regulation generates costs for buyers of the affected goods and services, and because regulation is often an instrument used to pursue non-economic – as opposed to sectoral – objectives, unilateral reform incentives may be larger than for trade in goods, and be less susceptible to roll-back, reducing the need to use international commitment mechanisms such as trade agreements.[7] Whether PTA policy commitments that *do not* reflect essentially unilateral reforms are applied on an MFN basis is an empirical question. Insofar as PTA commitments are 'additional' in the sense of going beyond the current national policies of a PTA member, much will depend on the feasibility of discrimination. In some areas discrimination may not be an option, so that PTA-based reform commitments will be multilateralizing. In others, multilateralization may not be automatic, but in principle may be feasible conditional on decisions by members to extend a certain discipline to non-members (or new members).

In the remainder of this section we briefly review both the border and several 'behind-the-border' policies that tend to be covered by PTAs: tariffs, product standards, services trade, investment and competition policy, IPRs, and enforcement provisions. Our discussion is interpretive and as far as possible concerns actual outcomes rather than legal agreements. A most useful quantitative analysis of the latter is given in Estevadeordal, Harris and Suominen (Chapter 7 of this volume).

30–60 per cent and FDI by 18–36 per cent. OECD (2005) estimates that greater convergence in regulatory regimes, and the removal of policy barriers to entry, could raise per capita GDP by over 3 per cent in the EU and the US.

[7] For example, allowing high-cost, low-quality services to dominate in a market will be detrimental to almost everyone in an economy, with large users having strong incentives to push for measures – such as deregulation, privatization and liberalization – that generate more competition in the provision of these upstream suppliers of inputs (Hoekman and Messerlin, 2000).

Tariffs

Preferential tariff reduction is the bread and butter of any PTA. In the area of tariffs it is clear what PTAs do – discriminate. From a multilateralization perspective, what matters is the extent to which preferential reductions in tariffs are also applied to non-members, either immediately, or following the implementation of the PTA with some lag. There is an enormous, mostly theoretical, literature analysing the incentives (and underlying political economy determinants) for PTA members to maintain, raise or lower external barriers.[8] Whether the economic forces for multilateralization of PTA-based merchandise trade liberalization are stronger than those working against this is an empirical matter.

Any PTA, when implemented, potentially generates trade diversion. This is especially the case for South–South agreements between countries that have relatively high external trade barriers. The costs associated with trade diversion provide a powerful force for multilateralization: lowering external barriers to trade will reduce such costs. Rigorous empirical research on the relationship between preferential and MFN tariffs over time is sparse as a result of data constraints – information on the implementation of preferential liberalization and the sequencing over time between unilateral and preferential tariff reduction is not available for many PTAs. In the case of Latin America, however, recent research by Estevadeordal, Freund and Ornelas (2008) concludes that the preferential tariff reduction following PTA formation in Latin America promotes subsequent external tariff reduction for those PTAs that do not involve the formation of a customs union. Bohara, Gawande and Sanguinetti (2004), focusing on the impact of preferential trade flows from Brazil to Argentina, find that greater imports from Brazil led to lower MFN tariffs in Argentina, especially in sectors where trade diversion occurred as a result of MERCOSUR.

Limão (2006a, 2006b) and Karacaovali and Limão (2005) have shown, on the other hand, that in the case of the EU and the US, PTAs may be a force working against multilateralization: they find that both the EU and the US made fewer (shallower) multilateral (MFN) liberalization

---

[8] See, for example, Schiff and Winters (2003) for a review of this literature. Incentives and likely outcomes differ depending on the type of PTA, free trade agreement or customs union, and on the extent to which trade policy is used by PTA members as an instrument to enforce cooperation in other policy areas (Limão, 2007).

commitments in the Uruguay Round on tariff lines where there were significant preference margins for imports from their preferential trading partners. Limão (2007) hypothesizes that this may reflect the use of market access as 'payment' for concessions by PTA partners in non-trade areas.

Thus rigorous empirical research reveals that PTAs may lead or retard non-discriminatory reductions in tariffs, and no general conclusions are possible. The fact that MFN tariffs have fallen significantly in almost all countries, whatever their participation in PTAs, suggests that unilateral decisions to liberalize have been paramount (World Bank, 2005; Martin and Messerlin, 2007). Indeed, a good case can be made that the spread of PTAs has done little to substantially reduce the extent to which trade flows are distorted by preferences, as most of the recent PTAs are either (a) between small countries, (b) between countries that have (very) low external protection and many zero-rated MFN duties, and/or (c) exclude those sectors where there is significant protection – for example, agriculture (Pomfret, 2007; Sen, 2006). Restrictive rules of origin further reduce the impact of many PTAs. The combination of the exclusion of agriculture and restrictive rules of origin is particularly important in EU PTAs with countries that are not accession candidates. The large export supply response following the implementation of preferential access agreements between the US and some African and Middle Eastern countries – for example, Lesotho and Jordan – illustrates the importance of including agriculture and using liberal rules of origin for labour-intensive manufactures such as apparel. Both Lesotho and Jordan have preferential access agreements with the EU but have not seen exports to the EU expand.[9]

Insofar as PTAs have only a limited impact in terms of preferential liberalization, the negative implications of discrimination for other developing countries will be attenuated, and there is less 'need' for multilateralization to undo potential trade diversion. To date there is little evidence outside the EU and the 'European neighbourhood' of the multilateralizing forces identified by Baldwin (2006). As noted by Gasoriek, Augier and Lai-Tong in Chapter 4 and Estevadeordal, Harris and Suominen in Chapter 7, the prospects for multilateralizing different rules of origin regimes are limited, although within specific regions there are incentives for convergence and cumulation. However, given that research suggests that the tariff equivalent of rules of origin and associated

---

[9] See Portugal-Perez (2007) on Lesotho and Al Khouri (2007) on Jordan.

enforcement procedures is in the 3–5 per cent range, and the fact that many MFN rates in major markets are less than that, rules of origin may not be as constraining as is sometimes argued.[10] Insofar as applied tariffs are low, firms are more likely to pay the tariff and/or push for the abolition of tariffs altogether than invest in efforts to reduce the restrictiveness of origin rules.[11] This may occur on a sectoral basis – along the lines of the WTO Information Technology Agreement. The implications of such multilateralization of PTAs for developing countries, should it occur, are discussed in Section 3 below.

Standards and technical regulations

Technical product standards, sanitary and phyto-sanitary measures, professional qualifications, and the processes and procedures that are used to certify that products and service providers comply with norms can have the effect of needlessly restraining trade. They are therefore subject to disciplines in both the WTO and many PTAs. In contrast to tariffs and quotas, the objective underlying mandatory standards is generally not to protect domestic producers from foreign competition, although standards can have that effect if compliance costs are higher for foreign producers.

Two approaches can be taken to reducing the costs for producers (and consumers) associated with differences in standards for the same/similar products across markets: harmonization and (mutual) recognition. The latter comes in two types: mutual recognition of substantive norms as being equivalent, and mutual recognition of conformity assessment and testing bodies.

Harmonization can be 'hegemonic' – reflecting convergence to the norms prevailing in the largest market; or 'cooperative' – reflecting the joint development and adoption of a specific norm. International standards, the adoption of which is encouraged by WTO rules in this area, are an example of the latter. In practice, PTA-based formal harmonization of mandatory technical regulations has not been very

---

[10] Firms that produce in enclaves such as export-processing zones – i.e. whose production does not enter into the customs territory of an importing country – are not affected by rules of origin at all. We are not aware of research on the proportion of total global production-sharing trade that operates under such exemptions.

[11] There is a long history of fruitless discussions and efforts dating back to the 1970s to harmonize rules of origin and to extend WTO disciplines to preferential rules of origin (see Hoekman and Kostecki, 2001).

prevalent. EU efforts to harmonize product standards were a failure and led to the shift to the mutual recognition principle (see e.g. Pelkmans, 2001). However, the EU has passed numerous regulatory norms (directives and regulations), including in the area of the environment and consumer health and safety, which imply harmonization of minimum norms that products and/or operators must satisfy. Recent examples are laws concerning the treatment of electronic waste products and the use of chemicals (Selin and Vandeveer, 2006).

Producers anywhere in the world that wish to sell to the EU must comply with EU requirements. Given the size of the EU market, this can give rise to *de facto* hegemonic harmonization. This may go beyond compliance with specific rules on the use of certain substances or the performance of products. An example is the use of the 'precautionary principle' by the EU in setting standards. This is central to the EU approach to standardization, but it is not something that can be – or is – imposed on their partners explicitly. *De facto*, however, the strong risk aversion that characterizes EU policy imposes constraints on partners, as they are precluded from using technologies and products that are not accepted in the EU – genetically modified organisms, for example – for fear of spillovers to the EU. This constraint is actually an MFN one, since it applies to anyone who wishes to export to the EU, but it more adversely affects PTA partners because they have invested most in such exporting.[12]

The harmonization of standards also occurs at the international level. For example, governments cooperate at the global level to define minimum standards through bodies such as the Codex Alimentarius Commission and the International Organization for Standardization (ISO). In addition, as far as product norms are concerned, significant harmonization occurs through the operation of market forces: firms have strong incentives to produce to the standards that prevail in large markets so as to realize economies of scale, whether these standards are mandatory or 'voluntary' – imposed by buyers as opposed to governments. In practice most harmonization occurs outside the ambit of specific PTA clauses and agreements.

The principle of mutual recognition – agreement that regulatory standards in two areas are essentially or substantively equivalent – can

---

[12] Contrary to what is sometimes claimed, the EU does not impose the *acquis communautaire* regarding product standards on partner countries, i.e. formally require that they implement the *acquis*.

do much to enhance the contestability of markets and reduce compliance costs by eliminating duplicative and redundant requirements. Achieving progress on this front requires mutual trust, understanding and acceptance of regulatory systems. A precondition is not just agreement on the equivalence or adequacy of the substantive norms that apply in each market, but also that these norms are enforced.

Outside the EU and EEA members, and the ANZCERTA, few PTAs appear to have made much progress through the vehicle of mutual recognition of standards and certification and conformity assessment entities. Pelkmans (2007) argues that this is not surprising, since MRAs require considerable trust and sophistication to be feasible. Indeed, MRAs do not *require* a PTA. Many MRAs and MRA discussions have taken place without the countries involved having a bilateral trade agreement. This was the case, for example, with the MRAs negotiated between the EU and the US in the second half of the 1990s.[13] One reason may be that the negotiations involved the relevant national regulatory agencies, as well as representatives from the industries concerned (under the auspices of the Transatlantic Business Dialogue; see e.g. Devereaux, Lawrence and Watkins, 2006). However, the prospects of recognition may be improved by the fact that many PTAs establish institutions that facilitate communication between national standards-setting bodies.

From a multilateralizing perspective it does not appear that PTA provisions in this area have major potential downsides. In an assessment of the coverage and approaches taken in PTAs with respect to standards, Piermartini and Budetta (2006) conclude that the majority of extant PTAs have provisions that conform to those found in the WTO: calling for transparency in the process of setting and enforcing standards,[14] and encouraging mutual recognition. There is little evidence of explicit harmonization.

As argued in Baldwin (2000), cooperation on standards will have fewer adverse effects – if any – on non-participants than the preferential removal of tariffs. Insiders may benefit from lower costs as a result of mutual recognition or the adoption of common standards, but this is also likely to benefit outsiders. Chen and Mattoo (2004) find that MRAs

[13] The agreements cover bilateral inspection, testing and certification for a variety of traded products, including medical devices, pharmaceuticals, recreational craft, telecommunications, electromagnetic compatibility (EMC) services, and electrical equipment.

[14] A number of PTAs establish joint bodies to deal with standards issues, and many – in particular those involving the US and Mexico – call for actions and specific bodies to increase the transparency of standards setting and enforcement.

of conformity assessment promote trade of *both* covered and excluded countries.[15] As Baldwin (2000) and Chen and Mattoo (2004) note, much depends on whether the MRAs contain restrictive rules of origin, i.e. apply only to goods produced in MRA members. Contrary to what is sometimes claimed, some MRAs do impose restrictive rules – for example, agreements between the EU and Australia and New Zealand. This implies that non-members cannot benefit from the MRA by having goods tested in MRA countries.[16]

The main concern for outside countries is the cost of compliance with prevailing norms, not discrimination per se. The appropriate response is a combination of assistance – 'aid for trade' – and increased scrutiny of the likely impact on developing countries of standards that are proposed/established in either the regional or international context. Here also, the primary focus should be on compliance cost. Relatively little attention appears to have been given to establishing alternative methods of determining compliance with a view to identifying least-cost approaches that can be used in developing countries.

Services policies

Most PTAs negotiated since the early 1990s include provisions on services. Although many early PTAs did not (and do not) go much beyond the GATS, agreements of more recent vintage often have a higher level of ambition, although none comes close to the EU. A recent assessment by Roy, Marchetti and Lim (2006) concludes that many of the trade agreements reported to the WTO since 2000 have a sectoral coverage that greatly exceeds the commitments the countries involved made in the GATS. This applies both to the existing GATS commitments and to the offers that were on the table in the Doha Round in mid 2006 when the talks were suspended. Roy *et al.* also conclude, however, that the substantive disciplines (rules) that are included in many of the agreements are similar to those in the GATS, i.e. the depth of the associated commitments often does go much beyond what PTA members committed to under the WTO.

Many agreements do entail some additional liberalization and commitments – for example, the EU–Chile agreement goes further than the

---

[15] Baller (2007) replicates these results.

[16] The scope for such 'free-riding' by shipping goods to a PTA testing facility for conformity assessment will be affected by transport and transaction costs and the level of MFN tariffs of PTA members in cases where temporary (duty-free) entry is not feasible.

GATS by locking in some liberalization of telecommunications and maritime services (Ullrich, 2004), and the DR–CAFTA requires Costa Rica to further open its telecommunications and insurance industries – but the 'additionality' is usually limited.[17] An in-depth analysis of services liberalization in PTAs in Asia by Fink and Molinuevo (2007) finds that there is great variance across PTAs in terms of coverage of services and depth of commitments, with more commitments made in sectors where countries have also made more extensive commitments in the GATS. Sensitive sectors, such as health, transport and financial services, as well as the movement of service suppliers (mode 4), tend to be subject to the fewest commitments. In areas where there are no WTO disciplines, there tend not to be PTA rules either – for example, safeguards, subsidies or procurement. The same is true as regards domestic regulation, with only one PTA establishing an across-the-board necessity test.[18]

An important conclusion by Fink and Molinuevo (2007) and Fink and Jansen (Chapter 6 of this volume) is that the rules of origin that are contained in the PTAs are mostly liberal, in that PTA benefits extend to non-member firms that are established (have a commercial presence) and have substantial business operations in a PTA member. While Fink and his co-authors and Baldwin, Evenett and Low (Chapter 3 of this volume) argue that such liberal rules of origin necessarily mean PTAs on services are multilateralizing in nature, we are less sanguine. One reason is that, if there are significant policy-based barriers to entry into a market, and thus significant rents, there are obvious incentives for firms in the PTA partners to seek to limit entry by non-member firms. Moreover, even liberal rules of origin will effectively exclude many potential services suppliers that do not have the capacity to establish a physical presence (engage in FDI). This will encompass many firms in developing countries. Insofar as policy barriers are maintained on cross-border supply and on mode 4, liberal rules of origin for mode 3 will primarily benefit large services multinationals that are generally present in markets in any event. They may also distort the choice of mode of supply that is used. Thus it is not the liberal rule of origin that matters,

---

[17] Houde, Kolse-Patil and Miroudot (2007) examine twenty PTAs and conclude that all are WTO-plus. They also point out that bilateral reciprocity is stronger than in GATS in that developing country PTA members (not surprisingly) make the greatest number of additional commitments relative to those made under the GATS.

[18] This is contained in the Trans-Pacific Economic Partnership Agreement, between Brunei Darussalam, Chile, New Zealand and Singapore.

but the removal of market access barriers. With the exception of the EU and a small number of agreements between high-income countries (e.g. Australia–New Zealand), most PTAs have not achieved much in terms of actual *additional* liberalization.

The difficulty experienced by the EU in fully liberalizing intra-EU services trade and creating a single market for services illustrates that in practice it is not straightforward to achieve liberalization through regional cooperation, even where there is a strong political commitment and common institutions that have a mandate to pursue the integration of markets. Progress towards a single market in services across the EU has encountered strong opposition when attempting to remove limitations on cross-border services trade and the temporary movement of personnel. Although the EC Treaty guarantees the freedom to provide services and the freedom of movement of workers between all EU countries, many governments have been unwilling to accept 'home country regulation'. A 1996 Directive on 'The Posting of Workers in the Framework of the Provision of Services' (96/71/EC) clarified that EU states must apply their local minimum terms and conditions of employment to workers from other EU members posted temporarily by their employer to work in their country, potentially vastly reducing the scope for benefits from cross-border services trade. The January 2004 draft Services Directive sought to go beyond this by requiring that sector-specific regulations of EU member states be non-discriminatory, objectively justified on the grounds of public interest, and proportionate. Many EU members opposed the associated 'competition in regulation' and the Directive that was eventually adopted allows countries to retain a number of policies that segment EU services markets.

As is true of the recent PTAs in Asia and elsewhere, there is a close correlation between sectors and policies where the EU members have agreed on internal liberalization, and the extent of external liberalization and commitments in the GATS. Thus the average level of specific commitments offered by the EU-15 on market access and national treatment in its Doha offer was 58 per cent (up from 46 per cent currently), a fairly high number compared to other WTO members.[19] The highest levels of commitment that were offered by the EU were in modes 2 (consumption abroad) and 3 (commercial presence): 88 and

---

[19] This index is a weighted average measure of the depth of the commitments on national treatment and market access, the maximum – no limitations and no exceptions – being 100 (see Hoekman, Mattoo and Sapir, 2007).

83 per cent, respectively. By far the fewest commitments were on offer for mode 4 (temporary movement of natural persons supplying services): 4.5 per cent. Mode 1 (cross-border trade) was in the middle: the coverage of the offer was 57 per cent. Not surprisingly, the EU's external trade policy reflects the constraints it confronts in achieving a fully integrated internal market for services. There is a strong revealed preference to commit to the liberalization of modes of supply that can be controlled by host country governments.

It is very much an open issue how much PTAs add to services liberalization and regulatory reform that has already been decided and implemented on a unilateral basis by PTA members. Most observers agree that PTAs are mostly mechanisms to lock in autonomous reforms. There is less agreement – and very little hard evidence – on the extent to which PTAs drive non-discriminatory reforms.

Investment policies

An increasing number of PTAs include investment provisions. In the case of US agreements these take the form of specific chapters, modelled on the NAFTA. These provide for national treatment and MFN, ban trade-related investment measures (TRIMs) such as performance requirements, guarantee capital transfers, and include provisions requiring compensation in cases of expropriation. Extensive dispute settlement provisions, including investor–state arbitration, are a core part of these agreements. These PTAs generally subsume and go beyond pre-existing BITs. They include broad definitions of investment, including not only FDI, but also portfolio flows, debt instruments and intangible assets such as intellectual property. The treatment of investment and capital flows in EU agreements tends to be less extensive than in US agreements. For example, the EU–Mexico agreement simply states that the existing restrictions on investment will be progressively eliminated and no new restrictions adopted, without specifying particular sectors or setting a timeline for liberalization. The language in the EU–Chile agreement is even more general, calling for 'free movement of capital relating to direct investments made in accordance with the laws of the host country'.

As is the case with services policies, there has been very significant unilateral reform of investment-related policies in most developing countries. Performance requirements are used much less than in the past, reflecting the recognition that they are either redundant or not conducive to attracting FDI. Indeed, in many countries policies have been put in place to attract or retain direct investment. This helps to explain why provisions banning investment performance requirements have become common in PTAs. However, insofar as policy reforms are unilateral, the same question arises as in the services context: do PTAs add much? To our knowledge there is no empirical work extant that documents whether there is additionality associated with the recent crop of PTAs. Instead, most analyses focus on the coverage and form of legal language embodied in the PTAs. One cannot infer from this whether PTAs are driving reforms, as sometimes seems to be implied (e.g. in Chapter 3 of this volume).

What can be inferred from the provisions of the PTAs is that they do not do much – if anything – to discipline the subset of investment-related policies that create negative spillovers on partner countries. Examples are investment subsidies and other incentives to attract or keep investors. One reason why progress on investment policies has not (yet) proved possible in the WTO or elsewhere (e.g. the OECD attempt to negotiate a multilateral agreement on investment) is that, from an economic perspective, it is these types of policies that matter most for developing countries (Hoekman and Saggi, 2000). An implication is that, from a multilateralization perspective, the PTA provisions on investment do not matter much – the policies that create negative spillovers are not covered.[20]

Although much of the investor-protection-related rules contained in PTAs may already have been in place through BITs, these provisions are only enforceable by firms that originate in signatory states. Non-parties do not have access to the arbitration and other enforcement provisions of BITs. This may be one reason for the finding by Egger and Pfaffermayr (2004) that a BIT has a statistically significant positive impact on the bilateral outward FDI stock: the BITs apply only to signatories. The introduction of BIT-type investment protection provisions into PTAs does not change their discriminatory nature – the associated enforcement disciplines apply only to investors that originate in PTA members in the sense that only they can invoke the associated enforcement mechanisms. Extending the disciplines to non-members on an MFN basis would be desirable; but doing so would also erode the value of preferences and increase effective competition, so it is far from an innocuous provision for members to swallow.

---

[20] Lesher and Miroudot (2007) conclude that investment provisions in PTAs do affect investment flows positively.

Competition policies

Competition policy (defined here as disciplines on the behaviour of firms and the ability of governments to provide financial assistance to firms) has played an important role in only a few PTAs. The EU is of course the 'gold standard' in terms of the extent and reach of the constraints that are imposed on member states regarding policies that may have an impact on intra-regional trade. Disciplines are imposed on state aid (subsidies), monopolies, government procurement practices, and the behaviour and size (via market dominance clauses) of firms. The various disciplines are enforced by supranational bodies (the European Commission and the European Court of Justice) as well as by national institutions. These various competition provisions were considered necessary in order to achieve the objective of creating an integrated European market. Thus the primary focus is to discipline measures (public and private) that may segment national markets or distort trade. The disciplines benefit any potential competitor – even one from outside the Union – so competition policy is potentially multilateralizing, in the sense of not discriminating.

Another PTA with far-reaching cooperation on competition policy is the Closer Economic Relations agreement between Australia and New Zealand, under which it was agreed that nationals of one state could be made the subject of an enquiry by the competition authorities of the other state, and be required to respond to requests for information. Anti-trust legislation in both countries was amended to extend its scope to encompass the behaviour of firms located in either market; courts were empowered to sit and serve orders in the other country; and judgments are enforceable in both countries. However, the application of anti-trust remedies remains strictly national.

Many – indeed, most – of the more recently negotiated PTAs have provisions on competition law. Most of these PTAs do not come even close to the depth of cooperation found in the EU/EEA or between Australia and New Zealand. This is the case even for EU PTAs, where competition provisions figure most prominently. Given the importance of common competition disciplines in the realization and functioning of the EU, it is not surprising that competition policy also figures on the agenda of EU PTAs. For example, the Association agreements with Mediterranean countries require them to adopt – after a transition period – EU rules relating to agreements between firms restricting competition, abuse of dominant position, the behaviour of public undertakings (state-owned firms) and competition-distorting state aids that have an effect on trade. However, these provisions are best regarded as of a 'best endeavours' nature. The type of cooperation that is called for is limited to consultation and weak forms of comity. Most US PTAs do not contain disciplines on competition law, and those that do have language on this subject explicitly exempt the relevant provisions from the dispute settlement mechanisms established to enforce the PTA. Such exclusions also apply in EU PTAs – this is the case, for example, in the EU–Chile PTA – and most Latin American PTAs (Sokol, 2007).

The EU is the outlier on the competition policy front in that, given the vigour with which it is pursued in bilateral relations, one might conclude that there is some hegemonic intent/hope in terms of the coverage, scope and style of competition policies. However, a distinct feature of EU competition law is that the focus is narrow: on practices that will distort the functioning or prevent the realization of an integrated market. This differs from the perspective that will be taken by national competition agencies, which are (should be) concerned with maintaining competition in domestic markets.

In general, there is not much evidence of hard law here, although in truth it is hard to detect exactly what is going on in most PTAs. As is the case for other policy areas discussed previously, unilateral action is arguably the dominant force behind the adoption and implementation of competition policies, not the negotiation of PTAs or the spread of similar provisions on competition in PTAs. Moreover, similar to the situation remarked upon with respect to investment disciplines in PTAs, cooperation does not extend to actions that consider more than national welfare narrowly construed. For example, PTAs do not require the competition authorities of member states to consider the impact of anti-competitive practices by 'their' firms on other jurisdictions – something that could benefit developing countries with weak enforcement capacity (see e.g. Hoekman and Saggi, 2007).

Intellectual property rights

The protection of intellectual property has long been the focus of international cooperation. International conventions and bodies dealing with this subject date back to the nineteenth century. The inclusion of intellectual property in trade agreements is largely driven by a desire on the part of rights holders to ensure implementation of international conventions, and to use the threat of trade sanctions as an enforcement mechanism.

There are significant differences across PTAs as regards the coverage of IPRs. With the exception of US agreements, most PTAs do not go beyond the substantive provisions of the WTO. The US is the major outlier. It includes IPRs in the definition of assets covered by the investment chapter of a PTA, and has negotiated TRIPS-plus disciplines (Fink and Reichenmiller, 2005). Access to investor–state arbitration under the PTA's investment provisions is considerably more powerful than the state-to-state provisions found in the WTO and EU PTAs. In the case of US PTAs, IPR provisions clearly involve an effort by the hegemon to impose its standards in the form of legally binding, enforceable norms. Whether this is done in a way that protects everyone's IP – that is, including non-members – is an open question, but in practice it is likely that the required legal changes and enforcement will be non-discriminatory. The EU tends to be much less prescriptive on the substance of IPRs, although some observers note that the EU may begin to use PTAs as a vehicle to impose its preferred approach to the definition and protection of geographical indications – especially if WTO agreement cannot be obtained.[21]

Multilateralization of WTO-plus disciplines is unlikely to occur, especially insofar as developing country PTA members have accepted such disciplines only because of specific 'compensation' offered by the US or EU, be it market access or something else. Thus there is much less reason to expect a 'march to the top' in IPRs than in other areas of regulation, such as EU environmental directives. Multilateralization that takes the form of weakening the prospect of WTO plus disciplines is more likely. The example of TRIPS and public health is illustrative – recent PTAs include language reaffirming the right of developing country signatories to impose compulsory licensing to address public health concerns.

Implementation, enforcement and dispute settlement

To be credible and meaningful, PTA commitments must be enforceable. Indeed, one reason why disciplines on domestic, 'behind-the-border' policies are being incorporated in PTAs rather than (in addition to)

---

[21] The EU and the US have agreed to cooperate in the enforcement of IPRs in third countries, including an agreement to make IPR enforcement a key focus in trade capacity-building technical assistance to third countries, and to improve the coordination of their efforts in this area with a view to avoiding duplication (see US Government, 2006).

being pursued through other forms of international cooperation, is because trade sanctions can be used to enforce commitments. Signing a PTA is one thing, but implementing it and then enforcing its provisions is quite another. Much of the literature on PTAs tends to focus on their content – the texts and coverage of disciplines. Very little attention is given to documenting implementation and determining 'additionality' (if any) over status quo policies. The reason is that these matters are extremely difficult to pin down. One might detect implementation in terms of legal statute, but quite often the PTA clauses do not require changes in statutes so much as in lower-level regulations, which are very hard to identify from outside the government or sector concerned. Enforcement is even harder to observe; something might be inferred from enforcement activity, but not too much is known about this even in the best-documented PTAs. Information can be gleaned from the dispute settlement provisions of the PTAs regarding which provisions are in principle binding (enforceable through actions), but ultimately what matters is the extent to which these are used.

By a long way, the US ('NAFTA'-type) PTAs are the most far-reaching in terms of dispute settlement provisions, not surprisingly in the areas where there are strong lobbies in the US – first and foremost IPRs and investment protection, but also in areas such as product standards and conformity assessment. The latter is actually rather asymmetric. In the CAFTA, signatories are subject to disciplines to enhance the likelihood that US certification of goods is accepted as equivalent, but there is no similar language on US acceptance of their certification. This is hegemonic multilateralization, given that US standards are applied by other countries too.

The seriousness of US implementation is reflected not just in terms of formal, binding dispute settlement, but also in terms of calling for – and setting up – bodies to monitor implementation. Thus the US seems to take implementation of agreed conditions in a PTA more seriously than others. For example, the USTR website has documents on compliance by partners, and the US PTAs call for and have established performance benchmarks and contact points through which interested parties (citizens) can raise perceived instances of non-compliance.[22]

---

[22] A noteworthy feature of recent US PTAs is that dispute settlement makes provision for compensation payments in lieu of implementation (or retaliation). In the US–Chile agreement, in the case of non-implementation of a panel finding, the losing party can offer to pay 50 per cent of the damage caused. This appears to be open-ended, as the text

A corollary of the focus on enforcement by the US is the care it takes to ensure that subjects on which it does not want to be bound – e.g. anti-trust – are excluded from dispute settlement. An example is the US–Chile PTA. None of this exists with EU or Asian PTAs, where diplomatic and political processes predominate, although there are some hints of it in the Latin American agreements. The latter probably represents evidence of multilateralization, as Mexico sought to use the models that it had adopted under NAFTA with its other partners, and so on to their partners.

Compared to the active case load of the WTO – over 350 cases adjudicated since 1995 – for most PTAs there is very little evidence of enforcement action, even for US-type PTAs.[23] In instances where countries are PTA members and could use the dispute resolution mechanisms of the PTA, they often choose to use the WTO. The US–Mexico Telmex dispute is an example. Piérola and Horlick (2007) provide other examples of when countries went to the WTO because PTA rules were ambiguous or non-existent, and conclude that case law under NAFTA and similar agreements has entailed 'little or no jurisprudential development' (2007: 891).

3 Interpreting experience: stocktaking and assessment

The bird's-eye overview of the coverage of recent PTAs reveals that there are major differences across agreements, and major differences in the extent to which cooperation in a PTA context is likely to give rise to discrimination against non-members. Such discrimination is most clear-cut in the case of tariffs. In principle, it could also arise in the case of contingent protection (anti-dumping, safeguards). As discussed by Baldwin, Evenett and Low (Chapter 3), most PTAs continue to allow members to use such instruments on intra-PTA trade flows, although in practice there is a marked reduction in the use of such instruments against partner countries (Prusa, 2006).

---

speaks of annual payments. This PTA also provides for monetary fines of up to US$15 million per year in the case of violation of labour/environmental provisions. Proceeds go into a fund earmarked for labour/green initiatives.

[23] Exceptions are MERCOSUR, with 543 disputes between 1993 and 2007, most of which were resolved before reaching the arbitration stage, and the Andean Community, with 385 disputes between 1980 and 2005. There were 173 disputes under NAFTA between 1989 and 2007 (disputes prior to 1994 were under the US–Canada Free Trade Agreement). See http://idatd.eclac.cl/controversias/index_en.jsp.

The implications of multilateralizing preferential tariff reductions for developing nations will depend on the type of channel that is used by PTA members. We are very doubtful whether harmonization of rules of origin across PTAs will be feasible, even on a sectoral basis. Similarly, seeking to agree to additional multilateral rules or disciplines on PTAs seems unlikely to be productive either, given the history of non-enforcement of GATT Article XXIV. The difficulty in agreeing to a set of *non*-preferential rules of origin in the World Customs Organization suggests that achieving this for preferential rules is highly unlikely.

In practice, as has been argued by Baldwin (2006), different systems of rules of origin are likely to emerge, anchored in the major regions – the EU, NAFTA and East Asia. Insofar as this is accompanied by a greater use of simple, non-restrictive rules that are permanent and not subject to uncertainty (e.g. by penalizing successful countries by tightening the rules), this will benefit all developing countries, as it increases the share of non-PTA value that is permitted in a specific product. Conversely, measures such as the adoption of diagonal cumulation for rules of origin along the lines of the Pan-European Cumulation System (PECS) can enhance trade diversion against non-PTA members.

The best form of multilateralization is to further lower applied MFN rates, as was done by East Asian members of the ASEAN free trade agreement. This has the advantage of enhancing access for all producers, reducing trade diversion costs and lowering the costs of rules of origin, whatever form these take. As far as small developing country members of PTAs are concerned, reducing MFN tariffs is unambiguously beneficial – these countries cannot influence their terms of trade in any event. However, it is precisely these countries for which the external pressures to liberalize are weakest – both multilaterally and bilaterally. Multilaterally, small countries are expected to contribute to the Rounds of collective liberalization, but their contributions are not scrutinized very carefully, and outside the Rounds more or less no one takes them to dispute settlement, or requests further tariff cuts. Within PTAs, a liberally inclined Asia is doing regionalism mostly for foreign policy reasons, and so is not held back by it; a unilaterally reformed Latin America has partially locked in its reforms through NAFTA-type deals; and the 'greater' EU is creating a 'European neighbourhood'. The missing areas are the small and poor – the Caribbean, the Pacific and Africa. Although the EU may be successful at getting these countries to liberalize preferentially, so as to create the EPAs, it has been quite explicit that Africa should expect no further liberalization, either in Doha or beyond. In other words, where the need is arguably greatest the pressure and external incentives are weakest, so that Baldwin's political evolution multilateralization seems least likely. Neither EU nor US governments, nor their private sectors, seem likely to be sufficiently exercised by trade frictions with Africa to address the issue robustly.

Views differ widely on the extent to which PTAs have imposed disciplines on domestic regulatory policies, relative to both the *status quo ante* and the commitments made by PTA members in the WTO. These differences in view relate both to the direction of causality and to the extent of discrimination implied by PTAs. Those who argue that PTAs are setting in motion multilateralizing effects point to the willingness of developing countries to make commitments, and to various factors suggesting that the associated policy changes are *de facto*, if not *de jure*, non-discriminatory.

In our view, the evidence that PTAs drive reform is not compelling. One can more convincingly argue that unilateral policy reforms and/ or exogenous developments (e.g. technological change) allow commitments to be made in the PTA context. This is the case, for example, in procurement, investment and competition policy, where drivers of policy are national, and/or cooperation has occurred outside the context of a PTA (e.g. procurement reforms tend to be driven by the multilateral development banks). Telling to us is the fact that the dimensions of these policy areas, where there are clearly negative spillovers associated with national policy, are not addressed in most PTAs. Examples in the area of competition and investment policies were mentioned above.

Why do developing countries sign PTAs with disciplines on policy areas that they are not willing to contemplate in the WTO? Presumably because there is a clear pay-off for them that is not on offer in the WTO – e.g. exclusive improvements in access to agriculture or apparel markets in the case of US-style PTAs, or development assistance in the case of the EU. In many cases the commitments that are made by developing countries in North–South PTAs largely reflect the status quo – governments have already decided or implemented reforms unilaterally. The major exceptions are intellectual property and in some instances specific service sectors. The former simply constitutes a price that must be paid; the latter may or may not involve a cost in terms of maintaining restrictions on access against non-members. The incentives for rent-sharing outcomes in sectors where competition has been restricted can be great, although, as noted above, there is little empirical evidence on the extent of discriminatory liberalization.

This suggests that attention should focus on two questions: (i) is there discrimination, *de jure* or *de facto*, in terms of outcomes in sectors where there are rents to be shared (e.g. telecoms or insurance in Costa Rica under DR–CAFTA)?; and (ii) are the US, the EU or other dominant partners in a PTA trying to create 'precedents' for hegemonic preferences in areas where there are no 'natural' reasons for other countries to emulate them? Examples are US efforts to impose limitations on the use of portfolio capital controls and WTO-plus disciplines on intellectual property, and the EU interest in getting countries to protect geographical indications.

Insofar as PTAs entail discrimination, the modalities we have at present – more PTAs or multilateral talks – seem to offer no obvious means for evolving spontaneously from a discriminatory to a multilateral form. A number of factors combine to make deep integration more complex and demanding than border restrictions in the goods sector. These reasons affect progress in the multilateral system as well as preferentially, but there is no compelling reason why they impinge less heavily on the latter.

As far as services liberalization is concerned, one relevant consideration is that large services firms that operate globally – most of them European or American – can meet local regulatory requirements relatively easily and cheaply by hiring locally certified professionals, which is something they would do anyway for good business reasons. These firms will also want to invest (establish) in the major markets in any event – and do so if permitted. This suggests that rules of origin are not an important factor – which may explain why 'liberal' rules are observed.

The firms that are most affected by regulatory differences are the smaller ones, but their characteristics – small, dispersed, etc. – and the high degree of uncertainty they confront regarding likely benefits of international expansion, make it difficult to organize effective lobbying for overseas market access. Equally, the greater cost of going global makes their existing national markets more important, and so increases the benefits of resisting liberalization at home. Given the important role of incumbent firms in the regulation of many sectors, this imbalance gives a strong bias towards inward-looking policy.

Another factor that will affect the power of bilateral cooperation to support national regulatory reform is that, while dealing with regulatory costs (and reducing the associated rents where these exist) will be good for consumers in the PTA, it may not do much to increase trade. Instead, the main effect may be to foster domestic entry into the markets concerned. In the case of many services, not only are there transaction costs associated with international competition, but the need to employ local labour and other factors of production in order to sell services – many of which remain difficult to trade via mode 1 – may imply that foreign firms will not have that much of an advantage over domestic firms in newly opened market segments. This will reduce the incentive for service firms to lobby for/support bilateral opening/cooperation. Such considerations may help to explain the limited progress that has been made to date in the EU–US transatlantic context in regulatory cooperation and mutual recognition of standards and professional qualifications.

A third possible factor is that the intersection of what needs to be done and what is politically feasible looks small. In the case of merchandise trade all WTO members have clear interests in improving access to export markets. Some countries are more diversified than others, and all have differential specific interests – but all countries are exporters of goods that are subject to trade barriers in partner country markets. Thus they have exporters that see potential benefits from reciprocal negotiations on tariffs affecting merchandise trade. The same is true for the rules of origin created by the proliferation of PTAs – these basically become another form of tariff barrier into PTA markets (the upper bound of any rule of origin is the MFN tariff).

Interests are less symmetric when it comes to services, investment, procurement and IPR policies. In the case of services, while many developing countries are significant exporters, the key sectors are often those in which the relevant policies are under the control of the government as opposed to trading partners – i.e. in which there is relatively little to be gained internationally. The most important is tourism, where the export revenue generated depends primarily on measures that the destination country puts in place itself. As far as cross-border trade in services via telecommunications networks is concerned (mode 1 GATS), developing countries have export interests, but this channel for trade is usually not constrained by policy in the importing country (at least at present): for example, business process outsourcing, call centres, etc. The one mode where developing countries confront particularly high barriers, and that is therefore of great relevance to potential exporters, is the temporary cross-border movement of service providers (natural persons) – mode 4. However, this is politically extremely sensitive, and insofar as exporters perceive little promise of progress, they will invest little in lobbying.

Turning to investment, few developing countries have significant 'offensive' interests – i.e. they do not have indigenous multinational service providers seeking better access to foreign markets. FDI is primarily of interest to firms based in high-income countries and large emerging economies. Likewise competition policy in their markets is unlikely to do much for small exporting firms from developing countries, as opposed to action on anti-dumping policies, which the developed countries have striven to keep in an entirely separate box in the negotiations. And most developing countries have little ability to generate intellectual property that can be internationalized or to influence standards much.

Regulatory cooperation that takes the form of recognition agreements implies that firms that are established in a market that is covered by the agreement will be able to contest the other market(s) more easily, whatever their 'nationality'. That is, firms from third parties that have established a commercial presence in a PTA member – and thus have satisfied the regulatory requirements prevailing in the host market – will also benefit. This will not necessarily be true for cross-border trade, as home-country regulation by third countries may not be accepted as equivalent by regulators in the markets that have recognition agreements. This implies that recognition agreements may generate a bias towards FDI as the channel through which to contest large PTA markets. As mentioned, the same is true for 'liberal' rules of origin for services. Insofar as firms in small countries (developing economies) cannot engage in FDI because the associated fixed costs are too high, they will not be able to benefit from an MRA between their trading partners.

All told, then, much of the PTA-focused deep integration agenda seems either of little interest, or beyond the reach of developing country trade negotiators. To the extent that it will make progress, it will require domestic constituencies to emerge to control domestic regulation, and PTAs will contribute mainly via these. National investments will be needed to improve regulatory infrastructure and capacity. Here development assistance – aid for trade – can play a beneficial role. If such aid is more likely to be provided in the context of a PTA – or is conditional on signing a PTA – there is a clear problem unless the focus is squarely on policies and areas that are national priorities. In general, there is a prima facie case for such assistance to be provided on a multilateral basis.

Finally, the characteristics of regulation – including product standards – complicate liberalization. Barriers to trade in goods apply at the border and are visible. In the case of regulation, trade is restricted by a mixture of explicit discrimination against foreign providers, and domestic policies that may result in *de facto* discrimination. The prevalence of regulation to address market failures due to asymmetric information, imperfect competition and network externalities greatly complicates international cooperation and integration efforts. Regulators may be concerned (for good or bad reasons) that trade liberalization will impede their ability to enforce domestic regulatory standards. Trade will bring with it regulatory competition if services suppliers from abroad are subject only to the norms and standards that apply in their home markets. A critical – and difficult – question is how to differentiate between legitimate concerns relating to quality and performance, and regulatory requirements that simply constitute barriers to entry, creating rents for incumbents. These are matters that can only be clarified through repeated exchanges and interactions, informed by analysis. In practice there is likely to be substantial pressure for *de facto* harmonization to the norms that prevail in a country's major trading partner – hegemonic harmonization – whether they have a PTA relationship or not. Similarly the harmonization of global norms – e.g. via international standards-setting bodies – may be acceptable just because it ensures a reduction in transaction costs over a wider domain than a PTA.

It is very difficult to design rules in a way that clearly separates or distinguishes between measures that are protectionist and measures that have good domestic efficiency or social equity rationales. Regulators may therefore be concerned that PTA negotiating dynamics could adversely affect their ability to design and implement regulatory norms that maximize national welfare. Given these political constraints, the prospect of deep integration multilateralizing spontaneously seems rather weak.

4 Liberalizing the temporary movement of labour – mode 4 of the GATS

We have just noted that a key area for many developing countries is the liberalization of the temporary movement of labour – including mode 4 of the GATS. Thus in this section we offer a brief case study of this very important policy area. The temporary movement of labour (TML) is simultaneously the most sensitive area of the WTO politically, and probably the one of greatest interest in terms of aggregate welfare for developing countries. To date progress in this area has been dominated by regional and bilateral approaches. While much of the story is *sui generis*, the experience with TML helps to shed light on the process of 'deep integration' in general, and the prospects for multilateralizing preferential agreements.[24] Our conclusion is that, while it is possible that experience with bilateral TML agreements will provide sufficient business enthusiasm and popular political comfort to permit an extension to multilateral forms, it is by no means inevitable.

Oye (1992) argued that PTAs could play a major role in liberalization when issues were too sensitive or too complex for multilateral processes to work. Using the 1930s as his principal example, he argued that the economic stakes were so high and suspicions so great that only the high degree of internalization provided by preferential approaches could overcome political resistance to liberalizing trade. In the event the regionalism of the USA's Reciprocal Trade Agreements Act was multilateralized after the Second World War, and so this process proved quite benign for goods trade. Can we expect the same for mode 4 of services trade or migration more generally?

The argument hinges around the fact that mode 4 involves people rather than things – people whose behaviour and welfare have to be considered in one form or another, even after they have entered a country, and which impinge on the behaviour and welfare of domestic residents in a much more basic way than the origin of the goods and services they consume. Is the additional dimension entailed in labour movement compared with goods and other forms of services trade an insurmountable barrier, or one that in time might be eroded? To answer this, we contrast various bilateral labour agreements with the multilateral norm as embodied in mode 4 of the GATS.

The architecture of the GATS contains several features that lie uneasily with policymaking in the field of migration. First, GATS mode 4 is explicitly stated to be only about trade and not about migration. We have written this several times ourselves, but suspect that merely reiterating it in a louder voice is not winning the argument. Electorates, politicians and immigration bureaucracies in host countries all perceive TML as raising issues such as national security, access to national or local public goods and acceptance of civic duties, and seem set to resist trade-type concessions until these are addressed. In source countries concerns are sometimes voiced about exploitation and the conditions under which workers serve. The GATS provides no instruments for

---

[24] Mode 4 agreements are restricted to mobility to provide services, but the discussion that follows covers all temporary labour agreements.

dealing with these non-trade dimensions, and indeed few ways of even bringing the competent authorities together.

Second, the GATS views TML solely as a matter of reciprocal market access – the host ('importing') nation relaxes its restrictions on entry in return for reciprocal market access concessions from its partner in the same or a different market. But while some labour does move both ways across many borders, the flows are usually very far from balanced, so there is no real equivalent to the intra-industry trade, or even the primaries-for-manufacturing trades found for goods. Within a TML negotiation, there is at present nothing that a source (exporting) country can do to encourage its destination partner to lower access barriers to particular classes of labour – e.g. there is no GATS provision for it to make binding commitments to, say, validate migrants' qualifications, provide security vetting or guarantee readmission for returnees. The best one can foresee under present rules is swapping concessions on skilled labour market access in developing countries for those on unskilled labour access in developed countries, but this is a huge political challenge, given their very different political interests and sectors of work within each economy. Thus, beyond this one possibility, we will probably need to invent new GATS modalities if the will to multilateralize TML suddenly arises.

Third, GATS calls for bindings – all-but-permanent commitments to market opening, backed up by an effective enforcement mechanism. Opening conditional on the state of the labour market, on experience with previous groups of migrants, on political peace, or on national security considerations, is not accommodated except via tacit commitments to renegotiate or turn a blind eye to infringements. Thus there is no way that source countries can share the risks that hosts perceive, and so help them along the way to making concessions.

Fourth, GATS is colour/race/culture-blind, but most societies have quite strong views about who belongs and who does not. For example, European countries are generally more open to residents of their former colonies, and most countries favour neighbours over more distant partners. We do not advocate discrimination even *ex ante*, and certainly not *ex post*, but one has to be realistic about the ways in which societies define themselves. In addition, 'regionalism as diplomacy' is probably stronger for TML than for goods trade: migration looks like an even stronger tool for influencing or trying to stabilize small countries in one's sphere of influence than preferential trade. Thus, for example, New Zealand has specific labour schemes for workers from the Pacific islands, with which it identifies closely. For both reasons, the GATS' MFN clause presents peculiar difficulties for TML.

The absence of modalities for cooperation in the GATS contrasts strongly with the large number of bilateral labour arrangements that exist on TML. These typically involve the negotiation of a good deal of action by the source country in return for the grant of a quota of places for temporary emigrants from that country alone. The sort of elements that enter such a deal are that the developed partner (i) accepts a quota of less-skilled or semi-skilled workers to specific segments of its labour market (but often with some rights to change employer), with the overall quota having some flexibility with respect to an economics needs test or an objective measure of labour market conditions; (ii) offers guarantees about the welfare of workers while abroad; and (iii) makes some commitment to encourage the return of workers at the end of their TML period.

In return the developing partner offers some of the following:

(a) security clearance or details and documentation on its nationals;
(b) some validation and possibly management of their qualifications;
(c) a commitment to accept its nationals back at the end of their TML period (or before, if conditions were breached), even if they no longer hold the appropriate documentation;
(d) facilities for recruitment in-country;
(e) pre-migration training courses for potential migrants;
(f) enhanced efforts to prevent migrants from absconding into undocumented migration – for example, by limiting the number of family members eligible for migration and coordinating social pressure on migrants to return by agreeing that if there is significant failure, future quotas may be reduced.

The important point about these actions is that they cannot, at least to some extent, to be monitored by the developed partner – (a) and (b) are, for example, expressly aimed at reducing the need for developed partner monitoring, while (f) is not measurable. For this reason they depend on mutual trust between the partners, and thus are likely to be feasible only for a subset of partners, at least at first.

Beyond this skeleton, there would still be myriad details to negotiate – for example, the transferability of health and pension rights, and whether or not to withhold part of their payment until the workers exit – and then to administer. Again these are much more feasible, and possibly only feasible at all, in the context of bilateral or regional agreements.

Experience suggests that business finds immigrant labour a considerable boon, so as long as the labour market remains buoyant, one can expect there to be pressure to maintain and probably extend access. For example, farms in the southern USA are quite clear how much they depend on undocumented labour from Mexico and beyond; and in Germany business advocated the guest-worker schemes in the 1960s and 70s. It is true that firms prefer to keep the same workers if they can – or to have them back season after season – so their support for temporary mobility is qualified, but their overall priority is likely to be obtaining access to any labour. Thus the question of multilateralizing bilateral labour agreements depends on other players – governments, labour organizations and society at large. From the contrast drawn above, we would conclude that these groups are unlikely to see much benefit in meeting the demand for labour by extending the number of countries that are covered by an agreement rather than increasing the quotas or length of stay for the subset already favoured. Moreover, any lessons learned from dealing with one set of labour partners will quite easily be dismissed as not being relevant to relations with another set. Thus while immigration numbers might be allowed to increase (which itself is not certain), it is unlikely to multilateralize.

The apparent advantages of bilateral over multilateral TML agreements are a major challenge for the multilateral trading system and its advocates like us. The defence that PTAs are just the first step towards multilateralism is attractive, but in our judgment it is not sufficiently well established in this area to be plausible. The necessary steps for such an evolution to occur are for the GATS to find a means of allowing source countries to make binding commitments on their side of the TML process, and for their capacity to honour these commitments to be boosted by technical assistance and other means. Once experience with bilaterals has defined developed countries' requirements of their partners in a fairly objective way, it might be possible to agree that *any* developing country that could meet those parameters would be eligible for a TML quota of a 'standard' kind. The parallel would not be MFN so much as the mutual recognition component of the WTO agreements on technical barriers and sanitary and phyto-sanitary measures.

In truth, however, such steps would be far from sufficient: the arguments about cultural affinities and potential assimilation would remain to be solved. One might look to the WTO to enforce them, for, after all, the MFN obligation in the GATS applies to all services trade whether scheduled or not (unless a measure has been explicitly made an exception from MFN, and even that is time-limited). This would be a major strain for the system as a whole, and we would not recommend it. One might be better off recognizing that treating TML as a purely trade issue is neither convincing intellectually nor effective practically. With its deep implications for national policy and identity, TML is perhaps not yet ripe for multilateralism; or, rather, multilateralism is not yet ripe for it.

TML is probably the area of bilateral liberalization least likely to be successfully multilateralized, but the case study has some lessons for other areas of deep integration. It illustrates the dampening effect of other non-trade bureaucracies and their concerns, whether substantive or turf-related. This is especially so if these concerns reflect deep-held social attitudes – for example, the European attachment to the pre-cautionary principle. It illustrates the way that modalities which allow potential exporters to bind themselves to particular actions to support an importer's grant of market access may permit bilateral deals that can be bilaterally withdrawn, as opposed to the more laborious business of altering a WTO-bound agreement. On the other hand, however, facilitating developing country concessions may just permit large developed partners to extract more of the rent from an agreement – indeed this could explain part of the EU and US penchant for bilateralism – and so applying this lesson multilaterally certainly requires some care.

5   Where to from here? Options to encourage welfare-enhancing multilateralization

This section contains a brief discussion of what makes sense in multi-lateralization from an economic development perspective, followed by some thoughts on how to help to bring it about. While there is some scope for PTAs to develop in multilateral directions in some areas of 'deep integration', there is a need for considerable caution about the strength and frequency of this effect and the desirability of its destination (outcome). There is also a strong case for helping the journey along through conscious intervention.

The objective

Simple multilateralization is fine from a welfare perspective for trade in goods: free trade is first best. This is not necessarily the case for services or regulation. Regulation is not, per se, a 'bad', although it can be bad. The implication is that we cannot just engage in the reciprocal mechanics of 'liberalization', defined as the removal of any policies that business argues restricts entry or raises their operating costs. One needs to weigh the relative benefits of regulation in solving market failures and improving competition against the costs and restraints they imply for business. And the trade-off will vary from sector to sector. It may also be affected by the geographical coverage and the credibility of the regulation, both issues on which PTAs and multilateral agreements may have an impact.

One rationale for deep integration may be to internalize pecuniary spillovers – for example, reflecting tax or incentive competition to attract FDI, generally a beggar-my-neighbour policy that ultimately primarily benefits multinationals. Developing countries therefore have an incentive to push for international disciplines on incentive policies. PTAs represent one potential vehicle for doing so, and multilateral agreements another, but in fact neither has yet proved effective in this regard. From a development perspective, the extension of PTAs to regulatory issues can be beneficial if it improves policy quality and/or credibility, thereby reducing risk premiums and helping to attract investment. Regional cooperation may be more effective in this regard than multilateral, for partners may be more similar (e.g. have common legal or administrative systems) than the world as a whole. North–South PTAs also tend to be associated with deeper transfers of finance and knowledge (technical assistance), potentially helping to reduce implementation and adjustment costs. Proponents of deep integration in North–South agreements often argue that bound disciplines in areas such as competition and investment policy are critical for integrating markets, and that it is easier to envisage enforcement among small groups than among large, because the classic public goods problems are weaker. Schiff and Winters (2003) discuss this case, noting the potential benefits, but also showing that they are far from automatic, and rather have to be consciously sought and designed *ab initio*.

Given the large asymmetries in size and power, the challenge for small and poor countries is to ensure that any negotiated outcome is in their interest. Such countries have very little scope to use their trade policies as an instrument to induce other countries to open up their markets, so quid pro quo 'payments' for preferential market access are likely to be sought in areas such as regulatory regimes, investment policy, etc. But the regulatory standards that are written into trade agreements generally start from the status quo prevailing in OECD countries, so that the lion's share of associated implementation costs – but presumably also the benefits – lies with developing country signatories. From a development perspective, the acid test is whether proposed rules will improve the business environment, lower costs and/or help achieve domestic non-economic objectives *in the developing country*. The credibility of the wrong policy is not an aid to development. The phenomenon here is hegemonic multilateralization; PTAs offer one route, but spontaneous and multilaterally negotiated multilateralization is more important. In fact, it is difficult to identify the additionality that PTAs bring in this dimension. Moreover, the politics are less asymmetric in the non-PTA cases – the spontaneous route entails no negotiation, while the multilateral one involves a much larger group (potential alliance) of developing countries to counter developed country demands – witness, for example, the rejection of three of the so-called Singapore Issues in the Doha Round, but their vigorous existence in recent and current PTA negotiations.

For non-participants (excluded countries), the key concern is whether deeper integration among PTA members has negative implications for them, for example by fostering trade diversion or creating a momentum towards inferior regulatory regimes. Ideally, the objective here, from a multilateralization perspective, is to satisfy the equivalent of the Pareto criterion: gains from the deeper integration of PTA members should not lower welfare in other developing countries. From a development perspective the issue therefore is not only to maximize the potential pay-offs of deeper integration for developing country members of PTAs, but to maximize the prospect that the desirable components of such integration be 'multilateralized', and thus benefit non-member developing countries as well.

The means

The discrimination caused by the preferential access that PTA members get to each other's markets is a negative for the rest of the world, and may sufficiently offset the advantages of trade creation that PTAs are detrimental to some of their members. The issues here are very well known, as are the means through which such downsides can be attenuated. Trade diversion may generate incentives for PTA members to lower MFN barriers as well as internal ones – see, for example, Estevadeordal, Freund and Ornelas (2008) – but, equally, it may not – Limão (2006a, 2006b, 2007). More generally, the WTO offers the instrument of MTNs through which to negotiate lower MFN barriers.

The case of PECS – one of Baldwin's (2006) examples of multi-lateralization in goods – is partly persuasive. For members it represented a large step forward and, to the extent that it created a domino effect (another of Baldwin's important insights about European integration), it spread that effect outside the original set of members. But PECS has done nothing for sub-Saharan Africa, the Americas or Asia – indeed, by making European neighbourhood internal trade more attractive, it may well have hurt them. Similarly, the ITA – Baldwin's other cause célèbre – was undoubtedly a useful innovation – and a largely multilateral one at that. But despite the enthusiasm for this modality, no further example has come close to fruition. It may be that the international community ought to try harder to repeat the experience, but it would be unwise to ignore the special features of that case and the fact that, by providing sectoral relief to an important constituency, the ITA effectively took a set of strong 'demandeurs' for general liberalization out of play.

Ensuring that deep integration benefits developing country PTA members requires that the specifics of regulation and cooperation reflect national circumstances. Regulatory standards and institutions need to be tailored to national circumstances to be effective and attain the desired objective. An increasing body of evidence has shown that a 'one size fits all' approach – including international 'best practice' norms – may not be appropriate. For example, Barth, Caprio and Levine (2006), in a comprehensive cross-country assessment of the impact of the Basel Committee's standards for bank regulation, conclude that there is no evidence that any single set of 'best practices' is appropriate for promoting well-functioning banks. They argue that a high degree of country specificity may be needed, rather than simply adopting international norms 'off the peg'.

All this suggests that what may be most appropriate from an economic welfare (development) perspective would be to create a framework for assisting governments to identify 'good policies', not a system that is premised on negotiated harmonization or convergence.[25] An important

---

[25] As we argued above, convergence is still likely to occur via the hegemonic route, as firms and countries internalize the advantages of minimizing transactions costs with their major markets. And much of this will be driven by the EU as the most active progenitor of standards and (usually) the progenitor of the highest (most binding) standards. But this is only very indirectly due to PTA relations. The EU's relationships with its suppliers in general owe nothing to the EU being a PTA. The only link is that one might argue that, as the administration of a PTA with few instruments of policy to control, the EU Commission has 'specialized' in standards and this has led to their proliferation and a

corollary of such an approach must be 'restraint' on the part of large industrialized partner countries in PTAs, and accountability for performance and outcomes. PTAs could help by creating/supporting institutional mechanisms to increase the transparency of policies and their effects (outcomes) through common (joint) monitoring and analysis. Creating a focal point for *constructive,* as opposed to adversarial, interactions between governments on the competitive (market segmenting) effects of regulation (or a lack of regulation), and the costs and benefits (incidence) of specific reforms, could do much to mobilize the needed support by constituencies in developing country PTA members. This is especially so if the high costs of adjustment and of subsequent compliance for developing country members is recognized through increased technical assistance and investment to upgrade facilities. This argument seems to suggest that PTAs will not generalize easily to multilateral forms, which so far have been rather adversarial in the trade domain.

Such an approach to deeper integration would benefit from expanded development assistance to help put in place and improve non-discriminatory regulation in developing countries. Much effort is already being put into technical assistance to help countries expand trade capacity. From a multilateral perspective the key concerns and constraints are that such aid should promote policies that are non-discriminatory in intent and effect and that it should be devoted to policies that are appropriate for the developing countries concerned – i.e. not WTO-plus except in a few well-defined cases.

The proposed approach is not that different from the one being pursued in the context of EU–US bilateral cooperation on regulatory matters (in the context of transatlantic dialogue) and the European Neighbourhood Policy. The latter offers neighbouring countries the opportunity for, but does not impose, the adoption of elements of the EU *acquis.* In the bilateral EU–US context, the Framework for Advancing Transatlantic Economic Integration stresses dialogue, learning and soft forms of cooperation: the establishment of joint mechanisms and processes to assess the impact of regulatory regimes and to enhance timely access to information on proposed regulations, and a Transatlantic Economic Council to guide the process and review progress.[26]

---

good deal of experience in negotiating them among sovereign states. In other words, creating standards may be an EU comparative advantage.

[26] However, only a number of issues relating to financial markets are mentioned as 'lighthouse priority projects' in the EU–US 2007 Summit: accounting standards ('mutual

A discussion of EU–US co-operation raises two obvious questions. First, why does deep integration need to be pursued through a PTA if US–EU co-operation does not need it? In fact, if the focus is on the implementation of non-discriminatory regulatory improvements and cooperation, there is no prima facie case to pursue it through a PTA. In practice, as mentioned above, and as discussed at greater length in Schiff and Winters (2003), 'deep integration' has often been pursued through other forms of cooperation. One possibility is that trade negotiations of a reciprocal kind are the only way to get at regulations with a protectionist intent, and that removing these is a precondition for being able to use 'soft law' cooperation to generate efficient regulation to address market failures and attain non-economic objectives.

The second question is, what if the US and EU *do* decide that they need to place their co-operation in a bilateral PTA context? Obviously much depends on the details, but the general point needs to be made that such a scheme could certainly be harmful to excluded countries, both via trade diversion and its impact on regulatory norms. If the EU and the USA were to agree to a series of norms, these would become very strong poles of harmonization for other countries, and unless great care were taken in designing them, it is far from sure that they would be suitable, still less optimal, for developing countries.

Efforts to ensure that PTA-based regulatory cooperation benefits members may also help to realize multilateralization if it enhances the prospects for the non-discriminatory application of reforms. However, the likelihood of such an outcome depends very much on the political economy forces that prevail in the PTA. Constituencies that perceive benefits from deeper integration may perceive less 'need' to discriminate against non-PTA members insofar as the costs of reform have already been incurred. Conversely, however, they may perceive a greater interest to keep non-PTA firms out of 'their' markets. This suggests that a key input into greater multilateralization is documenting where there are significant net benefits from doing so. This in turn suggests a need to do much more to monitor and analyse the effects of deep integration initiatives. In this respect our view strongly parallels the proposal made by Rollo (Chapter 14), although we see the need as being for continuing support, rather than a one-off exercise over the existence of the PTA.

recognition' of US GAAP and the IFRS to allow firms to dispense with expensive reconciliation of reports), auditor oversight, reinsurance regulation, and mutual recognition in the field of securities regulation ('where appropriate').

What role for the WTO? Transparency!

As is painfully obvious from this chapter, little is known (or at least publicly available) about what is actually being done by PTAs. To what extent are provisions implemented? Is deeper integration implemented in a discriminatory way in areas where this is not necessary in principle? What are the effects of specific instances of deeper integration? What are the estimated costs and benefits? What is the incidence of these effects?

The WTO could be a much more effective focal point for information on these types of questions. The absence of comprehensive information on the implementation of PTAs greatly impedes the analysis of their effects, in turn attenuating the accountability of governments that have negotiated them. A concerted effort by the major protagonists involved in PTAs – starting with the EU and the US – to agree to regular in-depth scrutiny of PTAs, and to finance the required data collection effort, would do much to remove the uncertainty that currently affects efforts to assess the extent and impacts of PTA-based deeper integration efforts.

Reforms require domestic constituencies to implement and sustain them – comprehensive data on the implementation of policies will allow think tanks, NGOs, industries and researchers to assess and analyse the effects of PTAs. While ideally pursued through the WTO, the collection, compilation and analysis of the required information should involve research and public interest bodies in the PTA members. These bodies can do much to help shed light and build consensus for better policies.

6   Concluding remarks

We have examined the prospects for multilateralizing regionalism from the point of view of developing countries – whether it is happening, whether it could happen, whether it should happen. Overall, our perception is less optimistic than that of many of our colleagues, and we certainly do not adhere to the view that PTAs are benign because they offer developing countries a good chance of embarking on a constructive path of deep integration. Some of the other chapters in this book, especially Baldwin, Evenett and Low (Chapter 3), paint a rosier picture than we think is appropriate. As ever, the big challenge and the big difference between authors lies in determining the counterfactual.

Much (most) reform to date is unilateral and there is very little direct evidence that PTAs do a lot more than unilateralism or drive reform.

One problem is to determine the direction of causality. One cannot infer from the spread of specific PTA disciplines ('templates') that PTAs are driving reforms beyond what governments had already decided was beneficial autonomously. Many of the disciplines currently embodied in PTAs are redundant or meaningless.

There is evidence that PTAs include more service sectors than countries have scheduled at the WTO, but it also suggests that their clauses do not move much beyond those in the WTO. That is, PTAs may broaden the coverage of commitments to lock in service liberalization, most of which has been implemented autonomously, but they do not deepen it. Moreover, in areas of key importance to the developing world – for example, the mobility of labour or disciplining the incentives offered to foreign direct investors – neither multilateral nor bilateral routes appear to have achieved much. We argue above that the bilateral route is more likely to yield fruit in the case of labour mobility, but we do not advocate PTAs as the modality so much as free-standing migration agreements. This is, however, one area where bilateral experience could usefully contribute to the design of WTO disciplines.

Most research in this area focuses on legal texts, not on the extent to which PTAs imply/require or result in changes in national legislation. It may well be that the source for reform has primarily been knowledge and information – the demonstration effects of successful countries or the general focus of academia and the international community on the benefits of deregulation, competition, etc. Maybe the IFIs, OECD, APEC, etc., which have been advocating better policies and more transparency for years, are the key: perhaps the World Bank's report (2008) has been a more potent driver of recent reforms than any PTA.

The current discussion pays too little attention to enforcement and dispute settlement. It is assumed that PTA disciplines are, or will be, enforced, but past experience suggests otherwise. Moreover, although most PTAs are too recent to have generated many disputes, so far there has been little PTA-specific enforcement. We see much more action in the WTO, even between PTA members. We do not follow Pauwelyn (Chapter 8) in advocating that the WTO should help to enforce PTAs – that is a bit like giving burglars the key to your door so that they commit burglaries without making so much mess – but rather conclude that the relative contributions of PTAs and the WTO are more in favour of the latter than is sometimes recognized. A necessary input into resolving this weighting definitively, however, is data: the international community desperately requires detailed studies not only of legal structures (which are starting to emerge), but of policy change and enforcement on the ground.

We also have to recognize that governments are not the only, or even the most important, players in some areas. In the case of standards, norms are much more driven by markets than governments – firms have clear incentives to comply, and governments to reduce compliance costs. Walmart may be much more of a player than any government in setting and enforcing standards (see Javorcik, Keller and Tybout, 2006).

Before conceding that PTAs represent a step in the right direction we would apply the basic tests: (i) 'Does the PTA go beyond what governments had already decided to do?' and (ii) 'Are the negative spillovers – for either the rest of the world or the developing country members – dealt with adequately?' Our belief is that in many areas – for example, investment or competition policies – and in most PTAs, the answer is 'No'. The fact that developing countries are adopting disciplines *and* applying them on an MFN basis – if that is indeed the case – does not imply that the norms concerned are beneficial for these countries. If they are not, multilateralizing a PTA is bad news! One example may be the US IPR regime. The general lesson is that we should not ignore the substance of the norms that are included in PTAs. Whether these are autonomously decided or externally imposed, what matters at the end of the day is whether they benefit the countries that adopt them *and* the countries that are affected by them (the non-members). From this perspective, another important priority is the establishment of institutions or other means to help developing countries take an informed view of what they are asked to do in PTA negotiations, and how neighbours' PTAs impact upon them.

Of course we recognize that PTAs do not occur in a vacuum. There may be important so-called non-economic dimensions to agreements between countries, and we have to take a holistic view of any PTA. Some preference between countries may be warranted by foreign policy considerations, but it should be conscious and justified, and not at the expense of the world community as a whole. Moreover, trade preference may not be the best modality. If PTAs are to become the ostensible route to multilateralism, we face the danger that they may transfer preferentialism to other sectors where it would not otherwise exist, such as aid flows and cultural and educational connections.

References

Al Khouri, R. (2007) 'National Security Aspects of Western-Middle East Free Trade Agreements', *Aussenwirtschaft* 62 (2): 175–92.

Baldwin, R. (2000) 'Regulatory Protectionism, Developing Countries and a Two Tier Trading System', in S. Collins and D. Rodrik (eds.), *Brookings Trade Forum 2000*, Washington, DC: Brookings Institution.

(2006) 'Multilateralising Regionalism: Spaghetti Bowls as Building Blocks on the Path to Global Free Trade', *The World Economy* 29 (11): 1451–518.

Baller, S. (2007) '*Trade Effects of Regional Standards Liberalisation: A Heterogeneous Firms Approach*', World Bank Policy Research Paper 4124, Washington, DC: World Bank.

Barth, J. Caprio, G. Jr., and Levine, R. (2006) *Rethinking Bank Regulation: Till Angels Govern*, Cambridge: Cambridge University Press.

Bohara, A., Gawande, K. and Sanguinetti, P. (2004) 'Trade Diversion and Declining Tariffs: Evidence from Mercosur', *Journal of International Economics* 64: 65–88.

Chen, M. and Mattoo, A. (2004) '*Regionalism in Standards: Good or Bad for Trade?*', World Bank Policy Research Paper 3458, Washington, DC: World Bank.

Devereaux, C., Lawrence, R. and Watkins, M. (2006) *Case Studies in US Trade Negotiation: Making the Rules*, Washington, DC: Institute for International Economics.

Egger, P. and Pfaffermayr, M. (2004) 'The Impact of BITs on FDI', *Journal of Comparative Economics* 32: 788–804.

Estevadeordal, A., Freund, C. and Ornelas, E. (2008) '*Does Regionalism Affect Trade Liberalisation Towards Non-Members?*', CEP Discussion Papers No. 868, London: Centre for Economic Performance.

Fink, C. and Molinuevo, M. (2007) '*East Asian Free Trade Agreements in Services: Roaring Tigers or Timid Pandas?*', Washington, DC: World Bank.

Fink, C. and Reichenmiller, P. (2005) '*Tightening TRIPS: Intellectual Property Rights in US Free Trade Agreements*', Trade Note No. 20, Washington, DC: World Bank.

Hoekman, B. and Kostecki, M. (2001) *The Political Economy of the World Trading System: The WTO and Beyond*, 2nd edn, Oxford: Oxford University Press.

Hoekman, B. and Messerlin, P. (2000) 'Liberalizing Trade in Services: Reciprocal Negotiations and Regulatory Reform', in P. Sauvé and R. Stern (eds.), *Services 2000: New Directions in Services Trade Liberalisation*, Washington, DC: Brookings Institution.

Hoekman, B. and Saggi, K. (2000) 'Assessing the Case for Extending WTO Disciplines on Investment Related Policies', *Journal of Economic Integration* 15: 588–610.

(2007) 'Tariff Bindings and Bilateral Cooperation on Export Cartels', *Journal of Development Economics*, 83: 141–56.

Hoekman, B., Mattoo, A. and Sapir, A. (2007) 'The Political Economy of Services Trade Liberalisation: A Case for International Regulatory Cooperation?', *Oxford Review of Economic Policy* 23 (3): 367–91.

Houde, M.-F., Kolse-Patil, A. and Miroudot, S. (2007) '*The Interaction between Investment and Services Chapters in Selected Regional Trade Agreements*', OECD Working Paper 55, Paris: OECD.

Javorcik, B., Keller, W. and Tybout, J. (2006) '*Openness and Industrial Response in a Wal-Mart World : A Case Study of Mexican Soaps, Detergents, and Surfactant Producers*', World Bank Policy Research Paper 3999, Washington, DC: World Bank.

Jensen, J., Rutherford, T. and Tarr, D. (2007) 'The Impact of Liberalizing Barriers to Foreign Direct Investment in Services: The Case of Russian Accession to the World Trade Organisation', *Review of Development Economics* 11 (3): 482–506.

Karacaovali, B. and Limão, N. (2005) '*The Clash of Liberalizations: Preferential vs. Multilateral Trade Liberalization in the European Union*', World Bank Policy Research Working Paper No. 3493, Washington, DC: World Bank.

Kee Hiau Looi, Nicita, A. and Olarreaga, M. (2008) 'Estimating Trade Restrictiveness Indices', *The Economic Journal*, forthcoming.

Konan, D. and Maskus, K. (2006) 'Quantifying the Impact of Services Liberalisation in a Developing Country', *Journal of Development Economics* 81: 142–62.

Kox, H. and Lejour, A. (2006) 'The Effects of the Services Directive on Intra-EU Trade and FDI', *Revue Économique* 57, 4: 747–69.

Lesher, M. and Miroudot, S. (2007) 'The Economic Impact of Investment Provisions in Regional Trade Agreements', *Aussenwirtschaft* 62 (2): 193–232.

Limão, N. (2006a) 'Preferential vs. Multilateral Trade Liberalization: Evidence and Open Questions', *World Trade Review* 5 (2): 155–76.

(2006b) 'Preferential Trade Agreements as Stumbling Blocks for Multilateral Trade Liberalization: Evidence for the United States', *American Economic Review* 96: 896–914.

(2007) 'Are Preferential Trade Agreements with Non-Trade Objectives a Stumbling Block for Multilateral Liberalization?', *Review of Economic Studies* 74 (3): 821–55.

Markusen, J., Rutherford, T. and Tarr, D. (2005) 'Trade and Direct Investment in Producer Services and the Domestic Market for Expertise', *Canadian Journal of Economics* 38 (3): 758–77.

Martin, W. and Messerlin, P. (2007) 'Why Is it so Difficult? Trade Liberalization under the Doha Agenda', *Oxford Review of Economic Policy* 23: 347–66.

OECD (2005) 'The Benefits of Liberalising Product Markets and Reducing Barriers to International Trade and Investment: The Case of the United States and the European Union', Economics Department Working Paper 432, Paris, OECD.

Oye, K. (1992) Economic Discrimination and Political Exchange: World Political Economy in the 1930s and 1980s, Princeton, NJ: Princeton University Press.

Pelkmans, J. (2001) European Integration: Methods and Economic Analysis, 2nd edn, Harlow: Financial Times–Prentice Hall.

(2007) 'Mutual Recognition in Goods. On Promises and Disillusions', Journal of European Public Policy 14 (5): 699–716.

Piermartini, R. and Budetta, M. (2006) 'A Mapping of Regional Rules on Technical Barriers to Trade', mimeo, Geneva: WTO.

Piérola, F. and Horlick, G. (2007) 'WTO Dispute Settlement and Dispute Settlement in the "North–South" Agreements of the Americas: Considerations for Choice of Forum', Journal of World Trade 41 (5): 885–908.

Pomfret, R. (2007) 'Is Regionalism an Increasing Feature of the World Economy?', World Economy 30: 923–47.

Portugal-Perez, A. (2007) 'The Costs of Rules of Origin in Apparel: African Preferential Exports to the EU and US', mimeo, University of Geneva.

Prusa, T. (2006) 'Preferential Trade Agreements and the Incidence of Antidumping Disputes', mimeo, Rutgers University.

Roy, M., Marchetti, J. and Lim, H. (2006) 'Services Liberalisation in the New Generation of Preferential Trade Agreements: How Much Further than the GATS?', WTO Staff Working Paper No. ERSD-2006-07, Geneva: WTO.

Schiff, M. and Winters, A. L. (2003) Regionalism and Development, Oxford: Oxford University Press.

Selin, H. and Vandeveer, S. (2006) 'Raising Global Standards: Hazardous Substances and E-Waste Management in the European Union', Environment 48 (10): 6–17, available at: http://www.heldref.org/env.php.

Sen, R. (2006) '"New Regionalism" in Asia: A Comparative Analysis of Emerging Regional and Bilateral Trade Agreements involving ASEAN, China and India', Journal of World Trade 40: 553–96.

Sokol, D. (2007) 'Why is This Chapter Different from Others? An Examination of Why Countries Enter into Non-Enforceable Competition Policy Chapters in FTAs', mimeo, University of Missouri School of Law.

Ullrich, H. (2004) 'Comparing EU Free Trade Agreements: Services', ECDPM Brief, European Centre for Development Policy Management, available at: www.ecdpm.org.

US Government (2006) 'U.S.–EU Working Together to Fight Against Global Piracy and Counterfeiting', available at: www.whitehouse.gov/news/releases/2005/06/20050620-6.html.

Winters, L. Alan (1999) 'Regionalism vs. Multilateralism', in R. Baldwin, D. Cohen, A. Sapir and A. Venables (eds.), *Market Integration, Regionalism and the Global Economy*, London: CEPR.

World Bank (2005) *Global Economic Prospects: Trade, Regionalism, and Development*, Washington, DC: World Bank.

(2008) *Doing Business 2008 Report*, Washington DC: World Bank.

Comment

PHILIP I. LEVY

This is a very useful chapter. It attempts to tackle some of the challenging analysis that lurks beyond more straightforward border barriers, such as tariffs and quotas. The authors note the limits to our knowledge of services, investment, standards and so forth, and demonstrate that there is a lot of conceptual work to be done.

Multilateralization

A first question, central to this entire project, is: What does multi-lateralization mean? The chapter addresses this somewhat obliquely. I do not really mean that as a criticism, since it is a ferociously difficult task to say something concrete when the underlying topic is so multi-faceted. The chapter describes three distinct paths whereby we start with heterogeneous rules in preferential trade agreements (PTAs) and end up with harmonization into a more coherent global trading system: first, "hegemonic multilateralization," in which a dominant power imposes its own restrictions, and everyone else is compelled to adopt those rules; second, the "convergence route", whereby there is competition between rules, and a common approach emerges; third, "political evolution," in which there are changes in countries' political economy that undermine opposition to competition.

I would suggest a complementary set of possibilities for multilate-ralization. Whereas the one in the chapter provides a good overview of the grand trajectory toward multilateralization, a much more frequent policy question is whether any given measure undertaken now will hinder or contribute to as yet unspecified future integration. One could categorize particular policies as "instantly available," "easily expandable," or "setting a precedent." An example of an instantly available policy would be a reform that allowed foreign retailers to set up in a particular country. This could be demanded by an FTA partner, but if the permission is non-discriminatory, we have instant multilateralization. An "easily expandable" policy would be a measure that allowed for exclusion, but inclusion is straightforward. Following the retailer example, PTA participants would enjoy the privilege, but new members could readily gain access for their retailers. Finally, a precedent-setting policy could be one that might create a model that could be widely adopted. Many of these issues have not been addressed in the multilateral setting, leaving plenty of room for innovation. A rule might spread once its efficacy is demonstrated. The effect is not instant, but it moves along as others adopt. An example would be the sort of spread that Baldwin, Evenett, and Low discuss in Chapter 3.

Of course, these are potential positive effects of PTAs on multilateralization, and some policies will be more conducive to this sort of spread than others. It could be interesting to delve into such ratings as a policy guide, outlining best practices for those who argue that regional agreements complement multilateral liberalization.

Political economy

A key question is how easy is it to make changes on these deeper integration measures. The general presumption is that it is hard. These are issues that move beyond the conventional trade issues and touch on the competencies of other groups within a legislature, or even within states or sub-regions in a federal system (e.g. the US regulation of legal or medical services).

But is there a fixed cost to every change, independent of the scope? Or does cost increase with partner size? With number of partners? I doubt there is a single answer, but these are the building blocks for even more detailed thinking about this.

The principal case study in the chapter is of mode 4 negotiations, concerning the movement of natural persons. One can hardly accuse the authors of taking on an easy issue to support an optimistic take. In fact, my initial reaction was that mode 4 is a wildly masochistic issue to illustrate prospects for multilateralization.

The reason, though, has to do with the political economy (at least in the United States). US inclusion of mode 4 abruptly ceased when Congress decided that this was an incursion into immigration policy and was inappropriate for trade agreements. It is in the nature of deep integration that it crosses such boundaries. It is worth thinking through how best to approach these issues, given those constraints. The answers are likely to come from careful examination of case studies.

Developing country perspective

Let me turn for a moment to the headline distinguishing topic of this chapter – the developing country perspective. First, I would argue that it was a strategic mistake for developing nations to keep these issues out of multilateral talks. In many ways, these deep liberalization negotiations in PTAs present a worst-case scenario for developing nations. They present difficult analytics. You have the standard imbalance in negotiating leverage. On top of that, you have an additional loss of leverage because of the developed powers' interest in standard-setting and harmonization.

Second, I disagree with the authors' assertion that there is little to gain for developing countries on these topics. They note that developing countries' "offensive interests" in services, investment, intellectual property and competition policy may be limited. I would argue that the distribution of offensive interests on trade issues is uneven, but the whole point of holding broader negotiations is to allow countries to undertake welfare-enhancing reforms in one sector (defensive), while crowing about concessions won in other sectors (offensive). These topics are clearly something developed countries care about, and that have the potential to benefit developing countries.

Constrained optimization

This raises the question of what will benefit developing countries. This is a very tricky area. The authors note the difficulty of differentiating between legitimate concerns relating to quality and performance versus barriers to entry.

My reaction was that this would be a wonderful set of areas on which the World Bank could do work – trying to develop an array of policies that could best serve the interests of developing countries. In doing so, I think it would be wise to keep in mind the pressure for multilateralization. That means that one would be looking at constrained optimization – what are the best set of policies to advocate for developing countries contingent upon existing standards and the ultimate goal of multilateralization?

14

The challenge of negotiating RTAs for developing countries. What could the WTO do to help?[1]

JIM ROLLO

1 Introduction

Preferential regional and bilateral trade agreements (RTAs is the WTO term for these, and that is used here) are on the increase (by how much is controversial – see, for example, Messerlin (2007)), and arguably affect less than 20 per cent of world trade by value (Medvedev, 2006). What is not controversial is that the top trade powers (notably the EU, the US, China and Japan) are actively pursuing such agreements at the same time as momentum in multilateral trade negotiations has, at best, slowed. It is also worth noting that developing countries are involved in 125 out of the 193 preferential agreements notified to the WTO Secretariat and in force as at March 2007 (see Table 14.1).[2]

Neither Article XXIV of the GATT nor Article 5 of the GATS exerts much discipline on the workings of RTAs between WTO members. In any case, discipline is exerted after rather than before the event, so the impact of any negotiating mistakes or adverse effects on third countries is unlikely to be corrected unless a dispute is brought, and so far this has not happened very often. The challenge for participants in any given bilateral or regional negotiation is thus to negotiate an outcome that maximizes benefits and minimizes costs for themselves and ideally also for non-members and the trade system (though it is hard to see who is there to argue for it in any given negotiation).

Bilateral agreements are intrinsically more difficult to evaluate than either multilateral or unilateral liberalizations because of their second-best nature, i.e. the balance of costs and benefits is not a given. Economic

[1] I am grateful to the British Department for Business, Enterprise and Regulatory reform for financial support. All views expressed and any errors are my own.
[2] By July 2007, 205 agreements had been notified and were in place. See www.wto.org/english/tratop_e/region_e/region_e.htm.

Table 14.1 *Preferential agreements notified to WTO by type, as at March 2007*

	Preferential arrangements[*]	Free trade agreements[*]	Customs unions[*]	Services agreements[*]	Total
South–South	18	22	5	16	61
North–South	0	40	1	20	61
North–North	0	15	8	8	31
Transition–Transition	0	33	0	0	33
North–Transition	0	4	0	0	4
South–Transition	0	3	0	0	3
Total	18	117	14	44	193

[*] Including later accessions to already notified agreements.

Source: derived from http://www.wto.org/english/tratop_e/region_e/eif_e.xls.

analysis can deal relatively straightforwardly with this through concepts of trade creation and trade diversion. Even for relatively simple trade barriers, such as tariffs, or those that can be expressed as tariff equivalents, however, measurement of these effects is not always straightforward and requires a relatively specialized set of economic analytical skills. This problem of measurement is further complicated because increasingly RTAs go beyond the simple dismantling of border barriers to trade in goods. Such agreements now include services and other elements of deep integration (regulatory liberalization in particular, but also competition policy, intellectual property protection and investment) where data are poorer, analytical tools less developed and the domestic legal implications of any agreement complex and potentially substantial. The wide ambit and intensity of liberalization, taken along with the necessity to cover substantially all trade and sometimes deal with many partners, suggests that individual RTAs could be, in principle, as difficult to negotiate as a WTO negotiation with 150 parties.

The bureaucratic stresses for developed countries with relatively well-resourced[3] administrations can be substantial.[4] For administrations in

---

[3] For example Directorate-General (DG) Trade in the EU Commission has five directors, and seven administrative units dealing directly with bilateral trade relations, plus a chief economist and a legal unit, plus advice feeding in from other DGs, notably Agriculture. And then there is the input from the EU member states' administrations in the Article 133 Committee.

[4] The Republic of Korea is reportedly deploying in excess of 200 officials in its negotiations on an EU–Republic of Korea FTA.

developing countries, where human capital is often the binding constraint, the resource demands of negotiating one or more RTAs alongside multilateral and unilateral trade policymaking are potentially much greater. For example, the EU–Egypt association agreement of 2004 runs to 165 pages, with a main agreement text of 37 pages, plus six annexes and five protocols taking up the rest, of which 63 pages cover detailed rules of origin. Even this pales into insignificance against the text of the US–Peru agreement,[5] in which the main text (in twenty-three sections and three annexes) runs to 599 pages, including 116 pages of rules of origin, 46 pages on investment, and 36 pages on government procurement. For the US negotiators – since they have a standardized approach to bilateral agreements – there is a clear element of learning by doing, and by now they are very familiar with the texts they are aiming to agree on. This is the power of the hegemon in such a context. Similar considerations apply for the EU in agreements with the ACP countries, or the countries covered by its neighbourhood policy. For individual countries negotiating with these or other hegemonic trade powers, agreements are one-off and extremely demanding. The one-off nature of such negotiations is a recipe for misunderstandings and mistakes about implications of specific policy changes demanded by a specific agreement, not least for economic and social development.

All of this is further complicated by the possibility that each RTA negotiated by any given country could differ markedly from other RTAs under negotiation or in operation by or in that country. The issue of different levels of preferences for products from different origins causes potential bureaucratic confusion at the frontier, as well as complex impacts on domestic production and consumption, economic welfare and income distribution.

Rules of origin (Baldwin, 2006; Gasiorek, Augier and Lai-Tong, Chapter 4 of this volume) are particularly damaging for the developing countries. Restrictive rules of origin are economically damaging, as they can prevent the integration of developing countries into global production structures through both trade and FDI (foreign direct investment). Irrespective of their restrictiveness, differences in rules of origin in different agreements signed by any one country are a recipe for confusion for customs authorities and traders, and contribute to the negative externality of the spaghetti bowl effect which is the focus of this

---

[5] See www.ustr.gov/Trade_Agreements/Bilateral/Peru_TPA/Final_Texts/Section_Index.html. Approved by US Congress in December 2007 and due to enter into force in 2009.

volume. The 'spaghetti bowl' effect is particularly damaging for developing countries because they lack the human resources in public and private sectors to analyse systematically these complexities and their implications for trade, investment and development.

Finally, the unambiguous losers from any given RTA are those excluded. First, they are discriminated against and any trade or investment diversion damages them, with no offsetting benefits from trade creation (unless some aspects of services or other regulatory liberalization in a given bilateral agreement are effectively *erga omnes*). Second, fear of preference erosion may make participants in RTAs reluctant to negotiate non-discriminatory trade liberalization multilaterally. Third, partners in an RTA may lobby against multilateral or unilateral MFN liberalization. Fourth, the human resource cost of negotiating and implementing RTAs may reduce engagement in multilateral or unilateral non-discriminatory liberalization.

2   What can be done to relieve human resource constraints and reduce potential costs?

Given what is known about the potential effects of RTAs from economic theory and experience of previous episodes of preferential liberalization (e.g. the formation of the European Union), it is possible to construct a systematic framework that could be used to assess the potential impact of any given agreement. The elements in such a framework would include:

(1) A systematic checklist for analysing what is in and what is out of any proposed RTA, and how that relates to WTO rules and any other agreements in force.

(2) A guide to the WTO and domestic legal and legislative requirements to implement individual elements of any agreement.

(3) Guidance on how to assess the potential economic impacts of any agreement as an aid to reducing costs and increasing benefits for partners and third parties. This is potentially complex, but:

    (a) It is possible to derive some rules of thumb about likely impacts on economic welfare on the basis of readily available diagnostic statistics (importance of trade in the economy, trade shares and trade patterns with potential partner(s) and third countries, similarities and differences in trade and production structures among potential partners, the level of MFN applied tariffs and size and pattern of tariff peaks, the importance and incidence of NTBs where available, the importance and type of intra-industry trade generally, and with potential partners).

(b) Although these rules of thumb are relatively easy to assess in the case of shallow integration (removal of border barriers), they are less useful in the case of deep integration where barriers derive from domestic regulation (notably, but not only, in services, intellectual property protection and foreign investment).[6]

(c) The framework could be designed to give guidance on how to identify products and services where deep integration is likely to be important in generating gains from specialization and integration into supply chains with potential partners. Such gains would in turn help to raise productivity and generate dynamic economic gains that can offset any trade diversion losses from shallow integration.

(d) Diagnostic statistics and case studies could help to identify industries most likely to expand and contract as a result of a given RTA, and hence some indications of where to look for social (e.g. regional employment effects, income distribution, gender, health) and environmental consequences, and the need for flanking domestic policies to maximize benefits and mini-mize costs.

(4) The extension of the economic assessment to include economic modelling (both general and partial equilibrium) to allow more precise quantitative assessments of overall welfare effects (general equilibrium), and of the potential impact on trade, production and consumption for particular products or industries (partial equi-librium). Both of these approaches could be used in conjunction with social accounting matrices and household surveys and other databases to explore potential social and environmental impacts in a more detailed way.

(5) An interactive electronic version, which could guide users through the checklist, calculate diagnostic statistics and even allow some modelling, would potentially reduce time and human resource cost.

To give a sense of what such an analytical framework might look like, the Annex to this chapter describes and discusses the Sussex Framework. This is an attempt to design such an aid for negotiators, developed at the

---

[6] See boxes 14.1 and 14.2

University of Sussex, UK, and which has been used to assess a number of actual and proposed RTAs involving developing countries (Evans *et al.*, 2006). This is included to demonstrate the feasibility and effectiveness of such an analytical framework.

3 What is the interest and potential role of the international community in helping developing countries negotiate RTAs effectively?

Interest

The international community's interest derives essentially in reducing the costs of the 'spaghetti bowl'; second, in minimizing the costs to those excluded from any given RTA; and, third, in defending the existing multilateral trading system as embedded in the WTO. The WTO is clearly in the front line of minimizing the costs of RTAs. Its rules on preferential liberalization in Article XXIV of the GATT and Article 5 of the GATS provide a first potential discipline. These rules clearly acknowledge that preferential liberalization is prima facie in breach of the principle of non-discrimination, but also that preferences are a fact, and hence require rules to minimize negative effects on the multilateral system. Given that, historically, preferential integration has been a major policy instrument of the membership – most notably the EU and NAFTA members – and given the increase in notifications of preferential agreements since the formation of the WTO (see www.wto.org/english/tratop_e/region_e/region_e.htm) – it is not surprising that negotiations on procedures and disciplines on RTAs were included in the Doha Mandate. The new transparency mechanism agreed (albeit provisionally) in December 2006 is the first product of that.

The difficulty with WTO rules on RTAs, however, is that they apply *ex post*. Even the new transparency mechanism only asks that countries in new negotiations on RTAs *endeavour* to notify the WTO, and that they notify the WTO of the provisions of any signed agreement *when they are made public*.

The problem is that RTAs generate substantive difficulties for the WTO. First, and as we have seen, RTAs create incentives for gainers from RTAs (notably the winners from trade diversion) to resist RTA members cutting their MFN tariffs in multilateral negotiations (or indeed unilaterally). The importance of preference erosion as an issue in the Doha Development Agenda points that up. Second, as RTAs proliferate they threaten to increase the number of disputes brought to the WTO by

countries which consider their MFN rights have been impaired, particularly if the transparency mechanism leads to non-members becoming
better informed of the content and hence likely impact of new RTAs.

Policies which threaten not only the dynamic of multinational liberalization, but also increased litigation within the system, suggests a
WTO institutional interest in actions *ex ante* which help to reduce both
risks, particularly where some countries are less able to negotiate
effectively because of resource constraints. Having an agreed standardized framework with which to assess RTAs would also give non-members of the RTAs, as well as academics, NGOs, parliamentarians,
business and the media, a means of scrutinizing proposed RTAs in a
consistent way. Such a framework would act not just as a negotiating
tool but also as an enhanced transparency mechanism.

What role might the international community play ex ante in preparing parties for RTA negotiations?

The WTO is obviously the first place to look. However, the very fact that
RTAs are bilateral negotiations between WTO members would make a
role for the institution and the Secretariat potentially more difficult.
Neither the WTO as an institution nor the Secretariat (individually or
collectively), could take or be perceived to take, implicitly or explicitly,
sides in any RTA negotiation between members. That constraint would
seem on the face of it to preclude helping any member to use a framework
such as the one outlined above, to prepare a negotiating position. This
prohibition would presumably apply equally to any other multilateral
organization (e.g. UNCTAD or the development banks).

There might be a list of actions that the WTO might undertake, such as:

(1) getting international agreement on the content and structure of a
    standardized analytical framework;
(2) delivering/sponsoring generic training on the implementation of
    such a framework in Geneva or in developing countries;
(3) certifying private providers (consultants, academics, NGOs) who
    could give training and technical assistance in preparing negotiating
    positions;
(4) managing a trust fund to fund or partially subsidize these activities
    in developing countries, perhaps supported by the Aid for Trade
    funds agreed at the Hong Kong WTO Ministerial;
(5) giving written and approved legal advice/guidance on how to
    'WTO-proof' any agreement on a without-prejudice basis as far as

the rights of any party to take disputes cases after implementation are concerned.

Even this, however, might be too much for the membership to accept, and it would take time to negotiate such a package. There are arguments that in any case much of this could be left to the private/non-profit sector to deliver.

Private versus public provision

There is already a limited private provision of such analytical services. Many consultancies, research institutes and academics provide trade policy advice to developed and developing countries. Such advice to developing countries is often provided via aid-funded technical assistance contracts. There is no reason why an analytical framework such as the one outlined above should not be marketed in this way and compete with other approaches (as indeed the Sussex Framework does).

There are three reasons for an element of public provision and/or regulation of quality. The first reason is asymmetric information. Just as countries without any depth of bureaucratic resources to assess FTAs might make errors in negotiation, so they might also make errors in their selection of expertise and analytical methods. Given that RTA negotiations tend to be lumpy and not often repeated, such mistakes might be costly and the market might take too long to discover the best framework and/or providers. Public provision of quality assurance and certification of providers could help reduce these costs of asymmetric information.

Second is the risk of creating international public 'bads' in the negotiation of any given RTA, and of 'spaghetti bowl' effects from the cumulative effect of many countries being members of many bilateral agreements. There is no incentive on the part of the negotiators for the interests of third parties to be taken into account. In the worst case, negotiators may be actively negotiating to maximize their gains from trade diversion in RTA partners' markets at the expense of third parties.

Third, there is the potential damage to the relevance and credibility of multilaterally negotiated trade rules and liberalization. The hard-won relevance of the WTO to the global trade system is potentially at stake.

An internationally agreed and sponsored framework which included provisions which encouraged more trade-system-friendly RTA agreements would bring major public benefits. These considerations constitute, prima facie, a case for the international public provision of analytical services to help negotiators from developing countries. Additionally, such an institution would build up expertise very quickly, and generate economies of scale in the provision of analysis and advice that match those built up by developed countries, notably the USA and the EU.

4   A proposal for an Advisory Centre on Regional Trading Agreements (ACORTA)

Accepting that there is a case for subsidized public provision of: (a) an approved analytical framework to assess the economic, legal and development implications of particular RTAs; (b) training in its implementation; (c) advice on the framework's application to a specific bilateral negotiation; (d) advice on the implications of its outputs for negotiating strategy; and (e) the accreditation of providers of such training and advisory services to human resource constrained developing country administrations engaged in negotiation of an RTA, there are potential difficulties in persuading 153 members of the WTO to agree to the organization taking on such a politically exposed role. This is also true of other multilateral or regional organizations (e.g. UNCTAD, the World Bank, regional development banks) because of potential conflicts of interest when two or more members are on opposite sides in the same negotiation. It then follows that there is a case for a new, small international organization to provide these services.

There is a precedent and model for such an organization in the Advisory Centre for WTO Law (ACWL) which was set up in July 2001 to provide advice and training for developing countries engaged in dispute settlement actions in the WTO. The situation is similarly one in which WTO members have different interests even though RTA negotiations are not necessarily adversarial in the way that WTO disputes, by definition, are. The ACWL was set up explicitly to level the playing field for developing countries in disputes to allow for their lack of experience and depth of expertise in WTO law and so allow them to act effectively in a dispute. If two developing countries are on the opposite sides of a dispute and request advice, then one (usually the higher-income one) is directed to a roster of external counsel (approved law firms and appropriately qualified individuals who charge at the same rate as the ACWL) to avoid a conflict of interest. Least developed countries (LDCs) that are also WTO members, or candidates for membership, get free access to ACWL advice on WTO law, and advice on cases in the WTO, subsidized down to 10 per cent of the standard ACWL hourly rate. In the case of a conflict of interest between ACWL members, LDCs get preferred access to ACWL lawyers. Other developing countries get access by joining the ACWL, contributing to the trust fund that underpins it, and paying on a sliding scale of hourly rates for legal advice in specific cases, again broadly based on income per head. Developed countries have no access to services, but contribute to the trust fund, and some developed members have agreed to contribute to the annual running costs of the organization for an initial period of five years. Current membership is ten developed countries[7] and twenty-seven developing countries[8] and rising. The institution is small – eight legal staff and two administrators – and is based in Geneva, where it has status as an international institution under Swiss law. It is governed by a management board of five, nominated from and reporting to a general assembly of the members.

This model seems to be relevant to the problems facing developing countries negotiating RTAs identified above. Notably the ACWL model deals effectively with the conflict-of-interest problem inherent in existing international organizations intervening on one side or the other of a live negotiation. The main differences are, first, that the ACWL is staffed by lawyers, while economists would dominate in the proposed centre, and, second, that the new centre would have to create its own agreed analytical framework. There is a substantial corpus of WTO trade law cases and specialist training in legal analysis of such cases in universities worldwide as well as training in generic legal representation skills. Any such organization dealing with the negotiation of RTAs would have to begin by getting agreement from its members on the analytical framework. There is also a smaller global community of trade economists than there are trade lawyers from which to draw expertise.

The analysis above suggests that there is a case for a new international institution provisionally called the Advisory Centre on RTAs (ACORTA) with a remit to:

- agree a framework to analyse economic and legal aspects of RTAs, with advice from a group of distinguished trade economists and lawyers and subject to ratification by members of ACORTA;

---

[7] Canada, Denmark, Finland, Ireland, Italy, Netherlands, Norway, Sweden, Switzerland and the United Kingdom.

[8] Bolivia; China; Chinese Taipei; Colombia; Dominican Republic; Ecuador; Egypt; El Salvador; Guatemala; Honduras; Hong Kong, China; India; Indonesia; Jordan; Kenya; Mauritius; Nicaragua; Oman; Pakistan; Panama; Paraguay; Peru; the Philippines; Thailand; Tunisia; Turkey; Uruguay; and Venezuela.

- provide advice to LDCs and developing country members of ACORTA who are negotiating RTAs based on the framework for agreed fees, commensurate with ability to pay;
- prepare and deliver training in the use of the framework;
- prepare or supervise the preparation of handbooks and electronic aids to assist;
- countries to apply the analytical framework themselves;
- certify other providers as competent to apply the agreed framework, advise countries directly, and deliver training.

This could be done with an initial staff of up to eight professionals, of whom six might be economists, and two lawyers. Over time these numbers might drop as demands from building the framework, preparing documentation, electronic aids and training modules, and certifying private providers dropped. Financially ACORTA could be supported by some combination of an initial trust fund, based on one-off membership fees from developed and non-LDC members, to give some stability to financing, income from fees and perhaps, as with ACWL, commitment from some or all of the developed country members to guarantee the running costs for an initial period while capacity is being built. Costs will depend on the number of staff and overheads but are unlikely to be less than two million Swiss francs a year, depending on location and status.

5   Conclusions

This chapter and its Annex on the Sussex Framework has examined the complexities of assessing the impact of RTAs on economic welfare and development, and the difficulties these might present to under-resourced negotiators in developing countries. It has demonstrated proof of concept on an analytical framework that could help negotiators assess the costs and benefits of shallow and deep integration at relatively low resource costs and without recourse to sophisticated and expensive analytical methods. It proposes that while private provision could deliver the necessary training and advice, there is a case, based on asymmetric information and the potential for damage to the international system, for an internationally financed Advisory Centre on Regional Trading Arrangements, to provide training, negotiating advice and accreditation for private providers based on an agreed analytical framework.

The Sussex Framework: can RTAs be analysed in a practical, reliable and economical manner?[9]

BOX 14.1 IDENTIFYING WHAT NEEDS TO BE EVALUATED	
Checklist	Issues
(1) Economic relationship between partners	Size, asymmetry, tariff levels, cost differences
(2) FTA or customs union?	Flexibility, rules of origin
(3) Overlap with other agreements?	Complementarities versus spaghetti bowl
(4) Expected difficulties in negotiation	Depth and scope of PTA, sensitive sectors, exceptions
(5) Barriers to trade	Tariffs, NTBs – incidence, levels, range
(6) Elements of deep integration?	Trade-facilitating institutions and policies: investment rules, competition policy, labour mobility, standards, property rights, dispute resolution
(7) WTO compatibility?	Important if third country could be affected
(8) Role of aid donors	Political motivation behind the agreements, presence of technical/ development assistance

The conceptual basis of the Sussex Framework is to consider the political, social and economic viability of a given RTA. Its likely economic impact will depend on a number of key factors, and we provide a checklist of issues to be systematically evaluated, summarized in Box 14.1.

The first step in applying the Framework is to consider the importance of each element in the checklist with respect to the proposed agreement. In the context of the Economic Partnership Agreements

---

[9] Rather than re-presenting the basic description of the Sussex Framework, this section is a lightly edited version of Evans *et al.* (2007), with the addition of a discussion of resource and training requirements. I am grateful to my colleagues for allowing me to use our joint work *in extensio*. The original study is Evans *et al.* (2006). While the framework was developed with DFID support the usual disclaimers apply – the views expressed are those of the author(s) and do not necessarily represent the view of DFID.

(EPA) proposed between the EU and members of the ACP group of countries, for example, it is immediately clear that there are substantial asymmetries between the EU and the proposed EPA country groupings; what is being proposed is a free trade area (FTA) where rules of origin will be important; and the introduction of elements of deep integration and issues of trade-related development assistance complicate the negotiations. However, the results may be potentially more beneficial and development friendly if they are correctly designed.

The second step is to consider the economic viability and consequences of a proposed agreement, including an assessment of the potential welfare consequences. Viability depends on the magnitude and distribution of benefits, both across and within countries. The overall welfare impact will depend on the extent of shallow integration, as well as on deep integration.

In the first instance, any RTA involves a process of shallow integration. We have known for more than half a century that the potential net benefits from lowering trade barriers in an RTA are inherently ambiguous, because they involve both trade creation and trade diversion. Trade creation arises whenever more efficiently produced imported goods replace less efficiently produced domestic goods. Trade is 'created' and yields welfare gains. Trade diversion occurs when sources of supply switch away from more efficient non-partner countries to less efficient partner countries. Trade diversion reduces welfare, and the net welfare impact of an RTA will depend on the relative size of the two effects.

There are a number of rules of thumb, which are well grounded in economic theory, that help in evaluating the relative importance of trade diversion and trade creation:

- The higher the initial tariffs, the greater the likelihood of both trade creation and trade diversion.
- The greater the number of RTA partners, and the more similar the product mix in the member economies, the more likely it is that there will be trade creation because there is more scope for specialization.
- The wider the differences in comparative advantage between partners and the higher the initial share of trade between them, the more likely it is that the RTA will be welfare-improving.

In addition to the potential, but once and for all, efficiency gains and losses, there could be welfare gains arising from growth effects induced by economic integration. There could be faster technical change and total factor productivity growth, and scale economies arising from

Table 14.2 *Some diagnostic indicators[1]*

	Average tariff (%)	Share of imports		Export similarity index[2] (%)
		EU (%)	US (%)	
Jamaica	15.20	8.20	8.00	45.00
Trinidad and Tobago	18.00	12.60	34.00	33.40
Egypt	18.40	27.00	12.00	34.40
India	28.30	25.00	6.00	24.00

[1] The data for Jamaica and Trinidad and Tobago are for 2003, for Egypt 2003, and India 2004 (Indian average applied tariffs have fallen substantially since 2004 and now stand at around 12 per cent after the budget of 2007).

[2] This is the Finger–Kreinin index, and is a way of measuring the degree of similarity between a pair of countries, trade or production structures. If they are identical the index is equal to 1; if they are completely different the index is equal to 0.

increased specialization, and/or positive externalities between firms and/or sectors. These dynamic gains are typically more likely to arise in the presence of deep integration. We then use a range of diagnostic indicators that shed light directly and indirectly on the welfare consequences of a given RTA. A number of these indicators are directly related to the rules of thumb outlined earlier, and thus help in evaluating the shallow integration consequences as well as distributional implications. There are no easy rules of thumb for evaluating the implications of deep integration. The economics of the transmission mechanisms between deep integration and economic growth is an emerging field, and the relationships are more complex and less well understood than with shallow integration. Nevertheless, there are some indicators, which are useful in considering deep integration.

Shallow integration

Consider, for example, Table 14.2, which provides indicators for four countries involved in actual or proposed agreements with the EU. On the export side for the partner countries there will already be low tariffs on manufactures – except for a few special cases, which may differ for each partner, while sensitive agricultural products are no doubt excluded. Typically, then, there is little improved market access to the EU. On the

BOX 14.2 SHALLOW AND DEEP INTEGRATION

Shallow, or negative, integration involves the removal of border barriers to trade, typically tariffs and quotas.

Deep, or positive, integration involves policies and institutions that facilitate trade by reducing or eliminating regulatory and behind-the-border impediments to trade, where these impediments may or may not be intentional. These can include issues such as customs procedures, regulation of domestic services production that discriminate against foreigners, product standards that differ from international norms or where testing and certification of foreign goods is complex and perhaps exclusionary, regulation of inward investments, competition policy, intellectual policy protection and the rules surrounding access to government procurement.

These are exactly the issues that form the heart of the EU single market for goods and services, and typically require a degree of harmonization or convergence of norms and standards, or mutual recognition of each other's regulatory processes and standards.

import side, most of the potential partner tariffs are high, particularly for India. If we link these measures to the pattern of trade, we see that the share of imports from the EU is lowest for the two Caribbean economies, while the US is an important supplier. This suggests considerable scope for trade diversion (switching away from the US to the EU as a supplier for an RTA with the EU) – especially for Jamaica. India has a higher share of imports from the EU, and a much lower share of imports from the US. However, with an EU import share of 25 per cent (which has been rapidly declining), the majority of imports are sourced from third countries. If we add the low degree of similarity in production structures as proxied by the similarity of export structures (24 per cent), this again suggests the likelihood of trade diversion over creation in an RTA with the EU. In comparison the similarity in the exports of the EU and the US is above 69 per cent.

Similarly, for Egypt the share of imports with the EU is only 27 per cent, with the US accounting for 12 per cent; the degree of export (or production) similarity is higher than for India. These figures suggest perhaps slightly less trade diversion for Egypt than for India, but nevertheless still allow considerable scope for this. Using the Sussex Framework we can explore these issues more fully by a more detailed and disaggregated examination of these indicators; by looking at further indicators, such as the relative competitiveness of partner countries, examining indices of trade intensity; and importantly by looking at the evolution of these indices over time. It is also worth pointing out that even when comparing two countries within a given grouping and proposed RTA – Jamaica, and Trinidad and Tobago – there are considerable differences between them, and therefore also between the likely impacts. Within the CARIFORUM EPA grouping, those differences then become much more pronounced when the other countries are added in, ranging from the tiny Organisation of Eastern Caribbean States to the Dominican Republic. This suggests that the impacts are likely to differ widely across countries, and that countries' priorities and agendas are thus likely to be different. Using the Sussex Framework these issues can be identified and analysed.

Deep integration

From the perspective of shallow integration the Sussex analysis indicates that the effects of RTAs between the EU and partner countries are complex, but that typically there is considerable scope for trade diversion. This result should make us cautious in concluding that the welfare effects are likely to be positive. The next step is to consider elements of deep integration. Welfare gains from a successful process of deeper integration are likely to be considerably higher than losses from shallow integration. Deep integration permits both more niche market specialization and the creation of stable value chains.

The possible range of further gains associated with deeper integration include technology transfer and diffusion, both through trade and FDI; pro-competitive gains from increasing import competition in an environment of imperfect competition, which may also allow greater exploitation of economies of scale in production and the greater use of intermediate inputs; the increased geographical dispersion of production through trade that supports the exploitation of different factor proportions for different parts of the production process, and/or local economies of scale through finer specialization and division of labour in production; and externalities arising from institutional changes that lead to a wide increase in productivity.

With the Sussex Framework, we argue that the potential for gains from deeper integration depends on the extent to which the FTA creates a 'common economic space' among partners. This common economic space requires both the removal of barriers to trade that operate behind borders (e.g. discriminatory taxes and regulations) and actions to undertake common policies needed for dealing with the existence of public goods and externalities. Of course, the impact of deep integration will clearly depend on whether the norms adopted are appropriate – i.e. generate positive externalities and promote trade.

Broadly speaking, adopting appropriate standards is synonymous with finding the appropriate institutional framework for dealing with externalities. Some of these elements can be done by the market through private contracting, but they may require a facilitating environment. Foreign direct investment is an important channel for productivity-enhancing deep integration via technology and know-how transfer, quality improvement and specialization. Hence any assessment of the potential for deep integration gains from an analysis of the investment regimes in place, of the levels and patterns of existing FDI flows, and of the possible clauses that could be negotiated in the context of an RTA which encourages further FDI.

A key indicator of existing and the potential for further deep integration is the degree to which intra-industry trade (IIT) is currently taking place. Broadly, IIT takes three forms. First, it is the exchange of similar but differentiated goods (the same trade heading) of broadly similar qualities and prices; second, it is the exchange of similar goods of different qualities and prices (first and second categories together are known as horizontal IIT); and, third, it is the exchange of goods within a trade classification that represents a vertically integrated supply chain (parts for finished or part-finished goods). The last of these clearly includes the cases of global or regional supply chains, which have had a large positive impact on trade and growth in East Asia.

Each of these forms represents a way in which economic integration can encourage niche specialization and generate productivity gains, as well as lead to trade-induced technological change. Such gains can yield increases in trade, and more than compensate for any trade diversion losses arising from shallow integration alone.

Our work on EU–Egypt IIT suggests that while IIT has been growing fast in Egypt it is still at a very low level and is unlikely to represent a high current potential for deep integration. Taken alongside FDI flows into Egypt, which seem focused on energy and domestic market access, the scope for deep integration to offset the bias towards trade diversion (indicated by the diagnostic statistics noted above) is relatively low (although there may be niches where the harmonization of standards and conformity testing can generate substantial gains and our work includes a suggestive case study on new potatoes[10]).

---

[10] See Evans *et al.* (2006: 196–8) for details.

Table 14.3 *IIT indicators for India and the EU*

	India–World		EU–India	
	1992	2004	1992	2004
Percentage of trade which is IIT	43	52	19	39
Percentage of trade which is vertical IIT	18	35	8	18

India, on the other hand, shows relatively high levels of and growth in IIT indices (see Table 14.3). Levels and growth rates are below but comparable with those of China and Brazil. Overall 52 per cent of Indian total trade in 2004 was in IIT, and some two-thirds of that was in vertically integrated IIT. India–EU IIT lags somewhat behind the India–world IIT shares. This suggests (particularly when taken with the fast-growing totals of inward and outward FDI) that deep integration in an EU–India FTA could potentially generate substantial gains and compensate for any trade diversion losses.[11]

Robustness

We have tested the Framework, the usefulness of the diagnostic statistics and the rules of thumb against more sophisticated and resource-intensive analytical methods, notably general equilibrium and partial equilibrium modelling on a potential EU–Egypt fully reciprocal FTA and an EU Caribbean REPA. Overall the Sussex Framework gives very similar predictions of likely economic welfare effects of these proposed agreements to the modelling work, with the added advantage of being able to drill down at sectoral or geographical level in a way that the models typically cannot do.

Practicalities

Experience in applying the Sussex Framework in the context of actual or potential negotiations suggests that it, and/or any equivalent analytical framework, does clarify the potential effects of any given RTA in a helpful way for negotiators, and helps prioritization of objectives in the negotiations.

---

[11] To see a self-standing example of the Framework used to assess a proposed FTA between India and the EU see Gasiorek *et al.* (2007).

In terms of implementation the checklist is relatively easy and straightforward. The questions and the required answers are qualitative. They are in essence the questions that any administration would need to ask to begin the process of writing a negotiating brief for ministers. The advantage of the checklist is that it is ready-made and coherent, and covers issues that experience of previous negotiations suggests are important. It reduces the risk of issues being overlooked because of lack of resources or expertise – not least if the country concerned has no depth of, or recent experience in, such a bilateral negotiation. Clearly not every issue on the checklist is relevant to every negotiation, but it allows particular issues to be put to one side as an act of deliberate policy rather than by accident.

The rules of thumb, and the diagnostic statistics which underlie them, require more expertise. The diagnostic statistics are designed to be calculated using the standard trade and tariff databases – WITS and TRAINS – which developing countries can download free from the World Bank website. They can be calculated using standard spreadsheets. The formulae need economic expertise to derive, apply and to interpret the results. Someone with a strong grounding in the economics of trade and trade policy – for example, with a Master's level of training – can with time work out how to apply them. After a week or so of training they could start to derive useful results within two to three weeks. Then, with some initial guidance, they could immediately begin to provide policy-relevant analytical judgements. We have now used the Framework in the context of RTAs involving the EU, Caribbean ACP countries, India, Egypt, ECOWAS and COMESA states, Russia and Ukraine. Each run has reduced the time to calculate the statistics and interpret them. A first draft of a handbook on the methods, plus two training modules, have been prepared for the UNCTAD Virtual Institute[12] which will help shorten some of the training and implementation periods for new users. Ideally an electronic version of the Framework would allow the checklist to be completed and the diagnostic statistics derived quite quickly. It could also allow some quantitative modelling to be undertaken, although that would require significantly more expertise, and also raise the cost significantly.

The discussion so far is very much in the context of shallow integration. The lack of a clear conceptual base, and hence of relatively easily

---

[12] Available at: http://vi.unctad.org/joomla/index.php?option=com_content&task=view&id=33&Itemid=65.

derived diagnostic statistics beyond measures of IIT and FDI, means that greater expertise is required to examine the prospects for deep integration. Above all the lack of fine-grained services statistics or easy ways of linking regulatory changes to improved performance of the services sector, and any externalities for wider economic performance, limit the ability to come to quick conclusions. This is why accumulated experience of looking at a range of economies within the analytical context of the Framework, combined with local knowledge of sectors, will help to identify which sectors are likely to benefit from deep integration with bilateral partners.

Experience to date suggests that investment in training and expertise in the use of the Framework, or something similar to it, could pay off for countries facing a number of bilateral negotiations, or, as in the case of the EPAs or FTAA, where there is both local regional integration with a number of local partners and bilateral North–South integration going on. For countries which may only face one bilateral agreement at a time, investment in standing analytical capacity may be uneconomic, particularly if there is a high staff turnover, and high-quality human capital is lured away to other public sector jobs or to the private sector. The question of the provision of analytical services in these circumstances, whether from private or public sectors, is examined in the next section.

Conclusions from research leading to, and application of, the Sussex Framework

- Bilateral and regional trade agreements are here to stay (and may represent the policy response to market-led trade integration at a regional level, notably in Europe, the Americas and East Asia).
- Agreements are complex and human-resource intensive to understand and negotiate, particularly as each may have special characteristics.
- For developing countries shallow integration is likely to generate trade diversion losses and hence put a premium on identifying potential gains from deep integration. This will particularly be so when implementing reciprocal bilateral and regional liberalization in the place of existing but asymmetric liberalization (notably regional EPAs and EU Neighbourhood FTAs).
- The Framework requires training in its use, and experience of its application, to extract the most from it, particularly in the more complex task of assessing any potential for deep integration gains that might offset any trade diversion losses.

- The Sussex Framework is a clear, coherent, consistent and robust framework for analysing a given proposed agreement with relatively light human resource requirements. In that sense it is a proof of concept for a standardized approach to complex negotiations, whether using the Framework or something developed from it.

References

Baldwin, R. (2006) 'Managing the Noodle Bowl: The Fragility of East Asian Regionalism', CEPR Discussion Paper No. 5561, London: Centre for Economic Policy Research.

Evans, D., Gasiorek, M., Ghoneim, A., *et al.* (2006) 'Assessing Regional Trade Agreements with Developing Countries: Shallow and Deep Integration, Trade, Productivity and Economic Performance', DFID Project No. 04 5881, University of Sussex, UK, available at: www.sussex.ac.uk/Units/caris/CARIS/DFIF-RTA-REPORT.pdf.

Evans, D., Gasiorek, M., Holmes, P., Robinson, S. and Rollo, J. (2007) 'Assessing Preferential Trading Agreements Using the Sussex Framework', CARIS Briefing Paper No. 1, University of Sussex, UK, available at: www.sussex.ac.uk/Units/caris/wps/Carisbp01.pdf.

Gasiorek, M., Holmes, P., Mukerjee, C. *et al.* (2007) 'Quantitative Analysis of a Potential Free Trade Agreement between the European Union and India', Sussex University, Centre for the Analysis of Regional Integration and Consumer Unity and Trust Society (CUTS), Jaipur.

Medvedev, D. (2006) 'Preferential Trade Agreements and their Role in World Trade', World Bank Policy Research Working Paper 4038, Washington, DC: World Bank.

Messerlin, P. (2007) 'Assessing EU Trade Policy in Goods', Jan Tumlir Policy Essay No. 1, Brussels: European Centre for International Political Economy.

~

Comment

CLAUDE BARFIELD

Jim Rollo's chapter presents a succinct but lucid description of the so-called Sussex Framework, a sophisticated, yet highly user-friendly approach and methodology for analyzing RTAs (regional trade agreements) by developing countries (or, more specifically, the trade bureaucracies and trade-related political appointees of those countries). The framework consists of several separate parts, or systems of analysis; and it makes a clear distinction between the elements related to two types of integration: shallow integration and deep integration. By shallow integration, Rollo means border barriers, where rules of thumb related to economic welfare consequences, including trade creation and trade diversion, can be ascertained through the use of available diagnostic statistics, such as trade shares and patterns with potential partners, similarities and differences in production structures, and levels of tariffs and tariff peaks.

Deep integration, on the other hand, largely involves barriers to open markets and behind-the-borders competition, including a potentially wide variety of policies and regulations, ranging from customs impediments, domestic services regulations, product, safety and health standards, to competition and foreign direct investment policy and government procurement, among others. Rollo candidly admits that "there are no easy rules of thumb" for assessing the "complex mechanism between deep integration and economic growth" but goes on to set forth certain guidelines revolving around the development of "common economic space," or actions taken by trading partners to foster positive externalities from the proposed agreement. Examples cited for these joint efforts include the encouragement of FDI, technology transfer as a result of the RTA, and the existence of, and future promotion of, intra-industry trade.

Finally, the chapter makes the case that the multilateral trading system has a strong interest in getting it right with regard to the substance

and structure of RTAs, not least because of the threat of the proliferation of disputes among WTO members over allegations that specific
rights and obligations in the Marrakesh Agreement have been violated
or ignored. Rollo, however, quickly points to difficulties inherent in any
attempt by the WTO councils or the Secretariat to deal with such disputes. The RTAs themselves are the product of negotiations by member
states, and these states would likely rebel at attempts by the Secretariat
(or even – though this is unstated in the chapter – dispute settlement
panels) to intervene and dictate changes in executed agreements.

After briefly discounting the possibility for the private provision of
these advisory services, Rollo concludes the chapter with an argument
for a new international organization, the Advisory Centre on RTAs, for
which the model is to be taken from the old Advisory Centre for WTO
Law that was set up in 2001 to help developing countries involved in
WTO trade disputes.

In evaluating the analysis and recommendations in the chapter,
I divide my comments into two areas: certain assumptions regarding
shallow versus deep integration, and the case Rollo attempts to make for
the proposed Advisory Centre for RTAs.

On the former point, the chapter makes the valid judgment that in
general deeper integration has the greater potential to produce productivity gains and enhanced growth. But a second assertion that this
will "compensate for any trade diversion losses" is more problematical.
First, there is the question of "losses" for whom – the country pushing
for the RTA may well benefit in the short (or even long) run from
diversion through shallow integration. Though not clearly stated, there
seems to be the assumption that the valid metric for judging "losses"
versus "gains" is from the perspective of world welfare. This is a
standard that has not been asserted for existing RTAs, nor is it likely to
find favor among national governments as they contemplate future
RTAs. Second, there could well be situations with regard to "deep
integration" RTAs where substantial trade diversion could occur – for
instance, assume that in a two-country RTA, one partner had highly
protected service sectors and opened these sectors only to the second
partner and not to other trading partners. In summary, these issues are
more complicated than the chapter acknowledges.

Regarding a public Advisory Centre for RTAs, though Rollo admits
that WTO bodies or the Secretariat could not be seen to be taking sides
in RTA negotiations, he does not explore similar dangers even for an
independent outside advisory body. The precedent cited in the chapter

is from the existing Advisory Centre for WTO Law. This center has had some success in advising developing countries in dispute settlement actions before WTO panels. An advisory center for RTAs, however, would find itself in a very different situation. First, the legal advisory center deals with a unified government position and an "us versus them" legal fight. In RTA negotiations, inevitably, there are strong contending domestic political interests, and an outside advisory group would be called upon to make judgments in a political minefield. While it could attempt to quietly render advice to government bureaucrats behind the scenes, this would vitiate its role in the process as an independent, objective outside voice. One alternative, not explored in the chapter, would be for the creators of the Sussex Framework (researchers at the University of Sussex) to create (possibly with an outside organization) a private consulting service that would be able negotiate terms of service with individual governments. Though this would proscribe its independence, at least the most important participant in the negotiation (i.e. the governing party or coalition) would benefit from the sophisticated framework analysis.

To conclude, I would argue that, despite some reservations about certain assumptions regarding particular issues, Rollo has made a solid case for the utility of the Sussex Framework. Here's hoping that he and his colleagues at the University of Sussex can devise a viable mechanism to promote its widespread use by developing countries.

INDEX